MW00996005

Handbook for SOCIAL JUSTICE in Counseling Psychology

With deep humility and respect, we dedicate this Handbook to all the individuals, families, communities, organizations, and institutions working toward social justice in all its many forms. Among the many notable efforts around the world, we reflect on two recent historical events as we submit this dedication: Hurricane Katrina and the recent passing of Kenneth B. Clark. In the wake of Hurricane Katrina, we honor those affected by the devastation, persons helping with survival and adjustment, and individuals striving to identify and eliminate the injustices that emerged as a result of this tragic sequence of events. Your sacrifices and unwavering courage inspire us to even more fervently pursue equality, justice, and a truly compassionate world. In this past year, we have also noted the legacy of Kenneth B. Clark as one of the first psychologists to influence national policy in the face of racial discrimination through research, scholarship, and legislative advocacy. His work and the work of Mamie Clark stand as examples of the power and role that individuals and psychologists can have in shaping this nation.

Rebecca L. Toporek: To my many mentors, students, and clients for their generosity, wisdom, and faith. To Kaiya, Dylan, Phil, Cynthia, Veronica, and Daniel for their patience and love. To my parents, Walter and Doreen, for their unwavering belief in the need for a just world.

Lawrence H. Gerstein: In memory of my parents, Helen and Melvin, who modeled the ideal in social activism.

Nadya A. Fouad: To Bob, Nick, Andrew, and Patrick, with love and thanks for all the support.

Gargi Roysircar: For my students sharing in tsunami outreach in Tamilnadu, India.

Tania Israel: For my parents, Mary and John Israel, my early role models for political activism, cultural complexity, and community involvement.

Handbook for SOCIAL JUSTICE in Counseling Psychology

Leadership, Vision, and Action

EDITORS

Rebecca L. Toporek
San Francisco State University

Lawrence H. Gerstein
Ball State University

Nadya A. Fouad
University of Wisconsin, Milwaukee

Gargi Roysircar
Antioch New England Graduate School

Tania Israel
University of California, Santa Barbara

For information:

Sage Publications, Inc.
2455 Teller Road
Thousand Oaks, California 91320
E-mail: order@sagepub.com

Sage Publications Ltd.
1 Oliver's Yard
55 City Road
London, EC1Y 1SP
United Kingdom

Sage Publications India Pvt. Ltd.
B-42, Panchsheel Enclave
Post Box 4109
New Delhi 110 017 India

Printed in the United States of America

Library of Congress Cataloging-in-Publication Data

Handbook for social justice in counseling psychology: Leadership, vision, and action/Rebecca L. Toporek . . . [et al.].
p. cm.
Includes bibliographical references and index.
ISBN 1–4129–1007–2 (cloth)
1. Counseling. 2. Social justice. I. Toporek, Rebecca.
BF637.C6H3115 2006
158.'3—dc22 2005018260

This book is printed on acid-free paper.

05 06 07 08 09 10 9 8 7 6 5 4 3 2 1

Acquiring Editor: Arthur T. Pomponio
Editorial Assistant: Veronica Novak
Project Editor: Beth A. Bernstein
Copy Editor: Liann Lech
Typesetter: C&M Digitals (P) Ltd.
Indexer: Teri Greenberg
Cover Designer: Janet Foulger

Contents

Foreword ix
David L. Blustein

1. Social Justice and Counseling Psychology in Context 1
Nadya A. Fouad, Lawrence H. Gerstein, and Rebecca L. Toporek

2. Ethics and Professional Issues Related to the Practice of Social Justice in Counseling Psychology 17
Rebecca L. Toporek and Robert A. Williams

PART I: TRAINING 35

3. Social Justice Training in Counseling Psychology: Needs and Innovations 37
Rebecca L. Toporek and Christopher J. McNally

4. Incorporating Social Justice in Counselor Training Programs: A Case Study Example 44
Regine M. Talleyrand, Rita Chi-Ying Chung, and Fred Bemak

5. Empowering Undergraduate Students to Be Agents of Social Change: An Innovative Service Learning Course in Counseling Psychology 59
Karen M. O'Brien, Sheetal Patel, Nancy Hensler-McGinnis, and Jennifer Kaplan

PART II: SCHOOLS 75

6. Prevention Work in Schools and With Youth: Promoting Competence and Reducing Risks 77
Gargi Roysircar

7. Prevention and Outreach With Underserved Populations: Building Multisystemic Youth Development Programs for Urban Youth 86
Elizabeth Vera, Brian Daly, Rufus Gonzales, Melissa Morgan, and Charu Thakral

8. Transformative Endeavors: Implementing Helms's Racial Identity Theory to a School-Based Heritage Project 100
Chalmer E. Thompson, Dorienna M. Alfred, Sherri L. Edwards, and Patricia G. Garcia

9. Promoting Social Justice Through Preventive Interventions in Schools 117
M. Meghan Davidson, Michael Waldo, and Eve M. Adams

10. A Theoretical and Practice Framework for Universal School-Based Prevention 130
Gargi Roysircar

PART III: MARGINALIZED COMMUNITIES 147

11. Marginalized Communities in the United States: Oppression, Social Justice, and the Role of Counseling Psychologists 149
Tania Israel

12. Seeking Social Justice for Victims of Intimate Partner Violence: Real-World Struggles in Pursuit of Systemic Change 155
Margret E. Bell and Lisa A. Goodman

13. Achieving Social Justice for College Women With Disabilities: A Model for Inclusion 170
Barbara J. Palombi and Alisa Matteson Mundt

14. Environmental Racism: A Call to the Profession for Community Intervention and Social Action 185
Azara L. Santiago-Rivera, Kristin Talka, and Amy W. Tully

15. The Unwarranted Pathologizing of Homeless Mothers: Implications for Research and Social Policy 200
Lisa Cosgrove

16. Diving Into the Hornet's Nest: Situating Counseling Psychologists in LGB Social Justice Work 215
David H. Whitcomb and Michael I. Loewy

17. Toward a Radical Feminist Multicultural Therapy: Renewing a Commitment to Activism 231
Susan L. Morrow, Donna M. Hawxhurst, Ana Y. Montes de Vegas, Tamara M. Abousleman, and Carrie L. Castañeda

PART IV: CAREER AND VOCATIONAL ISSUES 249

18. Social Justice in Career and Vocational Aspects of Counseling Psychology: An Overview 251
Nadya A. Fouad

19. Tools for Remodeling the Master's House: Advocacy and Social Justice in Education and Work 256
Ruth E. Fassinger and Susanna M. Gallor

20. Individual, Programmatic, and Entrepreneurial Approaches to Social Justice: Counseling Psychologists in Vocational and Career Counseling 276
Rebecca L. Toporek and Robert C. Chope

21. Social Justice Through Self-Sufficiency: Vocational Psychology and the Transition From Welfare to Work 294
Cindy L. Juntunen, Angela M. Cavett, Rhanda B. Clow, Venessa Rempel, Rachel E. Darrow, and Adam Guilmino

PART V: SOCIAL JUSTICE IN HEALTH CARE 311

22. Counseling Health Psychology's Collaborative Role in the Community 313
Gargi Roysircar

23. Working for Social Justice From Within the Health Care System: The Role of Social Class in Psychology 318
Joshua A. Hopps and William M. Liu

24. Community Health Promotion Curriculum: A Case Study of Southeast Asian Refugees 338
Uyen K. Huynh and Gargi Roysircar

25. Social Justice Related to Working With HIV/AIDS From a Counseling Health Psychology Perspective 358
Christa K. Schmidt, Mary Ann Hoffman, and Nicole Taylor

PART VI: COUNSELING PSYCHOLOGISTS IN THE INTERNATIONAL ARENA 375

26. Counseling Psychologists as International Social Architects 377
Lawrence H. Gerstein

27. A Social Justice Approach to International Collaborative Consultation 388
Sharon G. Horne and Susan S. Mathews

28. Couples Helping Couples: Consultation and Training in Peñalolén, Chile 406
Benedict T. McWhirter and Ellen Hawley McWhirter

29. Bringing Social Justice to International Practices of Counseling Psychology 421
Kathryn L. Norsworthy with contributions by Ouyporn Khuankaew

30. Counseling Psychology and Nonviolent Activism: Independence for Tibet! 442
Lawrence H. Gerstein and Doris Kirkpatrick

31. Moving From Contact to Change: The Act of Becoming Aware 472
Scott L. Moeschberger, Alicia Ordóñez, Jui Shankar, and Shonali Raney

PART VII: POLICY AND LEGISLATIVE CHANGE 487

32. Social Action in Policy and Legislation: Individuals and Alliances 489
Rebecca L. Toporek

33. Extending the Parsons Legacy: Applications of Counseling Psychology in Pursuit of Social Justice Through the Development of Public Policy 499
Sandra L. Shullman, Bobbie L. Celeste, and Ted Strickland

34. Confessions of an Abiding Counseling Psychologist 514
Robert H. McPherson and Clare Reilly

PART VIII: FUTURE DIRECTIONS 531

35. Future Directions for Counseling Psychology: Enhancing Leadership, Vision, and Action in Social Justice 533
Rebecca L. Toporek, Lawrence H. Gerstein, Nadya A. Fouad, Gargi Roysircar, and Tania Israel

Author Index 553

Subject Index 571

About the Editors 603

About the Contributors 605

Foreword

I was both delighted and humbled to be asked to write a foreword for this noteworthy and timely book. This important *Handbook,* edited by Rebecca Toporek, Lawrence Gerstein, Nadya Fouad, Gargi Roysircar, and Tania Israel, presents a map for our field that will transform the next generation of training, research, and practice for counseling psychologists. Moreover, this book underscores counseling psychology's role as a leader in professional psychology in advancing a perspective that is singularly unique, expansive, and visionary. One of the strengths of counseling psychology has been its role within the general psychological community in advocating for a careful and systematic consideration of gender and culture as critical factors in human development. In my view, this book will help to locate a broad and inclusive social justice mission on our collective radar screens, once again placing counseling psychology at the leadership role in advancing a more engaged and activist course for professional psychology.

The increasing focus on social justice in counseling psychology represents the logical culmination of our historic commitment to understanding the role of culture, race, gender, ability/disability status, and sexual orientation in counseling, training, prevention, and research. The editors and authors of this book have each thoughtfully developed their contributions on the shoulders of the brave and courageous leaders in our field who have shed light on the influences of sexism, classism, racism, and heterosexism in human development. As readers have no doubt observed if they have explored any aspect of counseling psychology in recent years, the focus on context as a frame for individual experience has increasingly defined one of our unique contributions to psychological discourse. By exploring the role of schools, communities, work/career, health care, and the broader international context, as well as graduate training and public policy advocacy, the authors of the chapters in this *Handbook* have articulated a clear vision of what is at stake, and possible, in our work. In short, our work as counseling psychologists takes us to the forefront of the boundary where individual experience encounters social and economic forces that powerfully shape people's lives. Without giving voice to these external factors and describing their impact in the lives of our clients, I believe that we collude with the status quo to sustain inequity. The editors and chapter authors of this groundbreaking book have provided us with the tools to turn our passion, anger, and empathy into effective, engaged action that can transform the context of our richly diverse communities.

By focusing on these pernicious aspects of the context, the editors and authors have created a compelling case that human behavior is inherently embedded in a complex web of cultures, political structures, socioeconomic affordances, and social systems. When considered collectively, the authors describe how differential access to resources and barriers so powerfully shapes the trajectory of human life.

One of the main themes that emerges in these chapters is the reality that life is not fair. Although this phrase has generated a great deal of interest from policy analysts and government leaders (as well as parents, who hear this from their kids ad nauseum), it also underscores a critical reality in our society. People are born into families that have widely disparate resources and equally diverse opportunities for the sort of self-concept implementation that has been so long espoused as an aspirational value for our clients. In my humble opinion, this book has the very real capacity to transform the nature of our work as counseling psychologists, encompassing all aspects of our diverse roles.

The book you are about to read is akin to the message heard in the music of Woody Guthrie, an American folksinger and icon during the Great Depression. I have always been impressed with the confidence and commitment reflected in Guthrie's work and his bold statement about the impact of his art. Like Guthrie, who exposed many of the social and political forces that kept people of color and the poor from reaching the "land of plenty," the editors and authors have created a body of work that will help to take the nascent social justice movement in our field to the next level of maturation and effectiveness. Much like Guthrie's work, the material in this *Handbook* articulates how social and economic forces constrain our natural striving for a healthy life of meaningful relationships, access to meaningful work, and the opportunity for a healthy expression of our inner spirit. I believe that this book will hold an equally significant place in our field's history, inspiring new generations of activist scholars and therapists.

A close examination of the organizing structure of this book reveals the editors' thoughtful ideas about the array of contextual factors that influence the trajectory of individual life experiences. By focusing on training at the outset of the *Handbook*, the editors have wisely positioned their contribution as playing a key role in educating the next generation of counseling psychologists and other counseling professionals. The chapters in the section on schools build on an emerging discourse in counseling psychology on the role of psychosocial supports in the academic enterprise, highlighting a challenge that has been woefully ignored in recent reform efforts. In the section exploring the role of counseling psychologists in marginalized communities, the authors push the envelope of our typical considerations by providing specific tools for counseling psychologists that help to expand the theoretical knowledge needed to create a fully engaged social justice agenda in counseling psychology.

In the vocational psychology section, the emphasis on social justice, which encourages readers to consider everyone who works, marks a noted change from the prevalent focus on the work lives of people with considerable choice and volition. The section on health care helps to link the social justice agenda to another critical human context, while also detailing the critical role of social class in the maldistribution of health resources in the United States.

The focus on the international context continues a healthy movement away from the insularity that characterized much of U.S. psychology during the 20th century. The underlying theme of this section is articulated in a thoughtful way in the final chapter of this section, which describes how the process of international collaboration is transformative for all of the participants, including clients, psychologists, and other change agents. The final section of the *Handbook* focuses on the contributions that counseling psychologists make in shaping policy and legislation.

When considered collectively, the chapters represent more than the sum of their individual parts. As the editors and chapter authors have conveyed in this *Handbook*, many people lead hard lives, with few, if any, reasons to hope for a better future. The ideas presented here, in my view, can help to change the sharp edges of social and economic forces that so powerfully constrain our access to dignified, healthy, and engaged lives. The editors of this *Handbook* have demonstrated considerable vision in mapping the terrain of the social justice agenda for counseling psychology. Similarly, the chapter authors rose to the occasion by developing clearly detailed ideas that can be easily adopted by readers. The potential for transforming the landscape of our field is detailed eloquently in these pages; it is now up to us, as readers, to assume the challenges that have been described in this landmark publication.

David L. Blustein
Boston College

CHAPTER 1

Social Justice and Counseling Psychology in Context

Nadya A. Fouad, Lawrence H. Gerstein, and Rebecca L. Toporek

Social justice may be defined as "the distribution of advantages and disadvantages within a society" (Webster's Dictionary, 2004). Related to the legal notion of equity for all within the law, social justice also connotes that the distribution of advantages be fair and equitable to all individuals, regardless of race, gender, ability status, sexual orientation, physical makeup, or religious creed. Social justice within the context of counseling psychology focuses on helping to ensure that opportunities and resources are distributed fairly and helping to ensure equity when resources are distributed unfairly or unequally. This includes actively working to change social institutions, political and economic systems, and governmental structures that perpetuate unfair practices, structures, and policies in terms of accessibility, resource distribution, and human rights. Social justice activities for counseling psychologists have included such actions as working to promote therapists' multicultural competence; working to combat racism, sexism, homophobia, and ageism; increasing access to educational and occupational opportunities; understanding and ameliorating career barriers for women; reaching out to work with homeless individuals; resolving ethnopolitical conflicts; nation building; empowering individuals, families, groups, organizations, and institutions outside of the United States; attempting to resolve border disputes between nations; advocating for the release of political prisoners; developing and implementing strategies

Authors' Note: We wish to express our appreciation to Gargi Roysircar and Tania Israel for their contributions.

to eliminate human rights abuses; striving to protect the environment; and influencing the legislative process.

Since its inception, the profession of counseling psychology has demonstrated an interest in social justice, action, and advocacy (Hartung & Blustein, 2002; Ivey & Collins, 2003; Kiselica & Robinson, 2001). This is not surprising given that social justice, action, and advocacy work require the conceptual knowledge and many of the core skills intimately tied to the foundation and identity of our profession. That is, we rely on developmental, growth-oriented, strength-based, multicultural models of human, organizational, and environmental behavior to address a host of concerns and issues reported by individuals, families, groups, organizations, and institutions. More often than not, such work also requires competencies in assessment, evaluation, consultation, group dynamics and intervention, outreach and prevention, field research, and psychoeducational programming. All of these competencies are considered to be integral to the identity of counseling psychologists and the scientist-practitioner framework of the counseling psychology profession.

The counseling psychology profession, therefore, has attempted to confront various injustices and inequality through a reliance on relevant theories and strategies in counseling and the entire discipline of psychology (Gerstein, 2002; Jackson, 2000; Kiselica & Robinson, 2001; Mays, 2000; Strickland, 2000). However, over time, this value has varied in the extent to which it has been recognized by counseling psychology scholars, researchers, educators, and practitioners. Counseling psychologists were concerned about social justice in working with veterans of World War II in the 1940s and 1950s, working with the homeless and disenfranchised in the 1960s, and advocating for civil rights and feminist changes in the 1960s and 1970s (Fouad et al., 2004). In the 1970s, the field of counseling psychology was also interested in preparing future mental professionals to be change agents equipped to prevent institutional racism (Lopez & Cheek, 1977). Yet, in the 1980s and 1990s, there was a shift toward advocacy for the profession and preference for medical models emphasizing individual and remedial therapy in light of a managed care environment.

Given the widespread increase in societal problems and the systemic root of such problems, it is critical that more counseling psychologists develop a sophisticated understanding of social justice, social action, and advocacy. Focusing on the root of such problems should not only lessen human suffering, but also prevent the maintenance and emergence of these problems.

In the past several years, there has been a resurgence of interest and attention to social justice and action as a critical and defining feature of counseling psychology as a profession. This *Handbook* has been developed to help bring together counseling psychologists currently implementing social justice work in their practice and scholarship. This chapter provides an overview of the role that social justice played in the development of counseling psychology as a field. We then discuss recent events that have supported and guided the reemergence of social justice as a core philosophy and guiding principle in counseling psychology. Finally, we set the context for the remainder of the *Handbook* by discussing its creation and intent as well as the application of social justice in various contexts as described throughout the *Handbook*.

Social Justice, Advocacy, and Counseling Psychology: 20th Century

Social justice and social advocacy have been a hallmark of counseling psychology since before it was a fully recognized specialty. The father of vocational psychology, Frank Parsons, worked toward social justice in the early 1900s in Boston. He was appalled by the living conditions of the impoverished young boys he encountered in his neighborhood, and, collaborating with other prominent social activists in Boston, he helped to develop the Breadwinners Institute to provide opportunities for training and employment. Writing in 1909, he noted, "Not till society wakes up to its responsibilities and its privileges . . . shall we be able to harvest more than a fraction of our human resources or develop and utilize the genius . . . in each new generation" (p. 165). Nearly a century later, Herr and Niles (1998) commented, "Counseling, and in particular, career counseling, . . . have become sociopolitical instruments . . . to deal with emerging social concerns such as equity" (p. 121).

Historically, counseling psychologists expressed their commitment to social justice and advocacy work by empowering individual clients to confront oppression, marginalization, human rights abuse, discrimination, and injustice. For example, in 1957, Donald G. Paterson, a pioneer in counseling psychology, wrote about his concerns with the underutilization of talents of disabled, minority, and elderly clients, emphasizing "the role of educational and vocational counseling in reducing and preventing occupational maladjustment in our society" (p. 134). Counseling psychologists' social justice concerns included more than just an interest in addressing the needs of individual clients; early counseling psychologists were also very concerned about helping to influence the clients' environments. Ivey and Collins (2003) cited Patterson, Darley, and Elliott's 1936 book *Men, Women and Jobs* as an early indicator of counseling psychologists' recognition of the need to focus on the system in which clients live, if counseling psychologists were to help clients make lasting changes.

Counseling psychologists' early social advocacy focused on the area of career and work because access to work was viewed as a major vehicle to social equity. Borow (1990) commented that the early years of counseling psychology at the University of Minnesota were characterized by a "concern that its activities have discernable [*sic*] consequences for the benefit of the state and of the broader society" (p. 290). Consistent with this characterization, during the Depression years of the early 1930s, Minnesota counseling psychologists worked on the Employee Stabilization project, which was designed to help people get back into the work force. Counseling psychologists at Teachers College, Columbia University worked with the Veteran's Administration, the Department of Labor, and the Vocational Rehabilitation Act to advocate for equity in work for minorities, women, and individuals with disabilities (Thompson, 1990). Counseling psychologists at Ohio State University and the University of Missouri–Columbia, as well as other institutions, were working in university counseling centers to not only help students make wise career decisions, but also determine the best type of college environment that would maximize their potential. Following World War II, counseling psychologists helped returning veterans adjust to civilian life, also advocating for them to receive educational benefits. In the 1960s, counseling psychologists were encouraged to use their skills to become involved in "movements that have to do with desegregation, voting rights, employment practices, housing, and minimum wages" (Samler, 1964, p. 66). In the 1970s, counseling psychologists were strong advocates for women to become more assertive (Jakubowski-Spector, 1973) at the same time they were advocating for equal pay for women in the workplace (Fitzgerald, 1973).

In addition to action in career and vocational counseling, counseling psychologists were also advocating for reform in the prisons (Geis, 1983) and in higher education. Such examples include addressing ways that counseling psychologists functioned as change agents within the university, addressing student services needs (Morrill, Oetting, & Hurst, 1974), and handling conflicts with students actively organizing against the Vietnam War (Shoben, 1969).

In part, the work of early counseling psychologists was heavily influenced by the growing sophistication of psychological measurement, which led to advocacy for women (e.g., Fitzgerald, 1973; Hansen, 1972) and racial/ethnic minorities (e.g., Anderson & Love, 1973; Sedlacek & Brooks, 1973). But Leona Tyler (1974), writing about the need to attend to individual differences among people, also noted that "in our haste to abolish the unjust and obsolete, we cannot afford to ignore the psychological realities that generated . . . [unfair] systems" (p. 5). Schlossberg and Pietrofesa (1973) were concerned about the sex bias in interest inventories that led to stereotyped occupations for women, and Williams (1971) sounded an alarm about the misuses of testing for African American children. Thirty years later, Helms (2004) continues to criticize the use of cognitive testing as a means of regulating access to education and opportunities, noting the inaccuracy of such instruments in measuring cognitive ability given varying cultural experiences.

As Counseling Psychology became a recognized specialty with divisional status in the American Psychological Association (APA), an early president of the then-Division of Counseling Psychology (Division 17), Milton Hahn, noted, "Our most nearly unique single function . . . [is] the casting of a psychological balance sheet to aid our clients to contribute to, and to take the most from, living in our society" (Hahn, 1954, p. 246). Furthermore, Whiteley (1984) commented that the development of the field was highly influenced by the context in which the field grew. Post–World War II years gave way to the civil rights movement and social upheaval of the 1960s, the war on poverty, and the growing recognition of social inequities among racial/ethnic minorities. Whiteley summarized the effect of this time period on counseling psychology, saying that "the social context for [this period in counseling psychology history was] a ferment of rising expectations within American society that previously had been disenfranchised" (p. 26). This continued through the 1970s as noted by Delworth's comment about counseling psychology as a field: "At our best, we are . . . prepared to deal with the serious social and moral issues of our society" (1977, p. 43).

But the 1980s and early 1990s saw a greater influence on the field related to the employment of counseling psychologists rather than counseling psychologists' advocacy for others. Fretz and Simon (1992) documented the strong influences on counseling psychology from medicine, psychiatry, clinical psychology, and managed care. Fouad, Helledy, and Metz (2003) summarized themes from the Division 17 presidential addresses, noting that many of these speeches in the 1980s and early 1990s targeted the market forces outside of counseling psychology that appeared to have influenced counseling psychology to focus on identity issues, and how to best position themselves as competitive private practitioners.

Not surprisingly, as a result of this focus, social justice concerns faded from prominent view. However, some counseling psychologists continued to demonstrate greater interest and commitment to social advocacy. A task force, chaired by Derald Sue (Sue et al., 1982) and appointed by then-Division 17 President Allen Ivey, developed the Cross-Cultural Counseling Competencies. As additional examples, Janet Helms (1986) applied her seminal work on racial identity to the counseling process, and Nancy Betz and Gail Hackett began to look at women's confidence as a variable preventing them from choosing math or science careers (Betz & Hackett, 1981; Hackett & Betz, 1981). However, most of the counseling psychologists involved in social advocacy work operated independently. At this time, there was no major, systematic emphasis on social justice and advocacy in the field of counseling psychology even though a call for such an emphasis was voiced at the Third National Conference for Counseling Psychology held in Atlanta in 1987. For example, the Professional Practice Working Group at this conference reported that one important focus of counseling psychology should be employing "strategies for change such as advocacy, political involvement, and direct teaching of skills relevant to promoting the psychological health of individuals, groups, and systems" (Kagan et al., 1988, p. 351).

By the late 1990s and the early years of the current century, greater efforts toward social justice became more visible in the profession. Major contributions in *The Counseling Psychologist* provided evidence of a movement for counseling psychologists to become more activist oriented, not just in their research but also in their practice. Counseling psychologists were encouraged to play a broader role in policy setting and in shaping societal responses in schools (Blustein, Phillips, Jobin-Davis, Finkelberg, & Roarke, 1997; Worthington & Juntunen, 1997), in prevention (Romano & Hage, 2000) and welfare reform (Edwards, Rachal, & Dixon, 1999), and in combating racism (Thompson & Neville, 1999), as well as employing their skills to establish and maintain communities of peace throughout the world (Gerstein & Moeschberger, 2003; Norsworthy & Gerstein, 2003). Furthermore, counseling psychologists who were concerned about multicultural competence began to advocate for greater involvement in community activism, including encouraging counselors to be able to "exercise institutional intervention skills on behalf of their clients" and "work to eliminate biases, prejudice and discrimination" (Sue, Arredondo, & McDavis, 1992, p. 483). These were operationalized by Arredondo et al. (1996) as including working at an organizational level to address racism and changing institutional policies to promote advocacy against racism. In fact, the Guidelines on Multicultural Education, Training, Research, Practice and Organizational Change for Psychologists (APA, 2003), an initiative spearheaded by counseling psychologists to promote culture-centered practices for psychologists, encouraged psychologists to become organizational change agents.

Similarly, social justice was the focus of Nadya Fouad's 2000–2001 Division 17 presidential initiative and a prominent theme of the 2001 National Counseling Psychology Conference in Houston, Texas, co-chaired by Nadya Fouad and Bob McPherson. Fouad et al. (2004) traced the development of the focus on social justice in the conference and the underlying philosophical assumptions, as well as the logistics of the planning for the conference. A notable aspect of the conference was that planners asked three counseling psychologists (David Blustein, Nancy Elman, and Larry Gerstein) to develop social action groups, which were originally conceived as a set of small groups that would operate parallel to the conference. Each group focused on a separate policy issue (e.g., combating racism, domestic abuse, ethics of managed care, community violence), and each was intended to develop an action plan that would extend social justice activities beyond the conference itself.

The initial plan was to include about 90 conference participants in the social action groups. However, when the conference registration materials were distributed, more than 400 of the 1,000 registrants signed up for one or more social action groups, although only 77 participated in all of the social action group activities throughout the conference. Clearly, counseling psychologists were ready to participate in social justice activities in one form or another. The final activity of the conference was a town hall meeting in which participants were asked to respond to a variety of questions. When asked how important social justice activities were to the field, 88% indicated strong support for their importance.

Following the conference, a number of activities continued to indicate an interest in social justice work. At both the 2001 (San Francisco) and 2002 (Chicago) annual meetings of the American Psychological Association, Division 17 sponsored symposia, roundtable discussions, and informal meetings on social justice and advocacy. In fact, at both of these conferences, there was extensive dialogue about forming a Special Interest Group in the Division on social justice. In addition, following the Houston conference, an Internet discussion list of those interested in social justice remained active.

There is additional evidence of the growing interest in social justice work among counseling psychologists after the Houston conference. Upon assuming editorship of *The Counseling Psychologist* in 2002, Robert Carter initiated a forum on social justice. In his introduction, he noted,

> It is my hope that articles in the forum would provide counseling psychologists with a way to build a base of knowledge and recognition of social and economic issues that affect the people we seek to help, understand, and for whom we should advocate. (Carter, 2003, p. 12)

Since then, two major issues of *TCP* have focused on social justice (Goodman et al., 2004; Speight & Vera, 2004).

Even with these collective efforts, there are still significant concerns raised regarding the ability and commitment of the profession to affect social justice (e.g., Baluch, Pieterse, & Bolden, 2004; Helms, 2003). Counseling psychologists have been criticized for focusing too much on the status quo (Hage, 2003) and not being critical enough of the structural systems in which we, ourselves, work.

Thompson and Shermis (2004) suggested that counseling psychologists need to know more about oppression in the communities in which they work, and these authors also advocated ethnographic approaches to gain such knowledge. Speight and Vera (2004) noted that social advocacy is "action linked with theory to alter the status quo" (p. 113). Prilleltensky and Prilleltensky (2003) argued that counseling psychologists writing about social justice are in danger of being insular and of needlessly reinventing the wheel, exhorting the field to act on ways to eliminate oppression. Palmer (2004) also encouraged counseling psychologists to be more multidisciplinary. Watts (2004) noted that counseling psychologists too often are comfortable staying within prescribed "safe" parameters of advocacy and change; he encouraged counseling psychologists to play more of an activist role. The message from these critics is that it is not enough to educate and empower our various clients; we must actively work to dismantle the oppressive environments, systems, and structures in which they live and work. In addition, we may need to help bring about change to our institutions and organizations as well as to the way we work. Thus, it is not enough, for example, to help women choose nontraditional occupations—we must also work to question an occupational system that disempowers women's work choices and provides inequitable pay.

Clearly, the counseling psychology profession has displayed a renewed interest in social justice and advocacy expanding its role and function to serve both individuals and the society at large (e.g., Gerstein & Bennett, 1999; Goodman et al., 2004; Hage, 2003; Lee, 1998; Lewis, Lewis, Daniels, & D'Andrea, 1998; Vera & Speight, 2003). Counseling psychologists are involved in designing and modifying theories, strategies, and methods to reduce, prevent, and scientifically investigate systemic, structural, technological, legal, and physical forms of, for example, oppression, discrimination, injustice, inequality, and ethnopolitical conflict. Currently, the counseling profession is providing greater opportunities for students to learn various principles, strategies, and research methods of social justice, social action, and advocacy. Goodman et al. (2004) defined this work as "scholarship and professional action designed to change societal values, structures, policies, and practices, such that disadvantaged or marginalized groups gain increased access to these tools of self-determination" (p. 795).

It is within this context of counseling psychology in the early part of the 21st century that we conceived of this *Handbook*. Our deeply held commitment and action in social justice were fueled by the initiatives of the Houston conference and provided the original impetus. The next section describes the circumstances leading to the concept of this *Handbook*, specifically identifying the activities of three sections of the Society of Counseling Psychology during and after the Houston conference.

The Impetus and Evolution of the *Handbook*

During the Society for Counseling Psychology's (Division 17) Houston 2001 conference, the Section for Lesbian, Gay, and Bisexual Awareness (SLGBA), the Section for Ethnic and Racial Diversity (SERD), and the Section for the

Advancement of Women (SAW) came together in the spirit of creating stronger coalitions and alliances around social justice issues affecting each of their constituencies. It was hoped that such an alliance would facilitate members' awareness of issues across groups, ultimately enhancing their ability to be active and knowledgeable allies. An underlying premise, and the impetus for the name of the group, was that rather than competing for the small amount of resources ("a slice of the pie") typically available for marginalized groups and issues, it was important to work together to increase the amount of "pie" available. Hence, the More Pie Initiative was created as a cross-sectional group within APA's Division 17.

The first official meeting of More Pie was held at the 2001 APA convention in San Francisco. At that meeting, it was decided that More Pie should continue as a coalition consisting of representatives from SERD, SAW, and SLGBA, rather than initiating a separate section. In addition, it was decided that there should be a liaison with the potential formation of a Division 17 Special Interest Group on Social Justice. Since that time, members of other sections, such as the Section for Vocational Psychology and the Prevention Section, have maintained some involvement in More Pie activities. Among the many ideas generated at the 2001 meeting was the recommendation that a proposal be submitted for a roundtable session on social justice in counseling psychology for the 2002 APA convention. The commitment to coalition building during the proposal process resulted in a team of counseling psychologists who represented Division 17, More Pie, and the Social Justice Interest Group. At the 2002 APA convention in Chicago, this team hosted a roundtable titled "Collaboration Among Counseling Psychologists—Linking Diversity, Oppression and Social Justice" that addressed a wide range of topics and issues. The resulting comments from participants and facilitators emphasized the need for more opportunities to hear and share stories of social justice work by counseling psychologists, and in particular, interdisciplinary efforts to address various forms of social injustice. As a result of this feedback, the chairpeople of the roundtable approached representatives from the previously mentioned organizations and created a team of editors to develop a *Handbook* that would provide models and examples of social justice work for a wide range of settings and populations. The editors also consulted with the leaders (David Blustein, Nancy Elman, and Larry Gerstein) of the social justice groups at the Houston conference who had previously considered a book that would document the plans and activities resulting from the Social Action Groups. The collective decision was to combine efforts into this *Handbook*. Clearly, social justice activities in counseling psychology had moved from individual efforts to an organizational imperative.

Rationale and Goals for the *Handbook*

The 2002 APA convention roundtable reaffirmed the need for counseling psychologists to develop a sophisticated understanding of social justice, social action, and advocacy. However, there was limited literature guiding counseling psychologists in implementing social justice in their work and training. This *Handbook*, therefore, was envisioned to provide a comprehensive resource with a strong theoretical and practical basis that would foster leadership, vision, and action among counseling psychologists engaged in and potentially interested in social justice. In order to accomplish this objective, the *Handbook* was designed to achieve the following goals.

1. Serve as a tool to help students, educators, researchers, and practitioners integrate social justice and action into their professional identity, role, and function.
2. Trace the history of social justice and social action in counseling psychology.
3. Reestablish social justice as a core component of counseling psychology and provide validation and a sense of legitimacy for counseling psychologists doing social justice work.
4. Provide a conceptual "road map" of social justice and social action by offering a host of models and suggestions, as well as discussions of barriers, solutions, and resources.
5. Present exemplary models of social justice/action work performed by counseling psychologists in a diversity of settings, with a diversity of issues, and reflecting a diversity of types of actions.
6. Foster the movement of counseling psychology and multicultural counseling beyond individual and traditional practice to macro-level conceptual models, policy development and implementation, systemic strategies of structural and human change, cultural empowerment and respect, advocacy, technological innovation, and third and fourth generations of human rights activities.
7. Establish and strengthen collaboration and alliances among counseling psychologists and professionals from other disciplines.

To this end, each of the sections of this *Handbook* contains chapters that use systems and structural paradigms of group and community behavior grounded in multicultural issues and dynamics and provide a theoretical base and model of social justice work attending to interdisciplinary influences, ethical issues, and research implications.

Overview of the *Handbook*

In this introductory chapter, we have attempted to provide a foundation that includes a brief historical perspective of social justice in counseling psychology and the impetus for this *Handbook*. To further enhance the foundation needed for a professional identity that includes social action, Rebecca Toporek and Robert Williams, in the second chapter of the book, examine specific ethical issues and guidelines related to practice, training, and research in the pursuit of social justice. The main body of the *Handbook* is comprised of seven sections: training, school interventions, marginalized communities, career and vocational issues, health care issues, the international arena, and policy and legislation. Each of these sections is introduced by an overview chapter providing a broad review of issues and literature related to that section and introducing the chapters presented.

In the training section, Rebecca Toporek and Christopher McNally provide an overview of the literature regarding doctoral-level training in counseling psychology and social justice. Two additional chapters highlight specific examples of implementation of social justice into training. Regine Talleyrand, Rita Chi-Ying Chung, and Fred Bemak candidly chronicle the transformation of a graduate counseling program infusing social justice principles and practices. Next, Karen O'Brien, Sheetal Patel, Nancy Hensler-McGinnis, and Jennifer Kaplan present a unique model for the implementation and evaluation of service learning for undergraduate students that serves as a social justice intervention and training tool addressing domestic violence. The results of their program evaluation provide important implications for the teaching of social justice and multicultural awareness.

In the school interventions section of the *Handbook*, Gargi Roysircar provides an overview highlighting theoretical foundations that support social justice implementation in schools and describes the importance of recognizing the potential impact counseling psychologists can have as collaborators with communities and schools. The chapters in this section exemplify prevention in various programs and populations as well as describe specific programs and apply ecological models to the school setting. Elizabeth Vera, Brian Daly, Rufus Gonzales, Melissa Morgan, and Charu Thakral illustrate the complexities of engaging in community-based program development by providing a specific example of collaboration with a public school in a poor, urban, largely Latino neighborhood: a multi-systemic program aimed at fostering positive youth development and promoting school retention. Chalmer Thompson, Dorienna Alfred, Sherri Edwards, and Patricia Garcia present a social action organization that is community-driven and ecological in its focus toward educating African American students. Opportunities for systemic change through prevention interventions are explored by Meghan Davidson, Michael Waldo, and Eve Adams. In the final chapter of the schools section, Gargi Roysircar advocates for the suitability of ecological models for instituting culturally relevant social change in schools.

A wide range of marginalized communities are addressed in the next section of the *Handbook* through chapters that focus on social justice efforts undertaken by counseling psychologists to address populations and issues that have historically received minimal attention. Tania Israel presents an overview providing a conceptual framework for understanding marginalization as a reflection of oppression. Intimate partner violence as the subject of efforts for systemic change are addressed by Margret Bell and Lisa Goodman. Barbara Palombi and Alisa Matteson Mundt focus on the issues of college women with disabilities and present a model advocating for inclusion. Azara Santiago-Rivera, Kristin Talka, and Amy Tully describe alliances formed between Native American communities and psychologists to confront environmental racism. An examination of social justice issues of homeless mothers and the role of psychologists is contributed by Lisa Cosgrove. David Whitcomb and Michael Loewy describe the role of counseling psychologists in advocating on issues of gay, lesbian, and bisexual human rights. In the final chapter in this section, Sue Morrow, Donna Hawxhurst, Ana Montes de Vegas, Tamara

Abousleman, and Carrie Castañeda describe individual counseling as a form of social justice using a feminist and multicultural framework.

Given the importance of vocational and career work in counseling psychology, the overview chapter by Nadya Fouad in this next section presents a historical context for the integral relationship between social justice and vocational and career counseling within the field of counseling psychology. The next chapter, by Ruth Fassinger and Susanna Gallor, focuses on advocacy and legislation needed to bring about fair and just schools and workplaces (e.g., the Employment Non-Discrimination Act, Title IX, etc.) in four areas of human diversity (race/ethnicity, gender, sexual orientation, and disability). Rebecca Toporek and Robert Chope describe individual and systemic approaches to social justice issues in the third chapter, including a model of individual career counseling using an illustrative case and programmatic approaches to social justice issues; Toporek and Chope also discuss a number of ethical issues that arise in social justice work. In the final chapter in this section, Cindy Juntunen, Angela Cavett, Rhanda Clow, Venessa Rempel, Rachel Darrow, and Adam Guilmino provide an introduction to welfare reform and describe ways that counseling psychologists may influence the quality and relevance of services provided to recipients of welfare. Juntunen et al. also discuss the successes and challenges that may arise in the implementation of a partnership between counseling psychologists and a community agency.

Social justice issues abound in health care, and Gargi Roysircar provides an overview emphasizing the need for contextual approaches toward equity and access in health care systems. In this section of the *Handbook*, Joshua Hopps and William Liu expose the interaction of social class and the health care system, and the implication of counseling psychologists as members of systems that are often hostile to marginalized individuals and communities. Gargi Roysircar and Uyen Huynh examine health care issues of Vietnamese and Cambodian refugees in depth and describe a multidisciplinary approach to health education with this population. In the final chapter of the health care section, Christa K. Schmidt, Mary Ann Hoffman, and Nicole Taylor explicate how social justice can play a role in health psychology, with particular emphasis on HIV and AIDS, and outline a model of university and community agency partnership.

The next section of the *Handbook* highlights notable work being done by counseling psychologists in the international arena. The overview chapter written by Lawrence Gerstein provides a brief background of the history of counseling psychologists working outside of the United States with a particular emphasis on social justice activities. This chapter also introduces a framework to comprehend the issues and projects described by the chapters in this section. Finally, this overview chapter stresses the need for a greater number of counseling psychologists on interdisciplinary teams providing a host of culturally appropriate and effective services around the globe. Following this introductory chapter, Sharon Horne and Susan Mathews apply a multicultural feminist approach for engaging in international, cross-cultural consultation around social justice issues, particularly in Eastern Europe. Benedict T. McWhirter and Ellen Hawley McWhirter have authored a chapter that describes an innovative program to mentor couples in Chile that is based in liberation theology and the empowerment model. The fourth chapter in this section was written by Kathryn L. Norsworthy with contributions by Ouyporn Khuankaew. This chapter reports on some creative consulting efforts in Southeast Asia that draw from postcolonial studies, feminist psychology, critical theory, liberatory education, and participant action research. The next chapter in this section, written by Scott L. Moeschberger, Alicia Ordóñez, Jui Shankar, and Shonali Raney, discusses some strategies grounded in an awareness and engagement model to reduce and prevent conflict in El Salvadoran gangs, address the consequences of the damming of the Narmada River in India, and lower tension among the people struggling to settle the dispute over Kashmir. The final chapter by Lawrence Gerstein and Doris Kirkpatrick focuses on how counseling psychologists, through a reliance on social psychological, organizational, and Buddhist principles, can contribute to establishing and maintaining peaceful communities around the world with specific attention paid to various efforts geared toward resolving the Tibet-China conflict.

The final section of the *Handbook* focuses on counseling psychologists' involvement in policy and legislation that address issues of inequality and injustice. As an overview, Rebecca Toporek highlights the multitude of counseling psychologists who have been involved in public policy and social justice efforts both through APA and outside the organization. Furthermore, she provides information and resources that readers may use to enhance their capabilities as social change agents and advocates for implementation and modification of policy and legislation. Two additional chapters in this section of the *Handbook* provide unique narratives chronicling the careers of four counseling psychologists who have a long history of working toward social justice at a systems level through influencing public policy. First, Sandra Shullman, Bobbie Celeste, and Ted Strickland describe the trajectory of their careers and the increasing role that politics and public policy have played in their work. Second, Robert McPherson shares his experiences as an active proponent of groundbreaking legislation for client rights in the face of managed care. Additionally, he provides insight into the evolution of a career that actively integrates legislative and policy concerns with academic and administrative responsibilities.

In the final chapter of the *Handbook,* we, the editors, reflect on the issues and examples presented by the many distinguished contributors and propose implications for future directions in the field. The goal of this concluding chapter is to stimulate readers to develop and take action in relevant social justice arenas as well as to begin to envision and understand the central role that social justice plays in the past, present, and future of the field of counseling psychology.

Conclusion

We have argued that social justice has been a fundamental guiding principle of the field of counseling psychology from the beginning, even though the commitment to such work has waxed and waned over the years. In this chapter, we briefly traced the roots of social justice in counseling psychology and provided a context for our current examination of social justice in counseling psychology in the 21st century. It is clear that, as a field, we have a fair ways to go if, indeed, we want to embrace social justice as a central core identifying feature of our profession. Given the rapid and extensive decay of our social structure here in the United States and the basic and urgent needs of many people outside of the United States, we believe it is critical and imperative that counseling psychologists develop the conceptual, applied, and empirical knowledge and skills to engage in culturally appropriate and effective social justice and advocacy work. Equipping students with such a repertoire of competencies will ensure that counseling psychologists of the future will be able to successfully contribute to the effort to help reduce, eliminate, and/or prevent injustices experienced by individuals, groups, organizations, institutions, and in some instances, even nations. With the proper coursework, training, mentoring, and field experiences, counseling psychologists can play a pivotal role as social architects confronting and revising systems and structures that reinforce oppression, discrimination, injustice, inequality, human rights abuses, and ethnopolitical conflict. Furthermore, as social architects, counseling psychologists can contribute to the construction and implementation of systems and structures that honor human dignity and human rights, advance opportunities for all people regardless of background and personal characteristics, affirm ethnoreligious beliefs and behaviors, and provide for the equitable distribution of resources among individuals and nations. In this 21st century, it will take a coordinated, systematic effort among not only our world political leaders, but also an interdisciplinary team of professionals (e.g., social scientists, life and medical scientists, architects, engineers, urban planners) with various talents to achieve such objectives. Counseling psychologists can make a unique contribution to this team. In fact, as mentioned in this chapter and as will become evident when reading the remainder of this *Handbook,* some counseling psychologists are already serving on these teams as effective social architects meeting the needs of people, organizations, institutions, and, in a few instances, nations.

In conclusion, we are very hopeful that this *Handbook* will help set the stage for further discussions among our counseling psychology colleagues who are practitioners, faculty members, trainers, consultants, and students entering the field. Additionally, it is our intent that by recognizing interdisciplinary collaboration and contributions, diverse individuals and communities will enhance their mutual engagement, and consequently their strength, in the service of social justice. Ultimately, such service will reduce widespread suffering throughout the world.

References

American Psychological Association. (2003). Guidelines on multicultural education, training, research, practice, and organizational change for psychologists. *American Psychologist, 58,* 377–402.

Anderson, N. J., & Love, B. (1973). Psychological education for racial awareness. *Personnel & Guidance Journal, 51,* 666–670.

Arredondo, P., Toporek, R., Brown, S. P., Jones, J., Locke, D. C., Sanchez, J., & Stadler, H. (1996). Operationalization of the multicultural counseling competencies. *Journal of Multicultural Counseling & Development, 24,* 42–78.

Baluch, S. P., Pieterse, A. L., & Bolden, M. A. (2004). Counseling psychology and social justice: Houston . . . we have a problem. *The Counseling Psychologist, 32,* 89–98.

Betz, N. E., & Hackett, G. (1981). The relationship of career-related self-efficacy expectations to perceived career options in college women and men. *Journal of Counseling Psychology, 28,* 399–410.

Blustein, D. L., Phillips, S. D., Jobin-Davis, K., Finkelberg, S. L., & Roarke, A. E. (1997). A theory-building investigation of the school-to-work transition. *The Counseling Psychologist, 25,* 364–402.

Borow, H. (1990). Counseling psychology in the Minnesota tradition. *Journal of Counseling & Development, 68,* 266–275.

Carter, R. T. (2003). *The Counseling Psychologist* in the new millennium: Building a bridge from the past to the future. *The Counseling Psychologist, 31,* 5–15.

Delworth, U. (1977). Counseling psychology: A distinct practice speciality. *The Counseling Psychologist, 7,* 43–45.

Edwards, S. A., Rachal, K. C., & Dixon, D. N. (1999). Counseling psychology and welfare reform: Implications and opportunities. *The Counseling Psychologist, 27,* 263–284.

Fitzgerald, L. E. (1973). Women's changing expectations: New insights, new demands. *The Counseling Psychologist, 4,* 90–95.

Fouad, N. A., Helledy, K. I., & Metz, A. J. (2003). Leadership in Division 17: Lessons from the presidential addresses. *The Counseling Psychologist, 31,* 763–788.

Fouad, N. A., McPherson, R. H., Gerstein, L., Blustein, D. L., Elman, N., Helledy, K. I., & Metz, A. J. (2004). Houston, 2001: Context and legacy. *The Counseling Psychologist, 32,* 15–77.

Fretz, B. R., & Simon, N. P. (1992). Professional issues in counseling psychology: Continuity, change, and challenge. In S. D. Brown & R. W. Lent (Eds.), *Handbook of counseling psychology* (2nd ed., pp. 3–36). Oxford, UK: Wiley.

Geis, G. (1983). Criminal justice and adult offenders: An overview. *The Counseling Psychologist, 11,* 11–16.

Gerstein, L. H. (2002, April). *Global social activism: Counseling psychologists reaching out.* Symposium presented at the annual Great Lakes Counseling Psychology Conference, East Lansing, MI.

Gerstein, L. H., & Bennett, M. (1999). Quantum physics and mental health counseling: The time is . . . ! *Journal of Mental Health Counseling, 21,* 255–269.

Gerstein, L. H., & Moeschberger, S. (2003). Building cultures of peace: An urgent task for counseling professionals. *Journal of Counseling & Development, 81,* 115–120.

Goodman, L. A., Liang, B., Helms, J. E., Latta, R. E., Sparks, E., & Weintraub, S. R. (2004). Training counseling psychologists as social justice agents: Feminist and multicultural principles in action. *The Counseling Psychologist, 32,* 793–837.

Hackett, G., & Betz, N. E. (1981). A self-efficacy approach to the career development of women. *Journal of Vocational Behavior, 18,* 326–339.

Hage, S. M. (2003). Reaffirming the unique identity of counseling psychology: Opting for the "road less traveled by." *The Counseling Psychologist, 31,* 555–563.

Hahn, M. E. (1954). The training of rehabilitation counselors. *Journal of Counseling Psychology, 1,* 246–248.

Hansen, L. S. (1972). We are furious (female) but we can shape our own development. *Personnel & Guidance Journal, 51,* 87–93.

Hartung, P. J., & Blustein, D. L. (2002). Reason, intuition, and social justice: Elaborating Parsons's career decision making model. *Journal of Counseling and Development, 80,* 41–47.

Helms, J. E. (1986). Expanding racial identity theory to cover counseling process. *Journal of Counseling Psychology, 33,* 62–64.

Helms, J. E. (2003). A pragmatic view of social justice. *The Counseling Psychologist, 31,* 305–313.

Helms, J. E. (2004). The 2003 Leona Tyler Award address: Making race a matter of individual differences within groups. *The Counseling Psychologist, 32*(3), 473–483.

Herr, E. L., & Niles, S. G. (1998). Career: Social action in behalf of purpose, productivity, and hope. In C. C. Lee & G. R. Walz (Eds.), *Social action: A mandate for counselors* (pp. 117–136). Alexandria, VA: American Counseling Association.

Ivey, A. E., & Collins, N. M. (2003). Social justice: A long-term challenge for counseling psychology. *The Counseling Psychologist, 31,* 290–298.

Jackson, J. (2000). What ought psychology do? *American Psychologist, 55,* 328–330.

Jakubowski-Spector, P. (1973). Facilitating the growth of women through assertive training. *The Counseling Psychologist, 4,* 75–86.

Kagan, N., Armsworth, M. W., Altmaier, E. M., Dowd, E. T., Hansen, J. C., Mills, D. H., Schlossberg, N., Sprinthall, N. A., Tanney, M. F., & Vasquez, M. J. T. (1988). Professional practice of counseling psychology in various settings. *The Counseling Psychologist, 16,* 347–365.

Kiselica, M., & Robinson, M. (2001). Bringing advocacy counseling to life: The history, issues, and human dramas of social justice. *Journal of Counseling and Development, 79,* 387–397.

Lee, C. C. (1998). Professional counseling in a global context: Collaboration for international social action. In C. C. Lee & G. R. Walz (Eds.), *Social action: A mandate for counselors* (pp. 293–304). Alexandria, VA: American Counseling Association.

Lewis, J. A., Lewis, M. D., Daniels, J. A., & D'Andrea, M. J. (1998). *Community counseling: Empowerment strategies for a diverse society* (2nd ed.). Pacific Grove, CA: Brooks/Cole.

Lopez, R. E., & Cheek, D. (1977). The prevention of institutional racism: Training counseling psychologists as agents of change. *The Counseling Psychologist, 7,* 64–69.

Mays, V. M. (2000). A social justice agenda. *American Psychologist, 55,* 326–327.

Morrill, W. H., Oetting, E. R., & Hurst, J. C. (1974). Dimensions of counselor functioning. *Personnel & Guidance Journal, 52,* 354–359.

Norsworthy, K. L., & Gerstein, L. H. (2003). Counseling and communities of peace. Special issue of the *International Journal for the Advancement of Counseling, 25,* 197–324.

Palmer, L. K. (2004). The call to social justice: A multidiscipline agenda. *The Counseling Psychologist, 32,* 879–885.

Parsons, F. (1909). *Choosing a vocation.* Boston: Houghton Mifflin.

Paterson, D. G. (1957). The conservation of human talent. *American Psychologist, 12,* 134–144.

Prilleltensky, I., & Prilleltensky, O. (2003). Synergies for wellness and liberation in counseling psychology. *The Counseling Psychologist, 31,* 273–281.

Romano, J. L., & Hage, S. M. (2000). Prevention and counseling psychology: Revitalizing commitments for the 21st century. *The Counseling Psychologist, 28,* 733–763.

Samler, J. (1964). Where do counseling psychologists work? What do they do? What should they do? In A. S. Thompson & D. E. Super (Eds.), *The professional preparation of counseling psychologists: Report of the 1964 Greyston conference* (pp. 43–68). New York: Teachers College Press.

Schlossberg, N. K., & Pietrofesa, J. J. (1973). Perspectives on counseling bias: Implications for counselor education. *The Counseling Psychologist, 4,* 44–54.

Sedlacek, W. E., & Brooks, G. C. (1973). Racism and research: Using data to initiate change. *Personnel & Guidance Journal, 52,* 184–188.

Shoben, E. J., Jr. (1969). Student unrest: The climate of protest. *The Counseling Psychologist, 1,* 15–66.

Speight, S. L., & Vera, E. M. (2004). A social justice agenda: Ready, or not? *The Counseling Psychologist, 32,* 109–118.

Strickland, B. R. (2000). Misassumptions, misadventures, and the misuses of psychology. *American Psychologist, 55,* 331–338.

Sue, D. W., Arredondo, P., & McDavis, R. J. (1992). Multicultural counseling competencies and standards: A call to the profession. *Journal of Multicultural Counseling & Development, 20,* 64–88.

Sue, D. W., Bernier, J. E., Durran, A., Feinberg, L., Pedersen, P., Smith, E., & Vazquez-Nutall, E. (1982). Position paper: Cross-cultural counseling competencies. *The Counseling Psychologist, 10,* 45–52.

Thompson, A. S. (1990). Teachers College and counseling psychology: Innovator and integrator. *Journal of Counseling & Development, 68,* 260–265.

Thompson, C. E., & Neville, H. A. (1999). Racism, mental health, and mental health practice. *The Counseling Psychologist, 27,* 155–223.

Thompson, C. E., & Shermis, S. S. (2004). Tapping the talents within: A reaction to Goodman, Liang, Helms, Latta, Sparks, and Weintraub. *The Counseling Psychologist, 32,* 866–878.

Tyler, L. E. (1974). *Individual differences: Abilities and motivational directions.* East Norwalk, CT: Appleton-Century-Crofts.

Vera, E. M., & Speight, S. L. (2003). Multicultural competence, social justice, and counseling psychology: Expanding our roles. *The Counseling Psychologist, 31,* 253–272.

Watts, R. J. (2004). Integrating social justice and psychology. *The Counseling Psychologist, 32,* 855–865.

Whiteley, J. M. (1984). A historical perspective on the development of counseling psychology as a profession. In S. D. Brown & R. W. Lent (Eds.), *Handbook of counseling psychology* (pp. 3–55). New York: Wiley.

Williams, R. L. (1971). Abuses and misuses in testing black children. *The Counseling Psychologist, 2,* 62–73.

Worthington, R. L., & Juntunen, C. L. (1997). The vocational development of non-college bound youth: Counseling psychology and the school-to-work transition movement. *The Counseling Psychologist, 25,* 323–363.

CHAPTER 2

Ethics and Professional Issues Related to the Practice of Social Justice in Counseling Psychology

Rebecca L. Toporek and Robert A. Williams

> *Psychologists respect and protect civil and human rights and the central importance of freedom of inquiry and expression in research, teaching, and publication. They strive to help the public in developing informed judgments and choices concerning human behavior. In doing so, they perform many roles, such as researcher, educator, diagnostician, therapist, supervisor, consultant, administrator, social interventionist, and expert witness. (American Psychological Association [APA], 2002)*

This statement, taken from the Preamble of the Ethical Principles of Psychologists and Code of Conduct (APA, 2002), hereafter referred to as the "APA Code," identifies a range of professional roles and responsibilities of psychologists. Many of the roles noted in this statement are reasonable avenues that, when practiced from a place of ethics and accountability, can contribute significantly to the elimination of injustice, inequity, and bias.

There have been calls for a clearer and more consistent social justice presence in counseling psychology (Carter, 2003; Fouad et al., 2004; Ratts, D'Andrea, & Arredondo, 2004). This *Handbook* is designed to provide readers with the opportunity to see the wide range of roles, social issues, and projects through which counseling psychologists are contributing to social justice. The first chapter (Fouad, Gerstein, & Toporek) provides historical and conceptual underpinnings for the topics and approaches contained throughout the book. As discussed in that chapter, social justice has fluctuated in its acceptance within the profession of counseling psychology. Given this fluctuation, attention to ethics and ethical issues particular to situations involving counseling psychologists and social justice has been scarce. A more explicit discussion of ethics is necessary for a thoughtful and intentional base for social justice in practice, training, and research.

The intent of this chapter is to examine existing ethics documents for their potential to provide guidance and support for social justice work. Our primary focus will be on the APA Code (2002). However, we will also draw upon language and content presented in the ethics codes of other disciplines and specialties that historically have maintained social justice as a central tenet. In the second part of the chapter, we highlight ethical issues that may arise when working toward social justice and provide a case example demonstrating how a psychologist might attend to these issues. Finally, we provide recommendations regarding future development of ethical guidelines for social justice.

Working Definitions of Social Justice

With the renewed emphasis on social justice in counseling psychology, there is a need for a shared understanding of definitions and constructs. Two particular resources anchor our discussion. First, the Social Justice and Ethics Social Action Group that convened at the National Counseling Psychology Conference (Houston, 2001) established the following working definition of "social justice":

> A concept that advocates engaging individuals as coparticipants in decisions which directly affect their lives; it involves taking some action, and educating individuals in order to open possibilities, and to act with value and respect for individuals and their group identities, considering power differentials in all areas of counseling practice and research. (Blustein, Elman, & Gerstein, 2001, p. 9)

Second, Toporek and Liu (2001) distinguished between the related concepts of advocacy, empowerment, social action, and social justice, and they helped to define the construct of social justice within the framework of the counseling profession. They described a model using client advocacy as a unifying construct with empowerment on one end of a continuum and social action on the other. Toporek and Liu provided the following definition for advocacy.

> [Advocacy is] action a mental health professional, counselor, or psychologist takes in assisting clients and client groups to achieve therapy goals through participating in clients' environments. Advocacy may be seen as an array of roles that counseling professionals adopt in the interest of clients, including empowerment, advocacy, and social action. (p. 387)

Empowerment was described as action taken with a client to facilitate his or her ability to act in the face of oppression, whereas social action was described as action taken by the counselor, external to the client, to confront or act on behalf of client groups (Toporek & Liu, 2001). These definitions, and the definition of social justice provided by the Social Justice Ethics Work Group of the Houston conference, provide anchors for our examination of the relevance and utility of existing ethical codes.

Ethical Codes and Guidelines

Ethics codes, guidelines, and decision-making models serve as tools for ethical behavior. Within the APA Code (2002), the language that addresses social justice most clearly may be found in the Preamble and Principles. It is important to note that the Preamble and General Principles are "aspirational goals to guide psychologists toward the highest ideals of psychology. Although the Preamble and General Principles are not themselves enforceable rules, they should be considered by psychologists in arriving at an ethical course of action" (p. 1061). As aspirational guidelines, these have the potential to facilitate decision making regarding issues that arise in the course of social action.

In our review of the APA Code (2002), as well as the Canadian Code of Ethics for Psychologists (Canadian Psychological Association [CPA], 2000), the Association of Black Psychologists's Ethical Standards of Black Psychologists (Akbar & Nobles, 2002), the Feminist Therapy Ethical Code (Feminist Therapy Institute [FTI], 1999), and the National Association of Social Workers Code of Ethics (National Association of Social Workers [NASW], 1999), three recurring constructs seemed relevant for ethical practice in social justice: respect, responsibility, and action. We will organize our examination of the ethical codes around these three themes, with particular attention to the APA Code. Within each section, we will also note criticisms that have been voiced and draw upon other ethical codes for guidance.

Respect

Respect for the integrity and strength of affected communities and clients is the core of any kind of work aimed at improving the conditions of oppressed groups. The APA Code (2002), Principle E, Respect for People's Rights and Dignity, asserts that it is imperative to respect cultural differences and take these into consideration when working with ethnic groups. Although this is laudable, clearer guidelines are needed regarding how this respect may be operationalized—for example, utilizing respect and awareness of a community's values and mores as determining forces in engaging in social justice interventions. A useful guideline for psychologists who are engaged in community work can be found in the CPA Code (2000), which states that psychologists must "acquire an adequate knowledge of the culture, social structure, and customs of a community before beginning any major work there" (Respect for

Society, Paragraph 1). This is strengthened by the assertion that psychologists must "convey respect for and abide by prevailing community mores, social customs, and cultural expectations in their scientific and professional activities" (Respect for Society, Paragraph 2). The inclusion of the need to "abide" by the community and cultural mores helps to secure the position of the community as a driving force in the intervention.

The Ethical Standards of Black Psychologists goes even further in its ethical standards, stressing that Black psychologists are expected to "give deference to the will and intent of Black people" (Akbar & Nobles, 2002, p. 8). This strengths-based perspective conveys the assumption that the intent of Black people and human beings is inherently toward growth rather than destruction. This is articulated with regard to research in the statement, "This research should be reflective of the psychological strengths of Black people and/or should be focused on the cultivation of strengths which will foster such improvement" (Akbar & Nobles, 2002, p. 7). This high level of respect is commensurate with the responsibility and political implications of one's role as psychologist of a given age, race, ethnicity, social class, gender, sexual orientation, and disability status.

Respect thus lays a foundation for social justice work by ensuring that the psychologist understands and abides by the community's strengths, goals, and determination.

Responsibility

In our reading of ethical codes, three issues seemed to reflect a construct we identified as "responsibility": ensuring equal access to psychology, minimizing the effects of bias and discrimination, and serving oppressed communities. First, the APA Code (2002), Principle D, Justice, states, "Psychologists recognize that fairness and justice entitle all persons to access to and benefit from the contributions of psychology and to equal quality in the processes, procedures, and services being conducted by psychologists" (p. 1062). This statement may be interpreted as a suggestion that the expertise held by psychologists should be shared with all who can benefit. The difficulty, however, lies in the condition that systemic injustice may hinder equal access and quality of care. There is a need for clearer directives regarding the role that psychologists might have in eradicating the injustice that limits access to services.

The second ethical issue related to responsibility is that of bias. Principle D, Justice, of the APA Code (2002) states, "Psychologists exercise reasonable judgment and take precautions to ensure that their potential biases, the boundaries of their competence, and the limitations of their expertise do not lead to or condone unjust practices" (pp. 1062–1063). In addition, Principle G, Human Relations, clearly states that psychologists should not engage in discrimination and harassment. These statements take important steps in acknowledging the responsibility that counseling psychologists have to eliminate their own biases. However, it appears that the extent of the responsibility is directed toward the psychologist's own behavior. Notably, some authors (e.g., Brown, 1997) have charged that this approach is reactive and does not go far enough in asserting the need for psychologists to actively rectify discrimination and other forms of oppression. If counseling psychologists are committed to social justice, there is a need for clearer statements encouraging prevention of unjust practices as ethical behavior. One example of such language is seen in the NASW (1999) ethical code, which states that social workers "are sensitive to cultural and ethnic diversity and strive to end discrimination, oppression, poverty, and other forms of social injustice" (Paragraph 2).

The third area of responsibility may be described as an expectation that professionals actively serve members of oppressed groups and, in doing so, acknowledge the complexities of the group and oppressive circumstances. This ranges from direct statements, such as the responsibility of Black psychologists to return their expertise to the Black community (Akbar & Nobles, 2002), to statements asserting responsibility to serve marginalized or vulnerable groups. As an example of the latter type of statement, the CPA Code (2002) states,

> Although psychologists have a responsibility to respect the dignity of all persons with whom they come in contact in their role as psychologists, the nature of their contract with society demands that their greatest responsibility be to those persons in the most vulnerable position. (Values Statement, Paragraph 3)

Similarly, Bowman (1991) asserted that not only should psychologists learn about the communities that they serve, but they should be a part of the development of "special safeguards" in research to ensure that "vulnerable race and class groups are not systematically selected because of their compromised position, their open vulnerability, and their manipulability" (p. 753). Such a stance conveys both respect and responsibility for both the individuals and the communities that are being served. Although the APA Code (2002), Principle E: Respect for People's Rights and Dignity, refers to "special safeguards," it appears that this was written specifically to "protect the rights and welfare of persons or communities whose vulnerabilities impair autonomous decision making" (p. 1063), and it is uncertain whether this is meant to generalize to populations who are not "impaired."

Responsibility has been described as having a duty to serve oppressed groups, eliminate oppression, and make efforts to be conscientious in how one engages and intervenes within a community. Respect and responsibility lead to the third area of ethical practice, social action.

Social Action

Ethics in social justice inherently invoke an explicit call to action. Ethical codes we reviewed for this chapter varied in the extent and nature of the action expected of the professional. Attention to social action appeared to be articulated in the APA Code (2002), primarily through Principle B: Fidelity and Responsibility, which states that "psychologists strive to contribute a portion of their professional time for little or no compensation or personal advantage" (p. 1062). This statement encouraging pro bono work may be important in serving communities with limited resources. However, there is no clear expectation that these are the communities that psychologists will serve or that part of the work will be toward eliminating injustice.

Payton (1994) expressed concern regarding the shift from a focus on human rights, present in earlier ethical codes, to "a need to protect psychologists" (p. 317). Similarly, other authors have charged that APA Codes are written with the intent to protect the consumer and the profession, and that this emphasis does little to facilitate active involvement in confronting injustice (e.g., Brown, 1997; Lerman & Porter, 1990; Payton, 1994).

It is possible that the roles outlined in the Preamble of the APA Code (2002) have been interpreted in such a way that limits counseling psychologists' view of the appropriateness and relevance of social action. A review of such language in ethics documents of other organizations illustrates how social action may be articulated more clearly in ethical guidelines. For example, the CPA Code (2002) provides a very brief but direct call to action, stating the expectation that psychologists "act to correct practices that are unjustly discriminatory" (Nondiscrimination, Paragraph 2). The NASW is more explicit in its principle of "Social and Political Action," which states,

> Social workers should engage in social and political action that seeks to ensure that all people have equal access to the resources, employment, services, and opportunities they require to meet their basic human needs and to develop fully. . . . Social workers should act to expand choice and opportunity for all people, with special regard for vulnerable, disadvantaged, oppressed, and exploited people and groups. (Social and Political Action, Paragraphs 1–2)

Finally, a variety of assertions regarding the multiple ways in which a feminist therapist may take social action are listed in a section of the Feminist Therapy Code of Ethics (FTI, 1999) explicitly titled "Social Change." Examples of these assertions include the following: "A feminist therapist seeks multiple avenues for impacting change, including public education and advocacy within professional organizations, lobbying for legislative action, and other appropriate activities" (Social Change, Paragraph 1) and "A feminist therapist actively questions practices in her community that appear harmful to clients or therapists. She assists clients in intervening on their own behalf" (FTI, 1999; Social Change, Paragraph 2). Similarly, counseling psychologists who endorse social justice as part of their practice must understand that social action is an inherent part of such practice. This action may be accomplished through a range of roles, including, but not limited to, overt political action (Toporek & Liu, 2001). For example, the events leading to *Larry P. v. Riles* (1984), which currently blocks intelligence testing in San Francisco public schools, exemplifies a group of Black psychologists that used its roles as expert witnesses, clinicians, educators, and researchers to engage in political action, policy development, and implementation.

Counseling psychologists have a unique mission, skill set, and field of expertise. That uniqueness does not preclude counseling psychologists from drawing on the experience of related fields to develop ethical guidelines that facilitate, support, and guide intentional and ethical social justice interventions. Furthermore, ethical decision making is facilitated by awareness of ethical complexities that may arise in social justice endeavors. Hence, we turn our attention now to a review of issues that may arise, presenting ethical dilemmas for counseling psychologists.

Ethical Issues, Social Justice, and Counseling Psychology

Several authors have identified ethical issues related to social justice and advocacy in counseling (e.g., Goodman et al., 2004; Kiselica & Robinson, 2001; Toporek & Liu, 2001). Although not exhaustive, six major themes can be distilled from a review of this literature: competence, assumptions and worldview, politics, roles and boundaries, informed consent, and "do no harm." On the surface, these themes reflect those generally found in ethics discussions. However, their meanings take on different levels of complexity when considered within a framework of social justice; so much so that traditional definitions and conceptualizations are inadequate. To explore this complexity, we will present dimensions of these six themes followed by a case vignette illustrating a therapist's attention to each of the themes.

Competence

Competence is identified as one of the key elements of the APA Code (APA, 2002). "In those emerging areas in which generally recognized standards for preparatory training do not yet exist, psychologists nevertheless take reasonable steps to ensure the competence of their work and to protect clients/patients, students, supervisees, research participants, organizational clients, and others from harm" (APA, 2002, p. 1064).

Because concentrated attention to social justice within counseling psychology is relatively recent, it is reasonable to consider it "an emerging area." Unfortunately, there has been little examination of what competence means with regard to the practice of social justice. Numerous psychologists have asserted that the profession of counseling and counseling psychology has tended toward individual approaches and intrapsychic explanations for clients' distress (Haverkamp, 1994; Lewis, Lewis, Daniels, & D'Andrea, 1998; Prilleltensky, Dokecki, Friedan, & Wang, in press; Toporek & Pope-Davis, 2005). Given this emphasis, counseling psychologists who work with clients experiencing distress due to external, structural forces run the risk of conveying the belief that the individual is at fault for the injustice he or she is experiencing. Prilleltensky et al. (in press) charged that the counseling profession has been deficient in systemic-level training and neglects the environment and sociopolitical context because of the overemphasis on intrapsychic interventions. It follows that competent practice requires that counseling psychologists need to be trained to recognize the role of external forces in clients' lives and initiating systemic interventions such as advocacy and social action (Toporek & Liu, 2001).

A second aspect of competence reflects professional limitations. Kiselica and Robinson (2001) noted that in order to adhere to the ethical principle of recognizing one's professional limitations, counselors involved in social justice work must avoid being overzealous and making "promises they can't keep" (p. 394). Furthermore, they cautioned that, at times, during activist activities, professionals may become overly enthusiastic and consequently exaggerate the cause. Ethical social justice practice requires that counseling psychologists accurately reflect the people and causes they represent. Similarly, counseling psychologists must be genuine about their ability to take an advocacy or social justice position and acknowledge the limits of their professional ability to do so. This concern may also be reflected by full informed consent (discussed later in this chapter) in that psychologists and clients need to be clear about the means by which, and extent to which, a psychologist may be acting on a client's behalf or acting as an independent professional or individual.

A third aspect of competence reflects the psychologist's awareness of his or her well-being and ability to perform. Dinsmore (as cited in Kiselica & Robinson, 2001) noted,

> There is often a high price to pay for being an activist, including feeling emotionally drained, being viewed as a troublemaker, placing your job in jeopardy, and becoming the target of backlash from colleagues at work or of harassment from intolerant individuals. (p. 393)

It is the responsibility of counseling psychologists to monitor and modify practice when their well-being or political situation may negatively affect their work, even when the negative effects result from the stress of challenging oppressive systems. The self-care aspect of competence influences a psychologist's ability to follow through with a course of action agreed upon by the community or client and the psychologist. In addition, competence and well-being may take on special meaning when systemic opposition distracts from client-centered intent and can influence the psychologist's perspective, for better or worse.

Worldview and Assumptions

> The virtuous agent [is] one who (a) is motivated to do what is good, (b) possesses vision and discernment, (c) realizes the role of affect or emotion in assessing or judging proper conduct, (d) has a high degree of self-understanding and awareness, and, perhaps most importantly is connected with and understands the mores of his or her community and the importance of community in moral decision making, policy setting and character development and is alert to the legitimacy of client diversity in these respects. (Meara, Schmidt, & Day, 1996, pp. 28–29)

The summary of virtuous characteristics provided by Meara et al. highlights some of the critical elements related to the theme of worldview and assumptions. In this context, we are specifically targeting the aspect of worldview that influences the psychologist's perspective of the integrity of the client or community and the assessment of the extent to which the community is able to act on its own behalf. Toporek and Liu (2001) noted that there has been historical criticism of client advocacy based on the assumption that advocating for clients reinforces clients' feelings of helplessness. They acknowledged that the potential for paternalism exists, particularly when a psychologist outside of an oppressed community acts on behalf of that community. However, they also suggested that the intentions of psychologists can moderate the conditions under which advocacy is enacted. This underscores the need for counseling psychologists to be aware of their motives while involved in social justice work as well as their place of privilege based on social class, educational opportunities, race, gender, or other attributes.

The theme of assumptions and worldview also reflects issues of awareness regarding beliefs about what is the "right" thing to do or the "right" way to solve a problem. Goodman et al. (2004) raised this in their discussion of self-evaluation as a tenet of social justice work. This tenet may raise awareness of ethical issues affecting practice, such as in cases of incongruent cultural values between a psychologist and client group.

Dual Roles and Professional Boundaries

Because social justice work often requires systemic interventions, counseling psychologists may be called upon to take on roles that vary from traditional individual counseling. Having engaged in a self-reflective process and illuminated one's intent and assumptions about the client's capabilities, the counseling psychologist is in a better place to assess the context and identify appropriate and effective roles. It is important to note that the issue of competence resurfaces given that training programs historically have provided narrow guidance for counseling psychologists regarding their role with clients with little attention to roles such as advocate, social activist, consultant, and others. Multicultural scholars have noted the need for role variation for some time and have provided models (e.g., Atkinson, Thompson, & Grant, 1993) to help psychologists determine the appropriate role given the client, locus of the problem, and goal of counseling.

In a related vein, current professional standards have also been criticized for the constraints imposed on relationships with clients without consideration of context and culture (e.g., Brown, 1997; Kiselica & Robinson, 2001). Kiselica and Robinson (2001) noted that the issue of boundaries, as traditionally defined in counseling, may need to be revisited when working with marginalized clients who may be uncomfortable or reluctant to seek services in traditional settings. Likewise, being involved in social justice issues may result in clients and psychologists working side by side on a cause, thus raising the issue of dual relationships. Kiselica and Robinson cautioned that although it is appropriate to question definitions of boundaries, it is also important to recognize the validity of the concerns that may arise regarding the best interests of the client.

Politicizing of Social Justice

Another theme raised in the literature is the acknowledgment that social justice is political. Toporek and Liu (2001) noted that critics have raised concerns that the emphasis on multicultural counseling and social causes in counseling and psychology are used to further political causes. The public interest directorate has reported receiving regular letters from APA members expressing negative reactions that the directorate is taking a political stance by advocating about issues ranging from homelessness to immigration (Tomes, 1997). Whereas psychology has historically held the belief that the field itself is apolitical, there have been criticisms by multicultural and feminist scholars who have argued that psychology has never been apolitical (e.g., Aanstoos, 1986; Marecek, 1995; Prilleltensky, 1994; Smith, 2000). Social justice perspectives openly acknowledge the implicit political nature of asserting that clients and communities have a right to fair treatment; human dignity; and equal access to health care, education, and other resources. When a counseling psychologist examines his or her worldview and considers the implications of various roles, the danger of political and religious proselytizing in professional settings (Kiselica, 2003) is minimized. This examination and reexamination may be enhanced by ongoing collaboration with the community as well as mentors and colleagues.

The political nature of social justice counseling may be seen in Goodman et al.'s (2004) examination of ethical issues relevant to two counseling goals: giving voice and consciousness raising. Giving voice to clients or communities who have traditionally been silenced regarding their experience of oppression represents one aspect of social justice counseling. Difficult decisions may arise when counseling psychologists must choose which voices are amplified through advocacy or even in the choices of research foci. This presents itself particularly when there are limited resources, dissenting perspectives, and goals that may seem self-destructive. Goodman et al. provided an example of a counseling trainee advocating to amplify the voice of a female adolescent who, in the process of counseling, made life choices that were potentially harmful. The ethical dilemma arose for the trainee regarding the balance of giving voice to the adolescent while also working toward her well-being.

Two ethical considerations relate to the goal of consciousness raising. First, Goodman et al. (2004) pointed out that the act of consciousness raising, a political act, suggests that the psychologist has achieved some level of critical consciousness that is superior to that of the client or group. This assumption calls upon the psychologist to examine his or her worldview and beliefs. A second ethical issue may develop as a result of raising a client's consciousness regarding his or her oppressive circumstances in the absence of strategies for coping with or addressing those circumstances. We would like to highlight the need for a partnership between social action and consciousness raising. Furthermore, consciousness raising, in and of itself, may not be sufficient or even desirable if there is no attention to the consequences of the newly acquired perspective and potential for positive action.

Informed Consent

Informed consent is a historically central aspect of ethical practice and research. However, this construct may take on different meanings in social justice counseling, particularly in light of the need to work at multiple levels of interventions. Ensuring informed consent is the practice of providing individuals with information regarding services and interventions, thereby allowing them to make informed choices regarding acceptance and participation in those activities. Pope (1990) identified several issues pertaining to informed consent in prevention work and suggested collaborative development of general agreements regarding the methods used in community interventions. In addition, he posed the following questions:

> Yet even in the cases of these "general agreement" goals, are we not ethically responsible for examining the implications of what we're asking people to adjust and adapt to? What are the values implicit in this adjustment and adaptation? What are we influencing people to give up and to move toward, and at what personal and social costs? Some methods must be developed for ensuring that the individual's right "to be left alone" is given due weight. (Acting Only With Informed Consent, Paragraph 4)

Similarly, Goodman et al. (2004) noted two specific questions that bring complexity to the issue when multiple individuals or groups are involved: "Whose consent was necessary to obtain?" and "What would we do if some participants did not consent?" (p. 822). These questions highlight intricacies of informed consent that are not often encountered in traditional counseling approaches. The construct of informed consent needs to be enhanced within training and practice to assist psychologists in considering the multiple questions that arise as well as help clients consider the potential consequences of intervention.

Do No Harm

As with accountability and informed consent, the axiom of "Do no harm" needs to be considered differently within the context of social justice. The method of determining the potential for harm may vary depending on the population involved and is complicated when multisystemic interventions are enacted. Pope (1990) discussed the complexity of determining whether a community is harmed by an intervention, including dimensions such as the influence of the intervention on the community's social ecology, natural leadership, cohesiveness, and sense of self-determination. This assessment is further complicated by considering the potential effects of cultural and social class differences between the counseling psychologist and the community. Pope also described the need to assess the impact of a social intervention on the relationship of the community with the larger society using the following example:

> For example, a project might be planned to minimize the incidence of serious depression, anxiety, and impulsive behavior in an economically-disadvantaged neighborhood. Yet the disorders to be prevented might be viewed by others than those undertaking the project as a natural response to severe poverty. Attempting to eliminate such reactions to poverty might be a subtle, perhaps unintended, form of social control helping people learn to adapt and adjust to desperate conditions. Such efforts may tend to "quieten" a community or "keep the lid on." They may hinder the community's ability to identify the true source of its suffering and take effective action. (Do No Harm, Paragraph 12)

Pope (1990) recommended the development of an "impact report" discussing the impact of the intervention on all aspects of community life. In addition, psychologists may need to work with the community to identify the problem and possible interventions, including the possible consequences of interventions, in order to ensure informed consent. Raising the consciousness of the community about the political context could be crucial.

The principle of Do No Harm may also be relevant when considering Goodman et al.'s (2004) discussion of another ethical question. They posited that building clients' strengths and facilitating empowerment may emphasize for the clients the degree of control they "should" have in an oppressive system. Goodman et al. questioned the ethics of working to help clients feel empowered when they are actually in an unresponsive and oppressive system.

The Practice of Social Justice: A Case Vignette

The following is a case vignette that demonstrates a therapist's effort at engaging in ethically sound social justice. Through this case study, we would like to illustrate several of the issues discussed in the above section, articulate how these may or may not have been addressed by the therapist, and conclude by reflecting on ways the therapist may enhance his or her response in light of these issues. This vignette is presented chronologically; thus, there were multiple decision points that could have resulted in different outcomes had the therapist chosen different routes. The reader should be curious about how the therapist engaged in ethical decision making, but should also wonder how he or she might have approached the same situation given age, race, ethnicity, social class, gender, sexual orientation, and disability status similarities or differences.

The Case of the Couple, Their Nephew, and the Justice System

A 20-something African American male therapist met with a middle-aged, heterosexual, African American couple, who presented because the husband was on a conditional release from the state mental health agency, after being found not guilty by reason of insanity. He had been released for more than 20 years, but had to maintain regular contact with a designated mental health agency. During the regular check-in with the therapist, the couple mentioned that they were distressed because their nephew was being prosecuted for a murder he did not commit. The couple believed their nephew was being truthful. In session, they lamented his fate and the racism that caused him to be jailed and possibly imprisoned.

At this point, the therapist felt that he had some training and competence in addressing sociopolitical forces. Thus, he felt it appropriate to include a social justice approach as an aspect of this case. It is noteworthy that neither the therapist nor the agency had a reputation for social advocacy or justice.

Initially, the couple seemed to be using the therapy time for validation of their feelings of hopelessness in the situation pertaining to their nephew. Thus, the therapist validated their feelings, without agreeing that the situation was hopeless. After the therapist felt satisfied that he had empathized with the couple, he shifted to collaborating with them on what to do next. The couple indicated that they wanted "justice" for their nephew. The therapist asked them to describe what the justice would look like. Their reply was that their nephew would be out of jail. The therapist asked the couple to talk about any solutions they had tried before. They conveyed that they had not tried anything and were resigned to the hopelessness of the situation.

The therapist assessed the couple's competency, assuming that they had already attempted solutions to the problem they described. Hearing that they had not tried any, the therapist began to shift toward collaborating on solutions, rather than paternalistically imposing solutions. At this point, the process of becoming aware of the couple's knowledge and worldview, as well as those of the therapist, allowed the therapist to make informed choices about empowering and appropriate roles. He was operating from his personal principle of "only do for a family what it cannot do for itself." The therapist, an African American male, who was from a more advantaged social class than the couple, felt it would have been inappropriate to assume that the couple "should" advocate for themselves in the same manner as other middle- and upper-class families might advocate for their relatives in the justice system.

The couple said that they would like to support their nephew in his court appearances and appeals. But they did not see themselves as having any other role in advocating for him. After asking the couple to offer any other ideas on how they could help, the therapist shifted from the role of collaborator to that of expert. He asked the couple if they had ever heard of the attorney general. Because they had not, he described the attorney general as the highest ranking lawyer in the state and explained that it was the attorney general's responsibility to look into concerns they might have about impropriety. The therapist suggested that the attorney general would listen if they, as state citizens, had a legitimate cause and that because the attorney general was an elected official, they had a way to let him know whether he was doing a good enough job.

In the above dialogue, the therapist began to shift away from collaborator and move toward expert because his assessment indicated that the couple was uninformed about their legal options. At the end of the interaction, the therapist became concerned that his advocacy could easily become a public matter, resulting in a possible newsworthy event, and considered how he could maintain appropriate boundaries while also seeing his advocacy reach a reasonable endpoint. This potential highlights the need for informed consent given possible consequences the couple might face if their actions resulted in public attention.

The couple indicated that they did not know what to do, so they were resigned to wait until the court dates. The therapist asked them what outcome they hoped for, to which they replied that their nephew would be home and justice would be served. The therapist obtained the couple's permission to collaboratively problem solve ways to make this possible.

Throughout this session, one can see that the therapist refrained from imposing his social justice agenda. In an effort to ensure informed consent, he sought permission to proceed at each step toward social justice. This is important because psychologists who are involved in social justice may forget that some clients have not given much thought to self-advocacy or may not feel entitled to do so. Thus, psychologists may need to introduce aspects of social justice progressively in an effort to accompany rather than lead clients to action.

Consistent with the principle of not doing more for families than what they can do for themselves, the therapist systematically and collaboratively worked with the couple toward initiating action beyond supporting their nephew in court appearances. This was done by asking the couple if they knew how to identify and contact appropriate government officials, then assisting them in this process using the telephone book to find the state attorney general and local district attorney. As a result of this in-session problem-solving and solution-finding task, the couple indicated that they felt that action was possible. The couple then role-played how they might talk to the attorney general or district attorney. The therapist offered the couple the opportunity to make the call from his office, but they decided to make the call on their own. From there, the couple and therapist checked in weekly regarding the matter. Although the wheels of justice were slow, the couple was able to facilitate their nephew's release on bail, pending a second trial.

Reflecting on the Vignette

In the above vignette, the therapist (a) engaged in social justice because he felt he had some competence and training in this area, (b) had an awareness of his beliefs and intentions and was therefore able to collaborate rather than patronize, (c) carefully chose appropriate roles given the context and strengths of the couple as well as established appropriate boundary separation between "behind the scenes" involvement versus more public advocacy, and (d) attempted to maintain informed consent throughout the process.

The therapist's postcounseling reflections suggested that it may have been helpful to inform the couple about additional resources and collaborate with them to discover published resources such as the NAACP Legal Defense and Education Fund, as well as other nonprofit organizations that provided legal advocacy. In addition, establishing complete informed consent would have involved educating the couple regarding any potential negative and positive implications of their advocacy actions as well as the possible duration of advocacy necessary. In the long run, the therapist's goal was to help the couple develop skills that they could generalize in any kind of social justice matter similar to the tenet of "leaving the clients tools for social change," as described by Goodman et al. (2004, p. 798).

Another ethical concern may result when a therapist encourages a client to engage in a particular action even when there is a good likelihood that the advocated position may fail. It is possible that a state attorney general would be less likely to listen to the above-described couple than an advocacy group. Thus, it can be equally important to realistically prepare the couple for possible response or lack thereof. This is an example of how complex the choices may be in terms of determining an appropriate role and intervention. At times, empowerment of the couple may be enough, whereas at other times, empowerment may be combined with independent action or advocacy on the part of the psychologist independent from the client (Toporek & Liu, 2001). On a final note, this vignette provided an illustration of the "both-and" principle, rather than the "either-or" principle. It is often thought that "either" one engages in social justice "or" one engages in psychotherapy. The therapist endeavored to provide "both" psychotherapy "and" social justice. This parallels literature that emphasizes the need to balance intrapsychic and extrapsychic interventions (e.g., Boyd-Franklin, 2003; Haverkamp, 1994).

Recommendations for Future Developments

In light of existing ethical codes and issues as described in the social justice literature, we propose several recommendations for future directions to optimize ethical behavior and decision making.

First, there is a need for clearer and more direct language in ethics codes regarding the professional responsibility of psychologists to address social injustice. Additionally, specific recommended competencies for social justice work would help guide counseling psychologists and increase informed principled behavior. Feminist, multicultural, and prevention perspectives have established language that may be useful. Several documents provide competencies that are relevant to social justice initiatives (e.g., APA, 1990, 2000). Additionally, other disciplines have developed guidelines that may be very relevant for social justice approaches in counseling psychology. For example, the American Counseling Association has articulated a set of advocacy competencies (Lewis, Arnold, House, & Toporek, 2001) that outlines competencies and goals for counselors at three different levels: client or student, school or community, and larger public arena. The goals include empowerment, collaboration, information, and advocacy. Although this document is specifically focused on advocacy, it offers guidance for defining similar competencies for social justice.

Second, guidelines that could be used for ethical decision making for social justice in individual and community interventions would be useful; for example, the model for ethical decision making described by Ridley, Liddle, Hill, and Li (2001). This model involves two dimensions: stages (critical reflection and creative problem solving) and process (ethical consideration of cultural data and the ethical resolution of cultural conflicts) integrating attention to cultural contexts and implications. This type of model may be useful in social justice counseling given its attention to external and contextual variables.

Third, training programs will need to adjust their curricula to incorporate social justice interventions in order to broaden counseling psychologists' competence. In contrast to Prilleltensky et al. (in press), we believe that counseling psychologists can practice social justice ethically and can develop a scope of competence in this arena. At the same time, we agree that practitioners, researchers, and educators need to be trained to recognize external and systemic forces of oppression and intervene appropriately.

Fourth, research is needed to examine the impact of different ethical decision-making models on clients and counseling psychologists particularly in light of the complexities presented in social justice interventions. In addition, research regarding the efficacy of counseling psychologists undertaking alternative roles would be useful. Qualitative and quantitative research that assists psychologists in developing models for appropriate balance between individual and structural conceptualizations and interventions in counseling could help increase the cultural relevance of work with clients facing a variety of oppressive contexts.

Conclusion

Although the APA Code (2002) notes areas of ethical concern that may be applied to social justice in counseling psychology, complexities exist that suggest that there is a need for clearer guidance. For counseling psychology to truly demonstrate a commitment to positive social change, ethical codes and guidelines should reflect the issues inherent in this work. Related professions, organizations, and specializations that have historically centralized social justice should be considered as resources in the pursuit of more relevant guidelines. Finally, there is a need for more directed training and research to facilitate greater social justice competence at both organizational and individual levels in the profession of counseling psychology.

References

Aanstoos, C. M. (1986). The politics of psychology. *Humanistic Psychologist, 14*(1), 3–4.

Akbar, N., & Nobles, W. (2002). Ethical standards of Black psychologists. *Psychological Discourse, 32*, 6–11.

American Psychological Association. (1990). *Guidelines for providers of psychological services to ethnic, linguistic, and culturally diverse populations.* Washington, DC: Author.

American Psychological Association. (2000). Guidelines for psychotherapy with lesbian, gay, and bisexual clients. *American Psychologist, 55*, 1440–1451.

American Psychological Association. (2002). Ethical principles of psychologists and code of conduct. *American Psychologist, 57*, 1060–1073.

Atkinson, D. R., Thompson, C. E., & Grant, S. K. (1993). A three-dimensional model for counseling racial/ethnic minorities. *The Counseling Psychologist, 21*(2), 257–277.

Blustein, D., Elman, N., & Gerstein, L. (2001, August). *Executive Report: Social Action Groups National Counseling Psychology Conference.* Houston, TX: Authors.

Bowman, P. J. (1991). Race, class and ethics in research: Belmont principles to functional relevance. In R. Jones (Ed.), *Black psychology* (3rd ed., pp. 747–766). Berkeley, CA: Cobb & Henry.

Boyd-Franklin, N. (2003). *Black families in therapy: Understanding the African American experience* (2nd ed.). New York: Guilford.

Brown, L. S. (1997). The private practice of subversion: Psychology as Tikkun Olam. *American Psychologist, 52,* 449–462.

Canadian Psychological Association. (2000). *Canadian code of ethics for psychologists* (3rd ed.). Retrieved July 19, 2005, from http://www.cpa.ca/ethics2000.html

Carter, R. T. (2003). *The Counseling Psychologist* in the new millennium: Building a bridge from the past to the future. *The Counseling Psychologist, 31,* 5–15.

Feminist Therapy Institute. (1999). *Feminist therapy code of ethics.* Retrieved November 6, 2004, from http://www.feministtherapyinstitute.org/ethics.htm

Fouad, N. A., McPherson, R. H., Gerstein, L., Blustein, D. L., Elman, N., Helledy, K. I., & Metz, A. J. (2004). Houston, 2001: Context and legacy. *The Counseling Psychologist, 32,* 15–77.

Goodman, L. A., Liang, B., Helms, J. E., Latta, R. E., Sparks, E., & Weintraub, S. R. (2004). Training counseling psychologists as social justice agents: Feminist and multicultural principles in action. *The Counseling Psychologist, 32*(6), 793–837.

Haverkamp, B. E. (1994). Cognitive bias in the assessment phase of the counseling process. *Journal of Employment Counseling, 31*(4), 155–167.

Kiselica, M. S. (2003). Insensitivity and anti-Semitism toward Jews by the counseling profession: A Gentile's view on the problem and his hope for reconciliation—A response to Weinrach (2002). *Journal of Counseling & Development, 81,* 426–440.

Kiselica, M. S., & Robinson, M. (2001). Bringing advocacy counseling to life: The history, issues, and human dramas of social justice work in counseling. *Journal of Counseling & Development, 70,* 387–397.

Larry P. v. Riles, F. Supp. 926 (N. D. Calif. 1979), aff'd in part, rev'd in part, 793 F. 2d 969 (9th Cir. 1984).

Lerman, H., & Porter, N. (1990). The contribution of feminism to ethics in psychotherapy. In H. Lerman & N. Porter (Eds.), *Feminist ethics in psychotherapy* (pp. 5–13). New York: Springer.

Lewis, J., Arnold, M. S., House, R., & Toporek, R. L. (2001). *Advocacy Competencies: American Counseling Association Task Force on Advocacy Competencies.* Retrieved July 19, 2005, from http://counselorsforsocialjustice.org/advocacycompetencies.html

Lewis, J. A., Lewis, M. D., Daniels, J. A., & D'Andrea, M. J. (1998). *Community counseling: Empowerment strategies for a diverse society* (2nd ed.). Pacific Grove, CA: Brooks/Cole.

Marecek, J. (1995). Gender, politics, and psychology's ways of knowing. *American Psychologist, 50*(3), 162–163.

Meara, N. M., Schmidt, L. D., & Day, J. D. (1996). Principles and virtues: A foundation for ethical decisions, policies and character. *The Counseling Psychologist, 24,* 4–77.

National Association of Social Workers. (1999). *Code of ethics of the National Association of Social Workers.* Retrieved July 19, 2005, from http://www.naswdc.org/pubs/code/code.asp

Payton, C. R. (1994). Implications of the 1992 ethics code for diverse groups. *Professional Psychology: Research and Practice, 25*(4), 317–320.

Pope, K. S. (1990). Ethics and malpractice: Identifying and implementing ethical standards for primary prevention [Electronic version]. *Prevention in Human Services, 8*(2), 43–64.

Prilleltensky, I. (1994). *The morals and politics of psychology: Psychological discourse and the status quo.* Albany: State University of New York Press.

Prilleltensky, I., Dokecki, P., Friedan, G., & Wang, V. O. (in press). Counseling for wellness and justice: Foundations, practice, and ethical dilemmas. In E. Aldarondo (Ed.), *Social justice and mental health practices.* Mahwah, NJ: Lawrence Erlbaum.

Ratts, M., D'Andrea, M., & Arredondo, P. (2004, July). Social justice in counseling: "Fifth force" in field. *Counseling Today,* 28–30.

Ridley, C. R., Liddle, M. C., Hill, C. L., & Li, L. C. (2001). Ethical decision making in multicultural counseling. In J. G. Ponterotto, J. M. Casas, L. A. Suzuki, & C. M. Alexander (Eds.), *Handbook of multicultural counseling* (2nd ed., pp. 165–188). Thousand Oaks, CA: Sage.

Smith, M. B. (2000). Values, politics, and psychology. *American Psychologist, 55*(10), 1151–1152.

Tomes, H. (1997). PI directorate is home to controversy. *American Psychological Association Monitor on Psychology, 28*(4), 4.

Toporek, R. L., & Liu, W. M. (2001). Advocacy in counseling: Addressing race, class, and gender oppression. In D. B. Pope-Davis & H. L. K. Coleman (Eds.), *The intersection of race, class, and gender in multicultural counseling* (pp. 285–413). Thousand Oaks, CA: Sage.

Toporek, R. L., & Pope-Davis, D. B. (2005). Exploring the relationships between multicultural training, racial attitudes, and attributions of poverty among graduate counseling trainees. *Cultural Diversity and Ethnic Minority Psychology, 11*(3); 259–271.

PART I

Training

CHAPTER 3

Social Justice Training in Counseling Psychology

Needs and Innovations

Rebecca L. Toporek and Christopher J. McNally

Commitment to social justice as a central focus of counseling psychology has fluctuated throughout the profession's history (Fouad, & Toporek Gerstein, chapter 1). As a result, it is not surprising that the notion of framing entire training programs around the subject of social justice remains a relatively new and, as of yet, less than universally affirmed phenomenon. Historically, the extent to which issues of social justice have been integrated into counseling psychology training has mirrored the early implementation of multicultural and feminist coursework and has depended greatly on the academic program, specific faculty, and voices of students.

One of the primary goals of this *Handbook* is to provide a comprehensive document that chronicles social justice leadership, vision, and action as evidenced by counseling psychologists and collaborators in a wide range of settings. It is hoped that professionals and students will find guidance and inspiration to further their own social justice efforts. Training is a critical element in increasing counseling psychologists' likelihood of engaging in social justice as well as their competence in doing so. Hence, every chapter in this *Handbook* explicitly discusses training within the framework of the particular issue or population addressed in the respective chapter. This section establishes a foundation with an overview of training and presents two chapters, each describing an example of the integration of social justice into the training environment.

Scope of the Section: Training in Counseling Psychology

Counseling psychologists are involved in a wide range of teaching and training roles through doctoral programs, master's-level counseling programs, undergraduate psychology courses, schools, industry, and community or adult education programs. In this section of the *Handbook,* we have chosen to focus our attention on two of these training arenas: master's-level training and undergraduate experiences. In addition, this overview chapter and Talleyrand, Chung, and Bemak (chapter 4) provide a brief review of current literature regarding doctoral-level counseling psychology training, highlighting two doctoral training programs that have specifically attended to social justice in the fabric of their curriculum. We begin with a discussion of interdisciplinary attention to social justice training as well as applicable training models within counseling psychology.

Setting the Context for Social Justice Training

It is important to recognize the contributions of ethnic studies, women's studies, teacher education, sociology, student affairs, and community psychology, where curriculum has addressed oppression since the mid-1960s (e.g., Adams, Bell, & Griffin, 1997; Levine & Perkins, 1997; Prilleltensky, 2001; Sarason, 1974). Drawing on the contributions of multiple disciplines, Bell (1997) provided a framework and definition of social justice education that helps to set a context for our discussion:

> We believe that social justice education is both a process and a goal. The goal of social justice education is full and equal participation of all groups in a society that is mutually shaped to meet their needs. . . . Social justice involves social actors who have a sense of their own agency as well as a sense of social responsibility toward and with others and the society as a whole. (p. 3)

Community psychologists contribute to the legacy of social justice education through their attention to oppression and liberation psychology (Watts & Serrano-García, 2003) as well as community-driven research and intervention. Simultaneously, contemporary discourse in community psychology provides insight into the struggle to bring social justice to the forefront of the profession (Prilleltensky, 2001).

With the educational and philosophical foundations provided by other disciplines, as well as a historical legacy of valuing social justice, the profession of counseling psychology has the tools for a more thorough implementation of social justice into training.

Applying Models of Training in Counseling Psychology to Social Justice

The integration of social justice perspectives into education and training in counseling and psychology can be conceptualized in a parallel manner to that of multicultural counseling. LaFromboise and Foster (1992) described the implementation of multicultural training as a continuum ranging from "separate course," to "area of concentration," to "interdisciplinary," to "integration" models. Given the relatively new status of social justice as an explicit component of training, this model seems to aptly describe the range of training approaches described in the literature. Corresponding examples of these include ways to address the issue of oppression in training (e.g., Kiselica, 1999), use of service learning as a tool for teaching social justice and multiculturalism (O'Brien, Patel, Hensler-McGinnis, & Kaplan, chapter 5), development of courses for social justice and oppression education (Adams et al., 1997), and counseling psychology training program design (Goodman et al., 2004; Talleyrand et al., chapter 4). Some programs incorporate a social justice perspective via annual events (e.g., the annual Social Justice Conference hosted by the University of Wisconsin's Department of Counseling Psychology), whereas other programs attempt to instill an overarching commitment to social justice throughout the curriculum via community-based research and practice (e.g., counseling psychology doctoral programs at Boston College and the University of Oregon).

Some authors have argued that the specialty of counseling psychology has remained somewhat comfortably ensconced in attempts to address social justice through lenses of diversity, multiculturalism, and population- or gender-specific theory (Watts, 2004). Reflecting long-standing areas of expertise within the field of counseling psychology, these are logical avenues for incorporating social justice perspectives because these courses address oppression and social justice as integral concepts. However, Goodman (2001) cautioned that efforts of this type emerge naturally within privileged groups that exhibit a commitment to social justice, representing admirable though ultimately limited characteristics of empathy, moral reasoning, and growthful self-interest. Other authors have asserted that a more genuinely transformative commitment to social justice demands increasingly engaged, self-reflective, and politicized approaches to knowledge, recognizing the value-laden nature of psychological intervention as well as the moral imperative that work in the social sciences may entail (Harris, 2003; Prilleltensky, 1997; Prilleltensky & Walsh-Bowers, 1993).

Addressing the question of social justice in broad fashion, the counseling psychology doctoral program of the University of Oregon devised a training program based on Bronfenbrenner's (1979) ecological model, with significant grounding in the community psychology tradition (Levine & Perkins, 1997) and a focus on the empowerment of trainees (McWhirter, 1998). Critical emphasis is placed upon trainees having a positive impact on environmental settings and assuming active roles in the shaping of cultural contexts. Focusing on research and practice within the community, students are encouraged to become critically conscious members of a larger system, growing to appreciate the significant impact of social, historical, cultural, and political contexts.

In their attempt to integrate a social justice perspective, the counseling psychology doctoral program of Boston College's Lynch School of Education takes a similar ecological approach, framing their unique First Year Experience (FYE) in terms of feminist and multicultural theory (Goodman et al., 2004). The FYE involves students in weekly work at various sites within the surrounding urban community. These sites offer opportunities for students to work in nontraditional advocacy roles in settings such as courts, public schools, community agencies, and departments of public health. Talleyrand et al. (chapter 4) highlight some other notable aspects, and Goodman et al. (2004) provide a thorough description of the Boston College training program.

With regard to the feasibility of social justice training, it is notable that both the University of Oregon and Boston College programs are housed in Colleges of Education, where openness to this type of curriculum is typically present and applicability is perceived to be more consistent with institutional mission than in more traditional Colleges of Arts and Sciences. Of the 11 doctoral programs in counseling psychology gaining accreditation within the past 5 years, 8 are located in Colleges of Education, with 1 located in an independent graduate department and 2 in Colleges of Arts and Sciences (APA, 2003). As many long-standing programs work to maintain their established roles in traditional humanities environments, newly accredited programs in more progressive academic settings may provide opportunity for the expression of fresh perspectives and the further pursuit of social justice training.

Challenges for Social Justice Training

In spite of these notable attempts to integrate social justice in counseling training, there remain significant challenges, including the continued prominence of the scientist-practitioner model, market demands of licensing and managed care, traditional academic tenure criteria, program accreditation criteria, and relative professional insularity.

Many voices from within both the counseling psychology specialty (Chwalisz, 2003) and the broader profession (Kendler, 2000, 2004) continue to affirm core components of the Boulder (scientist-practitioner) training model, traditionally emphasizing objective science, quantitative research methodology, diagnosis grounded in a medical model of illness, and the primary treatment of intrapsychic conflict (Baker & Benjamin, 2000). This emphasis has tended to neglect, and at times disapprove of, social justice roles for counseling psychologists. Alternatively, some authors have proposed an expanded "scientist-practitioner-advocate" model (Fassinger & O'Brien, 2000).

Helms (2003) provided a realist's perspective regarding attempts to address social justice in counseling psychology training environments, suggesting that counseling psychologists would perhaps do the most good by "honor[ing] a commitment to social justice work without necessarily promoting their own economic self-destruction" (p. 312). She specifically called attention to the reality of rigid managed care systems and competitive service delivery for practitioners, as well as the likelihood that academics will see their social justice work devalued and marginalized when tenure review and promotion opportunities occur. As Helms and her colleagues made clear in describing their own innovative training program (Goodman et al., 2004), a degree of latitude may result from circumstance, such as an academic program's fortuitous location within a religiously affiliated university, where social justice concerns are embedded within the larger mission of the institution itself.

Attempts to integrate a social justice perspective or to add coursework specifically addressing social justice are often hampered by the already extensive curriculum requirements of APA accreditation standards (Murdock, Alcorn, Heesacker, & Stoltenberg, 1998). Integration of a social justice perspective ideally benefits students and faculty, as well as the larger academic program and the surrounding cultural context. Yet even in highly successful settings, considerable thought must be given to cost-benefit for trainees, as students must exit their academic programs as competitive candidates for various internship placements, postdoctoral residencies, and eventual licensure, regardless of programmatic idiosyncrasies. Certain internship sites and postdoctoral opportunities such as APA's Congressional Fellowship Program may provide additional training in areas closely related to social justice. Early exposure to these possibilities may benefit students, particularly those who hope to qualify for them on an a priori basis when concluding their academic work.

Concurrent professional insularity and less than thorough acknowledgment of the relevant social justice work of other disciplines (Palmer, 2004; Prilleltensky & Prilleltensky, 2003) slows the integration of social justice in counseling training. Consequently, students are less likely to recognize how long-standing approaches to research, teaching, and therapy may actually reinforce the oppressive cultural status quo (Albee, 1986; Fox, 2003). By situating dialogue around social justice within the well-established framework of community psychology (Fondacaro & Weinberg, 2002; Prilleltensky & Nelson, 1997) and the recently emerging literature of critical psychology (Fox & Prilleltensky, 1997; Prilleltensky & Nelson, 2002), a number of counseling psychology training programs have begun to reflect an increasingly vital interdisciplinary awareness while also exemplifying the type of professional collaboration that social justice work ultimately demands.

Contributing to Social Justice Training in Counseling Psychology: Service Learning and Comprehensive Program Design

Given the array of methods for implementing social justice training, and the challenges inherent in doing so, the two chapters we have chosen for this section of the *Handbook* illustrate two quite different models. The first section, O'Brien et al. (chapter 5), describes the integration of social justice and multicultural training for undergraduate psychology students using a service learning model. Specifically, the program addresses students' awareness, knowledge, and skills within the context of domestic violence. In the process, the program facilitates greater understanding of oppression within families, as well as the systemic oppression of classism, sexism, and racism. This chapter provides a thorough examination of issues necessary for consideration in designing such an experience.

Talleyrand et al. (chapter 4), provides a detailed account of the total redesign and restructuring of a counseling master's and doctoral program to reflect social justice as the guiding construct throughout the entire program. Through a step-by-step description of mission statement development, faculty and student recruitment, curriculum design, internship and placement, and outcomes, necessary process elements and resources become clear for readers who may desire to initiate substantive changes in their own programs. The details of the substantive changes are enhanced by the authors' attention to the processes of self-reflection and personal examination required in such a transformation.

Summary

Attention to social justice in counseling psychology is at a historical pinnacle. However, the integration of this priority into training is still in its infancy. The following chapters in this section of the *Handbook* provide detailed descriptions of course and program development that serve as resources to enhance and encourage greater integration of social justice into counseling psychology training.

References

Adams, M., Bell, L. A., & Griffin, P. (Eds.). (1997). *Teaching for diversity and social justice: A sourcebook.* New York: Routledge.

Albee, G. W. (1986). Toward a just society: Lessons from observations on the primary prevention of psychopathology. *American Psychologist, 41,* 891–898.

American Psychological Association. (2003). Accredited doctoral programs in professional psychology. *American Psychologist, 58,* 1067–1080.

Baker, D. B., & Benjamin, L. T. (2000). The affirmation of the scientist-practitioner: A look back at Boulder. *American Psychologist, 55,* 241–247.

Bell, L. A. (1997). Theoretical foundations for social justice education. In M. Adams, L. A. Bell, & P. Griffin (Eds.), *Teaching for diversity and social justice: A sourcebook* (pp. 3–15). New York: Routledge.

Bronfenbrenner, U. (1979). *The ecology of human development: Experiments by nature and design.* Cambridge, MA: Harvard University Press.

Chwalisz, K. (2003). Evidence-based practice: A framework for twenty-first-century scientist-practitioner training. *The Counseling Psychologist, 31,* 497–528.

Fassinger, R. E., & O'Brien, K. M. (2000). Career counseling with college women: A scientist-practitioner-advocate model of intervention. In D. A. Luzzo (Ed.), *Career counseling of college students: An empirical guide to strategies that work* (pp. 253–266). Washington, DC: American Psychological Association.

Fondacaro, M. R., & Weinberg, D. (2002). Concepts of social justice in community psychology: Toward a social ecological epistemology. *American Journal of Community Psychology, 30,* 473–492.

Fox, D. (2003). Awareness is good, but action is better. *The Counseling Psychologist, 31,* 299–304.

Fox, D., & Prilleltensky, I. (1997). *Critical psychology: An introduction.* Thousand Oaks, CA: Sage.

Goodman, D. (2001). *Promoting diversity and social justice: Educating people from privileged groups.* Thousand Oaks, CA: Sage.

Goodman, L. A., Liang, B., Helms, J. E., Latta, R. E., Sparks, E., & Weintraub, S. R. (2004). Training counseling psychologists as social justice agents: Feminist and multicultural principles in action. *The Counseling Psychologist, 32,* 793–837.

Harris, C. (2003). Beyond multiculturalism: Difference, recognition, and social justice. *Patterns of Prejudice, 35,* 13–34.

Helms, J. E. (2003). A pragmatic view of social justice. *The Counseling Psychologist, 31,* 305–313.

Kendler, H. H. (2000). *Amoral thoughts about morality: The intersection of science, psychology, and ethics.* Springfield, IL: Charles C Thomas.

Kendler, H. H. (2004). Politics and science: A combustible mixture. *American Psychologist, 59,* 122–123.

Kiselica, M. (Ed.). (1999). *Confronting prejudice and racism during multicultural training.* Alexandria, VA: American Counseling Association.

LaFromboise, T. D., & Foster, S. L. (1992). Cross-cultural training: Scientist-practitioner model and methods. *The Counseling Psychologist, 20*(3), 472–489.

Levine, M., & Perkins, D. V. (1997). *Principles of community psychology: Perspectives and applications* (2nd ed.). New York: Oxford University Press.

McWhirter, E. H. (1998). An empowerment model of counselor education. *Canadian Journal of Counseling, 32,* 12–26.

Murdock, N. L., Alcorn, J., Heesacker, M., & Stoltenberg, C. (1998). Model training program in counseling psychology. *The Counseling Psychologist, 26,* 658–672.

Palmer, L. K. (2004). The call to social justice: A multidiscipline agenda. *The Counseling Psychologist, 32,* 879–885.

Prilleltensky, I. (1997). Values, assumptions, and practices: Assessing the moral implications of psychological discourse and action. *American Psychologist, 52,* 517–535.

Prilleltensky, I. (2001). Value-based praxis in community psychology: Moving toward social justice and social action. *American Journal of Community Psychology, 29,* 747–778.

Prilleltensky, I., & Nelson, G. (1997). Community psychology: Reclaiming social justice. In D. Fox & I. Prilleltensky (Eds.), *Critical psychology: An introduction* (pp. 166–184). Thousand Oaks, CA: Sage.

Prilleltensky, I., & Nelson, G. (2002). *Doing psychology critically: Making a difference in diverse settings.* Basingstoke, UK: Palgrave Macmillan.

Prilleltensky, I., & Prilleltensky, O. (2003). Synergies for wellness and liberation in counseling psychology. *The Counseling Psychologist, 31,* 273–281.

Prilleltensky, I., & Walsh-Bowers, R. (1993). Psychology and the moral imperative. *Journal of Theoretical and Philosophical Psychology, 13,* 90–102.

Sarason, S. B. (1974). *The psychological sense of community: Prospects for a community psychology.* San Francisco: Jossey-Bass.

Watts, R. J. (2004). Integrating social justice and psychology. *The Counseling Psychologist, 32,* 855–865.

Watts, R. J., & Serrano-García, I. (2003). The quest for a liberating community psychology: An overview. *American Journal of Community Psychology, 31*(1–2), 73–78.

CHAPTER 4

Incorporating Social Justice in Counselor Training Programs

A Case Study Example

Regine M. Talleyrand,
Rita Chi-Ying Chung, and Fred Bemak

Incorporating Social Justice in Counselor Training Programs: A Case Study Example

In the early 1900s, advocacy counselors such as Clifford Beers and Frank Parsons pioneered a social justice movement in the counseling profession (Kiselica & Robinson, 2001). Since then, traditional models of counseling and psychotherapy have largely focused on helping individuals without taking into consideration the ecological context that affects individuals. Within the past two decades, there has been renewed interest in challenging counseling psychology to replace its focus on individuals and individuals within groups with a commitment to addressing societal inequities (e.g., poverty, racism) from a macro-level perspective. For counseling psychologists to be effective for all people, issues of social justice, cultural democracy, and equity must be addressed in training, research, and practice (e.g., D'Andrea & Daniels, 1999; Helms & Cook, 1999; Lee & Walz, 1998; McDowell, Fang, Brownlee, Young, & Khanna, 2002; Parham & McDavis, 1987; Thompson & Neville, 1999; Toporek & Reza, 2001).

Although there is acknowledgment in the field that it is critical to incorporate social justice issues in training, in most cases, psychologists and counselors learn social justice skills, interventions, and strategies on the job. That is, there is a lack of emphasis in counselor training programs on preparing students to actively engage in systemic change processes and incorporate these issues into their professional identity (Vera & Speight, 2003). The goal of this chapter is to describe one approach to integrating social justice into training by examining the counseling graduate program at George Mason University (GMU). This program has transformed its central mission to train counselors about issues of social justice and, as a result, has redesigned the entire program. While different training programs have unique challenges, this chapter illustrates a process and provides general recommendations that may be useful for both counseling psychology and counselor education programs.

Before describing the program at GMU, we will first highlight several counseling psychology programs that have used a social justice agenda to guide their training, research, and practice. We have decided to focus on counseling psychology training programs since the field of counseling psychology has historically been rooted in and identified with prevention, multiculturalism, and social justice (Hage, 2003), and relates to counselor education programs as well. Next, we will present the steps we have taken to transform the GMU Counseling and Development counselor education program including a discussion on the development of our new social justice mission statement, new recruitment initiatives, curriculum revisions, program development, research, and local, national, and international partnerships. Finally, we will present the challenges encountered in the transformation process followed by recommendations for social justice training.

We are using Davis's (1996) definition that describes social justice as

> a basic value and desired goal in democratic societies and includes equitable and fair access to societal institutions, laws, resources, [and] opportunities, without arbitrary limitations based on observed, or interpretation of, differences in age, color, culture, physical or mental disability, education, gender, income, language, national origin, race, religion or sexual orientation. (p. 1)

Models of Social Justice Training in Counseling Psychology Programs

Few counseling psychology programs have incorporated social justice initiatives into their graduate training programs that go beyond offering an independent course on multicultural counseling to fulfill accrediting body requirements (e.g., American Psychological Association [APA], Council for the Accreditation of Counseling Related Education Programs [CACREP]). This next section will highlight several counseling psychology programs that have been genuinely committed to taking an innovative approach to implementing social justice initiatives into their training, research, and practice.

One social justice initiative that has been at the forefront of several counseling psychology programs has been the recruitment and retention of faculty and students of color to reach the level of "critical mass" recommended by Ponterotto, Alexander, and Grieger (1995). This "critical mass" refers to the belief that having 30% minority representation on predominantly White college campuses creates a psychologically safe environment for students of color. Given the fact that some researchers have found that students' educational experiences are enriched when a culturally affirming learning environment is created (Ponterotto et al., 1995), several counseling psychology programs have committed to diversifying their student and faculty populations.

Boston College, Penn State University, Ball State University, Loyola University Chicago, and Marquette University, to name a few, have developed mission statements and program climates that address cultural diversity and social justice issues (e.g., recruitment of students and faculty) in their counseling psychology training programs. In fact, Marquette University's Counseling Psychology Program has developed a three-pronged approach to minority student recruitment and retention:

> Identifying and implementing the best strategies for recruiting minority students, improving the physical and social environment in the department so that it is welcoming of diverse students, and developing policies and marketing materials aimed at increasing applications from qualified members of underrepresented groups. (Marquette University School of Education Web site: http://www.marquette.edu/education/pages/programs/coep/diversity)

Aside from incorporating a social justice philosophy into its mission statement and recruitment efforts, Boston College's counseling psychology program has endorsed a developmental contextual framework (Lerner, 1995) as a theoretical foundation for their training program. Their aim is to train their graduate students to conceptualize problems from individual, contextual, and developmental perspectives, so that students can learn to create treatment and prevention programs that address problems from an individual and systemic level. In their program, specific attention has been given to forming collaborations with various professionals (e.g., school administrators, social workers) in an effort to address and meet the needs of children and families in the local schools and communities (Brabeck, Walsh, Kenny, & Comilang, 1997). This type of approach typically has not been recognized within the counseling psychology profession, and consequently has not been endorsed in traditional counselor training programs.

An example of a social justice initiative is Boston College's "Tools for Tomorrow" intervention, which is a collaborative effort between teachers in the Boston public schools and Boston College counseling faculty and students (Hartung & Blustein, 2002). This intervention, led by faculty and graduate students from Boston College's counseling psychology program as well as teachers from the Boston public schools, is designed to complement existing school career programs by teaching inner-city ninth-grade students career decision-making skills that include a contextual perspective relevant to these students' life experiences. This initiative, inspired by Parsons's work in the early 1900s, clearly promotes a social justice agenda in that it provides at-risk students with equitable access to educational and career opportunities.

Boston College also houses the Institute for the Study and Promotion of Race and Culture (ISPRC), which is under the direction of Janet E. Helms, another pioneer in the field of social justice and a Boston College counseling psychology faculty member. This institute was developed to address societal, racial, and cultural conflicts in theory, research, and mental health practice on both a professional and a societal level. Beyond engaging in multiple research and practice initiatives, the ISPRC staff provides an opportunity for scholarly interdisciplinary social justice discourse and debate by hosting an annual Diversity Challenge Conference.

We have provided a few examples of specific efforts made by two counseling psychology programs to ameliorate social justice. Both of these programs have moved from "discourse to action" (Hartung & Blustein, 2002) in an effort to create a level playing field for all people. The next section will focus on describing a unique counselor education program that has infused social justice throughout its graduate program.

George Mason University's Social Justice Model

To provide a context for the program, it is first helpful to briefly describe George Mason University (GMU). GMU is the largest publicly funded university in the Commonwealth of Virginia, with 29,000 students and more than 100 degree programs. The university is located just outside Washington, DC, and has been identified by the Princeton Review as the second most diverse campus in the United States. The Counseling and Development (C&D) Program is housed in the College of Education and Human Development, which has 100 full-time faculty. The C&D program offers a doctoral degree through the Graduate School of Education, a master's degree with specialization in Community Agency Counseling and School Counseling, and post–master's degree certificate programs.

The C&D program at GMU differs from other graduate training programs in that it goes beyond simply culturally diversifying student and faculty. In contrast, GMU's program has included social justice as a part of the mission statement, emphasized contextual frameworks of social issues as a core for training, and built community and school partnerships that aim toward equity and equality. Therefore, GMU's program is unique in that it has included social justice in every aspect of its training program. This program has not only built social justice as a cornerstone of its mission and embedded concepts of social justice and human rights throughout the coursework while diversifying the faculty and student population, but it has also taken additional steps that included developing actual courses and internships in social justice and social change. In addition, the program has included an emphasis on interdisciplinary training that includes public policy, public health, political science, sociology, anthropology, and education as important components toward social justice work (Bemak, 1998). For example, potential internship sites include the Peace Corps, the American Counseling Association, the Center for Multicultural Human Services, the U.S. Committee for Refugees, and the American School Counselors Association. Therefore, in the GMU Counseling and Development Program, social justice is in the foreground in the training program.

This is unique in the counseling field and, to our knowledge, is being done in few, if any, counseling graduate training programs.

Five years ago, the program was in a state of transition given the departure of the three full-time faculty members. This left the Graduate School of Education (GSE) with a major decision—whether to continue or close the program. With the three full-time faculty gone, the GSE hired two interim visiting faculty to "hold up" the program while the administration decided about the future of the program. Although the two interim faculty were committed to the program, they were also overwhelmed. Eventually, the GSE administration made a decision to continue the program, recruit new faculty, and revitalize the program. Two senior faculty were recruited from Ohio State University (the second and third authors) to assume a leadership role in continuing the program. The GSE administration convinced them that there was unanimous support for revamping the entire program in their vision of social justice and multiculturalism, and the administration committed to additional faculty. In line with the GSE commitment, two additional faculty were hired, for a total of four full-time faculty. The two additional entry-level faculty each had significant experience in the field but a limited university background. This was an ideal situation in which four new faculty were beginning together, with administrative support for restructuring the program.

The philosophical belief held by the senior faculty members was that a significant program change would be far more effective with all faculty being on board and in agreement about the direction of the program. Therefore, during the first year, the four new faculty held three retreats, two of them overnight, to discuss a new program mission and direction. In addition, there were bimonthly, 2- to 3-hour Counseling and Development faculty meetings to maintain ongoing discussions about the new program. This initiated the energy and process of careful reflection and conversation about developing a new program mission and subsequent advancement of courses that would align with the new mission. It should be noted that administration never requested any information or reports by the Counseling and Development faculty, explicitly stating that they hired faculty because they "believed in them and trusted them" to do the best for the program. This resulted in a climate of complete support for the reorganization of what was generally agreed upon as an outdated and "stale" program.

During the first year, the program mission was redefined to include an emphasis on social justice, multiculturalism/internationalism, leadership, and advocacy. Examining the mission, in-depth discussions were held to align old and new courses with the new mission. Careful deliberations about how to infuse the new mission into existing classes were held, along with reflections about what new courses needed to be added. The creation of the new program created an atmosphere of excitement and creativity among faculty, students, and administration. Based on the evolution of the program and increasing student enrollment and national attention, the GSE administration decided to open a national search for an additional faculty member. Interviews included a comprehensive inquiry about applicants' beliefs about social justice and multiculturalism, and their commitment to join a faculty team that was in the midst of working on establishing a new and innovative program along these lines. The result of this search was the hiring of an additional faculty member who demonstrated an established commitment to cultural and social justice issues (the first author).

Theoretical Framework and Mission

The development of GMU's Counseling and Development Program mission statement was guided, and continues to be influenced, by the multicultural counseling competencies (e.g., Arredondo et al., 1996; Sue, Arredondo, & McDavis, 1992), the social justice literature (e.g., D'Andrea & Daniels, 1999; Helms, 2003; Helms & Cook, 1999; Ivey & Collins, 2003; Lee & Walz, 1998; Parham & McDavis, 1987; Vera & Speight, 2003), an examination of counselor efficacy and roles in a rapidly changing technological and global world, and our personal experiences. The aim was to provide a training environment that teaches counselors to embrace an ecological framework. This macro approach to counseling included the awareness, acceptance, acknowledgment, and understanding of the sociopolitical, historical, psychosocial, economic, physical, and spiritual health of individuals, families, communities, organizations, and systems, in order to contribute to the advancement of a global well-being.

The resulting program mission statement reads as follows:

> The program strives for national and international excellence in implementing a counseling perspective that provides a foundation in basic counseling skills and focuses on multiculturalism, social justice, leadership, and advocacy. It is our belief that a global perspective on development across the life span, and an understanding and appreciation of multiculturalism, diversity, and social justice, are integral to the preparation of professional counselors, requiring that they are prepared to assume leadership roles, be proactive change agents, and become advocates for social, economic, and political justice.

Teaching students to become aware of their worldviews and how these worldviews affect individuals, groups, communities, and the society at large continues to be an integral part of our mission because we believe that social change and advocacy taken without self-awareness can become oppressive. There are multiple methods for educating individuals regarding their worldviews (Helms & Cook, 1999; Pedersen & Hernandez, 1997), such as field-based experiences and intensive personal exploration through structured exercises. Equally important has been the need to create culturally diverse learning environments for all students and faculty so that the critical discourse necessary for social justice reform can take place. One of the efforts toward creating a culturally diverse training environment was to increase the recruitment and retention efforts of faculty and students of color, as well as place an emphasis on respecting differences of values, worldviews and attitudes, backgrounds, ethnicity, race, and sexual orientation.

Faculty and Student Recruitment

Given the desire for a culturally diverse learning environment, one of our primary goals was to increase the representation of students and faculty of color in our master's- and doctoral-level training programs. Since implementing the mission statement in 2001, our recruitment efforts for faculty and staff have been quite successful. With the addition of a new faculty member, the Counseling and Development Program full-time faculty has gone from being overwhelmingly European American (approximately 75%) to now having 50% full-time faculty of color. Simultaneously, the adjunct faculty pool has changed from being predominantly European American (95%) to approximately 50% faculty of color. Parallel to the commitment and changes in diversity among faculty, the ethnicity of the student body has changed dramatically, from approximately 98% European American females to about 30% students of color and 70% European Americans. Currently, the changes in faculty and student composition reflect the changes in the program's mission. Furthermore, as the program has gained recognition regionally and nationally, applications to the program have increased significantly, subsequently increasing the number of student of color applicants.

There also have been significant changes in our admissions procedures. Before the program began its transformation, traditional criteria for admissions had been used in the past with a heavy emphasis on test scores. Faculty reexamined the admission process, taking into consideration how traditional admission procedures could be biased toward particular groups (e.g., standardized scores/grades of students of color). Given the research on test biases (e.g., Helms, 1992), faculty decided to use alternative admission criteria without compromising the quality of students admitted to the program. Although test scores remained a part of the evaluation process, they were not the main criteria for admittance to the program. Instead, a more comprehensive approach was endorsed that included an examination of various aspects of the applicants' personal, social, educational, and work values and experiences. This approach eliminated the one-measure criterion of admittance and provided information on the broader personal, social, and educational values of applicants and hence the potential to be an effective social justice counselor.

In addition, the admissions process was revamped by using a changed procedure for faculty to evaluate students' applications whereby during the interview process, students were questioned about their attitudes, thoughts, beliefs, views, and perspectives on the program's mission statement. In addition, students were asked about their previous advocacy work and experience as well as to respond to the program's mission statement in the form of a writing sample.

Curriculum and Training

Early on in the transformation process, we recognized that in order to prepare our students to assume leadership roles; be proactive change agents; and become advocates for social, economic, and political justice, we would have to transform our coursework to align it with the mission statement. Initially, faculty met to reach consensus about the mission statement and course content. This was challenging given the different ideas and different teaching and learning styles among the faculty. Persistence and commitment were key elements during this phase. As a faculty, we initiated self-awareness activities and discussions regarding our own experiences, and we also reviewed each class syllabus to identify areas for growth with respect to social justice training, including changes in teaching styles, course objectives, textbook choices, and assignments.

A number of changes included the addition of new coursework into the curriculum as well as the revision of how we teach core classes in the curriculum. Our perspectives regarding the role of social justice in counseling were incorporated in the program's introductory courses. For example, we created a new course titled "Foundations in Counseling," a course that was open to students newly admitted to the program as well as those considering applying to the program. In this course, considerable time is spent introducing the program's mission statement and having students reflect upon and develop their worldviews. This process was challenging, particularly for students who had been trained to adopt a Eurocentric approach in their understanding of the world and the traditional viewpoint predominated by individual counseling. For example, in this class, students are introduced to the stark realities of social injustices, such as the correlation between mental health issues and other variables (e.g., poverty, racism, discrimination, public funding priorities, etc.). This is not what students typically expect in an introductory class, and it forces them to consider counseling within the context of larger social justice issues.

Although social justice and human rights issues were infused in all of the courses in the curriculum, we also believed that there should be an additional course that focused specifically on counseling and social justice. This is a required course for all students in the program. This new advanced-level course is separate from the multicultural counseling course and challenges students to move from discourse to action by providing hands-on experience. The format for the course is lecture and discussion, and it includes numerous field-based assignments and experiential class exercises. Given the location of GMU (15 miles outside of Washington, DC), it is an ideal situation for students to undergo field experiences in various federal, state, regional, and professional organizations.

One example of these field experiences has had students working in collaboration with a major national professional mental health organization's public policy and legislation committee. Students researched various social justice issues pertinent to counseling with the outcome of producing a white paper that might influence federal policy and legislation. Students were also given the opportunity to have input in the GMU Counseling and Development Program curriculum. They designed various social justice assignments for all courses in the program. Students' ideas and suggestions were shared with faculty, who in turn included these suggestions in their syllabi.

Another hands-on project involved students by collaborating with a national professional association in developing a multifaceted gang prevention program. The prevention program included a unit for counselors and educators in schools;

identified at-risk behavior for students, counselors, teachers, and parents; and developed prevention and intervention programs for school, community, and the home. The students who developed the program also had an opportunity to pilot the gang prevention unit at their internship sites.

A major aim of the fieldwork experience is the exposure to real-life issues related to social justice work. Students' responses to their fieldwork experiences have ranged from feelings of frustration and disappointment when they encountered barriers to social change, to excitement when they witnessed that the work they have undertaken as social justice counselors can make a difference. Students therefore experienced changing systems on multiple levels: within the GMU Counseling and Development Program, the university environment, local schools and communities, and federal policy and legislation.

Other curriculum revisions still in progress include changes in the core career counseling class. Typically, students enrolled in the career counseling class gain exposure to career theories and practice, including providing career counseling to paying clients who have been recruited from the community. Currently, we are establishing partnerships with leaders of various community agencies (e.g., domestic violence shelters) to provide career counseling outside of the traditional career counseling parameters (e.g., use of career tests in an office setting), potentially meeting the vocational needs of underrepresented groups in the community.

While the program was becoming focused on social justice in our core classes, there was parallel work being done by faculty in community agencies and schools. For example, as assignments in practicum and internships changed to include a focus on social justice (e.g., plan a prevention program that focuses on social justice), there was a shift away from having only traditional individual, group, and family counseling practicum and internship experiences. Therefore, the program faculty had to work carefully with placement agencies and schools to educate them about the rationale for engaging in other types of activities that were not historically included in these types of experiences. Regular meetings were held with schools and agency supervisors and administrators to discuss and present the "new" program and the changes in students' field experiences. In addition, as part of their classroom experiences, students engaged in case processing and supervision using a multisystems approach.

Within our doctoral program, we have developed three new classes that are specifically aligned with the program's mission statement and, to our knowledge, have never before been taught. These courses include an Advanced Internship in Social Justice, an Advanced Internship in Leadership, and an Advanced Internship in Multiculturalism. There is no counseling emphasis in these courses; rather, students are prepared to be leaders in the counseling field by taking on positions such as client, policy, research, or community and school advocates. As mentioned previously, given the proximity of GMU to Washington, DC, students are placed in various governmental, nongovernmental, and professional organizations (e.g., Peace Corps, U.S. Office of Refugee Resettlement). The aim of these courses, unlike the traditional counseling internship, is to provide advanced training in leadership, advocacy, and social change. Therefore, students have an opportunity to integrate their counseling skills with their social justice work in the real world.

Finally, throughout all of our coursework, we acknowledged the need to incorporate technology (Kiselica & Robinson, 2001) and ethics into our training. Specifically, we believed that Web-based technologies could offer our students opportunities to enhance their social justice cultural competencies through the use of instructional methods (e.g., blackboard discussions) that could allow for more in-depth and genuine interactions among students outside of the classroom (Talleyrand & Kitsantas, 2003). Simultaneously, we realized that ethical considerations are crucial in training, especially as we consider social justice work. Therefore, we designed an ethics course specifically geared toward incorporating counseling and social justice in the curriculum, including case studies, research papers, and assignments that emphasized dealing with inequities and unfair practices as they related to the practice of counseling. Examples of ethical issues include dealing with systematic prejudice in a community, addressing larger issues of poverty, the role of the psychotherapist in addressing gender discrimination, and so on.

In summary, major transformations have occurred in the program's curriculum and training, including the redesigning of 98% of the curriculum and the addition of six new courses: Foundations of Counseling, Counseling and Social Justice, Advanced Multicultural Internship, Advanced Internship in Social Justice, Advanced Internship in Counseling Leadership, and Advanced Group Counseling. We are training our students to use a multisystems and interdisciplinary perspective when working with clients and to use individual, group, and organizational change strategies; knowledge and use of technology and ethics; and assessment and research skills that are paramount to social justice reform (Kiselica & Robinson, 2001).

Research and Professional Development Activities

As social justice advocates, we realize that when attempting to create change in a traditional system, data are power. Therefore, the faculty is heavily involved in supporting research agendas that reflect the program's mission statement. For example, faculty in the program have published extensively in the fields of cross-cultural and multicultural psychology, working with at-risk youth, bullying behaviors, chronic illness, immigrant and refugee mental health, interethnic race relations, and racial and ethnic mental and physical health models. Furthermore, we have used both quantitative and qualitative research methods to fully capture the experiences of all individuals, their families, and communities. In addition, the second and third authors are currently writing a book on social justice and counseling from a global perspective (Chung & Bemak, 2004). Finally, students are strongly encouraged early in the program to participate in collaborative research projects with faculty. Along with participating in research projects, faculty and students collaboratively present social justice research initiatives at local, national, and international conferences. Furthermore, students in the program have also been appointed to state and national committees by presidents in the various professional organizations.

Local, National, and International Partnerships

From the creation of this transformation process, faculty were engaged on local, regional, state, national, and international levels of social justice work. Statewide, the program took a leadership role in advocating a larger voice for school counseling in the Virginia Department of Education. GMU faculty organized and led a School Counseling Leadership Team composed of faculty from surrounding universities and county School Counseling Directors to promote this agenda. As a result of meeting with high-level officials, a State Department of Education assistant superintendent was assigned as a liaison to the team. Further meetings with the president of the State Board of Education led to an actual position being created in the Virginia Department of Education. Three years later, this team still exists and works closely with the state and other regions to provide guidance and leadership about school counseling.

Concurrently, activities are going on at the national level. Two of the faculty (second and third authors) provided training to counselors and counselor educators at a Social Justice Day by the Counselors for Social Justice Division of the American Counseling Association. Through the Education Trust, another faculty member provided training and consultation focused on fair and equal education for all students, particularly low-income and ethnic minority students, to school districts around the country. Additionally, the second and third authors have been involved in developing a pilot international study regarding the relationship of social justice and counseling through the International Association for Counselling, a first in the mental health field. All three authors will be doing further work on this study.

Challenges in the Transformation

Spending several years transforming a traditional counselor education program into one that endorses social justice, multiculturalism/internationalism, leadership, and advocacy was not without challenges. First, as faculty of color in the program, the first two authors struggled to gain credibility among students, who had preconceived notions regarding what faculty of color should and should not teach. That is, some students reacted differently to and were more resistant to hearing straightforward yet sensitive information (e.g., dialogue on White privilege and cultural bias in testing) from faculty of color rather than from White faculty members. Second, although we admitted students who were proponents of our mission statement, some students endorsed the statement on different levels developmentally, creating unique and sometimes challenging discourse in the classroom. Third, finding practicum and internship sites and supervisors who shared values akin to our program's mission statement was a difficult task. We addressed this issue by meeting with supervisors in agency and school settings to educate them regarding our vision for our program and our students' training experiences. Finally, we encountered some difficulty ensuring that part-time adjunct faculty were on board with our mission statement and were comfortable with incorporating it into their teaching strategies and coursework. One solution was to hold special faculty meetings to discuss our mission statement with adjunct faculty and to create pairs between full-time faculty and part-time faculty who teach similar courses so that we could ensure that the mission statement was incorporated in all aspects of our training. This solution to address the training needs of adjunct faculty can be incorporated in both counseling psychology and counselor education graduate training programs.

It is important to comment on accreditation for our program and implications for other graduate-level psychology and counseling programs. In our review of the field, and an analysis of accreditation policies, we found that social justice was not a relevant issue to either APA or CACREP accreditation. Therefore, the GMU Counseling and Development program coursework meets CACREP standards and standards for state licensure and certification, but currently, the faculty has chosen not to become CACREP accredited. Consistency with meeting licensure requirements is challenging for counseling psychology and counselor education graduate training programs that are committed to social justice and include a social justice emphasis in their programs. Accreditation standards do not require social justice training, therefore necessitating graduate programs to add and go beyond current and acceptable training while conforming to the standards.

Recommendations for Social Justice Training

As we reflect on the process and our journey for the past 3 years, the following are recommendations we suggest for successfully implementing a social justice mission into counselor training programs. As we mentioned previously, although our recommendations are based on our experiences in developing a counselor education program, we believe that they also can be applied to counseling psychology programs because both types of programs share a commitment to training counselors and researchers (e.g., scientist-practitioner model) who are competent in prevention, multiculturalism, and social justice. Furthermore, we also suggest that the recommendations are applicable to other psychology or counseling training programs such as community or clinical psychology programs.

Faculty Retreats. It is important to utilize ongoing faculty retreats to process personal commitment to, and understanding of, social justice issues. Although most counselors would agree that social justice is an important issue in the counseling field, individuals have different ideas, perspectives, and views on the definition of social justice and how to operationalize social justice in their training/teaching, practice, and research. Similar to students, faculty can also be at different developmental levels in understanding the concept. Faculty retreats provide opportunities for faculty to discuss and exchange ideas on how social justice issues can be integrated into their teaching, as well as provide support and mentoring of faculty as they undergo the social justice journey.

Adjunct Faculty and Field Supervisors. Adjunct faculty or field supervisors often may be less committed to the program than full-time faculty. They may experience their work in isolation and have varied levels of connection to the program. To ensure that all adjunct faculty and practicum and internship supervisors are on board with the mission, they are told when hired that part of the course content must incorporate the mission of the program. They have discretion in line with academic freedom about how they include the mission in the delivery of the course material, and regular meetings are held to discuss issues such as this and keep adjunct faculty connected to the program's mission. Training also should be provided to bring them up to speed with the program's mission statement and new curriculum. Another way of ensuring that they understand and meet the needs of the mission, and hence maintain the quality of the program, is "pairing" between full-time and adjunct faculty. In addition to the faculty meetings, pairing faculty gives full-time faculty an opportunity to provide ongoing, one-on-one education and support to adjunct faculty.

Empowerment of Students. As mentioned previously, the social justice mission in the program is not just intended for training students, but also for students to have a voice in the program. Through student organizations (e.g., Chi Sigma Iota [CSI] National Honor Society), town hall meetings, and regular contact with faculty, avenues are created to provide open communication between faculty and students. It is important to note that these meetings are not for students to air their concerns regarding a particular faculty member or class, but rather a productive meeting focusing on overall program improvement. The town hall meetings are facilitated by CSI, which compiles an agenda based on the students' concerns, questions, or comments. Faculty attends the meetings, which are facilitated by the CSI leadership team. Another way of empowering students, as mentioned previously, is that faculty and students collaborate on social justice research and scholarship.

Partnership Building. Because social change does not happen in isolation, it is important to build partnerships at local, state, national, and international levels to address social justice reform globally. For example, faculty members are role models in forming partnerships with professional organizations, other universities, community agencies, schools, nongovernmental organizations, and so on.

Assessment and Evaluation. Evaluation of the program is also critical to ensure that the aim of the program and the needs of students are met. To assess the impact and quality of the program, it is important to develop measures that will provide both pre and posttest data measuring students' social justice competencies. To accurately assess students' academic experiences in the program and the program's relationship to their social justice development, both quantitative (e.g., surveys, questionnaires) and qualitative (e.g., semistructured interviews) research methodologies should be used. A follow-up assessment should be conducted with students who have left the program to assess whether they are incorporating and integrating social justice work in their profession.

Conclusion

Although there is growing recognition in the counseling profession that social justice should be addressed in all aspects of counseling training programs, few counseling programs have fully endorsed this mission. At GMU, we have been actively involved in creating a program that trains students to become social advocacy counselors and leaders. We have drawn from the multicultural competencies, social justice literature, an examination of counselor efficacy and roles in a rapidly changing technological and global world, and our personal experiences to develop a model that places an emphasis on oppression, privilege, social inequities, and social justice. We believe in empowering our students and having them become active participants in their learning process. We strive to teach our students to think more broadly about their professional roles in the counseling profession.

We realize that incorporating our mission statement throughout all aspects of our program (e.g., research, training, and practice) remains a work in progress. To date, we have increased substantially the number of students of color applying to the program and have created a pluralistic learning environment that promotes critical thinking skills and social justice action. We have also increased our numbers of faculty of color (full-time and part-time) and continue to receive inquiries regarding potential openings in our program. We encourage an ongoing assessment of our program through student and faculty dialogue and are currently in the process of operationalizing our social justice training efforts by developing a quantitative measure to assess students' social justice competencies. Although our transformed program is relatively new, we look forward to soon graduating students who are grounded in a solid theoretical and practical foundation in advocating for social justice in the counseling profession.

References

Arredondo, P., Toporek, R., Brown, S. P., Jones, J., Locke, D., & Sanchez, J. (1996). Operationalization of the multicultural counseling competencies. *Journal of Multicultural Counseling and Development, 24,* 42–78.

Bemak, F. (1998). Interdisciplinary collaboration for social change: Redefining the counseling profession. In C. C. Lee & G. R. Walz (Eds.), *Social action: A mandate for counselors* (pp. 279–292). Alexandria, VA: American Counseling Association.

Brabeck, M., Walsh, M. E., Kenny, M., & Comilang, K. (1997). Interprofessional collaboration for children and families: Opportunities for counseling psychology in the 21st century. *The Counseling Psychologist, 25,* 615–636.

Chung, R. C.-Y., & Bemak, F. (2004). *Social justice and multiculturalism: Application, theory and practice in counseling and psychotherapy.* Manuscript submitted for publication.

D'Andrea, M., & Daniels, J. (1999). Exploring the psychology of White racism through naturalistic inquiry. *Journal of Counseling and Development, 77,* 93–101.

Davis, K. (1996). What is social justice? *Perspectives on Multicultural and Cultural Diversity, 6,* 1–3.

Hage, S. (2003). Reaffirming the unique identity of counseling psychology: Opting for the "road less traveled by." *The Counseling Psychologist, 31,* 555–563.

Hartung, P. J., & Blustein, D. L. (2002). Reason, intuition, and social justice: Elaborating on Parsons's career decision-making model. *Journal of Counseling and Development, 80,* 41–47.

Helms, J. E. (1992). Why is there no study of cultural equivalence in standardized cognitive ability testing? *American Psychologist, 47,* 1083–1101.

Helms, J. E. (2003). A pragmatic view of social justice. *The Counseling Psychologist, 31,* 305–313.

Helms, J. E., & Cook, D. A. (1999). *Using race and culture in counseling and psychotherapy: Theory and practice.* Boston: Allyn & Bacon.

Ivey, A. E., & Collins, N. M. (2003). A long-term challenge for counseling psychology. *The Counseling Psychologist,* 31, 290–298.

Kiselica, M. S., & Robinson, M. (2001). Bringing advocacy counseling to life: The history, issues, and human dramas of social justice work in counseling. *Journal of Counseling and Development, 79,* 387–397.

Lee, C. C., & Walz, G. R. (Eds.). (1998). *Social action: A mandate for counselors.* Alexandria, VA: American Counseling Association.

Lerner, R. M. (1995). *America's youth in crisis: Challenges and options for programs and policies.* Thousand Oaks, CA: Sage.

McDowell, T., Fang, S.-R., Brownlee, K., Young, C. G., & Khanna, A. (2002). Transforming an MFT program: A model for enhancing diversity. *Journal of Marital and Family Therapy, 28,* 179–191.

Parham, T. A., & McDavis, R. J. (1987). Black men, an endangered species: Who's really pulling the trigger? *Journal of Counseling and Development, 66,* 24–27.

Pedersen, P. B., & Hernandez, D. (1997). *Decisional dialogues in a cultural context: Structured exercises.* Thousand Oaks, CA: Sage.

Ponterotto, J. G., Alexander, C. M., & Grieger, I. (1995). A multicultural competency checklist for counseling training programs. *Journal of Multicultural Counseling and Development, 23,* 11–20.

Sue, D. W., Arredondo, P., & McDavis, S. (1992). Multicultural counseling competencies and standards: A call to the profession. *Journal of Counseling and Development, 70,* 477–486.

Talleyrand, R. M., & Kitsantas, A. (2003). Multicultural pedagogy and web-based technologies. *Academic Exchange Quarterly, 7*(1), 23–28.

Thompson, C. E., & Neville, H. A. (1999). Racism, mental health, and mental health practice. *The Counseling Psychologist, 27,* 155–223.

Toporek, R. L., & Reza, J. V. (2001). Context as a critical dimension of multicultural counseling: Articulating personal, professional, and institutional competence. *Journal of Multicultural Counseling and Development, 29,* 13–30.

Vera, E. M., & Speight, S. L. (2003). Multicultural competence, social justice, and counseling psychology: Expanding our roles. *The Counseling Psychologist, 31,* 253–272.

CHAPTER 5

Empowering Undergraduate Students to Be Agents of Social Change

An Innovative Service Learning Course in Counseling Psychology

Karen M. O'Brien, Sheetal Patel, Nancy Hensler-McGinnis, and Jennifer Kaplan

Counseling psychologists are in a unique position to effect social change. The knowledge we generate as researchers, our skills as clinicians, and our work as teachers can be applied to improve the quality of life and the condition of society. The focus of this chapter is to provide a model of an innovative

Authors' Note: Gratitude is extended to Ms. Christel Nichols and Dr. William S. Hall for their commitment to a partnership between the House of Ruth in Washington, DC, and the University of Maryland Department of Psychology. Funding for the development of the service learning course was provided by the Office of the Dean for Undergraduate Studies, the Center for Teaching Excellence, and the Department of Psychology at the University of Maryland. Dr. Lisa Goodman was instrumental in envisioning a course that would prepare undergraduate students to be advocates of social change. The undergraduate students who completed this course contributed greatly to its success. Finally, Dr. David Petersen provided helpful comments regarding this chapter.

service learning course designed to engage undergraduate students in social change. In this two-semester course, students were educated about theory and research relevant to domestic violence and then provided with an opportunity to assist their community by volunteering in an agency that serves battered and homeless women and their children. A preliminary evaluation of this course will be described. Finally, suggestions for implementing service learning courses in counseling psychology will be discussed and recommendations for future research provided.

Service Learning as a Mechanism for Social Change

Social justice or social change work can be defined as actions that contribute to the advancement of society and advocate for equal access to resources for marginalized or less fortunate individuals in our society. Vera and Speight (2003) advocated for integrating social justice in the education and training of future counseling professionals. Others (e.g., Buckley, 1998) have suggested that students who receive an education infused with social justice will demonstrate an emotional understanding of social injustice, articulate the societal causes of human suffering, and develop skills to facilitate social change.

Service learning—teaching students by involving them in their communities—can be a mechanism for social change. Service learning is a form of experiential education in which service is informed by what is learned in the classroom and learning is enhanced by work in the community (Prentice & Garcia, 2000). Many disciplines (e.g., psychology, sociology, education, health education, social welfare) incorporate service learning in the training experiences of their students. Moreover, service learning as education has gained in popularity in recent years in academic institutions as a unique learning experience, and many colleges and universities are seeking to provide more service learning opportunities to their students (Jacoby, 1996). Two national organizations, Campus Contact and the Corporation for National Service, strive to increase service learning resources on college campuses.

Recently, studies investigating the efficacy of service learning reported a strong connection between service learning and multiple aspects of personal development (Eyler & Giles, 1999; Marullo, 1998). Researchers found service learning to affect self-knowledge, spiritual growth, altruism, and personal efficacy (Eyler & Giles, 1999), as well as citizenship, diversity awareness, leading abilities, moral development, and structural understanding of social problems (Marullo, 1998). Student teachers reported that service learning in urban schools resulted in positive academic, social, and personal outcomes (Wade, 1997). Moreover, service learning programs increased cross-cultural awareness and skills (GreyWolf, 1998), perhaps because service learning often moves students from the university into the community, allowing them to develop cultural competencies (Flannery & Ward, 1999). Specifically, stereotypes often are lessened and students become more tolerant and appreciative of other cultures (Eyler & Giles, 1999).

An Innovative Service Learning Domestic Violence Course

A two-semester service learning course was envisioned to assist students in being agents of social change through developing the knowledge base and skills necessary to be effective advocates with battered women and their children. Many service learning courses involve students in hands-on experiences during the same semester in which they learn about the issue being studied (e.g., Kretchmar, 2001; Strage, 2000). However, this course was designed to educate students about domestic violence in a comprehensive manner prior to having students volunteer in the community. We believed that providing students with a theoretical and empirical basis for understanding domestic violence during the first semester would allow them to be more effective advocates for battered women and their children in their shelter placements during the second semester. (Syllabi for both semesters' courses are available from the first author.)

During the first semester, didactic and experiential learning focused on the topics of domestic violence, helping skills, and cross-cultural competence. First, the students studied theory and research related to domestic violence and interventions with battered women. Films, guest lecturers from the local domestic violence community, and class discussions helped to educate the class about the dynamics of abuse, intergenerational transmission of abuse, societal constructions of gender and power, and community resources available to domestic violence victims.

Second, students were trained in the Hill and O'Brien (1999) Helping Skills Model, developed to teach beginning helpers the skills that research has shown to be effective in developing helping relationships and in assisting people to improve their lives. Students learned about the theoretical and research foundations for using basic helping skills to work effectively with battered women and their children. To facilitate their learning, students were guided in role-playing and mock interviewing. The students also wrote a final exam paper articulating their model of helping while incorporating domestic violence and cross-cultural issues.

The final focus of the didactic portion of the first semester was cross-cultural competence. This aspect of the training addressed beliefs and attitudes about culture and increased knowledge about institutional barriers that might hinder access to community resources for battered women and children of color. Students were asked to begin to examine issues related to their cultures and ethnicities, recognize the stereotypes and prejudices that they hold, and understand how cross-cultural issues affect their work in helping situations.

During the second semester, the students were assigned (in pairs) to volunteer for 4 hours per week in programs that served battered and homeless women and their children in Washington, DC. Most of the students who volunteered worked with children in the domestic violence shelter or in a transition home for families who experienced violence (e.g., facilitating teen support groups, homework clubs, and groups designed to enhance self-esteem or the healthy expression of feelings in children). Several students provided support groups for women struggling with homelessness and mental illness. Other students facilitated anger management groups or life skills groups for women struggling with addictions and trauma.

In addition to working in the shelter, students in this course completed several readings each week, wrote weekly service analysis reflection papers, and attended seminars twice a week in which they integrated their experiences at the shelter with related readings. Furthermore, the students wrote final papers that described their experiences at the shelter, their strengths and limitations as helpers, and the cross-cultural learning that occurred in their service work.

Finally, at the end of each semester, students completed service projects to give back to the community and to ensure that some of their work could continue once they left their placements. Examples of service projects included an annotated bibliography of books and toys with positive images of African Americans and women that was developed to encourage healthy self-image among women and children in shelters, an activity guide highlighting free and low-cost activities in the Washington, DC, area to encourage healthy and fun interactions between mothers and children, and a manual that describes all activities needed to replicate a 7-week anger management group for women living in the shelter. One student coordinated an educational toys-for-tots campaign that resulted in the donation of more than 50 educational toys for shelter use and several toys for every child in the shelter.

Initial evaluation of the course indicated that students were effective advocates for battered and homeless women and children as demonstrated by reports of the agency staff, the professor, and the students. Interestingly, several unexpected positive results of this course emerged. First, the work by the students was deemed so helpful by the agency that several of the undergraduate students who completed this course were hired in full-time positions by the agency. In addition, research projects were initiated as a result of the collaboration between the Department of Psychology and the community domestic violence agency. Moreover, a graduate service learning seminar on domestic violence was developed, and eight students completed this course. Finally, although the focus of the course was on domestic violence, many students indicated that their greatest learning and growth occurred relative to their understanding of multicultural issues (e.g., race, ethnicity, poverty, socioeconomic status, opportunity, and privilege).

Multicultural Education as Social Justice Work

This unexpected finding was of particular interest, as educating students about multicultural issues was seen as a critically important and valuable social justice endeavor. Multiculturalism, for the purposes of this chapter, is defined as respecting, embracing, and celebrating myriad ideas, values, beliefs, and worldviews that historically have not been acknowledged and are derived from the interactions of the multiple cultures that exist today (Rhoads, 1998). To date, many college students generally lack the cross-cultural awareness and skills necessary to adapt to and participate in the growth of our multicultural society (Parker, Archer, & Scott, 1992).

To assist students in understanding social justice concerns and succeeding in today's ethnically and culturally diverse America, university faculty have addressed issues related to marginalized individuals and diverse racial/ethnic groups by either integrating courses into existing disciplines (such as psychology, sociology, or education) or creating new disciplines such as ethnic studies or women's studies (Schmitz, 1992). Today, many colleges (approximately 30%) require coursework related to multiculturalism (Levine & Cureton, 1992).

Multicultural education combats race, ethnicity, gender, and social class oppression by teaching students the knowledge, awareness, and skills needed to transform oppressive educational paradigms and, thus, move society toward greater equality and freedom (Sleeter, 1991). In addition, multicultural education "challenges students to become knowledgeable of the social, political, and economic forces that have shaped their lives and the lives of others" (Rhoads, 1998, p. 41). Moreover, social action advocates of multicultural curriculum development believe that students should be taught not only social criticism and the inconsistencies between ideals and social realities, but also how they can become agents of social change and influence the social and political systems. Vera and Speight (2003) argued that multiculturalism needs to be infused with a focus on social change to diminish the inequities and powerlessness experienced by marginalized individuals. Thus, the goals of multicultural education should include enhancing multicultural awareness and self-awareness, and increasing cross-cultural competency while promoting social change.

Cross-cultural competency can be conceptualized as an awareness of one's attitudes toward ethnic minorities and the acquisition of cross-cultural communication skills (D'Andrea, Daniels, & Heck, 1991). Studies on cross-cultural training reported the strong success of alternative pedagogies over traditional academic learning styles. Researchers suggested that there are numerous ways to develop cross-cultural competencies, including interactions with people of various cultures, an academic course, and service learning (Flannery & Ward, 1999; Marullo, 1998; Rhoads, 1998).

Evaluation of Multicultural Learning in the Service Learning Course

Given the unexpected finding that the service learning class appeared to stimulate growth in multicultural awareness, we designed a pilot study to assess empirically the efficacy of this service learning course in advancing multicultural and self-awareness and cross-cultural competency. We hypothesized that students enrolled in this course would evidence enhanced multicultural and self-awareness and stronger cross-cultural competency because the course content addressed the experiences of battered women of color and because the service work required that students interact with battered and homeless women and children who were mostly low-income African American individuals. The following is a summary of the pilot study; for more specific information about the research, please refer to Patel (2001) and Patel, O'Brien, Hensler-McGinnis, Kaplan, and Goodman (2001).

Method

Participants were 15 undergraduate students enrolled in the two-semester service learning course. Qualitative and quantitative data were collected over 2 years. The first class consisted of seven women (one African American, two Asian American, three Caucasian American, and one Latina) and one biracial man, with a mean age of 20.87 (*SD* = 1.69). In the second class, eight women (seven Caucasian American and one Bermudan) whose mean age was 21 (*SD* = 1.41) were enrolled.

Students were invited to participate in a study on the effectiveness of the course. They were told that the questionnaires were anonymous, confidential, and voluntary, and that the professor would not know who chose to volunteer for the study. Of the 16 students enrolled in the course over 2 years, 15 chose to complete the questionnaires, resulting in a 94% return rate. These students completed surveys on domestic violence, helping skills, and cross-cultural issues three times over the course of the year: the beginning of the first semester, the end of the first semester, and the end of the second semester. Only the results involving cross-cultural issues are reported in this chapter. All of the students volunteered to share their weekly service analysis reflection papers for analysis.

Surveys were administered to assess level of multicultural awareness, knowledge, and skills (The Multicultural Awareness, Knowledge, and Skills Survey, or MAKSS) (D'Andrea et al., 1991); confidence in understanding one's values and biases in helping relationships (Awareness of Values subscale of the Counseling Self-Estimate Inventory, or COSE) (Larson et al., 1992); and confidence in cross-cultural competency (Cultural Competence subscale of the COSE) (Larson et al., 1992). Each student was asked to write a reflection paper that critically analyzed the service experiences and integrated these experiences with related course readings.

Scores on the three quantitative scales were plotted for each participant in the study, and trends within classes were examined. The preliminary analysis of the service analysis reflection papers involved three independent readers who read the papers (83 papers for the first wave of data collection [Group 1] and 106 papers for the second wave of data collection [Group 2]). Readers rated whether cultural issues were incorporated and, if so, also assessed the depth of analysis in reporting cultural issues. Those papers determined by at least one reviewer as having cross-cultural content were reread independently by the reviewers (30 for Group 1 and 22 for Group 2), and core ideas that reflected cross-cultural issues were identified. The team then worked to achieve consensus to ensure that the core ideas reflected the content of the papers. Each member of the team then independently sorted the core ideas into categories. The team met and, by consensus, developed the final eight categories that reflected the preliminary analysis of most of the papers containing cross-cultural content (29 papers for Group 1 and 13 papers for Group 2).

Discussion of Findings

The results of this study provide some support for the effectiveness of the service learning course in enhancing multicultural and self-awareness and increasing cross-cultural competency. Previous studies found that ongoing, direct experiences with cross-cultural communities were correlated with increases in multicultural awareness (Flannery & Ward, 1999; GreyWolf, 1998; Marullo, 1998; Myers-Lipton, 1996). Analyses of multicultural awareness scores indicated an increase for several students in the second year and no change in awareness for students in the first year. Students in the first year appeared to have prior knowledge of different cultural institutions and systems and how their cultures affect their interpersonal reactions and status in society. The students in the second year may have evidenced slight increases due to more limited previous exposure to cross-cultural issues than those students in the first group.

Analyses of the results from the two classes showed that confidence in dealing with their biases and values when working with clients increased during the academic seminar component of the course; this confidence leveled off or decreased during the service learning semesters. As found by Flannery and Ward (1999) and Eyler and Giles (1999), students' direct experiences with persons whose cultures and values differ from theirs may make them more tentative about their ability to remain objective in culturally charged interpersonal interactions. Moreover, it is possible that students underestimated the challenges involved when working with real clients. Previous research found that counseling students overestimate their counseling abilities until they are exposed to the realities of helping situations (Sipps, Sugden, & Faiver, 1988). In fact, counseling students may decrease in confidence after beginning to work with clients (Sipps et al., 1988).

Preliminary analysis of the service analysis reflection papers indicated that students addressed eight cross-cultural themes. A prominent theme found in the papers was awareness of the role of cross-cultural differences and similarities in establishing relationships with the women and children in the shelter, and awareness of themselves as culturally shaped beings. Students' work in the shelter consisted of creating helpful relationships with the women and children. Consistent with research by Flannery and Ward (1999), direct experiences and engagement in the process of forming these relationships challenged students to consider the impact of culture in interpersonal exchanges.

Another prevalent theme was an increased awareness on the part of students with regard to their cultures, selves, feelings, and personal issues as a result of their experiences in the shelter and classroom. For example, one student wrote,

> The most important aspect that I have learned this semester involves my perceptions and judgments of other people. Before taking this class and working at shelter, I tried to see everyone as a human being, plain and simple. I did not think about their backgrounds or the culture or look at the color of their skin, but simply thought about them as another person who experiences the same emotions that I do. Well, after working at shelter, I realize that you cannot take those differences in culture out of the picture. I once heard a Black woman say, "You will never know what it is like to be Black in this country," and I remember thinking to myself "Get over it, everyone has their own hardships to deal with, stop using your race as an excuse." Now that I can look back on that incident, I realize how naïve of a thought that really was! I know now that while I have had my share of ups and downs, I never will know what it was like to be born to an addicted mother or to be beaten as a child or even to experience racism.

As suggested by GreyWolf (1998), the weekly processing of feelings and thoughts about interactions with clients both in seminar and in the writing of service learning papers likely contributed to this heightened awareness. A second student commented,

> Another change I have experienced from working in shelter is that I have reconsidered the role of culture. It is a much bigger influence that I would have ever imagined. Some of the interactions I witness between the mothers and the children seem wrong to me because I was born and raised in the white, middle-class culture. I need to be on guard so as to avoid making judgments. As I realized the significance of culture, I have learned that I am not as comfortable being a minority as I thought I would be. Sometimes in shelter I feel glaringly white.

Thus, students, through their reflections, appeared to have increased in awareness of their personal values and cultural beliefs, particularly as they interacted with shelter residents with cultural backgrounds different from their own.

With regard to perceived cross-cultural competency, students' perceived ability to respond to ethnic and socioeconomic diversity in clients increased during the first semester both years the course was taught. Class readings and discussions that focused on general counseling skills and the need for sensitivity to the uniqueness of clients, as well as those addressing the intersection of domestic violence with issues like racism and poverty, appeared to lead to increased awareness of cultural issues and students' readiness to handle these issues. During the second semester, the first group appeared to decrease in cross-cultural competency, whereas the second group maintained its increased competency. One student shared the following:

> Without removing her eyes from Barbie's brown legs, [shelter child] said, "I wish I was white." . . . She did not want to say anything more on the subject, and seemed uninterested in hearing anything about it. . . . I feel as if I should have done something more, but at that point, I did not know what to do.

The students in the first class seemed to lose their perceived confidence in dealing with race-related issues with shelter residents. One possibility is that as these students became more aware of the complexities of culture while working in shelter, they became less confident in and more realistic about their abilities to respond to socioeconomic and racial diversity. Again, it is not unusual for counseling students to underestimate the challenges involved in actual helping relationships. The second group appeared to have lower levels of confidence at the start of the course and thus may have been more cautious (and realistic) about their self-perceived abilities to handle diverse client issues. Alternatively, perhaps the racial diversity of the first class (and previous experiences dealing with race-related issues) contributed to strong initial levels of confidence in addressing race-related issues. However, when confronted with the socioeconomic issues that arose in shelter work, students became less confident in addressing the concerns arising from the intersection of race and poverty (R. Toporek, personal communication, June 20, 2004). These findings lend support to the importance of addressing social class issues in multicultural and social justice training.

The analysis of the reflection papers also provided support for the development of cross-cultural competence in both groups. As found by other service learning researchers (e.g., Flannery & Ward, 1999; GreyWolf, 1998; Marullo, 1998; Williams, Youngflesh, & Bagg, 1997), papers written by students in service learning courses reflected attention to issues of ethnic and socioeconomic diversity at both societal and local levels. Students in this course wrote about societal issues like poverty and racism that contribute to domestic violence, as well as an interest in contributing to cross-cultural research and social and policy changes. The training received in the first half of the course on cross-cultural issues in domestic violence likely contributed to students' knowledge base and confidence in responding to issues of diversity. Themes in student papers also addressed diversity issues at the local level. Before beginning their volunteer experiences, students articulated concerns about how cross-cultural issues might affect their shelter work. Once in the shelter, students' conversations with residents made them aware of circumstances under which domestic violence occurs and is experienced at the personal level. As with Marullo's (1998) findings, these students were likely to reject individualistic explanations, and instead demonstrated a heightened awareness of how stereotypes, internalized oppression, and shared racism play a role in domestic violence in the lives of African American women and men. One student reflected:

> One of the women living in Herspace truly shocked my partner and I [me] with her views about why so many African American people live in poverty. . . . She blamed African American people for being lazy, and more interested in using drugs and having babies out of wedlock than pursuing an education and moving up in society. . . . It seemed to me this woman used these beliefs as a coping mechanism. The woman is in her twenties with four children and little money, living in a shelter, being beaten by the man she loved, and is obviously unhappy with her situation. Perhaps it makes her feel empowered to believe that there is no force so powerful out there that it can make it difficult for her to get out of her situation. . . . Thinking that racism does not exist might give her the courage, motivation, and strength she needs to overcome what life has presented her with.

Several students' papers reflected an enhanced understanding of how the larger societal issues (e.g., poverty, racism, gender, socioeconomic class, oppression, beauty standards) affect the lives of shelter residents. Marullo (1998) explains that the growth and development that result from service learning occur through observing, acting, analyzing, and reflecting. Thus, it can be suggested that the development of cross-cultural sensitivity in working with shelter residents reflected in these themes likely resulted from an ongoing interplay of working in the shelter, engaging in weekly seminars, and reflecting upon these experiences and conversations. The seminars became a forum to discuss the complicated issues occurring in the shelter, and the papers were an opportunity to reflect on experiences by incorporating discussions and relevant literature. Students' papers thus addressed an appreciation for the complex societal factors shaping individual shelter residents' lives.

A final group of themes reflected an increased sensitivity to discovering helpful ways to respond to diversity issues in domestic violence shelters and a belief in the importance of culturally sensitive services for domestic violence survivors. In addition, students articulated the importance and impressiveness of African American role models and survivors of domestic violence. In addition, students reported on knowing how to effectively respond to ethnic and socioeconomic diversity issues. Students also commented on the role of education in their commitment to researching cross-cultural issues and working for social and policy change. As explained by Rhoads (1998), personalizing experiences with underprivileged populations can empower individuals to believe in their capabilities to advance social change.

Ethical Issues Related to Service Learning

One ethical issue that arose centered on the university's inability to ensure the physical safety of the undergraduate students during their placements in inner-city shelters. The university lawyers required that students sign a detailed informed consent form approved by the attorneys prior to participation in the course. This form educates students about the risks inherent in their work in shelters. Students were required to work in pairs to minimize potential problems. In addition, students with cars were paired with students who did not have transportation so they could drive to their sites rather than rely on public transportation. Finally, each pair of students had at least one cell phone so they could call for help if a dangerous situation occurred.

The emotional and psychological safety of shelter residents and student volunteers also was of utmost concern. Before students began volunteering in the shelter, their projects and roles were clearly defined. Although coursework was designed to sensitize students to the effects of domestic violence and to increase students' confidence in working with individuals with trauma histories, student roles in all placements were defined clearly as support services rather than as counseling services to ensure that students practiced in accordance with their level of training; this distinction was communicated to all shelter residents and staff members. In addition, student volunteers were required to maintain professional boundaries with shelter residents, and the importance of not developing romantic relationships or close friendships with the battered women was addressed. Students also were taught that they could not promise to keep residents' secrets from shelter staff, and any instances of physical punishment from mothers to children were reported to the staff. Furthermore, students were supervised on site by shelter staff and off site by the course professor (first author), who remained in close communication with shelter staff at each placement location to ensure that any ethical issues that arose were addressed promptly.

Guidelines for Implementing Service Learning Courses in Counseling Psychology Programs

Although this course focused on domestic violence, we envisioned that the two-semester course would be taught by a variety of professors who were interested in a wide range of societal problems. Specifically, the course description was written broadly to include applied experiences in any community agency that addressed social justice issues (e.g., rape, poverty, mental illness, homelessness).

Based on what was learned after several iterations of this course, we make several recommendations to professors seeking to teach a similar course. First, the two-semester format of this course works well and should be retained. Students are educated thoroughly about the societal problem before they begin their work in community agencies. The staff of the community agency appreciated receiving students who were knowledgeable about the salient issues. The students, although hesitant when they first began their volunteer work, felt like they had a knowledge base from which to draw. Having students work in the agencies as they are learning about the issues is a less effective way of structuring this service learning course.

Second, carefully select the students who will work in the community agency. At our institution, we offer the first-semester domestic violence course to all psychology and women's studies students. About 30 students enroll in the class each semester. If students receive an A or B in the first course, they are eligible to participate in the second-semester course, where they volunteer in the community agency. By allowing only the most serious students to enter the second-semester course, we have minimized problems that might occur when students work in the community agency. Specifically, students who demonstrate mastery of the course material were informed about the broader contexts for domestic violence and the effects of relationship violence on survivors, both of which prepare students to engage sensitively with shelter residents. Also, students who exhibited the qualities of reliability, punctuality, and respect for others throughout the first semester would be expected to exhibit these characteristics once they began their work in the community agency. These characteristics, in turn, would increase the likelihood of the students being dependable volunteers who maintain the confidentiality of the shelter location, appropriately handle personal information about shelter residents, and treat the women and children with respect.

Third, meeting twice a week with students and requiring weekly reflection papers while they work in the community agency are absolutely necessary. The time spent processing the experience appeared to encourage the students to critically evaluate their reactions to their work and to incorporate relevant readings and theories into their work experiences. These meetings also enabled the professor to attend to any problems quickly and to provide extra assistance to students who appeared to be struggling.

Fourth and finally, the course cannot be successful without the close collaboration between the professor of the course and the director of the community agency. Forging bonds between the university and the community played a key role in the success of this course. The professor teaching this course serves on the board of directors for the domestic violence agency; this enhanced the collaboration and served to thank the agency for providing placements for our students.

Future Directions: A Call to Action for Research

Additional research is needed to evaluate the effectiveness of service learning courses in promoting social change. In this case, a replication of the pilot study across several campuses and several years (and with graduate students in counseling) is highly recommended. Moreover, the presence of a control group in a future study (e.g., one class learning from role plays and the other working in the shelter) would allow for a clearer indication of the role of the shelter experiences in changes in awareness of values and cross-cultural competencies.

In addition, there is a need for better measures to assess the development of critical thinking about cross-cultural issues and to capture the experiences of students in this course. Although this study documented changes over time, the changes were small, which could have been due to the actual impact of the course or the measures used to assess change. Finally, to investigate the lasting impact of the course in terms of students' development as social activists, the careers and volunteer work of students enrolled in the service learning course could be tracked across time. A focus could be placed on observing the careers and volunteer work of those not initially interested in social activism, and studying how these courses influence career and life paths.

Interestingly, our service learning course provided the impetus for several research projects at the domestic violence agency. In addition to this pilot study, which began as an undergraduate honors thesis, another undergraduate honors student studied the role of stress, coping strategies, and duration of service in predicting burnout among crisis workers (Salahuddin, 2001). A master's thesis investigated self-efficacy as a mediator between social support and adaptive coping among shelter workers (Baker, 2001), and a team of students collaborated with shelter staff to identify constructs and related measures that could be used to assess change among women and children receiving services at the community agency. Finally, four presentations at American Psychological Association conventions reported on research related to the course or subsequent studies.

Future Directions: Enhance Understanding of Systemic Contributions to Social Problems

Further development of service learning curricula that forge collaborations among professional, academic, and community organizations is increasingly important as educational institutions and workplaces adjust to a global marketplace in need of workers who are emotionally intelligent, sensitive to issues of diversity, and able to think critically while working on cross-functional and cross-disciplinary teams

(Van Slyke & Van Slyke, 1998). Moreover, students who understand systemic-level influences on societal problems and can generate comprehensive interventions to address these concerns could use their knowledge to contribute to lasting societal change.

The course provided an excellent forum for educating students about systemic-level interventions through collaborative efforts from university faculty and community agency staff. Attending to issues of power and oppression at the interpersonal level appeared to facilitate introspection among the students and enhance their understanding of systemic mechanisms that can either thwart or advance societal change. Moreover, through their interactions with shelter residents who often differed from them in race, culture, socioeconomic status, and educational level, students explored some of the basic issues addressed by multiculturalism: examination of privilege in interpersonal, social, cultural, and economic relationships; valuing of knowledge and experiences gained in nonmajority cultures; and engagement in identifying and exploring tensions that arise from difference to develop more productive relationships in local and global communities (Benishek, Bieschke, Park, & Slattery, 2004; Fassinger, 1997). Further attention to the development of service learning courses that address multicultural tenets and social change across academic disciplines could provide graduates with the basic tools from which they could develop solutions to complex societal and even international problems.

To conclude, immersing students in a challenging service experience, both intellectually and interpersonally, appears to promote social justice through multicultural education. Students gained multicultural and self-awareness that enhanced their sensitivity to the systemic issues of race, ethnicity, gender, and social class oppression in society, in themselves, and in the lives of victims of domestic violence and homelessness. In addition, the students enrolled in this service learning experience reflected an ability to go beyond studying diversity theoretically to confront the challenges of helping relationships in cross-cultural situations, and began to envision themselves as agents of social change. To end with the words of one student, "I continually realize my passion for helping bring about social change. Even if it is in a small way, I am excited about the opportunity."

References

Baker, L. (2001). *Self-efficacy as a mediator between social support and adaptive coping in shelter workers.* Unpublished master's thesis, University of Maryland, College Park.

Benishek, L. A., Bieschke, K. J., Park, J., & Slattery, S. M. (2004). A multicultural feminist model of mentoring. *Journal of Multicultural Counseling and Development, 32,* 428–442.

Buckley, M. J. (1998). *The Catholic University as promise and project: Reflections in a Jesuit idiom.* Washington, DC: Georgetown University Press.

D'Andrea, M., Daniels, J., & Heck, R. (1991). Evaluating the impact of multicultural counseling training. *Journal of Counseling & Development, 70,* 143–148.

Eyler, J., & Giles, D. E. (1999). *Where's the learning in service-learning?* San Francisco: Jossey-Bass.

Fassinger, R. E. (1997, August). *Dangerous liaisons: Reflections on feminist mentoring.* Paper presented at the 105th annual convention of the American Psychological Association, Chicago.

Flannery, D., & Ward, K. (1999). Service learning: A vehicle for developing cultural competence in health education. *American Journal of Health and Behavior, 23,* 323–331.

GreyWolf, I. (1998). Service-learning and cross-cultural psychology. In R. G. Bringle & D. K. Duffy (Eds.), *With service in mind: Concepts and models for service-learning in psychology* (pp. 171–177). Washington, DC: American Association for Higher Education.

Hill, C. E., & O'Brien, K. M. (1999). *Helping skills: Facilitating exploration, insight, and action.* Washington, DC: American Psychological Association.

Jacoby, B. (1996). *Service-learning in higher education: Concepts and practices.* San Francisco: Jossey-Bass.

Kretchmar, M. D. (2001). Service learning in a general psychology class: Description, preliminary evaluation, and recommendations. *Teaching of Psychology, 28*(1), 5–10.

Larson, L. M., Suzuki, L. A., Gillespie, K. N., Potenza, M. T., Bechtel, M. A., & Toulouse, A. L. (1992). Development and validation of the Counseling Self-Estimate Inventory. *Journal of Counseling Psychology, 39,* 105–120.

Levine, A., & Cureton, J. (1992). The quiet revolution: Eleven facts about multiculturalism and the curriculum. *Change, 24,* 25–29.

Marullo, S. (1998). Bringing home diversity: A service-learning approach to teaching race and ethnic relations. *Teaching Sociology, 26,* 259–275.

Myers-Lipton, S. J. (1996). Effect of service-learning on college students' attitudes toward international understanding. *Journal of College Student Development, 37,* 659–667.

Parker, W. M., Archer, J., & Scott, J. (1992). *Multicultural relations on campus: A personal growth approach.* Muncie, IN: Accelerated Development.

Patel, S. (2001). *Developing crosscultural competencies: An innovative service learning course.* Unpublished undergraduate thesis, University of Maryland, College Park.

Patel, S., O'Brien, K. M., Hensler-McGinnis, N., Kaplan, J., & Goodman, L. (2001, August). *Developing crosscultural competencies: An innovative service learning course.* Paper presented at the 109th annual convention of the American Psychological Association, San Francisco.

Prentice, M., & Garcia, R. M. (2000). Service learning: The next generation in education. *Community College Journal of Research & Practice, 24*(1), 19–27.

Rhoads, R. A. (1998). Critical multiculturalism and service learning. *New Directions for Teaching and Learning, 73,* 39–45.

Salahuddin, N. (2001). *Predicting burnout in women's crisis workers: The role of stress, coping strategies, and duration of service.* Unpublished undergraduate thesis, University of Maryland, College Park.

Schmitz, B. (1992). Cultural pluralism and core curricula. *New Directions for Teaching and Learning, 52,* 61–69.

Sipps, G. J., Sugden, G. J., & Faiver, C. M. (1988). Counselor training level and verbal response type: Their relationship to efficacy and outcome expectations. *Journal of Counseling Psychology, 35,* 397–401.

Sleeter, C. E. (1991). Introduction: Multicultural education and empowerment. In C. E. Sleeter (Ed.), *Empowerment through multicultural education* (pp. 1–23). Albany: State University of New York Press.

Strage, A. A. (2000). Service-learning: Enhancing student learning outcomes in a college-level lecture course. *Michigan Journal of Community Service Learning, 7,* 5–13.

Van Slyke, E. J., & Van Slyke, B. (1998). Mentoring: A results-oriented approach. *HR Focus, 75,* 14.

Vera, E. M., & Speight, S. L. (2003). Multicultural competence, social justice, and counseling psychology: Expanding our roles. *The Counseling Psychologist, 31,* 253–272.

Wade, R. C. (1997). Empowerment in student teaching through community service learning. *Theory Into Practice, 36*(3), 3–12.

Williams, D., Youngflesh, A., & Bagg, B. (1997). Enhancing academic understanding through service-learning: Listening to students' voices. *Expanding Boundaries: Building Civic Responsibility Within Higher Education, 2,* 74–79.

PART II

Schools

CHAPTER 6

Prevention Work in Schools and With Youth

Promoting Competence and Reducing Risks

Gargi Roysircar

"Be ashamed to die until you have won some victory for humanity," were the words of Horace Mann, the first president of Antioch College, Ohio, at his last Commencement speech (Straker, 1963, p. 42) More than 150 years ago, educator and social reformer Mann encouraged both respect for established knowledge as well as the courage to challenge it. His belief was that actual participation in community governance offers lived responsibility for policy decisions that affect a student's educational life. Similarly, counseling psychologists who are born of the tradition of social justice are committed to the principles of progressive social change and action. Among these are a few counseling psychologists who accept the challenge to initiate and test psychosocial prevention within public schools. These professionals are unique and rare owing to the fact that counseling psychologists by tradition work with adults and college students in university counseling centers and may be reluctant to work with those at lower developmental stages in a nontherapeutic milieu. Thus, we wanted to recognize and highlight the novel ways in which counseling psychologists and their graduate students step outside the academic university environs and strive to make changes in school settings where there are many disenfranchised, less privileged, minority, marginalized, and at-risk youth with few advocates. We present student-centered and value-based prevention projects because we feel a special obligation to ensure that counseling psychology graduates leave prepared for work in school communities of the 21st century and with an understanding of their roles as agents of social change in secondary education. Continued reflection and action are vital to this commitment because social justice work is, by nature, a demanding pursuit, and more so in a conservative public school setting, less open to change and with stretched resources, but that which is a microcosm of one's local community. It is the inherent responsibility of counseling psychologists with privilege to educate themselves and each other about their roles in a system of privilege and oppression, and to inspire each other toward transparency and equal access to information, compassion, participatory and inclusive decision making, security of person and protection from fear and violence, and accountability.

Risk and Protective Factors

Prevention work with the youth attends to both risk and protective factors in the identification of youth at risk or in promoting youth competence, as well as in the design of interventions. Risk factors are associated with greater incidence or severity of distress, whereas protective factors foster competence, well-being, or resilience under stressful circumstances (Cicchetti, 1984). Individual characteristics interact with environmental factors to form a risk constellation (Rutter et al., 1997), as illustrated by the stress-diathesis model. For instance, the diffused identity of adolescents (Marcia, 1980) who have not explored political, vocational, or interpersonal viewpoints is "activated" by parents and schools who fail to foster commitment to a coherent set of values. This person-environment interaction forms a risk constellation for youth disengagement from psychosocial development. Low socioeconomic status (SES) is a risk factor for a broad range of negative outcomes (National Center for Children in Poverty, 1990). Because a family does not have access to affordable primary care, a child may contract an illness for which immunization is available. SES may also function as a marker for influences more proximal than health care access, such as exposure to lead paint, inadequate parenting, and antisocial role models, which together influence eventual child conduct problems. A child's early intellectual capacity is predictive of educational and occupational achievement because cognitive ability gives one the advantage of good performance. However, achievement is also associated with opportunity advantages, which are protective factors. If a society cannot readily improve a child's inborn cognitive ability, it can still provide children with some of the opportunities, like Head Start, that are critical and proximal elements of the developmental pathway toward success.

Risk constellations or the intersection of various risk and protective factors is exemplified by Bronfenbrenner's (1977) ecological model, in which human development is subjected to simultaneous influence from concentric levels of the environment. The microsystem (immediate setting, such as family or classroom) is most proximal to the individual, with the exosystem (community and institutional practices) and macrosystem (larger social conditions and rules) being distal contexts within which individuals and families function. To illustrate the distal levels of influence, cultural acceptance of corporal punishment in certain ethnic immigrant communities is an exosystem risk factor for child maltreatment, and active community and neighborhood programs in immigrant enclaves (YMCA, temple-initiated social gatherings) represent an exosystem protective factor. At the macrosystem level, a shortage of affordable child care increases the risk for neglect, whereas a prosperous economy with a high rate of employment reduces risk. If preventionists wish to reduce teen smoking, their model might incorporate contributions to smoking behavior from teens' attitudes about smoking as well as from availability of cigarettes. The latter is a macrosystem variable that might involve removing cigarette vending machines or raising cigarette taxes. In the case of smoking cessation, macrosystem intervention might be more effective, provided that the community is prepared to accept restrictions. Features shared by members of a community are themselves important sources of risk (e.g., recent Asian immigrants' neglect of health care) and protection (their extended family kinship). The very act of defining communities is a necessary step in developing an understanding of risks and protections faced by their inhabitants.

Educational reform efforts target exosystem variables and the promotion of educational effectiveness for adolescents. Protective mechanisms include establishing small personalized learning communities, empowering decision making at each of the appropriate system levels, and holding high expectations and opportunities that promote success for all students. However, many counseling psychologists have elected not to operate within the exo- and macrosystem perspectives, but rather to target risk and protective factors that are considered to operate within individuals. Social justice-oriented psychologists are steeped in an ideology that emphasizes systemic over individual risk influences on behavior and often prefer to target the norms, structures, and practices of organizations or social units. Davidson, Waldo, and Adams, in their chapter "Promoting Social Justice Through Preventive Interventions in Schools," discussed the ways in which the concepts of social justice and prevention are deeply connected. They made the important point that not all prevention interventions can be viewed as social justice; that although most prevention efforts seek to eliminate risks for problems, they do not necessarily address underlying societal hierarchies that are the context for problems.

Universal Versus Selective Interventions

The classic public health typology (Commission on Chronic Illness, 1957) specifies prevention that is primary (incidence reducing, targeting whole communities); secondary (prevalence reducing, targeting high-risk groups); or tertiary (impairment reducing, targeting identified cases). There is controversy over whether tertiary care warrants prevention status (Cowen, 1996), because prevention arguably is restricted to interventions with individuals who are not symptomatic. Primary prevention and secondary prevention distinguish between "universal" interventions, which are offered to a whole population, and "selective" interventions, which are offered to select groups at risk for some problematic outcome.

Universal interventions are deemed to offer a favorable cost-benefit ratio to everyone in a population. For instance, the addition of iodine to table salt to prevent goiter or offering prenatal classes to all pregnant couples to prevent parent-child distress are examples of universal preventive measures. The benefits of selective interventions outweigh the costs only for subgroups of the population who are at elevated risk of developing a disorder. Individuals targeted by selective interventions are, however, presumed to demonstrate no risk manifestations other than membership in a risk group. "Indicated" preventive measures are suitable for individuals who are currently asymptomatic, but who present some individual-level characteristic (e.g., dieting by elementary school children) associated with high risk of developing a disorder (eating disorder). This renders the intervention justified, even if associated costs are relatively high. Widespread screening for persistent dieting by adolescents of normal weight, with referral of high-risk individuals for further assessment and counseling, constitutes an indicated intervention for the prevention of eating disorders. The target of indicated intervention is not an early symptom of a disorder because there is no assurance that the risk factor will develop into a disorder; this is what distinguishes indicated prevention from early treatment.

Given that multiple domains and levels, as indicated by Bronfenbrenner (1977), are implicated in risk constellations, it seems plausible that the most powerful and enduring effects would be obtained by targeting more than one domain and level (Conduct Problems Prevention Research Group, 1992). In a multicomponent preventive intervention, there is incorporation of both universal and selected prevention elements. The universal component of the interventions consists of a classroom-based interpersonal problem-solving curriculum beginning in first grade. The selected component, offered to a subset of children identified during kindergarten as at high risk for the persistence of conduct problems, adds much more intensive parent groups, child social training skills, case management, and academic tutoring. It involves multiple agents (child, parents, teachers, and peers) across home and school settings. For the universal intervention, goals include positive effects on classroom behavior and peer relations, and for the high-risk sample, goals include parenting, children's academic and social skills, peer relations, and disruptive behavior.

In chapter 7, Vera, Daly, Gonzales, Morgan, and Thakral, "Prevention and Outreach With Underserved Populations: Building Multisystemic Youth Development Programs for Urban Youth," presented a multimodal prevention program designed to meet the needs of urban, ethnically diverse populations. The program included components for students, teachers, and parents of seventh- and eighth-grade students. The prevention program incorporated three components: classroom psychoeducational instruction for students, workshops for parents, and consultation with teachers and administrators. Classroom instruction for students focused on decision making, peer pressure, career exploration, goal setting, and study and communications skills. Small group parent sessions addressed the challenges of parenting a teen, parental stress management, and adverse socioeconomic conditions affecting families. Teacher and administrative consultation focused on understanding cultural contextual factors and identifying the mental health needs of students. The program was completed over a three-month span.

Davidson et al. described counseling psychologists who promote social justice in school environments offering preventive interventions in multiple ways to a southwestern school system. These included service learning–based college coursework that provides outreach to public school students, helping teacher education students learn to refer students with mental health barriers, and consulting with school personnel on how they can affect their schools' policies and train their colleagues in knowledge and skills for preventing barriers to students' learning.

Using an integrative theoretical framework based on the nested ecological model, community prevention, and multicultural factors common to human diversity and organizational and practitioner competence, Roysircar envisioned a school–based universal prevention program. She also expanded the universal intervention to include selective secondary interventions for high-risk students and referrals of those with expressed symptoms for tertiary care. Program information was provided within the topics of mission statement, access, staffing and organization, evaluation, and limitations.

Wellness Promotion Versus Risk-Disease Prevention

Wellness programs attend to risks that are considered to be evenly distributed across the population and employ interventions of universal scope. In order to be beneficial universally, wellness promotion programs, for example, reduce low interpersonal problem solving, self-efficacy, or social confidence, by targeting protective mechanisms, such as, competence, resilience, or empowerment (Cowen, 2000). In schools, wellness promotion programs' universal interventions integrate coping skills, social skills (Elias & Weissberg, 2000), or vocational guidance education into school environments. Vera et al.'s outreach project at a racially diverse school in a large midwestern city used interventions that were strength-based and considered preexisting skills, talents, and social supports to cultivate protective factors.

Developing effective means of providing for the mental health needs of oppressed communities has received increasing attention in the past 25 years. Thompson, Alfred, Edwards, and Garcia, in their chapter, "A Transformative Endeavor: Implementing Helms's Racial Identity Theory to a School-Based Heritage Project," described a preventative to empower Black school students from Grades K–9 and their parents, teachers, and community members to collectively work through the racism manifestations in school settings. Using the rationale of liberation psychology, nationalism, and the application of racial identity theory to the classroom and school interactions, the authors posited that oppression causes ruptures in the development of healthy and socially engaging people. They proposed that racial-social activism among oppressed people is necessary to healing these ruptures. In this activism, efforts to build alliances among African Americans are important. An emphasis on heritage learning is shared by the topics of instruction (e.g., sense of beauty, examination of artifacts, dances). Teachers attend to basic skill enhancement in reading, writing, and arithmetic, as well as to critical pedagogy. Teacher training is provided to certified teachers and volunteers from the community, most of whom are African American. Workshops and consultations are held with principals and teachers from the city's public and private schools.

Unlike in the case of general wellness programs, risks concentrated within identifiable subgroups of a population call for interventions of a narrower scale, called selected or indicated prevention. Selective interventions are for high-risk populations that are readily identifiable, as are children of divorce, or those who are less obvious, such as maltreated children or adolescents with body image concerns.

Thus, there are both theoretical, and, subsequently, intervention differences in wellness enhancement and a risk-disease prevention approach. Wellness promotion advocates, however, wage a campaign on both theoretical fronts. On one hand, they insist there is more to life than absence of disease, and that our society should invest in competence and positive subjective states solely on their own merits (Seligman & Csikszentmihalyi, 2000). At the same time, they muster strong arguments in favor of wellness promotion as an illness prevention strategy. Wellness advocates counter that the disease-driven developmental models fail to recognize the global impact of positive states on mental health. Promoting wellness, they assert, constitutes disease prevention, offering protection against numerous problematic outcomes (Zigler, Taussig, & Black, 1992). Should it turn out that some types of disorder reduction can be better realized by a wellness enhancement than a risk-disease prevention approach, exclusive emphasis on the latter will act to obscure the former's potential for cutting down the flow of the very adverse conditions that a disease prevention strategy seeks to eradicate (Cowen, 2000). The wellness promotion advocates, however, need to attend to some weaknesses in their model. They need to provide clarification in their conceptualization, measurement, and determinants of psychological well-being. Also, universal interventions are feasible if relatively inexpensive and/or acceptable to the entire community.

Ethics of Prevention Work and Research

Prevention begins and ends in communities. At minimum, one must negotiate with a community to arrange access for basic and applied prevention research. Vera et al. discussed that logistics were a challenge to the successful implementation of their program in an ethnically diverse urban school. Logistical problems included difficulties with scheduling for parent and teacher meetings and classroom instruction, teacher involvement, management of unexpected crises, and working with the psychological issues of students in a nontherapeutic context.

Beyond logistical considerations, community outreach ideals need to encourage empowering community stakeholders and adapting to local needs. Vera et al. argued this point in their proposal that primary prevention may be effective in connecting with ethnically diverse populations because these constituents do not access traditional psychological services because of economic, institutional, and cultural barriers.

If prevention work is to have a lasting impact, researchers must either build long-term relationships with host communities or offer them ownership in the project so that the intervention remains in place after the investigators have vacated the community with their data. Psychology researchers are acutely aware of the challenges of recruiting and retaining individuals to participate in clinical studies; yet the recruitment of communities to support prevention intervention is an underdeveloped part of research methodology. Vera et al. explained that the procedures for community-based outreach and prevention for racial and ethnic minorities are based upon trust developed over time. Trust can be established through the creation of long-range collaborative initiatives based upon needs identified by the constituents themselves. The collaborative effort must include mutual goal setting, consideration of contextual causes and solutions, and the flexibility to accommodate the changing needs of the community. In the case of their prevention work, focus groups identified academic issues and school dropout rates as the primary concerns (Vera et al.).

Vera et al.'s recommendations for program evaluation and assessment methods take into consideration ethical and social justice issues. Similarly, Biglan (1995) has suggested practices to promote ethical social change research. Minimizing exploitation, coercion, and punishment is the highest priority. Traditional individualized informed consent is rarely practical in large-scale prevention research, but prevention researchers can nevertheless provide public information so that citizens can make informed choices about program participation or implementation in their communities. Preventionists need to submit intervention proposals to disinterested parties to ensure that the risks and benefits of research are appropriately distributed and communicated. They involve the target population in the design of the research itself. The involvement of stakeholders can improve participation as well as outcome. Preventionists maintain awareness of power imbalances among researchers, policymakers, and target populations.

There are numerous instances of prevention efforts whose proponents have either ignored or failed to provide empirical data. Well-meaning educators who initiated self-esteem programs assumed mistakenly that self-esteem is the cause rather than the effect of school failure or social rejection (Biglan, 1995). There are hundreds of prevention projects that rest on their face validity rather than evaluation of their efforts. For example, Project DARE instituted in more than half the nation's school districts despite evidence of minimal impact on drug use (Enner, Tobler, Ringwalt, & Flewelling, 1994). The failure to evaluate change efforts has been compared to a hospital abandoning the monitoring of vital signs on heart surgery patients because the past 100 operations have been successful (Biglan, 1995). Prevention and promotion efforts that are committed to and based on empirical evidence are more likely to succeed and to address the problems that incur the greatest social costs.

Vera et al. referred to their program evaluation design in their chapter. Their program evaluation proposed formative and summative assessment strategies, including pre- and posttests, verbal feedback, a student suggestion box, and a short survey of open-ended questions. These authors suggest that effective programs for disenfranchised populations should provide a multimodal and flexible format that can be adjusted based on feedback by the constituents, demonstrate participant satisfaction, and address effectiveness for both the scientific and real-world communities.

The costs of treatment are usually assessed against the immediate beneficiary of that treatment or some entity with a contractual obligation to the beneficiary. By contrast, the cost of prevention and promotion programs is typically borne by society at large, rather than individuals or third-party payers. Taxpayers are more likely to resist expenditures for intervention efforts as perceived urgency of the prevention service diminishes. Thus, those in prevention work and research need to continuously seek funding from diverse sources. Thompson et al. reported that their Heritage Project has a commitment of resources from Indiana University and its School of Education, which includes classroom space for Heritage School classes, parent meeting spaces, computer laboratories, and a library with a collection of children's books. Facilitators can also avail themselves of community centers and the local public library. The authors have established partnerships with civic organizations and businesses in the community.

Davidson et al. examined the barriers to doing prevention work. By examining some of the systemic barriers and how they have addressed them, the authors hoped to forestall the underutilization of prevention interventions within counseling psychology. With regard to training, the authors reminded readers that many counseling psychology students are interested in social justice and multiculturalism. If prevention is presented within the frameworks of multiculturalism and social justice, the authors said, students might be more interested in acquiring prevention experience. This is exactly the approach articulated by Roysircar in "A Theoretical and Practice Framework for Universal School-Based Prevention." Davidson et al. argued that while prevention work may not provide the same rewarding feelings for students as one-to-one counseling, if students feel they are correcting an injustice, they may feel compensated in a different way. Davidson et al. also added that if students are taught how to apply psychological theory to prevention interventions, they might find such service professionally meaningful. It is hoped that this Schools section overview, and chapters by Thompson et al. and Roysircar in the same section, can provide the theoretical grounding that counseling psychology students might be seeking.

The complex array of systemic and individual influences that guides human behavior makes the task of targeting prevention and intervention extremely complicated. Nevertheless, the chapters in this section provide reports on successful prevention programs in school settings.

References

Biglan, A. (1995). *Changing cultural practices: A contextualist framework for intervention research.* Reno, NV: Context Press.

Bronfenbrenner, U. (1977). Toward an experimental ecology of human development. *American Psychologist, 32,* 513–531.

Cicchetti, D. (1984). The emergence of developmental psychopathology. *Child Development, 55,* 1–7.

Commission on Chronic Illness. (1957). *Chronic illness in the United States* (Vol. 1). Cambridge, MA: Harvard University Press.

Conduct Problems Prevention Research Group. (1992). A developmental and clinical model for the prevention of conduct disorder: The FAST Track program. *Development and Psychopathology, 4,* 509–527.

Cowen, E. L. (1996). The ontogenesis of primary prevention: Lengthy strides and stubbed toes. *American Journal of Community Psychology, 22,* 149–179.

Cowen, E. L. (2000). Psychological wellness: Some hopes for the future. In D. Cicchetti, J. Rappaport, I. Sandler, & R. P. Weissberg (Eds.), *The promotion of wellness in children and adolescents* (pp. 477–503). Washington, DC: Child Welfare League of America.

Elias, M. J., & Weissberg, R. P. (2000). Wellness in schools. The grandfather of primary prevention tells a story. In D. Cicchetti, J. Rappaport, I. Sandler, & R. P. Weissberg (Eds.), *The promotion of wellness in children and adolescents* (pp. 539–553). Washington, DC: Child Welfare League of America.

Enner, S. T., Tobler, N. S., Ringwalt, C. L., & Flewelling, R. L. (1994). How effective is Drug Abuse Resistance Education? A meta-analysis of Project DARE outcome evaluations. *American Journal of Public Health, 84,* 1394–1401.

Marcia, J. E. (1980). Identity in adolescence. In J. Adelson (Ed.), *Handbook of adolescent psychology* (pp. 159–187). New York: Wiley.

National Center for Children in Poverty. (1990). *Five million children.* Washington, DC: Author.

Rutter, M., Dunn, J., Plomin, R., Simonoff, E., Pickles, A., Maughan, B., Ormel, J., Meyer, J., & Eaves, L. (1997). Integrating nature and nurture: Implications of person-environment correlations and interactions for developmental psychopathology. *Development and Psychopathology, 9,* 335–364.

Seligman, M. E. P., & Csikszentmihalyi, M. (2000). Positive psychology: An introduction. *American Psychologist, 55,* 5–14.

Straker, R. L. (1963). *Horace Mann and others: Chapters from the history of Antioch College.* Yellow Springs, OH: The Antioch Press.

Zigler, E., Taussig, C., & Black, K. (1992). A promising preventative for juvenile delinquency. *American Psychologist, 47,* 997–1006.

CHAPTER 7

Prevention and Outreach With Underserved Populations

Building Multisystemic Youth Development Programs for Urban Youth

Elizabeth Vera, Brian Daly, Rufus Gonzales, Melissa Morgan, and Charu Thakral

Identifying and addressing the mental health needs of historically oppressed communities have become increasingly important in the counseling field over the past quarter century. Despite the endorsement of multicultural guidelines (American Psychological Association [APA], 2003) and multicultural counseling competencies (Roysircar, Arredondo, Fuertes, Ponterotto, & Toporek, 2003) by professional organizations, there has been some debate as to how adequately such policies will improve the scope of service provision to underserved communities (Constantine & Ladany, 2000; Vera & Speight, 2003).

The current multicultural guidelines and multicultural counseling competencies have been developed around the assumption that counselors' primary roles are psychotherapists and diagnosticians. Members of historically marginalized communities who seek therapy will undoubtedly be better served by multiculturally competent counselors. Yet it is unlikely that competencies and guidelines that do not emphasize outreach will be sufficient to meet the needs of clients from underserved communities because of the underutilization of traditional services by such populations.

Accessibility of traditional psychological and counseling services to oppressed communities is a multifaceted social justice issue. In some racial and ethnic communities, the cultural stigma of seeking therapy is perceived as an admission of weakness or a violation of cultural norms regarding seeking help from outsiders. Help seeking may occur more informally in such communities or be targeted toward culturally sanctioned individuals (e.g., talking with a minister, elder, or folk healer) (Broman, 1987; Taylor, Harrison, & Chattes, 1996). Even if one's cultural norms permit the utilization of formal counseling services, such services are often sparse, especially in many poor communities. Furthermore, community members may distrust the local community mental health center, hospital, or university-based services even when such services are available (Sue & Sue, 1999).

Problems of access may also be due to institutional barriers such as inadequate health insurance, the cost of sessions, or a lack of evening and weekend appointments. For clients who have limited English-speaking skills in communities that lack bilingual professionals, counseling services may also be limited. Thus, relying on traditional counseling services, even when provided by multiculturally competent service providers, may be an ineffective way to address the needs of many oppressed communities.

If economic, institutional, and cultural barriers prevent underserved communities from seeking traditional mental health services, then it seems important to begin offering more nontraditional types of services, rather than solely focus on making our traditional services more culturally sensitive (Atkinson, Thompson, & Grant, 1993; Lewis, Lewis, Daniels, & D'Andrea, 1998; Thompson & Neville, 1999; Toporek & Reza, 2001; Vera & Speight, 2003). In several models of more broad-based mental health service provision (Atkinson et al., 1993; Lewis et al., 1998), prevention programs and community outreach have been identified as two professional approaches that might be particularly useful with underserved communities. Primary prevention in particular is guided by the goal of providing participants with skills and knowledge that will keep mental health problems from emerging (Romano & Hage, 2000; Vera & Reese, 2000). Prevention approaches are critical to decreasing the mental health disparities that exist in communities of color, because remedial approaches do nothing to eliminate the development of new cases (Albee, 2000).

Community outreach is another effective approach in that it brings resources to community members in their own environments through partnerships with schools, churches, or community centers. Outreach is defined as large-scale, direct services designed to address an existing or anticipated obstacle to psychological growth and well-being that takes place in the context of a community (Lewis et al., 1998). As the word implies, outreach work requires professionals to leave the office, hospital, or agency environment. Unfortunately, there are many challenges to engaging in successful outreach work that will be discussed later in the chapter.

In this chapter, we will illustrate a community outreach prevention program that was developed in response to the needs of an urban, predominantly Latino population in a large midwestern city. We will illustrate the ways in which our program was designed to be culturally responsive. We will also discuss the challenging aspects of designing, implementing, and evaluating such a program. Finally, we will discuss recommendations for doing such work in a variety of settings with diverse community participants.

Community-Based Program Outreach: The Challenge of Building Trust

Attempting to offer outreach and prevention services is greatly facilitated by being affiliated with a trusted community member (e.g., a minister, school principal, or community activist) or credible establishment in the community. As outsiders, we often have to work very hard to establish our credibility in the community in ways that differ from traditional counseling work. Credibility is based on trust formed over time and is often confounded by cultural differences. For example, members of universities or institutions may experience cultural mistrust from community members. This can be the case even when there is racial or ethnic similarity between the service practitioners and the participants. However, there are typically good reasons that communities distrust professional outsiders.

Underserved racial and ethnic groups have historically been taken advantage of by university researchers, often in the name of scientific progress that fails to benefit the community (Fairfax, 2000; Lerner, 2000; Reiss & Price, 1996). Often, such researchers gain access to the community under false pretenses, saying that they are there to address a community issue, claiming that data gathering will be part of an ongoing process that will culminate in some type of intervention. However, once the data have been obtained, the intervention never happens, or happens in a way that is much less rigorous than was true of the data collection. Communities who have felt taken advantage of through past experiences are understandably wary of initial offerings of outreach.

Building a trusting relationship with a community requires a reliance on personal integrity, not professional training and credentials, as proof of trustworthiness. One of the most meaningful ways to earn trust is to work toward developing long-range collaborative initiatives in the community and by avoiding "one-shot" interventions (Lerner, 1995). The only way to propose initiatives that have long-range potential is to engage in a great deal of listening, which can occur through formal and informal needs assessments. Community members are the best and most knowledgeable sources of information on resources and problems in the community. Successful outreach and prevention efforts respond to the needs of the community, as identified by the constituents themselves. When community participants feel that their opinions and perceptions are valued and reflected in the content of the program, then the "buy in," or engagement in the program, increases significantly (Reiss & Price, 1996).

In addition to being inclusive of community members' perspectives, it is critical to demonstrate flexibility to community members by exhibiting a willingness to accommodate the changing needs of the community, even when they fall outside the original design of the intervention (Lerner, 1995). For example, if an outreach program was designed to address violence prevention, it may be necessary to address unexpected events or crises in a particular iteration of the program if the community concern around such issues arises.

Although conversation and collaboration are the processes through which we establish relationships and assess needs, we must be able to modify our ideas to fit the realities of the community. This aspect of program development addresses cultural contexts and requires "cultural tailoring." Our perspective as professionals illuminates some aspects of what may be beneficial to a particular community. However, it is essential that our own ideas, hypotheses, or prejudices do not cloud important community goals. In an ideal collaborative relationship, both parties bring valuable expertise to the table and goal setting is mutual (Kenny & Gallagher, 2000).

Lerner (1995, 2000) also advocated the development of appropriate prevention and outreach initiatives by thinking contextually about the causes and solutions to community problems (i.e., developmental contextualism), including as many community voices as possible, and incorporating evaluation as an ongoing part of any intervention. Through collaborative processes of information gathering, program development, and continual feedback, the likelihood that prevention and outreach programs are supported by the community will increase. Paying insufficient attention to collaboration results in decreased relevance and success of such work (Kenny & Gallagher, 2000; Reiss & Price, 1996).

Outreach With Urban Communities: Program Rationale

Urban youth have been the focus of an overwhelming amount of mostly negative research in the past 50 years. This is due in large part to the toxic environments in which many urban American youth reside, which has placed them at increased risk for a variety of health and mental health problems (Garbarino, 2001). In the most recent adolescent prevention literature, one sees a shift in focus away from a purely etiological perspective where identifying predictors of specific problem behaviors is the goal. Instead, researchers are beginning to focus on aspects of positive development that foster healthy outcomes for youth and simultaneously prevent a host of mental health problems (Larson, 2000).

Advocates of this approach to prevention, called positive youth development, argue that even when youth do not exhibit diagnosable problems, there is no guarantee that they will grow up to become happy, productive adults (Catalano, Berglund, Ryan, Lonczak, & Hawkins, 1999). Positive youth development aligns itself with a primary prevention focus that is more universal and inclusive, rather than relying on knowledge of symptom predictors to identify youth who are at risk or in specific need of prevention interventions.

Positive youth development involves highlighting preexisting skills and talents and increasing competencies (Catalano et al., 1999). It uses a strength-building perspective to cultivate protective factors and characteristics of an individual, group, or community. For example, teaching communication skills to youth and families equips them with strategies for interpersonal interaction that may not only result in better relationships, but also prevent the need to rely on aggression and violence in times of conflict. In many cases, the etiology of problem behavior is not uniquely attributable to environmental stress, family dysfunction, or intrapersonal disturbance. Rather, the combination of these factors can result in suboptimal developmental life paths (Larson, 2000). Prevention efforts that focus on skill building and enhancing social support help to prepare individuals to become more productive and conscientious adults, regardless of what risk factors may exist in their environment.

Program Participants and Design

In our work with the urban adolescents, we designed a program with a positive youth development philosophy and with an understanding of the community that came from ongoing needs assessments and a long process of relationship development. The program focuses on approximately 200 youth each year who are 12–15 years old and in the seventh and eighth grades, as well as their families and the school community. The youth attend a public school in a large, urban, metropolitan area. More than 90% of the students in the school and in our program qualify for free breakfasts and lunches based on their family income levels. The majority (60%) of youth in the school and in the program are Latino, with most in this group being Mexican American. Ten percent of the students are African American, 10% are Asian American, and 10% are Caucasian, with another 10% being multiracial. The teacher participants consist of 6 seventh- and eighth-grade teachers, of which 4 are women and 2 are men. Racially, two of the teachers are White, two are African American, one is Latina, and one is Asian American. Of the parent participants, usually only 10 parents attend sessions, the majority being mothers. Invitations are sent out to all parents of seventh and eighth graders. Typically, the teacher and parent programs occur early in the morning, when space is available in the school. Both teacher and parent sessions were facilitated by the first author and one or two trainees.

Program goals and activities were designed based on a series of ongoing focus groups with students, teachers, and parents. The focus group participants expressed several sets of concerns. The first set of concerns had to do with keeping kids in school and away from the temptation to engage in risky activities (e.g., delinquency, sex, substance use) that would be potentially harmful to their futures. These risky behaviors appear in conjunction with another crisis in the community, dropping out of high school.

In particular, among Latinos and African American youth, drop-out rates are at epidemic proportions. For example, among Latino females, only 63% of those entering high school graduate, and only 49% of their male counterparts are successful (Harvard Civil Rights Project, 2004). The statistics for African Americans are comparable. In this community, there are ample opportunities for youth to join gangs, which may be especially attractive to kids who have dropped out of school and have few options. Monitoring the whereabouts of one's kids is also challenging to the parents in this community because many parents work multiple jobs during multiple work shifts.

Academic concerns were also expressed by parents and teachers. For some of the youth and their parents who are more recent immigrants, their English-language competency is a barrier to understanding the work. The school district's policy is that English-language learners receive 1 hour of language instruction per day while being mainstreamed into classes that are taught in English. Parental involvement in their kids' homework is often minimal because many of the parents have little formal education themselves. Thus, the teachers are constantly challenged to find effective ways to provide struggling students with additional help.

Addressing barriers to the academic and personal achievement of these youth became a priority for the community and, hence, the focus of our program. While these concerns in many ways are not culturally unique or developmentally unpredictable, the cultural contexts of these issues reveal social injustice issues. For example, the large numbers of youth who eventually drop out of school in this community create a different set of peer norms regarding the importance of education. The fact that many of the parents in this community are undereducated immigrants creates an economic context in which parents are working multiple shifts of jobs, sometimes 12–15 hours a day. This also creates familial burdens for the kids, who are often needed to supplement family incomes and to provide child care to their younger siblings. Bowman (1988) discusses the phenomenon through which distal economic and structural factors are distilled into psychological problems for youth and families. Furthermore, many of these parents were raised in nonurban contexts where the opportunities for gang and drug involvement were not prevalent. Thus, the parents often feel ill equipped to anticipate and manage the problems facing their children.

Program Curriculum

In response to all of this information, we developed three primary components to our prevention program: classroom-based prevention programming for the students, workshops for the parents, and consultations with the teachers and administrators. The curriculum developed for the students was psychoeducational in nature and relied on a variety of activities that helped youth explore the complexities of their worlds and strengthen their personal and academic competencies. Curriculum content included modules on decision-making skills, identification of ways to deal with peer pressure, identity and career exploration, goal setting, study skills, and communication skills. Each topic was covered in one session, and each was followed by take-home exercises for the students to work on out of school if they desired. The program activities included presentations from the facilitators; role-plays; small and large group discussion; and the use of worksheets, short writing projects, and journals. The student program was delivered to youth in their existing classrooms during the school day.

The program is designed to last 2 months, or 8 weekly sessions, occurring during the school day. The students receive the program in their classrooms during a negotiated class period, and the program staff consists of advanced graduate students in counseling psychology. Graduate students were trained to engage in preventive services through a course taken in their academic program. In addition to learning about the theories and skills involved in prevention work, trainees were also trained to implement the modules of the program, facilitate group discussions with the children, and attend effectively to classroom behavior management issues. Three trainees would deliver the program in one class, resulting in the need for at least nine trainees to deliver the program to three classrooms concurrently. Fewer trainees were required to deliver the teacher and parent components of the program because there were substantially fewer participants. The trainees were all supervised by the first author or by other licensed psychologists who assisted with the oversight of the program.

The program for parents involved three sessions, 1 hour each, held once a month for 3 months. Rather than use a formal curriculum with parents, the facilitators relied on small-group interactive sessions where parents discussed the challenges of raising teenagers in new cultural contexts amid the pressures of economic and personal struggles. Although some of the parent sessions were advertised as opportunities to discuss effective parenting strategies for adolescents, a more common theme that arose in the group discussions was parental stress management and addressing the adverse conditions under which many families live (e.g., low-paying jobs, poor child care options, discrimination, racism, and poverty).

The teacher consultations involved monthly 45-minute sessions before school. During these sessions, facilitators would help teachers identify the mental health needs of their students and help them to understand the cultural contextual factors involved in the development of academic and personal problems. Often, the session content was case example–based, where students discussed specific students, or types of students, about whom they were concerned.

Our evaluation strategy for student, teacher, and parent programs involves formative and summative strategies and a variety of data collection methods. For example, with regard to the student program, pre- and posttest assessments of the participants' skills and attitudes are used to detect changes that occur after the implementation of the program. We also asked for written feedback from the students (through the use of a "suggestions" box that stayed in the classroom) and verbal feedback from the classroom teachers every week to help us modify the program activities and content as necessary. Evaluation of the teacher and parent programs was summative, where participants were asked to answer open-ended questions on a short survey that asked for their perceptions of the program strengths and weaknesses.

Over the 8 years that we have been offering preventive services in this community, we have learned a great deal about the complexities of designing, implementing, and evaluating prevention and outreach programs. As an ongoing program in the community, there are many challenges to successful implementation that must be confronted from year to year. In the remainder of this chapter, we share insights and recommendations based on our current implementation of the program in the hope of benefiting those engaged in similar work.

Program Implementation Challenges

Before one can implement an outreach program, it is necessary to consider the existing community structure and address logistical challenges. In our case, we worked with seventh and eighth graders during their school day over several months in a school system that has many inflexible rules, in a community that has few external resources. We worked with parents who are underemployed, who struggle with providing for their families and keeping their children safe. All these social injustice factors have become relevant to the implementation of our program.

Scheduling challenges represent one of the first significant barriers faced when trying to integrate into an existing structure. The process of selecting a regular time and day for the program to be delivered to the students is important to initiate well before the program begins. Planning around teachers' preparation periods, lunch breaks, required academic classes that could not be interrupted, or the prior commitments of program staff (e.g., practicum, classes, jobs) can be quite difficult. During an academic year, there were also unavoidable blocks of time when significant interruptions in the program occurred, such as different spring break schedules for both participants and staff, in-service days, state-mandated testing periods, graduation practices, or eighth-grade picture day. Such inevitable gaps in program delivery represented continuity issues that were problematic for our goals regarding appropriate dosage and frequency of program delivery.

It was even more challenging to schedule events for parents and teachers because the school had little free space during the day. For example, teachers' meetings and events had to be held between 8:15 and 9:00, when school began, even though we would have liked to have longer sessions. Many teachers have after-school obligations (e.g., tutoring, after-school activities) that prohibited events from being held after the school day ended. It is important to converse with teachers and administrators regarding such issues well in advance in order to maximize participation.

Parent events have been the most difficult to implement. As always, there were logistics regarding when space was available, which often resulted in programs being offered first thing in the morning when parents walked their children to school. However, the most effective strategy we have found is to offer parent programs in conjunction with community/school events that draw the parents to the school. For example, there were times when the school's parent-teacher organization had events with which we partnered, such as a breakfast or book fair. Additionally, we took opportunities to offer programs during the report card pick-up day, when there was no school and parents or guardians were required to come to the school to receive their child's report card. Because this was an all-day event, we staggered our programs to repeat throughout the day in an effort to accommodate the parents' various work schedules. We also had to provide baby-sitting for parents who had preschool-aged kids in their care during the day or evening. Even after utilizing all these strategies, there were often times when parent participation was less than we had hoped for. This may be a reflection of the fact that parents have other priorities, and coming to a psychoeducational program may not have been a luxury available to them. These systemic factors reflect the constraints facing many urban parents and require a great degree of strategizing with those who know the community well (e.g., school administrators).

With regard to program content, for the youth programming, incorporating developmental differences is an important prerequisite to successful program design and implementation (Brooks-Gunn & Paikoff, 1993). Although grade-level differences in this case (seventh grade vs. eighth grade) appear to be relatively minor, the life events confronting these groups of students were often qualitatively different. For example, the eighth-grade students were focused on their upcoming transition to high school, which was anxiety-producing for many students. Additionally, many more of the eighth graders (especially the girls) were experiencing puberty and dealing with emerging identity issues than were their prepubescent peers. Developmentally focused programming is important to successful prevention and outreach programs in general, but it is particularly important when working with youth who are experiencing developmental transitions, such as adolescents.

Another challenge to effective implementation of programming was the level of teacher involvement and support of the program in the classrooms. The supportive teachers valued the interventions more, became involved in sustaining skill building with the kids, and during the program worked to maintain order in the classroom more often. In contrast, the more neutral or skeptical teachers were less engaged in the programming and often indicated their resentment with "losing" class time for a "nonacademic" program. The pressures facing teachers in urban public schools made these concerns understandable.

Teachers are facing increasing levels of pressure by parents, school administrators, and lawmakers to demonstrate satisfactory standardized achievement test scores and grades to facilitate advancement in grade levels. Although educational and psychological research suggests a significant relationship between socioemotional competencies and academic achievement (e.g., Masten & Coatsworth, 1998), some teachers believe that class time should be directed solely toward academic issues. Thus, the challenge for the interventionists involved validating the teachers' concerns while also educating them about the inherent value in school-based intervention programs. We found that, over time, the majority of teachers became very supportive, and evaluation data were useful in changing their attitudes. Ultimately, all teachers allowed us to work with their students. It is very important to elicit and address the concerns of teachers in this regard before implementing programs in schools.

Managing unexpected crises was a consistent challenge to successful implementation of the program. For example, when we offered the program in 1999, the Columbine High School shootings occurred in the middle of the program and the school community was in a crisis. Furthermore, the youth were worried about the potential for such an event to happen to them. It became necessary to temporarily shift our intervention focus to more of a debriefing approach that called for processing the event with the group, as well as discussing their fears about school violence, personal safety, and neighborhood violence. Deciding how and when to address these real-world incidents has been an ongoing challenge. Such events are likely to happen during any outreach experience, but in working with underresourced communities, it is often the case that the outreach team is the most accessible set of mental health professionals. This is especially true when school psychologists or on-site crisis teams may not exist or are insufficient in number. Although prevention science and the importance of program fidelity might caution against modifying one's intervention, common sense suggests that flexibility is essential to maintaining relationships within the school community.

Finally, several challenges emerged as a result of working with the participants on psychological issues in a nontherapeutic context. The instinctive inclination to probe deeper into a student's motivations for engaging in a particular behavior was difficult to resist at times. Additionally, we observed that some of the students were tempted to share things that were more personal and better suited to a therapeutic context. Ironically, some of the students would informally refer to our psychoeducational program as "therapy" (e.g., "Do we get to have therapy today?") even though the program was not psychotherapeutic in nature. Although we were able to attempt to refer individual students for therapeutic services when it was appropriate, we were also aware that in-school services of this nature were limited to assessment and referral.

Strategies for Successful Program Evaluation

Perhaps even more important in community outreach than in traditional psychotherapy, evaluating the outcome of one's efforts is critical. This is true because prevention and outreach activities may be seen as supplemental to traditional services, or they are grant-funded. Even when this is not the case, it is often possible to use evaluation data to influence public policy or to enhance capacity-building within the community. Examples might include helping organizations or schools to request budgets or write their own grants. Speer (1998) suggests that, in conducting an evaluation, one should consider the standpoint of several different stakeholders: the recipient, significant others, public gatekeepers, independent observers, and those who work directly with the recipient while executing the program. In our program, interventions and assessments were completed with youth, their parents, teachers, and administrators, as well as other community members. This gave us a broad range of information sources and helped us look at the overall program through the eyes of many different people who are personally invested in the current and future success of the youth.

Both formative and summative evaluations are important in prevention and outreach work. Formative evaluation allows for changes to be made during the intervention (e.g., learning that the students perceived journaling assignments to be ineffective because they were concerned about confidentiality), whereas summative evaluation is critical to generating evidence that programs are effective so that they can be continued. Yet differing levels of "evidence" are often needed for scientifically rigorous program evaluation and convincing the community that the program was a success. Such conflicts can create methodological dilemmas for outreach professionals, who may need to prove program effectiveness to both the scientific and the real-world communities.

In order to provide evidence that a program has resulted in changed attitudes, behaviors, or skills, it is critical to compare program participants with nonparticipants. But a social justice/ethical issue is raised when the community is underresourced, and withholding treatment, even if temporarily, may be highly undesirable to community leaders (e.g., school administrators). Creative solutions are often called for, such as the use of comparison groups, where students who are not in the program are receiving some alternative type of services. Delayed-treatment groups are often suggested as appropriate design strategies for community-based program evaluation. This option can be more or less possible depending on the resources available to implement such a condition.

For example, in our case, in order to implement a comparison condition or delayed-treatment group, it would be necessary to identify two separate 2-month blocks when we could implement the program to each group. Second, we would have to consider the effects of history in that some of the students might receive the program early in the school year and others before the end of the year. We would also be concerned about contamination effects in that the kids in each classroom interact with each other both in and out of school. Furthermore, given that the teachers attempt to keep all their students on the same academic curriculum schedule, it would be challenging to avoid interrupting students during important preparation periods (e.g., state testing) over such a long duration. Thus, the scheduling challenges involved in implementing one iteration of the program become twofold, and maintaining program fidelity in repeating the program becomes less and less feasible.

The use of resources in community outreach endeavors is in itself not without controversy. Often, program evaluation is either not conducted or not conducted well because researchers feel that funding would be better used to support the program itself (Dryfoos, 1990). Keeping evaluation a part of the program-planning process, including the designation of funds for evaluation, should be discussed with community participants from the beginning. The needs and requirements of funding agencies, when applicable, should also be considered early in the process. Often, these agencies have the power to discontinue prevention programming, so it is important to consider their expectations with regard to the evaluation. Even when allocating resources toward program evaluation is a shared priority, decisions about what constitutes sufficient evaluation data are not always clear.

Scientific outcomes must also be differentiated from participant satisfaction with the program, yet both should be valued (Speer, 1998). Although it is not technically necessary from an evaluation standpoint to have participant satisfaction data, addressing participant dissatisfaction can increase program success and prevent further dissatisfaction. Thus, addressing participant satisfaction is essential to increasing the community buy-in factor discussed previously in this chapter.

When deciding on appropriate variables to measure in program evaluation, it is important to note that many positive outcomes either do not occur immediately or cannot be assessed until a later time. In an ideal world, researchers have the time and resources to continue to measure participant progress longitudinally (e.g., in our case, when the students entered high school and throughout their high school careers). Evaluating a range of characteristics over a long period of time would provide the most accurate evaluation of most programs, but short-term indexes of program success must also be included. For example, in our program, we were able to measure constructs such as achievement motivation, social competencies, social self-efficacy, and optimism. In prevention work, it can be equally important to demonstrate that youth have gained something by participating in the program, not just that they avoided a particular problem.

To complicate program evaluation issues even further, there is a lack of consensus within the scientific community as to what minimal standards of rigor for evaluation research should be. Biglan, Mrazek, Carnine, and Flay (2003) suggest criteria for evaluating a program in the form of seven grades of effectiveness. The least stringent evidence for effectiveness is "endorsement based on clinical experience by respected authorities, description of programs, and case reports" (Biglan et al., 2003, p. 436). The most effective program evaluation would be characterized by "multiple, well-designed, randomized, control trials or multiple, well-designed, interrupted time-series experiments that were conducted by two or more independent researchers" (Biglan et al., 2003, p. 436) that also show effectiveness when executed in their intended settings. More established, long-term programs are probably in better positions to achieve this latter criterion. Newer programs must build their evaluation strategies to become more sophisticated over time. Yet the experimental approach has its limitations.

Practically, it is important to find alternatives to the experimental approach that are also ethically sound (Speer, 1998). Quasi-experimental alternatives, including single-cohort pretest-posttest, are often the first step in building program evaluation strategies. Once changes are detected from pretest to posttest, it is possible to pursue resources that allow for programs to be evaluated with comparison groups. Nonequivalent comparison groups may also be used to evaluate a program, especially in cases where participants cannot be randomly assigned to conditions, which is often the case in community settings (Speer, 1998). Ethical delivery of prevention services must be balanced with the need for quality program evaluation. Because there are no consistently accepted standards of rigor, the exploration of new and creative ways of determining the merit of a program is essential, particularly in community-based interventions. Rallis and Rossman (2003) advocate both a pragmatic and a mixed methodological approach to program evaluation. Using a combination of these distinct methods allows us to gain a more complete understanding of the impact of a program on a community than either method alone would be able to capture.

Conclusion

In this chapter, we have addressed the rationale for engaging in prevention efforts and community outreach as social justice–informed mental health practices. Many scholars have discussed recommendations for engaging in successful community-based prevention work, and we have summarized their writings as well. A multisystemic, positive youth development program for urban adolescents was presented to illustrate our work. In this illustration, we also attempted to present some of the challenges to engaging in successful prevention work and offer some recommendations for overcoming these challenges. In order for the counseling field to truly address the mental health needs of oppressed communities, it will be important to explore multiple methods of intervention. We believe that prevention and outreach represent effective strategies. However, it is also very important that as professionals, we do not neglect the importance of advocacy and public policy work in our efforts to confront the many social injustices that exist in our worlds and the worlds of our clients.

References

Albee, G. (2000). The Boulder model's fatal flaw. *American Psychologist, 55,* 247–248.

American Psychological Association. (2003). Guidelines on multicultural education, training, research, practice, and organizational change for psychologists. *American Psychologist, 58,* 377–402.

Atkinson, D. R., Thompson, C. E., & Grant, S. K. (1993). A three-dimensional model for counseling racial/ethnic minorities. *The Counseling Psychologist, 21,* 257–277.

Biglan, A., Mrazek, P. J., Carnine, D., & Flay, B. R. (2003). The integration of research and practice in the prevention of youth problem behaviors. *American Psychologist, 58*(6–7), 433–440.

Bowman, P. (1988). Post-industrial displacement and family role strains: Challenges to the Black family. In P. Voydanoff & L. C. Majka (Eds.), *Families and economic distress* (pp. 75–99). Newbury Park, CA: Sage.

Broman, C. L. (1987). Race differences in professional help seeking. *American Journal of Community Psychology, 15*(4), 473–489.

Brooks-Gunn, J., & Paikoff, R. (1993). Sex is a gamble, kissing is a game: Adolescent sexuality and health promotion. In S. P. Millstein, A. Petersen, & E. Nightengale (Eds.), *Promotion of health behavior in adolescence* (pp. 180–208). New York: Oxford University Press.

Catalano, R. F., Berglund, M. L., Ryan, J. A., Lonczak, H. C., & Hawkins, J. D. (1999). *Positive youth development in the United States: Research findings on evaluations of positive youth development programs.* Washington, DC: Department of Health and Human Services, National Institute for Child Health and Human Development.

Constantine, M., & Ladany, N. (2000). Self-report multicultural counseling competence scales: Their relation to social desirability and multicultural case conceptualization ability. *Journal of Counseling Psychology, 47,* 155–164.

Dryfoos, J. G. (1990). *Adolescents at risk.* New York: Oxford University Press.

Fairfax, D. (2000). From data raider to democratic researcher: Learning to become an academic-activist with the Merrimack Valley Project. In F. T. Sherman & W. R. Torbert (Eds.), *Transforming social inquiry, transforming social action* (pp. 11–36). Norwell, MA: Kluwer.

Garbarino, J. (2001). An ecological perspective on the effects of violence on children. *Journal of Community Psychology, 29,* 361–378.

Harvard Civil Rights Project. (2004). *Losing our future: How minority youth are being left behind by the graduation rate crisis.* Cambridge, MA: Author.

Kenny, M., & Gallagher, L. (2000). Service learning as a vehicle in training psychologists for revised professional roles. In F. T. Sherman & W. R. Torbert (Eds.), *Transforming social inquiry, transforming social action* (pp. 189–206). Norwell, MA: Kluwer.

Larson, R. (2000). Toward a psychology of positive youth development. *American Psychologist, 55,* 170–183.

Lerner, R. (1995). *America's youth in crisis: Challenges and options for programs and policies.* Thousand Oaks, CA: Sage.

Lerner, R. (2000). Transforming universities to sustain outreach scholarship: A communiqué from the front. In F. T. Sherman & W. R. Torbert (Eds.), *Transforming social inquiry, transforming social action* (pp. 37–56). Norwell, MA: Kluwer.

Lewis, J. A., Lewis, M. D., Daniels, J. A., & D'Andrea, M. J. (1998). *Community counseling: Empowerment strategies for a diverse society.* Pacific Grove, CA: Brooks/Cole.

Masten, A. S., & Coatsworth, J. D. (1998). The development of competence in favorable and unfavorable environments: Lessons from research on successful children. *American Psychologist, 53,* 185–204.

Rallis, S. F., & Rossman, G. B. (2003). Mixed methods in evaluation contexts: A pragmatic framework. In A. Tashakkori & C. Teddlie (Eds.), *Handbook of mixed methods in social and behavioral research* (pp. 491–512). Thousand Oaks, CA: Sage.

Reiss, D., & Price, R. H. (1996). National research agenda for prevention research: The National Institute of Mental Health report. *American Psychologist, 51,* 1109–1115.

Romano, J., & Hage, S. (2000). Prevention and counseling psychology: Revitalizing commitments for the 21st century. *The Counseling Psychologist, 28,* 733–763.

Roysircar, G., Arredondo, P., Fuertes, J. N., Ponterotto, J. G., & Toporek, R. L. (2003). *Multicultural counseling competencies 2003: Association for Multicultural Counseling and Development.* Alexandria, VA: AMCD.

Speer, D. C. (1998). *Mental health outcome evaluation.* San Diego, CA: Academic Press.

Sue, D. W., & Sue, D. (1999). *Counseling the culturally different* (3rd ed.). New York: Wiley.

Taylor, R. J., Harrison, C. B., & Chattes, L. M. (1996). Kin and nonkin as sources of informal assistance. In H. W. Neighbors & J. S. Jackson (Eds.), *Mental health in Black America* (pp. 130–145). Thousand Oaks, CA: Sage.

Thompson, C., & Neville, H. (1999). Racism, mental health, and mental health practice. *The Counseling Psychologist, 27,* 155–223.

Toporek, R., & Reza, J. V. (2001). Context as a critical dimension of multicultural counseling: Articulating personal, professional, and institutional competence. *Journal of Multicultural Counseling and Development, 29,* 13–30.

Vera, E. M., & Reese, L. E. (2000). Prevention interventions with school-aged youth. In S. D. Brown & R. W. Lent (Eds.), *Handbook of counseling psychology* (2nd ed., pp. 411–434). New York: Wiley.

Vera, E. M., & Speight, S. L. (2003). Multicultural competence, social justice, and counseling psychology: Expanding our roles. *The Counseling Psychologist, 31,* 253–272.

CHAPTER 8

Transformative Endeavors

Implementing Helms's Racial Identity Theory to a School-Based Heritage Project

Chalmer E. Thompson, Dorienna M. Alfred, Sherri L. Edwards, and Patricia G. Garcia

African-descended people have experienced injustices throughout their presence in what is now known as the United States (Franklin, 2000; Kelley & Lewis, 2000; van Sertima, 1987). For generations, Blacks had to endure constant reminders of their inferior sociopolitical status from a barrage of psychological assaults about their collective character. They also endured brute violence and the threat of murder, the likelihood of which increased when they openly resisted the treatment they received from Whites (Berry, 1995; Loewen, 1995). Decisions on whether to resist or not resist did not guarantee an improvement of one's lifestyle or even survival. Indeed, documented accounts of the experiences of African Americans throughout U.S. history reveal that Blacks developed a variety of strategies to respond to racism (Kelley, 1994; Kelley & Lewis, 2000). Evolved from historical events and dynamically informed by contextual forces, racism continues to shape African Americans' response to it.

In this chapter, we propose that racial-social activism is necessary in the obliteration of racism. Everyone influenced by racism will need to take part in this activism, particularly Whites. But in this chapter, we focus specifically on racial-social activism among Blacks. We present a framework for racial-social activism, namely Helms's Racial Identity Interaction Model, which describes key ingredients to facilitating positive change within communities. This model has been addressed in the psychological literature as a framework for promoting *individual* development among Blacks and other racial groups. However, we propose in this chapter that transformations on an individual level can be facilitated more optimally at group and community levels. We illustrate the application of Helms's model by describing the Heritage Project, one community's school-based social action efforts. We begin with a description of the frameworks that guide these efforts.

Helms's Racial Identity Theory and the Racial Identity Interaction Model

Racial identity refers to the perceptions that people have about their membership in socially defined "racial" groups. Racial identity theories refer to the frameworks that describe these perceptions in terms of patterned responses to racism. According to racial identity theorist Janet E. Helms (1995), "Racial identity theories do not suppose that racial groups in the United States are biologically distinct, but rather suppose that they have endured different conditions of domination or oppression" (p. 181). Helms developed four models that comprise her overarching theory of racial identity. In three of the models, Helms describes how different racial groups—Blacks, Whites, and People of Color—generally can develop increasingly more complex perspectives on racism relative to their own role and the role of racial others in its reproduction. The achievement of increasingly complex perspectives on racism is translated as the person's ability to appraise him- or herself and others as human. Such appraisals do not occur with the romantic insistence that people are merely human. Instead, the ability to humanize the self and others emerges when the individual discovers the need and the skill base to break free from these dehumanizing appraisals (see Thompson & Isaac, 2004). Therefore, racism is seen as a sociopolitical ill that profoundly influences the individual's way of life and his or her ability to simply be. Through racial identity development, the individual recognizes that racism, in its pervasiveness, inhibits healthy engagement with the world. It deters authenticity in human relationships, promoting fear and hatred, and under the "right" environmental conditions, it produces a propensity to conform to mass exploitation and violence (see Thompson & Annan, 2004). In each of the three models, advanced status characteristics include the resolve to engage in social action to help correct the ill of societal racism (Helms, 1995). Moreover, because racial identity development entails that the individual view people increasingly as more complex (human), the resolve for social action is not confined solely to racial matters. The individual achieves a level of commitment to eradicate the range of social ills that plague human and societal functioning.

Earlier, we emphasized that people *can* develop racial identity. In emphasizing the word "can," we are acknowledging the high likelihood that this development can be halted even at very early stages. Importantly, the likelihood that the individual develops heightened, more complex perspectives on racism is strengthened when an environment exists that nurtures this development; conversely, with no nurturance, this development is stalled.

In each of the three models, individual development involves an increasingly expansive repertoire of schemata that becomes part of a person's personality constellation. Helms (1995) stated, "The statuses may also have differing thematic content depending upon the person's racial membership group. However, the underlying cognitive-emotional information processing strategy (IPS) may be consistent across eras" (pp. 187–188). The IPS for individuals can range at earlier statuses from denial and obliviousness about racism and its impact, to hypervigilance and selective attention, to complex and flexible thinking. Helms theorizes that these perceptions influence the individual's ability to cope with racism. Racial identity statuses develop epigenetically; in short, each experience builds upon the previous experience.

Helms's Racial Identity Interaction Model is an explication of how maturation of racial identity can be fostered. She proposes that therapists can facilitate racial identity development in their clients. In the *progressive* relationship of this model, Helms proposes that therapists who are more advanced in their development than their clients are able to help their clients make sense of and address the problems that exist in various racial terrains (e.g., in the workplace, in the home, at school, etc.). These therapists are not seen as having achieved a state of perfection, but rather, as having developed an arsenal to identify the problems that arise from living in a racist society and the psychological means to address them meaningfully.

How does this individual-based conceptualization relate to broader, systemic change? We propose that the Racial Identity Interaction Model is based on a conceptual orientation that views human development as multilayered and constantly evolving. In developmental systems theories (Lerner, 2002), the ecology of human development is composed of multiple levels of organization that range from the biological and psychological at the individual level, to cultural, historical, and institutional levels. Interventions to promote human development can be implemented at any of the levels of human ecology because these levels are conceived as interconnected or integrated within the framework of developmental systems theories.

Helms's Racial Identity Interaction Model can be seen as couched within this conceptual framework because she insists that racial identity development best occurs in environments conducive to this development. In counseling and psychotherapy, this environment involves the therapist first acknowledging the pervasive existence and impact of racism and then facilitating the client's racial identity development. At other ecological levels, this environment includes any person or persons who have an influence over others and, similarly, are able to acknowledge racism and facilitate racial identity development in individuals. Thompson and Carter (1997) present illustrations of how racial identity development can be facilitated within group settings, organizations, and schools.

More pointedly, *relationism* is a defining feature of developmental systems theories: The bases for change lie in the relations that exist among the multiple levels of organization that constitute the substance of human life (Fisher & Lerner, 2005). Relating relationism to racial-social action among African Americans, to coalesce oppressed groups to engage in social action, is to promote racial identity development theory at various levels within a community. We also propose that within these communities, interventions related to antiracism strategies should be geared to removing the obstructions that prevent Blacks and other non-Whites from participating as fully in the social, political, and economic spheres of life in the United States. But more important, we propose that these interventions should be transformational in nature, taking into account the multiple ruptures that have been created as a result of structural oppression. Transformative endeavors that are consistent with Helms's advanced status descriptions reflect key elements to social action interventions: complexity in coping with racism and other structures of oppression, efforts to humanize people without absenting their race, and a commitment to social action.

On a concluding note for this section, we pause a moment to reflect on the efforts that could be considered nontransformational or superficial. We believe that Peller's (1995) description of what he perceives as the norm of Black activism reflects the more superficial of activism. In the following, Peller's comments about the contrast between integrationism and Black nationalism seem appropriate to this discussion on societal transformation:

> The embrace of integrationism as the dominant ethos of race discourse is the symbolic face of the new cultural "center" that was created in the context of the various ruptures of American society in the sixties. Relative to this center, black "militants" and white "rednecks" were defined together as extremists; comprehending racism as a form of "discrimination" meant that race could be understood as just another example of the range of arbitrary characteristics—like gender, physical handicap, or sexual preference—that right-thinking people should learn to ignore. For the cultural centrists, the concept of overcoming bias became the way to comprehend all the various challenges to mainstream culture in the sixties—movements by women, the poor, gays and lesbians, blacks, and young antiwar and leftist counterculturalists—as together representing the basic idea that bias should be overcome in favor of objectivity and neutrality. (p. 150)

Next, we examine how Black activism that aspires to do more than achieve "objectivity and neutrality" can be achieved. We look specifically at the matter of schooling.

Activism and the Schooling of Black Children

Despite improvements in educational access and opportunities for non-White citizens of the United States, current research suggests that irrespective of the school setting, African, Latino/a, and Native American students are achieving less academically than their White and Asian American counterparts, are experiencing disproportionately more disciplinary problems, and are disproportionately assigned to lower school "tracks" relative to their White counterparts (see reviews by Carnoy, 1994; Galster & Hill, 1992; Phillips, Crouse, & Ralph, 1998). In 1997, the College Board's National Task Force on Minority High Achievement found that at all social class levels, these racial/ethnic minority groups are chronically underrepresented among students who perform very high academically. Despite making up 30% of the total population, African, Latino/a, and Native Americans accounted for only 13% of the bachelor's degrees, 11% of the professional degrees, and 6% of the doctoral degrees awarded by U.S. colleges and universities (College Board, 1999). And more than 50 years after *Brown v. Board of Education*, America's schools are burdened with the separation of schoolchildren by race not only by school (Consortium for Policy Research in Education [CPRE], 1991), but also within the same school setting (Massey & Denton, 1993; Tatum, 1997a, 1997b).

Qualitative studies reveal some of the problems that students experience in academic settings. For example, Tatum (1997a) found that Black students in predominantly White schools experience a wide variety of cues from White teachers that convey the feeling that the presence of students of color is intimidating or unwelcome. In this same study, Tatum also found that some African American high school students at predominantly White schools acquired an oppositional identity that estranged them from academic achievement. Black students can encounter conflicts with students from similar racial/ethnic backgrounds who believe that racial/ethnic minority students on the whole deserve to be ostracized (see Fordham, 1996; Powell, Barry, & Davis, 1997; Tatum, 1997a). And even in racially segregated school settings, students can create hierarchies that have racial themes (Fordham, 1996).

Given the extent of problems, what strategies for social action would help disrupt the deep structure of racism in society? We contend that the strategies are not so mysterious. They have been used in the past by Blacks, but these representations of past activism by Blacks have not been easily transported to the contemporary context, at least not on a pervasive, mainstream level. We believe that in order for African Americans to engage constructively in social activism that is geared toward decolonialism, they must take into account the deep structure of racism. Efforts to build alliances among African Americans are important to this activism.

In reexamining Peller's (1995) quote on integrationism and Black nationalism relative to Helms's (1990) theory, people at earlier statuses can adopt integrationist approaches because they have colluded in a status quo that distorts ideas about race and racial beings. Raising racial consciousness would entail efforts to work through dehumanizing perspectives about Blacks. Perhaps ironically, the development of racial consciousness would require some attention to Whites, not just Blacks. This requirement does not mean that it is necessary to learn about Whites *for the purpose of* learning about Black culture. Rather, raising racial consciousness would entail the need to learn about events and details about Black people with some attention to the context in which they have lived (or currently live).

It is important to mention here that Blacks can hold on to integrationist approaches even as they engage in strategies to increase racial consciousness. This epigenetic feature of development lays the groundwork for potential change. For example, as Blacks develop a better awareness of the pervasiveness of racism, they can experience some discomfort (at best) or rage (at worst), which can trigger a need for change. One likely outcome that is consistent with the stage-like process of Helms's theory is that the individual relinquishes the integrationist approach in order to pursue Black nationalistic approaches more forcefully. When this occurs, the person will probably experience anger, even rage, and may be dismissive of those whom he or she perceives to be conformist (other Blacks or other People of Color) or racist (in reference to Whites). Helms views this shifting of the dominant schema as a "natural" progression to the malignancy of racism. Facilitation of highest-status sensibilities would involve ultimately addressing the idea of "othering" (perceiving certain groups or subgroups in demeaned ways) and strategies for overcoming it (see Thompson & Isaac, 2004).

Racial identity theory acts as a framework for explaining the contradictions that are presented as people are faced with racial matters. It also acts as a guide; consequently, its function is to demystify, nurture, and validate experiences against a background of dominant social forces that questions or diminishes the experiences. Its facilitation has to be pervasive to match the pervasiveness of societal racism. Consequently, with racial-social activism targeted to schooling, interventions that point to individual development of schoolchildren have to occur alongside interventions directed at school administrators and teachers, as well as at parents.

The Heritage Project (HP) is an example of community-driven intervention targeted at correcting the manifestations of racism in the local school district.

The Heritage Project

In its sixth year of operation, the HP is driven primarily by Black residents of Bloomington, Indiana, who have an interest in the quality of their children's education and socialization in the community. The HP is also a critical qualitative research study, a form of critical research that is "a transformative endeavor unembarrassed by the label 'political' and unafraid to consummate a relationship with an emancipatory consciousness" (Kincheloe & McLaren, 1994, p. 140). In conducting a study of change, our "transformative endeavor" is the co-establishment of the HP with families of color and a study of the shifts in thinking and behaviors that are observed by HP members as they work together to pursue social action (see Murry, 2001).

The HP seeks to (a) improve the school performance and psychosocial development of children of color (mostly Black and Latino/a) residing in a predominantly White U.S. midwestern community; and (b) establish a community climate where racism can be addressed constructively among students, teachers, parents, and community members across and within racial groups. In addition to the influence of Helms's racial identity theory on the implementation of all components of the HP, this intervention is also based on the community empowerment model of Paulo Freire (1970, 1994). In the widely known work *Pedagogy of the Oppressed*, Freire stressed the importance of school environments where students take an active part in their learning. Believing that oppression causes ruptures in the development of healthy and socially engaging people, Freire also contended that social action among oppressed people was necessary to healing these ruptures. These ideas are consistent with Helms's theory, as discussed previously.

The HP, with a membership of about 200 students, parents, volunteer teachers, and community participants, has been variously supported financially by the donations of HP members, local businesses, and grants from Indiana University.

On Saturdays for 2-hour sessions during the regular school year, the HP offers classroom instruction for children in grades kindergarten through 8. In 2004, this Saturday school format was replaced by a summer institute that also included ninth graders and was organized in association with the Mathers Museum of World Cultures. This first component of the HP, called the Heritage School, provides opportunities for children of color to engage in high-quality learning environments. Heritage School curricula include topics such as ideas of beauty across different cultures, an examination of artifacts from Africa and how to exhibit them for museum audiences, and dances from the African diaspora. What the topics share in common is an emphasis on heritage learning. In Heritage School classes, teachers also attend to basic skill enhancement (encouraging reading, writing, and arithmetic skills) and critical pedagogy (Freire, 1970). With regard to critical pedagogy, the Heritage School attempts to create learning environments where students are not only introduced to topics in which they can become actively involved, but also encouraged to discuss and ask questions related to aspects of the course content and its relevance to their observations about school or outside activities. The content and the reserved time for dialogue reflect opportunities for teachers to reinforce students' complex, flexible thinking about issues. These strategies also present teachers with the chance to discuss questions about the differences between what students may have learned heretofore and what they have learned during class. Classes are small, ranging in sizes from 4 to 12 students, therefore allowing for the development of cohesive classroom climates.

A second component of the HP is teacher training, provided by the first three authors. People who volunteer to teach Heritage School classes are provided with training and oversight in the development of age-appropriate lesson plans. Volunteers have been members of the community, licensed teachers, and preservice teachers at the university. The majority of teachers are African American. Other teachers have been Latino/a, Native American, and White. Teacher training involves information about racial identity theory and its application in the classroom (see Tatum, 1998). Volunteers are introduced to the theory and given opportunities to think about and role-play situations in which their students present with racial stimuli, or other stimuli that are suggestive of unfair social stratifications. Volunteers are also asked to keep journals of their experiences. In any given semester, there are six teachers of the Heritage School, and during one semester, these teachers, all of whom were preservice teachers, were given a nominal stipend for their participation. During another semester, they were offered semester credit.

The HP also helps to empower parents, teachers, and community members to collectively work through the racism manifestations in school settings. This third component is realized through workshops and consultations with principals and teachers of the city's public and private schools. Similar to the other components, racial identity theory is applied in this component through efforts to foster development in workshop settings. Thus far, the first author has been solely responsible for conducting these workshops. However, with future funding, there are plans to develop a facilitator training series for members of the community, parents, and teachers who are interested in conducting these workshops for various constituents.

Bloomington, Indiana, is the site of Indiana University (IU), a major research institution that houses one of the country's most technologically sophisticated and reputable schools of education. With a commitment of resources from Indiana University and its School of Education, the HP benefits from classroom space for Heritage School classes and parent meeting spaces. The school also has computer laboratories and a library with a collection of children's books. But in addition to using facilities at IU, HP facilitators can also avail themselves of community centers and the local public library. The director of the HP, the first author, coordinates volunteers and establishes partnerships with civic organizations and businesses in the community.

In the next section, we present more details about the strategies used by Heritage Project facilitators. We describe how these strategies reflect applications of Helms's Racial Identity Interaction Model with different groups in the Bloomington community.

Key Ingredients to Facilitating Racial Identity Development

With the use of the conceptual orientation of developmental systems theories as a backdrop for understanding the process of racial identity development, the HP functions to encourage community transformation by intervening with various groups in the community. It strives to alter racism manifestations of the community by coalescing Blacks and other racial allies to establish a collective, activist presence. In a community environment in which racism is frequently disguised yet pervasively present, the HP also strives to establish itself as a nurturing mediator: Facilitators make efforts to help the different constituents make sense of racism and to advance development through multiple outlets. The disequilibrium created by individuals not knowing how to make sense of racism can move them along the racial identity continuum when influential people can use informed skills to assist them.

Borrowing from Thompson's (1998) formulations on the key ingredients to the facilitation of racial identity, we describe key ingredients to this facilitation relevant specifically to racial-social activism. These ingredients include assessing the racial climate, maintaining a caring perspective, confronting dissonance, examining "othering," promoting heritage learning, and restoring historical memory. We illustrate these strategies using specific examples from the Heritage Project.

Assessing Racial Climate

The first ingredient to promoting development of racial identity in people involved in community activism is to become familiar with the dynamics in the community related to race and other intersecting forces of stratification. This assessment is important because facilitators need to anticipate the likely strains that arise from manifestations of racist ideology that are particular to the setting. They also need to know about past and existing coalitions and the triumphs that community members talk about proudly. Knowing about both positive and negative qualities related to social activism helps facilitators to acquire an appreciation of the community's strengths in combating injustice and the sources that frustrate the realization of the justice. A racial identity assessment would also include information about the demographics in the community and how different groups of people, racially similar and different, have convened to address the injustice in their community.

We conducted interviews of Blacks who were long-term residents in the community, as well as White allies, and recorded their stories about the challenges to their work and successes. This history is rich; in fact, one long-term resident who was interviewed wrote a book (Gilliam, 1985) that documents the presence of Blacks in Bloomington and the activism of several residents. In the future, we plan to include segments of these interviews on a Web page so that community members can have access to them and learn about this local history of activism directly from fellow residents.

We offer just a brief glimpse of our ongoing assessment of Bloomington. A northern state and a refuge for runaway slaves, Indiana's history is characterized by practices where citizens aided runaway slaves. A religious group called the Covenanters not only helped Blacks to settle in the area, but also encouraged Blacks to become members of their church (Beck, 1959). In a history all too familiar to many American communities, Bloomington was also known in the past for its practice of discrimination in hiring and housing opportunities (Gilliam, 1985). These practices were targeted against Blacks and Native Americans. Additionally, the savage presence and practices of the Ku Klux Klan served to instill terror among the Black residents of Bloomington in the late 1800s and throughout the 1960s. Ostensibly, Bloomington has changed over time. The city is considered to be politically liberal—a contrast to the surrounding rural communities.

Bloomington has a rich legacy of activism among African Americans. Over the years, Blacks have mobilized to face Klan activity and alleged police brutality, meeting primarily in churches. They also have organized community-wide picnics, formed Black women's social groups and Black men's reading groups, and have done so by cutting across socioeconomic backgrounds. Indeed, interviewers agree that in the 1960s and early 1970s, with the occurrence of activism, the sparse number of Blacks hired at the university were well incorporated into the Black community. This relative blurred distinction between "town and gown" is not as prevalent today, yet many Black Bloomingtonians attend many of the same churches (there are four Black churches in the community) and sit together on a variety of politically progressive committees (e.g., to build a multicultural library at a local community center). The HP is committed to forging alliances among Blacks across social classes, although this effort has not been without its challenges.

The university employs a majority of the population in the community. An aspect that fuels some of the usual tensions occasioned in college towns is that employees at the university who are not faculty or high-ranked administrators are paid poorly. For example, clerical staff and physical plant employees have salaries that are significantly lower than those of faculty. Moreover, the former group of employees is also largely White, whereas measures to diversify the upper ranks of the university have seen some degree of success in recent years. This configuration can fuel tensions among people across socioeconomic lines. The town is divided socioeconomically, and indicators of school success such as aptitude scores and school attendance are fairly dramatically different between the city's Eastside and Westside. Although there is no "Black side of town," most Blacks live in the less affluent Westside. Breakdowns in school performance based on standardized scores and rates of suspension (Skiba, Michael, Nardo, & Peterson, 2000) show that Black and Latino students earn lower scores and have higher rates of suspension than do their White and Asian student counterparts. All of these characteristics of the community are important to the racial identity facilitation and, indeed, to the initiation of the HP.

Maintaining a Caring Perspective

A second ingredient is to maintain a caring perspective in the facilitation of racial identity development. By caring, we refer to a sense of regard toward every person and an attendant willingness to endure the anticipated rage that people of color can experience as they become more aware of racism. Caring also involves a willingness to endure behaviors typically associated with racism. Although caring can be interpreted as "keeping the peace," we suggest instead that it means that facilitators persist in dialogues despite the probability that "race talk" can become heated. Yet facilitators do not attempt to demean or dismiss the various constituents with whom they interact as they attempt to inform people about the value of heritage learning and social action.

Not only will dialogues undoubtedly be heated, but facilitators will also be accused of being overly subjective or uncaring, or as having a preoccupation with racism. In one meeting on diversifying the public school curriculum in the county, one facilitator kept getting interrupted when she talked about the racism that families expressed experiencing when interacting with school officials, and eventually, the person interrupting, who was a member of the mayor's office, kept insisting on calling on experts to deal with the problem. All of the experts she named were White. On other occasions, the silencing was much more subtle. In speaking before a panel of principals of all of the schools in Bloomington, the HP director offered free confidential consultation about the problems that can arise between students of different races—problems that have been described vividly by families over the years. From several accounts, these problems have occurred frequently, and their resolution has met with little success. Although more than 3 years have passed since this invitation, no principal has contacted the director. Interviews of activists in the community have revealed that this avoidance has occurred over the years and with a variety of people availing themselves to assist with problems.

Persistence in leading and participating in dialogues about racism translates into a sense of caring for the people who are affected negatively by oppression. To maintain a caring perspective is to align oneself with the love that is required to triumph over adversity and evil. Withdrawing from the struggle to combat racism manifestations does not mean that there is an immediate resignation from *caring* about the problem. However, it could mean that the person feels personally attacked and defeated. Indeed, social justice work certainly requires periods of restoration and support from others. We believe that a future outgrowth of the HP, probably through the parent liaison group, is a support group for families and community members for allowing people to talk about the challenges and rewards of social justice work.

Confronting Dissonance

The facilitation of racial identity development requires in part the encouragement of people to confront contradictions. These contradictions are characterized on one hand by the individual's adoption of the hegemonic belief that racism is largely a relic of the past and that strivings for "objectivity and neutrality" are prudent. On the other hand, people may come to realize that these mainstream strivings fall short of the goal to address the trajectories of racist ideology. With the institution of teachers and in working with teachers, the question that inevitably arises in groups of participants after presentations about the myriad manifestations of societal racism is "Why have I, as someone with good intentions, been duped into participating in racism?" Preservice teachers, volunteers, and teachers, all from different racial groups, ask some of these questions. The expressions of each differ depending on their race and, hence, their different experiences with domination and exploitation. The other side of the contradiction is the realization that racism exists in myriad forms. The gap between not knowing and knowing has much to do with the acquisition of knowledge that was formerly lacking. This gap also has to do with the recognition, at some level, that this knowledge was not entirely unknown. For Blacks, this awareness can come with some anger, even rage, at doubting the inklings that something more existed. These were likely doubts about the capacity to read racial stimuli accurately and even doubts about others who identified the problem but whose perspectives were ignored or marginalized relative to alternative, more "acceptable" explanations. Individuals arrive at the realization that at various points in their lives, they likely dismissed their own perceptions and the perceptions of others whose marginality was being further decentered.

In the Heritage Project, our intent is to introduce content that could lead to dialogues about the contradictions. At younger ages, there is lesser likelihood of students harboring rage, shame, or regret over a history of discussing the contradictions as those have not been fully formed. Children also have a lesser commitment than adults to defend against shame because particularly at the kindergarten through fifth-grade levels, such feelings may not be firmed. Instead, children at all grade levels become intrigued instead by ideas about fairness and justice. They are especially excited about participating in action. In a fifth-grade class, the students learned about social movements and organized their own protest! At middle school ages, our experience has been that these students typically show the same level of intrigue. As mentioned earlier, teachers carve out time during sessions to talk with students about their reactions. Identity issues can be especially pronounced among the middle school students; consequently, extra attention is paid to them, especially about the perceptions they have about themselves and others who are similar to them or different in terms of race/ethnicity.

Examining "Othering"

In the preceding section, we talked about the identity issues that can be experienced by middle school students. In some cases, these issues are observed in HP classes. For example, these students may divide themselves according to social class. Not only are efforts made to enlist students across social classes, but we also try to encourage dialogue about the groups that can occur between these and other groups. To be sure, this is far from easy. However, one way of doing this is bringing up the topic of "othering"—that tendency to view marginalized groups in demeaning ways—an offshoot of which is for the marginalized group members to develop oppositional stances when they sense that others may view them negatively. While groups are not discouraged, we make efforts to have students think of each other in their immediate life where they have experienced othering, and the struggles they have used to cope with it. Typical strategies, and those emphasized by the facilitators as "natural" in consideration of the dehumanization that such othering elicits, include being with friends, praying to God, forgetting or denying that othering exists, or confronting the people who have made them feel poorly. We have observed in some classrooms that when children are introduced to topics such as the Underground Railroad or the origins of rhythm and blues music, they often talk about their desire to change how people are treated by making changes in the classroom. In one classroom, the students decided to talk about how each was interested in building a classroom community. These students share with each other descriptions of the qualities they believed to be important in building community. This racially and ethnically diverse classroom made an expressed pact to be a caring classroom.

Promoting Heritage Learning of Africans, African Americans, and Others, and Restoring Historical Memory

Because of the recency in social changes inspired by the civil rights movement of the 1950s and 1960s, there is ample print and audiovisual documentation of the storied lives of African Americans who lived through this era and whose lives were affected even when they were not boycotting buses or picketing the streets for fair housing. These changes also suggest that new generations of African Americans can listen to the stories of those who lived through this era. Sharing stories about a history of struggle and triumph can serve to equip the newer generations with tools for addressing evolved manifestations of racism. Yet there are challenges to the transmission of history.

Loewen's (1995) examination of history books prevalently adopted in mainstream schools presents a focused portrait of how these textbooks distort knowledge about events and people even with the appearance of inclusion in content. As Loewen states, racism is knottily woven into American history; consequently, accurate reporting of events and processes can engage students in learning about not only how this oppression has been rooted, but also about its treatment in different eras and with an increasingly diverse citizenry. These distortions extend even further back to knowledge about Africans. Thompson and Isaac (2004) state that in view of institutionalized racism, African-descended people can internalize the belief that their ancestry is vacuous, primitive, and inferior to White ancestry and culture. As with Loewen's (1995) observation, these beliefs are built not only on a relative absence of and distortion of knowledge about African culture, but also on incomplete and distorted knowledge about European or White culture. Thompson and Isaac reflect further on the impact of these distortions on the identity development of African Americans:

> People of all races who believe that African culture is either nonexistent or inferior to White or "universal" culture have colluded with the institutional structures that reinforce these ideas. We propose that when history about African culture and African American culture is restored, people can learn to appreciate the humanity of those from the past. We believe that the disconnection between this history and African Americans in contemporary society relates to a sense of dispossession. Stated another way, when the lives of Africans who helped build this nation and who struggled to survive amid horrific treatment are disregarded, so too are [*sic*] their humanity. Shrugging off the humanity of Africans is to internalize erroneous beliefs about the separation of the past from the present and to perceive Africans as unnecessary and disposable. . . . We believe this dissociation and suppression of history has bearing on how African Americans learn to make decisions about their perceptions of themselves, other African Americans, and non-African Americans as constituents of shared communities. (p. 135)

J. Diaz (1987), the director of the Integrated Corporation for Cultural and Social Development (Corporation Integral para le Desarrollo Cultural y Social) in Bogotá, Colombia, writes of *social literacy,* which, he argues, needs to accompany traditional literacy (learning to read and write) and functional literacy (mastery of an art or trade in order to work). In his description of the organization, Diaz's project sounds very similar to the Heritage Project (HP) and its mission. In both the Corporation Integral para le Desarrollo Cultural y Social and the HP, emphasis is placed on critical learning and the promotion of social action skills through heritage learning. Diaz (1987) explains further the use of these combined ingredients in his mission as director of the corporation:

> This pedagogy encourages people to recapture their own history. This has led to the understanding of one long term and specific program to enable people to recapture their own history at the micro and the macro levels, in the village,

> in the province, in the nation, and in the Andean Region. We have lost a great part of our historical memory. The inhabitants of a village no longer know their own origins, what their work has been, their art, their people, their glories, their sufferings, and frustrations. Thus, they cannot find the roots from which to develop an awareness of their own identity.
>
> The process of recapturing their own history in a village or in a province initiates a movement among the people, gives importance to the traditional, recognizes the popular knowledge, enriches the schools, and allows for an understanding of life as a whole in a more coherent way. (p. 52)

An inclusive teaching of history, including not only African Americans but all racial groups in the United States, can foster heightened racial consciousness. In fostering this consciousness, race can be seen as something that is not solely related to unpleasant, depressing aspects of history. In an interview about the theory, Helms (2003) spoke of the positive outcomes that have emerged as a result of Blacks' experiences with subjugation, outcomes that speak to the brilliance realized in enduring the subjugation and finding collective ways to humanize themselves in a dehumanizing society. These outcomes include the creation of dialects and various art forms such as blues and jazz music. Similar to the promotion of race consciousness espoused by Peller (1995), Helms believes that there needs to be an embracing of race. This embrace counters the integrationism perspective whose advocates "are committed to the view that race makes no real difference between people, except as unfortunate historical vestiges of irrational discrimination" (Peller, 1995, p. 13). bell hooks (1992) also describes the importance of Blacks discovering a love of Blackness as a necessary aspect of empowerment. She proposes that creating spaces for Blacks to gather together and to learn about Black history and culture is crucial to both group and personal empowerment.

Conclusion

Racism reduces the humanity of people, creating simplified images of complex lives for the purpose of justifying exploitation and violence. Variously, Black people can internalize these oversimplified images; dissociate themselves from other Blacks; or, in heroic fashion, celebrate the endurance that emerged throughout the generations when African-descended people faced racial adversities. Helms (1995) theorizes about the patterns of response to racism that manifest in daily living. In this chapter, we have attempted to describe how Helms's conceptualizations relate to racial-social action. We proposed that the Racial Identity Interaction Model is useful in both describing variance in Blacks' response to racism and promoting advanced development with various constituents in one community.

We also presented illustrations of how one organization addresses racial injustices in a community. The Heritage Project addresses these injustices in its activities with school-age children, local teachers and administrators, families, and other community members. In our involvement with this facilitation, we hope that individuals will increase their understanding about themselves and others as humans, and thus achieve more progressive, collective strategies for transforming their community. We proposed that by drawing on existing resources that already have served Blacks and other oppressed groups in combating injustice, people from all racial groups can learn more about their own complexity and the complexity of others.

The conditions for promoting this development can be challenged by a wall of distrust between and among groups, and a sense of hopelessness. Despite the fear of jeopardizing one's "place" along constructed hierarchies of human worth, we have witnessed how HP members have taken risks to speak for what they believe is right. This observation is especially heartened when this heroism is exemplified in children. Adults, whose strength is important to the cultivation of activism of children, must continue to use the legacies that have helped former generations to tear down the barricades of injustice and build cultures of peace and social action.

It is unlikely that unfair structures will ever be dismantled completely. To not acknowledge the formidable force of these structures is to believe idealistically that all that is needed to create change is individual fortitude and collective empowerment. Yet historically, social action has rubbed against the grain of social wrongs. The action is necessary, if not for the sake of witnessing immediate outcomes, then for outcomes that can be realized in the future. And in the end, people who refuse to accept violence, the obstruction of justice, and the exploitation of *any* group have also created a pathway, however minuscule, for discovering a more human and empowered self.

References

Beck, F. O. (1959). *Some aspects of race relations at Indiana University.* Unpublished master's thesis, Indiana University.

Berry, M. F. (1995). *Black resistance, white law: A history of constitutional racism in America.* New York: Penguin.

Carnoy, M. (1994). *Faded dreams: The politics and economics of race in America.* New York: Cambridge University Press.

College Board. (1999). *Reaching the top: A report of the National Task Force on Minority High Achievement: Executive summary.* New York: Author.

Consortium for Policy Research in Education (CPRE). (1991). *Equality in education: Progress in education: Progress, problems, and possibilities.* New Brunswick, NJ: Author.

Diaz, J. (1987). Learning through action in a violent environment: An experience of adult non-formal education at the grassroots level? In T. R. Carson & H. D. Gideonse (Eds.), *Peace education and the task for peace educators* (pp. 49–56). Bloomington, IN: World Council for Curriculum and Instruction.

Fisher, C. B., & Lerner, R. M. (2005). *Encyclopedia of applied developmental science, volume 1.* Thousand Oaks, CA: Sage.

Fordham, S. A. (1996). *Blacked out: Dilemmas of race, identity, and success at Capital High.* Chicago: University of Chicago Press.

Franklin, J. H. (2000). *From slavery to freedom: A history of African Americans* (8th ed.). Boston: McGraw-Hill.

Freire, P. (1970). *Pedagogy of the oppressed.* New York: Herder & Herder.

Freire, P. (1994). *Pedagogy of hope.* New York: Continuum.

Galster, G., & Hill, E. (1992). *The metropolis in Black and White.* New Brunswick, NJ: Center for Urban Policy Research/Rutgers University.

Gilliam, F. (1985). *A time to speak: A brief history of the Afro-Americans of Bloomington, Indiana, 1865–1965.* Bloomington, IN: Pinus Strobus.

Helms, J. E. (Ed.). (1990). *Black and White racial identity: Theory, research, and practice.* Westport, CT: Greenwood.

Helms, J. E. (1995). An update of Helms's White and People of Color Racial identity models. In J. Ponterotto, J. M. Casas, L. A. Suzuki, & C. M. Alexander (Eds.), *Handbook of multicultural counseling* (pp. 181–198). Thousand Oaks, CA: Sage.

Helms, J. E. (2003). *Janet E. Helms: An African American life review* [videorecording]. North Amherst, MA: Microtraining Associates, Inc.

hooks, b. (1992). *Black looks: Race and representation.* Boston: South End Press.

Kelley, R. D. G. (1994). *Race rebels: Culture, politics, and the Black working class.* New York: Free Press.

Kelley, R. D. G., & Lewis, E. (Eds.). (2000). *To make our world anew: A history of African Americans.* New York: Oxford University Press.

Kincheloe, J. L., & McLaren, P. L. (1994). Rethinking critical theory and qualitative research. In N. Denzin & Y. Lincoln (Eds.), *Handbook of qualitative research* (pp. 138–157). Thousand Oaks, CA: Sage.

Lerner, R. M. (2002). *Concepts and theories of human development* (3rd ed.). Mahwah, NJ: Lawrence Erlbaum.

Loewen, J. W. (1995). *Lies my teacher told me: Everything your American history textbook got wrong.* New York: Touchstone.

Massey, D. S., & Denton, N. A. (1993). *American apartheid: Segregation and the making of the underclass.* Cambridge, MA: Harvard University Press.

Murry, S. (2001). *Preparing African American pre-service teachers to teach students of color.* Unpublished doctoral dissertation, Indiana University, Bloomington.

Peller, G. (1995). Toward a critical cultural pluralism: Progressive alternatives to mainstream civil rights ideology. In K. Crenshaw, N. Gotanda, G. Peller, & K. Thomas (Eds.), *Critical race theory: The key writings that formed the movement* (pp. 127–158). New York: New Press.

Phillips, M., Crouse, J., & Ralph, J. (1998). Does the Black-White test score gap widen after children enter school? In C. Jencks & M. Phillips (Eds.), *The Black-White test score gap.* Washington, DC: Brookings Institution.

Powell, L. C., Barry, M., & Davis, G. Y. (1997). Facing reality in urban schools: Using racial identity theory in family group. In C. E. Thompson & R. T. Carter (Eds.), *Racial identity theory: Applications to individual, group, and organizational interventions.* Mahwah, NJ: Lawrence Erlbaum.

Skiba, R. J., Michael, R. S., Nardo, A. C., & Peterson, R. (2000). *The color of discipline: Sources of racial and gender disproportionality in school punishment.* Policy Research Report of the Indiana Education Policy Center, Bloomington.

Tatum, B. D. (1997a). Out there stranded? Black youth in White communities. In H. McAdoo (Ed.), *Black families* (3rd ed., pp. 213–233). Thousand Oaks, CA: Sage.

Tatum, B. D. (1997b). *Why are all the Black kids sitting together in the cafeteria? And other conversations on race.* New York: Basic Books.

Tatum, B. D. (1998, April). *A study of pre-service and in-service teacher training racial identity development.* Paper presented in symposium at the American Educational Research Association (AERA) conference, San Diego, CA.

Thompson, C. E. (1998, April). *Fostering racial identity development in schools and human service agencies: Chair's introduction.* Paper presented in symposium at the American Educational Research Association (AERA) conference, San Diego, CA.

Thompson, C. E., & Annan, J. R. (2004, November). *Applying racial identity theory to peace education in Uganda.* Paper presented at the African Studies Association Conference, New Orleans, LA.

Thompson, C. E., & Carter, R. T. (Eds.). (1997). *Racial identity theory: Applications to individual, group, and organizational interventions.* Mahwah, NJ: Lawrence Erlbaum.

Thompson, C. E., & Isaac, K. (2004). African Americans: Treatment issues and recommendations. In D. R. Atkinson (Ed.), *Counseling American minorities* (6th ed., pp. 125–143). New York: McGraw-Hill.

van Sertima, I. (1987). *African presence in early America.* New Brunswick, NJ: Transaction Books.

CHAPTER 9

Promoting Social Justice Through Preventive Interventions in Schools

M. Meghan Davidson,
Michael Waldo, and Eve M. Adams

Prevention and social justice are inextricably linked. Reducing social injustice is essential for preventing the myriad of problems that injustice spawns, and preventing problems among oppressed populations that lack resources for remediation promotes social justice. Public schools offer excellent contexts for promoting social justice through prevention; they are central to every community, in every social stratum, and in every geographic region in the United States (Dreyfoos, 1994). Schools serve the nation's children when they pass through developmental stages that make them both vulnerable to problems and receptive to efforts to increase their resilience (McWhirter, McWhirter, McWhirter, & McWhirter, 1998). This chapter will first discuss the ways in which the concepts of social justice and prevention are deeply connected. The chapter will then explore preventive interventions offered by counseling psychologists that promote social justice in school environments, such as (a) providing service learning–based college coursework that provides outreach to public school students, (b) helping teacher education students learn to refer students with mental health barriers, and (c) consulting with school personnel on how they can have an impact on their schools' policies and train their colleagues in knowledge and skills for preventing barriers to students' learning.

Social Justice and Prevention

In recent years, various voices within and outside of psychology have advocated for the overarching field of psychology to embrace a social justice agenda (Anderson & Christie, 2001; Fondacaro & Weinberg, 2002; Fouad et al., 2004; Hage, 2003; Jackson, 2000; Prilleltensky & Nelson, 1997; Strickland, 2000; Sue, Bingham, Porche-Burke, & Vasquez, 1999; Vera & Speight, 2003). Many of these same voices asserted that social justice is and has been a core value of psychology, and that we, as a field, need to return to our roots. For example, Fondacaro and Weinberg (2002) stated that social justice is the fundamental concept that "pervades and informs" (p. 474) the research and interventions in community psychology, and further articulated the need for a social ecological epistemology for fulfilling a social justice agenda. Anderson and Christie (2001) asserted that the struggle for social justice should be put at the center of psychology, and this assertion has been echoed by others, including Martín-Baró (1994) and Dawes (2001).

Although a great deal of social justice work ultimately might be viewed as prevention work because it seeks to thwart further inequalities in society, the converse is not necessarily true; not all prevention interventions can be viewed as social justice. Although most prevention efforts seek to eliminate suffering, they do not necessarily address underlying societal hierarchies. For example, the prevention of diabetes in general would not be a social justice intervention, whereas the prevention of diabetes for medically underserved communities would address social justice.

In her essay on oppression, Marilyn Frye (1983) expressed concern that oppression was viewed as synonymous with any suffering. She pointed out that the root of the word oppression is "press," meaning to reduce. Suffering means to endure something, whereas oppression is to be systematically restricted. Frye used the analogy of a cage to describe the experience of oppression where one has very few options of how to exist, and pathways for development have been reduced. The bars on the cage are "systematically related to each other" (p. 4) so as to immobilize the animal. However, if a person looks at only one bar, or even the space between the bars, then one might wonder what is keeping the animal in place. Frye stated that "one can study the elements of an oppressive structure with great care and some good will without seeing the structure as a whole" (p. 5). Therefore, for a prevention intervention to have a social justice focus, it must address systematic barriers in preventing a specific problem.

One critical way that the field of counseling psychology can advance a social justice agenda is through prevention. For example, Sue (1995) stated that counseling professionals often find themselves in the position of working with clients after they have been the victims of oppression, and he urged psychologists to take preventive and proactive roles to address both institutional and cultural bases of oppression. Vera and Speight (2003) asserted that "a meaningful synthesis of social justice and professional [psychological] practice can occur" (p. 262) via emphasizing both building on strengths and psychoeducational and developmental interventions; preventive efforts have at their core the principles of building on strengths and psychoeducational and developmental interventions. Additionally, Vera and Speight

(2003) implored counseling psychologists to embrace prevention efforts as a means toward working for social justice. They asserted that through "engaging in proactive (i.e., preventive) interventions directed toward social systems, institutions, and individuals," the following objectives are best achieved: (a) the promotion of mutuality, social obligation, and removal of oppression as key elements of a just society; (b) the use of interventions that change individuals and social systems; and (c) the promotion of a sense of community and emancipation of all people (Vera & Speight, 2003, pp. 262–263).

Others in the field of psychology have linked prevention and social justice. Ivey and Collins (2003) concluded that psychology does indeed need a social justice orientation, which requires greater attention to prevention as well as outreach, community service, and advocacy. In response to traditional mental health service systems failing to significantly reduce the effects of social and emotional distress in the vast majority of the U.S. population, Hage (2003) urged psychologists to more deeply affirm commitments to prevention, multiculturalism, and social justice. Grove McCrea, Bromley, McNally, O'Byrne, and Wade (2004) spoke of the emerging face of psychology such that social justice and the need for community-based, multidisciplinary, prevention-focused roles for psychologists are connected. In discussing the promotion of peace, perhaps the most fundamental of social justice issues, Anderson and Christie (2001) asserted that psychologists can play a pivotal role in establishing prevention as the treatment of choice. In discussing youth violence as a social justice concern, Elliott, Butler, and Gunther (2001) explicitly cited prevention, intervention, and resilience skills as critical in protecting youth from being perpetrators and/or victims of violence. Finally, Petrosino (2003) noted that research has demonstrated repeatedly that problems during childhood and adolescence generally manifest themselves later in adulthood, and that prevention programs could advance social justice by reducing the frequency of those problems.

Barriers to Prevention

Although prevention activities are plentiful, it is important to examine the barriers to doing prevention work. By examining some of the systemic barriers and how we have addressed them, we hope to forestall the underutilization of prevention interventions within counseling psychology.

Perhaps the biggest barrier is that prevention interventions are not reimbursed in the same manner as individual treatment (Helms, 2003). Although health insurance companies may not reimburse for prevention per se, many local, state, and national organizations provide resources for preventive interventions (Romano & Hage, 2000). Specifically, there are extensive grant monies to address social justice issues using prevention interventions from such federal agencies as the Health Resources and Services Administration and the U.S. Department of Education.

Another barrier to prevention interventions may be that many students who have chosen to get a degree in counseling psychology have done so in order to work with individuals. It is not that they did not know about social work, but more likely, they did not want to engage in case management and work with systems. However, many of these same students are interested in social justice and multiculturalism; if prevention work is contextualized in the frameworks of multiculturalism and social justice, students may be more interested in acquiring prevention experience, particularly if they are taught how to apply psychological theory to these interventions. Prevention work may not provide the same rewarding feelings of a working alliance with an individual client, but if students feel they are correcting an injustice, they may feel compensated in a different way.

Another barrier may be that counseling psychology programs are already filled with required coursework, so there is some resistance to finding space for a consultation and/or prevention course. Because consultation and public policy/advocacy are two of the core competencies of a psychologist ("Future Directions in Education," 2002), prevention should be a necessary element of any doctoral curriculum. Training for these competencies may be addressed adequately by infusing them in such courses as multicultural counseling, career counseling, health psychology, and any course that requires a systems perspective. Given the overlapping and complementary nature of prevention, multiculturalism, and social justice, it may be best not to have a separate course.

A related barrier to prevention activities involving consultation and advocacy is that such efforts require skilled interdisciplinary collaborations. A student's nascent professional identity as a counseling psychologist may create some insecurity when dealing with other professionals. In cross-listed classes, there often appears to be some discomfort with, and judgment about, the perspectives of students from other disciplines such as social work or school psychology. The ability to engage in interdisciplinary collaborations is, at best, a serendipitous occurrence in one's training and is probably more likely to occur in postdoctoral activities. Teaching counseling psychology trainees what they can bring to collaborations with various disciplines, as well as what they can learn from these disciplines, is an essential part of the professional socialization process. By creating greater student involvement in prevention efforts they will gain greater experience with interdisciplinary collaborations.

Clearly, agendas of social justice have given rise to a focus on prevention, and prevention activities and interventions have promoted social justice initiatives. There appears a history of the complementary relationship between prevention and social justice and a call for this relationship to propel our future work as counseling psychologists. Background information, assessment, and preventive interventions that have advanced social justice will be described below.

Pressing Needs for Prevention and Social Justice in New Mexico's Schools

Two of the authors have collaborated with other professionals to prevent problems and foster social justice for New Mexico's public school students. Their efforts have focused on furnishing direct service to students and providing both future and current teachers with training in the knowledge and skills they need to initiate preventive interventions promoting social justice.

Challenges facing families in New Mexico make prevention efforts in the schools particularly compelling vehicles for promoting social justice. New Mexico is an ethnically diverse (approximately 49% Anglo, 39% Hispanic, 9% Native American, 2% African American, and 1% Asian), rural state (12.5 persons per square mile) that has the largest number of children living in poverty in America (Annie E. Casey Foundation, 1999). These statistics are the warning signs of social injustice for New Mexico's children. Disparities in resources due to ethnicity, geography, and poverty make it unlikely that many New Mexico students will have access to and make use of mental health services compared to other groups. Low-income, rural, ethnically diverse populations show the lowest rates of mental health service utilization throughout the United States (Levy & Land, 1994; Steff & Prosperi, 1985; Stiffman, Earls, Robins, & Young, 1988). This pattern is certainly true in New Mexico, where the majority of students with problems are not receiving support or mental health interventions (New Mexico Department of Health, 1998). As a result, New Mexico is distinguished by ranking fifth in teen suicide, fourth in school dropout, and third in teen pregnancy in the United States (Annie E. Casey Foundation, 1999). New Mexico has been rated as one of the three worst states in which to raise children (Adelsheim, 2000). The discrepancy between children's needs and the services they are receiving argues for counseling psychologists to promote social justice by working to increase treatment resources and by providing prevention services to a larger segment of the population.

Needs and Resources Assessment

As a first step in designing preventive interventions that promote social justice, one of the authors collaborated with school psychologists, school nurses, teachers, parents, and students to develop a survey assessing barriers to students' learning (Grau, Waldo, Garcia-Vazquez, & Steiner, 2001). The survey asked students what problems interfere with their learning, to what extent they received help with those problems, and who helped them. Results from the survey revealed that fully one half of New Mexico high school student respondents experienced personal and/or social problems that they believed interfered with their learning (Grau et al., 2001). Problems included lack of academic/career goals (44%), depression/anger/anxiety/stress (64%), suicidal tendencies/self-injury (23%), violence (59%), threats/harassment (42%), and being treated poorly because of race or gender (33%). Less than 50% of the students who reported that they had problems said they received any help with those problems. Less than 10% of the students said they received help from agencies or social services outside the schools. The professionals from whom students most frequently reported receiving help were teachers (64%). Use of the same instrument with New Mexico middle school students yielded parallel results (Scullion, Silva, Steiner, & Waldo, 1999). The pattern of responses was the same, except that the high school students reported more problems, less help in general, and less help from mental health professionals; these findings suggest that conditions worsen as youth progress through school. The findings were used to target preventive interventions that promote social justice with students, preservice teachers, and school personnel. The preventive interventions will be described below.

Social Justice Service Learning Outreach to Public School Students

Lack of academic/career goals was cited by 44% of New Mexican students who completed a survey on barriers to their learning, and less than half of them (37%) indicated that they were receiving no help with this problem (Grau et al., 2001). In one of the authors' career counseling courses for counseling psychology students, there is a service learning project that requires all of the students to provide some sort of career intervention to an at-risk group. By "at-risk," we mean that the clients are at risk for being underserved by career development specialists and therefore are at risk for underutilizing their abilities. The service learning projects require that the students take action in promoting one of the social justice principles identified by Anderson and Christie (2001): "Reducing the wealth gap improves human well-being" (p. 176).

Students in the career counseling course initiated two service learning activities in public school settings. The first activity was to help all middle school students from one school district in a low-income county to access a computerized self-assessment tool. Master's and doctoral students went into classes with teachers and school counselors to help students begin considering their career aspirations based on the self-assessment results. The second project was to help selected students from an academically at-risk high school program discuss both their results on a computerized self-assessment tool and the perceived barriers they faced in implementing career decisions.

The career counseling students discussed their service learning experiences during class. Issues arising from lack of income, ethnicity, and English as a second language status became much more relevant to their understanding of career development. Through this project, public school students received services that were otherwise unavailable to them. Finally, both the department and the College of Education fostered positive public relations by fulfilling their service obligations to the community.

Promoting Prevention Through Social Justice Training in Teacher Education

As indicated above, 64% of New Mexican students who responded to a survey assessing barriers to learning indicated that depression/anger/anxiety/stress interfere with their learning (Grau et al., 2001). Again, less than half of these students (39%) indicated that they were getting any help with these problems. The survey also pointed out the importance of counseling psychologists working with teachers, because survey data suggested that teachers are the professionals to whom New Mexico students are most likely to turn for help. This finding suggested that counseling psychologists could promote problem prevention and social justice among youth by helping teachers acquire the knowledge and skills needed to help students overcome problems that pose barriers to their learning. In response to these data, the authors took advantage of opportunities within the College of Education in which they taught to empower future teachers to promote prevention and social justice.

Identification and Referral of Students With Barriers to Their Learning

Counseling psychologists changed the course content of their department's educational psychology course (which is required for all students preparing to be teachers) so that the course included training in the signs and symptoms of mental disorders that affect children and adolescents (Mayfield, Kaczmarek, & Waldo, 2000). In addition to lecture and videotaped demonstrations, preservice teachers received a manual addressing mental health issues in the classroom. The course was also modified to help the future teachers identify and advocate for mental health resources in their communities, and develop skills for facilitating the referral of troubled students to qualified mental health professionals. Pre- and posttesting of 112 teacher education students revealed significant increases in their knowledge about mental disorders affecting youth (Kaczmarek, Waldo, Mayfield, & Steiner, 2003). A second study (Scullion, 2003) was conducted on the class that employed random assignment of education students to either receive the training early in the semester (experimental condition, $n = 41$) or be placed on a wait list for training later in the semester (control condition, $n = 38$). Participants in the experimental condition showed significant improvement in their ability to communicate with students, teachers, and parents about student referrals, in comparison to those in the control condition.

Addressing Prejudice Through Multicultural Relationship Skills Workshops

Reducing violence and aggression in the schools has become part of contemporary U.S. education reform (Walsh & Galassi, 2002) and counseling prevention efforts in schools (Vera & Reese, 2000). Fifty-nine percent of surveyed New Mexican students reported concerns about violence and aggression, and less than half (33%) of them reported receiving help with these problems (Grau et al., 2001). Many of the organizations that are interested in creating nonviolent schools in the United States have a social justice agenda related to teaching young people how to confront prejudice and reduce hate crimes perpetrated by those who are intolerant of members of marginalized groups that are different from themselves (e.g., Southern Poverty Law Center and the Anti-Defamation League). Thirty-three percent of surveyed New Mexican students reported that being treated poorly because of race or gender interfered with their learning, and again, less than half of them reported receiving help (36%) (Grau et al., 2001).

Social justice prevention efforts addressing prejudice require multiple layers of intervention, because they are most effective if they target school personnel in addition to students (Peltier, 1998; U.S. Department of Education's Office for Civil Rights, 1999). Teaching future educators how to model effective communication skills when addressing prejudice and handling multicultural conflict situations could help prevent further incidences of prejudice-related violence (Peltier, 1998). Ideally, the reduction of violence in such situations also helps prevent secondary victimization in which individuals belonging to the same group as a primary victim also feel targeted and unprotected because the acts of violence are not handled appropriately by officials. For example, 36% of U.S. gay youth said that faculty never intervened when they heard homophobic remarks (Gay, Lesbian, Straight Education Network, 2003).

Counseling psychologists can collaborate with educators, many of whom are not comfortable addressing cross-cultural conflicts, by developing primary intervention programs aimed at training school personnel to effectively confront prejudice (Peltier, 1998). Addressing the social injustice of prejudice as both a person-centered intervention (i.e., teachers' growth) and an environment-centered intervention (i.e., the environment created by these teachers for their students who are directly harassed, and the students who are observing the harassment) increases the likelihood that prevention programs will create change (Vera & Reese, 2000).

In a preventive intervention conducted by two of the authors, Multicultural Relationship Skills Workshops were offered to teacher education students to help them develop interpersonal skills and cultural sensitivity. The teacher education students interacted with each other as members of different cultures who had different experiences related to prejudice (Adams et al., 2000). Counseling psychology graduate students served as workshop leaders. The workshops were an elective class activity within an educational psychology course. The workshops were based on Relationship Enhancement principles (Guerney, 1977) and were organized to maximize the beneficial impact of group dynamics (Waldo, 1985). The goal was to prepare future teachers to communicate effectively within their social justice/nonviolence advocate role with diverse students and parents when they assume positions in the public schools. Education students learned empathic listening and expressive speaking skills for addressing multicultural conflict situations.

An experimental evaluation of the workshops was conducted by randomly assigning 26 students to workshops early in the semester (experimental condition) and 22 students to workshops later in the semester (control condition). Comparison of the two groups showed significant gains in interpersonal skills for confronting prejudice in the experimental condition (Adams et al., 2003). This intervention is an example of Anderson and Christie's (2001) Principle 3 in promoting peace and social justice: "Violence can be prevented by constructive uses of conflict" (p. 177). We need to encourage others to speak and listen to one another.

Promoting Social Justice Through In-Service Prevention Training With School Personnel

In addition to offering training to preservice teacher education students, two of the authors have engaged in prevention to promote social justice in schools by consulting directly with school personnel. Two prevention consultation projects with school personnel are described below.

Safe School Project

One of the authors serves on the Board of Directors of the local Parents and Friends of Lesbians and Gays (PFLAG) chapter. PFLAG's national Schoolhouse Project seeks to make school environments safer for lesbian, gay, bisexual, and transgendered (LGBT) youth. PFLAG materials (PFLAG, 2001) and information from the Safe Schools Coalition Web site (2004), the APA LGB Healthy Student Web site (n.d.), and the GLSEN Web site (2003) were used to provide LGBT sensitivity training to five different groups of school personnel (school nurses, psychologists, social workers, counselors, and academic deans) at the elementary, middle, and high school levels. The prevention effort included information on confronting prejudice presented in the Multicultural Relationship Skills workshops described above; resources furnishing additional information on lesbian, gay, and bisexual youth; referral strategies; and "Safe Zone" posters that stated discrimination of any sort (including sexual orientation) would not be tolerated. The posters were displayed prominently and were, in many cases, the only visible sign to students that all sexual orientations were accepted by someone in the schools. The workshops may not have taken place if we had asked the upper administration of the public schools to let us provide this information; only by networking informally with a few staff members in each of the staff groups listed above were we invited to present. In the presentations, each participant was asked to think about who he or she could potentially influence with the information he or she received.

Supporting Teachers Supporting Students

One of the authors helped initiate a program for current teachers in which they were trained in the knowledge and skills needed to help students overcome barriers to their learning. Titled "Supporting Teachers Supporting Students," the program employed a "train the trainers" approach that has been demonstrated to be an effective and efficient method for disseminating preventive interventions in other settings (Waldo, 1989). Teachers and other school personnel (school counselors, social workers, nurses, principals, and case managers) were recruited from schools throughout New Mexico to serve as workshop leaders. These workshop leaders learned information and skills that they, in turn, could impart to their colleagues by leading workshops back in their schools. Some of the areas in which they were prepared to provide training included (a) prevalence and indexes of mental disorders among students, (b) impact of trauma on learning, (c) effects of poverty, (d) multicultural influences on learning, (e) effective communication with students and parents, (f) power and control issues in the classroom, (g) resiliency, and (h) establishment of referral networks.

The leaders received extensive training on workshop facilitation and a workshop leader's manual (Waldo & Liessmann, 2001). Workshop facilitation training covered potential benefits of workshop participation for members (universality, hope, catharsis, corrective reenactment, cohesion, altruism, feedback, information, modeling, techniques, and reality checks); dynamics associated with different developmental stages of groups (forming, storming, norming, performing, and adjourning);

and variations in leadership styles (executive function, emotional stimulation, caring, and meaning attribution) (Waldo, 1985). The workshop leaders learned and practiced two formats for running workshops: (a) a skill development format that involved them in describing, demonstrating, guiding participants' practice, and facilitating discussion of a specific skill; and (b) a discussion format based on theme-centered interaction for raising participants' awareness, motivation, and collaboration for addressing problems.

The workshop leaders offered two workshops for teachers and other school staff back in their own schools. During the first year of the program, there were 16 co-leader teams (32 leaders). Workshop attendance varied from 5 to 40 participants, with average attendance being 8 members. A total of 253 school personnel participated in the workshops, including teachers, special education staff, educational assistants, support staff, and administrators. The workshops were typically 1.5 hours in length. One of the authors attended a number of the workshops to serve as a consultant to the leaders.

Workshop participants evaluated the quality and usefulness of the workshops at the conclusion of the workshop meetings. An average of more than 90% of the participants agreed with positive evaluations of the workshops. For example, 98% of participants agreed that the objectives of the sessions were met and that the information presented addressed a need at their school. During the second year of the program, these numbers more than doubled (64 leaders, 640 participants), and again, more than 90% of the participants agreed with positive evaluations of the workshops. In its third year, the program once again more than doubled in size (132 leaders, 1,320 participants). At this rate of expansion, the program could offer a workshop to every teacher in New Mexico in 4 years, potentially benefiting all students in New Mexico public schools.

The "Supporting Teachers Supporting Students" program provided an excellent vehicle through which psychologists contributed to efforts to promote problem prevention and social justice for rural, poor, minority youth (Kenny, Waldo, Warter, & Barton, 2002). The counseling psychologists worked with a multidisciplinary steering team that included a teacher (experienced in both regular and special education), a child psychiatrist, and a counselor. The psychologists provided specific expertise on barriers to students' development, guidelines for workshop design, workshop leadership training, consultation with leaders while workshops were being offered, and a great deal of encouragement to school personnel who were uneasy about offering workshops for their colleagues. The psychologists were effective at promoting prevention and social justice in the schools through collaboration with school personnel.

Conclusion

Through this chapter, we attempted to clearly articulate theoretically how prevention interventions and strategies can foster social justice. Additionally, we attempted to provide concrete examples of various applied prevention activities that sought and achieved further social justice and social change in school environments. It is our hope that we have inspired readers to embrace prevention as a critical method to further the social justice agenda of psychology.

References

Adams, E. M., Waldo, M., Steiner, R., Mayfield, R., Ackerlind, S. J., & Castellanos, L. P. (2003). Creating peace by confronting prejudice: Examining the effects of a multicultural communication skills group intervention. *International Journal for the Advancement of Counseling, 25,* 281–291.

Adams, E. M., Waldo, M., Vazquez, L., Ackerland, S., Mayfield, R., & Stoltzfus, S. (2000). Empowering teachers to confront prejudice in borderland schools. *Border Walking Journal, 4,* 5–14.

Adelsheim, S. (2000). Addressing barriers to development and learning: School, family, community, and agency partnerships in New Mexico. *Counseling and Human Development, 32,* 1–12.

American Psychological Association. (n.d.). *Healthy LGB student project.* Retrieved April 26, 2004, from http://www.apa.org/ed/hlgb/

Anderson, A., & Christie, D. J. (2001). Some contributions of psychology to policies promoting cultures of peace. *Peace and Conflict: Journal of Peace Psychology, 7*(2), 173–185.

Annie E. Casey Foundation. (1999). *School-linked services community action report.* Boston: Author.

Dawes, A. (2001). Psychologies for liberation: View from elsewhere. In D. J. Christie, R. V. Wagner, & D. D. Winter (Eds.), *Peace, conflict, and violence: Peace psychology for the 21st century* (pp. 295–306). Englewood Cliffs, NJ: Prentice Hall.

Dreyfoos, J. (1994). *Full service schools: A revolution in health and social services for children, youth, and families.* San Francisco: Jossey-Bass.

Elliott, D., Butler, L. M., & Gunther, J. (2001). Adolescent violence: A family health and community challenge. *Violent Youth, 10*(1–2), 177–191.

Fondacaro, M. R., & Weinberg, D. (2002). Concepts of social justice in community psychology: Toward a social ecological epistemology. *American Journal of Community Psychology, 30*(4), 473–492.

Fouad, N. A., McPherson, R. H., Gerstein, L., Blustein, D. L., Elman, N., Helledy, K. I., & Metz, A. J. (2004). Houston 2001: Context and legacy. *The Counseling Psychologist, 32*(1), 15–77.

Frye, M. (1983). *The politics of reality: Essays in feminist theory.* Freedom, CA: Crossing Press.

Future directions in education and credentialing in professional psychology: Competencies Conference workgroup summaries. (2002, November). Scottsdale, AZ. Retrieved November 4, 2003, from http://www.appic.org/news/3_1_news_Competencies.htm

Gay, Lesbian, Straight Education Network. (2003). *National school climate survey: The school-related experiences of our nation's lesbian, gay, bisexual and transgender youth.* Retrieved April 26, 2004, from http://www.glsen.org/binary-data/GLSEN_ATTACHMENTS/file/300–1.PDF

Grau, N., Waldo, M., Garcia-Vazquez, E., & Steiner, R. (2001). Assessing barriers to learning in a borderlands high school. *Border Walking Journal, 5,* 1–18.

Grove McCrea, L., Bromley, J. L., McNally, C. J., O'Byrne, K. K., & Wade, K. A. (2004). Houston 2001: A student perspective on issues of identity, training, social advocacy, and the future of counseling psychology. *The Counseling Psychologist, 32*(1), 78–88.

Guerney, B. G. (1977). *Relationship enhancement.* San Francisco: Jossey-Bass.

Hage, S. M. (2003). Reaffirming the unique identity of counseling psychology: Opting for the "road less traveled by." *The Counseling Psychologist, 31*(5), 555–563.

Helms, J. E. (2003). A pragmatic view of social justice. *The Counseling Psychologist, 31*(3), 305–313.

Ivey, A. E., & Collins, N. M. (2003). Social justice: A long-term challenge of counseling psychology. *The Counseling Psychologist, 31*(3), 290–298.

Jackson, J. (2000). What ought psychology do? *American Psychologist, 55*(3), 328–330.

Kaczmarek, P., Waldo, M., Mayfield, R., & Steiner, R. (2003). Training borderland teachers to identify and refer students who may have mental health problems. *Border Walking Journal, 7,* 6–11.

Kenny, M., Waldo, M., Warter, E., & Barton, C. (2002). Theory, science, and practice for enhancing the lives of children and youth. *The Counseling Psychologist, 30,* 726–748.

Levy, A., & Land, H. (1994). School-based intervention with depressed minority adolescents. *Child and Adolescent Social Work Journal, 11,* 21–35.

Martín-Baró, I. (1994). War and mental health. In A. Aron & S. Corne (Eds.), *Writings for liberation psychology: Ignacio Martín-Baró* (pp. 108–121). Cambridge, MA: Harvard University Press.

Mayfield, R., Kaczmarek, P., & Waldo, M. (2000, August). *Teachers: An effective partner in an early warning system.* Paper presented at the annual meeting of the American Psychological Association, Washington, DC.

McWhirter, J. J., McWhirter, B. T., McWhirter, A. M., & McWhirter, E. H. (1998). *At-risk youth: A comprehensive response* (2nd ed.). Pacific Grove, CA: Brooks/Cole.

New Mexico Department of Health. (1998). *The status of children's mental health in New Mexico.* Santa Fe: Author.

Parents and Friends of Lesbians and Gays. (2001). *Our house to the school house: A recipe for safe schools.* Available from http://www.pflag.org/education/schools/ourhouse.html

Peltier, B. (1998). Reducing cross-cultural conflict with Choice Theory. In L. L. Palmatier (Ed.), *Crisis counseling for a quality school community: Applying William Glasser's Choice Theory* (pp. 355–379). Washington, DC: Accelerated Development.

Petrosino, A. (2003). Standards for evidence and evidence for standards: The case of school-based drug prevention. *Annals of the American Academy of Political and Social Science, 587,* 180–207.

Prilleltensky, I., & Nelson, G. (1997). Community psychology: Reclaiming social justice. In D. Fox & I. Prilleltensky (Eds.), *Critical psychology: An introduction* (pp. 166–184). Thousand Oaks, CA: Sage.

Romano, J. L., & Hage, S. M. (2000). Prevention and counseling psychology: Revitalizing commitments for the 21st century. *The Counseling Psychologist, 28,* 733–763.

Safe Schools Coalition. (2004). Retrieved April 26, 2004, from http://www.safeschools-wa.org/

Scullion, K. (2003). *Training prospective teachers to identify and refer students who show mental health concerns that may pose barriers to their learning.* Unpublished doctoral dissertation, New Mexico State University, Las Cruces, NM.

Scullion, K., Silva, D., Steiner, R., & Waldo, M. (1999, February). *Barriers to learning for borderland middle school students.* Paper presented at the Border Walking Conference, Las Cruces, NM.

Steff, M. E., & Prosperi, D. C. (1985). Barriers to mental health service utilization. *Community Mental Health Journal, 21,* 167–177.

Stiffman, A., Earls, F., Robins, L., & Young, K. (1988). Problems and help-seeking in high-risk adolescent patients of health clinics. *Journal of Adolescent Health Care, 9,* 305–309.

Strickland, B. R. (2000). Misassumptions, misadventures, and the misuse of psychology. *American Psychologist, 55*(3), 331–338.

Sue, D. W. (1995). Multicultural organizational development: Implications for the counseling profession. In J. G. Ponterotto, J. M. Casas, L. A. Suzuki, & C. M. Alexander (Eds.), *Handbook of multicultural counseling* (pp. 474–492). Thousand Oaks, CA: Sage.

Sue, D. W., Bingham, R. P., Porche-Burke, L., & Vasquez, M. (1999). The diversification of psychology: A multicultural revolution. *American Psychologist, 54*(12), 1061–1069.

U.S. Department of Education, Office of Civil Rights. (1999). *Protecting students from harassment and hate crime.* Available from http://www.ed.gov/pubs/Harassment/

Vera, E. M., & Reese, L. E. (2000). Preventive interventions with school age youth. In S. Brown & R. Lent (Eds.), *Handbook of counseling psychology* (pp. 411–434). New York: Wiley.

Vera, E. M., & Speight, S. L. (2003). Multicultural competence, social justice, and counseling psychology: Expanding our roles. *The Counseling Psychologist, 31*(3), 253–272.

Waldo, M. (1985). A curative factor framework for conceptualizing group counseling. *Journal of Counseling and Development, 64,* 52–58.

Waldo, M. (1989). Primary prevention in university residence halls: Paraprofessional-led Relationship Enhancement groups for college roommates. *Journal of Counseling and Development, 67,* 465–471.

Waldo, M., & Liessmann, C. (2001). *School Behavioral Health Training Institute manual* (2nd ed.). Albuquerque: New Mexico School Mental Health Initiative.

Walsh, M. E., & Galassi, J. P. (2002). An introduction: Counseling psychologists and schools. *The Counseling Psychologist, 30,* 675–681.

CHAPTER 10

A Theoretical and Practice Framework for Universal School-Based Prevention

Gargi Roysircar

School prevention programming is social justice work for counseling psychologists. Social justice, a collective value, forms the basis for the empowerment of schoolchildren; the integration of culturally different children, children at risk, or those experiencing maladjustment into the mainstream; and the promotion of the well-being of the whole school community. Rather than having "clients," we have partners in schoolchildren, their parents, teachers, the school staff, and volunteers and supporters in the larger community. These partners play an active role in the social justice paradigm. Counseling psychologists' power base is reformulated into power sharing and partnership processes. In addition to upholding the value basis of social justice, this chapter frames school prevention within an integrative theory of ecological setting, community psychology, and common multicultural factors that include organizational and provider multicultural competence. There is a brief discussion on ethics. A universal school prevention program is envisioned, accompanied by a mission statement, service delivery, and interventions. Issues of access, staffing and organization, evaluation, and challenges to school prevention are addressed. The purpose of the chapter is to present program development and evaluation, with the hope that it will stimulate ideas in counseling psychologists for school prevention work.

School-based programs offer three important assets to effective service delivery. First, almost constant access to the target population ensures greater contact and increases the possibility that unreported problems have a greater chance to be observed and addressed. Second, space in which services are delivered is geographically close to the population and readily available. And third, school outreach offers connections with local policymakers and community health professionals who can assist in collaboration with school officials (Sears, Evans, & Kuper, 2003). The stigma often associated with mental health problems may be lessened through the integration of interventions into school-based service (Sears et al., 2003). An integrative theoretical approach is recommended to guide the design of school-based community outreach programming. This approach is composed of three interwoven models: ecological setting, prevention services, and common multicultural factors.

An Integrative Theory: Ecological Setting

According to Snell-Johns, Mendez, and Smith (2004), underserved populations can be understood through a socioecological perspective in which individual, family, and community factors play a role. An ecological theory suggests that an individual develops and lives within a set of nested environmental systems (Bronfenbrenner, 1989). The microsystem is the setting that includes the person's family, peers, school, job, neighborhood, racial or ethnic associations, churches, and other places of worship. An adolescent's relative lack of primary adult socialization experiences because of scarce contact with parents who work long hours and because of minimal options for structured recreational outlets owing to constrained family finances are fundamental factors within the microsystem. The mesosystem involves relationships between the microsystems, such as a family's relations with the school. Gaps in communication between an adolescent's caregiver and the educational environment are particularly common for ethnic minorities and those of low socioeconomic status (SES) (Juntunen, Atkinson, & Tierney, 2003). The exosystem involves other social systems in which the individual does not have an active role, but that have an influence on what the individual experiences in an immediate context, such as a parent's employment status influencing a child's care. Also within the exosystem, the traditional counselor-client model of mental health care precludes access to treatment for the largely untreated population of adolescents (Cardemil, Reivich, & Seligman, 2002). The macrosystem involves the larger culture in which the individual lives, such as the dominant White American culture, which pressures immigrants to assimilate European-American values. All the gaps mentioned within the various systems are interconnected and interact throughout an individual's lifetime, and their joint impact becomes critical at certain important junctures, such as puberty.

An emphasis on the ecological setting also draws attention to how the individual perceives his or her notion of self within a specific frame of reference; racial or ethnic identity; sexual identity; gender; age; health; SES; institutional relationships; and the greater social, political, and historical context. In an effort to fully understand Bronfenbrenner's model, it must be recognized that individual risk factors (e.g., stresses of poverty contributing to disruptions in psychosocial development) (Campbell, Richie, & Hargrove, 2003) interact with environmental stressors (e.g., entry into high school, acculturation pressures, racism, and poverty). Historically, clinicians viewed racial and ethnic minorities from a deficit perspective; thus, they blamed social and psychological problems among minority clients on a presumed "cultural deficit" (Sue, Arredondo, & McDavis, 1992, p. 479). In contrast, within an ecological perspective, problems are analyzed in the context of social and environmental influences (Duffy & Wong, 2003).

The systems of care model, also called the wraparound model, as presented by Casas, Pavelski, Furlong, and Zanglis (2001), illustrates the application of the Bronfenbrenner nested environmental systems model for mental health care. Casas et al. suggest services that are community-based and that involve a continuum of care that includes home-based delivery and promotes Latino family participation. Although the family is considered central to the intervention and treatment process, individualized treatment to youth with severe emotional disturbance is included (Casas et al., 2001). The systems of care model has been shown to facilitate adjustment into mainstream society (Kamradt, 2000), in addition to providing high-quality, cost-effective services (Casas et al., 2001). Services such as these are particularly useful when working with a community's growing immigrant population and low SES clientele.

Community Psychology

The framework of outreach programming permits the introduction of protective factors relative to adolescent risk factors, such as parent-adolescent disconnection, alienation from the educational environment, and a lack of access to treatment, all contributing to and maintaining adolescent maladjustment. Outreach programs consist of interventions that are primary, secondary, and tertiary (Duffy & Wong, 2003). Primary interventions are preventive in nature; are designed to reduce incidence of a disorder (e.g., low social skills or social competence in adolescents); and target a wide population, whether symptoms are present or not. Primary prevention involves partnerships with local schools and community groups, including youth development organizations (e.g., YMCA), to ensure that teenagers are provided opportunities for engaging in structured activities (protective factors) comparable to those enjoyed by children of privilege. Involvement in extracurricular activities has been shown to have a positive impact on the psychosocial development of adolescents (Berk, 2004).

Secondary prevention interventions help to alleviate prodromal symptoms and offset severity and persistence of a disorder. In a school program, secondary prevention for youth who exhibit symptoms of maladaptive behaviors can combine participation in a structured prevention activity with individual or group counseling. The program design is intended to reduce feelings of apprehension that adolescents may have about psychological counseling by embedding the counseling program in a structured activity program. In a study, participation in structured activities reduced depressive symptoms in 14-year-olds who reported high levels of depression and detachment from their parents (Mahoney, Schweder, & Stattin,

2002). Tertiary prevention for youth who exhibit severe psychological or behavioral problems involves close collaboration with relevant mental health community agencies. Teachers and school counselors and social workers can be instrumental in identifying students in need of secondary or tertiary prevention.

Historically, however, adolescent utilization of tertiary interventions of social services has been low. The underutilization of mental health resources by racial and ethnic minorities is a prominent concern (Sue et al., 1992). Access to mental health care in rural areas is often blocked by social, geographical, and climatological factors, as well as by shame, fear, and stigma (Nordal, Copans, & Stamm, 2003). Snell-Johns et al. (2004) described several community factors interfering with access and utilization, specifically those related to rural areas. For example, rural areas typically have fewer specialized services; people must travel further for services; and people are socially isolated, which decreases the likelihood of initiating services. Snell-Johns et al. provided empirically validated strategies to reduce access barriers and increase the ability to reach underserved populations. Notable strategies included transportation and decreasing service costs.

Common Multicultural Factors

Access

There is a dearth of research on rural adolescents. This may be viewed as an extension of a more general lack of attention to rural health in community psychology (Duffy & Wong, 2003). Suicide rates among rural boys aged 15 to 19 are higher than among urban boys of the same age (Nordal et al., 2003). Residents have fewer options for employment, which may be related to a lack of sufficient services. Juntunen et al. (2003) suggest that in underserved areas, "local service organizations, PTA's, and church groups are all potential sources of help in program development" (p. 162).

Cultural Experiences

Asian and Latino cultures are the largest growing immigrant populations in the United States. First- and second-generation adolescent immigrants have multiple difficulties with which to cope, including depression, acculturative stress, low self-esteem, a feeling of being disconnected from parents and cohorts, and minimal social support (Roysircar, 2004; Roysircar-Sodowsky & Frey, 2002). Acculturative stress has been predictive of both depressive symptoms and suicidal behaviors in male and female Latino(a) high school students (Juntunen et al., 2003). Cross-cultural studies have consistently indicated a 2-to-1 sex ratio of women to men in rates of depression that becomes apparent in adolescence (Garber & Flynn, 2001). There is evidence suggesting that improved sense of community and social support is crucial in decreasing stress among immigrant adolescents (Roysircar & Maestas, 2002).

According to Bemak and Chung (2003), language is a major barrier for first- and second-generation adolescent immigrants. When working with Latino and Asian adolescents, culturally competent assessment involves taking into account the relationship between language and culture. For example, in the Spanish language, the connotation or meaning of words may be different when translated into English and can, therefore, influence clinical judgment. Bilingual providers will be a basic requirement to providing outreach service, especially for adolescents who use English as a second language. Because "language is a metaphor for cultural pluralism and promotes respect and receptivity to differences" (Bemak & Chung, 2003, p. 89), it is imperative to have multilingual staff members available for immigrants and their families. Additionally, members of the ethnic community can be used as educators and translators (Bemak & Chung, 2003; Juntunen et al., 2003). The ultimate goal for effective cross-cultural communication is the ability of all parties to similarly send and receive both verbal and nonverbal messages. Educational, vocational, and career goals are major concerns for minority adolescents, and they are more likely to use services addressing these goals as opposed to traditional "talk therapy."

Organizational Multicultural Competence

Dialogues regarding diversity in schools must lead to action and structural changes in order to be effective. Culture-bound values of the majority European American community population represented in the school system have the potential of acting as increased stressors on those students with variant cultural values and belief systems. Furthermore, use of standard English, as opposed to cognizance of diverse communication jargon and style, could potentially discriminate against low SES and language minority individuals. Care must be taken to have diverse representation within each prevention activity group that allows all participants equal voice and opportunity of expression. Facilitators need to be vigilant for overt signs of derogatory racial, ethnic, sexist, or classist comments, addressing them in the context of the prevention programs. Covert signs, such as exclusionary behavior or refusal to engage in activities with particular classmate(s), can be addressed in private meetings with a student or students involved. The bimodality of SES in schools reflects another area of concern. Class-bound values and assumptions are likely to be held not only by students, but also by teachers, facilitators, and the school staff, as well as being reflected in school policies.

Research suggests that many Latinos do not use community mental health services because such services are culturally unfamiliar (O'Sullivan & Lasso, 1992). In addition, cultural barriers such as language and the location of services have had a negative impact on service delivery (O'Sullivan & Lasso, 1992). Therefore, identifying a target area for the outreach service involves locating a neighborhood that is geographically proximal to where Latino families reside (Harachi, Catalano, & Hawkins, 1997). Ideally, this area is close to existing social networks (e.g., YMCA, local middle or high school) that allow easy access and referrals. In addition, after-school transportation services enhance retention and decrease dropout. Recruitment strategies consist of direct contact procedures facilitated by bilingual, Spanish-speaking members of the outreach staff. Direct contact involves contacting persons based on an existing relationship (e.g., a minister's spouse contacting and recruiting members of a congregation).

Provider Multicultural Competence

Dyche and Zayas (2001) believe that cross-cultural empathy is particularly useful in building collaborative relationships with populations that have often been disempowered and distrustful of services. They further state, "The capacity to face others with openness to their reality while simultaneously maintaining coherence in your own beliefs and sense of self is the dialectic process behind human attachment and social contract" (p. 257). Kottler (1991) emphasizes that regardless of the therapeutic approach, the development of a trusting, honest, caring relationship between the client and therapist is an essential condition for positive change. The client's perception that the therapist genuinely cares about him or her is of the utmost importance. Kottler also lauds the importance of humor as an integral part of the therapeutic relationship. These factors may have special significance in working with adolescents. In addition to creating a supportive environment, it is vital that the clinicians are aware of the developmental issues that face adolescents today. Precise understanding of the cognitive development of adolescents is needed to clarify psychosocial adjustment at an age when the distinction between "normal" and "abnormal" behavior is blurred.

Every effort needs to be made to ensure that counselors, facilitators, and teachers are multiculturally sensitive and aware of their own and student participants' worldviews as defined by the principles of multicultural counseling competencies (MCCs; Roysircar, Arredondo, Fuertes, Ponterotto, & Toporek, 2003) and the American Psychological Association's multicultural guidelines (American Psychological Association, 2003). MCC further requires clinicians to be aware of their own ethnic or racial backgrounds and to understand how their own attitudes and values influence their treatment of their clients (Roysircar, 2003). There must be awareness and understanding of the differences between and within cultures, and a sensitivity whereby positive and negative values are not attributed to the differences within and between cultures. From a social constructionist perspective, "The therapist makes every effort to learn the culture of the client as the client sees it" (González, Biever, & Gardner, 1994, p. 519). MCC workshops can be held for instructors and facilitators prior to their leading outreach activities. Weekly supervision and peer consultation can address multicultural issues as they arise throughout the duration of the program. Effectively engaging adolescents in a community program entails providers transcending barriers of age, race, ethnicity, and SES.

The American Psychological Association's 2002 Ethics Code specifically states that when working with diverse populations, psychologists must have knowledge and understanding of relevant factors related to the target group (American Psychological Association, 2002). Family dynamics must be understood within the context of the multiple systems in which the family exists. Parents may report that because of increasing financial pressures, they are forced to work longer hours. Work responsibilities make it difficult for them to monitor their children's behaviors and peer relationships. As opposed to neglecting their children, many working parents view working long hours as a way of ensuring their children's financial security and providing them with a better life. It is vital not to interpret that these parents do not desire to be more involved in their children's lives. For Latino and Asian parents, language, acculturation, and educational attainment often pose further limits on the range of available jobs.

Understanding the impact of ethnicity on identity formulation is a key prevention concern for adolescents. According to Berk (2004), "For teenagers who are members of minority groups, ethnic identity—a sense of ethnic-group membership and attitudes and feelings associated with that membership—is central to the quest for identity, and it presents complex challenges" (p. 386). A strong, positive ethnic identity is linked with higher self-esteem, self-efficacy, and optimism. Conversely, exposure to negative attitudes about one's cultural group can be especially detrimental to the self-esteem and self-worth of minority youth. Therefore, racial and cultural prejudice may be a factor in rates of maladjustment for Latino and Asian adolescents.

The concern for respecting diversity was extended and reinforced in the American Psychological Association guidelines for working with lesbian, gay, and bisexual clients (American Psychological Association, 2000). Developing a sexual identity is an essential part of ego identity development in adolescence. Stresses resulting from the social stigma surrounding homosexuality have been linked with increased risk for psychological distress, substance abuse, and suicide attempts (American Psychological Association, 2000). It is probable some teenagers who display maladjusted behaviors are struggling with a gay, lesbian, or bisexual identity. The American Psychological Association guidelines recognize that gay, lesbian, and bisexual individuals who are members of racial and ethnic minorities may face special challenges related to multiple and often conflicting cultural norms, values, and beliefs. The challenges may be exacerbated for minority youth who are in the process of exploring their sexual identity and orientation as well as their developmental transitions. The traditional gender role socialization characteristics of immigrant Latino families make exploring issues of sexual identity and orientation particularly sensitive and complex.

Additional Ethical Considerations

The American Psychological Association Ethical Principles (2002) include the general principles of "Justice" and "Respect for People's Rights and Dignity." The principle of Justice includes two parts: the psychologist must understand justice, and he or she must work to make sure that his or her own biases do not lead to or condone unjust practices. The principle of Respect for People's Rights and Dignity requires psychologists to respect the dignity and worth of all people and the rights of individuals to privacy, confidentiality, and self-determination. These general principles are but initial steps that need to be expanded from caring for individual justice to observing the collective value of social justice, which sees the community in a relational framework and inspires social change. Through long-term efforts in a community and positive relationships with its members, the initial mistrust of psychologists entering one's community can be diminished. Inequities that arise within organizations are not seen to be primarily due to poor communication, lack of knowledge, poor management, person-organization fit problems, and so forth, but to monopolies of power. Psychologists understand the impact of dismantling affirmative action and antibilingual education legislation; in addition, they understand the stigmatizing aspects of being a member of a culturally devalued group (in terms of the dominant culture's values) and its daily effects (American Psychological Association, 2003). Psychologists are able to encourage discourse among employers, professional organizations, and training institutions that promotes policy development regarding multicultural issues (American Psychological Association, 2003).

The most important subdivision of the ethical standard of "Competence" is "Boundaries of Competence" (American Psychological Association, 2002). Psychologists are ethically able to provide only those services that are within their competence, including age, gender, and race. Therefore, counseling psychologists need to gain competence in school prevention work. They can expand their competence through training, education, study, and experience in school prevention. In ethical decision making, our profession's principle ethics can be strengthened with virtue ethics and a psychologist's personal emotional investment in multicultural responsibility, which result in interpreting the general professional principles differently for each cultural context.

A Universal School Prevention Program: Mission Statement

Although all levels of intervention can be attended to, the main focus of the suggested outreach programming is on primary or preventive interventions. Because informed parental consent is necessary for student participation, parental cooperation, encouragement, and participation may further aid in student recruitment and retention. The mission statement of the school outreach program is the building and implementation of community-based services that promote the social, emotional, and physical well-being of a diverse student body. Thus, the goals of the program are to (a) strengthen the competencies of local youth, which in turn strengthens the community as a whole; (b) decrease the rate of adolescent maladaptive behaviors; (c) increase community awareness of adolescent needs; and (d) increase adolescent utilization of preexisting treatment and social service opportunities. The program's objectives can be to decrease adolescent stress, improve coping skills, and increase social support. The program promotes the following core values within all its components: diversity, empowerment, respect, responsibility, teamwork, and safety.

A Universal Program

A universal program for prevention can be inclusive of all ninth graders entering a high school. Activities can be designed after input from the students and may include art studios and exhibits; musical events; relevant vocational workshops; job fairs; ESL mentoring and tutoring; and peer group social interactions guided by semistructured, safe group methods. Workshops are preventive in nature and focus on substance abuse education and skills training. Education is focused on enhancing effective communication, interpersonal skills, negotiation, and problem solving, all cited protective factors against mental health disorders (Dumont & Provost, 1999).

Classes in dance, drama, poetry, music, and various other forms of art can be offered. The intent here is to give adolescents a social outlet to release their creativity, develop various artistic talents, explore vocational interests, and find and practice something that they are good at. Moreover, in addition to the promotion of adolescent personality development, socialization, and expression of the individual's spirit and social needs, adolescents learn and preserve their cultural heritage through social arts and education. Empirical research indicates that Latino adolescents often use social activities as a way of coping positively with personal stress (Roysircar-Sodowsky & Frey, 2002). Such activities have the potential to enhance overall feelings of self-esteem and perceived control, noted protective factors against adolescent depression and anxiety (Dumont & Provost, 1999). Finally, such a program can further allay the stigma associated with mental health services, which may prevent some children from attending a program without educational attractions. Therefore, an advantage of universal programs is that they minimize stigma for participants.

Just "hanging out" can also be encouraged. An after-school café can be established for students as a safe and attractive place to eat, socialize, and participate in various activities. Snacks and beverages can be free to all students to reduce any stigma that may result from lack of financial resources and to encourage participation. The menu can be determined, for the most part, by the students. Such a program can provide teenagers with a sense of community, a social network, and other acquired skills, all considered to be protective factors against adolescent substance abuse (Chassin & Ritter, 2001) and depression (Garber & Flynn, 2001). The various components offered create a safe haven where teenagers can occupy their free time. Consequently, parents are comforted in knowing that their children are being monitored while they are working late hours.

During adolescence, the struggle for identity comes to the forefront, and this struggle can have implications for an individual's future (Berk, 2004). In fact, taking pride in one's sense of self during this time often predicts good educational and lifelong experiences (Berk, 2004). Although culture is a large part of one's identity, individuals often do not understand the impact of it on their identity and character. To deal with issues of racism, which is related to the development of self, cultural identity groups (CIGs) can be used (Washington et al., 2003), because group work has been shown to be an effective modality with adolescents. Specifically, CIGs address youths' issues and anxiety around racism and prejudice through narrative discussions with their peers about identity, culture, and race in a safe and supportive atmosphere (Washington et al., 2003). Each student attends two groups. The first is with people of similar background in which students have the opportunity to share struggles and successes, and gain peer approval and companionship. The other group is mixed, involving students of both the dominant (European American/high SES) and minority cultures and low SES. By finding commonalities through racial, personal, and educational experiences, the students are more likely to be supportive of each other, and it is less likely that community isolation based on race and culture will persist (Washington et al., 2003). The primary goal of the CIG approach is for children to learn how to tell more positive stories about themselves, gain a greater sense of self-esteem, and feel acceptance by and toward other groups in the community.

The race and ethnicity of characters used as examples throughout the workshops, classes, and group work are reflective of the members of each group. In addition, the life problems that are targeted for discussion include a range of issues that apply to all cultural groups represented. Furthermore, teachers who are trained to implement the program receive multicultural training and practice at specifically weaving multiple culturally relevant situations into the fabric of the problem-solving aspect of the program.

In conjunction with prevention activities with school students, a second program can establish resources for adult community members and family services. The availability of resources for adult community members and families is vital for the children's well-being. For instance, research has shown that children of addicted parents have a higher risk of abusing alcohol (Ingram & Price, 2001). In families, symptoms present in one member of the family may be rooted in the dysfunction of the family, its boundaries, and its structure. Resources made available to adults include psychoeducational groups dealing with adolescent needs and difficulties, identification of symptoms of alcohol and drug use and depression, family acculturation issues, bicultural identity formation, time management, and parenting. A group can counter parent-child detachment by assisting parents in the promotion and reinforcement of resiliency in their children. Home-based interventions attend to the attitudinal and logistical issues that are often barriers to parental participation in their children's education and to access of care (Casas, Furlong, & Ruiz De Esparaza, 2003). These interventions include referral, advocacy, social modeling, and mediation (Juntunen et al., 2003).

Access

Research shows that universal programs have higher recruitment and retention rates than programs using a directed approach for a select group (Shochet et al., 2001). Additionally, adolescence is a stage in which peer group acceptance is of utmost importance (Berk, 2004). Targeting and labeling specific students for outreach services during this vulnerable age can be stigmatizing, have long-lasting effects, and discourage students' productive participation.

The question of retention is directly related to its relevance concerning issues of ethnicity and SES. Although school-based prevention programs have been successful in retaining participants in environments where middle-class values prevail (Shochet et al., 2001), retention in the proposed prevention program is clearly related to the experiences of low-income, ethnic minority students' experiences, and the program needs to be relevant to their real-life experiences. Consequently, care must be taken to prevent intervention experiences from imposing suburban, middle-class values or perspectives on the participants.

The first step is drawing students into a program of activities they can enjoy with their peers. Actively reaching out to teenagers and soliciting their input about activities, scheduling, and other relevant issues may lead to recruiting and retaining participants. Because the school is involved, teachers can survey students about their preferences and disseminate information about the program as it evolves. It is probable that the students who are most responsive to the program are those with a low risk for maladjustment. But it is also likely that their social networks include peers who are more in need of intervention. Informal peer networks as well as formal channels, such as the school and churches, can play a key role in recruiting both low-risk and high-risk teenagers into the program.

Because this after-school program is located in school, transportation is not a concern. On the other hand, school buses can be used to transport teenagers home from the after-school program. To increase access further, the majority of services are free of charge. However, preparation courses for standardized tests can be offered at heavily reduced rates. Offering incentives to participants helps to increase utilization by the underserved (Snell-Johns et al., 2004). When students sign up for a recreational event, they can receive a free T-shirt with the program's logo and mission statement on it. The T-shirts act not only as an incentive but also as an advertisement for the program, which is important for utilization. Snell-Johns et al. noted that advertising through the school system and general practitioners' offices is an effective strategy for rural areas. This strategy promotes utilization across the community. Staff members and participants use their creativity to develop slogans and handouts to attract diverse teenagers and their families to the program. A major recruitment strategy is to petition the school to promote the arts component of the program to interested kids who can then get their peers involved. Scholarships are awarded as an incentive to students who have exhibited artistic promise.

Staffing and Organization

The primary stakeholders in this school-based program are administrators, teachers, parents, and students. During the development stages of the intervention, meetings between school administrators and teachers, parents, and students are held. All participants are encouraged to help brainstorm ideas and comment on the initial plans.

The program provides an environment in which people want to work, volunteer, and be empowered to make decisions. This type of environment facilitates effective service delivery (Duffy & Wong, 2003). Implementation of programming requires coordination with school teaching and administration staff to ascertain the most efficient placement within the school and with psychologists who provide supervision and consultation. Community volunteers and parents are critical for school programming, and their help is actively sought to act as facilitators, volunteers, and tutors, and to provide transportation for field trips.

A mentoring program can be instituted based on the Big Brother/Big Sister model that matches, when possible, by race, ethnicity, and gender, adult members of the community with those adolescents at risk and those students who express an interest. School personnel are asked to identify students who might serve as role models and volunteers—an extremely valuable asset to a program operating on limited resources. A peer mentor program can be established with junior and senior students addressing academic issues, substance use and abuse, risky behaviors, and conflict resolution. Peer mentors receive training and supervision from the school counselor and local psychologists in subject areas and ethical issues, such as confidentiality.

The participation of community leaders provides a channel to inside informants who can offer valuable insights and volunteer activities. Enlisting the participation of community members not only increases the prospects of program success, but also exemplifies the principles of community empowerment (Duffy & Wong, 2003). Recruiting staff members who reflect the ethnicity of Latino and Asian families is an excellent strategy. Although minorities are underrepresented in the counseling profession (Sue et al., 1992), the multimodal nature of the program provides opportunities for staff members and volunteers who are not psychological counselors; these individuals can be racial and ethnic minorities. Minority adults and even peers who have successfully worked through acculturation demands and ethnic identity issues can effectively engage minority youth in self-esteem building and identity formation. In fact, teenage peers and young adults who are minorities may be particularly credible role models.

To address the underutilization of community mental health resources and secondary and tertiary intervention, culturally competent school counselors and psychologists can be available at the high school on a daily basis, with an open-door policy that can allow for on-site assessment and consultation. In addition, graduate psychology students doing practicum can provide another level of on-site care. They can pay special attention to gender-specific concerns, ethnicity, issues revolving around poverty, and comorbidity of adolescent difficulties.

The program is staffed with various levels of education. A college degree, however, is not required for the majority of volunteer opportunities. There are various internship opportunities for undergraduate students who are willing to work in an after-school prevention program. College students majoring in areas such as education, recreation therapy, and psychology can have valuable experience in working toward prevention. Furthermore, the school district's community-wide task force for the prevention program can work to determine how preexisting community jobs can be used to staff the after-school program. Lerner (2000) talks about the advantages of having nonschool personnel as program facilitators. By not relying on teachers or teachers' aides to implement a program, the students sometimes feel less inhibited because they perceive less punitive threat to their participation.

Even with a committed and competent group of professionals, organizational conflicts can undermine program success (Duffy & Wong, 2003). Respecting the expertise of professionals from different disciplines and ensuring that each one has a voice in the way that the program evolves simultaneously works to reduce conflict while expanding ideas for improving and enhancing the program design. School staff and community members are respected stakeholders whose contributions help to shape the program more effectively.

Evaluation

A formative evaluation, conducted with the aim of program improvement (Mertens, 1998), uses both quantitative and qualitative components. Qualitative assessment, based on the interpretive/constructivist paradigm, for instance, attends to the question of whether the program meets the expectations and criteria of the various stakeholders involved with the program (Mertens, 1998).

In addition, in keeping with the positivist/quantitative paradigm, evaluation of changes in assessment scores exhibited within a quasi-experimental format answers the question of quantitative change correlated with the completion of the proposed program. In effect, the practical question being asked in the quantitative aspect of the evaluation is whether the program is substantially better than no program, to justify the cost and effort of continuing to use it. Consequently, a control group or no-intervention group can be accessed from a different school system that is comparable in size and socioeconomic and ethnic group make-up as the school with the prevention outreach. The promise of sharing the control group data to facilitate baseline assessment as well as training in use of the prevention program is offered to the control group school. A pretest-posttest control group design is used (Mertens, 1998) in which there are two independent variables: intervention condition and time (pretest, posttest, follow-up) for each assessment measure (dependent variable). Because there is a mix of a between-subjects independent variable (intervention condition) and a within-subjects independent variable (time), a 2×3 repeated measures factorial analysis of variance is used to analyze the data.

Afterthought About the Proposed Program

Despite the constant access to the population being a primary advantage of school-based programs, the disadvantage is that often youth who need the most help are not reached because they attend school infrequently or have dropped out. The universities in which I have worked are located in college towns with rural surroundings. Therefore, my prevention work considers rural adolescents both in program conceptualization, as presented in this chapter, and in implementation (e.g., Roysircar, Gard, Hubbell, & Ortega, 2005). I need to emphasize that access to health and human services is not just a rural problem. A lack of sufficient services is problematic in both rural and urban environments, as are a lack of employment options. Relatedly, one goal for the envisioned program is to include increasing utilization of preexisting treatment opportunities (i.e., tertiary care). In the case where resources are insufficient in number or quantity, there will be advocacy effort on the part of the program to increase access. The suggestions regarding advertising, food, buses, and scholarships in conjunction with the program would obviously require considerable resources. Funds will need to be raised through state and federal grants; donations from community members, businesses, and university alumni/ae; and philanthropists who support multicultural projects.

In conclusion, health promotion efforts described in the proposed school-based prevention program were typically guided by assessing risk and protective factors.

References

American Psychological Association. (2000). The professional practice guidelines for psychotherapy with lesbian, gay, and bisexual clients. *American Psychologist, 55,* 1440–1451.

American Psychological Association. (2002). Ethical principles of psychologists and code of conduct. *American Psychologist, 57,* 1060–1073.

American Psychological Association. (2003). Guidelines on multicultural education, training, research, practice, and organizational change for psychologists. *American Psychologist, 58,* 377–402.

Bemak, F., & Chung, R. C.-Y. (2003). Multicultural counseling with immigrant students in schools. In P. B. Pedersen & J. C. Carey (Eds.), *Multicultural counseling in schools: A practical handbook* (2nd ed., pp. 84–104). Boston: Allyn & Bacon.

Berk, L. E. (2004). Emotional and social development in adolescence. In L. E. Berk (Ed.), *Development through the lifespan* (3rd ed., pp. 342–379). Boston: Allyn & Bacon.

Bronfenbrenner, U. (1989). Ecological systems theory. In R. Vasta (Ed.), *Annals of child development* (Vol. 6, pp. 187–251). Greenwich, CT: JAI.

Campbell, C., Richie, S. D., & Hargrove, D. S. (2003). Poverty and rural mental health. In B. H. Stamm (Ed.), *Rural behavior health care: An interdisciplinary guide* (pp. 41–51). Washington, DC: American Psychological Association.

Cardemil, E., Reivich, K., & Seligman, M. (2002). The prevention of depressive symptoms in low-income minority middle school students. *Prevention and Treatment, 5,* 1–27.

Casas, J. M., Furlong, M. J., & Ruiz De Esparaza, C. (2003). Increasing Hispanic parent participation in schools: The role of the counselor. In P. B. Pedersen & J. C. Carey (Eds.), *Multicultural counseling in schools: A practical handbook* (2nd ed., pp. 107–130). Boston: Allyn & Bacon.

Casas, J. M., Pavelski, R., Furlong, M. J., & Zanglis, I. (2001). Advent of systems of care: Practice and research perspectives and policy implications. In J. G. Ponterotto, J. M. Casas, L. A. Suzuki, & C. M. Alexander (Eds.), *Handbook of multicultural counseling* (2nd ed., pp. 189–221). Thousand Oaks, CA: Sage.

Chassin, L., & Ritter, J. (2001). Vulnerability to substance use disorders in childhood and adolescence. In R. E. Ingram & J. M. Proice (Eds.), *Vulnerability to psychopathology: Risk across the lifespan* (pp. 107–134). New York: Guilford.

Duffy, K. G., & Wong, F. Y. (2003). Schools, children, and communities. In K. G. Duffy & F. Y. Wong (Eds.), *Community psychology* (3rd ed., pp. 163–188). Boston: Allyn & Bacon/Pearson Education.

Dumont, M., & Provost, M. A. (1999). Resilience: Protective role of social support, coping strategies, and social activities on experience of stress and depression. *Journal of Youth and Adolescence, 28,* 343–363.

Dyche, L., & Zayas, L. H. (2001). Cross-cultural empathy and training the contemporary psychotherapist. *Clinical Social Work Journal, 29*(3), 245–258.

Garber, J., & Flynn, C. (2001). Vulnerability to depression in childhood and adolescence. In R. E. Ingram & J. M. Price (Eds.), *Vulnerability to psychopathology: Risk factors across the lifespan* (pp. 175–225). New York: Guilford.

González, R. C., Biever, J. L., & Gardner, G. T. (1994). The multicultural perspective in therapy: A social constructionist approach. *Psychotherapy, 31,* 515–524.

Harachi, T. W., Catalano, R. F., & Hawkins, J. D. (1997). Effective recruitment for parenting programs within ethnic minority communities. *Child and Adolescent Social Work Journal, 14,* 23–39.

Ingram, R. E., & Price, J. M. (2001). *Vulnerability to psychopathology: Risk factors across the lifespan.* New York: Guilford.

Juntunen, C. L., Atkinson, D. R., & Tierney, G. (2003). School counselors and school psychologists as school-home-community liaisons in ethnically diverse schools. In P. B. Pedersen & J. C. Carey (Eds.), *Multicultural counseling in schools: A practical handbook* (2nd ed., pp. 149–168). Boston: Allyn & Bacon.

Kamradt, B. (2000). Wraparound Milwaukee: Aiding youth with mental health needs. *Justice Journal, 7*(1). Retrieved July 16, 2004, from http://www.ncjrs.org/html/ojjdp/jjjnl_2000_4/wrap.html

Kottler, J. A. (1991). *The compleat therapist.* San Francisco: Jossey-Bass.

Lerner, R. (2000). Transforming universities to sustain outreach scholarship: A communiqué from the front. In F. T. Sherman & W. R. Torbert (Eds.), *Transforming social inquiry, transforming social action* (pp. 37–56). Norwell, MA: Kluwer Academic.

Mahoney, J., Schweder, A., & Stattin, H. (2002). Structured after-school activities as a moderator of depressed mood for adolescents with detached relations to their parents. *Journal of Community Psychology, 30*(1), 69–86.

Mertens, D. M. (1998). *Research methods in education and psychology: Integrating diversity with quantitative and qualitative approaches.* Thousand Oaks, CA; Sage.

Nordal, K. C., Copans, S. A., & Stamm, B. H. (2003). Children and adolescents in rural and frontier areas. In B. H. Stamm (Ed.), *Rural behavioral health care: An interdisciplinary guide* (pp. 159–170). Washington, DC: American Psychological Association.

O'Sullivan, M. J., & Lasso, B. (1992). Community mental health services for Hispanics: A test of the culture compatibility hypothesis. *Hispanic Journal of Behavioral Sciences, 14,* 455–468.

Roysircar, G. (2003). Counselor awareness of own assumptions, values, and biases. In G. Roysircar, P. Arredondo, J. N. Fuertes, J. G. Ponterotto, & R. L. Toporek (Eds.), *Multicultural competencies 2003: Association for Multicultural Counseling and Development.* (pp. 15–26). Alexandria, VA: AMCD.

Roysircar, G. (2004). Child survivor of war: A case study. *Journal of Multicultural Counseling and Development, 32*(3), 168–180.

Roysircar, G., Arredondo, P., Fuertes, J. N., Ponterotto, J. G., & Toporek, R. L. (Eds.). (2003). *Multicultural competencies 2003: Association for Multicultural Counseling and Development.* Alexandria, VA: AMCD.

Roysircar, G., Gard, G., Hubbell, R., & Ortega, M. (2005). Development of counseling trainees' multicultural awareness through mentoring ESL students. *Journal of Multicultural Counseling and Development, 33*(1), 17–36.

Roysircar, G., & Maestas, M. V. (2002). Assessment of acculturation and cultural variables. In K. S. Kurasaki, S. Okazaki, & S. Sue (Eds.), *Asian American mental health: Assessment theories and methods* (pp. 77–94). Dordrecht, The Netherlands: Kluwer Academic.

Roysircar-Sodowsky, G., & Frey, L. L. (2002). Children of immigrants: Their worldviews value conflicts. In P. Pedersen & J. C. Carey (Eds.), *Multicultural counseling in schools: A practical handbook* (2nd ed., pp. 61–83). Boston: Allyn & Bacon.

Sears, S. F., Jr., Evans, G. D., & Kuper, B. D. (2003). Rural social service systems as behavioral health delivery systems. In B. H. Stamm (Ed.), *Rural behavioral health care: An interdisciplinary guide* (pp. 109–120). Washington, DC: American Psychological Association.

Shochet, I. M., Dadds, M. R., Holland, D., Whitefield, K., Harnett, P. H., & Osgarby, S. M. (2001). The efficacy of a universal school-based program to prevent adolescent depression. *Journal of Clinical Psychology, 30,* 417–463.

Snell-Johns, J., Mendez, J. L., & Smith, B. H. (2004). Evidence-based solutions for overcoming access barriers, decreasing attrition, and promoting change with underserved families. *Journal of Family Psychology, 18*(1), 19–35.

Sue, D. W., Arredondo, P., & McDavis, R. J. (1992). Multicultural counseling competencies and standards: A call to the profession. *Journal of Counseling and Development, 70,* 477–486.

Washington, E. D., Crosby, T., Hernandez, M., Vernon-Jones, R., Medley, R., Nishimura, B., & Torres, D. (2003). Cultural identity groups and cultural maps: Meaning-making in groups. In P. B. Pedersen & J. C. Carey (Eds.), *Multicultural counseling in schools: A practical handbook* (2nd ed., pp. 26–42). Boston: Allyn & Bacon.

PART III

Marginalized Communities

CHAPTER 11

Marginalized Communities in the United States

Oppression, Social Justice, and the Role of Counseling Psychologists

Tania Israel

This section focuses on ways that counseling psychologists can support members of marginalized communities in the United States through social action. Tatum (1997) identified the "seven categories of 'otherness' commonly experienced in U.S. society" (p. 22) as race/ethnicity, gender, religion, sexual orientation, socioeconomic status, age, and physical/mental ability, with the respective oppressions of racism, sexism, religious oppression/anti-Semitism, heterosexism, classism, ageism, and ableism. Oppressed groups experience exploitation, marginalization, powerlessness, cultural imperialism, and violence, although the degree and form of these aspects of oppression may vary across different groups (Young, 1990). The chapters in this section address the situation of people who belong to one or more of these categories, the associated impact of oppression, and strategies counseling psychologists can use to advocate for these groups.

The Impact of Oppression on Individuals and Communities

Oppression is maintained through individual mechanisms such as discrimination and stereotyping, as well as through societal and structural systems. Although the United States was founded on principles of freedom,

> the democratic-free market blueprint in America has never applied equally to everyone. From the very beginning, indentured servants, slaves, Native Americans, women, and others were systematically excluded from both the protections of the Constitution and the opportunities of "free market" capitalism. (McNamee & Miller, 2004, p. 8)

Individuals from marginalized groups continue to experience inequities through institutional discrimination, or "actions, practices and policies embedded in the organization of society that have negative impacts on individuals and groups that have socially specified characteristics" (McNamee & Miller, 2004, p. 156). Institutionalized discrimination reflects and reifies existing prejudice and discrimination through major social institutions, such as law, religion, education, work, and housing. The negative impacts on marginalized individuals include occupational and educational disparities, violence and harassment, overrepresentation in the criminal justice system, and underrepresentation in positions of political and economic power (McNamee & Miller, 2004).

Although the exact form of oppression may differ for various disenfranchised groups, the relationship between dominant and subordinate groups is defined by certain dynamics, regardless of the type of otherness that marks the group as subordinate. For example, members of the subordinate group are labeled defective, members of the dominant group are ascribed characteristics that are highly valued, and exceptions to these rules are viewed as anomalies (Miller, 1976). Furthermore, members of dominant and subordinate groups have different socially constructed views of reality; in order to survive in an atmosphere of unequal power, members of subordinate groups tend to know more about the dominant groups than vice versa (Tatum, 1997).

Intersections among various types of oppression create unique situations for individuals who fall into multiple categories of disenfranchisement. For example, sexism and racism may intersect to particularly disadvantage women of color (McNamee & Miller, 2004). Alternatively, a European American, working-class, able-bodied, gay man may be advantaged because of his gender, ethnicity, and physical abilities, but experience oppression because of his socioeconomic status (SES) and sexual orientation. Oppression in the United States is characterized by similarities among experiences of disparate marginalized groups, as well as individual experiences that are multiply determined by both oppression and privilege. These dynamics reveal the interconnectedness of oppressions and the necessity of addressing multiple forms of oppression in order to overcome social injustices embedded in U.S. society.

As a result of oppression, members of marginalized groups are at increased risk for psychological stressors. For example, compared to men, women experience considerably higher rates of depression (Wells, Brack, & McMichen, 2003); lesbian, gay, and bisexual (LGB) adolescents have an increased risk for suicidality and substance abuse (Hershberger & D'Augelli, 2000); people with disabilities may experience low self-esteem and high stress (Nosek & Hughes, 2004); and a disproportionate share of people of color experience mental health concerns (Atkinson, 2004).

Because oppression likely contributes to marginalized individuals' vulnerabilities to mental health problems, individualistic interventions must be accompanied by societal and systemic solutions. Otherwise, psychologists can do little more than help individuals cope with the negative impact of marginalization and adjust to an oppressive system. Alternatively, social justice efforts can focus on altering the causes and conditions of oppression.

Armed with personal insight into the dynamics and consequences of oppression, members of marginalized communities have worked for systemic change. The labor movement; civil rights movement; women's movement; disability rights movement; and lesbian, gay, bisexual, and transgender rights movement are examples of social movements in the United States that have advocated for the rights of marginalized individuals (Goodwin & Jasper, 2003). Social activism may be an important piece of identity development for members of marginalized groups. In particular, the stages of dissonance and resistance may foster social activism for ethnic minority individuals (Atkinson, 2004), and the identity pride stage is characterized by involvement in social activism for lesbian and gay individuals (Cass, 1979). Individuals from dominant groups may engage in social activism as part of their process of identity development as well. White individuals may work against racism as a result of awareness, guilt, and shame (Rowe, Bennet, & Atkinson, 1994). Similarly, the focus on sociopolitical ramifications of heterosexuality during the stage of politicized heterosexuality may foster activism in LGB causes (Mohr, 2002).

Response of Counseling Psychology to Concerns of Marginalized Communities

Counseling psychologists have addressed issues of oppression through various mechanisms. Multicultural counseling may be the most prominent contribution of counseling psychology to addressing the needs of marginalized individuals. The Cross-Cultural Counseling Competency model (Sue et al., 1982) was initially presented in a Division 17 Position Paper and has received considerable attention and elaboration (Ponterotto, Fuertes, & Chen, 2000). Counseling psychologists have been instrumental in the development of guidelines for psychotherapy with girls and women (Nutt, Rice, Enns et al., 2003); guidelines on multicultural education, training, research, practice, and organizational change (American Psychological Association, 2003); and early efforts to describe affirmative therapy with lesbian and gay clients (e.g., Browning, Reynolds, & Dworkin, 1991; Buhrke & Douce, 1991).

The Society for Counseling Psychology (SCP) (Division 17 of the American Psychological Association) houses several sections that focus on the concerns of marginalized individuals in the United States. The Section for the Advancement of Women; the Section for Ethnic and Racial Diversity; and the Section for Lesbian, Gay, and Bisexual Awareness provide support for these communities through programming at APA, student awards, and participation in the development of professional guidelines and policies. These three sections have joined forces to discuss common concerns, achieve greater visibility, and promote organizational change. This collaboration, titled the "More Pie Initiative," seeks to create "more pie" rather than fight over pieces of the pie (Israel, 2003). In addition, SCP cosponsors the biannual National Multicultural Conference and Summit that addresses issues of race/ethnicity, sexual orientation, gender, SES, and disability.

In addition to involvement in Division 17, counseling psychologists are members of other divisions of APA that specifically address concerns of women (Division 35, Society for the Psychology of Women); LGB issues (Division 44, Society for the Psychological Study of Lesbian, Gay, and Bisexual Issues); and ethnic minority issues (Division 45, Society for the Psychological Study of Ethnic Minority Issues). Outside of APA, counseling psychologists can find professional support and development in organizations such as the Asian American Psychological Association; the Association of Black Psychologists; the National Latino/a Psychological Association; the Society of Indian Psychologists; the Association for Women in Psychology; and divisions of the American Counseling Association (e.g., American Multicultural Counseling Association; Association for Gay, Lesbian, and Bisexual Issues in Counseling).

Overview of This Section

The chapters in this section provide some models for the role that counseling psychologists can play in addressing disparities for marginalized individuals and communities. These models push beyond the limits of therapeutic interventions to demonstrate approaches to social and systemic change. Furthermore, they address a range of issues, including some that typically have not been at the forefront of counseling psychology (e.g., disability, poverty), and several chapters address unique intersections among various types of oppression.

Social action may lead counseling psychologists into new realms, such as collaboration and consultation with policymakers and service providers. Bell and Goodman describe their efforts to address intimate partner violence at a systemic level through interactions with professionals from other fields and settings. By sharing strategies for action, as well as barriers they faced in their work, these authors prepare counseling psychologists to widen their sphere of influence in addressing this multifaceted problem.

Although some approaches to social justice require counseling psychologists to adopt new roles, it is also possible to address concerns of marginalized individuals by being conscious of oppression when carrying out existing responsibilities. Palombi and Mundt present a model that college counseling centers can employ to attend to the needs of college women with disabilities. This chapter can help counseling psychologists who are in a traditional counseling psychology setting envision how to address the needs of a marginalized group by altering the physical environment, developing inclusive outreach programming, and using empowering approaches to counseling.

In addition to the impact of oppression on political and social contexts, marginalized individuals may experience negative effects from their physical surroundings. Santiago-Rivera, Talka, and Tully call attention to the problem of environmental racism. The authors introduce an ecological framework to demonstrate how counseling psychologists can use their skills to enhance community intervention and social action to combat this problem.

The combination of research and social action can help counseling psychologists have an impact on scholarship while they are providing support to marginalized communities. Cosgrove describes her use of participatory action research and discourse analysis to address the needs of homeless mothers. Her research exposes common assumptions about this population and emphasizes the importance of using a strength-based framework in designing research, public policy, and services.

Whitcomb and Lowey describe their own work and that of other counseling psychologists in advocating for LGB issues. They provide examples of actions that counseling psychologists can take to support LGB individuals through community activism, policy and legislation, and public opinion. Furthermore, they describe strategies to address the challenges of engaging in social action regarding LGB issues, specifically attending to challenges for LGB individuals, allies, and academic counseling psychologists.

Multicultural counseling will need to expand beyond current models of individual therapy in order to embrace a social justice agenda (Vera & Speight, 2003). Morrow, Hawxhurst, Montes, Abousleman, and Castañeda outline a model of radical feminist multicultural psychology that is grounded in activism. By articulating an approach to multicultural counseling that reflects an understanding of intersections among oppressions and focuses interventions at a systemic level, these authors move the field toward a new vision of multicultural counseling.

Counseling psychologists are clearly concerned about the needs of disenfranchised individuals. These chapters provide a blueprint for those professionals who want to address the needs of marginalized communities beyond the confines of a therapeutic setting. Challenging oppression through social and systemic actions will realize the potential of counseling psychology and move the United States toward a vision of a just society.

References

American Psychological Association. (2003). Guidelines on multicultural education, training, research, practice, and organizational change for psychologists. *American Psychologist, 58,* 377–402.

Atkinson, D. R. (2004). *Counseling American minorities* (6th ed.). Boston: McGraw-Hill.

Browning, C., Reynolds, A. L., & Dworkin, S. H. (1991). Affirmative therapy for lesbian women. *The Counseling Psychologist, 19,* 177–196.

Buhrke, R. A., & Douce, L. A. (1991). Training issues for counseling psychologists in working with lesbian women and gay men. *The Counseling Psychologist, 19,* 216–234.

Cass, V. C. (1979). Homosexual identity formation: A theoretical model. *Journal of Homosexuality, 4*(3), 219–235.

Goodwin, J., & Jasper, J. M. (2003). *The social movements reader: Cases and concepts.* Malden, MA: Blackwell.

Hershberger, S. L., & D'Augelli, A. R. (2000). Issues in counseling lesbian, gay, and bisexual adolescents. In R. M. Perez, K. A. DeBord, & K. J. Bieschke (Eds.), *Handbook of counseling and psychotherapy with lesbian, gay, and bisexual clients* (pp. 225–247). Washington, DC: American Psychological Association.

Israel, T. (2003). Integrating gender and sexual orientation into multicultural counseling competencies. In G. Roysircar, P. Arredondo, J. N. Fuertes, J. G. Ponterotto, & R. L. Toporek (Eds.), *Multicultural counseling competencies 2003: Association for Multicultural Counseling and Development* (pp. 69–77). Alexandria, VA: AMCD.

McNamee, S. J., & Miller, R. K. (2004). *The meritocracy myth.* Lanham, MD: Rowman & Littlefield.

Miller, J. B. (1976). *Toward a new psychology of women.* Boston: Beacon Press.

Mohr, J. J. (2002). Heterosexual identity and the heterosexual therapist: An identity perspective on sexual orientation dynamics in psychotherapy. *The Counseling Psychologist, 30,* 532–566.

Nosek, M. A., & Hughes, R. B. (2004). Navigating the road to independent living. In D. R. Atkinson & G. Hackett (Eds.), *Counseling diverse populations* (pp. 172–193). Boston: McGraw-Hill.

Nutt, R. L., Rice, J. K., Enns, C. Z., et al. (2003). Appendix: Guidelines for psychotherapy with girls and women. In M. Kopala & M. E. Keitel (Eds.), *Handbook of counseling women* (pp. 575–579). Thousand Oaks, CA: Sage.

Ponterotto, J. G., Fuertes, J. N., & Chen, E. C. (2000). Models of multicultural counseling. In S. D. Brown & R. W. Lent (Eds.), *Handbook of counseling psychology* (3rd ed., pp. 639–669). New York: Wiley.

Rowe, W., Bennet, S. K., & Atkinson, D. R. (1994). White racial identity models: A critique and alternative proposal. *The Counseling Psychologist, 22,* 129–146.

Sue, D. W., Bernier, J. E., Durran, A., Feinberg, L., Pedersen, P., Smith, E. J., & Vazquez-Nutall, E. (1982). Position paper: Cross-cultural counseling competencies. *The Counseling Psychologist, 10,* 45–52.

Tatum, B. D. (1997). *Why are all the black kids sitting together in the cafeteria?* New York: Basic Books.

Vera, E. M., & Speight, S. L. (2003). Multicultural competence, social justice, and counseling psychology: Expanding our roles. *The Counseling Psychologist, 31,* 253–272.

Wells, M., Brack, C. J., & McMichen, P. J. (2003). Women and depressive disorders. In M. Kopala & M. E. Keitel (Eds.), *Handbook of counseling women* (pp. 429–457). Thousand Oaks, CA: Sage.

Young, I. M. (1990). *Justice and the politics of difference.* Princeton, NJ: Princeton University Press.

CHAPTER 12

Seeking Social Justice for Victims of Intimate Partner Violence

Real-World Struggles in Pursuit of Systemic Change

Margret E. Bell and Lisa A. Goodman

In the past several years, a growing number of counseling psychologists have urged their colleagues to take action on the field's long-standing commitment to social justice (see, e.g. Blustein et al., 2001; Fouad, 2001; Vera & Speight, 2003). Although counseling psychologists in general appear receptive to these calls (Arredondo & Perez, 2003; Fouad et al., 2004; Fox, 2003; Ivey & Collins, 2003), two obstacles to action are ambiguity about what constitutes social justice work and confusion about how psychologists might engage in it.

In an attempt to address these issues, a previous paper by the second author and her colleagues conceptualized social justice work as "research and professional action designed to change societal values, structures, policies, and practices such that disadvantaged or marginalized groups gain increased access to these tools of self-determination" (Goodman et al., 2004, p. 795). That article described three ecological levels at which social justice work can take place: the micro level, with individuals and families; the meso level, with communities, institutions, and organizations; and the macro level, with social structures, ideologies, and policies (Bronfenbrenner, 1977; Moane, 2003).

Despite the fact that counseling psychologists have long included social contextual (meso- and macro-level) factors in our conceptualizations of individual difficulties, our models of intervention nevertheless have remained at the micro-level of analysis (Fox, 2003; Vera & Speight, 2003). These micro-level interventions, although tremendously important, do not address directly the systems, structures, ideologies, and policies from which individual difficulties often originate (Goodman et al., 2004). Ultimately, change in these systemic (meso and macro) levels is necessary if we hope to be successful in our work with individuals, not to mention in our promotion of social justice more generally.

We believe that, by and large, counseling psychologists already have the training, theoretical grounding, and skills necessary to have a greater impact on these levels. What the field lacks, however, are concrete examples of how counseling psychologists might meaningfully apply their skills to nontraditional contexts and efforts at systemic change. We need to begin conversations in which we share these types of examples, both to cultivate a collective sense of how to create and navigate research and intervention efforts that move beyond the individual level of analysis, as well as to provide forums in which to discuss and learn from each others' successes and failures.

This chapter seeks to begin one such conversation by describing three of our own experiences seeking systemic change for victims of intimate partner violence (IPV). Social justice work can be very rewarding, and it would be easy to center our examples on what we have gained from doing this type of work. Our goal, however, is to stimulate counseling psychologists to think about the sometimes difficult practicalities of acting on a commitment to social justice. Therefore, we have chosen to present projects that exemplify some of the real-world issues with which we have struggled in our systemic change efforts. The challenges we discuss are by no means exclusive to social justice work, nor do they embody a comprehensive list of such difficulties. They are challenges, however, that have come up repeatedly in our own systemically oriented work. They include (1) working collaboratively across disciplines; (2) acknowledging not just the benefits, but also the potential negative consequences of our work; and (3) handling shifts in roles and goals over the course of a project. First, however, we provide some background on intimate partner violence, particularly with regard to how systemic factors shape victims' experiences.

Intimate Partner Violence: Background and Systemic Issues

Based on sheer numbers, IPV is a problem of immense proportions in the United States.[1] According to the National Violence Against Women Survey, approximately 25% of all women will be physically assaulted and/or raped by a current or former husband or boyfriend over the course of their lifetimes (Tjaden & Thoennes, 2000). Although startling in and of itself, this figure does not include the stalking or ridicule, degradation, jealousy, restriction, isolation, damage to property, threats, and other forms of psychological abuse that commonly accompany physical violence (Follingstad, Brennan, Hause, Polek, & Rutledge, 1991; Sackett & Saunders, 1999).

Nor do these statistics convey the devastating physical and psychosocial aftereffects of battering. Physical abuse can lead to a wide range of injuries, including bruises, cuts, sprains, burns, broken teeth and bones, dislocations, internal injuries, wounds from knives or guns, and permanent disfigurement or brain damage (Acevedo, 2000). Ultimately, several thousand women are killed by a partner or former partner each year (1,414 known female victims in 1992; Bachman & Saltzman, 1995). Those who survive are likely to suffer from severe depression (Bell & Goodman, 2001; Goodman, Bennett, & Dutton, 1999), incapacitating anxiety (Follingstad et al., 1991), posttraumatic stress disorder (PTSD) (Kemp, Rawlings, & Green, 1991; Kocot & Goodman, 2003), or other mental health problems. To add to their burden, battered women often find themselves isolated from family, friends, and community supports, thus making it more difficult for them to obtain the resources they need to promote their safety (Lloyd & Taluc, 1999; Sullivan, Basta, Tan, & Davidson, 1992).

Even when they do manage to connect with sources of help, victims of IPV are still too often led to believe that they are somehow to blame for their experiences of violence. Voices as varied as a woman's abusive partner, her family and friends, clergy, and politicians continue to ask her what she did to provoke her partner, or even urge her to be more loving and forgiving (Miller, 1996; Rhodes & McKenzie, 1998). Alternatively, they ask her why she doesn't leave, but then fail to support her efforts to do so (Loseke & Cahill, 1984; Miller, 1996; Rhodes & McKenzie, 1998). In doing this, they fail to intervene with or even acknowledge the cultural and societal forces that keep her trapped in the abusive situation; the implicit assumption (and communication) of these types of responses is that the problem is located largely within victims themselves.

In contrast, feminists involved in the anti-domestic violence movement have long recognized that the struggles of individual battered women are in large part rooted in oppressive social, political, and cultural forces. So, too, must counseling psychologists committed to social justice attend to the ways in which various sociocultural factors contribute to the problem of IPV (Goodman et al., 2004). That is, a social justice perspective on IPV needs to consider how economic inequality, traditional gender roles, and religious and cultural practices that privilege men both promote men's use of violence and make it more difficult for women to escape such violence once it begins (Schechter, 1982; Yllö, 1988). For example, lower wages, poor employment opportunities, and child care responsibilities frequently leave women heavily dependent upon their male partners for money, housing, and transportation (Johnson, 1992; Rhodes & McKenzie, 1998). Compounding this material dependence, many women also have to wrestle with internalized societal dictates that they be self-sacrificing, defer to their partners, and preserve the family at all costs (Latta & Goodman, in press; LaViolette & Barnett, 2000). In combination, these two sets of obstacles often make it extremely difficult for battered women to take steps to end their relationship or to otherwise address the violence (Anderson & Saunders, 2003; Hendy, Eggen, Gustitus, McLeod, & Ng, 2003).

A counseling psychology perspective emphasizing social justice also needs to attend to the ways in which specific social institutions may contribute to and sustain the problem of IPV. For example, despite the numerous legal reforms championed by anti-domestic violence activists over the past 20 years, seeking help from the justice system is still a revictimizing experience for many battered women (Bennett, Goodman, & Dutton, 1999; Erez & Belknap, 1998). Some jurisdictions routinely refuse to charge misdemeanor offenders, implicitly or explicitly discourage women from pursuing criminal charges, or fail to enforce protection orders (Erez & Belknap, 1998; Zorza, 1992). Although well-intentioned, recent reforms that mandate arrest and/or prosecution may only recapitulate some women's sense of helplessness about the abuse—and perhaps even lead to an increase in abuse—by taking control and influence of the process out of their hands (Coker, 2001; Epstein, Bell, & Goodman, 2003; Ford & Regoli, 1992; Hirschel, Hutchison, & Dean, 1992).

Unfortunately, the criminal justice system is not the only institution to fail victims of IPV. For instance, until recently, government agencies responsible for welfare and immigration services did not consider a woman's history of IPV before making decisions about requirements for work or petitions for citizenship, thus ignoring the ways in which being monitored, threatened, and generally controlled by her partner might affect her ability to follow through on these requirements (Acevedo, 2000; Riger & Krieglstein, 2000; Tien-Li Loke, 1997). Strapped by lack of funding, even the network of feminist-run shelter programs often cannot provide adequate help to certain victims, including those with substance abuse or mental health problems, physical disabilities, or a limited ability to communicate in English (Donnelly, Cook, & Wilson, 1999).

Historically, the institution of counseling psychology has also responded inadequately to the problem of IPV, particularly in its reliance on psychotherapy and batterer treatment as the remedies of choice. Without question, these types of interventions are extremely important in terms of helping individual victims to recover and individual batterers to reform. Therapy provides an opportunity to learn about gender socialization, male privilege, and other contextual factors that predispose men to using—and women to experiencing—IPV. Batterer treatment, in spite of the questions that remain about its efficacy (Healey, Smith, & O'Sullivan, 1998), is likewise an invaluable source of education and consciousness-raising. However, given the sociocultural and institutional factors involved in sustaining IPV, it is clear that individually focused, micro-level interventions can only do so much; effectively addressing intimate partner violence also requires changes in our cultural, religious, medical, and political institutions that promote and maintain violence against women (Goodman, Koss, Fitzgerald, Russo, & Keita, 1993).

Happily, concurrent to promoting change through therapy and other micro-level interventions, counseling psychologists also have a meaningful role to play in effecting systemic change. Many of the traditional professional activities of counseling psychology—including program design and evaluation, research, and consultation—can be fruitfully applied to shape social policy and popular thinking. We next present several of our own efforts in this regard.

Our Experiences Seeking Systemic Change for Victims of Intimate Partner Violence

Although the nature of the tasks involved in seeking systemic change may be familiar to counseling psychologists, applying these skills to new contexts and ends often creates new challenges. For example, three difficulties that we have encountered repeatedly in our efforts to promote systemic change are (1) the need to negotiate divergent perspectives and value orientations among individuals involved in a collaboration; (2) the need to consider not just the potential benefits, but also the potential negative consequences of the work; and (3) the need to adapt to shifts in the nature of one's role or of the task itself.

To illustrate how we negotiated these challenges and, in doing so, drew upon our skills as counseling psychologists, we next present three recent systemically based research or intervention projects on which one or both authors have worked. Recognizing that there are no absolute, universal solutions to the difficulties we highlight in these examples, we name them and share our own responses to them in the hope that doing so here will provide at least a starting point for the field to begin discussing these and related issues. Likewise, the roles that we adopted in the projects we describe certainly do not represent the only ways in which counseling psychologists might have contributed to the work being done.

Communicating Across the Divide(s): Participating in the Victim-Informed Prosecution Team

In 1997, Lisa Goodman (the second author of this paper), then a faculty member at the University of Maryland, College Park, was conducting research on institutional responses to IPV when she met Deborah Epstein, a law school professor who was also Director of the Domestic Violence Intake Center at a local court. Joined in 1998 by Margret Bell (the first author of this paper, and at the time a doctoral student at the University of Maryland, College Park), the three of us began talking informally about the criminal justice system's increasing reliance on "mandatory" strategies that focused on securing arrests, prosecutions, and convictions—thus ensuring offender accountability—often without considering the victim's needs or whether a conviction would be the best way to promote her safety (see Epstein et al., 2003, for an extended discussion of this issue).

Soon thereafter, we had a chance to address these concerns when, through our ties to the local prosecutor's office, we became involved with an innovative program known as the Victim Informed Prosecution Project[2] (VIP). VIP is unique within the criminal justice system in that it redefines prosecutorial success as ensuring both offender accountability and victim safety. To accomplish these twin goals, each potential criminal case is handled by a coordinated team comprised of prosecutors, civil attorneys, and advocates from a local domestic violence agency. Instead of employing a cookie-cutter response to domestic violence—that is, seeking prosecution and conviction in all cases, even if it means going forward without the victim—the team meets regularly to discuss options that might best address each victim's particular situation. In these discussions, the victim's needs and wishes are central, although not entirely determinative (see Epstein et al., 2003, for a more detailed description of the program). Outside of these meetings, team members also make efforts to connect victims with relevant community agencies, provide help in obtaining civil protection orders, and be a source of emotional support and help with safety planning.

Part of VIP from its very inception, we helped shape the structure of the program by providing consultation about how the emotional and physical safety needs of battered women might affect their involvement with the court system. Part of this work involved sharing our thoughts on how the system might better account for and respond to these needs. More recently, we have been working with the VIP team members to conduct an outcome evaluation of the program's efficacy (Goodman, 2004). We also continue to sit in on team meetings and provide consultation on individual cases.

Although our experience with VIP has been a wonderful opportunity to address some of the systemic obstacles faced by IPV victims, particularly those marginalized by poverty, racism, and social isolation, it has also been extremely challenging to work across disciplinary boundaries. More specifically, although it is clear that team members all share a commitment to addressing the problem of domestic violence more effectively, each comes with a different institutional culture, disciplinary language, and overall perspective that, in concert, make the day-to-day business of collaborating very challenging.

For example, one "divide" that manifested itself early in the development of VIP was between the advocates and psychologists on one hand, and the legal agents (particularly the prosecutors) on the other. Each group had a different perspective on what, ultimately, would be the most effective deterrent to future violence. Not surprisingly, the prosecutors on the team believed that securing a conviction was the most important thing they could do to help victims. As such, they typically considered their work done—and the victim safe—once they had obtained a conviction. This made sense, given that the justice system as a whole generally defines its job as punishing a perpetrator's most recent violation of the criminal law, with little attention to anything else (Epstein et al., 2003). Adopting a more holistic, long-term view, we (from our perspective as clinicians), along with the advocates, felt that meeting participants' broader psychosocial needs was crucial if the team was to deter future abuse. That is, we felt that the effects of any given prosecution were deeply intertwined with—and thus inevitably affected by—the complexities of each particular victim's life.

This difference in perspective played out in a number of concrete ways. For example, given the prosecutors' focus on obtaining evidence that would secure a conviction, they were unlikely to gather or consider information about the context in which particular violent episodes were embedded. This context might include ongoing threats of retaliation by the abuser or his family members; a history of escalating abuse after previous court interventions; the victim's and her children's dependence on the abuser for money, housing, or other material supports; or a religious community from which the victim would be extruded should she be seen as responsible for sending her husband to jail. In contrast, we believed that attending to, accounting for, and even intervening with this larger picture was imperative, in that it shed light on how a criminal prosecution or particular sentencing option would be experienced by the victim and batterer. This, in turn, would determine what types of responses the prosecution might provoke and thus how effective the criminal justice intervention would be in the long run.

Although we were often able to pursue both sets of goals—that is, to seek a conviction while simultaneously addressing a victim's broader needs and concerns—this difference in perspective came to a head when we discussed how to handle the cases of certain participants for whom the consequences of prosecution seemed great. Believing that sacrificing full batterer accountability in these situations might ultimately promote victim safety, we sometimes urged prosecutors to drop cases altogether and rely on the services that other team members, such as the advocates, might provide. Finding our logic to be backward, and believing that batterer accountability through prosecution was the best way to ensure victim safety, prosecutors were frustrated by these requests. They felt that to do what we suggested would go against the training they had received and the justice system culture of which they were a part. Furthermore, they knew that they (rather than the team as a whole) would be the ones held responsible if even one woman whose abusive partner received one of these more lenient interventions was severely injured or killed. Illustrating their perspective, they asked us rhetorically, "Will you be there to defend us when this victim gets killed and our names are splashed all over the newspapers for failing to help her?"

Beyond this divide between clinicians and prosecutors, a second divide that manifested itself on the team was between the practitioners (advocates and lawyers) and us in our role as researchers. Although we deal with aspects of the researcher-practitioner split in more depth in our next vignette, these issues also arose during our evaluation of the VIP program. As researchers, we knew that conducting a valid evaluation would require that we develop—and stick to—specific criteria regarding which women could participate in the program. Although we had derived these criteria by group consensus, when it came to implementation, practitioners on the team occasionally wanted to include certain women simply because they had "an intuition" that they could benefit from the services, even though they did not meet the predetermined criteria. This repeatedly left us with the unpopular job of reminding team members about the methodological importance of adhering strictly to the screening protocol. In response, we encountered frustration and anger that the "research was getting in the way of helping people."

Over time, we learned to deal with these conflicts using a number of different strategies. The most important one was developing personal relationships with members of the team. This helped enormously to cut through rhetoric and create empathy across perspectives. A second strategy was to try to pick our battles, seek a middle ground, and make compromises wherever possible. A third was to make absolutely sure to create research and evaluation goals that would be useful and interesting to every single person at the table. When conflict arose, we were then able to remind team members of what they themselves would gain by sticking with the research methodology despite their legitimate concerns about it. A final strategy was to listen carefully for the reasonableness of each team member's perspective. When we stopped arguing for our point of view, we often heard their struggle much more clearly and came to appreciate the constraints and demands with which they had to work. Feeling heard, they were then often more able to hear our perspective, leading to more productive discussions and creative solutions.

For example, with respect to the divide between clinicians and legal agents over how to best pursue victim safety, it was only after we set aside our own deeply held opinions long enough to really hear the prosecutors' perspectives (and vice versa) that we were able to work out a creative compromise. Once we began to embrace the validity of both perspectives, we were able to agree to "defer sentencing" in certain cases—that is, suspend a batterer's sentence as long as he stopped his abuse completely. This solution kept the batterer accountable while hopefully avoiding some of the consequences that might result from his immediate imprisonment. With respect to how we addressed the second divide, that between practitioners and researchers over study protocols, we finally decided that if practitioners felt particularly strongly about including a woman in VIP who didn't meet the screening criteria, we would include her but not count her as a participant in the main body of the evaluation. We would, however, track this third (tiny) group of women separately in order to document outcomes for them compared to the participants selected in adherence with the study protocol.

Overall, our work on the VIP project taught us much about the extent to which disciplinary and professional backgrounds shape our assumptions concerning what are the "best" methods for reducing violence against women. Ultimately, by learning from each others' perspectives, examining our own biases, and reminding each other of our common goal of reducing rates of intimate partner violence, we were able to successfully find ways to bridge our various divides.

Biting the Bullet: Evaluating a Law School–Based Advocacy Intervention

As Margret began looking for a topic for her master's thesis in 1998, Lisa's ongoing research in the court system made her aware of the innovative work with IPV victims being done by a local university-based legal advocacy clinic. She also knew that the clinic director was interested in research and might be willing to collaborate on a project to examine the effectiveness of the program.

To provide some background, this clinic paired low-income victims of IPV seeking civil protection orders with specially trained law student advocates for 4 to 6 weeks (Bell & Goodman, 2001). Numerous studies have documented both the frustrations that battered women experience in seeking help from the justice system and the large proportion of women who simply drop out of the process before getting what they need (Bennett et al., 1999). Aware of these systemic difficulties, both of us (and the clinic director) were excited that the legal representation, emotional support, and connection to community resources provided by the clinic might help civil courts be more accessible and accountable to the victims seeking help from them. Furthermore, despite the widespread usage of IPV advocacy programs in a variety of settings, there continued (and continues) to be very little research on their effectiveness (Bell & Goodman, 2001; Goodman & Epstein, 2005). It was thus clear that, although documenting the efficacy of this particular program would be important in its own right, it would also be a key step in validating the effectiveness of advocacy programs more generally. This, in turn, could help promote the systemic changes necessary to improve women's experiences in the justice system.

Although new to the research process, the director and supervisors of the advocacy program were deeply committed to their work in the clinic, convinced of the intervention's positive effects for victims, and eager for empirical data to support these convictions. Although we shared this optimism and enthusiasm, we also recognized the realities and complexities of the research process, particularly as conducted in the community.

For example, an empirical research project, by necessity, can examine only a limited number of narrowly defined outcomes and questions. Choosing to focus exclusively on certain mental health or violence-related outcomes might cause us to miss any effects the intervention had on, say, victims' attitudes toward or ability to use the justice system. Likewise, although interviewing women multiple times over an extended period of time would be the optimal way to assess the true impact of the program, we knew we would be limited to one short-term follow-up given the time frame and financial resources available to us. We had to hope—gamble even—that whatever time frame and constructs we chose would be sufficient for us to see the impact of the program on participants' experiences. Failure to do so might lead others to conclude prematurely that the program had no effects.

Also potentially problematic, as noted in the previous example on VIP, was the fact that the conduct of research requires community programs—which are often geared toward helping the most at-risk victims of the moment in whatever ways they need most—to conform to a stable set of inclusion criteria and other protocols. We were concerned that in imposing controls to make their program "researchable," we might be mitigating the very specialized, targeted aspects of the intervention that made it effective. That is, rather than crafting individualized solutions, providing targeted referrals, and investing differential amounts of time with different clients, advocates might end up implementing a "one-size-fits-all" intervention that, because of its generality, was less effective. Although there were ways around some of these problems, such as using a qualitative design or employing specialized statistical analyses, they too had their limitations. Eventually, we had to recognize that no matter how well thought out our decisions and how vigorous our efforts, certain methodological limitations might ultimately determine the nature of the results we obtained.

Although frustrating in any research endeavor, the possibility that our study might not adequately assess the true impact of the program was particularly distressing given the real-world consequences of not finding significant, positive effects. That is, nonsignificant results, even if due to methodological limitations, could jeopardize the program's future efforts to secure funding and, nationally, could discourage the adoption of a potentially useful intervention. Moreover, the personal disappointment that less-than-positive results would bring to the director, the law student supervisors, and the law students themselves would be tremendous.

Nevertheless, for the reasons detailed previously, we believed in the importance of conducting a formal evaluation of the clinic program. The best we could do, we realized, was to acknowledge the potential for negative results, then "bite the bullet," be thoughtful and informed about our methodological decisions, and move forward.

Perhaps most important in the service of being thoughtful and informed in our methodological decisions were our efforts to help the clinic members understand research methods. This allowed two things: One, they were able to use their own expertise about the clinic to help us think through the impact of some of our choices about methodology; and two, we were, together, better able to avoid some of the methodological errors that might lead to nonsignificant results.

In addition, we also made careful efforts to balance optimism and guardedness in both ourselves and the clinic members throughout the course of the project. The clinic members were thrilled that their program was being evaluated and confident that we would demonstrate its effectiveness. We were also hopeful, but much less confident. Although the nature of this dynamic is sometimes different in community-based research—with program staff often more suspicious of and needing more encouragement about the research process than was the case here—there is nevertheless always a need to prepare stakeholders for the possibility that the study might produce results that are not what they want to hear. As such, we made sure to engage in a series of discussions about this issue, especially with respect to what their reaction to negative or even neutral results might be. Moreover, feeling the pressure to produce positive results, we carefully monitored our own actions and decisions to ensure we maintained adequate scientific rigor.

Ultimately, our findings were exciting in that we found that women receiving the advocacy intervention reported significantly lower levels of psychological and physical abuse and marginally higher levels of emotional support than did women in the comparison condition (Bell & Goodman, 2001). The clinic has since used these findings to apply for continued funding. The dissemination of the results through these grant proposals as well as through other outlets (journals, conferences, feedback to the law student advocates themselves) will hopefully encourage further investigation into and support for these types of interventions.

Although our ending was a happy one, resulting in positive, real-world changes, there was a very real chance that our findings might not have been so supportive of our hopes and convictions about the program's effects. Throughout the course of the study, we had to confront this possibility for ourselves and for the clinic members, delicately maintaining both the optimism to continue with the research and the realism to be prepared for whatever the results might show. Learning to sit with this ambiguity ourselves, as well as helping our research partners to do so, was thus a central task of this project.

Responding to Changes in the Road Map: Examining a City's IPV Services for Haitian Immigrant Women

In the fall of 2001, Lisa (now at Boston College) was approached by the director of the Violence Prevention Office (VPO) in a northeastern city long known for its progressive response to IPV. Concerned about the fact that only a small proportion of abused immigrant women seemed to be accessing the city's domestic violence services, the director wanted to learn more about why this was so.

Over the course of a few meetings, Lisa, Rachel Latta (a doctoral student at Boston College), and the director agreed that a qualitative needs assessment survey with a single immigrant group at a time (beginning with Haitian women) would be the best way to learn about the accessibility and usefulness of the city's domestic violence services. (The resulting study's methodology and findings are described in more detail in Latta & Goodman, in press.) We all agreed that our overall goal was systemic change: to develop a report that the director could use to inform service provision and policy.

We dove into the data collection and analysis process quickly and, based on our findings, began to develop recommendations for reform. Just as we began to anticipate the end of the project, however, the director who had commissioned the study left the VPO for another job, a not-uncommon occurrence in public sector or community-based agencies. Moreover, the city was unable to hire a replacement for her because of a city-wide hiring freeze that was lifted only recently (over a year later).

Given this turn of events, we were forced to re-evaluate the "map" that had guided our work on the project to that point. That is, we had begun the project as consultants to the director, who would herself be primarily responsible for advocating for the implementation of the study's results. With her departure, however, it was unclear whether any of the report's recommendations would even be read, much less implemented. This was obviously tremendously disappointing to us. Nonetheless, one option was for us to consider our work finished, since we had already turned in our report to the VPO and completed an article for publication. This would have been a reasonable course of action—and indeed, would have followed the well-marked course laid out by traditional research endeavors—given that we had fulfilled the obligations and commitments specified in our original map.

However, a central reason we had embarked on this project was the desire to effect systemic change that would improve the lives of a group of marginalized IPV victims. We felt that in this respect, our job was not yet done. To accept the added responsibility that had, by default, fallen in our laps of bringing the report to the attention of the city and advocating for its recommendations would require much more work than we had envisioned at the outset of the collaboration. But given that our commitment was to a cause and vision—not to certain static outcomes or predetermined obligations—we ultimately decided to extend our time and efforts on the project and find ways to continue to advocate for our report's conclusions.

Choosing to discard the original road map and/or lengthen the journey requires a great deal of flexibility and patience, but the need to do so is ultimately a defining challenge of systemically oriented social justice work. This work is both highly attentive to contextual influences and also highly dependent upon them. For example, in this project, we set out with a plan for addressing a problem in the community that, as a result of change in the surrounding context, changed the very way the problem needed to be addressed. Although this meant rethinking our time line, reexamining our commitment to the project, and reformulating our plan of action, so too did our roles and goals need to adapt along the way.

What Counseling Psychologists Bring to Systemic Change Efforts

Each of these projects drew heavily on our skills as counseling psychologists. Obviously, the evaluation of the law school advocacy program and the project on services for Haitian women victimized by IPV involved the use of traditional research conceptualization and design skills, albeit geared toward research in a community setting. As VIP continues to grow, program evaluation research will be a central piece of this project as well.

Traditional consultation skills are also essential to systemically based work. For example, in creating an official report and recommendations for the city on the results of the Haitian project, we had to consider how to acknowledge both the strengths and weaknesses of the current system, how to present our participants' ideas in a way that would be heard, and what might be the most feasible way to implement the study's results. Likewise, in working with the VIP team we contributed our knowledge of why, psychologically, certain victims might be reacting in the ways they were. This included sharing our thoughts on how prosecutors, advocates, and other team members might form stronger connections with the victims with whom they worked. Finally, drawing on our knowledge of assessment, we also shared with the team measures and protocols that they could use to more accurately assess each participant's mental health and history of abuse.

Perhaps less obvious, all three projects also engaged our counseling skills. Although each of the projects required sensitivity to issues involving ethnic and racial diversity, the project involving Haitian women in particular demanded that we consider deeply the meaning of cultural competence, examine our own biases and assumptions about Haitian culture, and consult with colleagues who knew more—all skills that we learned in our training as therapists.

These counseling skills were also crucial as we sought ways to collaborate across disciplinary boundaries. Although interdisciplinary collaboration presents enormous opportunities in terms of combining resources, knowledge, and effort (Cohen, Baer, & Satterwhite, 2002), it is not easy, especially given the tensions that have historically existed between professionals and activists, "insiders" and "outsiders," and academia and the "real" world (Gondolf, Yllö, & Campbell, 1997; Yllö, 1988). However, we believe that counseling psychologists have special skills to bring to bear in handling these tensions. Most critical is our ability to develop rapport and form relationships in which others feel safe and respected. Collaboration is by no means analogous to counseling, but still, our skills in conveying empathy, our capacity to listen to and hear differing viewpoints, and the ability to make sure everyone's voice gets heard are important both for resolving problems in the moment and for maintaining the group's ability to work together over the long haul. Considering that each of these projects took several years to complete, it was crucial to be able to foster, manage, and maintain relationships in this way.

Conclusion

The three projects outlined in this chapter represent just a few of the ways in which counseling psychologists can engage in social justice work and just a few of the struggles that may arise in doing this work. We hope that others will join us in describing the process, and not just the outcomes, of their work at the meso and macro levels of analysis. We believe that these kinds of descriptions are essential if counseling psychology as a whole is to translate its social justice aspirations into practical action. But fundamentally, if we truly hope to address the roots of social problems and, in turn, make the world a more just place for all, we must engage in change efforts that go beyond the individual level of analysis. Clearly, there is a great deal that counseling psychologists can contribute to these efforts.

Notes

1. Although we acknowledge that not all victims of abusive interpersonal relationships are women, we have chosen to discuss the experiences of battered women and to use the pronoun "she" throughout this chapter in recognition of the fact that the overwhelming majority of those who are victimized in this way are female (Bachman & Saltzman, 1995; Tjaden & Thoennes, 2000).
2. This program was originally named the Targeted Offender Program (TOP) and is referred to as such in the Epstein et al. (2003) article.

References

Acevedo, M. J. (2000). Battered immigrant Mexican women's perspectives regarding abuse and help-seeking. *Journal of Multicultural Social Work, 8*(3/4), 243–282.

Anderson, D. J., & Saunders, D. G. (2003). Leaving an abusive partner: An empirical review of predictors, the process of leaving, and psychological well-being. *Trauma Violence & Abuse, 4*(2), 163–191.

Arredondo, P., & Perez, P. (2003). Expanding multicultural competence through social justice leadership. *The Counseling Psychologist, 31*(3), 282–289.

Bachman, R., & Saltzman, L. E. (1995). *Violence against women: Estimates from the redesigned survey, August, 1995.* Washington, DC: Bureau of Justice Statistics.

Bell, M. E., & Goodman, L. A. (2001). Supporting battered women involved with the court system: An evaluation of a law school–based advocacy intervention. *Violence Against Women, 7*(12), 1377–1404.

Bennett, L., Goodman, L., & Dutton, M. A. (1999). Systemic obstacles to the criminal prosecution of a battering partner: A victim perspective. *Journal of Interpersonal Violence, 14*(7), 761–772.

Blustein, D., Jackson, J., Kenny, M. E., Sparks, E., Chaves, A. P., Diemer, M. A., Gallagher, L. A., Mullin, K., & Copman, S. (2001, March). *Social action within an urban school context: The Tools for Tomorrow project.* Paper presented at the 4th National Counseling Psychology Conference, Houston, TX.

Bronfenbrenner, U. (1977). Toward an experimental ecology of human development. *American Psychologist, 32*(7), 513–531.

Cohen, L., Baer, N., & Satterwhite, P. (2002). *Developing effective coalitions: An eight step guide.* Oakland, CA: Prevention Institute. Available: www.preventioninstitute.org

Coker, D. (2001). Crime control and feminist law reform in domestic violence law: A critical review. *Buffalo Criminal Law Review, 4,* 801–860.

Donnelly, D. A., Cook, K. J., & Wilson, L. (1999). Provision and exclusion: The dual face of services to battered women in three Deep South states. *Violence Against Women, 5*(7), 710–741.

Epstein, D., Bell, M. E., & Goodman, L. A. (2003). Transforming aggressive prosecution policies: Prioritizing victims' long-term safety in the prosecution of domestic violence cases. *Journal of Gender, Social Policy, & the Law, 11*(2), 465–498.

Erez, E., & Belknap, J. (1998). In their own words: Battered women's assessments of the criminal processing system's responses. *Violence & Victims, 13*(3), 251–268.

Follingstad, D. R., Brennan, A. F., Hause, E. S., Polek, D. S., & Rutledge, L. L. (1991). Factors moderating physical and psychological symptoms of battered women. *Journal of Family Violence, 6*(1), 81–95.

Ford, D. A., & Regoli, M. J. (1992). The preventive impacts of policies for prosecuting wife batterers. In E. S. Buzawa & C. G. Buzawa (Eds.), *Domestic violence: The changing criminal justice response* (pp. 181–207). Westport, CT: Auburn House.

Fouad, N. A. (2001). 2001 Division 17 presidential address: Dreams for 2010: Making a difference. *The Counseling Psychologist, 30*(1), 158–166.

Fouad, N. A., McPherson, R. H., Gerstein, L., Blustein, D. L., Elman, N. S., Ihle Helledy, K., & Metz, A. J. (2004). Houston 2001: Context and legacy. *The Counseling Psychologist, 32*(1), 15–77.

Fox, D. R. (2003). Awareness is good, but action is better. *The Counseling Psychologist, 31*(3), 299–304.

Gondolf, E. W., Yllö, K., & Campbell, J. (1997). Collaboration between researchers and advocates. In G. K. Kantor & J. L. Jasinski (Eds.), *Out of the darkness: Contemporary perspectives on family violence* (pp. 255–267). Thousand Oaks, CA: Sage.

Goodman, L. A. (2004, April). *Victim-informed prosecution: Initial findings.* Paper presented at the 1st International Research and Action Conference: Innovations in Understanding Violence Against Women, Wellesley, MA.

Goodman, L. A., Bennett, L., & Dutton, M. A. (1999). Obstacles to victims' cooperation with the criminal prosecution of their abusers: The role of social support. *Violence & Victims, 14*(4), 427–444.

Goodman, L. A., & Epstein, D. (2005). Refocusing on women: A new direction for policy and research on intimate partner violence. *Journal of Interpersonal Violence, 20*(4), 479–487.

Goodman, L. A., Koss, M. P., Fitzgerald, L. F., Russo, N. F., & Keita, G. (1993). Male violence against women: Current research and future directions. *American Psychologist, 48*(10), 1054–1058.

Goodman, L. A., Liang, B., Helms, J. E., Latta, R. E., Sparks, E., & Weintraub, S. R. (2004). Major contribution: Training counseling psychologists as social justice agents: Feminist and multicultural theories in action. *The Counseling Psychologist, 32*(6), 793–837.

Healey, K., Smith, C., & O'Sullivan, C. (1998). *Batterer intervention: Program approaches and criminal justice strategies.* Washington, DC: National Institute of Justice. Available: http://www.ncjrs.org/pdffiles/168638.pdf

Hendy, H. M., Eggen, D., Gustitus, C., McLeod, K. C., & Ng, P. (2003). Decision to Leave Scale: Perceived reasons to stay in or leave violent relationships. *Psychology of Women Quarterly, 27*(2), 162–173.

Hirschel, J. D., Hutchison, I. W., & Dean, C. W. (1992). The failure of arrest to deter spouse abuse. *Journal of Research in Crime & Delinquency, 29*(1), 7–33.

Ivey, A. E., & Collins, N. M. (2003). Social justice: A long-term challenge for counseling psychology. *The Counseling Psychologist, 31*(3), 290–298.

Johnson, I. M. (1992). Economic, situational, and psychological correlates of the decision-making process of battered women. *Families in Society, 73,* 168–176.

Kemp, A., Rawlings, E. I., & Green, B. L. (1991). Post-traumatic stress disorder (PTSD) in battered women: A shelter sample. *Journal of Traumatic Stress, 4*(1), 137–148.

Kocot, T. G., & Goodman, L. (2003). The roles of coping and social support in battered women's mental health. *Violence Against Women, 9*(3), 323–346.

Latta, R. E., & Goodman, L. A. (in press). Considering the interplay of cultural context and service provision in intimate partner violence: The case of Haitian women. *Violence Against Women.*

LaViolette, A. D., & Barnett, O. W. (2000). *It could happen to anyone: Why battered women stay* (2nd ed.). Thousand Oaks, CA: Sage.

Lloyd, S., & Taluc, N. (1999). The effects of male violence on female employment. *Violence Against Women, 5*(4), 370–392.

Loseke, D. R., & Cahill, S. E. (1984). The social construction of deviance: Experts on battered women. *Social Problems, 31*(3), 296–310.

Miller, S. L. (1996). The fatal flaw: Inadequacies in social support and criminal justice responses. In B. Sipe & E. J. Hall (Eds.), *I am not your victim: Anatomy of domestic violence* (pp. 245–257). Thousand Oaks, CA: Sage.

Moane, G. (2003). Bridging the personal and the political: Practices for a liberation psychology. *American Journal of Community Psychology, 31*(1/2), 91–101.

Rhodes, N. R., & McKenzie, E. B. (1998). Why do battered women stay? Three decades of research. *Aggression & Violent Behavior, 3*(4), 391–406.

Riger, S., & Krieglstein, M. (2000). The impact of welfare reform on men's violence against women. *American Journal of Community Psychology, 28*(5), 631–647.

Sackett, L. A., & Saunders, D. G. (1999). The impact of different forms of psychological abuse on battered women. *Violence & Victims: Special Issue: Psychological Abuse in Domestically Violent Relationships, 14*(1), 105–117.

Schechter, S. (1982). *Women and male violence: The visions and struggles of the battered women's movement.* Boston: South End Press.

Sullivan, C. M., Basta, J., Tan, C., & Davidson, W. S. (1992). After the crisis: A needs assessment of women leaving a domestic violence shelter. *Violence & Victims, 7*(3), 267–275.

Tien-Li Loke, N. (1997). Trapped in domestic violence: The impact of United States immigration laws on battered immigrant women. *Boston University Public Interest Law Journal, 6,* 589–614.

Tjaden, P., & Thoennes, N. (2000). *Extent, nature, and consequences of intimate partner violence: Findings from the National Violence Against Women Survey.* Washington, DC: National Institute of Justice.

Vera, E. M., & Speight, S. L. (2003). Multicultural competence, social justice, and counseling psychology: Expanding our roles. *The Counseling Psychologist, 31*(3), 253–272.

Yllö, K. (1988). Political and methodological debates in wife abuse research. In K. Yllö & M. Bograd (Eds.), *Feminist perspectives on wife abuse* (pp. 28–51). Newbury Park, CA: Sage.

Zorza, J. (1992). Symposium on domestic violence: Criminal law: The criminal law of misdemeanor domestic violence, 1970–1990. *Journal of Criminal Law & Criminology, 83,* 46–72.

CHAPTER 13

Achieving Social Justice for College Women With Disabilities

A Model for Inclusion

Barbara J. Palombi and Alisa Matteson Mundt

Social oppression, the systematically supported mistreatment and exploitation of one group by another, occurs when dominant members of society place pressure on a subgroup in order to stabilize and bolster their own claim to power, wealth, and status (Hanna, Talley, & Guindon, 2002). Individuals who have disabilities, such as physical, cognitive, hearing, and visual impairments, have historically experienced this form of oppression (Davis, 1997; Sue & Sue, 2003; Wendell, 1997). In today's society, those with disabilities continue to be oppressed by social stigma and are forced to live with this oppression as part of the environments in which they work, play, and socialize (Goffman, 1965; Wendell, 1997).

The present chapter moves beyond a discussion of the social oppression experienced by persons with disabilities in general to explore the unique experiences of women with disabilities and the societal manifestations of social oppression within this subgroup. Although men and women with disabilities may be similar in some respects, the focus of this chapter will be women with disabilities in order to address more fully their unique circumstances. A model for inclusion is presented to serve as a framework for this discussion. Examples and suggestions for clinical intervention with women with disabilities at a college level provide an illustration of the applicability of the model to one particular segment of this population.

Women With Disabilities and Social Oppression

Women with disabilities have been described in the literature as facing a double handicap—being female and disabled in a society dominated by able-bodied males. They have traditionally been stereotyped as child-like, dependent, and asexual, and often regarded by the nondisabled community as incapable of fulfilling adult social roles (Asch & Fine, 1997; Prilleltensky, 1996; Sue & Sue, 2003).

In U.S. society, women are typically seen as holding nurturing roles, including those of wife-companion, mother, sexual partner, and office worker-pleaser. Although these stereotypes are limiting for all women, they pose particular problems for women with disabilities. Members of the American culture often view women with disabilities as incapable of parenting or being a sexual partner (DeLoach, 1994). Women with disabilities are often seen as dependent people who must be the recipients rather than the providers of nurturance (Hanna & Rogovsky, 1992).

A woman's perception of the cultural beauty standard of her group, her perception of how she meets that standard, and her perception of the importance of meeting that standard also play a major role in the development of her identity ("Disability Cool," 2002). Whereas feminism quite legitimately decries the sexual objectification of women, disabled women often encounter what Hahn has called "asexual objectification," or the assumption that sexuality is inappropriate and/or absent in disabled people (Thomson, 1997). The judgment that the disabled woman's body is asexual and unfeminine created what Fine and Asch term "rolelessness," a kind of social invisibility and cancellation of femininity (Thomson, 1997). However, this example need not imply that negative attitudes toward women with disabilities are based on physicality alone. Negative attitudes are transferred to women with any type of disability, including cognitive, psychological, or any factor that identifies a woman as having a disability. This phenomenon is referred to as "central characteristic or spread" (Sue & Sue, 2003) and occurs when someone meets a woman with a disability and formulates an impression of her based primarily on her disability regardless of other characteristics, or that she may even belong to another diversity group (Olkin, 1999; Wright, 1983).

In addition to having to prove their sexuality, disabled women find themselves having to prove that their bodies and their minds are fit for motherhood (Asch & Fine, 1997). Whereas motherhood is typically seen as compulsory for women, disabled women are often denied access or discouraged from the arena of reproduction (Asch & Fine, 1997; Nosek et al., 1995; Thomson, 1997).

Women with disabilities have limited social options (Asch & Fine, 1997; Nosek & Hughes, 2003). Although marriage may not be a preferred status for an increasing number of women, it is a customary measure of social options and position. Generally, persons without disabilities are not accepting of intimate relationships with women of any type of disability (DeLoach, 1994; Goffman, 1965, 1997). Compared to nondisabled women, disabled women are more likely never to marry; to marry at a later age; and once married, to be divorced (Asch & Fine, 1997).

As members of two devalued minority groups and considered inadequate for fulfilling either the traditional nurturing female role or the role of independent worker, some disabled women may feel that they do not have a role to play in society. This systematic "rolelessness" places women with disabilities at a disadvantage psychologically, socially, and economically, and allows limited avenues for self-affirmation (Lonsdale, 1990). The limited recognition that disabled women historically have received from the disability rights movement and the feminist movement exacerbates this sense of the rolelessness (Asch & Fine, 1997; Hanna & Rogovsky, 1992; Nosek & Hughes, 2003; Solomon, 1993).

Results from the 1986 Americans with Disabilities census data reveal many of the consequences of the social oppression faced by women with disabilities (Hanna & Rogovsky, 1992). Women with disabilities are more likely to be socially isolated, poorly educated, unemployed or underemployed, and living on a low income (Asch & Fine, 1997; Hanna & Rogovsky, 1992; Nosek & Hughes, 2003; Solomon, 1993; Szymanski & Trueba, 1999). Studies have found that women with disabilities have fewer economic advantages than men with disabilities or women without disabilities (Hahn, 1997). For example, women with disabilities earn an average of $1,470 per month, whereas men with disabilities and women without disabilities earn an average of $2,170 per month (Berkeley Planning Associates, 1996). Among working-age women (16 to 64 years), only 30% of women with a disability participate in the labor force, compared to 75% of women without a disability. Furthermore, almost half of women with a severe work limitation are poor (Jans & Stoddard, 1999). Consequently, women with disabilities are more likely to live in low-income neighborhoods with higher rates of crime, which increases their vulnerability to victimization (Nosek, Howland, Rintala, Young, & Chanpong, 1997; Nosek & Hughes, 2003). Because of these factors, women with disabilities are more vulnerable to other types of abuses, including harassment, physical and sexual abuse, and abuse by other authority figures of the dominant culture (Hassouneh-Phillips & Curry, 2002; Nosek et al., 1997; Torkelson Lynch & Thomas, 1999; Watson-Armstrong, O'Rourke, & Schatzlein, 1999).

Thus, having a disability begins to transform the sense of each segment of the lifespan; it influences the experience of one's body, one's sense of self, and one's place in the world (Lisi, 1993; Sweet & Estey, 2003). These factors make it difficult for girls and young women to find any reason to take pride in their disability (Buchanan, 1999). For women with disabilities who are entering college, this means adding an additional developmental struggle to the already abundant array of normative developmental changes at this stage of the life span.

College-Level Women With Disabilities

The passage of the Rehabilitation Act of 1973, as amended by the Rehabilitation Act of 1992, and the Americans With Disabilities Act in 1990 ensured that students with disabilities have access to programs of higher education. Since the passage of these federal laws, the number of female students with disabilities on university campuses has increased. According to Gajar (1998), the number of students with disabilities has risen to 10.5% of the postsecondary population. These female students represent a variety of disabilities, including physical, psychological, visual, hearing, learning, and other impairments that limit their ability to participate fully in today's society (Stodden & Conway, 2003).

In addition to the psychological concerns and challenges faced by all university students, a number of additional issues affect women with disabilities as they work to become part of society. Counseling psychologists who are situated in college counseling centers as staff, administrators, or consultants are well positioned to assist women with disabilities in dealing with the social stigma and discrimination that they experience.

Counseling center professionals are involved in multiple missions, such as providing clinical service, supervision and training, consultation, teaching, and research (Fukuyama & Delgado-Romero, 2003). These multiple missions provide an opportunity for counseling center professionals to advocate for social justice in a number of different interventions and missions, and to implement multicultural counseling competencies. In the following section, we have used the community model of embeddedness, intradependence, interdependence, and evolution to explore how multiculturalism (collective), women (relational), and women with disabilities (personal) are connected to the realm of social justice in counseling centers, as well as the role that counseling center professionals can have in being advocates for women with disabilities in achieving social justice.

Development of a Model for Inclusion

A major concern for women with disabilities is the lack of a framework or model that allows them to be a viable part of the community, to be connected with other women, and to develop their own sense of personal identity as women with disabilities. Most models of diverse groups focus on identity development and emphasize gender, racial/ethnic, or lifestyle concerns (Cass, 1984; Cross, 1995; D'Augelli, 1994; Gilligan, 1982/1993; Helms, 1990; Phinney, 1990). These models do not acknowledge the fact that women with disabilities are regarded as invisible members of the society and therefore struggle with both having and defining their own personal identity. Without recognition of this important component, social justice cannot be realized fully.

Prilleltensky and Prilleltensky (2003) posit that in order to achieve social justice, especially for those with disabilities, the values and needs of society must be expanded to include three separate spheres of wellness and liberation: personal, relational, and collective. Personal need is defined as "a sense of mastery and control" and is promoted by values such as "empowerment and self-determination." The relational sphere includes such needs as "support and affective bonds." These needs are advanced by such values as "caring and compassion and respect for diversity." The collective sphere encompasses the needs for "economic security, shelter, and structural safety nets." These needs are met by such values as "social justice, equality, and emancipation." Yet practitioners neglect these values and jeopardize the attainment of social justice for those groups who are marginalized (Prilleltensky & Prilleltensky, 2003).

The Community Model of Embeddedness, Interdependence, Intradependence and Evolution (CMEIIE) presented in this chapter emphasizes the attainment of social justice (Palombi & Pace, 1996). This model parallels Prilleltensky and Prilleltensky's (2003) spheres of personal, relational, and collective and incorporates the underlying values of personal empowerment, self-determination, respect for diversity, social justice, and equality. The model encompasses each of these separate spheres and supports the incorporation of women with disabilities into the community (collective), develops a connection with other women (relational), and allows them to develop their own sense of personal identity (personal).

The CMEIIE is based on Morrill, Oetting, and Hurst's (1974) model of the Cube and the expansion of the Cube by Pace, Stamler, Yarris, and June (1996). The Cube classifies programs based on three dimensions: (a) target of the intervention—individual, group, institution, or community; (b) purpose of the intervention—remediation, prevention, or development; and (c) method of intervention—media, consultation and training, and direct service (Delworth, Sherwood, & Casaburri, 1974). In 1996, Pace et al. rounded out the Cube and expanded it to include a global model of intervention for counseling centers. Pace et al. (1996) emphasized the aspects of community, collaboration, and interdependence.

Community Model of Inclusion in the University Setting

The CMEIIE combines the aspects of the Cube and the evolution of the Cube into a model that can be used within a variety of settings (Palombi & Pace, 1996). This model allows flexibility in looking at specific groups and issues from both the micro and macro perspectives and can be used to create a process for counseling psychologists to promote social justice on a college campus.

Used as a basis for social justice, the model can be applied to a targeted group of students. Even when interventions are focused on a target group, such as women with disabilities, their specific needs and concerns can be overshadowed by larger groups, for example, students in general or female students. This model allows group members to be empowered to determine their own personal direction in achieving social justice. Social justice for women with disabilities needs to be (a) embedded as a priority within the university community; (b) interdependent in terms of how social justice for women with disabilities is related to other campus groups (e.g., women, persons of color); (c) interdependent in terms of having women with disabilities determining how they may become embedded into the university community, connected to and acknowledged as part of women in general, and developing within the group a stronger sense of identity; and (d) constantly evolving in such a way that allows flexibility to alter any parts of the process by the women with disabilities, women and students in general, and the university community. In the following section, we have used the CMEIIE (see Figure 13.1) to explore how multiculturalism (collective), women (relational), and women with disabilities (personal) are connected to the realm of social justice in counseling

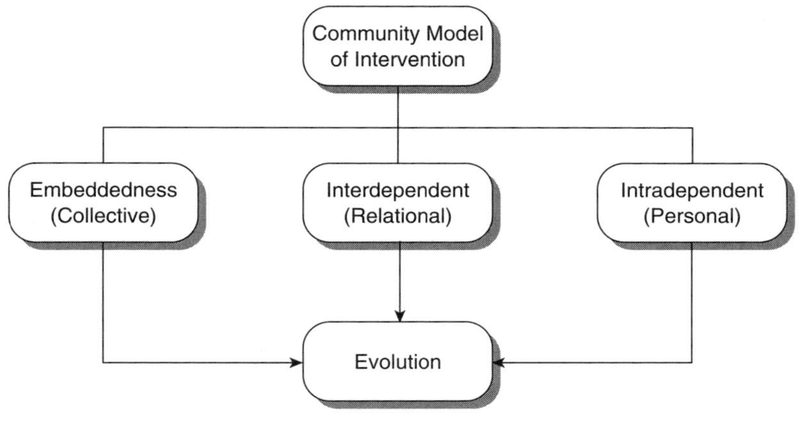

Figure 13.1 The Community Model of Embeddedness, Interdependence, Intradependence, and Evolution (CMEIIE)

centers and the role counseling center professionals can play in being advocates for women with disabilities in achieving social justice.

Embeddedness

The first component of this model is to "embed" women with disabilities into the university community. In achieving social justice, the first task is to define diversity in a manner that ensures inclusiveness (Hall & Greene, 1996). In 1964, the Civil Rights Act was passed to ensure that those in our society who had experienced discrimination and prejudice would be protected by the U.S. Constitution (Middleton, Rollins, & Harley, 1999). Yet groups protected by the civil rights law sometimes saw disability "as a dilution of civil rights on the grounds that people with disabilities were constitutively incompetent, whereas women and minorities faced discrimination merely on the basis of social prejudice" (Berube, 2003, p. 54). The passage of the Americans with Disabilities Act (ADA) in 1990 did add disability to the list of stigmatized identities covered by antidiscrimination (Berube, 2003; Middleton et al., 1999). Despite this, members of the society continue to be ignorant of the civil rights issues surrounding disability (Gold, 2002).

As counseling center professionals advocate for social justice and the advancement of oppressed groups, women with disabilities have not been recognized as having similar needs equal to those of other marginalized groups. Also, there is a lack of understanding of their social marginalization (Gold, 2002). It is important for counseling psychologists who advocate for multiculturalism to begin to view women with disabilities as members of society who experience prejudice and discrimination much the same as ethnic/racial minorities; women; and gay, lesbian, and bisexual individuals have experienced.

In this proposed model, women with disabilities would be "embedded" into all aspects of multiculturalism and psychological services (counseling, psychoeducational programming, and consultation services). Because the counseling center has multiple missions, it would be important for staff members to determine how issues associated with women with disabilities would be incorporated into its programs. Accessibility of the facility would need to be addressed. Women with disabilities need to feel welcome in order to ensure that they are embedded within counseling centers (Riger, 1994). Women with disabilities may scan a center to determine if needed accommodations are available. For example, advertising, brochures, policy statements, and emergency warnings need to be available in both visual and auditory formats. Large-print and audiotaped materials, tactile signage on doors in elevators within the building, closed-captioned video, signs to the nearest TTY, flashing emergency lights, and a lowered reception desk all signal signs of acceptance (Riger, 1994).

As clinical services have focused on specific groups of culturally diverse and underrepresented students, these same services need to be extended to women with disabilities. In the recently published multicultural competencies by the American Psychological Association (2002), mental health professionals are encouraged to understand the cultural competencies and recognize that lack of awareness may alienate clients. Esten and Willmott (1993), in their clinical work with women with disabilities, identified the following common mistakes that able-bodied therapists frequently make: (a) dispense the cure, (b) identify through personal experience, (c) have lower expectations for client, (d) provide meaningless encouragement, (e) propose too many helpful solutions, (f) participate in client's denial of disability, and (g) treat the client with special care or "just like anyone else." These types of clinical interventions continue to subtly perpetuate many of the social attitudes that prevent women with disabilities from having the confidence to empower themselves in achieving social justice. To embed women with disabilities into the missions of the counseling center, counseling center professionals need to be aware of both the environmental and the clinical skills needed to prevent women from being stigmatized.

Interdependence

The second portion of the model is interdependence, which emphasizes women's interdependence (relational) with other women, including women with disabilities. It may be easier for women to agree that all women share gender oppression than it is for them to acknowledge that they experience this oppression through their individual historical, social, political, economic, ecological, and psychophysical realities. To understand any woman, therefore, one must incorporate an understanding of many different aspects of her (Hall & Greene, 1996). Downing and Roush (1985) proposed a five-stage model of feminist identity development in which women move from the stage of denial of sexism to the final stage of a commitment to ending oppression. The goal of ending oppression would connect all women regardless of race/ethnicity, sexual orientation, or disability. The purpose of the interdependent component of the model is to determine what it means to be women across the historical, social, political, economic, ecological, and psychophysical realities. It is important for counseling center professionals to assist women with disabilities in developing their connection with other women.

Women with disabilities are faced with determining their relationship to the dominant culture and (a) whether to stress sameness or difference; (b) whether to place greater value on independence or dependence on other people; (c) whether to establish the goal of being integrated into the male-dominated/able-bodied society; and (d) whether to preserve some degree of separate culture, in which the abilities, knowledge, and values of women and women with disabilities are specifically honored and developed (Wendell, 1997). Counseling center professionals need to allow women with disabilities to explore each of these alternatives within the clinical work.

The consultation and outreach activities in which counseling psychologists are involved outside of counseling centers can assist women with disabilities in being connected to other women on campus. This may be accomplished in subtle ways, for example, programmatic activities that are primarily intended for female students can address issues that face women with disabilities, specifically. When counseling center professionals present workshops that explore women and body image, they commonly discuss the societal expectations placed on women to achieve a standard of physical perfection that is not possible. Typically, these workshops make no reference to women with disabilities who struggle to have their bodies valued as viable bodies (Prilleltensky, 1996). Counseling psychologists can take advantage of such opportunities to talk about the range of struggles faced by women.

In order to reach the final stage that is proposed in the Downing and Roush (1985) model of ending social oppression, women need to be bound as a collective group with an understanding of the sameness and differences that all women possess. In order to achieve this objective, women with disabilities could no longer be a group that remained silenced and marginalized. They would need to incorporate into the collective group labeled "women." If women with disabilities are to be fully integrated into society, counseling center professionals need to engage in activities that recognize the values of depending on others and being depended upon both within the center and the university community (Wendell, 1997).

Intradependence

The principle of intradependence underscores the need for women with disabilities to understand their unique experiences of belonging to multiple diversity groups, yet maintain a strong sense of identity as women with disabilities. The focus of much of the literature on social justice concerns those who have experienced discrimination based on race/ethnicity, gender, or sexual orientation. Attention only to these aspects of identity perpetuates the invisibility of women's disabilities (Alston & Mngadi, 1992). In the clinical setting, if a woman with a disability belongs to another oppressed group, the fact that she is disabled may be overlooked. For example, a woman with a disability who is also Hispanic may experience discrimination primarily due to her disability status, only to enter therapy and find that the focus is placed on her ethnicity and her disability is ignored.

It can be speculated that this phenomenon may be a by-product of the therapist's discomfort with disability issues. Regardless, the end result of such an experience can be invalidating to women with disabilities and does not permit them to acknowledge their disability (Sue & Sue, 2003).

According to Goffman (1965), women with disabilities behave in one of three ways: (a) They attempt to circumvent their stigmatized status by appearing nondisabled; (b) they attempt to surmount their stigmatized status by working to earn the acceptance of others; or (c) they attempt to come to terms with their stigmatized status by concluding, often through the use of rationalization, that social acceptance is not that important and by enjoying whatever gains are available in their situation. Most individuals with disabilities attempt to gain social acceptance by "passing" or denying their status as disabled persons (Hahn, 1997).

In Hershey's personal account of being a woman with a disability, she relates how she made a conscious choice to present a view of being healthy to others that downplayed her own needs arising from her disability (Hershey, 1993). According to Hershey (1993), this approach had several positive attributes. This approach emphasizes sameness, rather than difference, thus softening potential frictions. If women with disabilities have no disagreements, they avoid the "political responsibilities" made necessary by those differences and frictions. This approach focuses on making others more comfortable by keeping disability as a private problem, rather than a shared, social predicament (Hershey, 1993). Despite these apparent advantages to concealing one's disability, it is difficult for women with disabilities to regard themselves in a positive manner when they are not honest concerning personal limitations. Acknowledging personal limitations allows women with disabilities to develop a clearer idea of themselves and forces them to confront how they are not connected to others because of their dissimilarities (Hershey, 1993; Sweet & Estey, 2003).

Women with disabilities share positions of social oppression that separate them from the able-bodied (Sue & Sue, 2003; Wendell, 1997). These women share the physical, psychological, and social experiences of disability. Emphasizing differences from those who are able-bodied demands that those differences be acknowledged and respected. Furthermore, these differences challenge the able-bodied paradigm of the ideal person as being one who has the ability to walk, talk, hear, and see. Attention to the unique experiences of women with disabilities permits these women to develop cohesive relationships among themselves (Wendell, 1997).

The problems of being "the other" to a dominant group are complex. In the hope that the dominant group will recognize their rights and eventually assimilate them into the dominant culture, women with disabilities may emphasize similarities. Yet many women with disabilities are "tired of being symbols to the able-bodied, visible only for their disabilities" (Wendell, 1997, p. 272). Women with disabilities want to be seen as individuals, not as members of the group "the disabled" (Wendell, 1997). The road to self-acceptance for women with disabilities is to acknowledge, accommodate, and identify with a wide range of physical and psychological conditions (Wendell, 1997). Self-acceptance leads to liberation.

In therapy, clients may ascribe to the values of the therapist (Olkin, 1999). Counseling psychologists need to be cautious in encouraging clients to assimilate, or gain acceptance by passing, or settle for what accommodations may be available. Counseling center professionals aspire to accept and encourage gay, lesbian, and bisexual clients to be proud of their identity and support them in not wanting to be "changed" (Sue & Sue, 2003). It is unlikely that therapists would encourage African Americans or Latinos to reject their ethnic heritage. Because of society's ingrained prejudices and attitudes toward women with disabilities, it is difficult to understand when persons with disabilities say they do not want to be "changed" or "cured" (Gold, 2002). Counseling psychologists need to take an active role in assisting women with disabilities to value their physical and sensory differences and aid them in developing awareness of how these differences contribute to the university community (Sue & Sue, 2003).

Without a strong sense of self-identity, women with disabilities will continue to have difficulty in regarding themselves in a positive manner. This strong sense of identity is also important in women having a strong sense of self-efficacy, that they can influence their world and how they are perceived by others. Women with disabilities need to develop the ability to confront their oppressor and confront their own internalization of that oppression. Grappling with these issues provides women with disabilities the possibility of great personal growth and power (Healey, 1993).

Evolution

The last phase of the model emphasizes evolution. Research is a key component of the evolutionary nature of the field of psychology. Counseling center professionals broadly define research to include a variety of activities that reflect the profession's mission to achieve social justice for all members of society. Through a process of assessment, goal-setting, and outcome measures, relevant and appropriate clinical services and educational activities can be identified and implemented within society for women and women with disabilities (Palombi & Pace, 1996).

Social policy has tended to isolate women with disabilities, view them as different, and expect them to change or adapt to the norms of society (Torkelson Lynch & Thomas, 1999). In addition to personal variables, however, it is well recognized that environmental variables and social policy also affect the way in which women with disabilities are regarded and achieve their goals (Sue & Sue, 2003). It is important for researchers to carefully consider both the person and environmental/social policy variables. Mental health research within counseling centers can be more effective for practice when it emphasizes how people with disabilities have effectively used personal characteristics and the environment to achieve a desired outcome (Prilleltensky & Prilleltensky, 2003).

Counseling psychologists need to continue to educate themselves through reading and personal contact with persons with disabilities to recognize the normal emotional needs for a sense of inclusion, dignity, affirmation, autonomy, and competence. They can promote intellectual cross-fertilization by integrating disability issues in their work in related areas such as gender, social cognition, group dynamics, intimate relationships, and person-environment interactions (Riger, 1994).

To assist in the affirmation for social justice, counseling psychologists must validate women with disabilities, view their inclusion as important, and ensure the accessibility of the services and program that they sponsor and support (Sue & Sue, 2003). Just as counseling center professionals are changing to meet the demands of society and the world, the path to achieving social justice continues to evolve. As the demands of the psychological profession, community, society, and the world change, the model evolves to reflect these changes. Indeed, this degree of flexibility in the model is necessary to ensure that counseling center professionals are prepared for the many challenges and modifications created by the changing nature of the student community and the field of higher education.

Conclusion

Counseling psychologists who are committed to achieving social justice on college campuses must broaden the definition of those who experience discrimination and prejudice for the campus community (Brantlinger, 2001; Olkin, 1999; Sue & Sue, 2003). This will require work and commitment to look at the current definition of multiculturalism in a much broader perspective (Prilleltensky & Prilleltensky, 2003). People living with disabilities are the only oppressed group that anyone might join at any time (Gold, 2002; Olkin, 1999). Most people know little or nothing about living with long-term or life-threatening illness, or living with limitation, uncertainty, and pain (Wendell, 2001). Because of active lifestyles, changes in technology and longer life spans, more and more individuals are living with a disability. The problems stemming from having a disability should be shared throughout the society as much as we share the problems of love, work, and family life (Wendell, 2001). Counseling center professionals need to educate the members of the university community about the experience of disability (Sue & Sue, 2003). The lack of information continues to foster prejudice and discrimination.

Counseling psychologists need to acknowledge their own personal feelings concerning disability and those with disabilities (Sue & Sue, 2003). This process can begin by challenging one's own personal assumptions and realizing that disability is a natural part of life. Women with disabilities do not need to be "fixed" in order to fit into the norm—they are part of the norm (Gold, 2002).

In order to promote social justice, counseling psychologists must also support the civil rights struggles of women with disabilities (Sue & Sue, 2003). The "minority" civil rights model portrays people with disabilities as a minority group with clear rights and legitimate policy grievances (Olkin, 1999; Torkelson Lynch & Thomas, 1999). Just as the struggles for civil rights for people of racial/ethnic diversity; women; and gay, lesbian, and bisexual individuals have helped counseling center professionals to value diversity and difference, so too with the disability movement. Support of women with disabilities will help others to understand that disability is a normal experience, as is race/ethnicity, gender, and sexual orientation (Gold, 2002).

Oppressed groups face a dual task in confronting their oppressor and confronting their own internalization of that oppression (Healey, 1993). For their own survival, women with disabilities are forced to face issues that other members of society may also need to face but have the luxury to ignore. Counseling psychologists can assist women with disabilities in identifying and developing community and personal interventions that empower them and assist in their personal growth (Sue & Sue, 2003).

Counseling center professionals find themselves in a time when the university community of which they are a part is being challenged to embrace a broader range of diversity. They can be at the forefront of social justice for women with disabilities by embedding them into all dimensions of multiculturalism, including clinical service, supervision and training, consultation, teaching and research, and the future vision of social justice for all students. It is also important that the values as outlined by Prilleltensky and Prilleltensky (2003) that support social justice are integrated into the counseling center services and serve as the foundation for the future direction of counseling centers.

Finally, counseling psychologists need to ensure that women with disabilities are embedded as valuable members of the community; that their issues and concerns are embedded into multiculturalism; that women with disabilities are seen as interconnected to other women and therefore included in all dialogues, research, and interventions connected to women; that women with disabilities are encouraged to develop their own sense of identity and collegial relationships with other women with disabilities; and that their struggle to break through the barriers caused by society's prejudice and discriminations helps to create a society where social justice is the norm for all members.

References

Alston, R. J., & Mngadi, S. (1992). The interaction between disability status and the African American experience: Implications for rehabilitation counseling. *Journal of Applied Rehabilitation Counseling, 23*(2), 12–16.

American Psychological Association. (2002). *Guidelines on multicultural education, training, research, practice, and organizational change for psychologists.* Washington, DC: Author.

Americans With Disabilities Act of 1990, 42 U.S.C.A. 12101 et seq.

Asch, A., & Fine, M. (1997). Nurturance, sexuality, and women with disabilities. In L. Davis (Ed.), *The disability studies reader* (pp. 241–259). New York: Routledge.

Berkeley Planning Associates. (1996). *Priorities for future research: Results of BPS's Delphi survey of disabled women.* Oakland, CA: Author.

Berube, M. (2003). Citizenship and disability. *Dissent, 50*(2), 52–58.

Brantlinger, E. (2001). Poverty, class, and disability: A historical, social and political perspective. *Focus on Exceptional Children, 33*(7), 1–19.

Buchanan, S. (1999). No blood, it doesn't count. In R. P. Marinelli & A. E. Dell Orto (Eds.), *The psychological & social impact of disability* (pp. 187–190). New York: Springer.

Cass, V. C. (1984). Homosexual identity formation: Testing a theoretical model. *Journal of Sex Research, 20,* 143–167.

Cross, W. E., Jr. (1995). The psychology of Nigrescence: Revising the Cross model. In J. G. Ponterotto, J. M. Casas, L. A. Suzuki, & C. M. Alexander (Eds.), *Handbook of multicultural counseling* (pp. 93–122). Thousand Oaks, CA: Sage.

D'Augelli, A. R. (1994). Identity development and sexual orientation: Toward a model of lesbian, gay, and bisexual development. In E. J. Trickett, R. J. Watts, & D. Birman (Eds.), *Human diversity: Perspectives on people in context* (pp. 312–333). San Francisco: Jossey-Bass.

Davis, L. J. (1997). The bell curve, the novel, and the invention of the disabled body in the nineteenth century. In L. Davis (Ed.), *The disability studies reader* (pp. 9–28). New York: Routledge.

DeLoach, C. P. (1994). Attitudes toward disability: Impact on sexual development and forging of intimate relationships. *Journal of Applied Rehabilitation Counseling, 23*(1), 18–25.

Delworth, U., Sherwood, G., & Casaburri, N. (1974). *Student paraprofessionals: A working model for higher education: Vol. 17. Student Personnel Series.* Washington, DC: American Personnel and Guidance Association.

Disability Cool—Sexuality 'R Us. (2003, September 12). *Body beautiful/body perfect: Challenging the status quo. Where do women with disabilities fit in?* Retrieved from http://www.geocities.com/HotSprings/7319/sex.htm

Downing, N. E., & Roush, K. L. (1985). From passive acceptance to active commitment: A model of feminist identity development for women. *The Counseling Psychologist, 13,* 695–709.

Esten, G., & Willmott, L. (1993). Double bind messages: The effects of attitude towards disability on therapy. In M. Willmuth & L. Holcomb (Eds.), *Women with disabilities* (pp. 29–42). New York: Haworth.

Fine, M., & Asch, A. (Eds.). (1988). *Women with disabilities: Essays in psychology, culture and politics.* Philadelphia: Temple University Press.

Fukuyama, M. A., & Delgado-Romero, E. A. (2003). Against the odds: Successfully implementing multicultural counseling on a predominantly white campus. In G. Roysircar, D. S. Sandhu, & V. E. Bibbins, Sr. (Eds.), *Multicultural competencies: A guidebook of practices* (pp. 205–216). Washington, DC: Association for Multicultural Counseling and Development.

Gajar, A. (1998). Postsecondary education. In F. Rusch & J. Chadsey (Eds.), *Beyond high school: Transition from school to work* (pp. 385–405). Belmont, CA: Wadsworth.

Gilligan, C. (1993). *In a different voice: Psychological theory and women's development.* Cambridge, MA: Harvard University Press. (Original work published 1982)

Goffman, E. (1965). *Stigma: Notes on the management of spoiled identity.* Englewood Cliffs, NJ: Prentice Hall.

Goffman, E. (1997). Sections from *Stigma.* In L. Davis (Ed.), *The disability studies reader* (pp. 203–215). New York: Routledge.

Gold, S. (2002). Beyond pity and paternalism: Even progressive persons committed to social justice are unable to embrace the disability rights movement. Are we afraid of something? *The Other Side, 38*(5), 16–21.

Hahn, H. (1997). Advertising the acceptable employable image. In L. Davis (Ed.), *The disability studies reader* (pp. 172–186). New York: Routledge.

Hall, R. L., & Greene, B. (1996). Sins of omission and commission: Women, psychotherapy, and the psychological literature. *Women & Therapy, 18*(1), 5–31.

Hanna, F. J., Talley, W. B., & Guindon, M. H. (2002). The power of perception: Toward a model of cultural oppression and liberation. *Journal of Counseling and Development, 78,* 430–441.

Hanna, W. J., & Rogovsky, E. (1992). On the situation of African-American women with physical disabilities. *Journal of Applied Rehabilitation Counseling, 23*(4), 39–45.

Hassouneh-Phillips, D., & Curry, M. A. (2002). Abuse of women with disabilities: State of the science. *Rehabilitation Counseling Bulletin, 45*(2), 96–104.

Healey, S. (1993). The common agenda between old women, women with disabilities and all women. In M. Willmuth & L. Holcomb (Eds.), *Women with disabilities* (pp. 65–78). New York: Haworth.

Helms, J. E. (1990). *Black and white racial identity: Theory, research and practice.* New York: England Greenwood Press.

Hershey, L. (1993). Coming out in voices. In M. Willmuth & L. Holcomb (Eds.), *Women with disabilities* (pp. 9–18). New York: Haworth.

Jans, L., & Stoddard, S. (1999). *Chartbook on women and disability in the United States: An InfoUse report.* Washington, DC: U.S. Department of Education, National Institute on Disability and Rehabilitation Research.

Lisi, D. (1993). Found voices: Women, disability and cultural transformation. In M. Willmuth & L. Holcomb (Eds.), *Women with disabilities* (pp. 195–209). New York: Haworth.

Lonsdale, S. (1990). *Women and disability: The experience of physical disability among women.* New York: St. Martin's.

Middleton, R. A., Rollins, C. W., & Harley, D. B. (1999). The historical and political context of the civil rights of persons with disabilities: A multicultural perspective for counselors. *Journal of Multicultural Counseling and Development, 27*(2), 105–110.

Morrill, W. H., Oetting, E. R., & Hurst, J. C. (1974). Dimensions of counselor functioning. *Personnel and Guidance Journal, 53,* 354–359.

Nosek, M. A., Howland, C. A., Rintala, D. H., Young, E. M., & Chanpong, G. F. (1997). *National study of women with physical disabilities: Final report.* Houston: Center for Research on Women With Disabilities.

Nosek, M. A., & Hughes, R. B. (2003). Psychosocial issues of women with physical disabilities: The continuing gender debate. *Rehabilitation Counseling Bulletin 46*(4), 224–233.

Nosek, M. A., Young, M. E., Rintala, D. H., Howland, C. A., Foley, C. C., & Bennett, J. L. (1995). Barriers to reproductive health maintenance among women with physical disabilities. *Journal of Women's Health, 4,* 505–518.

Olkin, R. (1999). *What psychotherapists should know about disability.* New York: Guilford.

Pace, D., Stamler, V. L., Yarris, E., & June, L. (1996). Rounding out the cube: Evolution to a global model for counseling centers. *Journal of Counseling & Development, 74,* 321–325.

Palombi, B., & Pace, D. (1996). *Site report prepared for the American Psychological Association.* Allendale, MI: Grand Valley State University, Counseling and Career Development Center.

Phinney, J. S. (1990). Ethnic identity in adolescents and adults: Review of research. *Psychological Bulletin, 108,* 499–514.

Prilleltensky, I., & Prilleltensky, O. (2003). Synergies for wellness and liberation in counseling psychology. *The Counseling Psychologist, 31*(3), 273–281.

Prilleltensky, O. (1996). Women with disabilities and feminist therapy. *Women & Therapy, 18*(1), 87–97.

Rehabilitation Services Administration. (1993). Rehabilitation Act of 1973 as Amended by the Rehabilitation Act of 1992 (P.L. 102–569). Washington, DC: U.S. Department of Education.

Riger, A. (1994). *The disability friendly counseling center—What we stand for.* Unpublished manuscript, West Virginia University.

Solomon, S. E. (1993). Women and physical distinction: A review of the literature and suggestions for intervention. In M. Willmuth & L. Holcomb (Eds.), *Women with disabilities* (pp. 91–104). New York: Haworth.

Stodden, R. A., & Conway, M. A. (2003). Supporting individuals with disabilities in postsecondary education. *American Rehabilitation, 27*(1), 24–32.

Sue, D. W., & Sue, D. (2003). *Counseling the culturally diverse: Theory and practice* (4th ed.). New York: Wiley.

Sweet, S. G., & Estey, M. (2003). A step toward multicultural competencies: Listening to individuals with multiple sclerosis and cerebral palsy. In G. Roysircar, P. Arredondo, J. N. Fuertes, J. G. Ponterotto, & R. L. Toporek (Eds.), *Multicultural counseling competencies 2003: Association for Multicultural Counseling and Development* (pp. 103–117). Washington, DC: Association for Multicultural Counseling and Development.

Szymanski, E., & Trueba, H. T. (1999). Castification of people with disabilities: Potential disempowering aspects of classification in disability services. In R. P. Marinelli & A. E. Dell Orto (Eds.), *The psychological & social impact of disability* (pp. 195–211). New York: Springer.

Thomson, R. G. (1997). Integrating disability studies into the existing curriculum: The example of "Women and Literature" at Howard University. In L. Davis (Ed.), *The disability studies reader* (pp. 295–306). New York: Routledge.

Torkelson Lynch, R., & Thomas, K. R. (1999). People with disabilities as victims: Changing an ill-advised paradigm. In R. P. Marinelli & A. E. Dell Orto (Eds.), *The psychological & social impact of disability* (pp. 212–219). New York: Springer.

Watson-Armstrong, L. A., O'Rourke, B., & Schatzlein, J. (1999). Sexual abuse and persons with disabilities: A call for awareness. In R. P. Marinelli & A. E. Dell Orto (Eds.), *The psychological & social impact of disability* (pp. 275–289). New York: Springer.

Wendell, S. (1997). Towards a feminist theory of disability. In L. Davis (Ed.), *The disability studies reader* (pp. 260–278). New York: Routledge.

Wendell, S. (2001). Unhealthy disabled: Treating chronic illnesses as disabilities. *Hypatia, 4,* 17–33.

Wright, B. A. (1983). *Physical disability: A psychosocial approach* (2nd ed.). New York: Harper & Row.

CHAPTER 14

Environmental Racism

A Call to the Profession for Community Intervention and Social Action

Azara L. Santiago-Rivera, Kristin Talka, and Amy W. Tully

> *Wherever in the world environmental despoliation and degradation is happening, it is almost always linked to questions of social justice, equity, rights and peoples' quality of life in its widest sense.*
>
> —Agyeman, Bullard, and Evans (2003), p. 1

Proponents of environmental justice note that the degree of contamination of our land, air, and water is astounding. In the United States alone, 75,000 chemicals and more than a billion pounds of pesticides, herbicides, and fungicides are used on a regular basis (Pilisuk, 1998). Until recently, there was widespread dumping of more than 700 million tons of toxic substances, resulting in the identification of 50,000 hazardous sites in this country (Clark, Barton, & Brown, 2002). Because these sites are so pervasive, many communities have been exposed to a variety of hazardous materials in the environment.

Growing evidence suggests that exposure to toxic substances such as lead, mercury, pesticides, solvents, and polychlorinated biphenyls (PCBs) threatens the health and well-being of people in the United States (e.g., Lundberg & Santiago-Rivera, 1998; Santiago-Rivera, 2001). Attempts to address the human health risks associated with exposure to hazardous substances have resulted in national laws, regulations, and policies, as well as local grassroots movements across the country.

Heightened public awareness about environmental contamination, the creation of policies to reduce risks to humans, and the development of federal government funding sources to support research on health effects are noteworthy (e.g., Lundberg, 1998; Unger, Wandersman, & Hallman, 1992). However, little attention has been given to the impact of contamination on ethnic minorities despite the growing evidence that they are disproportionately exposed to hazardous materials because of their location, largely in urban settings, and economic status (Bullard, 1994; Santiago-Rivera, Morse, Hunt, & Lickers, 1998). *Environmental racism* is the term used to describe deliberate attempts to locate toxic waste facilities in ethnic minority communities, and the exclusionary nature of policies that deal with environmental contamination.

The purpose of this chapter is to (a) present an overview of environmental racism as it relates to health issues associated with exposure to hazardous wastes, as well as provide a brief historical perspective on the environmental justice movement; (b) describe the role of social justice and advocacy in environmental activism; and (c) outline ways in which counseling psychologists can play a major role in community intervention and social action. A number of theoretical perspectives on which to draw in developing a framework for environmental justice are presented.

Environmental Racism

In 1987, a landmark report produced by the United Church of Christ Commission for Racial Justice, titled, "Toxic Wastes and Race in the United States," claimed that ethnic minorities are more likely to live near hazardous waste sites and therefore are exposed to higher levels of pollution than Whites. Reverend Chavis, who issued the report on behalf of the Commission, was the first to coin the phrase "environmental racism," defined as

> racial discrimination in environmental policymaking, the enforcement of regulations and laws, the deliberate targeting of communities of color for toxic waste facilities, the official sanctioning of the life-threatening presence of poisons and pollutants in our communities, and the history of excluding people of color from leadership of the environmental movement. (Grossman, 1994, p. 278)

This term is now extensively used in describing the inequities in environmental protection and health.

A number of studies have confirmed that race is significantly and unequivocally related to environmental quality. The most striking evidence comes from Mohai and Bryant's (1992) review of 15 studies dating from 1971 to 1992 that examined a variety of environmental hazards such as air pollution, pesticide poisoning, and toxic fish consumption in primarily urban areas. Specifically, they reviewed these studies to determine the relative distribution of hazardous substances by race and income and found that race was the single most important factor. In support of this finding, Bullard (1994) noted that in the large metropolitan areas of Chicago and

Houston, African Americans and Latinos are disproportionately living near abandoned toxic waste sites compared to their White counterparts. Likewise, Latinos are twice as likely to be exposed to environmental lead compared to other ethnic groups (Wernette & Nieves, 1992). Because this body of literature reveals that, indeed, environmental inequality exists, it begs the question as to whether or not minority communities are at greater risk of suffering from physical and psychological effects of exposure to hazardous materials.

Environmental Contamination, Health, and Ethnic Minorities

A number of studies have shown that exposure to certain types of contaminants may increase the risk of contracting diseases such as lung cancer, chronic bronchitis, asthma, pulmonary edema, and other health maladies. For instance, symptoms of dizziness, diarrhea, and breathing difficulty have been linked with exposure to pesticides (Weiss, 1998). Additionally, exposure to a variety of contaminants has been shown to affect the autoimmune and reproductive systems (Arctic Monitoring and Assessment Programme, 1997).

Children are particularly vulnerable. The research in the area of behavioral neurotoxicology has found that children who have been exposed to mercury show symptoms of irritability, nervousness, and impaired memory (Weiss, 1998). Likewise, children exposed to lead paint in homes tend to exhibit detrimental effects in brain development (Needleman, Schell, Bellinger, Leviton, & Allred, 1990). Furthermore, the neurobehavioral effects of exposure to toxic solvents have been shown to promote cognitive deficits in memory, intelligence, and spatial relations, as well as increased sensitivity to food additives.

Exposure to environmental contamination not only may be related to harmful effects in physical health, but also may affect psychological well-being. In a study by Green, Lindy, and Grace (1994), a community in Fernald, Ohio, was exposed to radioactive materials by way of air and groundwater contamination that leaked from a nuclear weapons factory. These researchers found that residents reported a variety of psychological problems such as elevated levels of depression and anxiety, somatic complaints, obsessive thoughts, suspicion, and mistrust compared to their control group counterparts. Remarkably, these symptoms were not apparent until years after being exposed to the radioactive materials.

It is evident that the aforementioned studies increase our general understanding of the health risks associated with exposure to a variety of contaminants; however, limited information is available about its impact on specific ethnic and cultural communities. Nonetheless, a small but growing area of research examines this issue. One such body of research centers on the impact of environmental contamination in Native American communities. The landmark studies conducted by Palinkas and colleagues (e.g., Palinkas, Downs, Petterson, & Russell, 1993; Palinkas, Petterson, Russell, & Downs, 1993; Palinkas, Russell, Downs, & Petterson, 1992) provide important information about the detrimental effects of a sudden and unexpected technological disaster that affected a significant number of Alaskan communities.

Specifically, in 1989, a large tanker called *Exxon Valdez* spilled 11 million gallons of oil into the Prince William Sound, affecting a broad area. The environmental and economic impact was significant, with considerable efforts directed toward cleaning up the oil spill. Equally important, there was much concern about the effect of the oil spill on the traditional subsistence activities among the Alaskan Natives. In one of their studies, Palinkas, Downs et al. (1993) found that the Alaskan Natives exhibited more depressive symptoms than non-Alaskan Natives in a random sample of the high exposure group. More important, they noted that

> Native villages in general were the most heavily impacted by disruptions in subsistence activities. The reduction or cessation of subsistence activities affects not only food supplies but an entire set of social relations and practices that are an essential part of kin group and community integration. Interruption of the cycle of activity associated with subsistence has important symbolic significance for continuity in maintaining Native culture. (p. 7)

The Mohawk community at Akwesasne, a reservation located in northern New York, was also negatively affected by the disposal of a variety of toxic wastes such as fluoride, polychlorinated biphenyls (PCBs), cyanide, and metals that occurred during the 1950s through the 1970s. The insidious contamination of the land, air, and rivers over approximately a 20-year period significantly affected the traditional forms of their economy such as fishing and hunting. Residents could no longer sell their fish and produce to local markets. Most notably, the belief that the land is to be protected and respected, a core belief in indigenous peoples, was seriously threatened (Akwesasne Task Force on the Environment, 1997). When the Mohawk residents discovered that they had been exposed to these substances, they mobilized community leaders to seek environmental justice and requested an investigation into the potential health effects on the members of their community (Carpenter, 1995; Santiago-Rivera et al., 1998).

Attempts to investigate community concerns and potential sources of stress associated with environmental hazards are noteworthy. For instance, Adeola (1994) studied a random sample of Black and White residents in the Baton Rouge area known as "cancer alley" or the "toxic corridor," who live in close proximity to a large landfill site, oil refinery plants, or chemical and petrochemical plants. Aware of the potential health risks associated with exposure to high levels of toxic waste, Adeola (1994) set out to investigate residents' perceptions and concerns about their environment. As expected, he found that air and water pollution, and the presence of petrochemical waste, were the major concerns of the community respondents, and the majority reported that lung cancer, skin cancer, stomach cancer, miscarriage, and nervous disorders were perceived to be the greatest health risks associated with exposure. Similar to other studies, he also found that more Black than White residents lived closer to hazardous waste facilities.

As mentioned earlier, little research attention has been given to studying potential health effects even though there is general agreement that minority populations living near toxic waste sites may be at greater risk of developing health problems. The lack of research is related to a complex set of factors such as limited funding opportunities; the difficulties associated with determining a causal link between exposure to toxic elements and health problems; and environmental policies that, until fairly recently, overlooked the fact that minority communities are disproportionately exposed to hazardous substances.

Environmental Justice Movement

The struggle for environmental justice has a fairly long history dating back to the 1960s in the advent of the civil rights movement; however, the culminating event that brought the issue to the forefront was the 1982 protests in Warren County, North Carolina, where PCBs, a highly toxic substance, had been illegally dumped in a predominantly African American rural county. This was the first time that an African American community had not only received national attention, but took the lead in mobilizing what Bullard (1994) called "a broad-based group to oppose what they defined as environmental racism" (p. 6). The impact of this event was widespread. It triggered the formation of activist groups across the country consisting of people of African, Latino, Asian, and Native American heritage, and in 1991, the First National People of Color Environment Leadership Summit was held in Washington. According to Bullard (1994), the summit meeting provided the opportunity for ethnic minority community and national leaders to discuss and develop strategies to address the problem.

The summit resulted in the creation of 17 principles that brought to the forefront issues of environmental justice (Bryant & Mohai, 1992). Among these principles, a number of them relate to the importance of respecting cultural differences and empowering individuals to take action.

---

1. Environmental justice affirms the sacredness of Mother Earth, ecological unity and the interdependence of species, and the right to be free from ecological destruction.
2. Environmental justice demands that public policy be based on mutual respect and justice for all people, free from any form of discrimination or bias.
3. Environmental justice mandates the right to ethical, balanced and responsible uses of land and renewable resources in the interest of a sustainable planet for humans and other living things.
4. Environmental justice calls for universal protection from nuclear testing, extraction, and the production and disposal of toxic/hazardous waste and poisons that threaten the fundamental right to clean air, land, water, and food.
5. Environmental justice protects the right of victims of environmental injustices to receive full compensation and reparation for damages as well as quality health care.
6. Environmental justice must recognize a special legal and natural relationship of Native Peoples to the U.S. government through treaties, agreements, compacts, and covenants which impose upon the U.S. government a paramount obligation and responsibility to affirm the sovereignty and self-determination of the indigenous peoples whose lands it occupies and holds in trusts.

(Continued)

(Continued)

7. Environmental justice affirms the need for urban and rural ecological policies to clean up and rebuild our cities and rural areas in balance with nature.
8. Environmental justice calls for the education of present and future generations which emphasizes social and environmental issues, based on our experience and appreciation of our diverse cultural perspectives.

Since 1991, one of the main roles of the movement has been to ensure that the decision-making process in the development of policies dealing with environmental protection are more inclusive and represent all ethnic/cultural groups (Pinderhughes, 1996). Likewise, tribal lands were largely ignored in the nation's environmental movement until 1984, when the Environmental Protection Agency signed the Administration of Environmental Programs on Indian Reservations (Gaylord & Bell, 2001). The mobilization of Native Americans to challenge the location of hazardous wastes near their reservations has resulted in a variety of coalitions, such as the Indigenous Women of North America and Women of Color of North America, and the creation of the Agency for Toxic Substances and Disease Registry's Minority Health Initiative to address the impact of environmental contamination in minority communities (Harding & Greer, 1993).

The Role of Social Justice and Advocacy in Environmental Activism

Despite the growing awareness of the detrimental effects of environmental contamination, as well as the mobilization of various movements to address this situation, mental health professionals have not taken an active role in the process. We argue that counseling psychologists can not only expand their professional role to help individuals and families cope with the stress and fear that often exist when people learn that they have been exposed to hazardous substances, but also take a leadership role in working with individuals and communities for environmental justice.

In recent years, more attention has been directed toward the inclusion of social justice advocacy in the counseling profession (Chen-Hayes, 2001; Lewis & Bradley, 2000; Lewis, Smith-Arnold, House, & Toporek, 2004). An often-cited definition of social justice is proffered by Dr. King Davis (Teasley & Rice, 1996):

> Social justice is a basic value and desired goal in democratic societies and includes equitable and fair access to societal institutions, laws, resources, opportunities, without arbitrary limitations based on observed, or interpretations of, differences in age, color, culture, physical or mental disability, education, gender, income, language, national origin, race, religion, or sexual orientation. (p. 1)

In the following section, we outline various theoretical perspectives that provide a foundation for a social justice and advocacy framework to help counseling psychologists address environmental inequality in contemporary society. We describe these perspectives in the context of environmental activism.

Environmental Activism

Counseling psychologists are facing issues of social justice in their work with clients on a regular basis. A case can be made that social justice issues cannot be addressed adequately in individual and family counseling or psychotherapy alone, but need to be addressed at the community level as well, especially when working with ethnic minority groups (e.g., Hong & Ham, 2001; Parham, 2002; Santiago-Rivera, Arredondo, & Gallardo-Cooper, 2002; Sue et al., 1998; Trimble & Thurman, 2002). Past research has shown that many minority groups will identify themselves through their families and communities, a value that runs contrary to Western ideals of individualism (Sue et al., 1998). For example, Trimble and Thurman (2002) noted that when working on individual growth and development issues with American Indians and Alaska Natives, counseling psychologists must recognize the value and support provided by both their communities and family members. This notion was demonstrated by the work of the Akwesasne Task Force on the Environment (1997) discussed earlier. Therefore, it stands to reason that methods of environmental advocacy need to be implemented at the individual, familial, and community levels.

Sutton and Kemp (2002) noted that residential environments are central to the development of children and their families. The social networks and physical spaces of neighborhoods can help children and their families try out various social roles and engage in cultural practices and beliefs that, in turn, are believed to promote supportive interconnections between families, schools, and community organizations. In other words, the community and the environment are of great importance to the functioning of both the family and the individual. However, communities have been shown to be a source of inequality, especially for children (Brooks-Gunn, Duncan, Klebanov, & Sealand, 1993). When children and their families live in disadvantaged neighborhoods with inadequate housing, a lack of safe open spaces, poor schooling, and isolation from social networks, segregation ensues, along with deteriorating real estate values (Lynch, 1979). These downtrodden environments are believed to intensify the problems of those who are disadvantaged both psychologically and symbolically. In addition, Santiago-Rivera (2001) noted that there is an urgent need to address the greater environmental problems our society faces. Overall, these issues clarify the necessity of counseling psychologists to help improve the quality of their clients' lives by working with communities to promote healthier and sustainable living environments.

Gardner's (2003) research links social justice to environmental activism through the use of a feminist psychology framework that includes the following: (a) advocating for the public right to know and participate in discussions about environmental injustice; (b) working to strengthen the social justice mandate within environmental organizations; (c) defining and voicing environmental concerns from the needs and realities of a marginalized social group; and (d) building relationships, alliances, and a common cause across environmental and social justice sectors. By implementing such a framework, it is expected that environmental activism and change will substantially improve the overall well-being of individuals and their communities, which in turn will benefit future generations. Lubell (2002) posited that community citizens will engage in a collective endeavor when the expected value of their participation is positive, as described by what he calls the "collective interest model." The idea behind the collective interest model is to "incorporate the demand for the public good into an individual's utility calculus without violating the logic of free-riding" (Finkel, Muller, & Opp, 1989, p. 886). Translating this into counseling practice, clients may be more willing to become involved in environmental and community change when they perceive their contributions as positive without greater costs than benefits. In addition, Lubell (2002) hypothesized that citizens who believe they are threatened by environmental problems will be more likely to participate in environmental activism. Likewise, their participation in environmental regrowth will occur when they understand how economic and environmental conditions affect individual and community well-being. An important way of applying these theoretical perspectives in counseling is to provide clients with information about how their environment may be contributing to their presenting problems, as well as the costs and benefits of becoming involved in community and environmental change.

Finkel et al. (1989) proposed that a personal sense of efficacy is a strong predictor of environmental activism. This sense of efficacy is believed to be both internal and external. Internal efficacy is thought to relate to an individual's ability to understand and participate effectively in local community agencies and environmental groups. External efficacy is the belief that community agencies will, in turn, work with citizens to help bring about the necessary environmental and community changes. In essence, people are willing to cooperate if they trust others to cooperate. Counseling psychologists may help to build internal and external efficacy by teaching citizens the tools to work effectively with local government and environmental agencies. Furthermore, counseling psychologists may be instrumental in bridging the gap between community citizens and local agencies in order to foster a relationship that will bring about necessary environmental changes.

Toward a Framework for Social Action on Environmental Justice

Counseling psychologists have many resources upon which to draw in addressing the needs of individuals and communities facing the adverse effects of environmental racism. Some of these resources are inherent to the philosophical underpinnings and practice of counseling psychology, such as the focus on prevention as well as amelioration of problems, an ecological approach to case conceptualization (i.e., the impact of dynamic interactions between social systems on human behavior), and a commitment to multicultural competence in psychological research and practice (Arredondo et al., 1996). However, in order to meet the challenges of environmental racism, counseling psychologists need to broaden their scope and incorporate knowledge from disciplines such as social welfare, public health, and law. This can be accomplished, in part, by partnering with experts from these fields. However, counseling psychologists also need to be capable of adopting multiple roles in order to address the multidimensional problems associated with environmental racism.

Individuals, families, and communities carry the burden of psychological and physical symptoms related to environmental contamination. However, it is important to recognize the underlying problem when dealing with cases of environmental racism—unequal political power arrangements and an economic system that is characterized by racial oppression (Bullard & Johnson, 2000). Thus, in order for counseling psychologists to confront the problem of environmental racism at the source, we need to broaden our scope of understanding and impact. Clients' presenting problems need to be conceptualized in a larger, sociopolitical context in order to facilitate effective interventions.

Social justice has been the aim in developing and promoting multicultural competencies (Arredondo & Perez, 2003). As practitioners and client advocates, counseling psychologists can work to increase the psychological well-being of clients while addressing the macro-level issues of environmental racism, such as the need to eliminate policies that discriminate and create barriers (Arredondo et al., 1996). As stated earlier, psychotherapeutic interventions alone are likely to be insufficient when a client's symptoms are produced and maintained by his or her physical environment.

Counseling psychologists can adopt many roles in serving individuals and communities dealing with environmental contamination, including crisis counselor, educator, consultant, advocate, mediator, researcher, and collaborator with community leaders and other helping professionals. Additionally, counseling psychologists can use their expertise and experience to influence public policy decisions and legislation.

Counseling psychology may find it useful to draw upon systemic interventions from the field of social work (Vera & Speight, 2003). Social work interventions that seem particularly well-suited to problems of environmental oppression include (a) empowering clients to develop support systems (e.g., client action groups and agency coalitions); (b) promoting and developing public policies and programs addressed to populations at risk (e.g., advocating for clients in political and public arenas); and (c) providing case management to plan and orchestrate service delivery, and social planning/community organization (Hepworth & Larsen, 1990).

In an effort to address problems of environmental racism such as differential exposure and enforcement, Bullard (1994) articulated an environmental justice framework that focuses on a public health model of prevention (i.e., elimination of the threat before harm occurs), a method for shifting the burden of proof to polluters/dischargers (i.e., using a disparate impact or "effect" test as opposed to "intent" to infer discrimination), and a triage strategy for redressing the disproportionate impact of environmental contamination (i.e., targeting resources where environmental and health problems are the greatest). The purpose of this environmental justice framework is twofold: to eliminate unfair, unjust, and inequitable conditions and decisions, and to uncover the ethical and political questions of "who gets what, when, why, and how much" (Bullard, 1994).

In counseling psychology, it may be useful to adopt a similar framework for addressing environmental racism that extends the multicultural counseling competencies by integrating knowledge and skills from related disciplines such as public health and nursing (Clark et al., 2002) and social welfare (Reeser & Leighninger, 1990). For instance, counseling psychologists can work with public health nurses in conducting health assessments, as well as collaborate with epidemiologists, who have expertise in documenting the distribution of disease in groups affected by toxic substances. These approaches could clarify methods for integrating social justice–informed action into our professional roles when working independently with clients or in collaboration with professionals from other disciplines. For example, collaboration with other health specialists can facilitate articulation of the range and severity of biopsychosocial problems in communities affected by environmental racism. When advocating for government funds, services, and policy change, having this information readily available will have greater impact.

Although the advocacy role is important when working with individuals, families, and communities on issues related to environmental concerns such as exposure to toxic substances, we caution counseling psychologists not only to be sensitive to differing perspectives, but also to understand the complexity of the problem. For instance, Clark et al. (2002) noted that community members might believe that heightening public awareness about environmental health risks will lower their property values or that it will affect their health insurance coverage. Accordingly, families may be reluctant to take action because of financial consequences, or it may increase their feelings of anxiety, frustration, and helplessness. Therefore, they recommend that a more effective approach might be to serve in the role of "monitoring those responsible for environmental contamination and those responsible for cleanup to enforce adherence to mandated levels of safety and optimal efforts to communicate with the public" (p. 363). In other words, the counseling psychologist can serve as a voice for members of the community and work with individuals and their families in the provision of psychological services.

Although environmental racism can take many forms, there are common causes and effects that can be addressed systemically by counseling psychologists. Figure 14.1 provides a framework for conceptualizing the psychological and sociopolitical problems associated with environmental racism and possible interventions on micro and macro levels. The counseling psychologist's role is depicted as a sphere of influence that cuts across all systems. This reflects Martín-Baró's (1994) idea that a social justice–informed psychologist seeks to transform the world, not just to understand it. This diagram incorporates Neville and Mobley's (2001) ecological model for contextualizing multicultural counseling psychology processes. Their model outlines the recursive influence of individual and systemic factors on multiple, interconnected subsystems that influence human behavior. This ecological conceptualization seems particularly salient when planning multiculturally sensitive counseling interventions for individuals and communities affected by environmental racism because it reflects the complexity of the human experience in sociopolitical context.

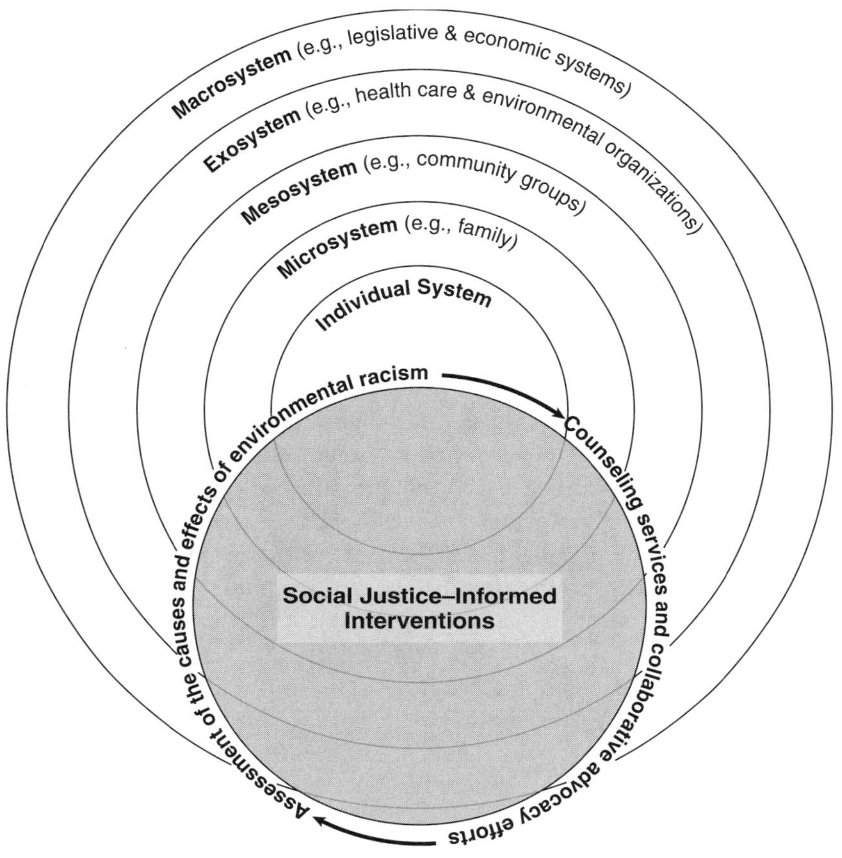

Figure 14.1

In Neville and Mobley's (2001) model, the following subsystems were identified: (a) the individual/person system, which includes general factors such as personality style and trauma experiences, and sociocultural factors such as social group identity and cultural mistrust; (b) the microsystem, which includes general factors such as family and neighborhood, and counseling-related sociocultural factors such as level of cultural competence of specific systems and the services they provide; (c) the mesosystem, which includes family and mental health professional interaction and sociocultural group organization and school interaction; (d) the exosystem, which includes health care and legal systems as well as social policies and social movements (e.g., civil rights); and (e) the macrosystem, which includes political and economic structures; social identity structures (e.g., class, race); sociocultural specific values; and dominant stereotypes about sociocultural groups. Neville and Mobley (2001) postulated that the macrosystem "structures all experiences and functions within the other subsystems" (p. 475).

In Figure 14.1, the concentric circles represent the systems described by Neville and Mobley (2001). The overlapping circle represents social justice–informed interventions that can have an impact on each of these systems. Additionally, the arrows outside of the circle represent a movement from understanding environmental racism to taking transformative action (Martín-Baró, 1994). An overlapping circle represents the interface of counseling interventions with environmental racism because the process is often not a linear one. For example, a counseling psychologist may first encounter the effects of environmental racism while working with an individual client or family. However, it is also possible that a counseling psychologist may first enter a community as a consultant or researcher. There are many possible points of intervention, and the counseling psychologist's role and scope of responsibilities may become broader as assessment and counseling interventions elucidate the need for collaborative advocacy efforts. Thus, a counseling psychologist can address problems associated with environmental racism by supporting individuals, families, and community-based organizations while confronting the industrial and government systems that caused or institutionally support environmental racism (e.g., by not providing equal protection and enforcing environmental laws, regulations, and policies). For example, individuals can be treated for depression; families can be provided with case management services; community groups can receive psychoeducation; community leaders and organizations can be consulted; and collaborative efforts can be coordinated with environmental policy experts and other professionals to advocate for clients (e.g., securing funding for environmental clean-up and health care, participating in legislative advocacy to prevent future problems).

Conclusion

Historically, environmental hazards such as oil spills, landfills, and PCB contamination have caused widespread problems in communities, affecting their local economies, shared living spaces, schools, real estate, and individual mental and physical health. Typically, the ethnic minority communities experience the majority of these environmental problems, and often have little or no say in how corporations or government agencies decide on where landfills will be placed or where dumping of contaminants will occur. Being mindful that one's environment affects overall psychological well-being, it is imperative that counseling professionals begin to integrate environmental advocacy in their work with clients. The model provided in Figure 14.1 helps to provide such a framework for counseling professionals. Although systemic environmental change may be challenging, we believe that counseling psychologists can have a central role in such an endeavor that will ultimately benefit our communities for years to come.

References

Adeola, F. O. (1994). Environmental hazards, health, and racial inequity in hazardous waste distribution. *Environment and Behavior, 26,* 99–126.

Agyeman, J., Bullard, R. D., & Evans, B. (Eds.). (2003). *Just sustainabilities: Development in an unequal world.* Cambridge: MIT Press.

Akwesasne Task Force on the Environment: Research Advisory Committee. (1997). Superfund clean up at Akwesasne: A case study in environmental justice. *International Journal of Contemporary Sociology, 34,* 269–290.

Arctic Monitoring and Assessment Programme. (1997). Pollution and human health. In *Arctic pollution issues* (AMAP Assessment Report, pp. 172–186). Oslo, Norway: Author.

Arredondo, P., & Perez, P. (2003). Expanding multicultural competence through social justice leadership. *The Counseling Psychologist, 31,* 282–289.

Arredondo, P., Toporek, R., Brown, S. P., Jones, J., Locke, D. C., Sanchez, J., & Stadler, H. (1996). Operationalization of the multicultural counseling competencies. *Journal of Multicultural Counseling and Development, 24,* 42–78.

Brooks-Gunn, J., Duncan, G. J., Klebanov, P. K., & Sealand, N. (1993). Do neighborhoods influence child and adolescent development? *American Journal of Sociology, 99,* 353–395.

Bryant, B., & Mohai, P. (Eds.). (1992). *Race and the incidence of environmental hazards: A time for discourse.* Boulder, CO: Westview.

Bullard, R. D. (1994). *Unequal protection: Environmental justice and communities of color.* San Francisco: Sierra Club Books.

Bullard, R. D., & Johnson, G. S. (2000). Environmentalism and public policy: Environmental justice: Grassroots activism and its impact on public policy decision making. *Journal of Social Issues, 56,* 555–578.

Carpenter, D. (1995). Communicating with the public on issues of science and public health. *Environmental Health Perspective, 103,* 127–130.

Chen-Hayes, S. F. (2001). Social justice advocacy readiness questionnaire. In M. E. Swigonski, R. S. Mama, & K. Ward (Eds.), *From hate crimes to human rights: A tribute to Matthew Shepard* (pp. 191–203). New York: Haworth.

Clark, L., Barton, J. A., & Brown, N. J. (2002). Assessment of community contamination: A critical approach. *Public Health Nursing, 19,* 354–365.

Finkel, S. E., Muller, E. N., & Opp, K. D. (1989). Personal influence, collective rationality, and mass political action. *American Political Science Review, 83,* 885–903.

Gardner, M. K. (2003). Linking activism and the self: The politics and practice of linking social justice to environmental activism. *Dissertation Abstracts International, 64*(4-A), 1173.

Gaylord, C. E., & Bell, E. (2001). Environmental justice: A national priority. In L. Westra & B. E. Lawson (Eds.), *Faces of environmental racism: Confronting issues of global justice* (pp. 29–40). Lanham, MD: Rowman & Littlefield.

Green, B. L., Lindy, J., & Grace, M. C. (1994). Psychological effects of toxic contamination. In R. J. Ursano, B. G. McCaughery, & C. S. Fullerton (Eds.), *Individual and community responses to trauma and disaster: The structure of human chaos* (pp. 154–176). Cambridge, UK: Cambridge University Press.

Grossman, K. (1994). The people of color environmental summit. In R. Bullard (Ed.), *Unequal protection: Environmental justice and communities of color* (pp. 271–297). San Francisco: Sierra Club Books.

Harding, A. K., & Greer, M. L. (1993). The health impact of hazardous waste sites on minority communities: Implications for public health and environmental health professionals. *Journal of Environmental Health, 55,* 6–9.

Hepworth, D. H., & Larsen, J. A. (1990). *Direct social work practice: Theory and skills* (3rd ed.). Belmont, CA: Wadsworth.

Hong, G. E., & Ham, M. D. C. (2001). *Psychotherapy and counseling with Asian clients: A practical guide.* Thousand Oaks, CA: Sage.

Lewis, J., & Bradley, L. (2000). *Advocacy in counseling.* Greensboro, NC: ERIC/CASS.

Lewis, J., Smith-Arnold, M., House, R., & Toporek, R. (2004). *American Counseling Association advocacy competencies.* Alexandria, VA: American Counseling Association.

Lubell, M. (2002). Environmental activism as collective action. *Environment and Behavior, 34,* 431–454.

Lundberg, A. (Ed.). (1998). *The environment and mental health: A guide for clinicians.* Mahwah, NJ: Lawrence Erlbaum.

Lundberg, A., & Santiago-Rivera, A. L. (1998). Psychiatric aspects of technological disasters. In A. Lundberg (Ed.), *The environment and mental health: A guide for clinicians* (pp. 57–66). Mahwah, NJ: Lawrence Erlbaum.

Lynch, K. (1979). The spatial world of the child. In W. Michelson, S. V. Levine, & E. Michelson (Eds.), *The child in the city: Today and tomorrow* (pp. 102–127). Toronto: University of Toronto Press.

Martín-Baró, I. (1994). *Writings for a liberation psychology.* Cambridge, MA: Harvard University Press.

Mohai, P., & Bryant, B. (1992). Environmental racism: Reviewing the evidence. In B. Bryant & P. Mohai (Eds.), *Race and the incidence of environmental hazards: A time for discourse* (pp. 163–176). Boulder, CO: Westview.

Needleman, H. L., Schell, A., Bellinger, D., Leviton, A., & Allred, E. N. (1990). The long-term effects of exposure to low doses of lead in children: An 11-year follow-up report. *New England Journal of Medicine, 322,* 83–88.

Neville, H. A., & Mobley, M. (2001). Social identities in contexts: An ecological model of multicultural counseling psychology processes. *The Counseling Psychologist, 29,* 471–486.

Palinkas, L. A., Downs, M. A., Petterson, J. S., & Russell, J. (1993). Social, cultural, and psychological impact of the Exxon Valdez oil spill. *Society of Applied Anthropology, 52,* 1–13.

Palinkas, L. A., Petterson, J. S., Russell, J., & Downs, M. A. (1993). Community patterns of psychiatric disorders after the Exxon Valdez oil spill. *American Journal of Psychiatry, 150,* 1517–1523.

Palinkas, L. A., Russell, J., Downs, M. A., & Petterson, J. S. (1992). Ethnic differences in stress, coping, and depressive symptoms after the Exxon Valdez oil spill. *Journal of Nervous and Mental Disorders, 180,* 287–295.

Parham, T. A. (2002). *Counseling persons of African descent: Raising the bar of practitioner competence.* Thousand Oaks, CA: Sage.

Pilisuk, M. (1998). The hidden structure of contemporary violence. *Peace and Conflict: Journal of Peace Psychology, 4,* 197–216.

Pinderhughes, R. (1996). The impact of race on environmental quality: An empirical and theoretical discussion. *Sociological Perspectives, 39,* 231–248.

Reeser, L. C., & Leighninger, L. (1990). Back to our roots: Towards a specialization in social justice. *Journal of Sociology & Social Welfare, 17,* 69–87.

Santiago-Rivera, A. L. (2001). Ecological violence: Impact of environmental degradation and contamination on psychological health and well-being. In D. Sandhu (Ed.), *Faces of violence: Psychological correlates, concepts and intervention strategies* (pp. 129–142). Huntington, NY: Nova Science.

Santiago-Rivera, A. L., Arredondo, P., & Gallardo-Cooper, M. (2002). *Counseling Latinos and la familia: A practical guide.* Thousand Oaks, CA: Sage.

Santiago-Rivera, A. L., Morse, G., Hunt, A., & Lickers, H. (1998). Building a partnership for community-based research: Lessons from the Mohawk Nation at Akwesasne. *Journal of Community Psychology, 20,* 163–174.

Sue, D. W., Carter, R. T., Casas, J. M., Fouad, N. A., Ivey, A. E., Jensen, M., LaFromboise, T., Manese, J. E., Ponterotto, J. G., & Vasquez-Nuttall, E. (1998). *Multicultural counseling competencies: Individual and organizational development.* Thousand Oaks, CA: Sage.

Sutton, S. E., & Kemp, S. P. (2002). Children as partners in neighborhood placemaking: Lessons from intergenerational design charrettes. *Journal of Environmental Psychology, 22,* 171–189.

Teasley, M., & Rice, J. (1996). What is social justice? *Perspectives on Multiculturalism and Cultural Diversity, 6*(2), 1.

Trimble, J. E., & Thurman, P. (2002). Ethnocultural considerations and strategies for providing counseling services for Native American Indians. In P. Pedersen, J. Draguns, W. Lonner, & J. Trimble (Eds.), *Counseling across cultures* (5th ed., pp. 53–91). Thousand Oaks, CA: Sage.

Unger, D. G., Wandersman, A., & Hallman, W. (1992). Living near a hazardous waste facility: Coping with individual and family distress. *American Journal of Orthopsychiatry, 62,* 55–70.

Vera, E. M., & Speight, S. L. (2003). Multicultural competence, social justice, and counseling psychology: Expanding our roles. *The Counseling Psychologist, 31,* 253–272.

Weiss, B. (1998). Behavioral manifestations of neurotoxicity. In A. Lundberg (Ed.), *The environment and mental health: A guide for clinicians* (pp. 25–41). Mahwah, NJ: Lawrence Erlbaum.

Wernette, D. R., & Nieves, L. A. (1992). Breathing polluted air: Minorities are disproportionately exposed. *Environmental Protection Agency Journal, 18,* 16–17.

CHAPTER 15

The Unwarranted Pathologizing of Homeless Mothers

Implications for Research and Social Policy

Lisa Cosgrove

The epistemic commitments one makes as a researcher affect all aspects of the research process; these commitments affect the questions asked, the design of the study, the analysis of the data, the findings generated, and the recommendations made. Despite the fact that counseling psychology is committed to a preventive and developmental model, many scholars have argued that the assumptions and epistemological framework of a pathology-oriented model continue to pervade our work. For example, Vera and Speight (2003) maintained that counseling psychologists need to rethink the assumptions that undergird their research if they are to transform psychology and make it more "conducive to justice enhancing work" (Fox, 2003, p. 299).

The call to challenge a pathology model and engage in justice-enhancing work is highly relevant to research on family homelessness. Specifically, when researchers rely on a discourse of deficit and victimization to study the causes of and solutions for family homelessness, they inadvertently contribute to the stigmatization of the homeless rather than depicting the depth and diversity of the lives of homeless people. In order to maximize the participation and activism of homeless people, researchers must not assume that people without homes are dysfunctional and incapable of participating in policy and programmatic decisions that affect their lives (Rosenthal, 2000). Thus, a significant issue for counseling psychologists is how to shift away from etiological and intervention models that rely on intraindividual factors to explain the causes of and solutions for homelessness. This shift is particularly important because most research on homelessness, including qualitative research, paints a picture of the homeless as a homogeneous group, uniformly disabled (Snow, Anderson, & Koegel, 1994). Because of problematic images of homeless and poor women in research, the media, and public policies, the United States has become one of the most dangerous democracies in which poor women and their children can live (Polakow, 1993).

Estimates of homelessness vary widely because it is difficult to operationalize the definition of homelessness; many people without homes are in precarious situations, "doubling up" and living, one step away from the streets, with friends or relatives. Another complicating factor with regard to generating statistics is that there is no standard methodology for measuring homelessness, and many individuals and families who live temporarily in makeshift housing, such as tents or cars, are not counted by researchers (National Coalition for the Homeless, 2002). These methodological difficulties notwithstanding, most researchers, as well as the media, use statistics from the well-respected Urban Institute Study (2000), which reported that there are 3.5 million people (approximately 1 million of whom are children) who are homeless in the United States. Although the public image of the homeless as a homogeneous group of male "skid row bums" continues to be pervasive, data from the recent U.S. Conference of Mayors (2003) contradict this image, indicating that 40% of the homeless are families (usually mothers with children). Unfortunately, assistance for precariously housed and homeless families has not kept pace with the growing number of families in need of help. In 2001, 52% of emergency shelter requests from families were denied, a 22% increase from 2000 (National Coalition for the Homeless, 2002).

Research on family homelessness inadvertently contributes to the stigmatization of the poor insofar as it fails to capture the lived experience, resilience, and interpersonal discrimination that homeless women face. The wealth of research on homelessness focuses on "demographics and disabilities" (Snow et al., 1994) and has been of modest use to participants. Numerous authors (e.g., Friedman, 2000; Liebow, 1993; Snow et al., 1994; Styron, Janoff-Bulman, & Davidson, 2000) attribute the distorting tendencies to a decontextualized and overly pathologized picture of homeless people. Explaining the etiology of homelessness by appealing to intraindividual factors reinforces negative stereotypes about the poor and contributes to the unwarranted pathologizing of homeless mothers. The images of women are particularly damaging as exemplified by studies that use comparative tests of group means. Comparing homeless mothers and low-income housed mothers on parenting practices (e.g., Koblinsky, Morgan, & Anderson, 1997), infant-mother attachments (Easterbrooks & Graham, 1999), and mental health and substance abuse problems (e.g., Bassuk, Buckner, Perloff, & Bassuk, 1998) sustains victim-blaming attitudes about the root causes of homelessness.

In light of the fact that many research studies use comparative tests of group means and focus on "demographics and disabilities," it is not surprising that most of the recommendations found in the psychological literature emphasize intraindividual, rather than structural, solutions. For example, a number of studies have "found" that homeless women tend to use dysfunctional or avoidant coping (Banyard & Graham-Bermann, 1998; for a more thorough critique, see Klitzing, 2003). However, psychological theories of coping assume a certain amount of privilege (Fine, 1992), and the instruments designed to measure coping reflect this privilege. Survey instruments that delimit coping categories (e.g., avoidant vs. problem-solving coping) have been harshly criticized for sustaining the belief that homeless women are incompetent and in need of "fixing" (e.g., see Klitzing, 2003). The conclusions reached and recommendations made often lead to the disciplining and regulation of homeless mothers. Recent state and federal welfare reform policies are founded on the idea that poor women are lazy and therefore need supervision and surveillance in order to "get off the system." Many states have adopted policies that create financial incentives for marriages and cut aid if a woman has a child while receiving benefits or if a child is truant from school (Fox-Piven, 1996; Perales, 1995). This punitive approach was summed up well by Connolly (2000), who wrote,

> [Women on welfare] are represented as incomplete, stranded in a child-like state. They are deemed "abnormal," deficient, and thus a drain on the government system. . . . They are wayward, rebellious adolescents in need of regulation and tough love. (p. 154)

Indeed, the Welfare to Work Act, a bill that Clinton signed in 1996 that essentially ended the 60-year program Aid to Families with Dependent Children, is an example of a federal policy that is grounded in racist and classist stereotypes of "the welfare queen" (Fox-Piven, 1996; Seccombe, 1999). One of the main criticisms of the recent welfare reform policies is that they are discriminatory because they fail to address the structural causes of poverty and they fail to address the complexities of the lives of single mothers, especially the difficulty in obtaining child care (Connolly, 2000; Perales, 1995; White, 1996).

Problematic media images also fuel public animosity by combining sexism, classism, and racism in subtle but powerful ways. George Will's (1990) vitriolic essay in *Newsweek*, "Mothers Who Don't Know How," is a classic example. Will wrote about "young unmarried mothers" living in inner cities whose "incompetent parenting" robbed their "ghetto children" of IQ points (p. 80). Unfortunately, many people share Will's beliefs. Researchers consistently find that attitudes toward the poor are significantly more negative than attitudes toward middle-class individuals, and that there is a strong tendency to blame the poor for their poverty (e.g., Cozzarelli, Wilkinson, & Tagler, 2001). Discrimination based on class, gender, and race is operationalized by the process of "Other-ing," that is, by denigrating and devaluing the experiences of members of marginalized groups (Bullock, 1999; hooks, 1990; Lott, 2002).

Ethical Issues Involved in Studying Homelessness and in Working With the Homeless

Challenging the victimization/pathology model necessitates an appreciation of the sociopolitical context in which homelessness occurs. One of the most pressing ethical issues in research on family homelessness is thus an epistemological one. That is, what beliefs about knowledge, knowledge making, and who gets to "count" as a knower inform the design of the study (see Harding, 1991; Nelson, 1993; Ussher, 1999)? Flyvbjerg's (2001) insightful interpretation of the Aristotelian concept of phronesis is helpful in responding to these epistemological questions. According to Flyvbjerg, the purpose of phronetic research is to "hold up a mirror to society thus encouraging and facilitating reflexivity. . . . Phronesis is that intellectual activity that is most relevant to praxis. . . . [Phronesis is] deliberation about values with reference to praxis" (pp. 64–65). Flyvbjerg argues that the concept of phronesis allows for an appreciation of context-dependent knowledge, although he notes that the term has no contemporary analogue. Insofar as phronetic research emphasizes the importance of reflexivity, context, and social action, participatory action research (PAR) can be seen as an example of phronetic research.

PAR helps psychologists avoid the "normalizing gaze" (Foucault, 1979) of the researcher, a gaze that all too often results in disciplinary effects. Specifically, PAR combines social investigation with action in order to improve the lives of those involved (Brydon-Miller, 1997; Gaventa, 1993; Yeich, 1996). The first step in participatory research—and one that sets it apart from traditional social science research—is for the researcher to engage in critical reflection on his or her epistemic commitments. Assumptions about the meaning of validity and objectivity in psychological research are called into question. The goal of PAR is to design studies that not only avoid objectifying participants but also foster a particular kind of interaction. In terms of doing research with homeless women, findings should be developed collaboratively, and they should be used to inform public policy and shelter programs. In the section below, I describe the research process and some of the themes that emerged from a participatory research project on family homelessness.

Homeless Mothers Talk About Their Needs and Experiences

Fifteen women were interviewed at two "strength-based" shelters in the northeastern United States.[1] Strength-based shelters are based on the assumption that the clients they serve are competent and that agencies should build on these strengths (Connolly, 2000; Friedman, 2000). The main goal of the study was to explore the lived experience of homeless mothers within the context of hegemonic cultural representations of homelessness and motherhood. Every attempt was made to avoid the role of researcher as "omniscient narrator" (Flyvbjerg, 2001) of participants' experiences; I did not assume that "homeless mothers" constituted a homogeneous category. Rather than approach the analysis of the data with the (implicit or explicit) question, "What are homeless mothers really like?" the focus was on identifying the material and interpersonal challenges that homeless mothers faced. Specifically, the thematic analysis centered on the following question: "How do 'ideologies of normative motherhood' (Connolly, 2000; Young, 1997) impact on women's experiences of parenting in shelters?" The themes that were identified from the interviews and the recommendations for changes in shelter policies and programs were developed in collaboration with both shelter guests and staff. Because most of the women had moved out of the shelters by the time the interviews and narrative analyses were completed, focus groups with current shelter residents were held. In collaboration with participants and shelter staff, the original list of themes and recommendations was elaborated on and modified.

All participants received services from the Department of Transitional Assistance (the welfare system administered by the state) as well as state-funded health care services. The majority also worked with providers from other agencies (e.g., for counseling). All of the women encountered negative stereotyping of the poor, and a major theme that emerged from the interviews was feeling stigmatized in subtle but powerful ways. Participants talked about the stress of trying to parent amidst the constant awareness that one is positioned as "aberrant Other." Women described how they felt "humiliated" and "disrespected," and they confronted dehumanizing stereotypes on a daily basis. One woman summed up the daily stigmatization in a very poignant way: "They [people] don't, they just don't respect you. *It's not by the words, it's just like they don't even look at you*" (italics added). Indeed, participants' experiences of interpersonal discrimination must be contextualized within their marginalized status as "welfare recipients," what Connolly (2000) has referred to as the stigma of the anticitizen as well as the antimother.

Although participants did not report feeling stigmatized by shelter staff, the myriad of ways in which they had been demeaned, avoided, and treated as contagion carried through to many aspects of shelter life. The shelters' explicit mission statements of hospitality and emphasis on women's strengths allowed for an atmosphere of deep respect to develop. Certainly, there were times when the sensitivity, patience, and flexibility demonstrated by the staff were not enough to compensate completely for the accumulated effects of cultural scapegoating. However, the caring relationships between staff and guests provided the structure and support necessary for shelter guests to negotiate the demands of communal living, and these supportive relationships were instrumental in helping women regain residential and financial stability.

One of the most striking aspects of this study was that all of the women identified numerous strengths and coping strategies. At the same time, however, they did not dismiss or discount their interpersonal struggles or mental health issues. Themes of self-efficacy, perseverance, resilience, and resistance were evidenced in the interviews, and all of the women stated explicitly that they planned to be employed, back in school, or in a training program in the near future. Unfortunately, however, many participants' active help-seeking behaviors were undermined by some of the state and federal policies. For example, many women reported great frustration over the difficulty in finding affordable child care. This difficulty was exacerbated by restrictions placed on subsidized or free child care. Although child care was provided when the women took the mandatory parenting classes, no child care was available for those women who had a high school degree or GED and who wanted to take classes at a local college. Women who were seeking employment ran into similar difficulties. Whenever possible, the dedicated staff at these two strength-based shelters assisted women, but there was no formal mechanism in place to allow women with children the opportunity to look for jobs or return to school.

As noted earlier, in participatory research, people are not seen as the objects of study; they are empowered to develop social change strategies (Gaventa, 1993; Yeich, 1996). All of the participants felt strongly that negative stereotypes about homeless women with children were pervasive, and they stated that policymakers do not understand the needs or experiences of the homeless. Participants were emphatic in their desire for policymakers to know that negative stereotypes and images of homeless mothers are untrue, and that the real causes of homelessness are low wages and the lack of affordable housing. A major problem encountered by participants was the inability to save enough money for even subsidized housing because of the limitations placed on the amount of money that could be earned before losing eligibility for shelter programs and health benefits. One woman, who worked as a teacher's aide prior to becoming homeless, summed up this point well, stating that it was impossible to make ends meet on her salary (she was making $7.25 per hour as a teacher's aide). She eventually had to quit her job in order to be eligible for food stamps and health benefits for herself and her daughters. "I don't think [policymakers] know this isn't what we want. We don't want to be in this situation. . . . If you work forty hours a week, you should be able to pay your rent and bills."

In keeping with the premise of phronesis, participatory and interpretive methods allow members of the community being studied to become actively engaged in the production of knowledge. Women were asked to identify their needs and to make suggestions for policymakers and shelter program personnel. The recommendations in Table 15.1 were developed in collaboration with all participants and with shelter, administrative, and professional staff.

Discourse Analysis of the Federal Policy on Homelessness

In addition to the interviews that were conducted, I reviewed the federal policy on homelessness. Thus, a discourse analysis of the policy on homelessness was combined with an examination of participants' experiences in an effort to see if the assumptions and rhetoric of the federal policy accurately reflected the needs and experiences of homeless mothers. The aim of discourse analysis is to interrogate the production of meaning in a text, whereby a "text" can be any discursive account, such as an interview, a newspaper article, or a conversation (e.g., see Burman & Parker, 1993;

Table 15.1 Policy and Programmatic Recommendations

Goals	*Objectives*
1. Provide more opportunity for women living in poverty to participate in decisions affecting their lives.	1. Institute roundtable discussions as a standard part of shelter programs. Invite community activists, researchers, and currently and formerly homeless individuals to these meetings. These discussions would allow for the development of specific social action plans.
2. Increase collaboration among university administrators and shelter administrators.	2. Provide tuition waivers to women in shelters. Have university faculty teach some classes at local shelters (e.g., GED or computer classes depending on need). In order to provide an impetus for teaching off-site, these classes could fulfill the university service requirement or be considered part of the regular courseload of faculty.
3. Provide vocational counseling and professional help with résumé writing and job searches.	3. Implement service learning models in universities. These models can serve as a mechanism through which graduate students (under faculty supervision) could provide needed services to homeless women in shelters.
4. Train staff who work with women living in poverty to avoid using deficit-oriented or victim-based models of intervention.	4. Train line and professional staff in a *social* analysis of homelessness. A social analysis emphasizes the ways in which structural impediments, inequities in the distribution of wealth, and gender inequality are implicated in the etiology of homelessness. Offer workshops, courses, and certificate programs for professionals working with homeless women and women living in poverty.
5. Increase awareness about the limitations of current psychological theories and assessment tools designed to measure "effective coping." Researchers and clinicians need to be more open to the myriad of ways that resilience can be manifest.	5. Use multimodal assessments and qualitative methodologies when identifying and assessing coping behavior. Behaviors that are typically seen as evidence of dysfunction (e.g., "avoidant coping style" as identified on a standardized coping assessment tool) in some contexts may be highly adaptive strategies.
6. Increase awareness about the pervasiveness of negative stereotypes of the poor and the impact of interpersonal discrimination. It is especially important for new staff to understand that for many women, the stigma carries over into shelter life. That is, the effects of unwarranted pathologizing and cultural scapegoating are felt *even in the supportive presence of shelter staff.*	6. Encourage women to document incidents of discrimination and educate women about their rights. Encourage women to discuss their experiences of interpersonal discrimination and share their respective strategies for coping. Include identification of strengths/coping skills as a standard part of the intake into the shelter system (Banyard & Graham-Bermann, 1998).

Goals	*Objectives*
7. Develop mechanisms by which shelter guests have more explicit input into the curriculum of parenting classes and groups. Provide multiple opportunities for shelter guests to talk about the conflicts that arise out of communal living situations, especially when guests feel that the rules of the shelter are not congruent with how they parented outside the shelter.	7. Staff and guests should review shelter rules and the curriculum of parenting classes on an ongoing basis.
8. Provide more affordable housing, wages on which one can live, and provide accessible child care.	8. Increase the supply of low-cost housing and keep it permanently affordable by keeping it out of the private sector (Timmer, Eitsen, & Talley, 1994). Raise the minimum wage, and offer state and federally subsidized child care.

Burr, 1995; Hollway, 1989; Potter & Wetherell, 1987; Wilkinson & Kitzinger, 1995). Using a discourse analytic method to "deconstruct" texts means "looking at texts [and] revealing how they contain 'hidden' internal contradictions, and making absent or repressed meanings present for the reader, showing how we are led by the text into accepting the assumptions it contains" (Burr, 1995, pp. 164–165).

It is important to note that there is no one formulaic method, because the label *discourse analysis* describes a set of approaches that can be used when working with texts (Marecek & Kravetz, 1998, p. 29). Content and meaning are addressed, but the assumption is that meaning does not exist prior to and apart from representational systems; meaning gets produced in complex and intricate ways. The discourse analyst tries to identify how particular meanings are constituted. It is in this sense that the analysis of the data is deconstructive: One tries to make explicit those views and beliefs that are repressed or marginalized. The researcher is interested in how his or her analysis might be used to shed light on the rhetorical and material practices by which truths and meaning are produced. As Burr (1995) noted,

> The goal [of discourse analysis] becomes a pragmatic and political one, a search not for truth but for any usefulness that the researcher's "reading" of a phenomenon might have in bringing about change for those who need it. Research thus becomes action research . . . and a political activity. For example, a study in which the researcher claimed that children in education are caught up in oppressive power relations would be evaluated . . . in terms of how useful and liberatory such an analysis might be to the children themselves. (p. 162)

A full analysis of the federal policy is being prepared (Cosgrove, 2005). What follows is an analysis of an excerpt from Priority: Home! (1993), an excerpt that is most germane to participants' experiences.

> The plan considers the cause and effect of a different destruction—devastation less sudden and obvious than that recently suffered by Los Angeles, yet more insidious in its nature. Urban areas throughout the nation have been consistently deteriorating with only periodic notice and episodic attention. Aging infrastructure, loss of businesses, failing school systems, increasing violence, dilapidated housing, lack of employment, and pervasive drug use define too many communities. Unlike the situation in Los Angeles, the Federal government cannot claim credit for repair, but instead bears joint responsibility for the decay. Failed attempts, scarce resources, and inaction have all contributed to the "silent earthquakes" that have slowly, yet forcefully, shaken the foundations of our communities.
>
> This plan is about the most visible victims of those silent earthquakes: the homeless. As with natural disasters, those resting on the weakest foundations with the frailest support structures have suffered most noticeably. Once reserved for areas predictable by the extent of urban ills, large-scale homelessness, the most manifest and obvious symptom of urban decay, is now spreading to rural and urban areas previously believed to be immune. (p. 1)
>
> A decade of research and practical experience has confirmed that there are many varieties of contemporary homelessness. Manifold in its causes, duration, consequences, and co-existing disabilities, its steady growth in the early 1980's reflected the confluence of a number of factors. . . . When fashioning measures to reach those who are currently on the street, personal problems that contribute to the prolongation of homelessness must be addressed. If stable residence is the goal of policy, appreciating the role of risk factors is essential. Psychiatric disability, substance abuse, domestic violence and chronic illness not only add to the likelihood that someone will be homeless, but complicate the task of re-housing someone already on the street. (p. 25)
>
> Solving homelessness will thus mean confronting traditional sources of impoverishment . . . and it will also mean confronting relatively new social phenomena that are adding to the costs of poverty. . . . Accordingly, a comprehensive approach will have to mount initiatives on a number of fronts simultaneously. Homelessness will not be solved simply by outlawing the most visible evidence of its presence on the streets. Solving homelessness will require durable means of arresting the sources of residential instability. (p. 35)

After reading and rereading this policy (the body of which is too lengthy to produce here in its entirety), I was struck by three main themes (see Table 15.2). I focus on what images are evoked via these themes, what alternative images are suppressed, and what function these particular themes and images serve. I begin by identifying key thematic elements in the passages cited above. Next, I describe in more detail the discourses evidenced in this policy statement and briefly discuss the implications of these discourses.

Table 15.2 Images Evoked in Priority: Home!

Terms That Suggest That the Etiology of Homelessness Is the Result of an Impersonal, Uncontrollable Event or Natural Disaster	*Terms That Suggest That Homelessness Is Best Characterized as a Disease*	*Terms That Encourage a Militarized or War-Like Response to Homelessness*
Devastation	Symptom	Confronting
Destruction	Immune	Mount initiatives
Deteriorating	Spreading	On a number of fronts
Aging infrastructure	Frailest	Outlawing the most visible evidence
Silent earthquake	Victims	Arresting the sources
Victims	Misdiagnosed	
Urban decay	Risk factors	
Damage	Psychiatric disability	
Rebuild	Substance abuse	
Crisis	Chronic illness	
	Urban ills	

Homelessness as Uncontrollable Event or Natural Disaster

The analogy made to the earthquake in Los Angeles, together with descriptors such as *devastation, destruction,* and *decay,* evoke clear images of nature and the unpredictability of a natural disaster. This is seen most obviously in the statement that likens the homeless to victims of "silent earthquakes." Although the plan begins with a statement that acknowledges that the federal government bears "joint liability," the extent of that liability is limited by comparing the homeless to victims of natural disasters such as earthquakes. However well intentioned such a comparison may be, it actually preserves the view of homelessness as being caused by circumstances beyond our control. The natural disaster analogy also allows the federal policy to be driven by a paternalistic rhetoric insofar as the implied course of action is to rescue rather than collaborate, to pity rather than empower. Making homelessness analogous to a natural disaster obscures the psychosocial implications of the growing disparity in wealth in the United States.

Homelessness as Disease

Homelessness is also metaphorized as a disease, as evidenced by the use of such terms as *risk factors, symptom, victims,* and *immunity.* Describing the increasing numbers of homeless as "spreading" is also congruent with a disease model. Such terms, which are interspersed throughout the narrative, subtly encourage a pejorative view that actually preserves the stereotype of the homeless as aberrant, as objects of contagion, as "abject Other." Appealing to a biopsychiatric discourse to explain the etiology of homelessness sustains the unwarranted pathologizing of the homeless. Use of this discourse and these images reinforces the erroneous belief that psychiatric problems (e.g., depression) or substance abuse are the cause and not the result of homelessness (e.g., see Blasi, 1990; McChesney, 1990; Shinn, 1992; Snow et al., 1994; Timmer et al., 1994). The image of homelessness as a disease invites a response of "treatment by experts" and thus undermines a collaborative approach. That is, solidarity work with the homeless is undermined insofar as the call for action is a call to act for—not necessarily with—homeless individuals (Mishler & Steinitz, 2001).

War-Like Solutions for the Problem of Homelessness

The language contained in this text creates the impression that it is possible to eradicate the problem of homelessness by using force. Phrases such as "arresting the sources of residential instability" and "outlawing the most visible evidence" suggest images of doing battle against an evil scourge or invader. Such imagery normalizes the view that the homeless are victims of an (outside) evil force with which we must contend—homelessness is something that (unfortunately) happened and it must be combated. Although the war-like imagery may appear to increase a unified response, military metaphors and images actually undermine the development of participative, collaborative, and empowering solutions.

Implications for Public Policy and for Creating Strength-Based Services

The importance of developing federal and state policies on homelessness based on a social analysis of homelessness rather than on negative stereotypes of the poor cannot be overstated. The 1992 amendments to the federal policy on homelessness (i.e., Priority: Home!) included the results of a survey in which homeless persons were asked to prioritize issues (via a questionnaire). This was a valiant first effort at true collaboration and respect for the homeless. Unfortunately, reading the policy does not provide insight into the lived experiences of homeless families. Although the amendments do reflect a changing view of homelessness (Foscarinis, 1995), future policy must build upon these initial collaborative efforts so that public policy truly gives voice to homeless women with children. Also, as demonstrated in this brief discourse analysis, the rhetoric used objectifies the homeless and casts them as Other. At best, the policy engenders a paternalistic response to "passive and needy" (Timmer et al., 1994) victims by "do-gooder" experts. The voices and recommendations of homeless activists, for example, are absent in the federal policy. As Timmer et al. (1994) noted, the rhetoric engendered by the "politics of compassion" too frequently obscures the inequities and policies that contribute to the creation of extreme poverty. Compassion is a necessary but insufficient condition for ending homelessness in the United States. High rates of homelessness are all but guaranteed when 18% of full-time workers fall below the poverty line (Polakow, 2003) and only 20% of the poor live in government-subsidized housing of any kind—*the lowest rate of assistance in any industrialized nation in the world* (Dreier & Atlas, cited in Timmer et al., 1994, emphasis added). In addition to the voices of homeless activists, the experiences of, and solutions for, interpersonal discrimination are missing from Priority: Home! Attempts to prevent homelessness will be extremely limited until we understand the ways in which homeless women's active help-seeking behaviors are thwarted by the very systems designed to meet their needs.

For example, as noted earlier, participants encountered three main problems: (a) interpersonal discrimination when negotiating the bureaucracy of state welfare systems; (b) lack of affordable child care, especially when looking for employment or when attempting to go back to school; and (c) the combination of low-wage jobs, lack of affordable housing, and unrealistic restrictions placed on wage earnings. This combination of factors puts women in a no-win situation: Either they continue working at low-wage jobs (e.g., for $7.25 an hour as a teacher's aide) and have insufficient funds to pay for food and health benefits, or they quit their jobs in order to become eligible for food stamps and health care. The rhetoric on which the federal policy is built fails to address these and other problems because the lived experience of homeless individuals, especially homeless families, is missing. Creating strength-based services necessitates insight into the needs, difficulties, and resilience of homeless women and their families. Public policy on homelessness determines the structure and philosophy of state and local programs (including, but not limited to, shelter programs). Thus, it is imperative that policy statements and the language of legislative bills reflect the reality of being poor rather than myths about the character of the poor or the causes of homelessness.

Conclusion

In order to develop public policies and strength-based programs that adequately reflect the lived experiences of homeless mothers, it is recommended that researchers stop designing studies that exaggerate the role of individual deficits (e.g., using primarily comparative analytic strategies), and instead design studies that are aimed at identifying strengths and coping strategies. In addition, more research on the stigmatization and interpersonal discrimination of poor and homeless women is needed. Such research is a necessary first step in eradicating stereotypes that fuel punitive public policies and social service programs, and these studies will also raise awareness about the injustices that homeless women must endure on a daily basis. Psychologists also need to work collaboratively with homeless women, activists, and the staff and administrators of successful strength-based shelters in an attempt to identify which aspects of these programs are most useful. Such collaboration would also invoke much-needed discussions about how shelter programs and social service systems can empower the women whom they serve.

Insofar as counseling psychologists use a preventive and strength-based model of human functioning, they have a critical role to play in transforming psychological research on homelessness. The concept of phronesis is a useful heuristic for psychologists committed to solidarity research with homeless individuals. Incorporating reflexivity, interrogating our epistemic commitments, and including the voices of poor women are necessary components of phronetic/justice-enhancing work. In contrast to a phronetic approach, research that is grounded in a positivist-empiricist model secures the science/politics binary and sustains relations of dominance. In order to challenge the status quo and be responsive to the needs of disenfranchised groups, humility—not epistemic arrogance—must be our starting point. Indeed, if our research is to be of genuine use to the communities with whom we collaborate, then we must start from the assumption that participants are capable individuals who are knowledgeable about the discourses, practices, and policies that affect their lives.

Note

1. This research project was supported in part by the funds given by the National Institute of Mental Health to the Henry A. Murray Research Center of the Radcliffe Institute for Advanced Study, Harvard University, Cambridge, Massachusetts. From 2002 to 2003, Cheryl Flynn (a graduate student at UMass–Boston) and I conducted a series of interviews with homeless women. I am most grateful for her assistance in and contributions to this research project. We also offer our heartfelt thanks to the shelter guests and staff who took the time to speak with us, and to Manisha Vijayaraghavan for her superb editorial assistance. Space constraints do not allow for a detailed description of the methodology. Please see Cosgrove and Flynn (in press) for a thorough description of the narrative analysis and a more detailed description of the results.

References

Banyard, V. L., & Graham-Bermann, S. A. (1998). Surviving poverty: Stress and coping in the lives of housed and homeless mothers. *American Journal of Orthopsychiatry, 68,* 479–489.

Bassuk, E. L., Buckner, J. C., Perloff, J. N., & Bassuk, S. S. (1998). Prevalence of mental health and substance use disorders among homeless and low-income women. *American Journal of Psychiatry, 155,* 1561–1564.

Blasi, G. L. (1990). Social policy and social science research on homelessness. *Journal of Social Issues, 46*(4), 207–220.

Brydon-Miller, M. (1997). Participatory action research: Psychology and social change. *Journal of Social Issues, 53,* 657–666.

Bullock, H. E. (1999). Attributions for poverty: A comparison of middle-class and welfare recipient attitudes. *Journal of Applied Social Psychology, 29,* 2059–2082.

Burman, E., & Parker, I. (Eds.). (1993). *Discourse analytic research: Repertoires and readings of texts in action.* New York: Routledge.

Burr, V. (1995). *An introduction to social constructionism.* New York: Routledge.

Connolly, D. (2000). *Homeless mothers: Face to face with women and poverty.* Minneapolis: University of Minnesota Press.

Cosgrove, L. (2005). *Discourse analysis of the federal policy on homelessness.* Manuscript in preparation.

Cosgrove, L., & Flynn, C. (in press). Marginalized mothers: Parenting without a home. *Analysis of Social Issues and Public Policy.*

Cozzarelli, C., Wilkinson, A. V., & Tagler, M. J. (2001). Attitudes toward the poor and attributions for poverty. *Journal of Social Issues, 57,* 207–227.

Easterbrooks, M. A., & Graham, C. A. (1999). Security of attachment and parenting: Homeless and low-income housed mothers and infants. *American Journal of Orthopsychiatry, 69,* 337–346.

Fine, M. (1992). *Disruptive voices: The possibilities of feminist research.* Ann Arbor: University of Michigan Press.

Flyvbjerg, B. (2001). *Making social science matter: Why social inquiry fails and how it can count again.* New York: Cambridge University Press.

Foscarinis, M. (1995). Shelter and housing: Programs under the Stewart B. McKinney homeless assistance act. *Clearinghouse Review, 29,* 760–770.

Foucault, M. (1979). *Discipline and punish: The birth of the prison* (Trans. A. Sheridan). Oxford, UK: Vintage.

Fox, D. R. (2003). Awareness is good, but action is better. *The Counseling Psychologist, 31,* 299–304.

Fox-Piven, F. (1996). Welfare and the transformation of electoral politics. *Dissent, 43,* 61–67.

Friedman, D. H. (2000). *Parenting in public: Family shelter and public assistance.* New York: Columbia University Press.

Gaventa, J. (1993). The powerful, the powerless, and the experts: Knowledge struggles in an information age. In P. Park, M. Brydon-Miller, B. Hall, & T. Jackson (Eds.), *Voices of change: Participatory research in the United States and Canada* (pp. 21–40). Westport, CT: Bergin and Garvey.

Harding, S. (1991). *Whose science? Whose knowledge? Thinking from women's lives.* Ithaca, NY: Cornell University Press.

Hollway, W. (1989). *Subjectivity and method in psychology: Gender, meaning and science.* Newbury Park, CA: Sage.

hooks, b. (1990). *Yearning: Race, gender, and cultural politics.* Boston: South End Press.

Klitzing, S. W. (2003). Coping with chronic stress: Leisure and women who are homeless. *Leisure Sciences, 25,* 163–181.

Koblinsky, S. A., Morgan, K. M., & Anderson, E. A. (1997). African-American homeless and low-income housed women: Comparison of parenting practices. *American Journal of Orthopsychiatry, 67,* 37–47.

Liebow, E. (1993). *Tell them who I am: The lives of homeless women.* New York: Free Press.

Lott, B. (2002). Cognitive and behavioral distancing from the poor. *American Psychologist, 57,* 100–110.

Marecek, J., & Kravetz, D. (1998). Putting politics into practice: Feminist therapy as feminist praxis. *Women & Therapy, 21,* 17–36.

McChesney, K. Y. (1990). Family homelessness: A systematic problem. *Journal of Social Issues, 46*(4), 191–206.

Mishler, E. G., & Steinitz, V. (2001). *Solidarity work: Researchers in the struggle for social justice.* Retrieved March 3, 2004, from http://www.coe.uga.edu/quig/proceedings/Quig01_Proceedings/mishler.html

National Coalition for the Homeless. (2002, September). *How many people experience homelessness?* Retrieved August 16, 2004, from http://www.nationalhomelessness.org

Nelson, L. H. (1993). A question of evidence. *Hypatia, 8,* 174–189.

Perales, N. (1995). A "tangle of pathology": Racial myth and the New Jersey family development act. In M. A. Fineman & I. Karpin (Eds.), *Mothers in law: Feminist theory and the legal regulation of motherhood* (pp. 250–269). New York: Columbia University Press.

Polakow, V. (1993). The other childhood: The classroom worlds of poor children. In M. A. Jensen & S. G. Goffin (Eds.), *Visions of entitlement: The care and education of America's children* (pp. 157–174). Albany: State University of New York Press.

Polakow, V. (2003). Homeless children and their families: The discards of the post-welfare era. In S. Books (Ed.), *Invisible children in the society and its schools* (2nd ed., pp. 89–110). Mahwah, NJ: Lawrence Erlbaum.

Potter, J., & Wetherell, M. (1987). *Discourse and social psychology: Beyond attitudes and behavior.* Newbury Park, CA: Sage.

Priority: Home! (1993). *The federal plan to break the cycle of homelessness* (Executive Order 12848 of May 19, 1993). Washington, DC: U.S. Government Printing Office.

Rosenthal, R. (2000). Imaging homelessness and homeless people: Visions and strategies within the movement(s). *Journal of Social Distress and the Homeless, 9,* 111–126.

Seccombe, K. (1999). *"So you think I drive a Cadillac?" Welfare recipients' perspectives on the system and its reform.* Boston: Allyn & Bacon.

Shinn, M. (1992). Homelessness: What is a psychologist to do? *American Journal of Community Psychology, 20,* 1–24.

Snow, D. A., Anderson, L., & Koegel, P. (1994). Distorting tendencies in research on the homeless. *American Behavioral Scientist, 37,* 461–475.

Styron, T. H., Janoff-Bulman, R., & Davidson, L. (2000). "Please ask me how I am": Experiences of family homelessness in the context of single mothers' lives. *Journal of Social Distress and the Homeless, 9,* 143–165.

Timmer, D. A., Eitsen, D. S., & Talley, K. D. (1994). *Paths to homelessness: Extreme poverty and the urban housing crisis.* San Francisco: Westview.

Urban Institute. (2000, February). *A new look at homelessness in America.* Retrieved August 16, 2004, from http://www.urban.org

U.S. Conference of Mayors. (2003). *Hunger and homelessness survey: A status report on hunger and homelessness in America's cities.* Retrieved August 16, 2004, from www.usmayors.org/uscm/hungersurvey/122003/onlinereport/HungerAndHomelessnessReport2003

Ussher, J. M. (1999). Commentary: Eclecticism and methodological pluralism: The way forward for feminist research. *Psychology of Women Quarterly, 23,* 41–46.

Vera, E. M., & Speight, S. L. (2003). Multicultural competence, social justice, and counseling psychology: Expanding our roles. *The Counseling Psychologist, 31,* 253–272.

White, L. E. (1996). On the "consensus" to end welfare: Where are the women's voices? *Radical America,* p. 26.

Wilkinson, S., & Kitzinger, C. (1995). *Feminism and discourse: Psychological perspectives.* Thousand Oaks, CA: Sage.

Will, G. F. (1990, April 23). Mothers who don't know how. *Newsweek, 115,* 80.

Yeich, S. (1996). Grassroots organizing with homeless people: A participatory research approach. *Journal of Social Issues, 52,* 111–121.

Young, I. M. (1997). *Intersecting voices: Dilemmas of gender, political philosophy, and policy.* Princeton, NJ: Princeton University Press.

CHAPTER 16

Diving Into the Hornet's Nest

Situating Counseling Psychologists in LGB Social Justice Work

David H. Whitcomb and Michael I. Loewy

Lesbian, gay, and bisexual (LGB) people are a minority group that has been systematically oppressed and discriminated against in societies throughout the world for much of recorded history. It was only a generation ago that the American Psychiatric Association removed homosexuality as a mental disorder from the *Diagnostic and Statistical Manual* (*DSM*). Since then, the mental health professions have increasingly advocated for changes in social policies with the aim of promoting the well-being of LGB people. Such work continues today.

In many ways, working to attain social justice for LGB people is like diving into the hornet's nest—it does not appear to be the logical thing to do. Even when approaching a hornet's nest with great care and strategy, one is likely to be stung sometimes—such is the case with doing this work. Yet, much like a hornet's nest, there is a lot going on in the field—it is teeming with activity, and there are intricate systems to decipher. Those interested in this challenging work are well advised to take risks, develop a thick skin, and have a sense of adventure.

The purpose of this chapter is to provide counseling psychologists with a framework from which to engage in social justice work on behalf of LGB people. This framework will be created first by briefly reviewing the history of oppression and discrimination against LGB people, including within the mental health professions; reviewing the more recent history of affirmation and advocacy for LGB people within the field of psychology; and finally, providing suggestions for how counseling psychologists can work in several major areas to help create greater social justice for LGB people. We draw upon the literature in psychology, the popular media, our own experience, and the work of many of our colleagues as we suggest ways to move forward with an LGB social justice agenda. In doing so, we hope that the ultimate benefits of taking the plunge into this hornet's nest will become evident.

Oppression of LGB Individuals

Unlike racial and ethnic minority groups who suffer institutional oppression in the United States, LGB people's oppression begins in the informal and intimate communications and values in the family (Matthews & Lease, 2000). It is also found in every formal political, commercial, and social institution. Even in families and churches where homosexuality is not openly condemned, the "liberal" tolerance of this human diversity is often accompanied by messages that heterosexuality is still better than homosexuality (Morrow & Beckstead, 2004). This isolation leaves a psychological legacy of internalized homophobia that most LGB people carry with them and struggle with in one way or another for their entire lives. In most families, homosexuality is never mentioned or discussed in any meaningful way. This silence communicates to children that it is not only bad, but so bad that it is taboo to even talk about it. LGB children grow up isolated from each other and thinking that they are the only ones to violate the social norm of heterosexual attraction and familialism (D'Augelli & Patterson, 2001; Patterson & D'Augelli, 1998).

When children leave the home to enter school, they continue to be confronted with these oppressive messages, which serves to further isolate them. Homophobia is so entrenched in our society that teachers as well as parents are afraid to broach the subject with children in any meaningful way, either in the formal curriculum or informally. However, as Weis and Fine (2000) point out, most of children's education takes place in the informal spaces outside the classroom. As such, a visit to any schoolyard will expose one to words such as "gay" and "faggot" being used as common and vicious insults (Human Rights Watch, 2001). In fact, in a 14-city study of gay, lesbian, and bisexual youth, 80% reported verbal abuse, 44% reported threats of attack, 33% reported having objects thrown at them, and 30% reported being chased or followed (D'Augelli & Hershberger, 1993). As a consequence, students beginning to identify as LGB are often erased from school life (Redman, 1994) or tormented to the point of extreme social isolation or suicide.

The government also acts as an instrument of social control. For example, the fear of homosexuality and homosexuals (i.e., homophobia) has led to banishing LGB people from the U.S. military (Melton, 1989); barring LGB people from adoption and foster care of children (Patterson & Redding, 1996); and banning marriage, or even nonmarital civil unions, through legislative action and constitutional amendments (Buhrke, 2003). Some of these proposed constitutional amendments, such as the one in North Dakota, go so far as to prohibit private corporations that already have domestic partner benefits in place from continuing to provide these benefits to their employees (Equality North Dakota, 2004). Except in the cities and states where nondiscrimination laws have been passed, it is perfectly legal to fire someone from his or her job for no other reason than that he or she is LGB (Chung, 2001).

Unfortunately, the mental health professions have also been one of the most effective instruments of oppression against LGB people. The second *Diagnostic and Statistical Manual of Mental Disorders* (*DSM-II*) (American Psychiatric Association, 1968) included homosexuality as a mental illness. The third edition removed this diagnostic category but still included "ego-dystonic homosexuality," which refers to the condition wherein someone feels incongruent with her or his homosexual orientation. As later study made clear that in a society that demonizes homosexuality and devalues LGB people, ego-dystonia is a normative developmental process in the identity development of LGB people. This diagnosis was removed in the *DSM-III-R* in 1987 (Rothblum, 2000).

Hershberger and D'Augelli (2000) also point out that one of the results of LGB oppression is that LGB youth are at higher risk for a range of mental health problems. Higher rates of suicide, alcoholism, and other antisocial and self-harmful adaptation strategies are understandable when one is faced with relentless psychological abuse because of personal characteristics that are not perceived to be under the control of the individual experiencing them (i.e., LGB orientation). As such, LGB people are more likely to seek counseling services than the general population. Unfortunately, those services are sometimes more harmful than helpful (Garnets, Hancock, Cochran, Goodchilds, & Peplau, 1991; Liddle, 1995, 1996, 1997, 1999). Even when services are provided that affirm a gay, lesbian, or bisexual identity, counseling LGB individuals will not be sufficient to eliminate the causes of the psychological stressors induced by oppression. We need to venture beyond our offices to become more effective agents of social change in the community and in our profession.

Models of Counseling Psychologists Engaged in LGB Social Action

In this section of the chapter, we illustrate the scope of social justice work that we and other counseling psychologists have been conducting, and provide examples of people who have successfully focused their research on social justice issues, using the results to have an impact on institutions. These counseling psychologists have been active in their communities and in the local and national media; have been instrumental in initiating, shaping, and affecting American Psychological Association (APA) policy; and have published scholarly books and journal articles that have supported their social justice efforts. Becoming familiar with exemplary work may help readers to see how their own work may relate to the efforts of others who have accomplished much in this field.

Community Organizing

LGB communities become stronger through activities with high visibility, such as Gay Pride celebrations, as well as targeted activism and the building of support networks. In presenting some examples of our own work in this area, we suggest strategies for other counseling psychologists who want to engage in community organizing and illustrate some of the pitfalls of embarking on such projects.

I (Michael Loewy) was very active in starting and building a vital local and regional LGB activist community during my undergraduate years, starting with the formation of a university student group and then producing the first LGB Pride celebration and regional LGB leadership conferences. My early LGB activism brought me into contact with seasoned feminist and antiracist activists who quickly taught me about the intersection of identities and the diversity of issues that affect LGB people.

It can be very challenging to ensure that, as an activist, you are truly representing the interests of the group you claim to represent. So, when doing LGB advocacy, you should be sure that your work is benefiting all LGB people, not just White, middle-class, out, gay men, for example. It is important to bring a diverse group of people to the table during the initial stages of organization building, not after the leadership and agenda have been decided. This can be accomplished by including the issues relevant to diverse groups of LGB people on your activism agenda. For example, in order to represent LGB individuals of lower socioeconomic status, issues of poverty must be prioritized by LGB activists. We included issues related to racial and gender discrimination in our LGB conference planning. We also confronted local LGB leaders, usually LGB business (bar) owners—who often funded our early LGB activism efforts—regarding racist and sexist practices that were common in Las Vegas at that time.

It becomes apparent that even deciding upon an agenda can be challenging. Grassroots activism is a long, arduous process. Moving from the parliamentary procedures and majority rule model, in which the dominant culture typically operates, to a consensus model, which has become more typical of activist groups, is an effective way to address these concerns.

To illustrate how it can be a challenge to maintain momentum and avoid burnout during uphill battles in an activist group, recently in North Dakota, a constitutional amendment to ban same-sex marriages and domestic partnerships was proposed, which prompted an opposition movement. The first comment made by a seasoned activist at the first meeting of a group of about 10 LGB faculty and students called together informally to begin to build the opposition was that this measure was sure to pass no matter what we did. Were it not for the fresh-faced energy of the students there, we would have all left feeling quite deflated. It could have been either of us who made that remark, as we were certainly thinking it. Voters ultimately passed the amendment by a 73% to 27% margin. It can be hard to stay focused on LGB activism in the face of so much defeat. However, despite this loss, we educated a lot of people in the Grand Forks area, raised awareness of what it means to be LGB for the whole community, and helped many young people come out and begin to advocate on their own behalf.

No matter what the perceived impact, we need to remember to honor and appreciate each other for the activism we do. Although activism is often motivated by self-interest, there is always an element of altruism in the work we do on behalf of our groups, hoping that things will be better for the next generation than it is for us now.

Influencing Social Policy and Legislation

Sheila Kuehl, a California legislator who is also a lesbian, observes that legislators need better access to information that psychologists discover and publish in order to advocate for social change (Kuehl, 2003). She advises that psychologists inquire of the staff of their legislator as to whether that legislator might be interested in a particular area of research. Psychological research continues to play a crucial role in social policy change; without its support, legislation to change social policy has little chance of passing.

For example, Douglas Haldeman's writings on the harmful effects of sexual orientation conversion or "reparative" therapies (Haldeman, 1991, 1994, 2001, 2002, 2003) have been instrumental in changing policy and law. Haldeman's work has been cited by the American Psychiatric Association (2000) in its Position Statement on Same Sex Unions. His articles were also cited in the 2003 Amici Curiae brief to the U.S. Supreme Court, submitted by the American Psychological Association, the American Psychiatric Association, the National Association of Social Workers (NASW), and the Texas Chapter of the NASW (Gilfoyle et al., 2003). This document was written to support the plaintiffs in *Lawrence and Garner v. Texas,* 539 U.S. 558 (2003); the Supreme Court's ruling in their favor led to a ban of antisodomy laws, which had been used for many years to persecute and intimidate individuals engaging in consensual same-sex sexual relations. Counseling psychologists can also have a direct impact on policy and legislation by working within the legal and political system. For example, Robin Buhrke served as advisor to Senator Paul Wellstone as the William A. Bailey AIDS Policy APA Senior Congressional Fellow, 1997–1998.

In contrast to earlier oppressive practices of psychologists, APA has been a national leader among mainstream professional organizations in promoting social justice and social policy change for LGB people. APA has been very active in developing amicus briefs for legislative and judicial purposes in relation to LGB issues. A look at the Public Interest Directorate Web site of APA reveals numerous policy statements regarding LGB political issues and guidelines for working with various LGB populations that are backed up by much psychological research. "Just the Facts About Sexual Orientation & Youth: A Primer for Principals, Educators & School Personnel" (American Psychological Association Public Interest Directorate, 1999) is one example of a user-friendly plan that can greatly assist counseling psychologists as we collaborate more with school counselors on community service issues (see Romano & Kachgal, 2004).

In 1991, putting its money where its mouth is, the organization even gave up revenue (and some membership) by declining advertising in the *Monitor* from one of its biggest advertisers, the U.S. military, because of its discriminatory practices toward LGB people (Fox, 1992). Through the Education Directorate and the Committee on Accreditation, APA has also been very influential in higher education and the training of psychologists. Although "Footnote 4" allows religious institutions to maintain accreditation despite prejudiced and unfair discrimination against LGB people (in the guise of freedom of religious expression), overall, the accreditation process helps to ensure that LGB concerns and appropriate therapeutic interventions are a part of the training of psychologists in the United States.

The public positions that APA has taken on LGB issues have often followed years of internal discussion and debate. At the highest levels of APA governance, Division 44's members of the Council of Representatives took the lead at the 2004 APA convention to pass the Resolution on Same Sex Marriage (American Psychological Association, 2004), which states that prohibiting same-sex marriage is unfair and discriminatory; as such, it encourages psychologists to act toward eliminating such discrimination. Division 17 Council Representatives played an important advocacy role in the unanimous passage of this resolution (L. Forrest, personal communication, August 2, 2004), but as with other LGB social justice issues, the impetus came from Division 44. There is certainly no need for efforts to be duplicated within APA, but a more formal liaison arrangement between 17 and 44 could maximize collaboration and ensure that the concerns of counseling psychologists are fully addressed in the social justice initiatives of organizations represented by many subdisciplines of psychology.

At a recent APA convention, I (David Whitcomb) observed one hour of the Council of Representatives meeting. Similar to watching C-SPAN on cable television, observing the political process can help one understand the procedures and protocol, the official activities being recorded, and the behind-the-scenes lobbying that was occurring. Joining the Section for Lesbian, Gay, and Bisexual Awareness (SLGBA) and similar organizations; reading psychological associations' newsletters (and then starting to contribute to them); lurking on and then becoming an active contributor to listservs; and, as discussed below, attending to the popular media are all important steps that would prepare someone to influence APA policy, public policy, and laws. In sum, as a pathway toward leadership, first observe (watch, read, listen); then participate; and selectively join groups when appropriate. The individuals who author the proposals that are brought to a vote, testify to the courts and legislatures, and become elected to top leadership positions have come up through the ranks. Essential work is nevertheless done at every level and every step of the process; working toward social justice is a team effort.

Influencing Public Opinion

In addition to his publications and APA offices, Douglas Haldeman, a counseling psychologist in private practice and at the University of Washington, has often been in the public eye as an advocate for lesbian, gay, bisexual, and transgender (LGBT) social justice. For example, he was interviewed in 2001 on ABC's *Good Morning*

America to critique the methodology of a controversial study on reparative therapy (Spitzer, 2003) 2 years before it was finally published.

Although we are not all asked to represent our views in the national media, most of us will have the opportunity to influence public opinion more locally. Recently, I (David Whitcomb) was invited by other social justice leaders outside of our professional discipline to speak with the editorial board of a local newspaper on the upcoming statewide referendum on same-sex marriage. The board was quite attentive as the group presented arguments against the constitutional amendment and sought information to help them formulate their editorial on the issue. In addition to personal insights, expertise as a psychologist was useful in informing the board how the proposed law could harm the emotional well-being of family members, including children. Sometimes, presenting at a professional conference feels like "preaching to the choir," whereas speaking about a similar topic in a community group can deliver a new message to an audience whose opinions may be more readily influenced to become more LGB affirmative.

When responding to requests from the media to speak as an expert on LGB issues, there are some important things to keep in mind. First, try to make sure that the interviewer is friendly to the cause, or at least unbiased and not unfriendly. There are too many examples of biased reporters twisting words or misquoting in order to make their point. Remember, an advocate knows a lot more about the topic than the interviewer. It is unlikely that a question will emerge for which one is totally unprepared.

Next, one should choose her or his words carefully in order to minimize the chance that what is said will be taken out of context or misquoted. LGB social justice issues are highly complex and controversial. When writing journal articles, carefully phrased footnotes or provisos about the terminology are included—yet such subtleties are typically lost in a newspaper column, and there is seldom the chance to elaborate in a recorded interview. The infamous "sound byte" most often does not adequately represent our stance on the issues, yet it is important to learn to speak the language in order to be represented to the broader public. In most instances, interviews require that one make points covered in the first couple of hours of an LGB 101 course. It is important work, but one often finds oneself having to start at the beginning by covering the basics.

Strategies for Surviving and Thriving in the Hornet's Nest: Staying Informed

When doing social justice work, it is important to keep up with current events on social injustices, efforts to right these wrongs, and projects intended to prevent unjust situations from occurring. In so doing, one will often rely not solely on the professional literature, but also on the popular media. Long before a phenomenon such as same-sex marriage is analyzed in a peer-reviewed journal or published in a book, advocates must keep apprised of these events by reading newspapers and magazines, visiting Internet sites, watching local and national news on television, and listening to the radio. In planning a response to counter the public backlash, for example, community organizers would rely on the popular media, not academic literature, to gauge public opinion and be alerted to any increase in "queer bashing" or other discrimination. Counseling psychologists can broaden the scope of data sources and methods of tracking them. For example, one can use one's training to explain to the public when numerical data from studies are being misrepresented or when skewed samples are used to draw conclusions in the popular media. By being adaptive in these ways, one can respond effectively to rapidly developing issues that require quick action to influence social policies.

Somewhere in between the domains of popular media and academic literature are Internet listservs, which range in purpose from professional to recreational. The Society of Counseling Psychology (SCP) listserv, for example, often contains postings that refer to social justice issues and more often refer the reader to Web sites in the popular media than to the academic literature. Because of APA's not-for-profit status, APA's listservs cannot include posts that endorse or criticize elected officials or those who are running for public office. This policy may interfere with open discussion regarding certain LGB-related policies that are associated with specific politicians. Thus, counseling psychologists who want to stay abreast of LGB social justice issues may want to join non-APA online discussions, such as http://groups.yahoo.com/group/lgbtactivist/ or http://www.outdemocracy.com/. In the examples of fighting injustices and proactive measures that follow, popular media sources are often cited for the most current information, supplemented by analyses in the professional literature that inevitably lag behind the work occurring on the frontlines. An excellent resource for scientific, educational, and policy matters related to sexual prejudice is social psychologist Gregory Herek's Web site (http://psychology.ucdavis.edu/rainbow/index.html), which also contains many documents written for the general public.

Finding Support Through Professional Organizations

APA has been one of the most supportive large professional organizations for LGB social justice. One can find many avenues through our professional organizations to advocate for LGB issues and will not risk ostracism or other negative results to one's career for engaging in LGB research or social justice activism. In fact, APA has most often been a salve for those hornet stings and an inspiration to carry on with this important work. Occasionally, there are turf issues, but there is strong support from many divisions, committees, and bureaus for activist work.

APA's annual convention provides many opportunities for professional gatherings, as does the biennial National Multicultural Conference and Summit, at which LGB issues are a major focus. Regional SCP meetings, such as the annual Great Lakes Conference, also feature top-quality research, but are of a size and pace (as well as distance and expense) that may be more comfortable for the newcomer. Individuals who want to engage in LGBT social justice can attend presentations given by the authors cited above or attend roundtable discussions on emerging issues, where the energy and insights of students, new professionals, and seasoned practitioners synergize with topics discussed by the authors from the literature. Following such conferences, we have often shared with colleagues how refreshed we feel, with new ideas and professional networks to help us pursue both the public service and research aspects of our social justice work.

Within APA, there are a few units that should be mentioned in terms of LGBT social justice. SCP contains numerous sections, one of which is the Section for Lesbian, Gay, and Bisexual Awareness (SLGBA). Currently, each year, the section is allotted an hour of convention-wide programming as well as 2 or more hours of SCP hospitality suite time, where a business meeting and small group discussions are held on issues such as LGB vocational psychology and integrating transgender issues into LGB issues. Current and past projects of SLGBA include a listserv for announcements and discussion; a student poster session; a newsletter, in which students, members, and officers may contribute commentary or a regular column; a mentorship program pairing students with counseling psychologists farther along in their careers; and ad hoc consultations. SLGBA is a welcoming organization that fosters professional development. Previous section leaders have generously provided mentorship to the current leadership, and past leaders have progressed to more visible leadership positions within APA, such as president of the Society for the Psychological Study of Lesbian, Gay, and Bisexual Issues (Division 44).

Even more than in SCP, LGBT social justice within APA is spearheaded by Division 44. Several past presidents of Division 44 are counseling psychologists, as are the current newsletter editor and her predecessor. Counseling psychologists can stay current with LGBT issues in the media and in the profession via their listserv and newsletters and by regularly attending their convention activities.

In order to remain relevant and inclusive, professional organizations must be responsive to emerging issues in the field. For example, resources are being developed to become more inclusive of transgender issues (see Carroll & Gilroy, 2002; Chung, 2003; Lev, 2004) in instances when oppression based on gender identity shares common ground with sexual orientation discrimination. Although "transgender" is not yet in Division 44's title ("bisexual" was added in the 1990s), the transgender task force was recently elevated to the status of a standing committee within the Division. Within SLGBA, transgender issues have been the topic of SCP hospitality suite discussion hours and convention-wide symposia (Cantor, Embaye, & Whitcomb, 2003; Kirby, Whitcomb, Israel, & Worthington, 2004).

In addition to APA, many counseling psychologists are active in other professional organizations, such as the American Counseling Association (ACA) and the Association for Counselor Education and Supervision. ACA has long been a vocal advocate for LGB social justice, as evidenced in its Code of Ethics; the content of its journal articles and convention presentations; and the work of the Association for Gay, Lesbian, and Bisexual Issues in Counseling, one of ACA's 19 divisions. Counseling psychologists work closely with counselor educators in ACA to promote diversity awareness; as with APA, many opportunities exist at every career level to foster the association's work for LGB social justice.

Navigating Conflicts Between Activism and Academia

In graduate school, I (Michael Loewy) started to focus my activism on counseling-related activities. Efforts such as becoming the trainer for a buddy program in AIDS outreach services, helping start a local ACT UP group to protest the government and corporate inaction in combating AIDS, and helping establish one of the first scholarship programs for LGB college students led to my being named "Man of the Year" by the LGB Center in 1989. In contrast to these accolades from the LGB community, my dissertation chair warned me to protect my time, give up the activism "for now," and focus on research. It can be a challenge for an early career academic to integrate his or her activism into graduate school and tenure-seeking activities.

Social justice activism most often falls into the part of the academic job description called service. Similar to our experiences as graduate students, we have found that for early- to mid-career academics, service is not very highly valued as compared to teaching and scholarship, especially in regard to tenure evaluation. Yet social justice work is very time-consuming, and for LGB academics, there is a lot of pressure from the LGB communities to do this work. LGB students seek us out for advising and support beyond our regular responsibilities. For clinicians, there is even less flexibility in the workday to fit in this kind of service—and, unlike in academia, where service is at least a small part of the job description, there is no remuneration at all.

Another issue to be aware of is institutional politics. Members of the academy are expected to protect it. If seen as loose cannons, members' career development could be halted or slowed down considerably. As someone who has a commitment to institutional change, it feels quite dissonant to benefit from the status quo at the same time. It can make one feel sometimes like one is part of the problem that she or he is trying to change. One way to navigate these treacherous waters is by seeking increasingly more visible and powerful leadership roles, such as administration, in the academy and our professional organizations. This can position one to understand the organizational culture better and to propose and implement the change one would like to see happen. It is important for academic counseling psychologists who are involved in community activism to be strategic about their career path and to choose their battles carefully.

Special Considerations for LGB Counseling Psychologists

LGB activism is a very public enterprise, and its leaders' names and pictures are often featured in the media. The sexual orientation of an activist working for LGB social justice therefore becomes a matter of public discussion, and there is an expectation to come out either as a LGB person or as an ally for the cause. This expectation can place a great deal of pressure on LGB persons who may want to promote LGB social justice but, for religious, cultural, or various personal reasons, may choose not to publicly disclose their sexual orientation.

Understanding models of gay and lesbian identity development can help us appreciate the place that coming out or not coming out has in community activism. Many of the most active members of the general public working to promote social justice are in what Cass (1979) has referred to as the Identity Pride stage of identity development. Persons at this stage feel empowered by having come out and may believe it is in the best interest of almost everyone to come out. Indeed, coming out plays an important role for many individuals, and for society as a whole, because persons who personally know gay and lesbian individuals are less likely to be biased against them (Herek & Capitanio, 1996; Simon, 1998).

Activism, however, is not a necessary part of lesbian and gay identity (McCarn & Fassinger, 1996), and the act of coming out is a very personal decision that is fraught with risk. To clarify, coming out is a culturally defined act that is not viewed or experienced similarly across different sociocultural groups (Boykin, 1996; Chan, 1997). If an LGB person's identity of origin is located in another oppressed group that has a history of devaluing LGB people (e.g., African American, Latino/Catholic), he or she may encounter a particularly excruciating double bind. For many people of color and people of faith, coming out means losing the only safe space available (Beckstead & Morrow, 2004; Chan, 1997; Greene, 1997).

It is imperative for counseling psychologists working as practitioners to help clients determine whether coming out would be liberating and empowering, or whether other ways to express one's same-sex attractions would be more appropriate. Similarly, in their work as activists, counseling psychologists can help organizations and task groups to respect each member's decision about coming out. We can help create and support roles for those who wish to be part of the cause without risking, for example, seeing their names printed in the local newspaper. The work that counseling psychologists are doing in developing the theories and techniques used to help people develop a positive LGB identity is very much social justice work at the grassroots level—one person at a time and in small groups.

Because LGB activism has been an integral part of identity development and identity pride for both of us, social justice work as LGB counseling psychologists has resulted in finding a supportive community. The opportunities are limitless, and the recognition for this work is just starting to grow. It is also important to point out that activism is fun and rewarding, and that activist allies, whether counseling psychologists or not, often grow into best friends.

For the counseling psychologist who is primarily a practitioner, one must be careful that one's activism does not scare away potential clients (again, one can be too visible for the comfort of some), and one should be prepared to let clients know that the calls for action one makes in public should not be considered as a directive for what the client needs to do in his or her life. An advantage for the practitioner is more lived experience to bring into the room with his or her clients. Having been on the front lines may help one to empathize with the challenges that oppressed clients are facing.

Heterosexual Allies

Heterosexual counseling psychologists have served in a variety of roles in social justice efforts for LGB people, and there is a significant need for more allies in our field (Bieschke, Worthington, Roysircar, & Perez, 2002). There are many opportunities and advantages associated with being a heterosexual counseling psychologist ally of the LGB communities. Part of being an ally is role modeling for students and colleagues the courage to advocate for a group of people who have fewer or different privileges from oneself.

Opportunities also exist for allies to become involved in community groups such as Parents, Family, and Friends of Lesbians and Gays (PFLAG). PFLAG is made up of family and friends who are allies looking for a way to be supportive and those who are struggling to understand and learn about their loved one's homosexuality or bisexuality. PFLAG groups often look to counselors and psychologists to help them cope and better understand their role and their lesbian, gay, or bisexual loved one. Heterosexual counseling psychologists are poised to help people with psychoeducational approaches to coping with and combating sexual prejudice.

In a similar way, an advantage to being an ally is the opportunity for disclosing one's own relationships with LGBT friends and family. Some people find it liberating to come out as allies and to be able to openly support people in their lives whom they care about. A heterosexual ally demonstrates that one does not have to give up one's own privileges to advocate for LGBT people to have the rights enjoyed by heterosexual persons (e.g., marrying the person you love and with whom you want to share your life).

Roger Worthington, an associate professor in the University of Missouri's counseling psychology program, is an example of an ally who has been involved in LGB leadership within SCP as a member of the board of SLGBA. He is also a frequent presenter for Division 44 at APA. He conducts research to better understand the process of becoming an ally (Dillon et al., 2004) as well as sexual orientation as a psychological construct (Worthington, 2003; Worthington & Mohr, 2002). He is very public about his advocacy for LGB people and shares information relevant to LGB issues in counseling psychology on several listservs. He is the mentor for many LGB graduate students, and almost all of his heterosexual doctoral students enter the profession with solid identities as allies to LGB people. His example suggests that academic training programs can benefit from actively recruiting and including allies as well as LGB professionals and students in our affirmative action considerations in both admissions and hiring decisions. Programs can also make sure that their Web sites and all their published materials include LGB affirmation.

There are some disadvantages and barriers to being an ally. Clients, colleagues, supervisors, and the general public may assume that you are LGB, which may lead to interesting choices of whether and how to come out as heterosexual. Many people still assume that if one is advocating for LGB rights, then that person must be LGB her- or himself. The heterosexual ally is often put into the position of confronting his or her own heterosexual privilege—and the ramifications of losing that privilege (Israel, 2004).

Similarly, LGB individuals may not readily trust and welcome the help of allies and may suspect that they are helping only to fulfill some ulterior motive, such as working out their own sexual orientation issues. Allies may need to work harder and longer to demonstrate their genuine interest and the value of their contributions toward LGB social justice. Even if generally accepted by the LGB communities, there may be perceived or actual instances of LGB people marginalizing allies, such as including them on some projects, special events, and private information but not others. Still, in all, heterosexual counseling psychologists have many opportunities to make both micro-level (i.e., therapeutic) contributions as well as macro-level (i.e., research and institutional change) contributions to LGB liberation.

Conclusion

The work that has been done over several decades to affirm the worth and dignity of LGB people and to secure civil rights for this oppressed minority group has gradually gained acceptance as being consistent with the valuing of human diversity in the field of psychology (see American Psychological Association, 2002). Counseling psychologists have long been important contributors to this work, but until recently, most of our work in harm prevention, community-level interventions, and advocacy for LGB people has not been articulated in terms of social justice. A main goal of this chapter has been to provide a variety of examples of the work that counseling psychologists do to advance LGB social justice.

At times, engaging in work that can situate us at the center of many of the major political, religious, and moral controversies of our time feels like diving into the hornet's nest—there is no escape without being stung. As we learn lessons about more and less effective means of influencing social policy and public opinion, however, we can share our knowledge; develop a professional support network to soothe our stings and rejuvenate our spirits; and use the science and practice of counseling psychology to make the world a more just place for lesbian, gay, and bisexual people.

References

American Psychiatric Association. (1968). *Diagnostic and statistical manual of mental disorders* (2nd ed.). Washington, DC: Author.

American Psychiatric Association. (2000). *Position statement on same sex unions.* Washington, DC: Author. Retrieved December 10, 2004, from http://www.aglp.org/ pages/position.html

American Psychological Association. (2002). Ethical principles of psychologists and code of conduct. *American Psychologist, 57,* 1060–1073.

American Psychological Association. (2004). *Resolution on sexual orientation and marriage.* Washington, DC: Author. Retrieved December 10, 2004, from http://www.apa.org/releases/gaymarriage_reso.pdf

American Psychological Association Public Interest Directorate. (1999). *Just the facts about sexual orientation & youth: A primer for principals, educators & school personnel.* Retrieved July 31, 2004, from http://www.apa.org/pi/lgbc/publications/justthefacts.html

Beckstead, A. L., & Morrow, S. L. (2004). Mormon clients' experiences of conversion therapy: The need for a new treatment approach. *The Counseling Psychologist, 32,* 651–690.

Bieschke, K., Worthington, R., Roysircar, G., & Perez, R. (2002, August). In J. O'Brien (Chair), *The grit and grace of becoming an ally for LGB concerns.* Symposium presented at the 110th annual meeting of the American Psychological Association, Chicago.

Boykin, K. (1996). *One more river to cross: Black and gay in America.* New York: Anchor.

Buhrke, R. (2003). Honoring and protecting relationships. In M. R. Stevenson & J. C. Cogan (Eds.), *Everyday activism: A handbook for lesbian, gay, and bisexual people and their allies* (pp. 171–192). New York: Routledge.

Cantor, J., Embaye, N., & Whitcomb, D. H. (2003, August). In J. O'Brien (Chair), *Where do we stand? Locating transgender issues in psychology.* Symposium presented at the 111th annual meeting of the American Psychological Association, Toronto.

Carroll, L., & Gilroy, P. J. (2002). Transgender issues in counselor preparation. *Counselor Education and Supervision, 41,* 233–242.

Cass, V. C. (1979). Homosexual identity formation: A theoretical model. *Journal of Homosexuality, 4,* 219–236.

Chan, C. (1997). Don't ask, don't tell, don't know: The formation of a homosexual identity and sexual expression among Asian American lesbians. In B. Greene (Ed.), *Ethnic and cultural diversity among lesbians and gay men* (pp. 240–248). Thousand Oaks, CA: Sage.

Chung, Y. B. (2001). Work discrimination and coping strategies: Conceptual frameworks for counseling lesbian, gay, and bisexual clients. *Career Development Quarterly, 50,* 33–44.

Chung, Y. B. (2003). Career counseling with lesbian, gay, bisexual, and transgendered persons: The next decade. *Career Development Quarterly, 52,* 78–86.

D'Augelli, A. R., & Hershberger, S. L. (1993). Lesbian, gay and bisexual youth in community settings: Personal challenges and mental health problems. *American Journal of Community Psychology, 21,* 421.

D'Augelli, A. R., & Patterson, C. J. (2001). *Lesbian, gay, and bisexual identities and youth: Psychological perspectives.* Oxford, UK: Oxford University Press.

Dillon, F. R., Worthington, R. L., Bielstein Savoy, H., Rooney, S. C., Becker-Schutte, A. M., & Guerra, R. (2004). On becoming allies: A qualitative study of LGB affirmative counselor training. *Counselor Education and Supervision, 43,* 162–178.

Equality North Dakota. (2004). *Text of North Dakota Measure #1.* Retrieved December 14, 2004, from http://www.equalitynd.org/marriage.html

Fox, R. E. (1992). Proceedings of the American Psychological Association, Incorporated, for the year 1991: Minutes of the annual meeting of the Council of Representatives. *American Psychologist, 47,* 893–934.

Garnets, L., Hancock, K. A., Cochran, S. D., Goodchilds, J., & Peplau, L. A. (1991). Issues in psychotherapy with lesbians and gay men: A survey of psychologists. *American Psychologist, 46,* 964–972.

Gilfoyle, N. F. P., McHugh, J. L., Ogden, D. W., Wolfson, P. R. Q., Liazos, T. C., Polowy, C. I., & Taranto, R. G. (2003, January). *Brief for amici curiae in the Supreme Court of the United States.* American Psychological Association, American Psychiatric Association, National Association of Social Workers (NASW), & Texas Chapter of NASW. Washington, DC: Authors. Retrieved October 17, 2005, from http://www.lambdalegal.org/cgi-bin-iowa/news/resources.html?record=945

Greene, B. (1997). Ethnic minority lesbians and gay men. In B. Greene (Ed.), *Ethnic and cultural diversity among lesbians and gay men* (pp. 216–239). Thousand Oaks, CA: Sage.

Haldeman, D. C. (1991). Sexual orientation conversion therapy for gay men and lesbians: A scientific examination. In J. C. Gonsiorek & J. D. Weinrich (Eds.), *Homosexuality: Research implications for public policy* (pp. 149–160). Newbury Park, CA: Sage.

Haldeman, D. C. (1994). The practice and ethics of sexual orientation conversion therapy. *Journal of Consulting & Clinical Psychology, 62,* 221–227.

Haldeman, D. C. (2001). Therapeutic antidotes: Helping gay and bisexual men recover from conversion therapies. *Journal of Gay & Lesbian Psychotherapy, 5*(3–4), 117–130.

Haldeman, D. C. (2002). Gay rights, patient rights: The implications of sexual orientation conversion therapy. *Professional Psychology: Research and Practice, 33,* 260–264.

Haldeman, D. C. (2003). The practice and ethics of sexual orientation conversion therapy. In L. D. Garnets & D. C. Kimmel (Eds.), *Psychological perspectives on lesbian, gay, and bisexual experiences* (2nd ed., pp. 681–698). New York: Columbia University Press.

Herek, G. M., & Capitanio, J. P. (1996). "Some of my best friends": Intergroup contact, concealable stigma, and heterosexuals' attitudes toward gay men and lesbians. *Personality & Social Psychology Bulletin, 22,* 412–424.

Hershberger, S. L., & D'Augelli, A. R. (2000). Issues in counseling lesbian, gay, and bisexual adolescents. In R. M. Perez, K. A. DeBord, & K. J. Bieschke (Eds.), *Handbook of counseling and psychotherapy with lesbian, gay, and bisexual clients* (pp. 225–248). Washington, DC: American Psychological Association.

Human Rights Watch. (2001). *Hatred in the hallways: Violence and discrimination against lesbian, gay, bisexual, and transgender students in U.S. schools.* New York: Author.

Israel, T. (2004). Conversations, not categories: The intersection of biracial and bisexual identities. *Women and Therapy, 27,* 173–184.

Kirby, K. M., Whitcomb, D. H., Israel, T., & Worthington, R. L. (2004, July). In D. Whitcomb (Chair), *Cultural competency in LGBT counseling: Applying lessons from multicultural psychology.* Symposium presented at the 112th annual meeting of the American Psychological Association, Honolulu, HI.

Kuehl, S. J. (2003). Seeing is believing: Research on women's sexual orientation and public policy. In L. D. Garnets & D. C. Kimmel (Eds.), *Psychological perspectives on lesbian, gay, and bisexual experiences* (2nd ed., pp. 786–795). New York: Columbia University Press.

Lawrence and Garner v. Texas, 539 U.S. 558 (2003).

Lev, A. I. (2004). *Transgender emergence: Therapeutic guidelines for working with gender-variant people and their families.* Binghamton, NY: Haworth.

Liddle, B. J. (1995). Sexual orientation bias among advanced graduate students of counseling and counseling psychology. *Counselor Education & Supervision, 34,* 321–331.

Liddle, B. J. (1996). Therapist sexual orientation, gender, and counseling practices as they relate to ratings of helpfulness by gay and lesbian clients. *Journal of Counseling Psychology, 43,* 394–401.

Liddle, B. J. (1997). Gay and lesbian clients' selection of therapists and utilization of therapy. *Psychotherapy, 34,* 11–18.

Liddle, B. J. (1999). Recent improvement in mental health services to lesbian and gay clients. *Journal of Homosexuality, 33,* 123–132.

Matthews, C. R., & Lease, S. H. (2000). Focus on lesbian, gay, and bisexual families. In R. M. Perez, K. A. DeBord, & K. J. Bieschke (Eds.), *Handbook of counseling and psychotherapy with lesbian, gay, and bisexual clients.* Washington, DC: American Psychological Association.

McCarn, S. R., & Fassinger, R. E. (1996). Revisioning sexual minority identity formation: A new model of lesbian identity and its implications for counseling and research. *The Counseling Psychologist, 24,* 508–534.

Melton, G. B. (1989). Public policy and private prejudice: Psychology and law on gay rights. *American Psychologist, 44,* 933–940.

Morrow, S. L., & Beckstead, A. L. (2004). Conversion therapies for same-sex attracted clients in religious conflict: Context, predisposing factors, experiences, and implications for therapy. *The Counseling Psychologist, 32,* 641–650.

Patterson, C. J., & D'Augelli, A. R. (Eds.). (1998). *Lesbian, gay, and bisexual identities in families.* New York: Oxford University Press.

Patterson, C. J., & Redding, R. (1996). Lesbian and gay families with children: Public policy implications of social science research. *Journal of Social Issues, 52,* 29–50.

Redman, P. (1994). Shifting ground: Rethinking sexuality education. In D. Epstein (Ed.), *Challenging lesbian and gay inequalities in education* (pp. 131–151). Buckingham, UK: Open University Press.

Romano, J. L., & Kachgal, M. M. (2004). Counseling psychology and school counseling: An underutilized partnership. *The Counseling Psychologist, 32,* 184–215.

Rothblum, E. (2000). "Somewhere in Des Moines or San Antonio": Historical perspectives on lesbian, gay and bisexual mental health. In R. M. Perez, K. A. DeBord, & K. J. Bieschke (Eds.), *Handbook of counseling and psychotherapy with lesbian, gay, and bisexual clients* (pp. 57–80). Washington, DC: American Psychological Association.

Simon, A. (1998). The relationship between stereotypes of and attitudes toward lesbians and gays. In G. M. Herek (Ed.), *Stigma and sexual orientation: Understanding prejudice against lesbians, gay men, and bisexuals* (pp. 62–81). Thousand Oaks, CA: Sage.

Spitzer, R. L. (2003). Can some gay men and lesbians change their sexual orientation? 200 participants reporting a change from homosexual to heterosexual orientation. *Archives of Sexual Behavior, 32,* 403–417.

Weis, L., & Fine, M. (Eds.). (2000). *Construction sites: Excavating race, class, and gender among urban youth.* New York: Teachers College Press.

Worthington, R. L. (2003). Heterosexual identities, sexual reorientation therapies and science. *Archives of Sexual Behavior, 32,* 460–461.

Worthington, R. L., & Mohr, J. J. (2002). Theorizing heterosexual identity development. *The Counseling Psychologist, 30,* 491–495.

CHAPTER 17

Toward a Radical Feminist Multicultural Therapy

Renewing a Commitment to Activism

Susan L. Morrow, Donna M. Hawxhurst,
Ana Y. Montes de Vegas, Tamara M. Abousleman,
and Carrie L. Castañeda

Feminist counseling and psychotherapy, having emerged from the Women's Liberation Movement of the late 1960s and 1970s, would appear to be naturally situated in the social justice arena in counseling psychology. However, many of the qualities that characterized feminist therapy as it emerged from its grassroots origins (e.g., radical critique of mental health systems and psychotherapy, consciousness raising, political analysis and activism, and commitment to social transformation as integral to work with clients) have faded into the background as feminist therapy has become more mainstreamed and feminist therapists have focused increasingly on individual solutions to human problems (Marecek & Kravatz, 1998b; Morrow & Hawxhurst, 1998). In addition, for a significant period in the herstory of feminist therapy, multicultural perspectives were included unevenly and have been centralized only recently in an integrative feminist multicultural therapeutic approach (Bowman & King, 2003; Bowman et al., 2001; Brown, 1994;

Authors' Note: Correspondence concerning this chapter should be addressed to Susan L. Morrow, University of Utah–Educational Psychology, 1705 E. Campus Center Dr. Rm. 327, Salt Lake City, UT 84112–9255. Electronic mail may be sent via Internet to morrow@ed .utah.edu.

Comas-Díaz, 1994; Espín, 1994; Israel, 2003; Landrine, 1995). This chapter will review the evolution of feminist multicultural psychotherapy, identify theoretical underpinnings for its ongoing development, and propose a social justice agenda for feminist multicultural therapy in counseling psychology. In addition, we provide two examples from our work as feminist multicultural counselors for social justice.

Herstory and Evolution of Feminist Multicultural Counseling

Feminist and multicultural counseling perspectives emerged from the social and political unrest of the 1960s. As disenfranchised groups began pressing for social change, counselors and other mental health professionals found themselves stranded without the tools to address cultural differences and oppression (Atkinson & Hackett, 2004). Feminist and multicultural scholars and practitioners began to criticize traditional therapies for their racist and sexist underpinnings. Mainstream psychology, particularly through the diagnostic process, pathologized women, people of color, and others for qualities and behaviors that were outside of the White, male, heterosexual norm. In addition, "symptoms" arising from victimization (e.g., battered women's syndrome; anger or fear responses to racism, sexism, heterosexism, etc.) were often labeled as personality defects (e.g., borderline personality disorder, paranoia) instead of being understood in the context of trauma theory as a reasonable consequence of intolerable and oppressive circumstances.

Another criticism of traditional therapies was their exclusively intrapsychic focus (McLellan, 1999). McLellan also argued that traditional therapies assume that all people have equal access to choice and power and that each individual is responsible for her or his own life circumstances and unhappiness, failing to recognize the ways in which oppression limits choice and power.

The impetus for multicultural counseling came from increasing attention to cross-cultural counseling and cultural diversity emerging from ethnic and cultural movements of the 1960s and 1970s. The 1973 American Psychological Association (APA)–sponsored conference on clinical psychology in Vail, Colorado, was an important turning point for the profession of psychology when it was declared unethical to provide counseling services if the provider lacked the appropriate cultural competence to do so (Korman, 1974). Multiculturalism in psychology and counseling was not easily accepted in the field given the predominantly intrapsychic focus and the view that human distress was primarily psychophysiologic in nature. In response to this resistance, Smith and Vasquez (1985), in their introduction to a special issue of *The Counseling Psychologist* on cross-cultural counseling, wrote the following:

> We believe that the doctrine of color blindness in mental health and counseling psychology has outlived its usefulness. Therapists are not color-blind. Culture is a major factor in the life development of individuals, and ethnicity is a major form of identity formation and group identification. (p. 532)

Over the years, the multicultural competency (MCC) literature has focused on five major themes: "(a) asserting the importance of MCC; (b) characteristics, features, dimensions, and parameters of MCC; (c) MCC training and supervision; (d) assessing MCC; and (e) specialized applications of MCC" (Ridley & Kleiner, 2003, p. 5). Early training in multicultural counseling stressed the importance of knowledge, awareness, and skills in working with diverse populations; this trifold objective remains central in the training literature today. The multicultural counseling literature has moved from a focus on merely appreciating and celebrating diversity (as important a beginning as this was) to an insistence on examining the underpinnings of privilege, power, and oppression, particularly as they relate to groups of people who have been marginalized (Liu & Pope-Davis, 2003). The recent adoption by the APA (2002) of Guidelines on Multicultural Education, Training, Research, Practice, and Organizational Change for Psychologists was a stunning victory for the profession and provided psychologists with aspirational goals to guide their work with ethnic minority individuals.

Feminist therapy grew out of political activism in the United States in the 1970s and was conceived of as a political act in and of itself (Mander & Rush, 1974). From its inception, feminist therapy was a response to feminist critiques of traditional therapy practices that were identified as harmful to women (Chesler, 1997). Its goals were twofold: to engage women in a process of political analysis geared to raising their awareness of how interpersonal and societal power dynamics affect their well-being, and to mobilize women to change the social structures contributing to these harmful power dynamics (Ballou & Gabalac, 1985).

The first decade of feminist therapy was characterized by "a critical examination of mental-health services to women, feminist consciousness-raising groups as an alternative to psychotherapy, an activist and grassroots orientation to therapy for women, an emphasis on groups as opposed to individual psychotherapy, and assertiveness training" (Morrow & Hawxhurst, 1998, p. 38). In the second decade, feminist therapists worked to further define feminist therapy by identifying and describing its goals, its processes, and the skills needed to practice it (Enns, 1993). Books and articles about feminist therapy proliferated during this time, as did critiques from within and outside the discipline (Morrow & Hawxhurst, 1998).

As feminist psychotherapy became increasingly mainstreamed and professionalized, radical feminist writers such as Kitzinger and Perkins (1993) sounded the alarm that feminist therapy—along with therapy in general—served a domesticating, depoliticizing function. Instead of the "personal being political," the political was being inexorably whittled away until it was once again privatized, individualized, and personal. In a special issue of *Women and Therapy* (1998) on "Feminist Therapy as a Political Act," researchers and practitioners addressed this problem in a number of ways. Hill and Ballou (1998) found that feminist therapists addressed power issues in the client-counselor relationship and helped clients examine oppression and the sociocultural causes of distress; in addition, some therapists actively worked for social change by advocating for their clients and teaching clients to advocate for themselves. However, Marecek and Kravatz (1998a, 1998b) found very little in their study of feminist therapists that distinguished the therapists as uniquely feminist. Most of the characteristics espoused by participants in the study were characteristic of humanistic or New Age therapies (McLellan, 1999).

In addition, prominent women of color in psychology and social work spoke out, bringing to light some of the omissions that characterized the predominantly White feminist therapy movement (Comas-Díaz, 1994; Espín, 1994). These authors provided an analysis of how feminist therapy, as it existed then, was harmful to women of color and to other women who were marginalized because it ignored important dimensions of their identities and life circumstances (Brown, 1991, 1994). Women of color have historically—and justifiably—viewed feminism as ethnocentric and class-bound and have challenged the centrality of gender oppression espoused by many Euroamerican feminists (Bowman et al., 2001). Alternatively, Espín (1994) recognized the potential value that feminist therapy could have for women of color if it were to recognize ethnicity as a major component of oppression along with gender. In describing her own journey of evolution as a feminist therapist, Brown (1994) referred to her earlier practice as "monocultural" (p. 75) and articulated the importance of considering each client's unique constellation of identity dimensions and life circumstances rather than having her or him choose one aspect of identity on which to focus in counseling. This process of self-reflection has characterized multicultural and feminist endeavors with increasing honesty and success over time.

A particular example of the ongoing integration of feminism and multiculturalism arose at a working conference of the APA Division 17 Section for the Advancement of Women (SAW), where conference organizers had been explicit in their planning for a feminist multicultural agenda of a project that was intended to result in significant scholarly contributions in a number of areas of feminist multicultural research and practice. Although organizers and working group leaders embraced the terminology of "feminist multicultural" and working groups were recruited for diversity across race/ethnicity, international status, sexual orientation, gender, and professional/student status, issues emerged surrounding whose voices were privileged. The SAW conference became a microcosm for working with issues of privilege and voice. Feelings ran high, and the ensuing months led to conversations (informally, through presentations and discussion hours at APA, and through writing and publication), most particularly about the integration of racial/ethnic multiculturalism and White feminism. Following the conference, Bowman et al. (2001) provided a particularly powerful critique questioning the "real meaning of integrating feminism and multiculturalism" (p. 780). These conversations continue to be an important venue through which feminist and multicultural scholars and practitioners move toward greater integration. This does not necessarily imply that the road is straightforward or easy. A core challenge to this integration is to resolve a multicultural commitment to respect diversity of cultural values while simultaneously holding a feminist value that women's subservience to men is something to be overcome. The complexity of working to empower women when their cultural or religious beliefs dictate certain limits on their behavior is something that needs to be addressed continually in order to continue the dialogue.

Gradually, feminist and multicultural counseling principles and practices have been integrated into a form of therapy in which client and counselor analyze power dynamics on an interpersonal and societal level and include in this analysis the ways that the various aspects of the client's identity and privilege (e.g., gender, race/ethnicity, sexual orientation, age, socioeconomic status, religious affiliation, ability/disability status, etc.) affect these power dynamics. Scholarship has continued to emerge in this integrated field and promises to guide feminist multicultural practice (e.g., Asch & Fine, 1992; Bowman et al., 2001; Landrine, 1995; Palmer, 1996; Russell, 1996; Wangsgaard Thompson, 1992). Critical analyses of feminism by scholars such as Bowman and King (2003) continue to challenge the assumptions of White feminists, particularly around issues related to separatism and apparently contradictory identities, while at the same time raising questions about the dilemma faced by women of color when they are asked to "join with the struggle against racism and subordinate any feelings of discrimination by sex for the greater good of saving the race" (p. 60). Integrative work such as that by Israel (2003) identifies the importance and challenge of integrating multiple identities such as race, ethnicity, gender, and sexual orientation. As feminist multicultural counseling and psychotherapy move forward in the 21st century, several contemporary influences have import for our commitments to social justice.

Concepts and Principles Related to Radical Feminist Multicultural Counseling for Social Justice

Situated at the beginning of the 21st century, philosophical and political writings from critical theories, liberation psychology, and recent writings in counseling for social justice and third-wave feminist psychotherapy converge. The relevant concepts and principles from these approaches provide strong underpinnings toward enhancing the possibilities of feminist multicultural counseling and therapy for social justice.

Critical Theories

Critical race theory (CRT) is defined as a "radical legal movement that seeks to transform the relationship among race, racism, and power" (Delgado & Stefancic, 2001, p. 144). The CRT movement began in the 1970s and was largely influenced by critical legal studies and radical feminism; however, it has been used in education and other fields (e.g., Delgado Bernal, 2002) and is applicable to feminist/multicultural education, counseling, outreach, and research. Critical race theory and its associated perspectives seek to better understand divisiveness that surrounds issues of race and other forms of oppression and are strongly driven by activism (Delgado & Stefancic, 2001). From this perspective, then, for many feminist multicultural therapists, traditional forms of psychotherapy fall short in empowering clients, especially those who are oppressed or marginalized. One reason for this shortfall is that traditional therapies have been built on a European American worldview. Alternatively, critical race-gendered epistemologies emerge from numerous worldviews without regarding a White, Euroamerican, male lens as the standard by which other perspectives are measured (Delgado Bernal, 2002). Thus, CRT and other critical theòries help to understand the complexities with which clients are confronted.

"Critical race theorists have built on everyday experiences with perspective, viewpoint, and the power of stories and persuasion to come to a better understanding of how Americans see race" (Delgado & Stefancic, 2001, p. 38). This understanding is facilitated by the use of counterstorytelling, the hallmark method of CRT. Counterstorytelling is writing that attempts to critically analyze "accepted premises" held by the majority (Delgado & Stefancic, 2001, p. 144). Thus, storytelling becomes a tool to better engage and involve clients in therapeutic work.

CRT's emphasis on narrative analysis supports much of the work in which feminist and multicultural psychotherapists engage their clients (McLellan, 1999). CRT is also a powerful tool to train professionals who not only are empathic to a diverse clientele, but also strive to more fully understand the complexities of clients' lives that go beyond the immediate assumptions and who are genuinely attempting to meet clients' individual needs. Client experiences may not neatly fit the theories and textbook descriptions traditionally studied in graduate training; thus, the process of telling and listening to stories can lead client and counselor to an understanding of the complexities of their lives. CRT maintains that stories "serve a powerful psychic function for minority communities" because stories are opportunities to voice discrimination and also serve to uncover shared experiences of discrimination (Delgado & Stefancic, 2001, p. 43).

The quest to more fully understand individuals from diverse communities has led critical race theorists to focus on the specific experiences and needs of diverse communities. Some of the offshoots of CRT include feminist critical theory (FemCrit), Latina/o critical theory (LatCrit), and critical theory drawn from queer theory (QueerCrit). Feminist critical theory (FemCrit) is an important critical perspective that relates to feminist multicultural counseling. Specific to FemCrit is the deconstruction of the concept "that there is a monolithic 'women's experience' that can be described independently of other facets of experience like race, class, and sexual orientation" (Harris, 1997, p. 11). Overall, CRT and its offshoots seek to address the braidings of racism; sexism; heterosexism; and other forms of privilege, power, and oppression (Wing, 1997). These movements offer feminist multicultural counselors and therapists an opportunity to move beyond previous, more simplistic understandings of oppression to embrace the complexities that are necessary to understand in order to promote social justice.

Liberation/Critical Psychology

Like critical race theories, the basic premises of liberation psychology are to take a critical view of and challenge the accepted assumptions in the field of psychology. Liberation psychology had its genesis in liberation theology in Latin America, in which Biblical scriptures were reinterpreted with a focus on the poor ("a preferential option for the poor") and on social justice. In the field of education, Paolo

Freire (1970) insisted that this pedagogy "must be forged with and not for the oppressed" (p. 48), emphasizing a core principle that the work of those with privilege is not to liberate those who are oppressed but to join with them. This is best illustrated in the words of an Aboriginal woman, who said, "If you are coming to help me, you are wasting your time. But if you are coming because your liberation is bound with mine, then let us work together" (Instituto Oscaro Romero, n.d.).

Asserting that traditional psychology serves to maintain the status quo in society, Prilleltensky (1989) charged psychologists to become aware of their ideological constraints and to deliberate on "what constitutes the 'good society' that is most likely to promote human welfare" (p. 799). A core strategy for achieving this goal is conscientization, "the process whereby people achieve an illuminating awareness both of the socioeconomic and cultural circumstances that shape their lives and their capacity to transform that reality" (Freire, 1970, p. 51). Prilleltensky (1997) proposed an emancipatory communitarian approach "that promotes the emancipation of vulnerable individuals and that fosters a balance among the values of self-determination, caring and compassion, collaboration and democratic participation, human diversity, and distributive justice" (p. 517).

Counseling for Social Justice

Counseling psychology's growing commitment to a social justice agenda parallels the rise in critical perspectives across a number of disciplines, including CRT and critical/liberation psychology. A commitment to social justice implies that counselors and psychologists look past the traditional narrow focus on counseling and psychotherapy and address societal concerns such as discrimination and oppression, privilege and power, equity and fair distribution of resources, liberty, and equality (Vera & Speight, 2003). Social justice work has long been on the agenda for feminist and multicultural therapists, despite the mainstreaming and professionalization of feminist therapy described above. "A social justice–informed psychologist seeks to transform the world, not just understand the world" (Vera & Speight, 2003, p. 261). Vera and Speight further suggested that such a transformation will require that psychologists rethink their training models, question their overdependence on "individual factors to explain human behavior" (p. 261), and expand the scope of their interventions beyond individual counseling. In particular, counseling psychologists need to reclaim our historical roots of prevention, person-environment interaction, and a focus on strengths; attend to larger-scale interventions in institutions such as schools and social systems; work to influence public policy; and engage in psychoeducation, community outreach, and advocacy.

Third-Wave Feminist Psychotherapy

The third wave of feminism in the United States is characterized by a generation of young women—and men—who have been raised with expectations of greater gender equality and freedom from oppression than women of the first and second waves experienced, along with greater awareness of diversity (Bruns & Trimble,

2001). Many second-wave feminists have expressed concerns that their efforts will have been in vain, that their "hard-won gains will be lost and the women's movements of the twentieth century eliminated from the history books or relegated to the margins of history" (Kaschak, 2001, p. 1). Today's young have learned about feminism in the halls of academe in women's and gender studies courses rather than through the personal call to action initiated by incidents of overt discrimination—what second-wave feminists called the "click." Believing that their consciousnesses had already been raised and that equal rights were a practical reality, third-wave feminists have been "shocked and amazed when affirmative action was first overturned and abortion rights challenged" (Bruns & Trimble, 2001, p. 27). Third-wave feminist psychologists and therapists have identified a number of issues that have implications for feminist multicultural counseling and psychotherapy. Among them are the rejection of an economic model of power in which there are "haves" and "have-nots" in favor of one that is relational (i.e., power is shared), the incorporation of diverse narratives and experiences, and the need for mentoring from second-wave feminists (Bruns & Trimble, 2001). Rubin and Nemeroff (2001) wrote of "embodied contradictions of feminism's third wave" (p. 92) in which young women are addressing the many contradictions of their lives (e.g., viewing gender inequality as a thing of the past while at the same time experiencing an antifeminist cultural backlash). In addition, as third-wave feminists identify their own feminist agendas, they "aim to disrupt, confuse, and celebrate current categories of gender, sexuality, and race" (p. 93). Bodies and body image are central issues in which the third-wave feminist movement is grounded.

Critical race/gender theories, liberation psychology, counseling for social justice, and third-wave feminism have in common an unapologetic analysis of power and oppression and a commitment to advocacy and activism. Together, they enhance current multicultural and feminist agendas and move the field closer to actualizing its social justice agenda.

Toward a Radical Feminist Multicultural Model of Counseling and Psychotherapy for Social Justice: Implementing Feminist Multicultural Counseling

The practice of feminist multicultural therapy for social justice integrates historic and contemporary feminist theory and therapy with increasingly complex understandings of multiculturalism, critical theories, and radical perspectives. It involves feminist multicultural perspectives on assessment and diagnosis; the personal as political, including consciousness-raising, conscientization, and demystification; an analysis of power in psychotherapy—power dynamics between client and therapist as well as issues of privilege and power in the life of the client; the importance of group work to empower clients; and political action and activism.

Feminist Multicultural Perspectives on Assessment and Diagnosis

How can we work in academe or mental health systems that characterize the dominant culture without participating in the conventional wisdom of mainstream counseling and psychotherapy practice? Brown (1994) identified the "master's tools" (Lorde, 1984) as

> expressions of dominant attempts to control and define the process of healing so that it does not threaten patriarchal hegemonies. These are the techniques used to classify people, to impose social control . . . tools that a feminist therapist may find herself required to learn about and use. (p. 179)

Diagnosis is one powerful example of such a process and system of techniques presented in the context of science and medicine as reality. As feminist multicultural therapists working for social justice, it is essential to call into question psychiatry's sacred scripture (i.e., the *Diagnostic and Statistical Manual of Mental Disorders* [*DSM-IV*]) (American Psychiatric Association, 1994) and other "master's tools" to which we continue to subscribe.

Sinacore-Guinn (1995) proposed an approach to assessment and diagnosis that is culture- and gender-sensitive and that provides an alternative to traditional diagnostic models. She also provided a useful training model designed to assist students in learning how to make culture- and gender-sensitive diagnoses. Sinacore-Guinn proposed four broad categories that can be used to understand a client's presenting problem(s): (a) *Cultural systems and structures* are considered broadly and include such variables as "community structure, family, schools, interaction styles, concepts of illness, life stage development, coping patterns, and immigration history" (p. 21); (b) *Cultural values* have five value orientations: time (focusing on past, present, or future), activity (doing, being, or developing and growing), relational orientation (individualistic, communal, or hierarchical), person-nature orientation (in harmony with, control over, or subjugated to), and basic nature of people (innately good or evil); (c) *Gender socialization* concerns what is considered gender-appropriate across cultures and how gender variance is pathologized; (d) finally, *trauma* is a far-reaching and life-changing event that must be considered within its social environmental and sociopolitical context. Trauma must be considered both in its more acute forms (e.g., sexual abuse and assault) as well as in its more insidious and chronic forms such as racism or homophobia.

A failure to explore the above-mentioned categories in depth with a client could easily lead to an inappropriate diagnosis or a misdiagnosis by *DSM-IV* standards. Misunderstanding a cultural value could result in misdiagnosis (e.g., a child whose culture is oriented toward "being" rather than "doing" might meet many of the criteria for attention deficit-hyperactivity disorder). In addition, counselors need to consider the possibilities of bicultural struggles or conflicts that could lead to misdiagnosis, recognizing that, as cultural variables are more diverse (e.g., multiple oppressions based on gender, race, class, sexual orientation, gender expression), the struggle is more complex. It is troubling to speculate about the numbers of clients who are diagnosed and pathologized using *DSM* criteria when the presenting "symptoms" or problems could be explained and understood from the perspective of one's cultural context, bicultural conflicts, and history and nature of trauma. From this broad perspective, a client's "symptoms" may actually be a culturally appropriate, nonpathological management of cultural conflict. Only after an in-depth cultural analysis, which includes a consideration of bicultural conflict and trauma, can a diagnosis be made. Even then, it is important to call into critical question the existing systems of diagnosis and treatment, examining ways that they perpetuate oppression and injustice.

The Personal as Political, Including Consciousness-Raising, Conscientization, and Demystification

Consciousness-raising or conscientization engages people in an analysis of their sociocultural realities in such a way that they become better able to transform that reality. Part of this process involves demystification. Mystification was defined by McLellan (1995) as "the deliberate use [by the dominant group] of mystery, deceit, lies and half-truths for the purpose of presenting a false reality" (p. 146) in order to ensure the continued dominance of that group. Thus, consciousness-raising in the counseling setting engages clients in demystifying their experiences (e.g., workplace discrimination) so that they understand the systemic forces that affect them. Ideally, this process occurs in a group setting, whether the group is a political discussion forum such as those of the civil rights and feminist movements of the 1960s and 1970s, a political action project (e.g., Freire), or feminist multicultural group counseling.

Analysis of Power in Psychotherapy

Feminist multicultural therapists examine with the client power dynamics between client and therapist as well as issues of privilege and power in the life of the client. Thus, differing statuses related to privilege and power in the therapy dyad—those related to gender, race/ethnicity, culture, class, sexual orientation, and so on, as well as those related to the therapist-client hierarchy itself—are raised by the therapist in order to provide a context for understanding how dynamics of oppression may operate in the therapy relationship. It is important that this examination take into account not only the therapist's relative power but the client's as well if, for example, the counselor is a person of color and the client is White.

In addition to examining power in the therapy relationship, feminist multicultural therapy assists clients in analyzing power in their lives at the personal, interpersonal, and sociopolitical levels. Morrow and Hawxhurst (1998) defined empowerment as "a process of changing the internal and external conditions of people's lives, in the interests of social equity and justice, through individual and collective analysis and action that has as its catalyst a political analysis" (p. 41). They argued that empowerment involved both analysis and action, similar to Freire's (1970) notion of praxis, which combines reflection and action. Thus, consciousness-raising is accompanied by action taken on one's own behalf in the interest of freedom.

The Importance of Group Work to Empower Clients

The centrality of group work for feminist therapists emerged, in part, from the consciousness-raising movement of the early 1970s. Groups help to reduce the power discrepancy between client and counselor, and group dynamics serve to better facilitate clients challenging the power and mystique of the facilitator. A basic assumption of feminist group work is that "women need to carve out their own space in what is essentially a hostile environment" (Butler & Wintram, 1991, p. 16). The same can be said about members of any oppressed group. Thus, a core aspect of feminist group work is safety and trust, which needs to be established early and revisited. The isolation of women, people of color, lesbian/gay/bisexual/transgender (LGBT) people, as well as abuse survivors, people with eating problems, and the like, is potentially alleviated in the group setting. One of the most powerful aspects of participating in a group is finding out one is not alone. Groups also provide support and friendship and are a door to creating community. Although this goal may seem at odds with counseling approaches that discourage contact among members outside of group sessions, we believe that providing the option for group members to meet outside of group helps to reduce dependency on group leaders as well as empowering members by providing them the opportunity to give and receive support as well as build a social network and community. Groups themselves are microcosms of societal dynamics; thus, issues of privilege, power, and oppression can be dealt with in an open environment in the group, with facilitators modeling intercultural communication and respect. When people are able to successfully address their experiences of isolation, alienation, and oppression within the group setting, they are empowered to take steps on their own behalf and that of others in the world outside.

Political Action and Activism

Of all the components of feminist multicultural counseling, counselors and therapists—even feminist therapists—struggle most with the idea of political action and activism. We propose two foci for activism: activism on the part of the therapist and action/activism on the part of the client. The two can converge in powerful ways.

Counselors and psychotherapists earn their living trying to heal the wounds inflicted by an unjust society. Feminist multicultural therapists consider it unethical to do so without taking steps to change social systems that oppress our clients. The Feminist Therapy Code of Ethics (Feminist Therapy Institute, 2000) states that the feminist therapist seeks avenues to effect social change and "recognizes the political is personal in a world where social change is a constant." Many feminist therapists have removed themselves from political action in the feminist community in order to avoid overlapping relationships. Although feminist psychologists have led the way over time in the move to protect clients from therapists' abuses, there are situations in which these overlaps can be empowering if processed carefully. When client and counselor work together to create sociopolitical change, some of the mystique surrounding the therapist is reduced and the client sees herself or himself as capable and competent.

Client action and activism occur on a number of levels. It may be necessary for many clients to take their first steps as activists on behalf of themselves or their families before it is realistic for them to engage in larger social, institutional, community, or political change. Although it is not necessary for all clients to engage at a larger political level, it is important to understand the exceptional potential for empowerment and transformation that accompanies participating in social change, both for oppressed people and for their allies. When activist efforts converge on the part of a client-counselor dyad in which one is a marginalized group member and the other a dominant group member, the consequences can be astounding for both. For example, when a heterosexual counselor and a lesbian or bisexual woman client work together for gay rights, the counselor's commitments become more apparent, and the client is viewed by herself and her counselor as "the expert" in the activist work. Traditional therapeutic boundaries are challenged in an appropriate manner, and power in the counseling relationship moves toward a more egalitarian frame.

Feminist Multicultural Counseling for Social Justice in Action

At the heart of feminist multicultural counseling for social justice is the premise that this work is not restricted to the one-to-one psychotherapy hour. The examples below demonstrate the integration of research, practice, and community-based social change (in Example 1) and of counseling, prevention, education, and community action (in Example 2).

Finding Voice: The Music of Battered Women

The first author of this chapter, Sue Morrow, was privileged to consult with a faculty member in music therapy, Elizabeth York, at a nearby university, on York's qualitative investigation of the efficacy of music therapy and creative arts interventions with women who were part of a support group at the Community Abuse Prevention Services Agency (CAPSA). Dr. York took a feminist research standpoint, which she defined as "women speaking their truth" (York, 2004, p. 3). The researcher conducted participatory action research in which she and the regular CAPSA support group facilitator engaged with client participants using "women's music" over a period of 9 months. The 40 women who participated contributed their original songs, stories, and poems and took an active part in creating an ethnographic performance piece in order to share their experiences of domestic violence with shelter workers and the public. Fifteen of the original 40 women took part in a transformation from "therapy group" to "performance group" (York, 2004, p. 11). The profound healing and empowerment experienced by these women were accompanied by physical improvement in posture and coordination, "vocal projection, emotional expression, and eye contact" (p. 12). In addition to seven public performances as of this writing, the "Finding Voice" group has produced a book of poetry and a CD of the performance.

Co-author Sue Morrow interviewed Beth York during the writing of this chapter to discuss the feminist multicultural aspects of this project, and Beth's responses were thought-provoking. All of the women were White and English-speaking, ages 18–58, and all but one were members of the Church of Jesus Christ of Latter-day Saints (LDS or Mormon Church). Their socioeconomic statuses ranged from working to middle class. Beth described her process of dealing with her own biases—based on being a non-LDS woman in a predominantly LDS community—that led her to expect that these women would likely have accepted cultural norms and messages to remain in their marriages and that these women would have a more difficult time leaving battering relationships than non-LDS women. Beth dealt with the conflict between her feminism and wanting to respect the religious values of her participants. She shared with me her anger at the church for having inflicted these values on the women, but she took care to examine and manage her feelings by journaling; debriefing with her cofacilitator, who was LDS; and, as she put it, having a "crash course" in Mormonism. This raises again the issue of the potential conflict between feminism and multiculturalism and demonstrates how one woman managed this conflict in a social justice project.

University of Utah Women's Resource Center

The University of Utah's Women's Resource Center (WRC) offers a feminist therapy field practicum for graduate students in counseling psychology, professional counseling, and social work to receive training in feminist multicultural counseling. Co-authors Donna Hawxhurst, Ana Montes de Vegas, and Tamara Abousleman have worked together integrally with this practicum as trainer and students. The staff and practicum counselors at the WRC represent a broad diversity of ages, ethnicities, cultures, socioeconomic origins, and sexual orientations. The WRC has had a commitment over time to a multicultural agenda and has formed strong relationships with the University's Center for Ethnic Student Affairs (CESA) and the Lesbian, Gay, Bisexual, Transgender (LGBT) Resource Center. Over time, its multicultural perspective has moved from a focus on multiculturalism as race/ethnicity to one that is more inclusive. A turning point was reached as the WRC staff (including support staff) and practicum counselors moved into a shared commitment to a process that includes social justice as a major part of its mission and a regular self-reflective process in which individuals present their biases in a context of self-reflection, communication, feedback, and critical honesty.

Feminist multicultural therapy training includes not only bias awareness, but also a critical consideration of traditional therapy issues such as diagnosis and assessment. Sinacore-Guinn's (1995) model, described above, provides a framework for assessment and diagnosis at WRC, with trainees learning to look critically at traditional assessment modalities. Training staff and practicum counselors engage in this process by starting with themselves, looking at cultural issues and cross-cultural dilemmas, examining their own cultural values, identifying coping strategies, and looking at gender and trauma (including direct, indirect, and insidious) in preparation for assessing clients. In conjunction with WRC, co-author Tamara Abousleman has developed a feminist multicultural outcome assessment tool for use specifically in feminist multicultural counseling environments.

Counselors are trained not just to provide individual counseling, but to conduct groups. Groups at WRC are open to community members as well as students, faculty, and staff at the university. In addition, a significant component of the training program involves outreach, prevention, and social action programs designed to make changes in the university or the larger community environment. The WRC partners with CESA, the LGBT Center, and the International Student Center to create programs and groups that will meet the needs of women who fall outside the groups traditionally served by campus women's centers—predominantly White, middle-class women who are either nontraditional students (women returning to education) or already feminists. These partnerships have led to an International Women's Support Social hosted at WRC for international women students and wives of international male students, a movie series for young lesbian and bisexual women, and a focus group for women of color to explore issues related to campus climate.

One example of the integration of therapy training, outreach, prevention, and programming is in the area of violence against women, where the WRC takes a multifaceted approach. In addition to specific training in feminist therapy seminar in working with victims and survivors of sexual abuse, sexual assault, and domestic violence, staff and practicum counselors participate in Peers Educating to End Rape, most recently implementing a 40-hour on-campus training for sexual assault crisis advocacy training with a particular focus on involving campus services to students who might be at risk or unlikely to seek help. The training is designed to develop competencies in dealing with victims of sexual assault and to raise the consciousness of the university community about violence against women. This program is especially important because it creates partnerships with men who become involved as allies by working with young men on campus in prevention outreach, calling into question male socialization to perpetuate violence. In addition, the WRC partners with community agencies such as the Utah Coalition Against Sexual Assault and the YWCA's Women in Jeopardy Program for battered women in collaborative efforts to end violence against women and serve the needs of female victims and survivors.

In conclusion, feminist multicultural counseling for social justice offers a unique perspective to the development of counseling psychology in which the complexities of an increasingly diversified population and important social needs call for something more than "talking therapy." As counseling psychology revisits its roots in prevention and psychoeducation, feminist therapists must reclaim their roots as activists and multicultural counselors must move beyond knowledge, awareness, and skills to social action. Feminist multicultural counseling for social justice offers the potential to bring the best of all three traditions into alignment to contribute to meaningful and lasting change.

References

American Psychiatric Association. (1994). *Diagnostic and statistical manual of mental disorders* (4th ed.). Washington, DC: Author.

Asch, A., & Fine, M. (1992). Beyond pedestals: Revisiting the lives of women with disabilities. In M. Fine (Ed.), *Disruptive voices: The possibilities of feminist research* (pp. 139–171). Ann Arbor: University of Michigan Press.

Atkinson, D. R., & Hackett, G. (Eds.). (2004). *Counseling diverse populations* (3rd ed.). Boston: McGraw-Hill.

Ballou, M., & Gabalac, N. W. (1985). *A feminist position on mental health.* Springfield, IL: Charles C Thomas.

Bowman, S. L., & King, K. D. (2003). Gender, feminism, and multicultural competencies. In D. B. Pope-Davis, H. L. K. Coleman, W. M. Liu, & R. L. Toporek (Eds.), *Handbook of multicultural competencies in counseling and psychology* (pp. 59–71). Thousand Oaks, CA: Sage.

Bowman, S. L., Rasheed, S., Ferris, J., Thompson, D. A., McRae, M., & Weitzman, L. (2001). Interface of feminism and multiculturalism: Where are the women of color? In J. G. Ponterotto, J. M. Casas, L. A. Suzuki, & C. A. Alexander (Eds.), *Handbook of multicultural counseling* (2nd ed., pp. 779–798). Thousand Oaks, CA: Sage.

Brown, L. S. (1991). Antiracism as an ethical imperative: An example from feminist therapy. *Ethics & Behavior, 1*(2), 113–127.

Brown, L. S. (1994). *Subversive dialogues: Theory in feminist therapy.* New York: Basic Books.

Bruns, C. M., & Trimble, C. (2001). Rising tide: Taking our place as young feminist psychologists. *Women and Therapy, 23*(2), 19–36.

Butler, S., & Wintram, C. (1991). *Feminist groupwork.* London: Sage.

Chesler, P. (1997). *Women and madness* (25th anniversary ed.). New York: Four Walls Eight Windows.

Comas-Díaz, L. (1994). An integrative approach. In L. Comas-Díaz & B. Greene (Eds.), *Women of color* (pp. 287–318). New York: Guilford.

Delgado Bernal, D. (2002). Critical race theory, Latino critical theory, and critical race-gendered epistemologies: Recognizing students of color as holders and creators of knowledge. *Qualitative Inquiry, 8,* 105–126.

Delgado, R., & Stefancic, J. (2001). *Critical race theory: An introduction.* New York: New York University Press.

Enns, C. Z. (1993). Twenty years of feminist counseling and therapy: From naming biases to implementing multifaceted practice. *The Counseling Psychologist, 21*(1), 3–87.

Espín, O. M. (1994). Feminist approaches. In L. Comas-Díaz & B. Greene (Eds.), *Women of color* (pp. 265–286). New York: Guilford.

Feminist Therapy Institute. (2000). *Feminist therapy code of ethics.* Retrieved November 22, 2004, from http://www.feministtherapyinstitute.org/ethics.htm

Freire, P. (1970). *Cultural action for freedom.* Cambridge, MA: Harvard Educational Review.

Harris, A. P. (1997). Race and essentialism in feminist legal theory. In A. K. Wing (Ed.), *Critical race feminism: A reader* (pp. 11–17). New York: New York University Press.

Hill, M., & Ballou, M. (1998). Making therapy feminist: A practice survey. *Women and Therapy, 21*(2), 1–16.

Instituto Oscaro Romero. (n.d.). *Krysallis: Internet resource for liberation psychology, theology, and spirituality.* Retrieved November 22, 2004, from http://www.krysallis.com/index.html

Israel, T. (2003). Integrating gender and sexual orientation into multicultural counseling competencies. In G. Roysircar, P. Arredondo, J. N. Fuertes, J. G. Ponterotto, & R. L. Toporek (Eds.), *Multicultural counseling competencies 2003: Association for Multicultural Counseling and Development* (pp. 69–77). Alexandria, VA: AMCD.

Kaschak, E. (2001). The next generation: Third wave feminist psychotherapy. *Women and Therapy, 23*(2), 1–4.

Kitzinger, C., & Perkins, R. (1993). *Changing our minds: Lesbian feminism and psychology.* New York: New York University Press.

Korman, M. (1974). National conference on level and patterns of professional training in psychology: Major themes. *American Psychologist, 29,* 301–313.

Landrine, H. (Ed.). (1995). *Bringing cultural diversity to feminist psychology.* Washington, DC: American Psychological Association.

Liu, W. M., & Pope-Davis, D. B. (2003). Moving from diversity to multiculturalism: Exploring power and its implications for multicultural competence. In D. B. Pope-Davis, H. L. K. Coleman, W. M. Liu, & R. L. Toporek (Eds.), *Handbook of multicultural competencies in counseling and psychology* (pp. 90–102). Thousand Oaks, CA: Sage.

Lorde, A. (1984). The master's tools will never dismantle the master's house. In A. Lorde, *Sister outsider: Essays and speeches* (pp. 110–113). Santa Cruz, CA: The Crossing Press.

Mander, A. V., & Rush, A. K. (1974). *Feminism as therapy.* New York: Random House.

Marecek, J., & Kravatz, D. (1998a). Power and agency in feminist therapy. In I. B. Seu & M. C. Heenan (Eds.), *Feminism and psychotherapy: Reflections on contemporary theories and practices* (pp. 13–29). Thousand Oaks, CA: Sage.

Marecek, J., & Kravatz, D. (1998b). Putting politics into practice: Feminist therapy as feminist praxis. *Women and Therapy, 21*(2), 37–50.

McLellan, B. (1995). *Beyond psychoppression: A feminist alternative therapy.* Melbourne, Australia: Spinifex.

McLellan, B. (1999). The prostitution of psychotherapy: A feminist critique. *British Journal of Guidance & Counselling, 27,* 325–337.

Morrow, S. L., & Hawxhurst, D. M. (1998). Feminist therapy: Integrating political analysis in counseling and psychotherapy. *Women and Therapy, 21*(2), 37–50.

Palmer, P. (1996). Pain and possibilities: What therapists need to know about working class women's issues. *Feminism & Psychology, 6*(3), 457–462.

Prilleltensky, I. (1989). Psychology and the status quo. *American Psychologist, 44,* 795–802.

Prilleltensky, I. (1997). Values, assumptions, and practices: Assessing the moral implications of psychological discourse and action. *American Psychologist, 52,* 517–535.

Ridley, C. R., & Kleiner, A. J. (2003). Multicultural counseling competence: History, themes, and issues. In D. B. Pope-Davis, H. L. K. Coleman, W. M. Liu, & R. L. Toporek (Eds.), *Handbook of multicultural competencies in counseling and psychology* (pp. 3–20). Thousand Oaks, CA: Sage.

Rubin, L., & Nemeroff, C. (2001). Feminism's third wave: Surfing to oblivion? *Women and Therapy, 23*(2), 91–104.

Russell, G. M. (1996). Internalized classism: The role of class in the development of self. *Women and Therapy, 18*(3/4), 59–71.

Sinacore-Guinn, A. L. (1995). The diagnostic window: Culture- and gender-sensitive diagnosis and training. *Counselor Education and Supervision, 35,* 20–31.

Smith, E. M. J., & Vasquez, M. J. T. (1985). Introduction. *The Counseling Psychologist, 13,* 531–536.

Vera, E. M., & Speight, S. L. (2003). Multicultural competence, social justice, and counseling psychology: Expanding our roles. *The Counseling Psychologist, 31,* 253–272.

Wangsgaard Thompson, B. (1992). "A way outa no way": Eating problems among African-American, Latina, and White women. *Gender & Society, 6*(4), 546–561.

Wing, A. K. (Ed.). (1997). *Critical race feminism: A reader.* New York: New York University Press.

York, E. (2004). *Finding voice: The music of Utah battered women.* Unpublished manuscript.

PART IV

Career and Vocational Issues

CHAPTER 18

Social Justice in Career and Vocational Aspects of Counseling Psychology

An Overview

Nadya A. Fouad

Social justice activities have long been applied through individuals' rights to work, advocacy about equality of work, and equal access to work for all. Indeed, vocational or work psychology had its very roots in social justice activities. Frank Parsons, the father of the field, began the vocational guidance movement with his work in Boston in the early 1900s. He established the Vocations Bureau, in which he helped young adolescent boys to find work at a time when public high schools were not available and child labor was common (Zytowski, 2001). He spoke passionately to various civic groups about the gap between the wealthy and the poor, and about the need to adequately prepare the young street boys (many of whom were orphans) for a career (Hartung & Blustein, 2002). O'Brien (2001) noted that Parsons "challenged inequity, called for moral actions, and ardently argued for . . . shared responsibility and ownership" (p. 73).

Parsons was involved with helping young boys make good career decisions, working with them individually, but he was also a social and political advocate as well, setting the stage for a long line of vocational psychologists interested in social justice. For example, counseling psychologists specializing in work-related issues developed the Employment Stabilization Project in the early 1930s, designed to help men find work during the Great Depression. Vocational psychologists were active after World War II in helping returning soldiers become trained for a career, and vocational psychologists and counselors were active in helping to develop career education programs in schools through the 1960s, 1970s, and 1980s.

While many vocational psychologists and counselors were effectively conducting individual counseling to help people (most often students) make work and career decisions, others were actively advocating for programmatic work-related interventions. For example, in the 1990s, the School to Work movement resulted in legislation designed to help students make the transition from school to work more effectively. Although some vocational psychologists were directly involved in school-based interventions (e.g., Fouad, 1997; Hains & Fouad, 1994; Solberg, Howard, Blustein, & Close, 2002), others were writing about the need to be more proactive at the legislative level (e.g., Worthington & Juntunen, 1997). Still others were advocating for the American Psychological Association to be more active with congressional representatives to include the psychological knowledge base in the legislation. In 1999, a multidisciplinary School to Work task force was established to synthesize the psychological literature related to School to Work transitions, and recommendations for policy at the congressional level were advocated. Unfortunately, the funding for School to Work programs was discontinued shortly after this task force published its report.

Currently, counseling psychologists' advocacy in the vocational and career realm is occurring at many levels. Vocational psychologists have been among the strongest advocates for expanding counseling psychology's traditional research base to increase our understanding of career issues for traditionally underserved populations: women (e.g., Betz & Fitzgerald, 1987; Cook, Heppner, & O'Brien, 2002; Fitzgerald, Fassinger, & Betz, 1995; Fitzgerald & Harmon, 2001); racial/ethnic minorities (Bowman, 1993; Cheatham, 1990; Fitzgerald & Betz, 1994; Fouad & Bingham, 1995; Fouad & Byars-Winston, 2004; Leong, 1995; Leong & Hartung, 2000); and gays and lesbians (Chung, 1995, 2003; Croteau, Anderson, Distefano, & Kampa-Kokesch, 2000; Elliott, 1993; Fassinger, 1995, 1996; Pope, 1995; Prince, 1995). A decade ago, Richardson (1993) exhorted vocational psychologists to attend to the work issues of all individuals, noting that too much vocational research focused on middle- and upper-middle-class individuals. More recently, Blustein (2001) echoed that concern, also calling for vocational psychologists to broaden the field and examine factors related to work for those poor or working-class individuals whose choices may be limited by opportunity or circumstances. He noted that "an inclusive psychology of working will help to broaden the impact of our scholarship with the overall intention of improving the conditions of work and of enhancing opportunities for the poor and working class" (p. 179).

Vocational psychologists have also encouraged programmatic interventions to increase an individual's access to work and to ensure equality in that access. Because work is often an avenue through which individuals can escape poverty and increase their ability to provide for their families, the social justice activities related to work and career psychology have typically emphasized eliminating barriers to work, equalizing the opportunities for preparation for work, and reducing prejudice and discrimination at work. Because work-related policies often have unequal implications for women and racial/ethnic minorities, vocational psychologists have also attempted to influence those policies.

The three chapters in this section are excellent examples of social justice activities in vocational psychology. Fassinger and Gallor provide a context for rethinking some of our fundamental assumptions about work and equity. Taking the metaphor of building a house, they suggest that the entire house (society's assumptions about work and equity) needs to be dismantled and rebuilt, but that we cannot use the original tools (assumptions) to do the dismantling or rebuilding. In other words, the very occupational structure of the United States economy is based on patriarchal hierarchies that serve to maintain the inequity in the workforce. Fassinger and Gallor present a compelling argument that more knowledge is needed, assumptions that blame the victim of discrimination need to be challenged, and policies need to be examined that maintain the status quo. They also advance the belief that we should extend our counseling psychology models to train scientist-practitioner-advocates. They encourage students to learn that science is not value-free, but that the very questions students ask in their research have social consequences.

The second chapter, by Toporek and Chope, traces the range of social justice interventions in vocational psychology, ranging from working with individuals to working as an institutional change agent. They provide two specific examples in which vocational psychologists worked systemically as agents of social justice, with the homeless and with individuals with disabilities in a large urban setting. Their chapter also provides an excellent review of some of the ethical issues that may arise as counseling psychologists embed social justice in their vocational work. For example, they point out that informed consent sometimes means considering how the community in which a client resides may be affected by the work of psychologists and, thus, may also need to be approached for informed consent. Two additional ethical considerations, limits of competence and adherence to client goals, are also discussed.

The third and final chapter in this section, by Juntunen, Cavett, Clow, Rempel, Darrow, and Guilmino, also provides an example of a programmatic vocational intervention but is a more in-depth examination of the development and maintenance of a partnership between the university and a community agency to support participants in a welfare-to-work program. Juntunen et al. provide a thorough review of the welfare reform movement, noting that, as a discipline, counseling psychology has been remarkably absent from involvement in this movement. They also provide a description of the program they developed, and they are refreshingly candid about the inevitable problems that arise in university-community partnerships and the ways they solved the problems.

The chapters in this section, then, contribute to our understanding of counseling psychology's approach to social justice in the work and vocational arena in several ways. All three chapters provide unique perspectives on policy and social implications of advocacy related to work. All three also provide a glimpse into how three sets of scholars, working in distinctly different corners of the United States, would "push the envelope" in vocational psychology to use their expertise and knowledge for the greater good.

References

Betz, N. E., & Fitzgerald, L. F. (1987). *The career psychology of women.* San Diego, CA: Academic Press.

Blustein, D. L. (2001). Extending the reach of vocational psychology: Toward an inclusive and integrated psychology of working. *Journal of Vocational Behavior, 59,* 171–182.

Bowman, S. L. (1993). Career intervention strategies for ethnic minorities. *Career Development Quarterly, 42,* 14–25.

Cheatham, H. E. (1990). Africentricity and career development of African Americans. *Career Development Quarterly, 38,* 334–346.

Chung, Y. B. (1995). Career decision making of lesbian, gay, and bisexual individuals. *Career Development Quarterly, 44,* 178–190.

Chung, Y. B. (2003). Career counseling with lesbian, gay, bisexual, and transgendered persons: The next decade. *Career Development Quarterly, 52,* 78–85.

Cook, E. P., Heppner, M. J., & O'Brien, K. M. (2002). Feminism and women's career development: An ecological perspective. In S. G. Niles (Ed.), *Adult career development: Concepts, issues and practices* (3rd ed., pp. 168–189). Columbus, OH: National Career Development Association.

Croteau, J. M., Anderson, M. Z., Distefano, T. M., & Kampa-Kokesch, S. (2000). Lesbian, gay, and bisexual vocational psychology: Reviewing foundations and planning construction. In R. M. Perez, K. A. DeBord, & K. J. Bieschke (Eds.), *Handbook of counseling and psychotherapy with lesbian, gay, and bisexual clients* (pp. 383–408). Washington, DC: American Psychological Association.

Elliott, J. E. (1993). Career development with lesbian and gay clients. *Career Development Quarterly, 41,* 210–226.

Fassinger, R. E. (1995). From invisibility to integration: Lesbian identity in the workplace. *Career Development Quarterly, 44,* 148–167.

Fassinger, R. E. (1996). Notes from the margins: Integrating lesbian experience into the vocational psychology of women. *Journal of Vocational Behavior, 48,* 160–175.

Fitzgerald, L. F., & Betz, N. E. (1994). Career development in cultural context: The role of gender, race, class, and sexual orientation. In M. L. Savikas & R. W. Lent (Eds.), *Convergence in career development theories: Implications for science and practice* (pp. 103–117). Palo Alto, CA: CPP Books.

Fitzgerald, L. F., Fassinger, R. E., & Betz, N. E. (1995). Theoretical advances in the study of women's career development. In W. B. Walsh & S. H. Osipow (Eds.), *Handbook of vocational psychology: Theory, research, and practice* (2nd ed., pp. 67–109). Hillsdale, NJ: Lawrence Erlbaum.

Fitzgerald, L. F., & Harmon, L. W. (2001). Women's career development: A postmodern update. In F. T. L. Leong & A. Barak (Eds.), *Contemporary models in vocational psychology: A volume in honor of Samuel H. Osipow* (pp. 207–230). Mahwah, NJ: Lawrence Erlbaum.

Fouad, N. A., & Byars-Winston, A. M. (2004). Work: Cultural perspectives on career choices and decision-making. In R. T. Carter (Ed.), *Handbook of racial/cultural psychology.* New York: Wiley.

Fouad, N. A., & Bingham, R. (1995). Career counseling with racial/ethnic minorities. In B. Walsh & S. Osipow (Eds.), *Handbook of vocational psychology* (2nd ed., pp. 331–366). Hillsdale, NJ: Lawrence Erlbaum.

Fouad, N. A. (1997). School to work transition: Voice from an implementer. *The Counseling Psychologist, 25,* 403–412.

Hains, A. A., & Fouad, N. A. (1994). The best laid plans: Assessment in an inner city high school. *Measurement and Evaluation in Counseling and Development, 27,* 116–124.

Hartung, P. J., & Blustein, D. L. (2002). Reason, intuition, and social justice: Elaborating on Parsons's Career Decision-Making Model. *Journal of Counseling & Development, 80,* 41–47.

Leong, F. T. L. (Ed.). (1995). *Career development and vocational behavior of racial and ethnic minorities.* Hillsdale, NJ: Lawrence Erlbaum.

Leong, F. T. L., & Hartung, P. J. (2000). Adapting to the changing multicultural context of career. In A. Collin & R. A. Young (Eds.), *The future of career* (pp. 212–227). New York: Cambridge University Press.

O'Brien, K. M. (2001). The legacy of Parsons: Career counselors and vocational psychologists as agents of social change. *Career Development Quarterly, 50,* 66–76.

Pope, M. (1995). Career interventions for gay and lesbian clients: A synopsis of practice knowledge and research needs. *Career Development Quarterly, 44,* 191–203.

Prince, J. P. (1995). Influences on the career development of gay men. *Career Development Quarterly, 44,* 168–177.

Richardson, M. S. (1993). Work in people's lives: A location for counseling psychologists. *Journal of Counseling Psychology, 40,* 425–433.

Solberg, V. S., Howard, K. A., Blustein, D. L., & Close, W. (2002). Career development in the schools: Connecting school-to-work-to-life. *The Counseling Psychologist, 30,* 705–725.

Worthington, R. L., & Juntunen, C. L. (1997). The vocational development of non-college-bound youth: Counseling psychology and the school-to-work transition movement. *The Counseling Psychologist, 25,* 323–363.

Zytowski, D. G. (2001). Frank Parsons and the Progressive Movement. *Career Development Quarterly, 50,* 57–65.

CHAPTER 19

Tools for Remodeling the Master's House

Advocacy and Social Justice in Education and Work

Ruth E. Fassinger and Susanna M. Gallor

Counseling psychology as a profession has a long history of association with advocacy and social justice in the arenas of education and work—directly through the legacy of pioneers such as Frank Parsons and Leona Tyler, and indirectly through the valuing of human strengths and the emphasis on educative interventions for difficulties in negotiating normative educational and vocational developmental tasks. Moreover, the rise of attention to diversity and multiculturalism in the profession has provided new opportunities and challenges for social action in education and work, and individual counseling psychologists are beginning to become more public and vocal about their social justice aims and activities (e.g., see Kiselica & Robinson, 2001).

This chapter focuses on broad-based social advocacy within the vocational arena (including both educational institutions and workplaces). The underlying assumption (well-supported in the literature) is that educational institutions and workplaces are embedded in societal structures that function—implicitly or explicitly—to advantage some and disadvantage others. Therefore, this chapter outlines necessary legal, policy, and professional changes aimed at creating schools and workplaces that are healthy and rewarding for all people. Because of space constraints, rather than presenting a detailed analysis of advocacy issues particular to every group marginalized by existing sociopolitical conditions (e.g., women, people of color, lesbian/gay/bisexual/transgender [LGBT] people, poor people, and people with disabilities), we focus here on general ideas, using specific groups simply for illustration. In addition, we write this chapter in the first person, in order to give voice to our recognition that taking a proactive stance in regard to social justice work is a deeply personal commitment.

To organize our ideas, we borrow a metaphor from the preeminent feminist scholar Audre Lorde, who asserted that "the master's tools will never dismantle the master's house" (Lorde, 1984, p. 112). The master's house consists of the patriarchal structures that frame our society and function to regulate entry and access to the resources within. An example is the occupational opportunity structure that marginalizes workers based on gender, race/ethnicity, class, sexual orientation, and disability, preventing them from full and free participation in the entire range of occupational possibilities. The master's tools are the methods and strategies—direct and indirect, explicit and implicit, deliberate and ubiquitous—systematically used to maintain those structures and repair them when they are compromised. An example of a strategy that buttresses the exclusionary occupational opportunity structure might be the "scientific" discourse around racial differences in intelligence, which seems to re-intensify during times of apparent educational and vocational advancement for people of color.

Lorde's argument, of course, is that oppressive structures cannot be torn down by using the very tools that built those structures in the first place. If the goal is dismantling racist educational practices, for example, engagement in discourse that rests, at its core, on a racist foundation will be a waste of time, as Lorde argues: "[The master's tools] may allow us temporarily to beat him at his own game, but they will never enable us to bring about genuine change" (1984, p. 112). Similar arguments have been made by other scholars; for example, Prilleltensky (1997) has asserted that one of the shortcomings of the seemingly positive empowerment model of psychological practice is that, despite its attention to context, its focus on personal rights keeps it firmly rooted in the very tradition of individualism to which it has been offered as a corrective. This illustrates the enormous difficulty in disrupting existing schematic structures when any of the assumptive underpinnings of those structures are maintained.

However, no matter how desirable, it is seldom feasible—in terms of skills, time, and resources—to tear down the existing house to the foundation and start rebuilding from scratch. And even if this were possible, the renovation would depend on using the same tools that were used to build the original house, because those are the only tools available. Of course, one could, theoretically, reinvent both the concept of what a house is and create the unique tools needed to build it, but that level of social change is well beyond what most of us as individual professionals can accomplish within our limited spheres of influence. So what is to be done with a pile of seemingly useless tools and a house that badly needs massive structural changes?

Measure Twice, Cut Once

It is critically important that the relevant knowledge base be sound before the dismantling of existing structures can begin, and, more specifically, that the recognition of oppression and power dynamics constitute an integral part of that knowledge—establishing what Prilleltensky (2003) refers to as "epistemic psychopolitical validity." The need for accurate information may seem obvious to those of us whose lives are organized around the acquisition of knowledge, but there is a great deal of myth and misinformation among those we seek to influence in our advocacy efforts, and fluctuations in the social and political climate are highly influential in determining the kinds of information that are pursued and merit credibility in the public eye (the attempts of the Bush administration to control scientific inquiry by imposing funding restrictions is a case in point). Moreover, much of the blatant educational and occupational oppression of the past has been replaced by more subtle forms of marginalization and discrimination, leaving the public (and perhaps even some of us) convinced that genuine change has occurred, while those who remain disadvantaged are even more prone to the self-blame of internalized oppression when they fail at enacting their plans and dreams (Fassinger, 1998, 2000, 2002; Fassinger & O'Brien, 2000). Using women as an example, we examine a few current workplace realities.

Despite some fairly radical social change during the past several decades, the work lives of most women in the United States today are still characterized by (a) pervasive difficulties in entering work environments dominated and controlled by men, (b) the notable absence of women in many career fields, and (c) persistent segregation into a narrow range of work roles characterized by less compensation and opportunity than roles afforded to men (see Fassinger, 2002, 2005). For example, White men make up approximately one third of the U.S. population, but they are still 85% of tenured professors, 86% of members of Congress, 85% of partners in law firms, 97% of Fortune 500 CEOs, and 100% of U.S. presidents. There are 73 (13.6%) women in the U.S. Congress at this writing, only 18 (24.7%) of them women of color. Of the 18 million people employed in administrative support (including clerical) positions in the United States, 79% are women, whereas 91% of the 14 million people employed in more lucrative precision, production, craft, and repair occupations are men. Even in fields traditional for women, such as education, men predominate at the top ranks. In the mid-1990s, women at Dartmouth and MIT held only 13% of managerial posts with salaries greater than $55,000, and only 6 out of 94 presidents of private PhD-granting universities were women. Approximately 97% of school superintendents in the mid-1990s were men.

Certainly, there has been dramatic change in women's entry into nontraditional careers in recent decades. The number of women with doctorates in science/technology/engineering/mathematics (STEM) fields, for example, has increased more than fivefold over the past quarter century. In the early 1960s, women represented only 3% of scientists in the United States (less than 1% were engineers), but had climbed to 20% by 2003 (14% of them engineers) (Government Accountability Office [GAO], 2004). Female science and engineering graduate student numbers increased from 35% in 1992 to more than 41% in 2002, and the number of science and engineering master's degrees earned by women has tripled since 1975. The participation of women and people of color in the scientific workforce is a critical issue in the United States at present because of vast gaps in projected growth rates in STEM fields (to 2.2 million jobs by 2010, a growth rate of 47%) as compared to steady declines in STEM degrees—the number of science and engineering doctoral degrees, for example, has declined by 6% since 1998, and bachelor's degrees in engineering and mathematics have decreased since 1990 by 8% and 20%, respectively (National Science Board [NSB], 2004). Because women and people of color represent the largest current and projected increases in labor force participation, their entry into scientific careers is thought to be crucial to the continued leadership of the United States in the scientific arena (NSB, 2004).

However, STEM fields remain overwhelmingly populated by men, and the intransigence of this problem can be seen in academic chemistry. In 1980, several of the top chemistry departments in the United States (Harvard, Stanford, MIT, University of Chicago, Columbia) contained either no female faculty or one woman; in 1997, these same departments all had one female faculty member, suggesting very little progress in almost 20 years. Similarly, the proportion of female faculty in medical schools at the rank of professor was below 10% in 1996, the same as it was in 1980. Hopkins (2004) projected that, at MIT, where it has taken a decade for women's numbers to increase from 8% and 7% in the sciences and engineering, respectively, to 14% in both areas, it will take fully 75 to 95 years to achieve equal numbers. Private institutions tend to lag behind public institutions in recruiting and retaining women in STEM fields, but overall, in the top 50 chemistry departments, women hold only 12% of all tenure track positions. In 1999, although women made up almost half (47%) of the college-degreed labor force, they represented less than one fourth (24%) of the STEM workforce, with women of color constituting less than one fifth of the female STEM workforce and only 4% of the overall STEM workforce (National Science Foundation [NSF], 2002a, 2002b). Although women now constitute the majority of college students, in 2000, they represented only two fifths of science undergraduates and less than one third of science graduate students (GAO, 2004).

In addition, women remain segregated in pockets of the STEM workforce. Of the 43% of STEM doctorates earned by women in 1999, 42% were in the social and behavioral sciences, 41% in biological sciences, but only 12% in engineering, 15% in computer sciences, and 21% in physical sciences; moreover, the engineering percentages represent an increase of less than 1% since 1966 (NSF, 2002a, 2002b). Patterns of STEM field location are similar for White and minority women, except that the proportion of Asian American women in the social sciences remains quite low; this is a consequence of larger patterns of ethnically based STEM field segregation, where African Americans, Hispanics, and Native Americans collectively constitute approximately 7% of the STEM workforce but are disproportionately likely to earn social science degrees and work in social services occupations, whereas Asian Americans, who compose 11% of the STEM workforce, are found primarily in engineering and computer science, with only 4% in the social sciences (NSF, 2002a, 2002b).

Field segregation and decreasing representation of women with advanced degrees in STEM fields indicate a well-documented "pipeline" problem for women—the further along in education, occupational entry, and career advancement, the fewer the numbers of women. For example, research suggests that women are now entering some STEM fields in numbers similar to men, but even when their academic preparation is equal or superior to that of men, women show a greater tendency to abandon STEM majors in college, both at the undergraduate and graduate levels. In 1999–2000, the numbers of women attaining bachelor's as compared to doctoral degrees were 47% versus 25% in mathematics, 40% versus 26% in the physical sciences, and 20% versus 16% in engineering (NSF, 2002a, 2002b). For women who remain in academe, the pipeline problem persists. In 1997, 12% of women were full professors, 25% were associate professors, and 37% were assistant professors and instructors; in 2002–2003, women in academe represented 56% of lecturers and instructors, but only 27% of full professors (NSF, 2002a). In grant support (critical for tenure and promotion in academic science), twice as many men as women applied for National Institutes of Health (NIH) first awards from 1988 to 1997, and although women were as successful as men in receiving first grants and competitive renewals, the overall percentage of NIH awards earned by women increased only slightly (18% to 22%) over the decade (NSF, 2002b). Fewer than 200 women are included in the prestigious 2,400-member National Academy of Sciences, most of them concentrated in biologically related sciences and very few in chemistry, physics, or engineering.

In industry, the largest employer of STEM-degreed workers, women are less likely than men to be employed (51% of women in 1999 vs. 68% of men) (NSF, 2002a, 2002b), and women largely are absent from managerial and leadership positions. For example, in 2004, of 42 publicly traded chemical companies, only 11.9% of members of their boards of directors were women, an average of 1.2 female directors per company. Only 6.3% of women were in executive officer positions (an average of 0.6 per company), and no women were serving as chief executive, operating, or financial officers ("Women in Industry," 2004). Moreover, projected increases of women in corporate leadership roles suggest very slow growth rates; 17% female corporate officers by 2005 were predicted in 2000 (Davis, 2000), a number that seems highly unlikely given current figures.

Salary discrepancies also persist, particularly with increasing levels of experience (NSF, 2002a, 2002b). Overall, 4.4% of female workers in the United States (vs. 2.8% of men) earn less than $10,000 per year, and only 5.5% of women (vs. 15.8% of men) earn salaries greater than $75,000; in 2002–2003, male faculty in academe earned more than women at every institutional level, in both private and public institutions, where the wage gaps were $13,972 and $11,155, respectively (U.S. Census Bureau, 2002). Wage gaps exist in STEM fields as well. In 1999, the median annual salary for female scientists and engineers ($50,000) was about 22% less than the median salary for men ($64,000); salary patterns for women of color in STEM fields are similar to those of White women, except for Asian American women, who fare slightly better because of their greater representation in computer science and engineering (where women's salaries are 12% less than men's) than in the social and life sciences (where women's salaries are 23% less than men's) (NSF, 2002a, 2002b). In the business sector, only 28 of the 755 senior executives of the top 150 Silicon Valley companies are women, and in 1990, only 6% of White women and 4% of women of color who were full-time salaried managers earned incomes in the top 20% of their field (Corcoran, 1999). Moreover, of the 100 best compensated Silicon Valley executives, only two were women; the average compensation package (including salary, bonuses, options) for men was $1.4 million compared to $830,000 for women. These figures do not even meet the minimum of $0.77 for every dollar earned by men that currently characterizes the salaries of women in the overall workforce. Women in different age and ethnic groups face different wage ratios, with the greatest disparities for older, Hispanic, and African American women.

Why are these disparities in participation, representation, and compensation so intransigent? A voluminous literature documents widespread systemic barriers to women's career development—terms like "glass ceilings" and "sticky floors" articulate the hidden but enduring structural nature of these barriers and fit nicely with our metaphor of the master's house. Modern sexism largely has replaced the overt discrimination of the past, where denial that discrimination exists combines with deeply entrenched nonconscious ideologies regarding women's roles, creating a series of micro-inequities that may seem insignificant in isolation, but add up over time to produce tangible cumulative disadvantage (Valian, 1998). Computer simulation research has been useful in illustrating this concept: The study of promotion practices in a hypothetical corporation demonstrated that small-scale gender bias—accounting for only 1% of the variability in promotion—resulted in 65% males at the top of an eight-level hierarchy after repeated promotions (Martell, Lane, & Emrich, 1996).

The specific kinds of micro-inequities that women face have been well documented in the literature and include occupational stereotypes; educational discrimination (including classroom practices, climate issues, exclusion, and lack of financial support); "chilly" workplace climates (including overt and covert sexism, racism, ableism, and homonegativity); lack of mentors; exclusionary "old boy" networks; occupational segregation and job tracking; double standards for behavior and accomplishment; unfair evaluation practices; inequities in the distribution of workplace resources (including salary and benefits); the added burden of "shadow jobs"; harassment and violence; tokenism; bias in vocational testing and counseling; norms and policies that complexify the home-work interface; multiple role conflict; and internalized oppression resulting in poor self-concept and low outcome expectations (for more detailed discussion, see Betz, in press; Fassinger, 2001, 2002, 2005; Phillips & Imhoff, 1997). Moreover, these problems often are exacerbated for women of color, lesbians, working-class women, and women with disabilities because of the interactive effects of multiple systems of oppression (e.g., racism, heterosexism, ableism, classism).

These kinds of inequities characterize the vocational lives of other marginalized groups as well, firmly attached to the "isms" that buttress the master's house. We share here some examples: Studies of LGB workers have documented that between 16% and 44% of them (more than one third of African American and more than one half of White LGB workers) reported workplace discrimination at some point in their careers, and more than one quarter of a recent sample of student affairs professionals reported discriminatory experiences in the job search process, particularly if they revealed their sexual orientation; one survey of 191 employers indicated that 18% would fire, 27% would refuse to hire, and 26% would refuse to promote a person perceived to be gay (American Psychological Association [APA], 2002). Studies of people with disabilities have indicated that only 20% of men and 11% of women with disabilities are employed full-time, compared to 80% of men and 54% of women without disabilities; in 2000, the employment rate among working-age adults with disabilities was only 24.5%, and people with disabilities are less likely than their nondisabled peers to be employed in jobs considered "optimal," with the biggest gaps at the lowest levels of education (Bruyere, 2000).

Salaries of people of color provide yet another example of inequity, as they still lag far behind those of their White counterparts, even when such factors as education, experience, occupation, and geographic region are equivalent. African Americans and Hispanics continue to be about twice as likely as Whites to be unemployed, and the median weekly earnings for employed African Americans and Hispanics ($468 and $396, respectively) are far less than the earnings of employed Whites ($591) (U.S. Census Bureau, 2002). Working White men are more likely (at 29.2%) than African American (18.5%) or Hispanic (11.4%) men to be managers or professionals; similarly, White women are more likely (at 33.4%) to be managers or professionals than African American (24.8%) or Hispanic (17.8%) women. Interestingly, the presence of a few highly placed people of color or women in the workplace appears to interact with the tendency for people to believe in a just world, resulting in the widespread misperception that the vocational meritocracy functions fairly for all (Valian, 1998).

Clearly, the existing knowledge base suggests that massive changes are needed in educational and occupational opportunity structures. But do legal and policy changes really make a difference in educational and workplace equity for people of color, women, LGB workers, and people with disabilities? We examine a few examples here.

The Glass Ceiling Gets More Pliable When You Turn Up the Heat

The battle over affirmative action provides a fertile ground for analyzing the effects of legal and policy efforts in promoting an agenda of equity and social justice for people of color. Many institutions of higher education instituted affirmative action policies in the 1970s, and enrollment of students of color changed dramatically. In the period from 1976 to 1993, the numbers of African Americans, Hispanics, Asian Americans, and Native Americans attending college increased 37%, 160%, 274%, and 62%, respectively (APA, 1999); the proportional representation of Hispanics in college doubled (from 3.6% to 7.4%); and the representation of Asian Americans nearly tripled (from 1.8% to 5.1%). From 1980 to 2001, the number of high school students of color who attended college increased from 2 million to 4.3 million, with African American student enrollment growing 56% to more than 1.7 million and Asian American and Hispanic enrollment tripling to 1 million and 1.5 million, respectively. Interestingly, the numbers of White students in college also increased by 18% during this time, undercutting the charge that affirmative action college admissions processes benefit some groups at the expense of others (APA, 1999).

It might be assumed that such changes would have occurred despite affirmative action, but the numbers suggest otherwise. Following the decision by the University of California Regents to eliminate race and ethnicity as one of the factors to consider in admissions, the Berkeley campus witnessed a dramatic 55% drop in minority admissions, and UCLA experienced a drop of 36%. In addition, the enrollment of underrepresented minorities in California medical schools declined 32% in 1998 (from its peak in the mid-1990s). In Texas, which also swept away affirmative action, African American enrollment in medical schools dropped 54% in 1997. A recent survey of 93 major research institutions found significant declines in minority enrollment in graduate science programs between 1996 and 1997; for example, the first-year enrollments of African American graduate students declined 30% and those of Hispanic students dropped 23% (APA, 1999). Although there may be additional factors accounting in part for these declines, it seems safe to conclude that affirmative action has had a dramatic effect on the participation of students of color in higher education.

The societal backlash regarding affirmative action is indicative of both its success and widespread misunderstanding about its aims of combating discrimination and fostering fair education, hiring, and advancement of qualified individuals. Opponents' charge that affirmative action creates preferences and quotas and thus results in reverse discrimination against White males highlights the power of accurate information in shaping public perceptions: One public opinion survey demonstrated that 59% of voters stated support for affirmative action after hearing a definition as "programs that expand access to jobs and education by creating a broader pool of applicants" (APA, 1999). The 2003 Supreme Court decision to uphold the University of Michigan's use of affirmative action in law school admissions decisions should be helpful in this regard, as it represents a clear legal affirmation of a compelling state interest in diversity in education, the military, and the workforce. Moreover, the pair of Michigan decisions (including the one striking down the university's point system used to implement affirmative action in undergraduate admissions) offers guidance for the defensible implementation of affirmative action policies. These decisions are likely to have far-reaching effects as institutions of higher education struggle to define "narrowly tailored" admissions programs and ensure that their policies are constitutional; in our own university, for example, the entire undergraduate admissions process is being reassessed and reorganized at this writing as a result of the legal counsel's interpretation of the Supreme Court's Michigan decision.

Another example of the effects of legal change is found in the battle over the extension of workplace benefits (e.g., health insurance, emergency and family leave, pension plans, use of recreational facilities, etc.) to unmarried or "domestic" partners. Same-sex couples have been at the forefront in this battle because they cannot obtain such benefits through legal marriage in any state except Massachusetts at this writing. Because benefits packages can comprise almost 40% of overall employment compensation (Mills, 2000), they are a tangible as well as symbolic step toward equal pay and equal rights for lesbian and gay workers.

In 1982, the first U.S. employer offered domestic partner (DP) benefits, but throughout the 1980s, fewer than two dozen other companies followed suit. In

1991, Lotus Corporation became the first publicly traded company to offer DP benefits, and many other companies in the high-tech sector followed. However, little change occurred outside this sector, and by 1995, only about 300 companies nationally offered DP benefits that included health insurance. Then, in 1997, San Francisco enacted the Equal Benefits Ordinance, requiring any employer under contract to the city or county to offer all employees the same benefits. Of 1,281 U.S. employers that added DP benefits in 1997, 1,228 were the result of the San Francisco ordinance; in 1998, 882 of the 964 employers adding DP benefits were attributable to this ordinance. It is also important that the San Francisco Human Rights Commission monitors compliance with the law; Los Angeles, which enacted a similar law in 1999, does not monitor, and as of July 2000, only 197 L.A. firms had been in compliance (Mills, 2000). In higher education, where approximately three quarters of the country's major research institutions currently offer domestic partner benefits, some of the change can be attributed to legal intervention; at the University of Pittsburgh, for example, where DP benefits are just being offered for the first time at this writing, university officials admitted that their decision was, in part, a fiscal response to a costly 10-year litigation brought about by several of their employees (Wilson, 2004). These examples suggest that enforceable legal mandates are critical in bringing about workplace equity.

Another example of the power of legislative change can be seen in the results of Title IX, which prohibits sex discrimination in any educational program or activity receiving federal funding; the most immediate and obvious application of this legislation was the requirement for schools to provide athletic support for women that was comparable to that of support for men. In 1972, when the legislation was enacted, 1 in 27 girls and women was involved in school athletics; now 1 in 3 is involved (Vasquez, 2002). Although data indicate that there are still major disparities between men's and women's sports participation and support, the dramatic influence of Title IX is undeniable. And lest sports participation be dismissed as irrelevant to career development, it is important to note that athletic scholarships historically have been a critical means of support for higher education for males; women's exclusion from sports thus circumscribes their structure of educational and occupational opportunity. Recently, there have been attempts to weaken or dismantle Title IX (e.g., the challenge by the National Wrestling Coaches Association, charging that Title IX requires quotas for female sports participation and thus results in the demise of many male sports programs), but the law has been upheld consistently (e.g., in 2003 by both a U.S. District Court and the presidential administration). In addition, there is increased attention at this writing to the applications of Title IX in the sciences; a recent GAO study of four federal science agencies that administer grants, for example, criticized the monitoring of compliance related to gender equity in both report form (GAO, 2004) and in public hearings.

Title IX also has been invoked in lawsuits related to safe educational environments for lesbian, gay, bisexual, and transgender (LGBT) youth. Recent research indicates that more than 80% of a national sample of LGBT youth had experienced verbal harassment over the past year, 42% had experienced physical harassment or violence, 25% reported hearing antigay slurs from faculty or school staff, and 30%

reported missing at least one day of school in the past month out of fear for personal safety (Cianciotto & Cahill, 2003). In terms of legally mandated protection, only eight states and the District of Columbia have passed laws banning discrimination or harassment of students on the basis of sexual orientation, five additional states have adopted antiharassment or nondiscrimination regulations pertaining to sexual orientation, and only three states prohibit discrimination and harassment based on gender identity and/or expression (Cianciotto & Cahill, 2003); thus, lawsuits based on other arguments are the only avenue of redress for many LGBT students and their families. In addition to Title IX, legal arguments have rested on the equal protection clause of the U.S. Constitution and the Equal Access Act of 1984; as of 2003, at least 15 lawsuits brought by students against their school districts for failing to stop harassment they were experiencing had been successfully litigated or settled, resulting in total damages of $2.3 million (Cianciotto & Cahill, 2003). There also are less reactive ways to engage educational institutions in social change; one example of the power of a more proactive stance in supporting LGBT students can be found in the state of Massachusetts. In 1995, Massachusetts instituted a statewide educational program designed to make schools safe for LGBT youth. From 1995 to 2001, the percentage of LGBT students reporting being threatened or injured at school dropped from 33% to 18%, despite better reporting (unfortunately, recent fiscal exigencies have eliminated or curtailed this program in many school districts, an example of the fragility of many social justice initiatives).

A final example of the powerful effects of legislation is found in the Americans with Disabilities Act, enacted in 1990, designed to prohibit discrimination based on disability, and requiring employers to make "reasonable accommodations" in order to hire qualified disabled workers. In one study of 1,000 disabled workers, results indicated that from 1990 to 1995, almost half (43%) of the participants moved into more integrated employment settings, and the proportion of individuals in competitive employment more than doubled (from 6% to 15%) during this period, suggesting positive impact of the ADA (Bruyere, 2000).

We have been arguing thus far for the importance of legal change in mandating educational and workplace equity. However, formal policy changes within organizations also can have tremendous impact, especially if initiated and supported at the top levels. An example of dramatic change was provided recently in the *Harvard Business Review* in a case study of a top law firm that successfully closed its gender gap in turnover through the committed efforts of its CEO. Using strategies such as holding educational workshops for all partners and managers, instituting a flexible system of accountability, accepting and promoting balance in the home-work interface, ensuring that women received premier assignments, mentoring, linking managerial compensation to performance appraisals that incorporated equity goals, and enlisting an external advisory council to monitor progress, the firm succeeded in nearly eliminating the gender gap in turnover and increased its percentage of female partners from 5 in 1991 to 14 in 2000, the highest among the "Big Five" firms (McCracken, 2000).

Returning to our earlier point that a sound knowledge base is a critically important foundation for legal and policy change, we emphasize here the proactive role that researchers can play in supporting advocacy goals. An example is provided by researchers at the University of Michigan, whose work influenced the Supreme Court decision upholding affirmative action. Gurin and her colleagues (cited in APA, 1999) analyzed national data collected from more than 9,000 students across 200 colleges and universities, as well as 1,300 students from the University of Michigan. The researchers found that both minority and nonminority students who reported greater classroom diversity and informal interactions with students from different backgrounds exhibited more complex thinking, greater intellectual self-confidence and engagement, greater motivation to understand the perspectives of other people, greater motivation to achieve, higher levels of interest in obtaining graduate degrees, and higher levels of citizenship. These results are consistent with other studies demonstrating that racially diverse educational environments are associated with positive intellectual and social outcomes for college students (e.g., Antonio et al., 2004), and that there are measurable performance benefits in the workplace when work groups can learn from members' different racial experiences (Lagace, 2004). More important, this research had a clear and strong impact on the decision making of the Supreme Court justices, and the ruling itself cites the work of Gurin and her colleagues.

Although research can support advocacy goals in innumerable ways, perhaps most convincing to some audiences are demonstrations of fiscal benefit. For example, there is mounting evidence of the tangible benefits of instituting child care programs. A cost-benefit analysis by one large banking firm of their limited policy of providing 20 days of back-up child care in emergency situations saved the company $825,000 in reduced absenteeism in only one year, suggesting that such policies are fiscally sound (Bond, Galinsky, & Swanberg, 1998). As another example, research indicates that domestic partner benefits are ranked the number one recruiting incentive for executives, that DP benefits increase the likelihood that gay employees will remain in an organization, and that DP benefits are, in fact, a very economical way to win the "talent war" currently being waged in the workplace (Mills, 2000). At IBM, for example, which instituted DP benefits in 1996, less than 1% of its 150,000 U.S. workers have requested the benefits; similar observations have been made regarding the potential effects of increased DP benefits prompted by same-sex marriage, the fiscal impact of which is projected to be negligible on most businesses and the federal government (i.e., more than 96% of businesses will have no additional costs related to health care DP benefits) (Badgett & Gates, 2004). As yet another example, this kind of research can challenge misperceptions of the Americans with Disabilities Act that it places unfair financial burden on employers in fighting expensive discrimination suits and providing costly accommodations; research indicates that employers prevail in discrimination suits 92% of the time, that 91% of employers do not believe that making accommodations is unduly expensive, and that actual costs of accommodation are under $1,000 in four out of five cases and no cost at all in one out of five cases (Bruyere, 2000). A final example of the possibilities of using research on fiscal issues to bring about social change is contained in recent provocative findings ("Women in Industry," 2004) regarding the financial performance of 350 Fortune 500 companies, in which companies with the highest average representation of women manifested a 35% greater return on equity and 34% higher total returns to shareholders than those with the lowest representation of women; although causal linkages cannot be assumed from these limited data, it seems safe to predict that researchers will be enlisted to explore these patterns, and subsequent studies might help to further illuminate the importance of women's presence in the workplace.

Clearly, legislative mandates, organizational policy implementation, and research that supports advocacy efforts all are critically important in prying loose the inequality embedded in the structure of educational and occupational opportunity. But exactly what are the changes we need to address, and where do we begin in making schools and workplaces more welcoming to all?

The Ornament of a House Is the Friends Who Frequent It

Many legal and policy changes exist that can open doors to the full inclusion and participation of all people in educational institutions and workplaces; we use the example of LGBT students and workers for illustration here. We also note that the American Psychological Association has issued numerous policy statements and amicus briefs in support of safer, more inclusive schools and workplaces, modeling quite clearly the professional responsibility of psychologists to engage in advocacy aimed at social justice goals.

In the LGBT arena, probably the most important legislative battle involves passage of the Employment Non-Discrimination Act (ENDA), a law that would prohibit workplace discrimination based on sexual orientation (APA, 2002). There is, at this writing, no federal protection from discrimination based on sexual orientation or gender identity/expression, leaving LGBT workers subject to an uneven patchwork of state and local laws in which only about one quarter of them are protected throughout the United States (Obear, 2000). Currently, only 14 states and the District of Columbia have antidiscrimination laws that explicitly name sexual orientation (an additional 11 states prohibit discrimination in their own public workforces), as well as 285 cities, counties, and government organizations; of those, 152 extend protection to employment in the private sector. Only four states and the District of Columbia, as well as a total of 153 public and private employers, explicitly prohibit discrimination based on gender identity/expression, and seven states have interpreted existing law to include some protection to transgender people (National Gay and Lesbian Task Force [NGLTF], 2004). Although many workplaces (e.g., 72% of Fortune 500 companies) have voluntarily instituted nondiscrimination policies specifically regarding sexual orientation, few also include gender identity/expression; a 2003 survey (Human Rights Campaign, 2003) of 120 companies gleaned from the Fortune 500 as well as *Forbes's* list of the 200 largest privately held firms indicated that although 95% had nondiscrimination policies covering sexual orientation, only 9% had policies including gender identity/expression. Although support for the much-needed ENDA is growing—in 2002, the number of companies endorsing it rose 50% (from 60 to 90, including 43 major corporations) (APA,

2002)—it has languished in Congress for years and is unlikely to gain momentum given the current conservative administration. In fact, in a recent alarming turn of events, the Office of Special Counsel ruled that LGBT federal employees will have no recourse if they are fired because of sexual orientation, and proceeded to remove information regarding sexual orientation from many government Web sites (APA, 2002).

A second important front for advocacy efforts in the LGBT arena is the ongoing fight for DP benefits, and we note that the extension of DP benefits (particularly health coverage) is much more than a convenient luxury, but rather a critical element of economic survival for many same-sex couples. At the current time, nine states and the District of Columbia, as well as about 5,700 U.S. employers (including about 70% of Fortune 500 companies) extend DP benefits, and it should be noted that DP benefits do not affect only LGBT workers—in 1998, of the 5.9 million unmarried partner households in the United States, only 1.7 million (28%) were composed of same-sex couples (Mills, 2000). Unlike heterosexual couples, however, most same-sex couples cannot legally marry in order to obtain benefits, so DP benefits provide critically important support while legislative battles are being waged on yet another important front: the legalization of same-sex marriage.

Like DP benefits, marriage rights are tied to economic survival, and there are more than 1,000 federal statutory provisions alone (e.g., social security, family medical leave, federal taxation, immigration policy) in which marital status is a factor in the determination or receipt of benefits and rights for (same-sex) couples and families (APA, 2005). For example, more than 1 in 10 same-sex couples include someone over 65 years of age, and nearly one quarter include a partner over the age of 55 (U.S. Census Bureau, 2002); the inability to marry poses threats to economic security for these aging same-sex couples due to discriminatory practices in monetary benefits (e.g., not receiving social security benefits, being taxed on inherited 401Ks and IRAs from one's partner) that are taken for granted by legally married (heterosexual) couples (U.S. Census Bureau, 2002).

At this writing, Massachusetts is the only state to have declared the restriction of legal marriage to heterosexual couples to be unconstitutional (thereby allowing same-sex couples to marry), but a recent ruling in that state expressly prohibits performing marriages for same-sex couples from other states. Moreover, 39 states explicitly prohibit same-sex couples from marrying with laws modeled after the 1996 federal Defense of Marriage Act (DOMA), which allows states to ban same-sex marriage, and 35 states introduced legislation aimed at preserving the traditional definition of marriage as a union between a man and a woman after the Massachusetts ruling and the contemporaneous spate of marriages performed in local jurisdictions (e.g., San Francisco, Portland) as a form of civil disobedience (Leonard, 2004). Together, these patterns suggest the existence of powerful forces of backlash, and the debate over same-sex marriage has been compared by some (e.g., Cooperman, 2004) to the debate over abortion in terms of its capacity to generate political controversy. Although the Federal Marriage Amendment (an attempt to define traditional heterosexual marriage as a constitutional issue) was defeated recently, the federal Marriage Protection Act was passed in the U.S. House of

Representatives a week later; it strips the federal courts of jurisdiction over challenges to DOMA, essentially blocking the courts from declaring the DOMA unconstitutional (the outcome of this legislation is unclear, as it also must be voted on by the Senate) (Peterson, 2004).

Another avenue for same-sex couples to establish at least limited claim to rights and benefits is through civil unions, and Vermont is the only state at this writing to grant civil unions. Unlike legal marriage, however, which is portable (i.e., those recognized as married in one state are recognized in every other state) and confers the broadest array of federal and state benefits, civil unions are restricted in both recognition and benefits to the state in which they are performed (i.e., unions performed in Vermont have not been recognized in other states, and benefits are limited to state benefits only) (NGLTF, 2004). Moreover, although Vermont's civil union legislation requires employers to provide the same insurance benefits to workers in legal marriages and civil unions (and insurance carriers have been mandated to write inclusionary policies), it remains unclear what the impact of Vermont's civil union law will be, especially on private employers. The only other state that provides marriage-like privileges at this writing is California, which has a domestic partner registry conferring state-level marriage benefits; however, a recent ruling of the California Supreme Court also nullified the nearly 4,000 marriage licenses that had been issued to same-sex couples in San Francisco in deliberate violation of state law (Peterson, 2004). Overall, legislative initiatives regarding legal protection of same-sex unions, as well as public opinion on the issue, are in a state of enormous flux, rendering it highly unlikely that LGBT workers will obtain benefits equal to those of their heterosexual counterparts through the mechanism of legal unions any time in the near future.

Because in many workplaces (e.g., most schools) conviction on a felony is grounds for dismissal, another important work-related legislative issue in the LGBT arena is the sodomy laws. Although the Supreme Court ruling in *Lawrence v. Texas* successfully overturned the Texas sodomy law (and rendered unconstitutional similar laws in 12 other states), citing its violation of privacy rights protected under the 14th Amendment, legislative backlash already has occurred. In Rhea County, Tennessee, for example, lawmakers attempted to introduce legislation amending the state criminal codes so that gays can be charged with crimes against nature, a frightening reminder that continued vigilance is needed to maintain the most basic rights and safety for LGBT people.

A final important front for legislative action in the LGBT arena involves the protection of LGBT youth in schools. As we noted previously, few states offer legal protection in schools from discrimination or harassment based on sexual orientation or gender identity/expression; moreover, five states expressly prevent the discussion of homosexuality in schools or mandate that references to it be exclusively negative (Cianciotto & Cahill, 2003). Dozens of states have parental notification laws with opt-out provisions (allowing parents to excuse their children from classes or assemblies dealing with sexuality), and at least one state (Massachusetts) is considering a bill that would convert its opt-out policy to a more restrictive opt-in law. Finally, the 2002 No Child Left Behind Act poses danger to LGBT youth in a number of its provisions, particularly its promotion of school vouchers for attendance at religious schools, which usually are exempt from nondiscrimination policies and also may be more likely to promote negative views of homosexuality (Cianciotto & Cahill, 2003). All of these legislative problems beg for intervention, and a policy statement from APA (issued in conjunction with the National Association of School Psychologists) (DeLeon, 1993) explicitly advocates for school environments that promote understanding and self-acceptance for LGB youth—a bold call to action for psychologists interested in social justice and change.

Lay Me on an Anvil, O God

"Lay Me on an Anvil, O God, Beat me and hammer me into a crowbar, Let me pry loose old walls, Let me lift and loosen old foundations . . ." Prilleltensky (2003) argues that social justice involves "transformative psychopolitical validity," what Kiselica and Robinson (2001) refer to as "advocacy counseling"—the involvement in personal and interpersonal action to bring about structural change and liberation. We consider here some specific actions counseling psychologists might take to tear down walls of inequality and oppression in education and the workplace (for more detailed discussion, see Fassinger, 2002).

Clearly, legislative efforts are crucial to equity goals. We must keep abreast of ballot initiatives at the federal, state, and local levels, and participate in lobbying activities, letter-writing campaigns, and other attempts to influence legislators (this is easy to do by joining a listserv in which policy updates and requests for help are routinely sent, are highly structured, and often require no more than signing a petition or sending a message electronically). As researchers, we can make our knowledge base more accessible and applicable to policymakers and the public, for example, through writing editorials and articles for these audiences in local and national publication venues. We also can obtain training to provide expert testimony in courtrooms or in the media, and those of us who enjoy leadership positions might run for local political office or the school board. At the very least, we can actively support those legislators who are friendly to our social justice issues (and let them know why we are supporting them). We can establish or become involved in local chapters of organizations such as the Human Rights Campaign in order to form a base of support for group efforts at lobbying and political action. Those of us who are very brave can challenge existing laws and policies as they affect us personally.

Policy changes at the institutional and organizational level also are crucial targets for our intervention. First and foremost is the need for nondiscrimination and antiharassment clauses in the policies, documents, and public relations materials of any organizations or institutions in which we are involved. Other critical policy issues to pursue that are related to the full inclusion of women, people of color, LGBT people, poor people, and people with disabilities in educational institutions and workplaces include mandatory on-site child care; liberal family leave policies; flexible work arrangements (e.g., flextime, job sharing, time-out tenure tracks); DP benefits for all unmarried employees with partners; handicapped-accessible physical structures and practices (e.g., scheduling meetings so that colleagues in wheelchairs may recover adequately from travel); required career, diversity, and sex education in schools; Internet use policies that address online hate and harassment; and inclusion of information about diversity in all possible contexts. To maximize our effectiveness as shapers of policy, we might start working collaboratively in institutions in which we already are active or have support (e.g., PTAs, church vestries, scout troops), and then move into other community organizations, strategically enlisting top leaders in change efforts. Simply providing resources also is an effective way to support organizations that are pursuing social justice aims (e.g., donating money to charities) or to shape institutional practices (e.g., leading an effort to donate or purchase books for the local library or establishing Web sites that offer online information). In terms of resources, we also can work to ensure that our monetary investments (e.g., retirement funds) are being used in socially responsible ways.

Education is another important way of engaging in advocacy. We can offer education to individuals (e.g., through mentoring programs such as Big Brother/Big Sister), and we also can provide our expertise (including pro bono services) to groups through interventions in workplaces, educational institutions, and community organizations, collaborating with them in providing workshops and educational programs, organizing panels, and creating other public events. We can organize or support ally groups, advise student groups, or serve as an omsbuds or equity officer in our workplace. In addition, we can support the efforts of our students and clients who want to engage in similar organizational change activities. As professionals, we need to direct energetic efforts toward preservice and in-service training—both of professionals outside our field (e.g., clergy, physicians, counselors, teachers, police officers, etc.) as well as our colleagues and students in our own graduate training programs. This last point leads us to our final area of consideration for advocacy efforts, but one that may be the most amenable to our immediate individual influence.

If All You Have Is a Hammer, Everything Looks Like a Nail

Perhaps one of the most salient reasons for the lack of overt involvement in advocacy and social justice work by counseling psychologists is that most of us receive little or no training in the roles and skills that would enable us to engage effectively in these activities. We end up embracing and enacting—whether through science or practice—decontextualized, intrapsychic approaches to the amelioration of difficulties that are presented to us as problematic (rather than engaging in proactive attempts to radically alter the status quo of disadvantage and restricted opportunity) because that is what we have been taught to rely on as our main professional role and that is where we have been permitted to develop tools for intervention. But such narrow training constrains our scientific imagination and clinical acumen, forming a nonconscious professional ideology that prevents us from seeing outside the confines of the structures and tools with which we are familiar. If all we know is the intrapsychic and the individual, then that is what we will see in our clients, students, and research participants, and we will continue to hammer away ineffectually at individual change when liberation needs to occur in a much broader social context.

In addition, there is evidence that our students are not being adequately trained to deal with most kinds of human diversity. Mintz and colleagues (Mintz, Rideout, & Bartels, 1994) found that more than half of a national sample of internship-level doctoral counseling and clinical students had never heard of the Principles for the Counseling and Therapy of Women (despite their publication in 1978 and subsequent wide dissemination), that only about 15% of their sample had taken a graduate-level course in counseling women or the psychology of women, that most (83%) of that 15% reported that the course had been an elective, and more than half (58%) of the total sample reported that no course related to women or gender was even offered in their training program. Similarly, a study by Phillips and Fischer (1998) of more than 100 clinical and counseling graduate students revealed that the modal number of hours of didactic training in LGB issues and LGB clients seen in practica was zero, almost three fourths of the sample reported never having had a supervisor with expertise in LGB issues, half of the respondents had never been encouraged to explore their heterosexist biases in coursework or supervision, and most reported that there were no visible LGB faculty or faculty with LGB expertise in their programs. Probably even less attention is given to disability and social class in most graduate programs. We pose the question that, if we are not training our students adequately in the very basics of human diversity, how can we train them in advocacy and social justice?

On previous occasions (Fassinger, 1998, 2000, 2002; Fassinger & O'Brien, 2000), Ruth Fassinger has argued for the radical reconstruction of our field, one that would augment our much-endorsed scientist-practitioner model into a scientist-practitioner-advocate (SPA) model of training and professional contribution. In doctoral programs, coursework necessary for the implementation of the SPA model would include legal and policy issues, consultation, forensics, and program development and evaluation. In addition to stand-alone courses, advocacy and social justice concerns would be infused throughout all courses; for example, individual client cases in practica could be analyzed for policy and social justice implications, counseling and vocational theories could be examined for their compatibility with advocacy goals, and ethics courses could include material on the ethical issues involved in advocacy and social justice work. Faculty and supervisors in most programs would need in-service training, because they are unlikely to be prepared to develop and implement such courses or strengthen existing courses with this material. While curricular changes are being made (and afterward), guest speakers might fill in knowledge gaps.

Within the research realm of the SPA model, students would learn that science is not value-free; that it is a political act with social consequences; and that there are social and policy implications of research, whether intended or not. They would learn to do research using populations other than introductory psychology students. They would learn to do large-scale, multisite collaborative studies, undertaken by diverse teams of researchers, including community members and other stakeholders. They would learn techniques for shifting the dominant discourse in their areas of interest to ensure inclusion and equity (e.g., studying the home-work interface as not just a women's issue, but one that also affects men; studying White privilege alongside racial/ethnic issues). They would learn to disseminate their work to diverse audiences, and journal policies would include the expectation that published research document social and policy implications of the findings.

In the future, assessing competence in students would be linked not only to knowledge regarding human diversity, but also to skills regarding advocacy. These issues would be incorporated into site visit criteria and accreditation requirements, and eventually linked to certification and licensing requirements. While programs undertake the massive change needed to help all students develop basic competencies regarding advocacy, doctoral programs and postdoctoral training sites could, at minimum, offer advocacy tracks (supported by both inside and outside experts) for those who want to pursue these activities more centrally in their careers. In short, students would learn that the privilege of their advanced professional training brings with it the obligation to use that training for social justice goals, and they would be given more appropriate intervention tools to use in those efforts.

Old Houses Mended, Cost Little Less Than New Before They're Ended

In conclusion, we note that home remodeling teaches an important truth: that any project undertaken will take far more time, effort, and resources than ever anticipated. Social change is like that as well. In part, our expectations are unrealistic, a problem exacerbated by our advanced education and relatively isolated work environments. We often assume that the world thinks much like we do, and that a little reasoned argument is all that is needed to bring about opinion—and thus policy—change. However, social change is slow, labor-intensive, and inefficient. Every new plank put into place can be torn down by fear and backlash, and we often have to build and rebuild over and over again, intrapersonally as well as interpersonally. We become tired and discouraged.

Our strength for the ongoing struggle can be found in collaboration and coalition. Together, we can shape policy, we can educate others, and we can use our professional credibility to tear down ignorance and discrimination. Together, we can bring our analysis of gender, sexuality, race, ability, and power to use as a crowbar for dismantling structures that marginalize and oppress. Together, we can build schools and workplaces that protect and shelter all who enter.

References

American Psychological Association. (1999). *How affirmative action benefits America.* Washington, DC: Author.

American Psychological Association. (2002). *Testimony submitted by the American Psychological Association to the U.S. Senate Committee on Health, Education, Labor, and Pensions for the hearing on Employment Non-Discrimination Act (ENDA).* Washington, DC: Author.

American Psychological Association. (2005). *Examining the Employment Non-Discrimination Act (ENDA): The scientist's perspective.* Washington, DC: Author.

Antonio, A. L., Chang, M. J., Hakuta, K., Kenny, D. A., Levin, S., & Milem, J. F. (2004). Effects of racial diversity on complex thinking in college students. *Psychological Science, 15*(8), 507–510.

Badgett, M. V. L., & Gates, G. (2004). *The business cost impact of marriage for same-sex couples.* Washington, DC, and Amherst, MA: Human Rights Campaign and Institute for Gay and Lesbian Strategic Studies.

Betz, N. E. (in press). Basic issues and concepts in the career development and counseling of women. In W. B. Walsh & M. Heppner (Eds.), *Handbook of career counseling for women.* Mahwah, NJ: Lawrence Erlbaum.

Bond, J. T., Galinsky, E., & Swanberg, J. (1998). *The 1997 national study of the changing workforce.* New York: Families and Work Institute.

Bruyere, S. M. (2000). Civil rights and employment issues of disability policy. *Journal of Disability Policy Studies, 11*(1), 18–28.

Cianciotto, J., & Cahill, S. (2003). *Education policy: Issues affecting lesbian, gay, bisexual, and transgender youth.* New York: The National Gay and Lesbian Task Force Policy Institute.

Cooperman, A. (2004, July 26). Gay marriage as "the new abortion." *Washington Post,* p. A03.

Corcoran, E. (1999, January 23). Women in technology compare experiences, challenges at meeting. *Washington Post.*

Davis, S. (2000, May). *An oddity no longer: Women scientists in the chemical industry.* Presented at the Chemical Sciences Roundtable, National Research Council, Washington, DC.

DeLeon, P. (1993). Proceedings of the American Psychological Association, Inc., for the year 1992: Minutes of the annual meeting of the Council of Representatives August 13 and 16, 1992, and February 26–28, 1993, Washington, DC. *American Psychologist, 48,* 782.

Fassinger, R. E. (1998, August). *Gender as a contextual factor in career services delivery: A modest proposal.* Paper presented at the annual meeting of the American Psychological Association, San Francisco.

Fassinger, R. E. (2000). Gender and sexuality in human development: Implications for prevention and advocacy in counseling psychology. In S. Brown & R. Lent (Eds.), *Handbook of counseling psychology* (3rd ed., pp. 346–378). New York: Wiley.

Fassinger, R. E. (2001). Women in non-traditional occupational fields. In J. Worrell (Ed.), *Encyclopedia of gender* (Vol. 2, pp. 1169–1180). San Diego, CA: Academic Press.

Fassinger, R. E. (2002). Hitting the ceiling: Gendered barriers to occupational entry, advancement, and achievement. In L. Diamant & J. Lee (Eds.), *The psychology of sex, gender, and jobs: Issues and solutions* (pp. 21–46). Westport, CT: Greenwood.

Fassinger, R. E. (2005). Theoretical issues in the study of women's career development: Building bridges in a brave new world. In W. B. Walsh & M. L. Savickas (Eds.), *Handbook of vocational psychology* (3rd ed., pp. 85–124). Mahwah, NJ: Lawrence Erlbaum.

Fassinger, R. E., & O'Brien, K. M. (2000). Career counseling with college women: A scientist-practitioner-advocate model of intervention. In D. Luzzo (Ed.), *Career development of college students: Translating theory and research into practice* (pp. 253–265). Washington, DC: American Psychological Association.

Government Accountability Office. (2004, July). *Gender issues: Women's participation in the sciences has increased but agencies need to do more to ensure compliance with Title IX* (Report No. GAO-04-639). Washington, DC: Author.

Hopkins, N. (2004, July 22). Comments delivered at U.S. Senate news release of GAO report on Title IX compliance, U.S. Capitol building, Washington, DC.

Human Rights Campaign. (2003, June 22). *Corporate equality index.* Available: http:// www.hrc.org/Template.cfm?Section=About_HRC&CONTENTID=23128&TEMPLATE=/ContentManagement/ContentDisplay.cfm

Kiselica, M. S., & Robinson, M. (2001). Bringing advocacy counseling to life: The history, issues, and human dramas of social justice work in counseling. *Journal of Counseling and Development, 79,* 387–397.

Lagace, M. (2004, June 21). *Racial diversity pays off.* Available: http://hbswk.hbs.edu/item.jhtml?id=4207&t=strategy

Leonard, A. S. (2004, July 22–28). Dubious GOP marriage bill. *Gay City News, 3*(330). Available: http://www.gaycitynews.com/gcn_330/dubiousgopmarriage.html

Lorde, A. (1984). *Sister outsider.* Freedom, CA: The Crossing Press.

Martell, R. F., Lane, D. M., & Emrich, C. (1996). Male-female differences: A computer simulation. *American Psychologist, 51*(2), 157–158.

McCracken, D. (2000, November/December). Winning the talent war for women: Sometimes it takes a revolution. *Harvard Business Review.* Retrieved from http://harvardbusinessonline.hbsp.harvard.edu/b02/en/common/item_detail.jhtml?referral

Mills, K. I. (2000). GLBT employees make gains in workplaces nationwide. *Diversity Factor, 9*(1), 8–11.

Mintz, L. B., Rideout, C. A., & Bartels, K. M. (1994). A national survey of interns' perceptions of their preparation for counseling women and the atmosphere of their graduate education. *Professional Psychology: Research and Practice, 25,* 221–227.

National Gay and Lesbian Task Force. (2004). *Ways to protect same-sex relationships: A comparison.* Available: www.thetaskforce.org/downloads/MarriageDifferences.pdf

National Science Board. (2004). *An emerging and critical problem of the science and engineering labor force.* Arlington, VA: Author.

National Science Foundation (2002a). *Science and engineering indicators: 2002.* Washington, DC: Author.

National Science Foundation. (2002b). *Women, minorities, and persons with disabilities in science and engineering: 2002.* Arlington, VA: Author.

Obear, K. (2000). Best practices that address homophobia and heterosexism in corporations. *Diversity Factor, 9*(1), 26–30.

Peterson, K. (2004, August 26). *50-state rundown on gay marriage laws.* Available: http://www.stateline.org/live/ViewPage.action?siteNodeId=136&languageId=1&contentId=15576

Phillips, J. C., & Fischer, A. R. (1998). Graduate students' training experiences with lesbian, gay, and bisexual issues. *The Counseling Psychologist, 26*(5), 712–734.

Phillips, S. D., & Imhoff, A. R. (1997). Women and career development: A decade of research. *Annual Review of Psychology, 48,* 31–59.

Prilleltensky, I. (1997). Values, assumptions, and practices: Assessing the moral implications of psychological discourse and action. *American Psychologist, 52*(5), 517–536.

Prilleltensky, I. (2003). Understanding, resisting, and overcoming oppression: Toward psychopolitical validity. *American Journal of Community Psychology, 31*(1–2), 195–201.

U.S. Census Bureau. (2002, March). *Current population survey.* Available: http://www.census.gov/apsd/techdoc/cps/cps-main.html

Valian, V. (1998). *Why so slow? The advancement of women.* Cambridge: MIT Press.

Vasquez, M. (2002, August). *Extending the ladder of opportunity: Breaking through the colored glass ceiling.* Presidential address at the annual meeting of the American Psychological Association, Washington, DC.

Wilson, R. (2004, September 2). Pitt to offer health benefits to same-sex partners, ending a decade's defiance. *Chronicle of Higher Education.* Available: http://chronicle.com/daily/2004/09/2004090202n.htm

Women in industry. (2004, August 9). *Chemical & Engineering News,* pp. 18–19.

CHAPTER 20

Individual, Programmatic, and Entrepreneurial Approaches to Social Justice

Counseling Psychologists in Vocational and Career Counseling

Rebecca L. Toporek and Robert C. Chope

Over the past 50 years, the U.S. economy has seen a dramatic change from manufacturing to service and technology, resulting in a gradual loss in the income-producing power of the people who have been titled "working class" (Leach & Chakiris, 1985). Globalization of manufacturing and service occupations, as well as the offshoring of many other jobs identified as working class, will continue to have an impact on the workforce (Niles, Herr, & Hartung, 2002; Peterson & Gonzalez, 2000). Economic and employment disparities have been exacerbated by the creation of a digital divide where some workers have serious problems developing upward mobility because of a lack of rudimentary computer skills (Ford & Whaley, 2003; National Telecommunications and Information Administration, 1999). In addition, public policy aimed at reducing public financial assistance for families living below the federal poverty level, lack of health care policies, and minimal resources for child care have also increased the difficulty faced by low-income and less educated workers (Rice, 2001; Welfare Law Center, 2002). It is within this climate that we have seen a glimmer of renewed attention to the link between social justice and counseling psychology (Fouad, 2001; Hansen, 2001; Hartung & Blustein,

2002; Herr & Niles, 1998). Two recent events demonstrate the growing rejuvenation of the role of social justice as a notable force in counseling psychology: Nadya Fouad's presidential address to Division 17 of the American Psychological Association (Fouad, 2001) and Editor Robert Carter's initiation of a regular social justice forum in *The Counseling Psychologist* (Carter, 2003). The significance of these two public commitments has given support for a more thorough integration of social justice as a central role in counseling psychology. Although the increased discussion regarding social justice in counseling psychology is occurring across all specializations, prime examples are seen in the vocational domain.

The field of vocational guidance, later termed career counseling, emerged in the United States during the latter part of the 19th century during a time characterized by social upheaval, political reform, and economic change, resulting in a general feeling of insecurity, poor employment opportunities, and displacement throughout the United States (Pope, 2000). It was during this time that Frank Parsons emerged as a socially responsible practitioner of the new field of vocational counseling, establishing the first career counseling center in the United States and a settlement house for young people who were displaced from their homes and sporadically employed or unemployed (Pope, 2000). As a social justice activist and counselor, Parsons's work demonstrated the essence of a scientist-practitioner-advocate model. He set the stage for moving beyond the framework of the individual counselor to create institutions, systemic change, and interconnections between disciplines (Davis, 1969). The career of Leona Tyler stands as another model of a social change agent through her work serving on local and state boards of peace organizations, providing counseling for conscientious objectors, and founding a veteran's counseling service at the end of World War II, later to become the counseling center at the University of Oregon (Sundberg & Littman, 1994).

In addition to the careers of notable psychologists such as Frank Parsons and Leona Tyler, there has been service and literature addressing a variety of social problems. Early efforts included the Employment Stabilization Research Institute (Darley & Paterson, 1934; Paterson & Darley, 1934), addressing widespread Depression-era unemployment, as well as Super's (1954) interest in manpower utilization in underdeveloped countries. Thompson, Super, and Napoli (1955) collaborated with Columbia University's Teachers College and the Veteran's Administration Hospital in metropolitan New York to create a model training program to provide counseling services to returning veterans.

More recently, counseling psychologists have contributed to literature regarding vocational barriers (e.g., Lent, Brown, & Talleyrand, 2002; Luzzo & McWhirter, 2001) and discrimination in the workplace based on gender, race, and sexual orientation (e.g., Liddle, Luzzo, Hauenstein, & Schuck, 2004; Root, 2003) as well as culturally relevant approaches to career counseling and development (e.g., Fouad & Bingham, 1995; Leong, 1995). In addition, there have been counseling psychologists involved in addressing the influence of social class (e.g., Fouad & Brown, 2000); welfare reform (e.g., Juntunen, chapter 21); and school-to-work transition (e.g., Blustein et al., 2002; Worthington & Juntunen, 1997), helping to increase the opportunities for people who have traditionally had difficulty moving into the workforce.

These efforts serve as beacons of commitment by individual counseling psychologists and vocational programs. However, there is a need for more coordinated efforts linking social justice and counseling psychology. We believe that if the integration of social justice and counseling psychology is to take place more consistently in the vocational domain, counseling psychologists need to see clearly how their roles and work can promote social justice regardless of the domain. In this chapter, we will focus on social justice approaches for counseling psychologists who work in vocational and career counseling by first laying a foundation suggesting some areas of critical knowledge and discussing a sample of ethical issues. We will then highlight individual and programmatic applications, presenting examples and considerations for implementation. Throughout the chapter, we use the phrase "social justice work" to refer to work that has, as its central mission, a focus on alleviating injustice and oppression of individuals and groups.

Foundations for Practicing From a Place of Social Justice

Whether the counseling psychologist is practicing individual career counseling, vocational program development, or consultation, an informed approach begins with a consideration of pertinent knowledge and potential ethical issues. We have identified four areas of foundational knowledge: interdisciplinary contributions, cultural competence, complex roles, and social justice resources. First, numerous disciplines outside counseling psychology have a history of addressing social problems (e.g., social work, social psychology, public health, community psychology, anthropology, sociology, education, law) and have been involved in practice, research, and public policy regarding poverty, discrimination, and other forms of institutional oppression. Partnerships that combine counseling psychologists' expertise in vocational psychology with the unique assets of other disciplines have the potential to better serve client populations, increase creativity used in approaching problems, minimize redundancy of services, develop strong and lasting political alliances, create a broader net for funding, and improve the visibility of counseling psychologists as change agents. In order to build interdisciplinary relationships, counseling psychologists need to become familiar with the work of other fields regarding the target problem, community, or population. They need to invest time in developing relationships both with the community and with other professionals with similar interests and goals. Finally, counseling psychologists need to have a clear sense of their potential contribution above and beyond the work that is already being done. Central to this notion is the ability to communicate outside the field regarding the profession of counseling psychology as well as the psychologist's role and potential assets.

As a second foundation for implementing social justice, psychologists must be working toward greater cultural competence, particularly as it relates to the clients' issues and background. Hargrove, Creagh, and Kelly (2003) proposed a guide for multicultural counseling competencies in career counseling based on Sue, Arredondo, and McDavis's (1992) tripartite model of awareness of own beliefs and attitudes, client's worldview, and culturally relevant interventions. As with multicultural competence, we believe that social justice work requires that counseling psychologists are aware of their own beliefs, values, and biases regarding work, money, career identity, and social responsibility. For example, it is important for a psychologist to understand the investment she or he may feel in having clients choose careers that the psychologist views as "socially responsible" and how the psychologist's values influence the extent to which interventions are consistently in the best interest of the client. In addition, numerous documents delineate competencies for working with different groups, such as women; ethnic minority individuals; gay, lesbian, and bisexual individuals; and individuals with disabilities.

The third foundation area reflects the breadth of roles for counseling psychologists working in vocational arenas. In addressing social problems and working with clients experiencing systemic injustice, counseling psychologists need to consider how their role may need to vary given situations presented. For example, Atkinson, Thompson, and Grant (1993) proposed a model that identified a range of appropriate roles for the psychologist given a client's level of acculturation, locus of problem etiology (internal or external), and the goal of counseling (prevention or remediation). Social justice issues, by their nature, have an external etiology, although they may manifest as internal distress or behavioral dysfunction. It is insufficient for counseling psychologists to work only toward alleviating clients' feelings of distress or dysfunction without addressing external problem sources. Applying Atkinson et al.'s model to a vocational situation, if a counseling psychologist is working with a client who is experiencing racial discrimination on the job (external etiology of the problem), the client is not acculturated to the dominant U.S. culture and has very limited English-language skills, and the goal of counseling is remediation, a reasonable counseling role would be that of advocate. Atkinson et al. identified three additional roles (i.e., change agent, adviser, and consultant) that are relevant when addressing problems that have an external etiology and when level of client acculturation and counseling goals vary. Similarly, in a discussion of the need for psychologists and counselors to integrate advocacy into their work, Toporek and Liu (2000) described a range of counseling roles and goals on a continuum from empowerment (individual and small scale) to social action (systemic and large scale). They proposed that psychologists intervene from any point along that continuum based on the nature of the situation, the client, and the expertise or strengths of the psychologist and client. Building on these models, we believe that where social justice issues are concerned, flexibility in roles is needed to strike a balance between situational, contextual, cultural, and ethical needs.

A fourth foundation is provided by adequate knowledge of resources that can address clients' needs, such as financial resources, advocacy resources, affiliation resources, and others. This includes knowledge of laws related to employment (e.g., Equal Employment Opportunity Act [Title VII], Age Discrimination Act); education (e.g., Higher Education Act [Title IX]); and disability (e.g., Americans with Disabilities Act), as well as familiarity with organizations that inform and enforce these laws and acts (e.g., U.S. Civil Rights Commission, Equal Employment Opportunity Commission, State Department of Civil Rights). Using an approach that integrates legislation and policy conveys a proactive and supportive stance to clients and reinforces the validity of the client's worldview.

Ethical practice is as important, and no less complex, in social justice as any other arena of psychology. Although a more comprehensive discussion of ethical issues in social justice work is available (see Toporek & Williams, chapter 2), we would like to highlight three issues: informed consent, adherence to client goals, and limits of competence. First, informed consent in a systemic approach means that the psychologist must not only provide adequate information to the identified client regarding possible interventions and outcomes, but also consider the system within which the client exists. If the psychologist is striving for systemic change, he or she may need to consider the extent to which the community might need to give informed consent or at least receive adequate information regarding the psychologist's work and how the community may be affected (Pope, 1990). Consider the following example.

> Dr. Lee is a counseling psychologist who has been hired as a consultant for a community career center serving recent immigrants with a lot of job transition. After meeting with several clients, she begins to suspect that some of the local employers have a pattern of terminating employees of certain ethnic backgrounds. Dr. Lee meets with a group of clients and begins to discuss ways they may band together as advocates to confront these employers. As a result of the confrontation with one of the employers, conflict within the community rises and tension mounts between neighbors given allegiances to the employers or the advocates.

This example suggests that although systemic interventions or community empowerment may be an appropriate alternative, clients need to have the opportunity to consider the potential ramifications of taking such action. By including a discussion and consideration of how the community may be affected, the psychologist provides more comprehensive informed consent and increases the likelihood that interventions will be more appropriate for the community.

Second, one aspect of competence reflects the psychologists' willingness to work cooperatively with other agencies, providers, or researchers to best address a client's or community's needs. There may be times that the goals of providers from different disciplines (e.g., law, social work, public health) seem to be at odds. In these cases, the client's best interest may be facilitated by ensuring that the client is clear about the role of the different agencies and by the psychologist taking a mediating role if appropriate and desired by the client. At times, the ethical course of action is to consider involving or referring to professionals in other fields to provide more competent interventions.

Third, in order to practice ethically, it is necessary for the counseling psychologist to maintain the client's goals in the forefront and navigate a balance when there is a conflict between the client goals and social change. If the client chooses to refrain from taking action in the face of injustice, the psychologist must respect those decisions, within legal constraints. For example, if a client is experiencing sexual harassment in the workplace and in the course of due process decides to discontinue fighting the sexual harassment, the psychologist must adhere to the client's wishes. However, the psychologist may choose to find an alternative way to address the issue as a systemic one provided that the client is not implicated or involved and privacy is maintained.

When an organization is the client and at the same time is a perpetrator of injustice, the complexity increases. In these cases, balancing between the ethical obligation to adhere to the client's goals and the greater good of others involved may be difficult. For example, if, in the course of providing training for a company's employees around motivational issues, the psychologist observes covert systematic racial discrimination within the organization, he or she needs to consider the charge from his or her client, the organization, and the welfare of the employees. Based on consultation and careful consideration of the impact of the problem, the psychologist can develop a range of alternative responses, such as informing the organization of the psychologist's observations, and recommend corrective actions.

The discussion regarding pertinent knowledge and ethical issues is intended to provoke critical thinking regarding potential issues that may arise in the vocational arena. Although we have not provided an exhaustive review, we would like the reader to consider these and other issues as we shift the focus to highlight applications of social justice in individual and programmatic career interventions.

Facilitating Clients Through Dilemmas of Social Justice: Individual Approaches

A variety of situations that may arise in individual career counseling are appropriate for a social justice approach, including harassment or discrimination on the job, barriers to employment, whistle-blowing, and decision-making dilemmas regarding social justice career choices. In this section, we have chosen to focus on two types of situations that have come up relatively frequently in our work providing career counseling in college, university, and private practice settings: workplace discrimination and career choice dilemmas. We will use the following case vignette to set the stage and then delineate considerations in each area.

> Jolenna, a 24-year-old single mother of two, expressed a desire to major in social work because she was "fed up" with the welfare system and believed there needed to be a change. She had seen her family, her parents, and her friends "beaten down by the system." Throughout her education, she had been challenged daily to balance family, school, and poverty. Jolenna discontinued counseling to focus on school but indicated that she would return after final exams. During her first session back in counseling, she reported feeling discouraged and disheartened. She disclosed that social work was not a realistic option because she needed to find a career and major that would provide more money for her family, and soon. She would not sacrifice her children's security just because she wanted to make a difference in the world. Besides, even if it was a viable career option, she was so aggravated by the sexist behavior of her internship supervisor that she was not even sure she wanted to be in this field.

Helping Clients Deal With Discrimination and Harassment

Experiences of discrimination or harassment based on gender, race, sexual orientation, religion, age, and disability status may take place in a variety of career-related venues, such as the workplace, government agencies (e.g., public assistance or immigration), educational institutions, or in the job search process. It is clear that these are social justice issues. What is often not clear to individual practitioners is the role that they might play in helping clients resolve these issues. Traditionally, the field in counseling psychology has emphasized internally focused interventions. Toward social justice, we believe that a wider range of roles may be necessary and should be considered after reviewing relevant information. We want to reinforce that throughout the process outlined below, the psychologist should implement basic counseling and multicultural competence in helping the client to deal with the effects of the discrimination or harassment. Often, people who are the recipients of persistent discrimination and harassment experience psychological, emotional, and physical distress that may manifest as depression, anxiety, posttraumatic stress disorder, and other mental health issues (Ibrahim & Ohnishi, 2001; Root, 2003). The following briefly describes a course of action that may be helpful for addressing discrimination and harassment when they arise as counseling issues.

Gain Familiarity With Relevant Documents

As we discussed in the Foundations section of this chapter, counseling psychologists should be familiar with relevant law and social policy regarding issues such as discrimination. In Jolenna's case, it may be helpful to partner with her to also become familiar with relevant policies and due process procedures within her training program and internship site.

Understand the Context and Gather Information

It is important to attempt to fully understand Jolenna's experience and the context in which the discrimination or harassment has taken place. In this process, it is important to proceed in a way that does not imply that she must "prove" her experience is real. Familiarity with types of harassing or discriminatory behaviors and strategies (Root, 2003) helps increase understanding of the client's experience. Helping Jolenna to develop tools and skills such as documenting offenses using specific behavioral and observable descriptions can serve her as well as provide the psychologist with needed information.

Determine Appropriate Role(s) and Provide Intervention

Two models discussed earlier, the three dimensional model (Atkinson et al., 1993) and the advocacy model (Toporek & Liu, 2001), can provide guidance using criteria about a client and situation. If empowerment or self-advocacy is the goal, then the role of the psychologist may involve helping the client to clarify what action the client might want to take (if any), understand relevant policies and due process procedures, possibly role-play the client's chosen course of action, and identify sources of support either from the organization or his or her community. Alternatively, an advocate role may be appropriate when the psychologist has access to power, beyond that of the client, that is critical in resolving the problem. When using the advocate role, it is important that the psychologist has a clear rationale for the need to be involved directly (Toporek & Liu, 2001). Most often, if advocacy is an alternative chosen, we also believe it should be in concert with the client's self-advocacy actions. A third role is that of a social change agent, wherein the psychologist acts on behalf of an issue, not a specific client. This type of action is typically implemented at institutional, systemic, or legislative levels.

As reported by Jolenna, her supervisor's sexist behavior was causing distress and contributing to her ambivalence about choosing a career option that she had hoped would lead to social change. At the same time, the conflict between her values and needs were creating further dilemmas that influenced her persistence in her chosen career path.

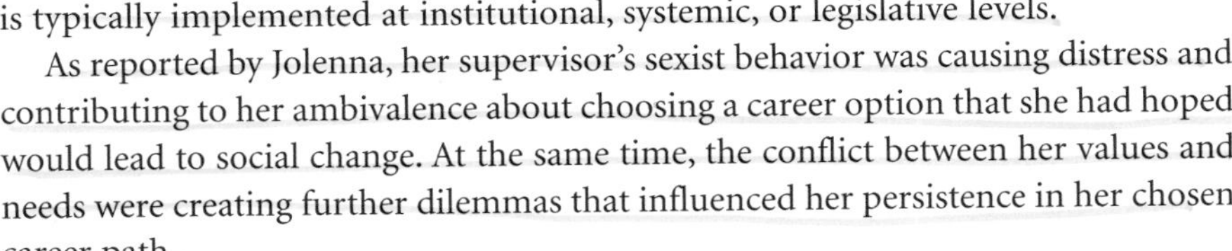

Helping Clients to Consider Becoming Professional Social Change Agents

In our work with clients who are struggling to make a career in social justice a reality, we have found that some critical areas do not seem to be addressed directly in most traditional theory. Many recent contributions to career counseling theory have widened the scope to make career counseling more relevant to previously neglected populations (e.g., Bingham & Ward, 1996; Cook, Heppner, & O'Brien, 2002; Fouad & Bingham, 1995; Leong, 1995). Nonetheless, we believe that there is a need for more explicit attention to the realities for low-income clients in identifying and reaching career opportunities and goals. Examples include individuals who have passion to change systemic injustice in society in their work but, because of financial realities, feel unable to follow this passion.

The case of Jolenna provides a context for discussing a framework that we have found useful in helping clients with limited economic resources and whose career goals, particularly those that are social justice related, often do not promise significant financial rewards.

Understand the Client's Contextual Cultural Framework

Numerous multicultural counseling theories attend to the client's cultural framework (e.g., Bingham & Ward, 1996; Fouad & Bingham, 1995; Hargrove et al., 2003; Sue et al., 1992). In addition, we believe that focused attention needs to be given beyond general cultural variables to attend to Jolenna's immediate financial needs, family obligations, and other responsibilities and how these influence her view of her future. Her cultural context is expansive, including competing demands, her view of her own degree of power in confronting larger systems (e.g., welfare system), and the extent to which she believes she may accomplish her career goals. A fuller understanding of her experience with her internship supervisor would be useful.

Develop a Plan for Contextual and Cultural Support, Including Affiliation and Basic Needs

Jolenna has clearly identified financial stability and commitment to her children as high priorities. At the same time, she has expressed the desire to contribute to the well-being of the community. Counseling can help Jolenna find ways to meet her basic needs through resources such as study groups, cooperative child care, scholarships and other sources of financial support, as well as finding others in the community with similar goals and beliefs. This respects the reality of her priorities and moves her closer to seeing that her goals are achievable. In addition, advocacy or empowerment (see Toporek & Liu, 2000) may be necessary regarding problems encountered with the social services system and with the discrimination Jolenna may be experiencing at her internship site.

Identify Life Goals and Career Options

Jolenna's life goals may be fluid yet can help to begin to draw a picture of the criteria she may want to consider when evaluating career options. Life goals may include desired or existing caregiving roles, geographic location, income, status, type of community, and role in community. Although some clients may need some help identifying "work that needs doing" (Hansen, 2001, p. 49), Jolenna knows her passion but may benefit from finding resources offering profiles of organizations involved in social change (e.g., Cowan, 1991), Internet Web sites for social justice organizations, and service organizations such as Vista and AmeriCorps for concrete information regarding career options.

Identify Mentors, Role Models, and Allies

The impact of Jolenna's experience in her internship has increased her hesitance to follow this career path. Conversely, positive role models, mentors, and allies enhance resilience and success in careers and educational endeavors (Allen, Eby, Poteet, Lentz, & Lima, 2004; Bahniuk, Hill, & Darus, 1996). This is especially relevant for individuals engaged in careers in which few colleagues reflect the individual's own background, culture, gender, values, and goals (Kalbfleisch & Davies, 1991; Thomas & Alderfer, 1989). Given that social justice work tends to confront status quo, entrenched systems, or emotionally complex situations, developing alliances can normalize difficulties, strengthen political power, and create new ways of looking at problems and solutions.

Develop Strategies for Increasing Opportunities and Decreasing Barriers

Getting involved in internships, shadowing, and part-time work can help Jolenna see realistic perspectives of the range of ways that she may address the problems she sees in the welfare system (Krumboltz, 1996). Combining these experiences with an examination of her perceived barriers and ways of addressing the barriers can help her to develop more career self-efficacy (Lent & Brown, 2002). Counseling can help Jolenna consider that change in the welfare system may be addressed through a variety of career options and academic majors (e.g., law, psychology, social work, or political science).

Develop Strategies for Strengthening Resilience

Confronting injustice, although sometimes rewarding, may lack a sense of accomplishment when working with very entrenched systems and difficult problems. Career counseling can help clients to develop clear and realistic indicators of career and life success, and exploring a client's life history and motivation for pursuing social justice may provide strength as well as challenge in the client's career. In Jolenna's case, she had stated that she was motivated to change the welfare system because she was "fed up." As well as providing strength, her motivation may also be fueled by unresolved experiences that could potentially hinder her success, self-efficacy, and satisfaction in a particular career.

Strengthening Jolenna's resilience for the difficult path balancing family and training as well as the likely demands of later social justice work could be done by helping her identify and enhance naturally occurring protective factors such as her sense of humor, self-esteem, self-efficacy, positive future expectations, and availability and use of external support systems (Garmezy, 1993).

Counseling psychologists may be called upon for a variety of social justice issues that arise in individual counseling. Although career counseling can make a significant contribution to the work of individuals, the extent of social injustice demands greater measures. We now turn our discussion to several examples of interventions that aim to influence greater numbers of individuals and communities.

Focusing on Institutional Change

It has become more evident that even if psychologists hold social justice as a core value, their influence is limited if they focus only on individual clients and not institutional change (Hall, 1997). Counseling psychologists may make a variety of contributions in the vocational arena at programmatic, institutional, or policy levels. In this section, we will focus specifically on programmatic interventions and begin by discussing issues in vocational program development oriented toward social justice. We will then highlight examples of two different types of programs: (a) a program integrating counseling training and job search services for homeless individuals; and (b) a social entrepreneurship approach providing job training, substance abuse counseling, and housing through self-sustainable endeavors.

Although vocational programs may differ dramatically in terms of their funding sources (public vs. private), service learning potential, and infrastructure, there are similar tasks in creating ecological models to address social concerns. The first task is to determine the needs of the population and community as well as existing resources and assets. Engaging community members as partners in goal setting and planning is critical and often a long process (LaFromboise, 2003). The extent to which the community is involved in the project may vary from intensive governing involvement to consultative involvement. Second, reviewing existing programs and research can lead to identification of programs and interventions that have been successful with similar problems in similar communities. As is true in individual counseling, a plan must be created that takes into account the demanding social context that some marginalized clients experience. Cultural considerations are paramount because interventions that may be very appropriate in one community may be wholly ineffective for another community. In developing a plan, a realistic estimation of the financial and personnel requirements needs to be made. Personnel must be attracted to the project for more than financial remuneration, and therefore strong "psychic" income must be made aware to the service providers and volunteers. Counseling strategies need to be developed that go beyond the traditional office experience, taking place on street corners and in the hallways of shelters and agencies. Finally, staff and the community served must meet regularly to adjust the program to meet the ever-changing demands of the clientele.

To illustrate vocational program services designed to ameliorate social problems (e.g., poverty, homelessness, substance abuse, etc.), we have chosen to highlight two programs that both provide vocational services but differ along significant dimensions. The first program was designed as a service learning "in the streets" program. The second was designed as an intricate, self-sustainable system.

The Roving Résumé Writers: Service Learning on the Street

The Roving Résumé Writers was an employment advocacy, service learning, and peer education project developed and run by students and faculty in the Counseling Department at San Francisco State University as a way to address local issues of homelessness and poverty. The project was started by a graduate student in the program, Henry Ostendorf, when he found himself disregarding the presence of homeless individuals in his daily life. The project's mission was to provide employment-seeking assistance for very difficult-to-reach clientele by pairing counseling graduate student volunteers with people who were either homeless or very low income. Meeting clients in their own environment, students provided résumé and job search assistance through workshops and individual counseling at community agencies, homeless shelters, and community- and church-related job programs, as well as street corners. The program served hundreds of unemployed veterans, homeless adults in shelters, battered women, runaway youth, ex-offenders, and impoverished families and job seekers in San Francisco.

Necessary components of the project included training and basic operations resources. The training component of the project had several aspects. The volunteer training consisted of a 3-hour orientation session, beyond the students' career counseling coursework, and learning about the volunteers' responsibilities and available community resources. In terms of content, the volunteers were trained in conducting 3-hour skill assessment interviews and assisting clients in clarifying employment objectives and work experiences, resulting in a résumé. The training also addressed volunteers' beliefs and assumptions about the population, and special attention was given regarding counseling skills needed for working with people who had difficulty with verbal communication, limited English skills, or problems with rudimentary hygiene. In addition, the training aimed to increase volunteers' understanding of the unique problems for individuals who did not have a permanent home and were often living on the streets, as well as the challenge of inconsistent employment records. These were clients who were unlike many of the individuals discussed in most of the career counseling literature and unlike most with whom graduate students had personal experience.

In terms of the operations component of the project, significant effort was expended to obtain necessary resources and support. A graduate student coordinator held primary responsibility, and a faculty sponsor served as an advisor. The project procured the assistance of the local phone company, which provided clients with a voicemail phone number to list on their résumés, often a serious barrier for homeless individuals seeking employment. Monies for incidentals (i.e., paper) were obtained through a small stipend from a San Francisco grant titled the Bay Area Homelessness Project.

The Roving Résumé Writers was successful in its mission for 7 years. Unfortunately, it did not remain viable because the primary funding agency, a local agency encompassing many efforts beyond the Résumé Writers, was defunded, and alternative sources of income were not identified. In addition, the commitment and availability of volunteers fluctuated given the ongoing turnover inherent in a 2-year graduate program. In addition, the faculty sponsor was absent for a year due to sabbatical and no other faculty had the agency network contacts or academic interest to maintain the program. Although the program was successful in meeting its immediate goal—providing employment service to homeless individuals—it was unable to maintain this success because it was not institutionalized.

Helms (2003) noted that one historical and structural problem in integrating social justice in counseling is that it most often relies on pro bono and volunteer work, or going beyond the scope of one's duty. Although many vocational counseling psychologists do this, it is difficult to sustain long-term efforts this way. Finding and applying for financial resources, developing contacts, training volunteers, and pioneering creative interventions requires multilevel skills and more than part-time effort. As an alternative to the volunteer model, social justice efforts have been successful with the creation of innovative, entrepreneurial, and self-sustainable organizations. The Rubicon Programs, Inc. provides an illustration of an enterprise that blends the efforts of psychologists with entrepreneurial and social justice outcomes.

Rubicon Programs, Inc.: An Example of Social Entrepreneurship

Organizations founded on principles of social entrepreneurship serve the public and sustain their efforts by becoming financially prudent organizations that are not dependent upon financial or volunteer contributions to exist. Social entrepreneurship or social capitalist ventures are similar to nonprofit organizations but differ in that they strive for economic self-sufficiency by providing a product or service for fee. These types of ventures typically utilize the expertise of business with other disciplines such as education, public policy, community health, and psychology. Counseling psychologists offer a unique perspective because of their expertise in working with the health and well-being of whole individuals.

The Rubicon Programs, Inc., are social entrepreneur programs in the San Francisco Bay Area that provide employment in exchange for housing, career counseling, substance abuse counseling, job training, mental health, and other supportive services to individuals who have disabilities, are homeless, or are otherwise economically disadvantaged (Rubicon Programs, 2005). In 1973, a psychologist, Rick Aubry, left therapeutic counseling and founded The Rubicon Program in an effort to address social problems on a broader scale (Overholt, 2004). A bakery and a landscape services company, the central and most profitable industries of Rubicon Enterprises, are staffed and managed by participants in the program. New employees are trained in basic work skills and evaluated on a regular, closely monitored basis throughout the program and then periodically after leaving the program.

Rubicon Programs has grown dramatically since its inception and now includes five different programs (Rubicon Programs, 2005). Rubicon Employment Services, one of the programs, provides job readiness services, basic skill classes, direct placement, and work experience/job skills training. Services are available for adults who (a) are out of the workforce, (b) have little or no work history or problems of interrupted employment, (c) have deficiencies in basic education skills, (d) are not able to get competitive employment without assistance, and/or (e) are low income. Fifty percent of the funding is derived from income gained through Rubicon Enterprises. Donations and grants provide the remaining resources. In addition, the program partners with community and governmental agencies regarding housing, employment, and other services. In 2003, 800 people received job training and 400 were placed in new jobs outside the Rubicon Programs.

The Roving Résumé Writers and Rubicon Programs, Inc., provide examples of two avenues through which counseling psychologists may support programmatic approaches to social justice issues. Although these programs provide examples of psychologists founding and directing programs, there are many other significant roles that psychologists may play in such endeavors. At the individual level, psychologists may provide a range of direct services to clients receiving career and vocational services. Moreover, counseling psychologists have expertise that they may contribute at organizational levels. Although ventures in social entrepreneurship have been dominated by individuals in business disciplines, counseling psychologists may serve as consultants, board members, and senior staff in such organizations given expertise in career development, multicultural counseling, training, and life-span development. In addition, counseling psychologists who work within educational institutions may be able to offer volunteer graduate students, training curriculum, grant resources, and institutional collaborations.

Implications for Theory, Training, Practice, and Research

For integration of social justice into the professional fabric and identity of counseling psychology, new and existing theory will need to be examined through a prism that considers the ability of each theory to address and contribute to resolving social justice issues. Multicultural theory has initiated this type of examination, and we suggest that counseling psychology, as a field, needs to go further.

Training in career development and vocational counseling needs to include more attention to the needs of clients in impoverished and difficult circumstances. Counseling psychology programs need to expand the scope of practice training to include skills for consulting with organizations and engaging in social action at organizational and legislative levels. Topics in career development and vocational counseling courses could include fairness in hiring practices, preventing workplace violence, confronting discrimination, working with institutional whistle-blowers, and facilitation of systemic change. Students benefit from the ability to access interdisciplinary skills and knowledge to help them form alliances with various types of service providers and scholars in the areas of community and social psychology, business, law, social work, public health, and others. Hence, efforts to develop practicum, externships, and internships in organizations that are addressing social justice issues in multidisciplinary ways would be fruitful. Finally, training in ethics should provide students with skills to examine roles such as change agents or bystanders in social justice concerns. Furthermore, standards of competence for working with specific populations must be considered an ethical practice and integrated into ethics, practicum, and internship experiences.

In practice, collaboration and competence are two central themes. Socially conscious counseling psychologists need to develop formidable alliances and strong support systems for real social change. The creation of new linkages between government agencies or between agencies and the private sector can lead to more creative joint efforts. For those providing individual career counseling, it is important to be competent in serving the specified population and be informed about resources and career trends pertinent to the populations or issues that are the focus of the psychologist's work. In addition, it is crucial to stay informed about political and legislative issues that may affect the community or population.

Another area of competence involves agencies and populations with which the psychologist has limited experience. One way to increase competence is to collaborate with a community agency that is providing direct service to this population, offering the counseling psychologist's expertise in exchange for consultation regarding the specific community. It is important that the community perceives the program and the psychologist as consistent and reliable, putting the needs of the community at the forefront. If a research agenda or university's goals take precedence, the community may question the extent to which the program can be trusted.

For those counseling psychologists interested in engaging in social entrepreneurship, a variety of resources are available, such as David Bornstein's (2004) *How to Change the World: Social Entrepreneurs and the Power of New Ideas*; organizations such as the Social Enterprise Alliance, which serves as a resource for nonprofit organizations working on self-sustainability; and Internet resources such as *Fast Company's* Social Capitalism Resource Center.

There is a need for research in many areas of social justice and counseling psychology, specifically, the role of social justice in counseling psychologists' work, the efficacy of social justice orientations in individual counseling and programmatic ventures, and the usefulness of different training models for raising students' awareness regarding social justice in vocational concerns. Given the scarcity of attention to social justice in counseling research, qualitative methods may be useful in assessing psychologists' work climate for receptivity and support for social justice interventions. This can help training programs to better prepare graduates for taking such a stance.

Generally, there is a need for research that examines how vocational psychologists integrate attention to social justice issues in their work. Baluch, Pieterse, and Bolden (2004) pointed out that while there has been a shift in the attempt of counseling psychologists and ultimately career counselors to be more inclusive of people who have been historically marginalized, there is a need for research on the impact of the change in service delivery. The framework for individual career counseling described in the first part of the chapter could be empirically examined to determine its comprehensiveness and usefulness for clients. Qualitative and quantitative research examining the effectiveness of social entrepreneurship in addressing social problems would be helpful, particularly in providing longitudinal data.

Finally, there is a need for counseling psychologists to more consistently consider research on social justice issues as a potential resource for informing social and public policy. Reporting research findings should go beyond academic journals and put forth implications in public forums such as popular media as well as judicial and legislative hearings.

Conclusion

Our goal in writing this chapter was to present concrete examples of implementation of social justice in vocational applications of counseling psychology. We believe that social justice is at the core of the profession yet has received minimal attention in terms of guidance for its actual application. Every counseling psychologist has the potential to make a significant and positive change in ameliorating the injustice incurred daily by people who are abused, discriminated against, and disenfranchised. Fortunately, there are inspired interventions that allow us to reconceptualize how we see our roles as counselors and social justice advocates and provide support for the important work at hand.

References

Allen, T. D., Eby, L. T., Poteet, M. L., Lentz, E., & Lima, L. (2004). Career benefits associated with mentoring for protégés: A meta-analysis. *Journal of Applied Psychology, 89*(1), 127–136.

Atkinson, D. R., Thompson, C. E., & Grant, S. K. (1993). A three-dimensional model for counseling racial/ethnic minorities. *The Counseling Psychologist, 21,* 257–277.

Bahniuk, M. H., Hill, S. E. K., & Darus, H. J. (1996). The relationship of power-gaining communication strategies to career success. *Western Journal of Communication, 60*(4), 358–378.

Baluch, S. P., Pieterse, A. L., & Bolden, M. A. (2004). Counseling psychology and social justice: Houston . . . we have a problem. *The Counseling Psychologist, 32,* 89–98.

Bingham, R. P., & Ward, C. M. (1996). Practical applications of career counseling with ethnic minority women. In M. L. Savickas & W. B. Walsh (Eds.), *Handbook of career counseling theory and practice* (pp. 291–315). Palo Alto, CA: Davies-Black.

Blustein, D. L., Chaves, A. P., Diemer, M. A., Gallagher, L. A., Marshall, K. G., Sirin, S., & Bhati, K. S. (2002). Voices of the forgotten half: The role of social class in the school-to-work transition. *Journal of Counseling Psychology, 49*(3), 311–323.

Bornstein, D. (2004). *How to change the world: Social entrepreneurs and the power of new ideas.* New York: Oxford University Press.

Carter, R. T. (2003). *The Counseling Psychologist* in the new millennium: Building a bridge from the past to the future. *The Counseling Psychologist, 31,* 5–15.

Cook, E. P., Heppner, M. J., & O'Brien, K. M. (2002). Career development of women of color and white women: Assumptions, conceptualization, and interventions from an ecological perspective. *Career Development Quarterly, 50*(4), 291–305.

Cowan, J. (Ed.). (1991). *Good works: A guide to career in social justice.* New York: Barricade Books.

Darley, J. G., & Paterson, D. G. (1934). Employed and unemployed workers: Differential factors in employment status. *Bulletin: Employment Stabilization Research Institute, University of Minnesota, 3,* 7–26.

Davis, H. V. (1969). *Frank Parsons: Prophet, innovator, counselor.* Carbondale, IL: Southern Illinois University Press.

Ford, D. L., & Whaley, G. L. (2003). The digital divide and managing workforce diversity: A commentary. *Applied Psychology: An International Review, 52,* 476–485.

Fouad, N. (2001). Dreams for 2010: Making a difference. *The Counseling Psychologist, 30,* 158–166.

Fouad, N. A., & Bingham, R. P. (1995). Career counseling with racial and ethnic minorities. In W. B. Walsh & S. H. Osipow (Eds.), *Handbook of vocational psychology: Theory, research, and practice* (2nd ed., pp. 331–365). Hillsdale, NJ: Lawrence Erlbaum.

Fouad, N. A., & Brown, M. T. (2000). The role of race and class in development: Implications for counseling psychology. In S. D. Brown & R. W. Lent (Eds.), *Handbook of counseling psychology* (3rd ed., pp. 379–408). New York: Wiley.

Garmezy, N. (1993). Children in poverty: Resilience despite risk. *Psychiatry, 56,* 127–136.

Hall, C. (1997). Cultural malpractice: The growing obsolescence of psychology with the changing U.S. population. *American Psychologist, 52,* 642–651.

Hansen, L. S. (2001). *Integrative life planning: Critical tasks for career development and changing life patterns.* San Francisco: Jossey-Bass.

Hargrove, B. K., Creagh, M. G., & Kelly, D. B. (2003). Multicultural competencies in career counseling. In D. B. Pope-Davis, H. L. K. Coleman, W. M. Liu, & R. L. Toporek (Eds.), *Handbook of multicultural competence for counseling and psychology* (pp. 392–405). Thousand Oaks, CA: Sage.

Hartung, P. J., & Blustein, D. L. (2002). Reason, intuition, and social justice: Elaborating on Parsons's Career Decision-Making Model. *Journal of Counseling & Development, 80,* 41–47.

Helms, J. E. (2003). A pragmatic view of social justice. *The Counseling Psychologist, 31*(3), 305–313.

Herr, E. L., & Niles, S. G. (1998) Career: Social action in behalf of purpose, productivity, and hope. In C. C. Lee & G. R. Walz (Eds.), *Social action: A mandate for counselors* (pp. 117–136). Alexandria, VA: American Counseling Association.

Ibrahim, F. A., & Ohnishi, H. (2001). Posttraumatic stress disorder and the minority experience. In D. B. Pope-Davis & H. L. K. Coleman (Eds.), *The intersection of race, class and gender in counseling psychology* (pp. 89–126). Thousand Oaks, CA: Sage.

Kalbfleisch, P. J., & Davies, A. B. (1991). Minorities and mentoring: Managing the multicultural institution. *Communication Education, 40*(3), 266–271.

Krumboltz, J. D. (1996). A learning theory of career counseling. In M. L. Savickas & W. B. Walsh (Eds.), *Handbook of career counseling theory and practice* (pp. 55–81). Palo Alto, CA: Davies-Black.

LaFromboise, T. D. (2003). Walking through collages. In J. G. Ponterotto, J. M. Casas, L. A. Suzuki, & C. M. Alexander (Eds.), *Handbook of multicultural counseling* (2nd ed., pp. 14–21). Thousand Oaks, CA: Sage.

Leach, J. J., & Chakiris, B. J. (1985). The dwindling future of work in America. *Training & Development Journal, 39*(4), 44–46.

Lent, R. W., & Brown, S. D. (2002). Social cognitive career theory and adult career development. In S. G. Niles (Ed.), *Adult career development: Concepts, issues and practices* (3rd ed., pp. 76–97). Columbus, OH: National Career Development Association.

Lent, R. W., Brown, S. D., & Talleyrand, R. (2002). Career choice barriers, supports, and coping strategies: College students' experiences. *Journal of Vocational Behavior, 60*(1), 61–72.

Leong, F. T. L. (1995). *Career development and vocational behavior of racial and ethnic minorities.* Hillsdale, NJ: Lawrence Erlbaum.

Liddle, B. J., Luzzo, D. A., Hauenstein, A. L., & Schuck, K. (2004). Construction and validation of the Lesbian, Gay, Bisexual, and Transgendered Climate Inventory. *Journal of Career Assessment, 12*(1), 33–50.

Luzzo, D. A., & McWhirter, E. H. (2001). Sex and ethnic differences in the perception of educational and career-related barriers and levels of coping efficacy. *Journal of Counseling & Development, 79*(1), 61–67.

National Telecommunications and Information Administration. (1999, November). *Falling through the net: Defining the digital divide.* Retrieved September 10, 2004, from http://www.ntia.doc.gov/ntiahome/digitaldivide/factsheets/income.htm

Niles, S. G., Herr, E. L., & Hartung, P. J. (2002). Adult career concerns in contemporary society. In S. Niles (Ed.), *Adult career development: Concepts, issues and practices* (3rd ed.). Columbus, OH: National Career Development Association.

Overholt, A. (2004, January). Social capitalists: Profiles [Electronic version]. *Fast Company, 78,* 51.

Paterson, D. G., & Darley, J. G. (1934). Occupational guidance in the public employment office. *Mental Health Observer, 2,* 3.

Peterson, N., & Gonzalez, R. C. (2000). *The role of work in people's lives.* Belmont, CA: Wadsworth/Thomson Learning.

Pope, K. S. (1990). Ethics and malpractice: Identifying and implementing ethical standards for primary prevention. *Prevention in Human Services, 8*(2), 43–64.

Pope, M. (2000). A brief history of career counseling in the United States. *Career Development Quarterly, 48,* 194–211.

Rice, J. (2001). Poverty, welfare and patriarchy: How macro-level changes in social policy can help low-income women. *Journal of Social Issues, 57*(2), 355–374.

Root, M. P. (2003). Racial and ethnic origins of harassment in the workplace: Evaluation issues and symptomatology. In D. B. Pope-Davis, H. L. K. Coleman, W. M. Liu, & R. L. Toporek (Eds.), *Handbook of multicultural competencies in counseling psychology* (pp. 478–492). Thousand Oaks, CA: Sage.

Rubicon Programs. (2005). Available: http://www.rubiconprograms.org/

Sue, D. W., Arredondo, P., & McDavis, R. J. (1992). Multicultural counseling competencies and standards: A call to the profession. *Journal of Counseling and Development, 70*, 477–486.

Sundberg, N. D., & Littman, R. A. (1994). Leona Elizabeth Tyler (1906–1993). *American Psychologist, 49*(3), 211–212.

Super, D. E. (1954). Guidance: Manpower utilization or human development? *Personnel & Guidance Journal, 33*, 8–14.

Thomas, D. A., & Alderfer, C. P. (1989). The influence of race on career dynamics: Theory and research on minority career experiences. In M. B. Arthur & D. T. Hall (Eds.), *Handbook of career theory* (pp. 133–158). New York: Cambridge University Press.

Thompson, A. S., Super, D. E., & Napoli, P. J. (1955). Developing a VA counseling psychology training program: A case history of university-hospital cooperation. *American Psychologist, 10*, 283–288.

Toporek, R. L., & Liu, W. L. (2000). Advocacy in counseling psychology: Critical issues of race, class, and gender. In D. B. Pope-Davis & H. L. K. Coleman (Eds.), *The intersection of race, class and gender in counseling psychology* (pp. 385–413). Thousand Oaks, CA: Sage.

Welfare Law Center. (2002). *Welfare Law Center: Annual report.* Retrieved on September 10, 2004, from http://www.welfarelaw.org/annualReport/annualReport03.pdf

Worthington, R. L., & Juntunen, C. L. (1997). The vocational development of non-college-bound youth: Counseling psychology and the school-to-work transition movement. *The Counseling Psychologist, 25*, 323–363.

CHAPTER 21

Social Justice Through Self-Sufficiency

Vocational Psychology and the Transition From Welfare to Work

Cindy L. Juntunen, Angela M. Cavett, Rhanda B. Clow, Venessa Rempel, Rachel E. Darrow, and Adam Guilmino

In 1996, the Personal Responsibility and Work Opportunity Reconciliation Act (Public Law 104–193) was signed into law, with apparently widespread bipartisan support and the purported ability to "end welfare as we know it." Now well into the eighth year of welfare reform, the consequences of that change are far from clear and abundant opportunities remain for psychologists to use their professional skills to support a positive transition from welfare to self-sufficiency. Although Edwards, Rachal, and Dixon (1999) called several years ago for increasing attention to welfare by counseling psychologists, there remains an absence of multifaceted psychological and consultative services in the current welfare reform system.

The purpose of this chapter is to provide an introduction to welfare reform and the opportunities to engage in social justice by improving the services provided to recipients of welfare. To that end, we will first present an overview of welfare reform and its known consequences, followed by a description of the current services included in welfare-to-work programs. The responses of the American

---

Authors' Note: Portions of this chapter were previously presented in Juntunen (2002). Project HOPE was funded (2000–2003) by the Otto Bremer Foundation of Minneapolis.

Psychological Association to issues of welfare and poverty will be discussed briefly, as will the emphasis on social justice and change within the field of vocational psychology. Next, we will present the findings of a study that sought to understand the needs of welfare recipients, and the transformation of those findings into a curriculum designed to meet the psychosocial, self-efficacy, and job skills training needs of welfare recipients in a specific community. The chapter will conclude with the outcome of that curriculum, addressing both the successes and challenges of initiating such a community-based program.

Historically overlooked, families living in poverty are in critical need of support. Many have psychological stressors requiring responses that psychologists are uniquely trained to provide. The opportunity to make a difference exists in each interaction with an individual moving toward self-sufficiency. Beyond that, with increased knowledge of welfare reform and the systems that support it, psychologists can create real social change by educating the policymakers and institutions that enforce welfare policy about strategies to improve access to self-sufficiency for every family.

Welfare Reform

The Personal Responsibility and Work Opportunity Reconciliation Act (PRWORA) of 1996 resulted in two major changes to previous welfare policy. First, it ended the entitlement to cash welfare that was previously provided in the program known as AFDC (Aid for Families with Dependent Children). Instead, it awarded two block grants to states. The first grant supports families transitioning out of welfare as long as the parent(s) is (are) verifiably seeking work and avoiding out-of-wedlock births. States can also use money from this block grant to encourage marriage and the formation of two-parent families. The second block grant is designed to support child care needs for families receiving or at risk for returning to welfare.

The second major change in PRWORA was that cash welfare was disallowed to several groups of people, including noncitizens, children who are classified as disabled strictly because of age-inappropriate behavior, people addicted to substances (part of Public Law 104–121), and any family that had received more than 60 months of assistance. This 60-month lifetime time limit was not in place for previous welfare assistance programs and resulted in Temporary Aid for Needy Families (TANF) programs, which are part of the first block grant awarded to states and replaced the previous AFDC programs (for a thorough summary of PROWRA, see Committee on Ways and Means, 1996).

It is important to note that although the receipt of TANF support is linked to seeking work and job training, it is also connected to personal behaviors such as pregnancy and marriage. In fact, of the 10 findings that supported the bill in its passage through the legislature, none refers to work (U.S. Congress, 1996). Instead, the findings focused on the importance of marriage, the need to prevent out-of-wedlock births, and the importance of having two parents present for children.

Also important is the fact that states were given discretion in the ways in which they use their block grants, as long as they observed the fairly broad objectives established by PRWORA. On one hand, this is useful in that it allows states to develop programs and plans most suitable for their local populations. Recipients of welfare-to-work grants have indicated that the flexibility of program options and the ability to tailor programs to meet local needs are particular strengths of welfare reform (Nightingale, O'Brien, Egner, Pindus, & Trutko, 2003). On the other hand, such flexibility makes it more difficult to determine the overall effect of welfare reform on low-income and poverty-level families, because there is a great deal of variation across state programs and outcomes.

Evaluating the outcome of welfare reform is further complicated by the fact that this major policy change coincided with a period of strong economic growth in the United States. Even in the absence of any other changes, the decreased unemployment rate, increased real income, and other improvements in the labor market of the mid-1990s would have been expected to both lower the welfare rolls and increase employment rates (Blank, 2001).

Indeed, the welfare rolls decreased dramatically following the implementation of PRWORA. In 1996, more than 12 million people (many of them children) were receiving social assistance benefits. By June 1999, that number had decreased by almost 44%, to 6.9 million (Pavetti, 2000). These findings indicate that welfare reform was a nationally successful initiative, although little information was available about the state-to-state differences for families on welfare and there was no ability to control for sociocultural factors such as labor market cycles.

A closer look at these outcomes suggests a less successful picture for many families who left the welfare rolls. Loprest (2001) found that 40% of families were moving from welfare to poverty, and more than 20% returned to welfare. In a national survey of families leaving welfare, Cheng (2002) found that 58% of the families were classified as poor in their first postwelfare year, and their household income averaged 67% of what it had been while they still received welfare. Also, only 35% of families were both off of welfare assistance and not poor during that first year, and the authors concluded that that was largely due to having an additional source of income (from a working spouse or other source), as the income from the previous welfare recipient accounted for only 35% of their household income.

In a similarly complex set of findings, Hill and Kauff (2001), in a survey of 401 families that left TANF in 1999, concluded that most experienced an increase in household income, employment rates, and earnings. However, the poorest of families experienced worsening financial situations. In fact, there is evidence that the number of families in "deep poverty," defined as household income of 50% below the federal poverty line, has increased (Haskins, Sawhill, & Weaver, 2001). The families that fall into this category are facing extreme hardships, such as hunger and homelessness. Furthermore, they are likely to encounter multiple barriers to employment, including addictions, disabled children, emotional illnesses, domestic violence, lack of work experience, and poor education. Haskins et al. (2001) conclude that not much is known about how to help such families, identifying an area of social justice research ripe for attention by counseling, vocational, and family psychologists.

Welfare-to-Work Programs

Numerous outcome studies have been (and continue to be) conducted on welfare programs since the 1996 passage of PRWORA. The breadth of that research is well beyond the scope of this chapter, and the interested reader is referred to the Manpower Demonstration Research Project (http://www.mdrc.org/); Mathematic Policy Research, Inc. (http://www.mathematica-mpr.com/); and the Urban Institute (http://www.urban.org/), as well as the U.S. Department of Labor Employment and Training Administration (http://www.doleta.gov/) for a more thorough introduction to the extant literature. This section will briefly address general points and highlights relevant to existing welfare-to-work programs.

In the attempt to address the educational and vocational deficits of welfare recipients and enhance their employability, welfare-to-work programs have focused their efforts predominantly on providing basic education, skills training, and postsecondary education. Few programs have adequately addressed underlying issues that interfere with the attainment of adequate work intended to improve economic well-being (Edwards et al., 1999). In fact, the time limits in TANF may serve to force many program recipients into work (or at least off of the welfare rolls) when they remain unprepared (Cheng, 2002).

Two major evaluations (Gueron & Hamilton, 2002; Hamilton, 2002) of multiple welfare-to-work programs compared three types of programs: those that emphasize job search activities (called job-first programs) with little attention to the nature of the work or pre-employment training, those that emphasize education and training prior to searching for a job, and those that use a mix of education and job search activities in an attempt to match individual client needs.

In both studies, it was found that the best results came from programs that used a mix of initial activities. Gueron and Hamilton (2002) offered three conclusions based on their findings: (a) there is no evidence to support a rigid education-or-training-first policy; (b) there is a clear role for skills-enhancing activities in welfare reform; (c) programs should include training that fosters career advancement, integrates basic education and skills training, and engages local employers. Hamilton (2002) further noted that the most successful of the 11 programs included in her 5-year study of 40,000 participants also encouraged participants to hold out for higher-paying, more stable work positions, rather than taking the first job that was available. Overall, the participants in the 11 programs examined demonstrated increased employment and less reliance on welfare than did control samples, but did not increase material gains or decrease poverty. Indeed, similar to findings in other studies (Cheng, 2002; Hill & Kauff, 2001), some of the most disadvantaged participants were actually worse off financially after leaving welfare.

There are multiple factors that contribute to some recipients of welfare having a more difficult time making the transition to work, or at least to work that will support them financially beyond the level of welfare assistance. The possible factors and relationships between them are complex and have yet to be thoroughly understood. But there are several indications that mental health concerns are likely to be relevant, emphasizing the need for psychologists to become more involved in developing, implementing, and evaluating welfare-to-work programs. In Hamilton's (2002) multisite evaluation, for example, the only subgroup that did not show benefits in response to participating in a welfare-to-work program was people at risk of depression.

Substance abuse is another mental health issue frequently identified as a barrier in making the transition from welfare to work. There is evidence that substance abuse is related to welfare assistance, poverty, and homelessness (Anderson, Shannon, Schyb, & Goldstein, 2002; Bush & Kraft, 2001). One frequently overlooked aspect of PRWORA is the provision of discontinued disability payments for substance abuse disorders, resulting in reduced benefits for addicts. That has triggered concern that people addicted to substances will be less likely to obtain services and maintain housing, and more likely to be unemployed, engaged in criminal activities, and vulnerable to continued substance abuse (Anderson et al., 2002).

Despite the apparent importance of attending to mental health concerns, very few welfare-to-work programs adequately address the interaction of mental health and successful employment. In one exception, Anderson and Martinson (2003) describe a work retention program designed to meet the needs of hard-to-serve populations, including those with substance abuse and disability issues. It is clear that psychology can make a contribution to the design of successful welfare-to-work programs by addressing the interface of mental health concerns with employment and self-sufficiency goals. Greater attention is finally being paid to this need, as described in the following section.

Psychology's Response to Welfare Reform

Over the past several years, the American Psychological Association (APA) has produced several policy papers and documents that have closely examined problematic aspects of existing welfare legislation (APA, 1998, 2000, 2001, 2004; APA's Urban Initiatives Office, 1999). Through these papers, APA has presented detailed recommendations for reforming the welfare system specifically, and the work environment as a whole in ways that benefit both welfare recipients and the working poor. Recommendations fall into six major categories: the role of adequate health care, domestic violence, child care, education and training, service delivery systems, and future research.

In the recommendations for health care, APA includes mental health and substance abuse services, both of which are seen as playing a crucial role in efforts to improve people's quality of life (APA, 1998, 2000, 2001, 2004; APA's Women's Programs Office, 1998). The authors of these policy statements argue for the necessity of mental health parity, higher levels of health care coverage for both people on welfare and the working poor, prioritizing children's mental health, and greater access to all forms of health care.

Acknowledging a population that is frequently ignored in the discussion of poverty and employment, APA's Urban Initiatives Office (1999) has also called for improved training for all service providers in the detection of domestic violence, which frequently hampers a person's ability to maintain steady employment (APA, 1998, 2001). This stance is supported by several very recent studies and position papers published by counseling psychologists, primarily in the vocational psychology literature (Brown, Reedy, Fountain, Johnson, & Dichiser, 2000; Chronister & McWhirter, 2003; Chronister, Wettersten, & Brown, 2004; Wettersten et al., 2004).

A comprehensive national child care policy has been promoted by APA as a crucial element of welfare reform (APA, 1998). The need for more flexible child care hours is a necessity because of lower-skilled jobs that typically do not operate on an 8–5 schedule (APA, 2000, 2004; APA's Urban Initiatives Office, 1999). Furthermore, it is difficult to find child care for children with special needs, and most child care centers and providers are not able to pay wages sufficient to support staff with advanced training in special needs.

Although few psychologists appear to be actively involved in training and education related to the transition from welfare to work, psychological theory has a role in improving the training programs available. The fact that many clients of welfare programs are placed in lower-skilled jobs that provide few benefits, little opportunity for career advancement, and low job security is presented as evidence of the importance of taking a "human-capital" (investing in education and training) as opposed to a "work first" approach to training (Rice, 2001, p. 356). Such a paradigm shift would support several critical policy changes that APA is working to publicize.

The 1998 APA document "Making 'Welfare to Work' Really Work" highlights the importance of flexibility and collaboration among service delivery systems, acknowledging the uniqueness of each client and the importance of interagency cooperation. Furthermore, it is necessary to recognize the larger social context within which each client operates and develop service delivery systems that are culturally sensitive.

Finally, the APA's Resolution on Poverty and Socioeconomic Status (2000) provides numerous directives for future research, including research on the causes of poverty, prejudicial attitudes toward the poor, and special populations (e.g., immigrants, rural populations, children). Other areas for future research were highlighted by the APA's Urban Initiatives Office (1999), which voiced the need for research that will examine the shame and stigma attached to poverty and the utilization of welfare services.

Vocational Psychology and Social Justice

Vocational psychology is particularly suited to address the complexity of issues and barriers encountered in moving from welfare to work because of its roots in social action (Parsons, 1909) and the obvious interaction of psychological, economic, and employment barriers at play. In fact, O'Brien (2001) asserts that over the past century, career and vocational psychologists have been engaged in social action work through individual career counseling, intervening in the schools, working with special and underserved populations, and conducting research that furthers all of these efforts. She concludes by calling on vocational psychologists to "challenge societal ills and work for social reform" (p. 73).

Unfortunately, vocational psychology has been relatively slow to answer the need of people confronting the transition from welfare to work, but the tools to do so are certainly present. The vocational research literature strongly recommends developing and implementing multifaceted programs that (a) address a diversity of concerns and barriers that welfare recipients and poverty-level individuals face, and (b) deliver interventions that encompass a wide array of modalities (e.g., career counseling, psychoeducation, skills training, job coaching) (Edwards et al., 1999). This comprehensive approach could go further to meet the needs of transitioning welfare recipients than the exclusively work skills and training models presently implemented in most communities.

Such an effort is further supported by the recent increased attention within the field of vocational psychology to economic justice. As Blustein (2001) notes, "We need to ground our study of vocations in a broader understanding of social issues, with a focus on how interventions can help empower clients and change inequitable systems" (p. 174). More than a decade ago, Richardson (1993) warned that vocational psychology ran the risk of allowing classism to serve as a stumbling block in the study of work, and called for a theory of work that was more inclusive than traditional career theory. Efforts to implement this increased emphasis on social and economic justice can be found in research on the career development of women (Betz & Fitzgerald, 1987), the school-to-work transition (Blustein, Juntunen, & Worthington, 2000), work-bound youth (Herr & Niles, 1997), and numerous other traditionally disenfranchised groups. Similar attention must be paid to people struggling to make the transition from welfare to work, whose concerns have been only minimally addressed (Lent, 2001).

A Welfare-to-Work Program Grounded in Vocational and Counseling Psychology

The remainder of this chapter will describe the process of developing, implementing, and evaluating a work preparation program for welfare recipients in a medium-sized city of a rural state. The process had four primary components: assessing the needs of potential participants through qualitative interviews, developing and delivering a curriculum, creating partnerships with community providers who served potential participants, and evaluating the impact of the program.

The Voices of Welfare Recipients

We initially conducted qualitative interviews with six participants in the Family Self-Sufficiency program, a program of Housing and Urban Development (Juntunen, Cavett, Clow, & Suzen, 2000). All of the participants were long-term recipients of social assistance who were approaching or making a transition into full-time employment. Although each participant had a unique story to tell, four consistent themes emerged and were saturated through six interviews. These themes were self-efficacy, ambivalence about welfare assistance, mental health concerns, and a cluster of logistical barriers.

Participants had low self-efficacy for living on their own without the safety net provided by social assistance. Furthermore, the welfare system, which many recipients reported made them feel "treated like children," sometimes served to reinforce the lack of self-efficacy of recipients. Although their self-efficacy for leaving social assistance was low, participants were ambivalent about being "in the system." The statements of many participants also showed their desire to be free of the system and to be independent, self-sufficient, and employed, while recognizing that they needed assistance for the present at least. Most participants expressed negative feelings related to the stereotype of welfare recipients and differentiated themselves from unknown "others" who were seen to be misusing or even cheating the system, supporting other research (Nelson, 2002).

Two major categories of barriers to self-sufficiency were identified. The first was mental health issues, as all but one participant revealed that they had been diagnosed with a mental illness. Furthermore, they identified mental health concerns as contributing to their reliance on welfare. Participants also noted several challenges encountered because they could not afford the resources that most citizens of the United States take for granted. Primary among these logistical barriers were quality child care, accessible and flexible transportation, health care, and secure housing.

A Community-Based Work Preparation Program

Based on the above findings, our research team developed a career preparation program titled Project HOPE (Honoring Occupational and Personal Empowerment). The program was designed to include approximately 30–36 hours of contact time, during which participants met in a group. The content and activities of that curriculum were organized around four basic stages.

Stage 1 focused on self-exploration, goal setting, and work aspiration activities. The primary purpose was to reinforce or foster greater self-efficacy, both for work-related skills and for moving off of welfare. Specific activities included interest assessments and exploration activities, values clarification activities, identification and reinforcement of the importance of skills used in daily life, and matching of interests and skills to potential work areas. All of these areas were integrated in group discussion and resulted in each individual setting preliminary goals.

In Stage 2, each individual participant identified the various concerns that he or she thought might get in the way of achieving or moving toward his or her goals. This was done individually through a Barrier Log and in group discussion, in which participants helped each other identify barriers and, ultimately, brainstorm ideas for overcoming those barriers. Members of the group were also very helpful in addressing their peers' interpersonal presentation (particularly low self-efficacy and low self-esteem) and challenging them to make changes to overcome those barriers.

During Stage 3, we implemented a variety of skills-training strategies to overcome barriers. Many of these were consistent with the so-called soft skills, transferable skills, or "SCANS skills" recommended by the Secretary (of Labor)'s

Commission for Achieving Necessary Skills (SCANS, 1992). Specifically, the group practiced strategies for improving communication, developing assertiveness, setting boundaries, dealing with problematic work situations, and solving problems. Each activity conducted during this stage focused on some specific skills or strategy for overcoming identified barriers. Together, the goal of Stage 3 was to develop readiness to implement work-related behaviors in real-world settings.

In the final stage, the participants were responsible for implementing work-relevant behaviors by carrying out a variety of specific job search or work exploration tasks, such as job-shadowing assignments, developing or refining a résumé, and practicing interview skills. This led to the final step, which was the development of an exit plan. In the exit plan, each participant met with a group facilitator and reviewed the next steps he or she would take to meet his or her long-term goals. Typically, these steps included educational and job application plans. However, many participants also noted strategies for obtaining driver's licenses, securing reliable child care, and continuing to work on mental health and interpersonal needs.

Community Partnerships

Partnership was key to the success of Project HOPE, because the project was designed to complement programs delivered by local agencies, including Job Service and the local Housing Authority Family Self-Sufficiency Program. The academic staff from the University of North Dakota's Department of Counseling (who made up Project HOPE staff) and the service delivery staff from the local Job Service office collaborated for the duration of the program.

Forming teams that involve university-community relationships poses some unique challenges (Lynn, 2000). However, we used a number of different strategies to improve the partnership and reduce the likelihood of disruption. First, we explicitly discussed the ideological differences between our agencies. Second, because minimizing the duplication of services is a necessary task for collaborators, our agencies decided to identify a specialty within the range of services offered and then referred individual clients to various partner agencies to obtain those services. Finally, we relied heavily on regular communication between Job Service and HOPE staff. Without this kind of daily cooperation at the level of service delivery staff, many participants would have simply slipped through the cracks of the referral process.

Partnering across community-agency lines provided numerous opportunities. First and foremost, it resulted in more comprehensive services for clients by creating a holistic and contextual picture of each client. Second, the partnership provided valuable support for team members and maximized the resources available to all partners. This was particularly useful because of the different restrictions (or lack of restrictions) in the Job Service and HOPE programs. Federal programs such as those provided by Job Service often have very clear restrictions on services available to clients. However, HOPE had no such restrictions. In a supportive role, HOPE staff could often provide services that Jobs Service staff believed would be helpful but were not able to offer. Finally, the partnership created greater collective strength to work for social change, as well as more ability to seek and obtain greater external funding for social change efforts.

Outcome: The Impact of HOPE

The HOPE curriculum had a demonstrated impact on depression and on work-related skills. At the time of intake, 40% of the sample had Beck Depression Inventory (BDI) (Beck & Steer, 1987) scores of greater than 16 (indicating clinical levels of depression). Because of significant attrition in the sample, only 31 participants were administered the BDI a second time. However, within that subsample of 31, BDI scores decreased after completion of Stage 1 HOPE activities, and only 16% of the sample had BDI scores at or above the clinical level.

The relatively high levels of depression in this sample are certainly a significant factor to consider when working with individuals who are required to pursue work activities. In many situations, TANF recipients may be forced to pursue work activities even when that might be contraindicated from a mental health perspective. Increasing education about the impact of depression and other mental health concerns, and specifically increasing understanding of the impact of mental health concerns among providers and policymakers concerned with welfare, is an action that vocational psychologists could pursue for long-term impact.

Vocational identity was assessed with the My Vocational Situation (MVS) (Holland, Daiger, & Power, 1980), which measures the extent to which respondents believe that they are able or ready to make vocational decisions and the extent to which they need additional information or assistance in doing so. There was no significant change in the MVS score between the first and later administrations for HOPE participants, indicating that the activities in HOPE may not have addressed vocational identity. Importantly, a negative relationship was found between BDI and MVS scores. This suggests a relationship between depression and vocational identity that warrants further exploration. Specifically, it may be that vocational identity increases as depression decreases, which suggests that interventions that affect depression might also affect vocational identity, and vice versa. Although a small number of earlier studies have considered the relationship between depression and vocational identity (Heppner, Cook, Strozier, & Heppner, 1991; Saunders, Peterson, Sampson, & Reardon, 2001; Sweeney & Schill, 1998), no previous studies were found to consider this relationship among recipients of welfare.

In addition to the assessment-based data, HOPE participants assessed a total of 18 group objectives. These objectives fell into three broad categories: self-exploration, exploration of the world of work, and development of transferable skills. The objectives that participants evaluated as most important were exploring values, setting goals, bonding with other group members, managing stress, and working on self-confidence. Self-exploration and transferable skills–related activities did appear to have the most importance for these participants, although there was also an indication that some of the job exploration activities, particularly conducting informational interviews, had the potential to help them meet their future goals.

Finally, a qualitative analysis of the discussions held in six HOPE group sessions (Clow, 2004) offers additional insight into the impact of the HOPE curriculum. The interactions that occurred within the six sessions indicated that participants demonstrated increased awareness of interests and skills, change in future work and personal goals, and improved communication skills. Clow (2004) further concluded that Project HOPE's approach to career counseling helped to resolve some of the defensiveness and frustration with which the participants approached the task, especially for those recipients who attended many or all of the sessions. Reports from their case managers in assistance agencies confirmed positive changes in attitude toward the agency professionals, including increased cooperation and engagement.

Challenges and Opportunities

The community-based participation research involved in Project HOPE presented numerous challenges and opportunities for our research team. We began the project with a fairly naïve perspective—our belief that we had something unique to offer a population that was not receiving adequate services carried us into this effort with minimal recognition of the potential difficulties we would encounter. Subsequently, we encountered a substantial number of barriers to both service delivery and evaluation. However, those barriers, or challenges, provided the opportunity to develop new strategies for both service and research.

The first challenge was an unexpected relationship with federally funded agencies. We had planned to make HOPE a completely voluntary activity, connected to the social service system only by referrals. However, because of the needs of our community partners to demonstrate that TANF recipients were receiving appropriate work experiences, and because of their strong belief that HOPE was of value to those clients deemed hardest to serve, many of the HOPE participants were ultimately required to attend HOPE sessions as part of their work requirements. Therefore, we became much more a part of the social service system than we had ever intended. Ultimately, this challenge presented some excellent opportunities to have an impact on the well-being of assistance recipients in our region. By forging solid community partnerships with a number of agencies, we were able to infuse some of the values of vocational psychology into the ongoing discussion of service delivery for welfare recipients.

Beyond the need to be more integrated into the social assistance system, a variety of issues contributed to the difficulty of delivering and evaluating the HOPE curriculum. First among these is attrition and the transient nature of the population. Attrition and lack of participation are common phenomena in welfare-to-work programs (Hamilton, 2002), and for numerous reasons, many of the HOPE participants were unable to complete the entire group experience. In some cases, there were potentially positive changes, such as increased employment, a return to school as a full-time student, or some other event that resulted in financial self-sufficiency. In other instances, logistical barriers disallowed program attendance. In an attempt to counter the logistical barriers, we provided a program for children to address child care needs. We also had a contract with a local taxi company to transport participants who did not have a car or a driver's license. However, other issues such as health concerns, time conflicts, and family obligations could not be resolved as easily. Finally, we were frequently unable to contact many participants after our initial meetings. In these cases, the individual may have given up or lost his or her telephone service, moved in with a friend or family member, or left the community.

The long-term group structure of the program also proved to be a deterrent for a significant portion of participants, involving too much time and too long of a commitment. In response to this, we developed a series of workshops appropriate for provision through the local Job Service and Adult Learning Center. These workshops addressed the goals of HOPE in a more concise and discrete fashion, allowing participants to tailor their experience to meet their needs. These were only moderately successful, with a large number of participants showing up for the first such offering and dwindling numbers participating in the workshops scheduled over the remaining months. The feedback from sessions was positive, and the reasons for decreasing attendance are not clear, but they do suggest a need to carefully target the audience and tailor the topics to meet the specific needs of specific groups.

Mental health concerns affected the delivery of the HOPE curriculum as well, because a primary characteristic of the participants referred to HOPE by Job Service was the presence of significant mental health concerns. Depression and substance use were primary among these, although other issues were also present. Although this certainly presented some additional challenges to implementing vocational interventions, it was also an opportunity to better understand the very close relationship between unemployment and mental health problems in a population of welfare recipients. The curriculum was adjusted to integrate mental health and work issues for both the adult and youth groups. Furthermore, recognition of this relationship increased significantly among the staff at Job Service, who implemented some initial strategies for evaluating and referring for mental health concerns as an initial step in the intake process. In fact, mental health services became identified as an eligible part of the work requirements, in response to a special pilot program initiated by the local Welfare Reform Task Force.

Implications for Training and Research

The experience with Project HOPE suggests several considerations for counseling psychology training and research. First, it is essential to expose students to the unique issues encountered by recipients of welfare and challenge the barrier of classism (Lent, 2001) that can deter students from understanding this underserved population. We had two team members who were themselves recipients of welfare, which provided the opportunity for the HOPE staff to carefully question their own assumptions, but even so, negative stereotypes emerged and had to be confronted.

The outcomes of this project also highlight the integration of work and mental health needs, and identify the need to train counselors and counseling psychologists to both expect and be prepared to respond to combined work and personal issues in their practice. For welfare-to-work transitioning clients, mental health issues should not be assumed, but careful assessment of the interplay between work success and mental health is required.

Increased attention to consultation and partnerships is also essential for preparing students to work with recipients of welfare or any population whose well-being is affected by governmental and policy mandates. Training needs to identify ways in which institutions affect individuals, demonstrate how psychologists can affect such institutions, and provide students with strategies for making effective partnerships. This will better prepare psychologists to effect change at the organizational level, in turn improving situations for the individuals affected by the organization.

Research in the area of welfare reform and the impact on well-being can also be furthered in many ways. As demonstrated through the HOPE experience, outcome and evaluation research of such community-based projects is challenging. An important development in this area would be the dissemination of action research methodological strategies, inclusion of more community-based research in professional empirical research journals, and discussions of ways to more effectively include the real-life experience of marginalized populations in empirical work.

Additional research addressing the needs of recipients of welfare can also be expanded in several ways. The initial outcomes of Project HOPE present some intriguing questions about the relationship between depression and vocational identity, and suggest further examination of the preventive value of fostering earlier vocational identity. Also, a large number of participants stopped attending after the first stage of the program, which focused on self-efficacy and self-exploration. Although it is difficult to know what contributed to attrition at this point, it would be worthwhile to look closely at the role that self-efficacy and self-exploration play in the transition from welfare to work. Finally, the qualitative study of the welfare experience needs to be extended to quantitative work with larger samples, to better understand the factors that both predict a successful transition off of welfare and serve as barriers to that transition.

Conclusion

The passage of the Personal Responsibility and Work Opportunity Reconciliation Act will continue to affect the lives of millions of Americans living in poverty and low-income situations. The efforts of Project HOPE were designed to increase access to the reward and opportunity structure among people who have been discouraged from believing that they have a right to that access. There are some indications that a program such as this can be successful, and certainly we can identify several families who achieved financial security far beyond what they ever expected, at least in part due to their work in Project HOPE.

However, like many vocational interventions, Project HOPE goes nowhere near as far as it needs to in order to effect real and lasting change for people who rely on welfare. In large part, this is due to the fact that we are largely constricted, through the goal of serving recipients, to focus on the personal responsibility aspect of the PRWORA. The next step, and the one essential for establishing real change, is to tackle the world of work opportunities. Too often, government, social service, and even psychologically based programs place the responsibility for change squarely on the people who are the least empowered. Instead, we need to shift our focus to the responsibility of employers, policymakers, and community leaders. Reliance on welfare is not necessarily the failure of the individual to be self-sufficient. It is equally the failure of a society to provide sufficiently for its people. The allocation of wealth in our nation virtually ensures that a large minority of people will not have what they need to lead a full and contributing life. Rather than suggesting additional ways in which individuals can change, it is time for counseling psychology to identify ways to change the system that oppresses them.

References

American Psychological Association. (1998). *Making "welfare-to-work" really work.* Retrieved March 27, 2004, from http://www.apa.org/pi/wpo.html

American Psychological Association. (2000). *Resolution on poverty and socioeconomic status.* Retrieved March 27, 2004, from http://www.apa.org/pi/urban/povres.html

American Psychological Association. (2001). *Mental health issues in TANF reauthorization.* Retrieved March 27, 2004, from http://www.apa.org/pi/urban/tanfreg.html

American Psychological Association. (2004). *Briefing paper on work and family policy: New directions in work and family policy.* Retrieved March 27, 2004, from http://apa.org/ppo/issues/workandfam.html

American Psychological Association's Urban Initiatives Office. (1999). *Forgotten voices: Conversations with women on welfare.* Retrieved March 27, 2004, from http://www.apa.org/pi/urban/forgottenvoices.pdf

American Psychological Association's Women's Programs Office. (1998). *Mental health and substance abuse problems among women on welfare.* Retrieved March 27, 2004, from http://apa.org/pi/wpo/mhsaproblems.pdf

Anderson, J., & Martinson, K. (2003). *Service delivery and institutional linkages: Early implementation experiences of employment retention and advancement programs.* New York: Manpower Demonstration Research Council. Retrieved March 25, 2004, from http://www.mdrc.org/project_24_9.html

Anderson, T. L., Shannon, C., Schyb, I., & Goldstein, P. (2002). Welfare reform and housing: Assessing the impact to substance abusers. *Journal of Drug Issues, 32,* 265–295.

Beck, A. T., & Steer, R. A. (1987). *Manual for the revised Beck Depression Inventory.* San Antonio, TX: Psychological Corporation.

Betz, N. E., & Fitzgerald, L. F. (1987). *The career psychology of women.* San Diego, CA: Academic Press.

Blank, R. M. (2001). What causes public assistance caseloads to grow? *Journal of Human Resources, 36,* 85–118.

Blustein, D. L. (2001). Extending the reach of vocational psychology: Toward an inclusive and integrative psychology of working. *Journal of Vocational Behavior, 59,* 171–182.

Blustein, D., Juntunen, C. L., & Worthington, R. L. (2000). The school-to-work transition: Adjustment challenges of the forgotten half. In R. L. Lent & S. Brown (Eds.), *Handbook of counseling psychology* (3rd ed.). New York: Wiley.

Brown, C., Reedy, D., Fountain, J., Johnson, A., & Dichiser, T. (2000). Battered women's career decision-making self-efficacy: Further insights and contributing factors. *Journal of Career Assessments, 8,* 251–265.

Bush, I. R., & Kraft, M. K. (2001). Self-sufficiency and sobriety: Substance-abusing women and welfare reform. *Journal of Social Work Practice in the Addictions, 1,* 41–64.

Cheng, T. (2002). Welfare recipients: How do they become independent? *Social Work Research, 26,* 159–170.

Chronister, K. M., & McWhirter, E. H. (2003). Women, domestic violence, and career counseling: An application of social cognitive theory. *Journal of Counseling and Development, 81*(4), 418–424.

Chronister, K., Wettersten, K. B., & Brown, C. (2004). Vocational research for the liberation of battered women. *The Counseling Psychologist, 32,* 900–922.

Clow, R. B. (2004). *Experiential career exploration: Qualitative examination of a group-based intervention.* Unpublished doctoral dissertation, University of North Dakota.

Committee on Ways and Means, U.S. House of Representatives. (1996). *Summary of welfare reforms made by Public Law 104-193: The Personal Responsibility and Work Opportunities Reconciliation Act and associated legislation.* Retrieved September 6, 2005, from http://www.access.gpo.gov/congress/wm015.txt

Edwards, S., Rachal, K., & Dixon, D. (1999). Counseling psychology and welfare reform: Implications and opportunities. *The Counseling Psychologist, 27,* 263–285.

Gueron, J. M., & Hamilton, G. (2002, April). *The role of education and training in welfare reform.* New York: Manpower Demonstration Research Council. Retrieved March 25, 2004, from http://www.mdrc.org/publications/158/policybrief.html

Hamilton, G. (2002). *Moving people from welfare to work: Lessons from the national evaluation of welfare-to-work strategies.* New York: Manpower Demonstration Research Council. Retrieved March 25, 2004, from http://www.mdrc.org/publications/52/summary.html

Haskins, R., Sawhill, I., & Weaver, K. (2001). *Welfare reform reauthorization: An overview of problems and issues* (Brookings Institution Policy Brief 2). Washington, DC: The Brookings Institution. Retrieved April 1, 2004, from http://www.brookings.edu/wrb

Heppner, P. P., Cook, S. W., Strozier, A. L., & Heppner, M. J. (1991). An investigation of coping styles and gender differences with farmers in career transition. *Journal of Counseling Psychology, 38,* 167–174.

Herr, E. L., & Niles, S. (1997). Perspectives on career assessment of work-bound youth. *Journal of Career Assessment, 5,* 137–150.

Hill, H., & Kauff, J. (2001). *Living on little: Case studies of Iowa families with very low incomes.* Washington, DC: Mathematica Policy Research.

Holland, J. L., Daiger, D., & Power, P. G. (1980). *My vocational situation.* Odessa, FL: Psychological Assessment Resources.

Juntunen, C. L. (2002, August). Welfare to work transition: Evaluating a vocational intervention. In K. Wettersten (Chair), *Community, Work, and Social Justice: Integrating Vocational Interventions and Research.* Symposium conducted at the annual meeting of the American Psychological Association, Chicago.

Juntunen, C. L., Cavett, A. M., Clow, R. B., & Suzen, D. (2000, April). *A qualitative study of career concerns for welfare recipients.* Poster presented at the Great Lakes 2000 Conference of Division 17 of the American Psychological Association, Muncie, IN.

Lent, E. B. (2001). Welfare-to-work services: A person-centered perspective. *Career Development Quarterly, 50*(1), 22–32.

Loprest, P. (2001). *How are families that left welfare doing? A comparison of early and recent welfare leavers.* Washington, DC: The Urban Institute.

Lynn, F. M. (2000). Community-scientist collaboration in environmental research. *American Behavioral Scientist, 44,* 649–663.

Nelson, M. K. (2002). The challenge of self-sufficiency: Women on welfare redefining independence. *Journal of Contemporary Ethnography, 31,* 582–614.

Nightingale, D. S., O'Brien, C. T., Egner, M., Pindus, N., & Trutko, J. (2003). *Welfare-to-work grants programs: Adjusting to changing circumstances.* Washington, DC: The Urban Institute. Retrieved March 31, 2004, from http://aspe.hhs.gov/hsp/wtw-grantseva198/adj03/report.pdf

O'Brien, K. M. (2001). The legacy of Parsons: Career counselors and vocational psychologists as agents of social change. *Career Development Quarterly, 50,* 66–76.

Parsons, F. (1909). *Choosing a vocation.* Boston: Houghton Mifflin.

Pavetti, L. (2000). Welfare policy in transition: Redefining the social contract for poor citizen families with children. *Focus, 21,* 44–50.

Rice, J. K. (2001). Poverty, welfare, and patriarchy: How macro-level changes in social policy can help low-income women. *Journal of Social Issues, 57,* 355–374.

Richardson, M. S. (1993). Work in people's lives: A location for counseling psychologists. *Journal of Counseling Psychology, 40,* 425–433.

Saunders, D. E., Peterson, G. W., Sampson, J. P., Jr., & Reardon, R. C. (2000). Relation of depression and dysfunctional career thinking to career indecision. *Journal of Vocational Behavior, 56,* 288–298.

SCANS. (1992). *Learning a living: A blueprint for high performance: A SCANS report for America 2000.* Washington, DC: Author.

Sweeney, M. L., & Schill, T. R. (1998). The association between self-defeating personality characteristics, career indecision, and vocational identity. *Journal of Career Assessment, 6,* 69–81.

U.S. Congress. (1996). Personal Responsibility and Work Opportunity Reconciliation Act of 1996 (Public Law 104–193). Retrieved September 6, 2005, from http://www.ssa.gov/OP_Home/comp2/F104-193.html

Wettersten, K. B., Rudolph, S., Faul, K., Gallagher, K., Transgrud, H., Adams, K., Graham, S., & Terrance, C. (2004). Freedom through self-sufficiency: A qualitative examination of the impact of domestic violence on the working lives of women in shelter. *Journal of Counseling Psychology, 51,* 447–462.

PART V

Social Justice in Health Care

CHAPTER 22

Counseling Health Psychology's Collaborative Role in the Community

Gargi Roysircar

Prevention can move counseling health psychologists, if motivated by social justice, outside the human service bubble. Although hospitals, health care providers, and university psychology departments are located in the community, they do not necessarily have a focus on community change by reaching out to low-income individuals, groups at risk for HIV/AIDS, or racial and ethnic minorities with prevention interventions. The community is constructed as the location of professional practice rather than social justice. Insurance providers and health professionals socialized in a capitalist society and aiming for corporate and personal wealth do not typically address larger social and economic determinants of health, such as conditions of poverty, pollution, employment, housing, and education. Although many health service organizations, particularly those guided by a religious mission, emphasize the value of caring and compassion and use the charity model of intervention, few emphasize collaboration with potential service users or the need for social justice for the impoverished or less privileged.

In the social justice orientation, the community is seen as part of a health problem and, thus, a necessary part of any solution to improve the lives of people. The community is identified as the consumer in answer to questions of Whose interests will be served? Is there congruence between the worldview of the change agent and those whom he or she will be serving? Social justice–oriented clinicians consider psychoeducation, skills training, consultation, action research, rehabilitation, and psychosocial competence when asked the question, What form will the intervention take? To uphold the value of distributive justice, community members can be asked how a health organization should allocate its resources. One purpose of this question is to find out whether the agency should increase its commitment to prevention compared to that of treatment. Incorporating the value-based social justice framework can move health service organizations along a continuum from exclusive focus on remediation to a focus on social and community transformation.

When a social justice orientation (Fouad et al., 2004) is combined with health psychology, societal and policy issues associated with the health status of the underserved are assessed and addressed. Differential health status across diverse communities is carefully examined and offered equity and access. The integration of the APA multicultural guidelines (APA, 2003) in service delivery makes it imperative for health psychologists, when working with diverse populations, to become familiar with indigenous beliefs and health practices and to respect these. An expanding body of evidence, as reviewed by Hopps and Liu (chapter 23) "Working for Social Justice From Within the Health Care System: The Role of Social Class in Psychology," and by Huynh and Roysircar (chapter 24) in "Community Health Promotion Curriculum: A Case Study on Southeast Asian Refugees," shows the changing complexion of prevention orientation from visions and ideals to hard facts and pragmatics about the lack of access and availability to large segments of people in the United States. Social justice and multicultural prevention may no longer have to compete for priority in the public health agenda, which traditionally has favored the amelioration of disease and mental disorder.

Take, for instance, the case of obesity, which from the medical model has historically been seen as excess weight associated with heart disease, lending justification for an extraordinary investment of resources in weight loss efforts in the United States. Recently, it has been argued that focusing on weight may obscure important risks (e.g., level of physical activity) that are (a) not necessarily addressed by weight loss, (b) more amenable to influence through prevention than weight status, and (c) less fraught with iatrogenic risks to physical and psychological well-being (Wei et al., 1999). As empirical support for this view of cardiac risk accumulates, a few promising prevention interventions are drawing attention from weight status and seeking instead to enhance physical activity; decouple self-esteem from weight; and reduce eating disorders, including repetitive eating (McFarlane, Polivy, & McCabe, 1999). This changed view about health and interventions parallels the advent of the biopsychosocial model (Engel, 1977).

From a biopsychosocial perspective, understanding how people respond to chronic or terminal illness is essential in the treatment of individuals. Health psychology recognizes that a biopsychosocial perspective is necessary to appropriately assess and address psychological issues associated with health status (Engel, 1977; Hoffman & Driscoll, 2000). The biological component of mental health historically has been given short shrift in counseling psychology, which, however, is attended to by counseling health psychology. Physical illness can have a large effect on the mental health and well-being of individuals as they traverse the difficulties related to diagnosis, treatment, recovery, or death.

The integrative model of health psychology framed within a social justice, multicultural, and biopsychosocial framework acknowledges the need for prevention, intervention, and management efforts within the sociocultural contexts of clients.

With regard to prevention, the history of public health provides compelling evidence for the relative efficiency of preventive versus reparative interventions. No disease or disorder has ever been eliminated by treating those who have it. Success stories in public health involve preventive victories such as eradicating smallpox and polio, halting epidemics of cholera and dysentery, and dramatically reducing infant mortality. There will never be a sufficient number of trained clinicians to provide treatment for all diagnosable cases of mental disorders. Therefore, counseling health psychology places strong emphasis on prevention. These principles are illustrated in various degrees by Hopps and Liu, Huynh and Roysircar, and Schmidt, Hoffman, and Taylor ("Social Justice Related to Working With HIV/AIDS From a Counseling Health Psychology Perspective").

The understanding of psychosocial effects of chronic or terminal illness has largely focused on patients or their significant others. However, the chapters in this section examine group or macro-level effects. They focus on community engagements or agency-based services for prevention and treatment and describe community-based action research projects that include the collaboration of psychology departments in universities with local health and human services (Huynh & Roysircar, chapter 24; Schmidt et al., chapter 25). Projects exemplify a globalized methodology (e.g., trauma and AIDS at the international level), but their presentation is grounded in the local community's knowledge base and culture. Additionally, educational initiatives to decrease health risks are discussed. All chapters review public policy regarding treatment of disease, promotion of health, and utilization of health services. They describe the process for evaluating the status quo in health care and recommend interventions for prevention and promotion. The chapters review the barriers of culture, economics, and stigmatization to effective care.

Understanding the protective mechanism behind positive adjustment to illness, such as health care and gaining confidence in health maintenance, is an interest of the authors in this section. Counseling psychology, which emphasizes positive adjustment and personal strengths, provides a framework for such an orientation to health psychology. Furthermore, the positive psychology movement (Lopez & Snyder, 2003) encourages researchers to investigate the sources of strength and well-being in times of crisis.

Hopps and Liu review the inverse relationship between social class and health. In their search of the literature, they found extensive evidence for the explanatory effects of health behaviors, psychosocial factors, and graded effects of medical conditions across social class levels, but all of these factors, they found, had an individual, or micro, focus. They found a somewhat less programmatic literature that considered systemic or macro factors such as the health care system and social structures that may perpetuate inequality such as classism. Hopps and Liu's chapter addresses the micro/macro distinction, and the literature is reviewed within this framework. Recommendations for interventions and research at the macro level are made.

Huyhn and Roysircar discuss that the public health literature indicates that Vietnamese and Cambodian refugees have poor physical and mental health. Leaving their countries to seek political asylum in the United States, many have met the criteria for surviving trauma. Yet they cannot easily access adequate health care because of sociocultural and environmental barriers. In general, these barriers are low English proficiency; low socioeconomic status or unemployment; lack of knowledge of Western health care; inadequate low-cost, community programming in ethnic languages; and service providers' lack of multicultural competence. Asian cultural attributions and values also lead to underreporting and underutilization. The authors served as a health promotion coordinator and as a program evaluator, respectively, with the Harvard Program in Refugee Trauma (HPRT). Vietnamese and Cambodian organizations recruited participants using different methods: word of mouth; flyers; and advertisements posted in local Southeast Asian print matter (e.g., community newspapers, newsletters, and health bulletins at local community health centers). Under the auspices of HPRT, the authors were involved in a pilot health promotion curriculum for Southeast Asian trauma survivors. It was a disease prevention model that used a teacher-student learning process. The curriculum presented information on physical and mental health concerns that are common to Southeast Asian populations, along with basic general health education. Community health educators, assisted by translators, provided instruction in Vietnamese and Kru/Khmer. Initial outcome results indicated that the pilot health promotion intervention was important for Southeast Asian refugees in Massachusetts, where there has been little, if any, community health education programming. A traditional walk-in clinic for medical crisis could have been an alternative possible intervention, but it would have been more expensive and would have offered remediation rather than prevention.

Professionals in psychology have witnessed how health epidemics, such as HIV/AIDS, have far-reaching effects beyond biomedical symptoms. Physical health and disease also have profound effects on psychosocial, cultural, and political facets of individual communities. Schmidt et al. have selected HIV/AIDS to illustrate how a social justice approach to counseling health psychology can be integrated into university research and training programs. They illustrate the impact of HIV/AIDS on individuals, communities, and societies, which provides the backdrop for counseling psychologists' work with this particular global health concern from a social justice perspective. Discussed in detail is the authors' vision for a University and Community Agency Partnership (U-CAP) program, designed for counseling psychology students to work with individuals suffering from HIV/AIDS. This model includes recommendations specifically designed for counseling psychologists concerned with social justice. U-CAP encourages universities to partner up with community agencies focused on HIV/AIDS work to create practicum and research opportunities for training purposes. Students who work in an agency offering services for HIV/AIDS have the unusual opportunity to explore not only health and overall functioning, but also sexuality and sexual behaviors, substance use and abuse, stigma, discrimination, sexual orientation, social class, race, ethnicity, access to health care, and an intersection of numerous other variables that have defined this pandemic. As a result, this exposure allows for this particular disease to serve as a template because a number of these topics can be explored in graduate coursework, such as ethics and multicultural classes. The proposed U-CAP program also encourages research on HIV/AIDS, especially as partnerships with community agencies and organizations.

Collaborations such as the U-CAP and HPRT models provide a reciprocal, mutually beneficial opportunity for primary and secondary intervention on the individual and community levels of HIV/AIDS and war trauma of political refugees, as well as in the social justice training of counseling psychology graduate students. These partnerships place the core values of social justice into action within the framework of counseling health psychology. The manner in which HIV/AIDS and the HPRT health promotion curriculum are addressed can serve as a template for social justice training in counseling psychology programs for future critical social issues.

Before concluding, I need to refer to a landmark, essential reading on mental health disparities. The Surgeon General's report (U.S. Department of Health and Human Services, 2001), which is a supplement to the 1999 report, documents the existence of several disparities affecting the mental health care of racial and ethnic minorities when compared with Whites:

Minorities have less access to and availability of mental health services.

Minorities are less likely to receive needed mental health services.

Minorities in treatment often receive a poorer quality of mental health care.

Minorities are underrepresented in mental health research.

Disparities impose a greater disability burden on the underserved. It is imperative that psychologists design preventive interventions that will reduce this burden for the underserved.

References

American Psychological Association. (2003). Guidelines on multicultural education, training, research, practice, and organizational change for psychologists. *American Psychologist, 58,* 377–402.

Engel, G. (1977). The need for a new medical model: A challenge for biomedicine. *Science, 196,* 129–136.

Fouad, N. A., McPherson, R. H., Gerstein, L., Blustein, D. L., Elman, N., Helledy, K. I., & Metz, A. J. (2004). Houston, 2001: Context and legacy. *The Counseling Psychologist, 32,* 15–77.

Hoffman, M. A., & Driscoll, J. (2000). Health promotion and disease prevention: A biopsychosocial model of health status. In R. Lent & S. Brown (Eds.), *Handbook of counseling psychology* (Vol. 3, pp. 532–567). New York: Wiley.

Lopez, S. J., & Snyder, C. R. (Eds.). (2003). *Positive psychological assessment: A handbook of models and measures.* Washington, DC: American Psychological Association.

McFarlane, T., Polivy, J., & McCabe, R. E. (1999). Help, not harm: Psychological foundation for a non-dieting approach toward health. *Journal of Social Issues, 55,* 261–276.

U.S. Department of Health and Human Services. (2001). *Mental health: Culture, race, and ethnicity—a supplement to mental health: A report of the Surgeon General.* Rockville, MD: Author.

Wei, M., Kampert, J. B., Barlow, C. E., Nichaman, M. Z., Gibbons, L. W., Paffenbarger, R. S., Jr., & Blair, S. N. (1999). Relationship between low cardiorespiratory fitness and mortality in normal-weight, overweight, and obese men. *Journal of the American Medical Association, 282,* 1547–1553.

CHAPTER 23

Working for Social Justice From Within the Health Care System

The Role of Social Class in Psychology

Joshua A. Hopps and William M. Liu

Social class is an enduring cultural phenomenon that has only recently begun to receive attention as a psychological variable (Frable, 1997; Liu, Ali, et al., 2004; Ostrove & Cole, 2003). All of the constructs comprising social class (e.g., income, education, occupation, wealth) are intertwined with central components of life, such as (a) the physical environment and exposure to environmental hazards; (b) the social environment and exposure to violence or support; (c) socialization of personality, mood, and affect management; and (d) health behaviors (Adler et al., 1994). To this list can be added institutions with which individuals must interact to function in society, such as local, state, and federal government agencies, law enforcement officers, and health care systems. These institutions must be considered because they participate in constructing an individual's experience of society and his or her situation within that society. Understanding the interface between individuals and societal institutions can provide an instructive paradigm for exploring the impact these institutions can and do have, thereby providing an intervention point for a social justice–oriented systemic change. In order to achieve a more acute focus, we examine one specific type of institution that plays an indisputably vital role in the life of every individual: the health care system. This is a fruitful area because there has been a great deal of research in the area of health care and demographic variables in general, whereas individuals' interactions with governments and law enforcement have been examined less extensively.

To build the case for the utility of the interface between systems and individuals as a fruitful area of social justice–minded intervention, we will first provide an overview of social class as a psychological construct and the need for psychologists to integrate social class into practice. Second, we will present trends in the literature on the relationship between health and social class. It will be argued that the relationship in question can be discussed by focusing on two areas: individual and systemic contributions. There is an extensive literature on the former, whereas the latter is just beginning to be acknowledged by social science researchers. The data on individual factors will be reviewed, followed by an examination of systemic factors. This is a useful distinction because it is important to account for the variance in health that is contributed by each party. Because the purpose of the chapter is to scrutinize the interface between individuals and systems, it is important to attempt to gauge what each contributes to the equation. What results will allow the isolation of the systemic factors that can impede access to health care or differential health outcomes for different social class groups?

Social Class as a Psychological Construct

Social class permeates virtually all aspects of our lives. Yet for psychologists, it is one of the most difficult cultural constructs to understand and integrate into practice (Frable, 1997). Usually, social class is considered the amalgamation of one's income, education, and occupation (Liu, Ali, et al., 2004; Liu, Soleck, Hopps, Pickett, & Dunston, 2004). Based on these three criteria, it is not clear how social class is derived. That is to say, if a psychologist were given the income, education, and occupation of an individual, how is social class constructed? Furthermore, how do psychologists make sense of a person's income, education, and occupation as pertinent experiences or characteristics of the client? Current explanations fall far too short to be helpful in clinical practice.

Typically, individuals are stratified into preexisting categories of lower, middle, and upper social class, to name a few. Using various levels of the three objective indicators, a social class position is created. Several problems and assumptions arise from this procedure. First, it is assumed that once a person is placed in the "social class," the individual is similar to others in the same social class (i.e., perceives the world similarly). The extant research literature, which is far too extensive to review fully in this chapter, suggests vast subjectivity (i.e., intragroup variation) even among those in the same or similar objective social class (Bullock & Limbert, 2003; Kuriloff & Reichert, 2003; Ostrove & Cole, 2003). Second, there has not been any agreed-on formula for how to place a person in a social class, or on the social class structure (Oakes & Rossi, 2003). Therefore, without consensus on how social class should be operationalized, classification into any stratification system might be problematic for psychologists.

One issue that plagues a psychological understanding of social class is the confusion between social class and socioeconomic status (SES). Oakes and Rossi (2003) posit that the difference between the two constructs has not been clearly defined, and there is conceptual overlap between the two. Power, privilege, income, education, life opportunities, and occupation, for instance, are used in both social class and SES. Regardless of the terminology used, the construct should be linked to some theoretical understanding of how social class functions, and more important, it should be linked with classism (Liu & Pope-Davis, 2003; Liu, Ali, et al., 2004; Liu, Soleck, et al., 2004). This last point, although conceptually simple, has not been done consistently in psychology (Lott, 2002; Ostrove & Cole, 2003). Even though research suggests that classism is related to how people perceive themselves, their experiences, and their psychological well-being (Carter, 2003; Croizet & Claire, 1998; Grella, 1990; Liu, 2002), psychologists have infrequently examined both social class and classism as co-dependent constructs (Liu, Ali, et al., 2004). Throughout this chapter, we will use the term *social class* because it is conceptually easier to link it with classism. For us, social class represents a person's self-perceived social standing, and the individual's recognition that some people are higher, similar, and lower than the individual is currently. Because of the differences in perceived social class, it is likely that the individual will experience classism from others but also enact classism as a means to maintain his or her social class (Liu, Ali, et al., 2004; Liu, Soleck, et al., 2004).

Currently, several authors have suggested the need for psychologists to address classism (Liu, Ali, et al., 2004; Lott, 2002), examine the subjective experiences of social class (Adler, Epel, Castellazzo, & Ickovics, 2000; Liu, Soleck, et al., 2004; Ostrove & Cole, 2003), and connect social class with various experiences and psychological constructs (Ostrove & Cole, 2003) rather than treating it as a nuisance variable or demographic characteristic. Research has begun to explore the intersections of people's lives in areas such as schooling (Kuriloff & Reichert, 2003), work (Liu, 2002), and different racial groups (Clark, Anderson, Clark, & Williams, 1999; Cole & Omari, 2003). Just as important, research has examined how social class, access to health care, and self-perception are associated with health behaviors and help-seeking attitudes (Boyle & Lipman, 2002; Chen, Matthews, & Boyce, 2002; Cockerham, 1990; Cooper, 2002; Gallo & Matthews, 2003; Krieger, Willains, & Moss, 1997).

Background: Foundational Literature

In the past 30 years, research in the area of health and social class has blossomed into an expansive literature. Several approaches have been taken: (a) examination of the impact of living below the poverty line (e.g., Haan, Kaplan, & Camacho, 1987); (b) the graded effects of social class across the stratification range (e.g., Logue & Jarjoura, 1990); and (c) biopsychosocial mechanisms and pathways (e.g., Lantz et al., 2001). Research initially relied a great deal on longitudinal correlational data, mainly drawing associations between morbidity, mortality, and SES (we will use SES when necessary to accurately represent the original research). Several prominent examples warrant brief exploration. Kitagawa and Hauser (1973) linked death records with education and occupation information for the 1960 U.S. census and found that although mortality rates were dropping for the entire population, higher SES groups enjoyed a mortality decrease that was 60% greater than that of the lower groups. A strong inverse relationship was found between mortality and SES, a finding that has been echoed repeatedly. A full 5-year difference in life expectancy was found between the most and the least educated, and a strong link was found between heart disease and SES (Kitagawa & Hauser, 1973). Silver (1972) sampled all states in the United States from 1959 to 1961 and gathered data on median income in the area, household income, marital status, smoking, psychological stress, climate, air pollution, public health expenditures, and physician distribution. His conclusions reinforced those of Kitigawa and Hauser, finding a negative correlation with mortality for several variables: income, education, stress, and smoking.

In the United Kingdom, the Black Report (Townsend, Davidson, & Whitehead, 1988) and the Whitehall Studies (Marmot, Shipley, & Rose, 1984; Marmot et al., 1991) examined inequalities in the six SES stratifications in the United Kingdom. Mortality was twice as high for the lowest group as for the highest, even after controlling for race and age. On parallel with findings in the United States, there was evidence that the gap was expanding because of a more rapid decline in mortality among those in the upper classifications. As health care improves in quality and accessibility, the disparities between social class groups widen, because these benefits accrue differentially for upper- and middle-class groups, whereas those less privileged continue to be left behind. Similar evidence has been found in other western and eastern nations (e.g., Scandinavia, France, Japan) (Feinstein, 1993). Back in the United States, researchers added to the evidence for an expanding gap in mortality rates between SES groups (Feldman, Makuc, Kleinman, & Cornoni-Huntly, 1989). For White men aged 65–74, the difference between highest and lowest SES groups (measured by education) increased from 10% in 1960 to 100% in 1971–1984. This was mostly attributed to a sharp decline in heart disease among the most educated, whereas rates remained steady for the least educated. Among European American women, the gap between mortality of the highest and lowest educational groups was more pronounced than for their male counterparts. Logue and Jarjoura (1990) added to the complexity of the picture by increasing the focus on the middle of the social class range. In their U.S. sample, when compared with the upper middle class, the lower middle class had twice the mortality rate, and the working class had four times the mortality rate.

The U.S. Department of Health and Human Services (USDHHS, 2003) recently released a comprehensive report detailing disparities in health care in the United States. The National Healthcare Disparities Report details inequalities for members of racial and ethnic minority groups and lower social class groups across the entire health care system. These include limited access to primary care and specialized referrals, different recommendations for tests and interventions, disparate exposure to preventative efforts, and many similar findings, although the scope of the report cannot be encapsulated here. The Department of Health and Human Services has made an important step in making the commitment to annually compile data on health care disparities and track changes over time.

The inverse relationship between health and social class has been replicated across the life span: Neonatal adjustment has been shown to relate to social class

(Field et al., 2002), as has adolescent physical and emotional well-being (Brady & Matthews, 2002; Goodman, 1999; Starfield, Riley, Witt, & Robertson, 2002). Adult health risk behaviors are consistently related to poor socioeconomic conditions in childhood (Lynch, Kaplan, & Salonen, 1997). Among seniors, morbidity, mortality, poor quality of life, and cognitive functioning have shown to be inversely related to social class (Bassuk, Berkman, & Amick, 2002; Long, Ickovics, Gill, & Horowitz, 2001; Martikainen, Stansfeld, Hemingway, & Marmot, 1999; Turrell et al., 2002). Furthermore, there is evidence that social class hardship can accumulate across the life span, affecting health, psychological adjustment, self-care ability, and cognitive functioning (Lynch, Kaplan, & Shema, 1997; Turrell et al., 2002).

Not surprisingly, race is highly conflated with social class because of the history of oppression of people of color and continued economic disadvantage. In one study, Williams and Rucker (1996) found that one third of African Americans and 29% of Latinos were below the poverty line compared to 12% of European Americans. African Americans have higher rates of mortality, disease, and disability than do European Americans (Hayward, Crimmins, Miles, & Yang, 2000). Latinos and African Americans are more likely than European Americans to label their health as poor and more likely to report a compromise in the ability to perform activities of daily living (Ren & Amick, 1996). Hayward et al. (2000) found that socioeconomic conditions primarily accounted for the racial gap in health to the exclusion of health behaviors. However, these constructs remain difficult to separate. The Health Disparities Report of the USDHHS analyzed economic disadvantage and race separately and found that when disparities were found, they frequently co-occurred for both of these groups, although there are exceptions to this (e.g., findings of effect of race on health care). Factors such as limited proficiency in English and cultural differences from the provider specifically affect individuals from minority groups, whereas these are much less likely to be the case for majority group members of lower social class groups. Research that could directly address this question by targeting middle-class members of racial and ethnic minority groups is lacking.

Because of the social and methodological complexity of the constructs involved, no single factor is likely to account for all of the variance in the relationship between health and social class. Several theories have emerged about the social class-health relationship with varying amounts of explanatory power. One theory that has fallen out of favor is the drift hypothesis, which states that rather than social class causing poor health outcomes, the opposite is true. Because of poor health and concomitant economic and psychosocial repercussions, individuals slide down the social class scale. However, support never emerged from data, and this explanation has generally fallen from favor (Adler et al., 1994; Haan, Kaplan, & Syme, 1989). Adler and co-workers (1994) have proffered an alternative theory: "SES affects biological functions that in turn influence health status" (p. 17). Because of difficulty operationalizing and conceptualizing social class, we know little about the pathways that affect this relationship. In the next section, a distinction is made in etiology, function, and level of effect that may serve to clarify this matter.

Definitional Issues

An important distinction will be made when discussing the literature from this point forward: Putative causal mechanisms and pathways for the inverse relationship between social class and health will be divided into macro and micro levels. This will be done for two reasons: (a) because of different etiology for macro and micro pathways, these two pathways cannot be assumed to be unitary (Feinstein, 1993); and (b) the potential for different types of interventions to occur on a macro (i.e., community, societal) or micro (individual) level (Seeman & Crimmins, 2001). Macro-level mechanisms are defined as extrinsic, systemic factors outside the control of the individual that play a role in determining their socioeconomic and cultural milieu. Some examples of this are the structure of the health care system, attributes of the community, and racial and social class segregation. Micro mechanisms are those that are intrapsychic, psychosocial, or behavioral in origin. These are intrinsic personal attributes or are purportedly under the control of the individual. Although it can be argued that aspects of personality are determined by one's surroundings, especially during formative years, in order to present a cogent description, personality variables will be placed in the micro or individual domain. However, data on the psychological concomitants of low social class and economic hardship will be presented below. Examples of micro-level variables include health risk behaviors such as smoking, and psychological variables such as locus of control. Although the literature on the contributions of micro-level variables is quite robust, the conceptualization and condensation of macro-level variables as systemic in origin is relatively new (Seeman & Crimmins, 2001).

A number of pathways have emerged from literature as mediating the relationship between health and social class across the social class continuum (Goldman, 2001). The most prominent of these are (a) patterns of health risk behaviors; (b) feelings of control, security, and ability to cope; (c) social support; (d) access to stress-mediating resources; (e) exposure to stress; (f) access to preventive and curative medical care; (g) exposure to poor environmental conditions; and (h) access to health risk and health care information/education opportunities. These pathways can be divided into micro (individual) and macro (systemic) factors with the first four categorized as micro; the fifth straddling micro and macro; and the sixth, seventh, and eighth categorized as macro. Because exposure to stress can come from both systemic (e.g., classism, racism, economic deprivation) and individual (e.g., risk taking, poor life decisions, relationship discord) factors, the fifth pathway straddles the division between macro and micro causal pathways. These pathways will be expanded upon in the next two sections.

Micro Pathways

Research has, in part, turned from describing societal patterns to describing individual effects and risk factors, focusing on investigations of diseases and health conditions. This allows inferences to be made about the impact of these conditions on resiliency, morbidity, and mortality on an individual, or micro, level.

Potential Mechanisms: Causes and Contributors

Many health conditions have shown a now familiar inverse relationship with social class, such as obesity (Everson, Maty, Lynch, & Kaplan, 2002; Wardle, Waller, & Jarvis, 2002), cardiovascular disease (Singh & Siahpush, 2002; Smith & Hart, 2002; USDHHS, 2003), diabetes (Everson et al., 2002; USDHHS, 2003), fetal development (Field et al., 2002), poor traumatic brain injury prognosis (Hoofien, Vakil, Gilboa, Donovick, & Barak, 2002), subjective health rating (Cohen, Kaplan, & Salonen, 1999; Franks, Clancy, Gold, & Nutting, 1993), subjective life expectancy (Mirowsky & Ross, 2000), and difficulty with activities of daily living (Lynch, Kaplan, & Shema, 1997). Health behaviors have also received a great deal of focus over the past 30 years, but especially so in the past decade. Although behaviors such as smoking, lack of physical activity, alcohol consumption, and poor diet are associated with poor health outcomes (Lantz et al., 1998; Lantz et al., 2001; Logue & Jarjoura, 1990; Lynch, Kaplan, & Salonen, 1997; Marmot et al., 1984; Simon, van de Mheen, van der Meer, & Mackenbach, 2000), they account for only a portion of the variance in the relationship between SES and health, leaving questions about what is the dominating explanation for differences (Lantz et al., 2001). Many behaviors classified as a health risk are often intractable and difficult to change, and even if remediation occurred, the social class imbalance would remain (Lantz et al., 1998). This is not to say that focusing on remediation of health risk behaviors is fruitless. On the contrary, it is the intervention of choice on an individual, micro level. However, broader changes are necessary in order to address all of the factors involved.

Furthermore, psychological factors have been shown to play a role in differential resiliency, adjustment, and coping. Malatu and Schooler (2002) conclude that general psychological distress accounts for a notable amount of the variance in the inverse relationship between SES and health. Higher social class individuals experience relatively fewer life stressors and rate events as less stressful than do lower class groups (Adler et al., 1994; Carroll, Bennett, & Davey-Smith, 1993; Stronks, van de Mheen, Looman, & Mackenbach, 1998). Upper-class individuals experience less stress and are better able to cope with what stress they do experience. Exposure to higher levels of stress results in increased activation of the physiological stress response. Chronic elevation in levels of stress hormones and neurotransmitters, such as cortisol and catecholamines, can result in higher levels of chronic stress, poorer response to acute stressors, and poorer health status. Less privileged groups have been found to be higher than their upper-class counterparts in depression (Adler et al., 1994), hostility (Ranchor, Bouma, & Sanderman, 1996), cynicism and trait anger (Haukkala, 2002), poor self-esteem (Twenge & Campbell, 2002), poor sense of mastery (Williams & Rucker, 1996), and mental status decline (Long et al., 2001).

Social support has proven to be a complicated factor because of graded effects across the scope of SES. Social networks of lower-class individuals may be less supportive than those with relatively more social status, or if supportive, they are more likely to be a significant source of stress as well (Williams & Rucker, 1996). Among married couples, low SES was highly associated with joint experience of health problems (Wilson, 2001).

Macro-Level Factors

Access to health care is determined by several factors (Feinstein, 1993): (a) existence and quality of health insurance coverage, (b) provider/treatment variables, and (c) ability to navigate the system. Those at the lower end of SES are less likely to have health insurance and more likely to have poor subjective health status and medical conditions, a particularly difficult combination (Franks et al., 1993). Insurance plans are likely to be restricted for type of pharmaceutical treatment and physician (Feinstein, 1993; USDHHS, 2003). Shi and Starfield (2001) found an inverse relationship between primary care physician supply, income inequality, and mortality. Lower-income individuals may be more likely to use primary care under a universal health care system, but after controlling for health need, these individuals visited specialists less than their middle- and high-income counterparts (Dunlop, Coyte, & McIsaac, 2000). In an investigation of the influence of physician attributes on clinical decisions, McKinlay, Lin, Freund, and Moskowitz (2002) found that while patient demographic variables had no impact on treatment decisions, provider characteristics did. That is, extraneous attributes of the physician influenced health care decisions. Van Ryn and Burke (2000) found that physicians perceived lower- and middle-class individuals more negatively than upper-class individuals on variables such as personality, abilities, and behavioral tendencies. The USDHHS report found that individuals from lower-income and ethnic/racial minority groups were more likely to report poor communication and problems in their relationship with their primary care physician. These individuals were also less likely to receive referrals to specialists as well as certain interventions and diagnostic procedures.

Health literacy, or the ability to achieve a level of comprehension about health care to allow knowledgeable participation in decision making and treatment, has gained currency as a way to draw attention to the importance of full participation of the individual receiving treatment. It is conceived as part of what the treated individual brings to the interaction with the health care system. Therefore, if an individual is somewhat less than assertive in verifying understanding, or has difficulty conceptualizing medical problems, his or her health literacy can be a liability. One third of elderly patients and 80% of patients at public hospitals had poor or marginal health literacy, and this is related to poorer health status, higher hospitalization rates and costs, and reduced use of prevention efforts (Andrus & Roth, 2002; Williams, Davis, Parker, & Weiss, 2002). According to current measures of health literacy, 48% of Americans fall below adequate levels (Andrus & Roth, 2002). Because this is an astoundingly high number, the shortcoming appears to be on the part of the health care industry rather than individuals. Any failure on that scale should be remediated at the source, which is failure to communicate and check that those individuals receiving treatment understand their treatment. Using the example of individuals with diabetes, Schillinger and colleagues (2003) found that even though almost half of the information conveyed by physicians is not retained after a visit, understanding was assessed in only 20% of visits and about 12% of new concepts. Those individuals whose physicians did perform this type of assessment had better markers of adherence with the health care regimen in laboratory results. Schillinger and colleagues recommend that physicianss assess for levels of understanding of treatment concepts and tailor subsequent information to the individual's level of health literacy. This is especially important for those from lower social class groups as they appear to have particular difficulty with access to and understanding of health care information (USDHHS, 2003).

There is extensive evidence that lower social class groups have poorer experiences at all levels of health care: preventive, diagnosis and entry, treatment efficacy, and follow-up and readmission. These poor experiences include later diagnosis and admission, poorer prognosis following diagnosis, lower levels of compliance, and more difficulty navigating HMOs and finding nursing home care (Feinstein, 1993; USDHHS, 2003). Individuals from the lower end of the SES hierarchy are more likely to be passive when it comes to managing their own health care, and place the responsibility on the health care system (Cockerham, Lueschen, Kunz, & Spaeth, 1986).

Additionally, access to health risk information and health care educational opportunities can have a significant influence on health outcomes. In an examination of the interaction of social class and racial factors with cancer, limited knowledge, misinformation about cancer, and mistrust of the health care system were related to poorer adjustment and health care behaviors (Matthews, Sellergren, Manfredi, & Williams, 2002). O'Malley et al. (2001) found that women from lower social class groups were significantly less likely to receive a provider recommendation for a mammogram, which reduces the likelihood of receiving this type of preventive care. It is vital that health care providers engage in education and communication across the gamut of social class groups.

Exposure to poor environmental conditions beginning in childhood can also cause disadvantages to accumulate across the life span. Because housing options are restricted as social class decreases, those in lower social class groups are more likely to live in areas with higher crime and violence rates; pollution problems (e.g., hazardous waste, pesticides, industrial chemicals, air pollutants) (Evans, 2004; Seeman & Crimmins, 2001); and poorer drinking water (Anderson & Armstead, 1995; Ewart & Suchday, 2002; Lantz et al., 1998). Lower-class individuals are also more likely to have jobs that increase exposure to dangerous situations or hazardous materials (Feinstein, 1993), and prolonged exposure to poor material conditions is related to poor perceived health (Stronks et al., 1998). Living in areas in which there is a lack of investment in social capital (fewer resources spent on education, transportation, etc.) can have an erosive effect on health and social class advancement (Seeman & Crimmins, 2001). In a study of a large urban area, Haan et al. (1987) found that living in a poverty area was predictive of mortality even after controlling for SES and health factors. In other words, living in inner-city poverty conditions adds additional hardship to an already disadvantaged social class group.

As mentioned above, none of these factors in isolation will be sufficient to fully explain the gradient relationship between social class and health. Examining factors by the macro and micro etiologies allows for parsimonious exploration of a sizeable literature and opening a discussion of interventions on a macro level to supplement the micro-level interventions used on individual factors, such as psychotherapy and education.

Social Justice Intervention

A contradiction exists in the literature in the discussion of the meaning of the above findings for designing and delivering interventions. For example, Lantz et al. (1998), citing the inability of health risk behaviors to account for more than a modest amount of the variance in SES and health, cautioned that public health policies aimed at reducing health risk behaviors, although still indicated, would not eradicate the socioeconomic disparities in health. Designing a mass remediation program for intransigent health risk behaviors would indeed be shortsighted, but community-level preventive and educational initiatives have different goals. The difficulty arises when the sole point of intervention or prevention activity occurs in the sphere of the individual. This ignores the contribution of health care systems and places the onus on people, who may not be facile at operating within an often overwhelming system. It is our contention that although interventions at the individual level must be conducted, and are indeed essential in many cases, a system that is inflexible to the needs of consumers and unaware of its own shortcomings will inevitably fail. Systems must include sufficient flexibility to adapt to the needs of individuals in order to achieve equivalent levels of treatment across social class groups. This flexibility can occur at a policy level within institutions, but, perhaps most important for our purposes here, can also be implemented at the level of the health care provider.

Several of the studies reviewed above give indications not only about where the system fails those within it but also about how those failures can be averted or remediated. In general, lower social classification is related to poorer experiences at all levels of health care, leading to later diagnosis and admission, poorer prognosis, and poor compliance. However, two specific findings will be discussed from the perspective of mental health care providers interested in social justice interventions that are feasible even while working from within, or from without, the system.

First, social class can be predictive of poor knowledge and understanding of, and even misinformation about, medical conditions. Lack of understanding can be an important ingredient in poor compliance with the recommendations of health care professionals. If an individual does not grasp the importance of the health care regimen, he or she may be somewhat less than conscientious about adhering to each aspect. Also, if patients are not informed of the potential pitfalls of adhering to the prescribed treatment, they may be unprepared when the inevitable challenge arises, and compromise their compliance (Rapoff, 1999). Treatment goals may conflict between the provider and the patient (e.g., a different focus on pain, quality of life, etc.), and in such cases, adherence to treatment regiments is vulnerable (Clay & Hopps, 2003). These concerns can be addressed by health care providers by asking questions about specifics of what an individual understands about his or her condition, hopes to gain from treatment, and can reasonably adhere to without undue distress. Prescribing a treatment that is effective but beyond the scope of the individual's behavioral resources is tantamount to no treatment at all. A quick assessment can give the provider an idea of a feasible treatment plan. (For further discussion of treatment adherence related to individual and systemic factors and accommodation of treatment to an individual's lifestyle, see Clay & Hopps, 2003.) A lack of knowledge of preventive medicine can also be a problem. The illustrative example mentioned above was fewer mammograms for women from lower social class groups. This is disturbing because this was due to not only a lack of awareness of the usefulness of breast cancer screening, but also an apparent reluctance among physicians to make this referral.

Health literacy research focused on this issue has found that nearly half of individuals operating within the health system have inadequate understanding of their health care. With such a deficit, individuals cannot fully participate in their own health care, in decision making or in adherence to their prescribed treatment. This doubtless affects their health outcomes, and is at a level that clearly implicates a failure of the health care system to communicate effectively with its consumers. This is an important distinction to maintain, because it shifts the burden onto the entity providing the care, rather than those receiving care. Health care providers should check for understanding of concepts as they are introduced. They should also assess understanding across visits to minimize drift in treatment adherence. Open-ended questions such as, "Do you understand?" may not be useful because the patient may feel overwhelmed or may not want to appear uninformed. Specific probing questions about information conveyed should target key concepts and should serve to check for comprehension and provide a repetition of vital points from the visit. These can easily be phrased to avoid a paternalistic stance: "I've thrown a lot of information your way today and want to make sure we're on the same page about some important points. What do you remember about . . . ?"

Although mental health providers are infrequently able to make direct referrals within health care systems, they can take steps to facilitate their clients'/patients' access to care. Psychoeducation should be a holistic endeavor that not only emphasizes mental health, but also acknowledges the mind-body relationship. Once individuals are more familiar with this relationship, mental health providers can discuss important steps, preventive and remediative alike, that their clients/patients should consider, such as mammograms and prostate exams. Psychotherapy, and virtually every other psychological intervention, involves a great deal of education, and the concepts discussed above apply equally. Checking for memory of material across contacts can give practitioners an idea of what the individual views as important from sessions and also highlight areas that may not be addressed at a deeper level. Education is an inherently empowering endeavor, and its importance should never be underestimated. Aiding an individual in increasing his or her agency within the health care system, or in any setting, can empower a person to operate more competently within a system that may have objectives not entirely compatible with his or her own.

Second, passivity in managing health care is a common way of coping among lower social class groups, and these individuals find it increasingly difficult to navigate HMOs and find nursing home care. Indeed, there is a tendency to place the responsibility of health care on the health care system, a dangerous prospect in a system geared to lower costs rather than advocate for individuals. It is at this point when individuals slip through the cracks, an all too common phrase among those employed in health care.

Again, when direct referrals are not possible, mental health care providers still have options to pursue in advocating for their clients/patients. It is important to reemphasize a biopsychosocial focus on mental and physical health with clients and patients. This should include an assessment of physical well-being and encouraging a visit to a primary care physician when possible. If an individual has known health problems, these should not be seen as beyond the purview of the mental health provider. These problems should be tracked across client contacts, and signs of slipping through the cracks should be noted and addressed with the client. If possible, the mental health provider can request the client's permission to consult with the health care provider. The information available to different providers can often benefit all parties in treatment planning and implementation. In addition, the consultation can include diplomatically worded education of physicians, nurses, and other health care providers about social class issues as they relate to health and health care in general and specifically relate to the client or patient. Consultation may reveal or convey that the individual receiving treatment is not as aware of his or her treatment as desired, and strategies across providers can be designed to boost adherence to medical and psychological treatment. Given the evidence that health care providers' attributes, such as job satisfaction (DiMatteo et al., 1993) and perception of their patients (van Ryn, 2002; van Ryn & Burke, 2000), can influence their decision making and patient outcome, education of providers within the system is vital for systemic change. To achieve a social justice orientation, it is vital that the mental health provider construe his or her helping influence as extending beyond the traditional boundaries of the 50-minute session within the four walls of the consultation room.

Interventions at the Community Level

Social justice interventions at the community level have been shown to be effective in reducing social class disparities in health. In fact, Seeman and Crimmins (2001) cite community efforts to change unhealthy living conditions as some of the most successful public health interventions to date. For example, Syme (1978) conducted a study that made use of community resources for education by training community members to deliver educational information, rather than using standard health care outlets. Community members supplied direct assistance, support, and referrals, and overall compliance with medical regimens was boosted. However, there has been a lack of communication between research and practice in the area of community-level intervention. A more recent example is a program in Houston, Texas (Holleman, Bray, Davis, & Holleman, 2004), developed primarily for homeless individuals and families, most of whom had never had a primary care physician. All individuals beginning the program received an hour with a physician who collaborated closely with psychologists and family therapists to make appropriate physical and mental health referrals. Psychoeducation of the participants was highly emphasized in programs on medication management, and it was highly integrated into support groups and individual psychotherapy, as well as career and family building skills. The emphasis on collaboration—both interdisciplinary and patient-provider—was especially salient for all involved because it allowed for relatively seamless care of the biopsychosocial needs of the participants.

Health promotion theory has focused on both primary and secondary prevention efforts. These preventive steps occur at different points of access, one at the community level and another at the level of an individual health care professional and his or her client. Secondary prevention, or preventive medicine, occurs at the individual level and focuses on screening, educating, and counseling individuals about risky behaviors. There has been a disconnection between these two types of preventive efforts, with conflicting research findings and recommendations to health care providers (Dibble, 2003). This may have resulted in diminished referrals to community organizations focused on primary prevention and less of a focus on social and behavioral issues. Moreover, economically disadvantaged individuals are less likely to have a relationship with a primary care physician, thereby missing both primary and secondary prevention (USDHHS, 2003).

In their review of health promotion theory, Best and colleagues (2003) also noted a disjointed approach and classified current theories as focusing on one of the following, to the exclusion of the others: empowerment, reduction of risk behavior, or structural organization. Each of these theories is grounded in a wealth of theoretical and empirical scholarship in public health; but each contains only a segment of the issue of health disparities within its purview and alone is limited in its ability to comprehensively address current concerns. Best and colleagues argue that to optimize effective implementation of the research, it is vital that all of these be addressed. They propose community partnering as such a model because it allows for empowerment of the community by incorporating its members and establishing a structure that involves local practitioners in multiple disciplines as well as large state, provincial, and local organizations. It also facilitates interventions at the various levels where barriers exist: policy, systemic, and individual. In designing these interventions, it is vital that there be practical and theoretical rapprochement among researchers and practitioners from multiple disciplines. Diversity in theory and discipline is important in order to promote collaboration and maximize theoretical breadth, and to integrate separate but parallel knowledge bases from literature in different disciplines: public health, preventive medicine, nursing, health psychology, social work, and more. The program for homeless individuals described above (Holleman et al., 2004) is an example of an intervention with both breadth and depth at the community and individual levels, focusing on empowerment, education, behavior modification, and training on how to negotiate the health care system.

Communities often have organizations focused on concerns that are specific to their neighborhood, such as social class, race, crime, environmental conditions, and so on. Neighborhood associations are relatively common structural manifestations of a consensus of concern, and thus are often the conduit for political action that communities take about social issues. Although there is a wide degree of variability in the form and activity level of these groups, it is essential that this resource be accessed when designing and implementing interventions at the community level. In fact, neighborhood associations may be more active and more likely to focus on political issues in disadvantaged neighborhoods than in middle-class communities (Lenk, Toomey, Wagenaar, Bosma, & Vessey, 2002). However, the voice generated by these disadvantaged communities may have less clout than those with more resources (Mesch & Schwirian, 1996). By aligning with poorer neighborhoods, researchers and practitioners may directly affect the efficacy of neighborhood associations by providing additional attention to vital issues and improving social and policy-related networks. When professionals work with disadvantaged individuals, there should be a commitment to the community with concrete, planned results to avoid the appearance of exploitation for a research or policy agenda (Sue & Sue, 2002).

Specific Interventions

Making an intervention on a systemic level can strengthen ties and increase individual members' investment in the community. When health risk behaviors occur on such a wide scale, both macro- and micro-level interventions are necessary to address the scope and depth of the problem. Grzywacz, McMahan, Hurley, Stokols, and Phillips (2004) argue that the next era in rectifying health disparities involves intervention at these different levels using empirically derived "promising strategies" (p. 8). At the public policy level, some of the known examples of appropriate starting points for the systemic aspect of health risk behavior prevention and intervention are housing; environmental conditions; and the availability of alcohol, cigarettes, and fatty foods (especially to adolescents). At the level of the health care system, it is important to extinguish unnecessary barriers to health care access, including improving access to transportation; evaluate the cultural competence of all those within the health care system, including administrative staff; and eliminate institutional policies that may be inadvertently racist and/or classist. At the community level, working through established neighborhood associations not only improves the credibility of health care workers, but also can serve to strengthen community networks and establish more accessible care for hard-to-reach individuals. At the individual level, it is important that the targeted audience is known and that all outreach materials are appropriately designed. A biopsychosocial approach is important at the individual level because health status has ramifications for all aspects of human experience. Incorporation of research findings on patient education, like those mentioned above, on an individual and a systemic level is vital if those less skilled in operating within a daunting system are to be incorporated. Further investigation of how providers can facilitate this process is also warranted.

Research would do well to begin to test interventions that navigate at the policy level, the systemic (community and health care system) level, and the individual level. Although such programs are massive undertakings, it is vital that there be an integration of data and experience across disciplines. Continued research on micro-level contributions to the health/social class gradient is necessary, but neglecting the exploration of systemic contributions is tantamount to blaming the victim.

Although the interrelationship between social class and race has thus far proven elusive, it is an important question that should be addressed. An examination of health status and experiences within the health care system of middle- and upper-class racial/ethnic minorities will be an important step.

Conclusion

Social justice is clearly an aspirational goal for mental health providers. We have argued that systemic social justice interventions are possible at the individual level if practitioners extend beyond the comfort zone of the office and face-to-face client contact, and reconceptualize their helping role in a broader fashion. We chose the health care system as an example for such attempts because of the extant disparities in social class and health, and we emphasized a focus on clients' health, education of clients and other providers, and advocacy of clients who are all but invisible on the systemic level. This is certainly beyond what is required and probably what is asked. Overwhelmed with droves of needful patients and their own struggle for autonomy and a helping role within a complex system, many providers may be disinterested in either making or receiving such attempts. To persevere in reaching these providers, exactly those we would like to reach, is easy to ask when preaching to the choir.

References

Adler, N. E., Boyce, T., Chesney, M. A., Cohen, S., Folkman, S., Kahn, R. L., & Syme, S. L. (1994). Socioeconomic status and health: The challenge of the gradient. *American Psychologist, 49*(1), 15–24.

Adler, N. E., Epel, E. S., Castellazzo, G., & Ickovics, J. R. (2000). Relationship of subjective and objective social status with psychological functioning: Preliminary data in healthy White women. *Health Psychology, 19,* 586–592.

Anderson, N. B., & Armstead, C. A. (1995). Toward understanding the association of socio-economic status and health: A new challenge for the biopsychosocial approach. *Psychosomatic Medicine, 57*(3), 213–225.

Andrus, M., & Roth, M. (2002). Health literacy: A review. *Pharmacotherapy, 22*(3), 282–302.

Bassuk, S. S., Berkman, L. F., & Amick, B. C., III. (2002). Socioeconomic status and mortality among the elderly: Findings from four U.S. communities. *American Journal of Epidemiology, 155*(6), 520–533.

Best, A., Stokols, D., Green, L. W., Leischow, S., Holmes, B., & Buchholz, K. (2003). An integrative framework for community partnering to translate theory into effective health promotion strategy. *American Journal of Health Promotion, 18*(2), 168–176.

Boyle, M. H., & Lipman, E. L. (2002). Do places matter? Socioeconomic disadvantage and behavioral problems of children in Canada. *Journal of Consulting and Clinical Psychology, 70,* 378–389.

Brady, S. S., & Matthews, K. A. (2002). The influence of socioeconomic status and ethnicity on adolescents' exposure to stressful life events. *Journal of Pediatric Psychology, 27*(7), 575–583.

Bullock, H. E., & Limbert, W. M. (2003). Scaling the socioeconomic ladder: Low-income women's perceptions of class status and opportunity. *Journal of Social Issues, 59,* 693–710.

Carroll, D., Bennett, P., & Davey-Smith, G. (1993). Socio-economic health inequalities: Their origins and implications. *Psychology & Health, 8*(5), 295–316.

Carter, P. L. (2003). "Black" cultural capital, status positioning, and schooling conflicts for low income African American youth. *Social Problems, 50*(1), 136–155.

Chen, E., Matthews, K. A., & Boyce, W. T. (2002). Socioeconomic differences in children's health: How and why do these relationships change with age? *Psychological Bulletin, 128,* 295–329.

Clark, R., Anderson, N. B., Clark, V. R., & Williams, D. R. (1999). Racism as a stressor for African Americans: A biopsychosocial model. *American Psychologist, 54,* 805–816.

Clay, D., & Hopps, J. (2003). Treatment adherence in rehabilitation: The role of treatment accommodation. *Rehabilitation Psychology, 48*(3), 215–219.

Cockerham, W. C. (1990). A test of the relationship between race, socioeconomic status, and psychological distress. *Social Science and Medicine, 31,* 1321–1326.

Cockerham, W. C., Lueschen, G., Kunz, G., & Spaeth, J. L. (1986). Social stratification and self-management of health. *Journal of Health & Social Behavior, 27*(1), 1–14.

Cohen, S., Kaplan, G. A., & Salonen, J. T. (1999). The role of psychological characteristics in the relation between socioeconomic status and perceived health. *Journal of Applied Social Psychology, 29*(3), 445–468.

Cole, E. R., & Omari, S. R. (2003). Race, class and the dilemmas of upward mobility for African Americans. *Journal of Social Issues, 59,* 785–802.

Cooper, H. (2002). Investigating socio-economic explanations for gender and ethnic inequalities in health. *Social Science & Medicine, 54,* 693–706.

Croizet, J. C., & Claire, T. (1998). Extending the concept of stereotype threat to social class: The intellectual underperformance of students from low socioeconomic backgrounds. *Personality and Social Psychology Bulletin, 24,* 588–594.

Dibble, R. (2003). Eliminating disparities: Empowering health promotion within preventive medicine. *American Journal of Health Promotion, 18*(2), 195–199.

DiMatteo, M. R., Sherbourne, C. D., Hays, R. D., Ordway, L., Kravitz, R., McGlynn, E., Kaplan, S., & Rogers, W. (1993). Physicians' characteristics influence patients' adherence to medical treatment: Results from the Medical Outcomes Study. *Health Psychology, 12*(2), 93–102.

Dunlop, S., Coyte, P. C., & McIsaac, W. (2000). Socio-economic status and the utilization of physicians' services: Results from the Canadian National Population Health Survey. *Social Science & Medicine, 51*(1), 123–133.

Evans, G. (2004). The environment of childhood poverty. *American Psychologist, 59*(2), 77–92.

Everson, S. A., Maty, S. C., Lynch, J. W., & Kaplan, G. A. (2002). Epidemiologic evidence for the relation between socioeconomic status and depression, obesity, and diabetes. *Journal of Psychosomatic Research, 53*(4), 891–895.

Ewart, C. K., & Suchday, S. (2002). Discovering how urban poverty and violence affect health: Development and validation of a neighborhood stress index. *Health Psychology, 21*(3), 254–262.

Feinstein, J. S. (1993). The relationship between socioeconomic status and health: A review of the literature. *Milbank Quarterly, 71*(2), 279–322.

Feldman, J., Makuc, D., Kleinman, J., & Cornoni-Huntly, J. (1989). National trends in educational differentials in mortality. *American Journal of Epidemiology, 129,* 919–933.

Field, T., Diego, M., Hernandez-Reif, M., Schanberg, S., Kuhn, C., Yando, R., & Bendell, D. (2002). Prenatal depression effects on the foetus and neonate in different ethnic and socio-economic status groups. *Journal of Reproductive & Infant Psychology, 20*(3), 149–157.

Frable, D. E. S. (1997). Gender, racial, ethnic, sexual, and class identities. *Annual Review of Psychology, 48,* 139–162.

Franks, P., Clancy, C. M., Gold, M. R., & Nutting, P. A. (1993). Health insurance and subjective health status: Data from the 1987 National Medical Expenditure Survey. *American Journal of Public Health, 83*(9), 1295–1299.

Gallo, L. C., & Matthews, K. A. (2003). Understanding the association between socioeconomic status and physical health: Do negative emotions play a role? *Psychological Bulletin, 129,* 10–51.

Goldman, N. (2001). Social inequalities in health: Disentangling the underlying mechanisms. In M. Weinstein & A. I. Hermalin (Eds.), *Annals of the New York Academy of Sciences: Vol. 954. Population health and aging: Strengthening the dialogue between epidemiology and demography* (pp. 88–117). New York: New York Academy of Sciences.

Goodman, E. (1999). The role of socioeconomic status gradients in explaining differences in U.S. adolescents' health. *American Journal of Public Health, 89*(10), 1522–1528.

Grella, C. E. (1990). Irreconcilable differences: Women defining class after divorce and downward mobility. *Gender & Society, 4,* 41–55.

Grzywacz, J., McMahan, S., Hurley, J., Stokols, D., & Phillips, M. (2004). Serving racial and ethnic minority populations with health promotion. *American Journal of Health Promotion, 18*(5), 8–12.

Haan, M., Kaplan, G. A., & Camacho, T. (1987). Poverty and health: Prospective evidence from the Alameda County study. *American Journal of Epidemiology, 125,* 989–998.

Haan, M., Kaplan, G. A., & Syme, S. L. (1989). Socioeconomic status and health: Old observations and new thoughts. In J. T. Bunker, T. S. Gomby, & B. H. Kehrer (Eds.), *Pathways to health* (pp. 76–135). Menlo Park, CA: The Henry J. Kaiser Family Foundation.

Haukkala, A. (2002). Socio-economic differences in hostility measures: A population-based study. *Psychology & Health, 17*(2), 191–202.

Hayward, M. D., Crimmins, E. M., Miles, T. P., & Yang, Y. (2000). The significance of socioeconomic status in explaining the racial gap in chronic health conditions. *American Sociological Review, 65*(6), 910–930.

Holleman, W. L., Bray, J. H., Davis, L., & Holleman, M. C. (2004). Innovative ways to address the mental health and medical needs of marginalized patients: Collaborations between family physicians, family therapists, and family psychologists. *American Journal of Orthopsychiatry, 74*(3), 242–252.

Hoofien, D., Vakil, E., Gilboa, A., Donovick, P. J., & Barak, O. (2002). Comparison of the predictive power of socioeconomic variables, severity of injury and age on long-term outcome of traumatic brain injury: Sample-specific variables versus factors as predictors. *Brain Injury, 16*(1), 9–27.

Kitagawa, E. M., & Hauser, P. M. (Eds.). (1973). *Differential mortality in the United States: A study in socioeconomic epidemiology.* Cambridge, MA: Harvard University Press.

Krieger, N., Willains, D. R., & Moss, N. E. (1997). Measuring social class in public health research: Concepts, methodologies, and guidelines. *Annual Review of Public Health, 18,* 341–378.

Kuriloff, P., & Reichert, M. C. (2003). Boys of class, boys of color: Negotiating the academic and social geography of an elite independent school. *Journal of Social Issues, 59,* 751–770.

Lantz, P. M., House, J. S., Lepkowski, J. M., Williams, D. R., Mero, R. P., & Chen, J. (1998). Socioeconomic factors, health behaviors, and mortality: Results from a nationally representative prospective study of U.S. adults. *Journal of the American Medical Association, 279*(21), 1703–1708.

Lantz, P. M., Lynch, J. W., House, J. S., Lepkowski, J. M., Mero, R. P., Musick, M. A., & Williams, D. R. (2001). Socioeconomic disparities in health change in a longitudinal study of U.S. adults: The role of health-risk behaviors. *Social Science & Medicine, 53*(1), 29–40.

Lenk, K., Toomey, T., Wagenaar, A., Bosma, L., & Vessey, J. (2002). Can neighborhood associations be allies in health policy efforts? Political activity among neighborhood associations. *Journal of Community Psychology, 30*(1), 57–68.

Liu, W. M. (2002). The social class–related experiences of men: Integrating theory and practice. *Professional Psychology: Research and Practice, 33,* 355–360.

Liu, W. M., & Pope-Davis, D. B. (2003). Understanding classism to effect personal change. In T. B. Smith (Ed.), *Practicing multiculturalism: Internalizing and affirming diversity in counseling and psychology* (pp. 294–310). New York: Allyn & Bacon.

Liu, W. M., Ali, S. R., Soleck, G., Hopps, J., Dunston, K., & Pickett, T., Jr. (2004). Using social class in counseling psychology research. *Journal of Counseling Psychology, 51,* 3–18.

Liu, W. M., Soleck, G., Hopps, J. A., Pickett, T., & Dunston, K. (2004). A new framework to understand social class in counseling: The social class worldview and modern classism theory. *Journal of Multicultural Counseling and Development, 32*(2), 95–122.

Logue, E. E., & Jarjoura, D. (1990). Modeling heart disease mortality with census tract rates and social class mixtures. *Social Science & Medicine, 31,* 545–550.

Long, J. A., Ickovics, J. R., Gill, T. M., & Horowitz, R. I. (2001). The cumulative effects of social class on mental status decline. *Journal of the American Geriatrics Society, 49*(7), 1005–1007.

Lott, B. (2002). Cognitive and behavioral distancing from the poor. *American Psychologist, 57,* 100–110.

Lynch, J. W., Kaplan, G. A., & Salonen, J. T. (1997). Why do poor people behave poorly? Variation in adult health behaviours and psychosocial characteristics by stages of the socioeconomic lifecourse. *Social Science & Medicine, 44*(6), 809–819.

Lynch, J. W., Kaplan, G. A, & Shema, S. J. (1997). Cumulative impact of sustained economic hardship on physical, cognitive, psychological, and social functioning. *New England Journal of Medicine, 337*(26), 1889–1895.

Malatu, M. S., & Schooler, C. (2002). Causal connections between socio-economic status and health: Reciprocal effects and mediating mechanisms. *Journal of Health & Social Behavior, 43*(1), 22–41.

Marmot, M. G., Shipley, M. J., & Rose, G. (1984). Inequalities in death: Specific explanations of a general pattern. *Lancet, 331,* 1003–1006.

Marmot, M. G., Smith, G. D., Stansfeld, S., Patel, C., North, F., Head, J., White, I., Brunner, E., & Feeney, A. (1991). Health inequalities among British civil servants: The Whitehall II study. *Lancet, 337,* 1387–1393.

Martikainen, P., Stansfeld, S., Hemingway, H., & Marmot, M. (1999). Determinants of socioeconomic differences in change in physical and mental functioning. *Social Science & Medicine, 49*(4), 499–507.

Matthews, A. K., Sellergren, S. A., Manfredi, C., & Williams, M. (2002). Factors influencing medical information seeking among African-American cancer patients. *Journal of Health Communication, 7*(3), 205–219.

McKinlay, J. B., Lin, T., Freund, K., & Moskowitz, M. (2002). The unexpected influence of physician attributes on clinical decisions: Results of an experiment. *Journal of Health & Social Behavior, 43*(1), 92–106.

Mesch, G., & Schwirian, K. (1996). The effectiveness of neighborhood coalition action. *Social Problems, 43,* 467–483.

Mirowsky, J., & Ross, C. E. (2000). Socioeconomic status and subjective life expectancy. *Social Psychology Quarterly, 63*(2), 133–151.

Oakes, J. M., & Rossi, P. H. (2003). The measurement of SES in health research: Current practice and steps toward a new approach. *Social Science & Medicine, 56,* 769–784.

O'Malley, M. S., Earp, A. L., Hawley, S. T., Schell, M. J., Mathews, H. F., & Mitchell, J. (2001). The association of race/ethnicity, socioeconomic status, and physician recommendation for mammography: Who gets the message about breast cancer screening? *American Journal of Public Health, 91*(1), 49–54.

Ostrove, J. M., & Cole, E. R. (2003). Privileging class: Toward a critical psychology of social class in the context of education. *Journal of Social Issues, 59,* 677–692.

Ranchor, A. V., Bouma, J., & Sanderman, R. (1996). Vulnerability and social class: Differential patterns of personality and social support over the social class. *Personality & Individual Differences, 20*(2), 229–237.

Rapoff, M. A. (1999). *Adherence to pediatric medical regimens.* New York: Kluwer.

Ren, X. S., & Amick, B. C., III. (1996). Race and self-assessed health status: The role of socioeconomic factors in the USA. *Journal of Epidemiology & Community Health, 50*(3), 269–273.

Schillinger, D., Piette, J., Grumbach, K., Wang, F., Wilson, C., Daher, C., Leong-Grotz, K., Castro, C., & Bindman, A. B. (2003). Closing the loop: Physician communication with diabetic patients who have low health literacy. *Archives of Internal Medicine, 163,* 83–90.

Seeman, T. E., & Crimmins, E. (2001). Social environment effects on health and aging: Integrating epidemiologic and demographic approaches and perspectives. In M. Weinstein & A. I. Hermalin (Eds.), *Annals of the New York Academy of Sciences: Vol. 954. Population health and aging: Strengthening the dialogue between epidemiology and demography* (pp. 88–117). New York: New York Academy of Sciences.

Shi, L., & Starfield, B. (2001). The effect of primary care physician supply and income inequality on mortality among Blacks and Whites in U.S. metropolitan areas. *American Journal of Public Health, 91*(8), 1246–1250.

Silver, M. (1972). An econometric analysis of spatial variations in mortality rated by age and sex. In V. Fuchs (Ed.), *Essays in the economics of health and medical care* (pp. 161–227). New York: Columbia University Press.

Simon, J. G., van de Mheen, H., van der Meer, J. B., & Mackenbach, J. P. (2000). Socioeconomic differences in self-assessed health in a chronically ill population: The role of different health aspects. *Journal of Behavioral Medicine, 23*(5), 399–420.

Singh, G. K., & Siahpush, M. (2002). Increasing inequalities in all-cause and cardiovascular mortality among U.S. adults aged 25–64 years by area socioeconomic status, 1969–1998. *International Journal of Epidemiology, 31*(3), 600–613.

Smith, G. D., & Hart, C. (2002). Life-course socioeconomic and behavioral influences on cardiovascular disease mortality: The collaborative study. *American Journal of Public Health, 92*(8), 1295–1298.

Starfield, B., Riley, A. W., Witt, W. P., & Robertson, J. (2002). Social class gradients in health during adolescence. *Journal of Epidemiology & Community Health, 56*(5), 354–361.

Stronks, K., van de Mheen, H., Looman, C. W., & Mackenbach, J. P. (1998). The importance of psychosocial stressors for socio-economic inequalities in perceived health. *Social Science & Medicine, 46*(4–5), 611–623.

Sue, D. W., & Sue, D. (2002). *Counseling the culturally diverse: Theory and practice.* New York: Wiley.

Syme, S. L. (1978). Drug treatment of mild hypertension: Social and psychological considerations. *Annals of the New York Academy of Sciences, 304,* 99–106.

Townsend, P., Davidson, N., & Whitehead, M. (1988). *Inequalities in health.* London: Penguin.

Turrell, G., Lynch, J. W., Kaplan, G. A., Everson, S. A., Helkala, E., Kauhanen, J., & Salonen, J. T. (2002). Socioeconomic position across the lifecourse and cognitive function in late middle age. *Journal of Gerontology Series B: Psychological Sciences & Social Sciences, 57B*(1), S43–S51.

Twenge, J. M., & Campbell, W. K. (2002). Self-esteem and socioeconomic status: A meta-analytic review. *Personality & Social Psychology Review, 6*(1), 59–71.

U.S. Department of Health and Human Services, Agency for Healthcare Research and Quality. (2003). *National healthcare disparities report.* Rockville, MD: Author.

van Ryn, M. (2002). Research on the provider contribution to race/ethnicity disparities in medical care. *Medical Care, 40*(Suppl.), I140–I151.

van Ryn, M., & Burke, J. (2000). The effect of patient race and socio-economic status on physicians' perceptions of patients. *Social Science & Medicine, 50*(6), 813–828.

Wardle, J., Waller, J., & Jarvis, M. J. (2002). Sex differences in the association of socioeconomic status with obesity. *American Journal of Public Health, 92*(8), 1299–1304.

Williams, D., & Rucker, T. (1996). Socioeconomic status and the health of racial minority populations. In P. M. Kato & T. Mann (Eds.), *Handbook of diversity issues in health psychology* (pp. 407–423). New York: Plenum.

Williams, M., Davis, T., Parker, R., & Weiss, B. (2002). The role of health literacy in patient-physician communication. *Family Medicine, 34*(5), 383–389.

Wilson, S. E. (2001). Socioeconomic status and the prevalence of health problems among married couples in late midlife. *American Journal of Public Health, 91*(1), 131–135.

CHAPTER 24

Community Health Promotion Curriculum

A Case Study on Southeast Asian Refugees

Uyen K. Huynh and Gargi Roysircar

There are many barriers to the health and health care of American racial and ethnic minorities. These include poverty, low education, immigrants' limited use of English, value differences, prejudice and discrimination, and lack of a culturally sensitive health care system. In response to pervasive health disparities, and in envisioning "one America," President Clinton set forth the goal of eliminating racial and ethnic (henceforth called "minority") disparities in health as part of his Initiative on Race (U.S. Department of Health and Human Services [USDHHS], 1998). The USDHHS's Healthy People 2000 initiative report (USDHHS, 2001b) aimed at promoting health or preventing disease and provided data on all Americans, including minority populations' access to health care. Around the same time, the U.S. Congress commissioned the Commonwealth Fund study (Collins et al., 2002). The Commonwealth Fund study revealed that minorities have benefited less than White Americans from overall improvements in health care over the past century. Both reports revealed that American minorities suffered disproportionately from preventable and treatable conditions, such as cardiovascular disease, diabetes, asthma, cancer, and HIV/AIDS.

Authors' Note: Uyen Huynh completed her postdoctoral clinical work at Association for the Help of Retarded Children in New York City in the Department of Adult Day Services and Traumatic Brain Injury, 200 Park Avenue South, New York, NY 10003. She is now studying public health policy at the London School of Economics. Gargi Roysircar is professor of clinical psychology and director of the Multicultural Center for Research and Practice at Antioch New England Graduate School, 40 Avon Street, Keene, NH 03431–3516.

Community Health Promotion Curriculum: A Case Study on Southeast Asians

According to the Commonwealth Fund study (Collins et al., 2002), Asian Americans frequently stand out as among the least served by the health care system. The Commonwealth Fund study's disaggregated data on smaller ethnic groups (e.g., Vietnamese) helped to better explain cultural and minority status linkages to health. Important factors that contribute to minority disparities in equality of health care and low levels of utilization are briefly outlined in the pages to follow, along with the justification for and description of a community-based health promotion curriculum that targets the health care of Vietnamese and Cambodian refugees in the United States. The program involves an interdisciplinary collaboration between health care personnel, psychiatrists, counseling and clinical psychologists, and community leaders. The first author, who is a clinical psychologist, served as the health promotion coordinator for the Harvard Program in Refugee Trauma prevention outreach for Southeast Asian refugees in Massachusetts. The second author, a counseling psychologist, engages in primary and secondary community outreach in her training activities with psychology graduate students (e.g., Roysircar, 2004a, 2004c; Roysircar, Arredondo, Fuertes, Ponterotto, & Toporek, 2003; Roysircar, Gard, Hubbell, & Ortega, 2005). A pilot pre-post study of the program is included, followed by suggestions for a more complete program evaluation of a community health promotion outreach. First, we present select factors that contribute to minority health disparities.

Poverty and the High Cost of Health Care

Low income affects adequate health insurance, thereby limiting access to medical care, service from qualified health care professionals, and the availability of an overall good quality of care. Vietnamese Americans ranked among the top Asian minorities to have reported the highest rates of poverty (two thirds lived below 200% of the federal poverty level) and the lowest rates of health insurance coverage (Collins et al., 2002). Although some low-income Vietnamese patients have health insurance, their access is limited to the care that is available to indigent people. Being poor or not having health insurance results in less access to regular sources of care and fewer choices.

Lack of Health Care Prevention Service

Access to public health services includes health education, which provides information on prevalent diseases and educates on the prevention as well as care of such diseases. Asian Americans are reported to be among the least likely minority groups to receive preventive health services because health education programs do not exist in their respective ethnic languages (Collins et al., 2002). The Commonwealth Fund study found that many Vietnamese refugees turned to friends and family for health information; that about 50% of Asian Americans, in general, referred to books and other printed materials regarding health; approximately 38% turned to their pharmacists; and about 11% went to community health fairs for information regarding health (Collins et al., 2002).

Education, however, is considered important in the value systems of many Asians (Sodowsky, 1991; Sodowsky & Lai, 1997). Therefore, it is expected that Asian Americans will avail themselves of health education if it is available. Education leads to empowerment and is a strong tool of development for a community (Knight & Camic, 1998). Lacking empowerment, ethnic minority groups, we believe, suffer poor health; have low confidence in their ability to maintain health; and feel a loss of control over events in their lives, including their well-being. We propose that health education will help minorities feel empowered through information, resources, and a language-appropriate forum to ask questions of a qualified instructor.

Cultural Misunderstandings and Poor Communication With Health Care Providers

The Commonwealth Fund study found that 22% of Asian American adults needed an interpreter when seeking health care services. Many Asian Americans also felt their doctors misunderstood their needs for medical attention owing mainly to cultural differences (Collins et al., 2002). For example, an Asian American patient might prefer antibiotics and pain relievers, yet their doctors recommend x-rays of potentially affected organs. An elderly individual might choose to live with broken teeth or no teeth rather than undergo invasive dental surgery and be fitted with dentures or implants. Individuals with diabetes might want to control their disease with moderate medication and diet, refusing to check their sugar levels daily with monitors and insulin shots. An Asian American may be unable to give up rice, a staple food, but might be persuaded to reduce the quantity of rice intake. When doctors are not flexible about their state-of-the-art electronic treatment and referrals to specialists, their Asian American patients might discontinue treatment. When health care providers fail to understand attitudinal and worldview differences between themselves and their patients, communication and trust suffer (Roysircar, 2003, 2004b, 2004c). A breakdown in communication and trust leads to patient dissatisfaction, poor understanding of illness, low adherence to medication and health promotion strategies, and poor health outcomes (Collins et al., 2002). Uninformed patients' low confidence in their overall health maintenance as well as in their health care providers contraindicates good medical outcome.

Low Confidence in Overall Health and Health Care Provider

The Commonwealth Fund study found that 40% of Vietnamese Americans rated their health as fair or poor compared with 11% of Chinese Americans. Vietnamese patients were less likely than other Asian Americans to have high confidence in their doctors. Collins et al. (2002) linked the low confidence of Vietnamese people in their health care providers to their practice of indigenous health care, such as acupuncture and herbal medicines. This attribution of Collins and colleagues revealed, in our opinion, their value bias against indigenous health care. When we learned that 63% of all Asian Americans reported using alternative therapies (Collins et al., 2002), we remained hopeful, thinking that those who did not have consistent health insurance might at least practice alternative ways to treat their symptoms, such as applying turmeric paste, an Indian cooking spice, over a cut, should an antiseptic cream not be immediately available, or drinking hot tea mixed with crushed ginger root to treat common cold, rather than orange juice, or using cough suppressants and nasal decongestants.

Southeast Asian Refugee Health Problems

In addition to being poor, many Vietnamese refugees carry with them a trauma history such as that experienced as a result of the Vietnam War (Kinzie et al., 1990). In the 1960s and 1970s, the Vietnam War resulted in more than 2 million casualties for both Vietnam and the United States (Jamieson, 1995). Successful and unsuccessful attempts to escape Vietnam were compounded with war trauma that included bombings of villages and homes; the confiscation of personal property; witnessing deaths of family members; intimidation by soldiers; cannibalism, rape, and separation of wives, husbands, and children during escapes by boat; and incarceration in foreign refugee camps (Kinzie et al., 1990). Vietnam's problems with communist China continued through the 1980s, resulting in the Cambodian Holocaust. In its earlier history, Vietnam endured dramatic political upheavals, including cruel leadership and government takeovers, causing horrific violations against its own peoples. A high prevalence rate of posttraumatic stress disorder (PTSD), major depression, and anxiety has been found among Vietnamese and Cambodian refugees (Kinzie et al., 1990), which, we suggest, may also be due to an intergenerational transmission of trauma. The diagnostic criteria from the *DSM-IV-TR* (American Psychiatric Association, 2000), however, do not address in their delineation of trauma the effects of oppression across time and generations for minority populations.

Vietnamese refugees arrived in the United States carrying a multitude of infectious diseases, such as tuberculosis (TB), hepatitis B, malaria, dengue fever, and gastrointestinal infections (Centers for Disease Control & Prevention, 1990). The incidence of TB is 40 times higher among Southeast Asians than among the total U.S. population (Nolan & Elarth, 1988). After entering the United States, Southeast Asian immigrants markedly increase their intake of fats and decrease their intake of fiber, elevating their average total serum cholesterol level and putting them at further risk for cardiovascular illnesses (Bates, Hill, & Barrett-Conner, 1989). These factors are compounded by the relatively high incidence of childhood hypertension (Munger, Gomez-Marin, Prineas, & Sinaiko, 1991).

Fifty-six percent of Vietnamese men smoke, compared to 32% of the general U.S. population (Jenkins, McPhee, Bird, & Bonilla, 1990). According to the American

Lung Association (2002, 2004), the highest rates of current daily or occasional smoking for males were among people born in Vietnam, Laos, or Cambodia (43.6%), and the lung cancer rate is 18% higher among Southeast Asian men than among White males. The living cancer rate is more than 12 times higher among Southeast Asians than in the White population (Jenkins et al., 1990). A greater-than-average incidence of nasopharynx, stomach, and liver cancer has been documented in Vietnamese people (Ross, Bernstein, Hartnett, & Boone, 1991; Swerdlow, 1991). Men have high rates of penile neoplasms, whereas women have an increased incidence of cervical cancer and choriocarcinoma (Ross et al., 1991; Swerdlow, 1991). The elevated incidence of stomach cancer is possibly related to dietary factors, whereas hepatitis B is involved in the development of liver cancer (Ross et al., 1991). Vietnamese refugees report other health problems, such as asthma, diabetes, high blood pressure, obesity, anxiety, depression, and PTSD (Hauff & Vaglum, 1994; Kinzie et al., 1990). All of the conditions described above are among the most frequent causes of death in the United States. Mental health problems reported by the Vietnamese may have higher rates of incidence, considering that Asian Americans underreport mental illness owing to cultural values of stigma and loss of face (Nguyen, 1985).

Upon their arrival in the United States, Vietnamese refugees struggled with adjusting to a new country and rebuilding their lives from scratch. As with many other refugees, the Vietnamese encountered many barriers to establishing the foundation of their future prosperity. Acculturative stresses related to limited knowledge of American customs, English-language proficiency, financial means, transportation, and access to adequate health care increase susceptibility to illnesses (Lin, Masuda, & Tazuma, 1984; Roysircar-Sodowsky & Maestas, 2000).

Vietnamese Refugees' Health Knowledge and Practices

Many Vietnamese refugees lack knowledge about health and the behaviors that can result in poor health. One study (Jenkins et al., 1990) reported that 27% of patients surveyed did not know that smoking causes cancer. These patients also had limited knowledge of hepatitis B and AIDS transmission modes (Hinton et al., 1993; Jenkins et al., 1990). Another study reported that 37% of Vietnamese women surveyed did not know that a breast lump could be cancerous or that irregular menstrual bleeding could be a sign of malignancy (Pham & McPhee, 1992). Among these women, 74% were not aware that having multiple sex partners would increase their risk of developing cervical cancer (Pham & McPhee, 1992).

Health is defined in the United States as a state of complete physical, mental, and social well-being and not merely the absence of disease (World Health Organization, 2004). On the other hand, traditional Vietnamese people view health as a state of harmony with nature or freedom from symptoms (Purnell & Paulanka, 1998). The most common belief employed by rural Vietnamese is that the body is composed of air, fire, water, and earth, which have cold, hot, wet, and dry characteristics, respectively. To prevent sickness, many Vietnamese use traditional herbal remedies, tonics, avoidance of excess, and massage to maintain good health (Purnell & Paulanka,

1998). For Vietnamese villagers, symptoms do not merit a visit to the doctor; rather, they subscribe to home remedies such as *thuoc bac* or *thuoc nam,* or Chinese health practices such as moxibustion and acupuncture (Purnell & Paulanka, 1998). The notion of anxiety and headaches as indicators of any sort of mental illness would be a frightening idea. If that was the case, then the "average" person could have mental illness (Purnell & Paulanka, 1998). Vietnamese people's high regard for Buddhist practice and the supernatural, however, does not infer a duality between spirituality and science and between philosophy and pragmatics in their worldview.

The Need for Group Prevention Service for Southeast Asian Refugees

The current health data (Collins et al., 2002; USDHHS, 2001a, 2001b) on existing minority health disparities provide a strong argument for the need of societal institutions to address both cultural and financial barriers to the health care of Southeast Asian refugees. Culturally competent individual therapy is relatively new and occurring at a few mental health centers, such as the university hospital at the University of California at San Francisco; Kaiser Permanente Group, San Francisco, CA; and the Sunset Park Family Health Center Network of Lutheran Medical Center, Brooklyn, NY. Individual, tertiary care for immigrants is rare as well as costly. On the other hand, when working from a group prevention model, providers have the option to initiate culturally competent health education that specifically targets a particular minority group. There is very little community programming for Asian populations, especially that which addresses preventive health services. We offer the following reasons for implementing a health promotion program for Southeast Asian refugees:

1. Asian Americans are more likely to participate in a free health education course that is culturally competent to meet their needs.
2. Asian Americans are more likely to share the sentiment that it is better to take care of one's own health than go to a doctor who is expensive and also suspected to be culturally insensitive.
3. Preventive care that involves education is empowering for Asian Americans, prevents illness, strengthens the local ethnic community, and is cost effective because it is expected to reduce emergency hospitalizations.
4. Finally, education on health care can develop a link between indigenous health practices and Western models of health care.

Ethical Considerations

Americans have often been wary of large-scale efforts to influence their behavior, particularly, it seems, when the rationale invokes behavioral science. The suspicion is not without basis, particularly when considering the horrific abuses of minorities in the name of science, such as experimentation on Jews by the Nazis and the notorious Tuskegee study on the natural course of syphilis. Influence attempts that are overt, such as those of advertisers, are broadly accepted. Preventive interventions are not always evident to the persons whose behavior is targeted for modification. To the extent that prevention research targets systems-level variables or individual-level variables without a participant's awareness, researchers risk exacerbating the public's mistrust of science.

Efforts of behavioral scientists to "engineer" healthy behaviors or to eradicate unhealthy ones can be perceived as paternalistic manipulations, for example, Chomsky's (1971) attack on Skinner's reinforcement of positive behaviors. Even though we were conscientious investigators and preventionists, our proposed model of psychoeducational intervention for Southeast Asian refugees was subjected to close scrutiny by our university's internal review board. Our application for the proposed project was rejected twice. We appeared in person with our third application in order to be available for an interview with the board. To get permission, we evaluated potential risks to vulnerable participants who were trauma and torture survivors; responded to issues of the power differential of interventionists, educators, and scientists, whose power and prestige are at constant risk for abuse; showed evidence of language translations of the informed consent form and assessment measures that were used; and needed to be convincing that the projected benefits of the program outweighed its risks.

In addition to self- and institutional monitoring prior to program implementation, we offer a few comments on certain ethical challenges highlighted during the course of treatment. Health programs should ensure that conflict and grievance resolution processes are culturally and linguistically sensitive and capable of identifying, preventing, and resolving cross-cultural conflicts or complaints by patients. Health programs are encouraged to regularly make available to the public information about their progress and successful innovations and to provide public notice in their communities about the availability of this information (Federal Register, 2000; also see http://www.omhrc.gov/CLAS/; http://www.hsc.harvard.edu/~epihc/; http://www.diversityrx.org/).

The Biopsychosocial Model Applied to Southeast Asian Refugee Service

We conceptualized our health promotion program within the biopsychosocial model (Engel, 1977) because this model encompasses the psychosocial contexts of health and illness. In this model, nurses, physical therapists, psychologists, social workers, and many others, all viewed as effective providers of health (Engel, 1977), join physicians. Engel's biopsychosocial approach encompasses a whole system. This system includes individuals living in a psychosocial context of the family, community, culture, society, and biosphere. Furthermore, the model focuses on how clients communicate symptoms within psychological, social, and cultural contexts. Therefore, information is gathered about clients' beliefs, attitudes, values, culture, prior knowledge, and practices regarding their health. Health care providers who have these understandings, it is assumed, can better diagnose and treat illness. Finally, the model assumes multiple causes and multiple effects, and, therefore, addresses both micro- and macro-level processes in understanding health. For example, in the case of most Vietnamese refugees, the risk of chronic cardiovascular and gastrointestinal diseases, at least initially, is largely due to their cultural attitudes toward health care, lack of knowledge, institutional barriers to accessing care, and inaccurate diagnosis or underdiagnosis.

Engel's (1977) model rejects the biomedical model's assumption of a mind/body dualism and focuses on prevention, such as education, which helps to empower patients as the primary source of responsibility for health care (Huff & Kline, 1998). Giving patients important resources, such as basic knowledge as well as increased health care practice through strong relationships with their health care providers, can be very beneficial (Purnell & Paulanka, 1998). Patients with a better understanding of disease, multiple causes of disease, and intervention may feel better able to promote and manage their health.

At the macro level, from a public health point of view, the potential for community-wide disease warrants comprehensive surveillance, detection, and treatment of refugees upon their arrival and in their process of settling in the United States (Collins et al., 2002). Although resettled refugees are a relatively small population, their health and illness patterns can have a great effect on the larger community's health (Purnell & Paulanka, 1998) that might lead to poor and worsening outcomes for their community's future generations. Yet for refugees, it is often an uphill battle to get support for mental and physical health outreach efforts in their ethnic communities (Purnell & Paulanka, 1998). The physical and mental health status of Southeast Asian refugees requires a public health response, such as educational programming.

Harvard Program in Refugee Trauma (HPRT)

The physical and mental health needs of Southeast Asian refugees led to the development of the Health Promotion Curriculum (HP Curriculum), designed by the Harvard Program in Refugee Trauma (HPRT) under a federal grant from the Office of Refugee Resettlement. In this chapter, we describe the HPRT's HP Curriculum, an ongoing, year-round, grant-funded research project. We discuss its pilot implementation and initial pretest-posttest evaluation. The intent of the HP Curriculum's pilot implementation was to address the physical and psychological health of Southeast Asian refugees in the greater Boston area. It was based on the philosophy that by promoting health knowledge and education, the refugees would have increased confidence in their ability to achieve and maintain improved health standards.

The HPRT, founded in 1981, is a multidisciplinary, multinational program that has been pioneering the health and mental health care of refugees and civilians who are survivors of conflict/postconflict and natural disasters. Working in the United States and overseas, HPRT provides curriculum training to direct-care health providers and primary care practitioners in screening, treating, and providing prevention services to victims of torture and trauma in local clinics, hospitals, and community centers. HPRT works closely with Ministries of Health throughout the world, and its bicultural/international partnerships have resulted in culturally effective, sustainable programs that rely primarily on local human resources and indigenous healing systems. HPRT's current efforts in research, policy development, and primary and secondary prevention include the Bosnia Reconstruction Program, the Torture Survivors Program, the U.S. Terrorism Recovery Program, and the Kobe Earthquake Program. Each of these programs serves as a global model to be replicated worldwide.

The first author co-developed in a multidisciplinary team an HP Curriculum that was tailored to Vietnamese refugees in Dorchester, Massachusetts, and Cambodian refugees in Lowell, Massachusetts. The HP Curriculum's multidisciplinary team also included a licensed social worker, a psychiatric nurse, a community leader, and a psychiatrist. The second author consulted on the design, evaluation, and written report on the HP Curriculum's pilot implementation, which is summarized here. Although the pilot implementation was to address the health care needs of Southeast Asian trauma survivors, the HP Curriculum's overall goal was to have a program that might be generalized to trauma survivors in other parts of the world (e.g., Afghanistan, Bosnia, Iraq, South Africa, etc.).

Health Promotion Curriculum

HPRT developed a health education curriculum that fits within Engel's (1977) biopsychosocial model of understanding both medical and psychological conditions of Vietnamese refugees. The overall goal was that Southeast Asian refugees who took its classes would understand better their illnesses, medical procedures and treatments, medications, and preventive ways that would maximize the medical and social resources that are available to them. For the pilot implementation, the hypothesis was that through such learning, Southeast Asian refugees would self-report improved confidence in managing their health. The HP Curriculum instructors, who had training in psychiatry, addressed medical and psychological conditions that have high prevalence in Southeast Asian refugee communities and built working alliances with civic organizations, the Vietnamese American Civic Association (VACA), and the Cambodian Mutual Alliance Association (CAMAA) of Massachusetts. The hospital-ethnic community collaboration was expected to inform local ethnic community leaders on the need to promote health in their community members and to give community leaders an educational tool that specifically targeted their ethnic compatriots.

Culturally Competent Community Programming

Instructional teams were composed of a health professional (psychiatrist or psychiatric nurse) and a translator. Each instructor had contributed research to the field of refugee mental health and developed manuals and handbooks for clinicians who treat torture and trauma survivors. The instructors had previously worked with Southeast Asian refugee populations at the Indochinese Psychiatric Clinic in the Boston area during the 15 years of its operation.

The instructors addressed medical and trauma issues within a cultural context consistent with the biopsychosocial model (Engel, 1977), with recommended practitioner cultural competencies (Daniel, Roysircar, Abeles, & Boyd, 2004; Roysircar et al., 2003), and with the community outreach model for primary and secondary prevention (Duffy & Wong, 2003). For instance, they respected patients' view of their illness and listened to those who chose to volunteer case examples of their medical history. They offered a cultural model of health by referring to a patient's family, background, culture, history, and environment. As medical practitioners, they gave basic health information on a particular illness and related symptoms, and offered prevention and treatment plans. As community practitioners, they involved the patient as an essential part of prevention and treatment and offered community health resources available to guide the patient, if necessary.

The HP Curriculum was broken down into 6 weeks of instruction, with each 90-minute session addressing health issues that were prevalent among the target population. Health care teaching materials, which included pamphlets that corresponded to a week's given topic, addressed diabetes, cancer, heart disease, PTSD, exercise, nutrition, and vitamins.

Participants

The HP Curriculum was piloted with 25 Vietnamese and Cambodian refugees, who were 64% men and 36% women. Of these, 48% met the criteria for PTSD ($n = 12$) and depression ($n = 13$) individually, and 36% met the criteria for both PTSD and depression, indicating co-morbidity. The diagnoses were made on the basis of the HPRT Depression/Torture Screening Instrument (Mollica & Caspi-Yavin, 1991). During the first meeting of the HP Curriculum classes, each participant answered this measure, as well as the HPRT Health Promotion Confidence Evaluation Form (Mollica, Reczycki, & Lavelle, 2000), which measured the refugees' level of confidence in their health. With the help of the Health Confidence Questionnaire, instructors developed a sense of the level of knowledge the refugees had about their health prior to instruction.

HP Curriculum Syllabus

In the first class, participants were given a general overview of the curriculum. Instruction addressed the definition of good health (defined in a previous section, Southeast Asian Refugee Health Problems) versus bad health (explained in the same previous section) and the importance of health care knowledge and preventive practices. Additional instructional time was allotted for references to specific conditions (referred to in the same previous section) that are more endemic in Southeast Asian refugee populations. The second half of the instruction addressed the doctor-patient relationship and its importance in maintaining good health and well-being.

The second week's instruction was on heart problems, the most common disorder of Southeast Asian refugees. Instructors described different kinds of heart problems and disease and their relative occurrence among Southeast Asian refugees. Instruction also addressed other heart-related problems, such as high blood pressure and cholesterol. Participants were told how and where they could get blood pressure readings and cholesterol counts in the local community. Handouts translated in both Vietnamese and Kru/Khmer described heart-related conditions.

The third week's topics included other medical conditions most common among Southeast Asian refugees: high blood pressure and cholesterol, liver disease, stomach cancer, nasopharyngeal cancer, and TB. An overview of each medical condition was provided in terms of course of illness, epidemiology, symptoms, diagnosis, treatment, and prevention. Additional resource information on hepatitis B and C screening and related health information was distributed as handouts. Although all classes allowed questions and answers, this class was particularly open to address questions from participants, so that the instructors and the HP Curriculum could be culturally sensitive to cues and symptom presentations from culturally different learners.

The fourth week addressed interventions on nutrition, exercise, relaxation, and dental care. Topics related to high-risk behaviors, such as smoking and drinking, were addressed. Given data on the high degree of smoking and lung cancer among Southeast Asian refugees, it was important to integrate the topic of smoking into the HP Curriculum. Instructors introduced gentle exercises that could be done at home, such as taking short walks and practicing basic t'ai chi movements. They guided the participants in a group breathing exercise to demonstrate its effects. Because Vietnamese and Cambodians tend to present psychosomatic problems, these examples of gentle exercises were considered useful in helping patients relax in both mind and body. Handouts covering instruction on diet and exercise were distributed at the end of class.

The fifth week specifically addressed the topic of mental health. The topic of mental health was scheduled for a later class because Asian Americans tend to be less psychologically minded than White Americans (Sue & Morishima, 1982), and it was feared that the Southeast Asian participants might reject such information. Extensive discussions on physical health in previous classes prepared the path to discussing mental health. Instructors were sensitive and cautious when they talked about psychiatric disorders related to the Vietnam War and Cambodian Holocaust. They knew about the issues of underreporting, high prevalence, and cultural stigmatization of mental health problems among Asian Americans. Initially, education was geared toward discussing the physical side effects of psychological distress because Asian Americans are more familiar and comfortable with discussions on physical health concerns. Specifically, participants were told that they could show physical scars, fractures, and other disabilities related to trauma (Nguyen, 1985). Physical effects might be found in every system, such as the heart, immune system, and lungs. Fainting spells, insomnia, and agitation were related to previously experienced traumatic events.

Instructors discussed case examples of people who had been exposed to trauma and its effects (American Psychiatric Association, 2000) and asked participants whether or not they would like to share their particular story. Most important, instructors wanted participants to understand the high prevalence of PTSD, depression, and anxiety among Vietnamese and Cambodian refugees, the importance of diagnosis, and the possibilities of treatment. They discussed ways to treat mental illness. They described both psychopharmacology and psychotherapy as two different techniques commonly used to treat psychiatric disorders. Additional time was allotted for questions, and handouts related to the three specific psychiatric disorders were distributed.

This class also addressed the beliefs and attitudes that are popularly held by Southeast Asians about mental illness. It is known that culture helps to shape the expression and recognition of psychiatric problems (Dana, 2000; Roysircar, 2005; Sue & Morishima, 1982). Eastern beliefs (e.g., Buddhism) discourage open displays of emotion and pain. As such, Southeast Asian refugees' common attitudes regarding mental health are denial, avoidance, tolerance, and suppression of distress (Nguyen, 1985). Therefore, this denial of experience and expression of emotions can manifest itself in psychological distress expressed through the body rather than the mind. Southeast Asian refugees commonly experience psychosomatic illness in the form of sleep and appetite problems, muscular pain, and backaches and are more likely to exhibit somatic complaints of depression than are Whites (Nguyen, 1985).

When addressing psychological problems, the instructors emphasized the significant impact that trauma and torture have on mental health. The psychological impact of trauma and torture was described as the feeling of powerlessness and lack of control (United Nations High Commission on Refugees, 1998). Participants were told that both physical and psychological torture might result in long-term sequelae. However, it was explained that the detrimental, invisible signs of disability were psychological effects, commonly manifested in the symptoms of PTSD, depression, and anxiety (Kinzie et al., 1990).

The sixth and final week of the program addressed taking medication correctly. Case examples of health problems (e.g., arthritis, diabetes of participants in the class and their medications) were presented. For example, one participant stated that he used his medication only when he felt an oncoming physical symptom. His example was related to his arthritic condition, which developed when there was a change in weather. Instructors discussed how taking medication regularly would help to manage and control arthritic pain overall, instead of remedying occasional acute pain. Participants learned how medication taken over time would accumulate into long-acting levels in their body, thus avoiding the sudden incidence of physical discomfort. Handouts explaining the proper use of medication were distributed after case examples were demonstrated in class.

This final class reviewed any unanswered questions that the class participants had from previous weeks. In this last class, post-symptomatology and health confidence questionnaires were distributed to each participant and completed. The health confidence information is provided in the next section. Post-symptomatology information may be obtained from Richard Mollica, MD, of HPRT, who is directing the HP Curriculum projects in Massachusetts.

Evaluation of Participant Confidence in Health Promotion

Pretest and posttest health promotion confidence levels were examined in relation to the following hypothesis: After attending the HP Curriculum program, the full sample of Vietnamese and Cambodian participants from both VACA and CAMAA was expected to report increased confidence in health status, knowledge, and overall preventive care.

Measurement of participant confidence was collected with a self-report instrument, the Health Promotion Confidence Evaluation (Health Confidence Questionnaire) developed by HPRT (Mollica et al., 2000). This measure assesses level of confidence in the following health concerns: communication with health care providers; influences of diet, nutrition, medication, and exercise; and confidence in improving one's health. The Health Confidence Questionnaire was developed for the HP Curriculum pilot program in Massachusetts and had never been used previously. A pretest and posttest analysis was conducted to determine the level of confidence the participants reported. Cronbach's alpha for the 12-item Confidence Questionnaire for the 25 pilot participants was .83 at pretest and .80 at posttest. Participants' confidence was calculated by summing twelve 4-point Likert items and then dividing the sum total by 12 to arrive at a mean rating. Composite confidence scores can range from 12 to 48, 12 representing the highest reported level of confidence, and 48 representing the lowest reported level of confidence in one's health. Therefore, high scores indicate low confidence and low scores indicate high confidence. The range of observed scores was 13 to 39. For the full sample, the pretest mean was 25.80 (SD = 6.88) and posttest mean was 20.52 (SD = 6.95). Means and standard deviations of observed scores for specific demographic and diagnostic groupings are presented in Table 24.1.

Table 24.1 Means and Standard Deviations of Health Confidence Scores

Variables	*Pretest CON M*	*SD*	*Posttest CON M*	*SD*
Full Sample	25.80	6.88	20.52	6.95
Vietnamese	23.86	6.26	19.40	6.82
Cambodian	28.70	7.05	22.20	7.17
Female	25.19	6.88	19.44	5.08
Male	26.89	7.12	21.33	8.21
PTSD Diagnosed	26.58	7.40	21.50	7.91
Depres Diagnosed	27.25	7.21	22.00	7.51

Note: Full Sample n = 25; Vietnamese n = 15; Cambodian n = 10; Female n = 9; Male n = 16; PTSD Group n = 12; Depression Group n = 13. CON = Health Confidence Scores. Depres = Depression. Higher Health Confidence scores indicate less confidence in health promotion; lower scores indicate more confidence. Higher scores on PTSD and Depression indicate higher self-reported mental health disorders and lower scores indicate decreased levels.

Table 24.2 Within-Subjects Repeated Measures Analysis of Variance on Pretest and Posttest Health Promotion Confidence

Source of Variation	*SS*	*df*	*MS*	*F*	η^2
Time	360.80	1	360.80	19.75***	.46
Time × Ethnicity	12.40	1	12.40	.70	.0
Erro	421.12	23	18.27		

Note: ***$p < .001$.

A repeated measures analysis of variance was performed with Time 1 (pretest Confidence Level) and Time 2 (posttest Confidence Level) as the within-subjects factor and Vietnamese versus Cambodian group as the between-subjects factor. A nonsignificant effect for Time X Group was found, Pillai's Trace $F(1, 23) = .70$, $p > .05$, $\eta^2 = .03$. For within-subjects, a significant effect for time was found, Pillai's Trace $F(1, 23) = 19.75$, $p < .001$, $\eta^2 = .42$. (Between-subjects effects were Intercept [$df = 1$, MS = 26602.08, $F = 361.41$, $p < .001$]; Group [$df = 1$, MS = 174.80, $F = 2.38$, $p > .05$, $\eta^2 = .09$]). See Table 24.2 for sources of variability.

Although the small sample size lacked sufficient power, the results nevertheless indicated statistical effects in pretest and posttest changes in the positive direction in levels of confidence in health promotion for the full sample. The changed scores occurred immediately following the end of a series of classes. Follow-up tests were not conducted for the HP Curriculum's pilot implementation. Given the pilot results, it is hypothesized that with a larger sample size within each ethnic group, data analysis would suggest a possible stable trend, indicating that health education can positively affect Vietnamese and Cambodians' levels of confidence in their health. Using the same argument, it is hypothesized that the interaction of Time with Group would show that Cambodians might improve even more than the Vietnamese in health promotion confidence. Such a prediction means that a future report needs to address the history of Cambodian refugees and their health status with more specificity than what we have provided in our literature review. The shared features of PTSD and major depression (American Psychiatric Association, 2000) might explain similar responses from participants of both diagnostic groups to the health education classes (see Table 24.1). In addition, 36% of the Vietnamese and Cambodian participants had the dual diagnosis of PTSD and major depression, which might have prevented specific findings for each diagnostic group.

Summarizing the rationale for the HP Curriculum, many health promotion programs and literature target the general population, failing to address the important community-based and cultural factors necessary to succeed with minority groups. Therefore, the Harvard Program in Refugee Trauma recognized the potential success of developing a culturally competent Health Promotion Curriculum, offered through primary and secondary outreach, that addressed physical, psychological, and medical conditions. The pretest-posttest results from the Health Confidence Questionnaire of a small sample of Vietnamese and Cambodians for the pilot implementation was, at its best, minimal summative evaluation. What follows is a recommended program evaluation that can be used by HPRT to evaluate the HP Curriculum.

A Suggested Program Evaluation Model for the HP Curriculum

Community health programs are increasingly under pressure to evaluate their activities and to demonstrate the value of what they do. Conducting process (formative) and outcome (summative) evaluations are important for community health programs, which frequently must market themselves in a public arena, solicit members to participate, and secure funding. To do so, developers of community programs need to assess the cultural, sociopolitical, and community needs and the outcome of their programming to secure continued support and eventual changes in mental health policy. Once HPRT can determine the success of its HP Curriculum through improved evaluation processes, other communities in the United States can replicate its prevention program for Southeast Asian refugee communities.

Although HPRT has been actively involved in the greater Boston area, caring for the health needs of Southeast Asian refugees, its program efforts can be enhanced further by developing process/formative and outcome/summative evaluations. A comprehensive program evaluation can understand, verify, and increase the impact of the HP Curriculum on participants. Process and outcome evaluations can identify the HP Curriculum's strengths and weaknesses, assess whether the targeted goals have been achieved, ensure that the program is being implemented as planned, and determine the shape and direction of future program developments.

Process or Formative Evaluation

Process evaluations are most often desired by program management and staff, whose major concerns are operating a program efficiently, meeting programmatic goals, and satisfying clients (Royce, Thyer, Padget, & Logan, 2001). Questions that a community-based psychoeducation program must address are as follows: What are the specific needs of a particular group of refugees, including individual refugees? What are the needs of their respective communities? How can a refugee group benefit from the HP Curriculum classes? How can its communities benefit from a community health program? Determining a needs assessment involves forming an advisory board, typically made up of community leaders, program participants, health care educators, and administrators. An advisory board consults with program developers on the specific needs of its targeted audience through its use of focus groups, surveys, and public forum meetings. Advisory boards also provide feedback, support, and resources for program activities (Royce et al., 2001).

HPRT subscribed to the above assumption of process evaluations. During the initial development phase, HPRT was able to ensure that an advisory board for both Vietnamese and Cambodian communities determined the needs for health education. The advisory board for the pilot implementation of the HP Curriculum was composed of the directors from both VACA and CAMAA, assigned health educators for each site, Vietnamese and Kru/Khmer translators, a psychiatric nurse, a psychiatrist, a social worker, and the first author. We recommend that in the future, focus groups be held with community members, in addition to an advisory board of leaders, to develop a broad-based understanding of the health needs of a refugee community. The advisory board can also include some community members who will attend the program development meetings. Once the HP Curriculum program is in progress, the compelling questions of the evaluation are concerned with whether the program is operating as expected. Interviews can be conducted with program staff and community stakeholders. Good management and organization also need to be verified.

Key questions, based on the recommendations of Royce et al. (2001), for evaluating a community-based health promotion program are as follows: (a) Is the HP Curriculum program reaching all members of a refugee community? (b) Is HPRT implementing the health program as planned? and (c) Are participants satisfied with their experience? An example of how to address these questions is through the use of satisfaction surveys, which can assess the class topics, teaching styles, materials, and format. It is recommended that HPRT develop satisfaction surveys for these teaching components to better assess effectiveness. Course evaluations are needed for various aspects of instruction and the topic areas. HPRT can facilitate small focus groups that include both class participants and program staff, following the HP Curriculum classes, to obtain feedback about the classes. Cultural centers like VACA and CAMAA can distribute surveys to assess the community's public opinion about the HP Curriculum program. Process or formative evaluations are supplemented with outcome or summative evaluations.

Outcome or Summative Evaluations

Outcome evaluations examine whether or not a program accomplished its goals and objectives (Royce et al., 2001). Royce et al. stated that a strong design for outcome evaluation of community programs is one that compares the outcome in the program community to the outcome in a similar community that did not receive the program. In a quasi-experimental design, this would involve a comparison community. A neighboring, similar community may collaborate if baseline data from the program community are shared with it, so that the neighboring community could start its own health promotion program. When conducting an outcome evaluation, important questions to ask are the following: (a) Is the program having the effect it is designed to have? (b) Is any good resulting from this program? and (c) Are the participants better off than they were before the community program started?

Outcome measures can have more than one measurable outcome. These outcome measures can be conducted in a longitudinal study (i.e., a 1-year follow-up with the HPRT Health Confidence Questionnaire and the HPRT Depression/Torture Screening Instrument). In addition to increased confidence after education and decreased symptomatology, HPRT can have other measurable outcomes, such as changes in the number of physician office visits (i.e., an increase in annual physical exams, cancer screenings, visits to the dentist, etc.), as well as change in the number of psychiatric consultations by participants after the implementation of the HP Curriculum. Another possible measurable outcome would be increased enrollment in classes in English as a Second Language and other civic community classes. HPRT could also measure the number of returning participants for subsequent health classes following the pilot HP Curriculum classes.

HPRT could provide an understanding of outcomes with a developmental orientation. For instance, there may be a few participants who do not report mental health problems. At posttest and follow-up, it could be verified whether those who report good health show more confidence than those given a mental disorder diagnosis. Thus, the outcomes of a healthy normative group could provide the benchmark for clinically significant improvement for those diagnosed with a disorder and provided with intervention. The health education program also needs to address the within-group diversity of a refugee community.

The pilot group was composed of older particpants with an average age of 62 years. Younger refugees like children of war, the youth, and young adults need to attend HP Curriculum classes. Such developmental, preventive programming might positively affect the overall mental and physical health of a refugee population. What follows are concluding remarks on public policy implications for eliminating health disparities as related to the role of psychologists.

Conclusion

The reasons for health disparities for minorities are multifold and complex. Federal health initiatives that address health disparities highlight the importance of understanding how culture affects and interacts with health care (USDHHS, 1998, 2001a, 2001b). For Vietnamese Americans, cultural influences include language barriers, religious beliefs, lack of understanding of physical and psychological illnesses, traditional customs and health care practices, and a history of horrific sociopolitical and war trauma unfamiliar to most people in the United States. Generally speaking, culture influences (a) the manifestation and course of health problems, (b) the prevalence of health problems, (c) patterns of participation in the health care system, and (d) patterns of health-seeking and health-promoting behaviors (Huff & Kline, 1998; Roysircar, 2005).

Refugee health concerns call for a public health response. There is limited study in the area of refugee health, and particularly how researched information may be used to improve health policies and programs for specific refugee groups. It is critical that health care services meet the needs of an increasingly diverse society and health care system and that providers respond to their patients' cultural and linguistic needs. Enhanced efforts should be targeted at preventing disease, promoting health, and delivering culturally appropriate care in order to improve minority health outcomes.

It is important for psychologists to become increasingly involved in the development, implementation, and evaluation of public policy decisions that affect the overall health of people (Lorion, Iscoe, DeLeon, & Van den bos, 1996). Psychologists are uniquely able to understand the integration of biological, cultural, emotional, cognitive, and psychosocial dimensions of behavior. For instance, psychologists can formulate policies that better integrate mental health services into the health care system so that the physical manifestations of psychopathology can be addressed (Lorion et al., 1996). By doing so, health care providers can treat individuals more comprehensively with better understanding of how psychological illness can affect physical illnesses and vice versa.

Despite PTSD's known prevalence in the refugee population, little appears to be known about its presentation by non-Western populations. Herman (1992) states, "The current formulation of post-traumatic stress disorder fails to capture either the protean symptomatic manifestations of prolonged, repeated trauma or the profound deformations of personality that occur in captivity" (p. 119). Although refugees present with many characteristic symptoms of PTSD, depression, and other defined disorders, it is clear that other symptoms (e.g., somatization) are being presented that are not characteristic of these disorders. It is apparent that research determining other prevalent symptoms related to PTSD is needed. Cultural factors play a key role in making the diagnosis of PTSD. However, Marsella, Friedman, Gerrity, and Scurfield (1996) argued that ethnocultural differences in the expression of traumatic stress may not conform to the diagnostic criteria in the *DSM*. Furthermore, because of differences in cross-cultural expressions, the construct validity of PTSD assessment may be limited in its usefulness with a refugee population. A majority of the current refugee research does not take cultural factors into consideration during assessment, diagnosis, and treatment. Thus, the concept of PTSD assessment as both a diagnostic tool and a model of Western treatment for refugees is questionable. The exploration of the psychological consequences of trauma for refugees, aside from those known to be related to PTSD, may help to broaden the range of criteria known as posttraumatic and increase the validity of PTSD as an appropriate diagnostic category for non-Western populations.

References

American Lung Association. (2002). *Trends in tobacco use among minority populations.* New York: Author.

American Lung Association. (2004). *Asian American/Pacific Islanders and lung disease fact sheet.* Retrieved on December 30, 2004, from http://www.lungusa.org/site/pp.asp?c=dvLUK90OE&b=36054

American Psychiatric Association. (2000). *Diagnostic criteria from the DSM-IV-TR.* Washington, DC: Author.

Bates, S. R., Hill, L., & Barrett-Conner, E. (1989). Cardiovascular disease risk factors in an Indochinese population. *American Journal of Preventative Medicine, 5,* 15–20.

Centers for Disease Control and Prevention. (1990).

Chomsky, N. (1971, December 31). The case against B. F. Skinner. *The New York Review of Books,* pp. 18–24.

Collins, K. S., Hughes, D. L., Doty, M. M., Ives, B. I., Edwards, J. N., & Tenney, K. (2002). *Diverse communities, common concerns: Assessing health care quality for minority Americans: Findings from the Commonwealth Fund 2001 health care quality survey.* Washington, DC: Author.

Dana, R. H. (Ed.). (2000). *Handbook of cross-cultural and multicultural personality assessment.* Mahwah, NJ: Lawrence Erlbaum.

Daniel, J. H., Roysircar, G., Abeles, N., & Boyd, C. (2004). Individual and cultural diversity competence: Focus on the therapist. *Journal of Clinical Psychology, 25*(4), 255–267.

Duffy, K. G., & Wong, F. Y. (Eds.). (2003). Community psychology (3rd ed., pp. 163–188). Boston: Allyn & Bacon/Pearson Education.

Engel, G. (1977). The need for a new medical model: A challenge for biomedicine. *Science, 196,* 129–136.

Federal Register. (2000). Vol. 65(246), 80865–80879.

Hauff, E., & Vaglum, P. (1994). Chronic posttraumatic stress disorder in Vietnamese refugees: A prospective community study of prevalence, course, psychopathology, and stressors. *Journal of Nervous and Mental Disorders, 182,* 85–90.

Herman, J. (1992). *Trauma and recovery.* New York: HarperCollins.

Hinton, W. L., Chen, Y. J., Du, N., Tran, C. G., Lu, F. G., Miranda, J., & Faust, S. (1993). *DSM-III-R* disorders in Vietnamese refugees. *Journal of Nervous and Mental Disorders, 182,* 113–122.

Huff, R., & Kline, M. (1998). *Promoting health in multicultural populations: A handbook for practitioners.* Thousand Oaks, CA: Sage.

Jamieson, N. L. (1995). *Understanding Vietnam.* Berkeley: University of California Press.

Jenkins, C. N., McPhee, S. J., Bird, J. A., & Bonilla, N. T. (1990). Cancer risks and prevention practices among Vietnamese refugees. *Western Journal of Medicine, 153,* 34–39.

Kinzie, J. D., Boehnlein, J. K., Leung, P. K., Moore, L. J., Riley, C., & Smith, D. (1990). The prevalence of posttraumatic stress disorder and its clinical significance among Southeast Asian refugees. *American Journal of Psychiatry, 147,* 913–917.

Knight, S. J., & Camic, P. M. (1998). Health psychology and medicine: The art and science of healing. In P. M. Camic & S. K. Knight (Eds.), *Clinical handbook of health psychology: A practical guide to effective interventions* (pp. 3–15). Seattle, WA: Hogrefe & Huber.

Lin, K. M., Masuda, M., & Tazuma, L (1984). Adaptational problems of Vietnamese refugees: IV: Three-year comparison. *Psychiatric Journal of the University of Ottawa, 9,* 79–84.

Lorion, R. P., Iscoe, I., DeLeon, P. H., & Van den bos, G. R. (1996). *Psychologists in public policy: Balancing public service and professional need.* Washington, DC: American Psychological Association.

Marsella, A. J., Friedman, M. J., Gerrity, E. T., & Scurfield, R. M. (1996). *Ethnocultural aspects of posttraumatic stress disorder: Issues, research, and clinical applications.* Washington, DC: American Psychological Association.

Mollica, R. F., & Caspi-Yavin, Y. (1991). Measuring torture and torture-related symptoms. *Psychological Assessment, 3*(4), 581–587.

Mollica, R. F., Reczycki, M., & Lavelle, J. (2000). *Health Promotion Confidence Form.* Statewide network of local care to survivors of torture funded by the federal Office of Refugee Resettlement, Harvard Program in Refugee Trauma, Department of Psychiatry, Massachusetts General Hospital, 22 Putnam Avenue, Cambridge, MA 02139.

Munger, R. G., Gomez-Marin, O., Prineas, R. J., & Sinaiko, A. R. (1991). Elevated blood pressure among Southeast Asian refugee children in Minnesota. *American Journal of Epidemiology, 133,* 1257–1265.

Nguyen, D. (1985). Culture shock: A review of Vietnamese culture and its concepts of health and disease. *Western Journal of Medicine, 142,* 409–412.

Nolan, C. M., & Elarth, A. M. (1988). Tuberculosis in a cohort of Southeast Asian refugees: A five year surveillance study. *American Review of Respiratory Disorders, 137,* 805–809.

Pham, C. T., & McPhee, S. J. (1992). Knowledge, attitudes and practices of breast and cervical cancer screening among Vietnamese women. *Journal of Cancer Education, 7,* 305–310.

Purnell, L., & Paulanka, B. (1998). *Transcultural health care: A culturally competent approach.* Philadelphia: F. A. Davis.

Ross, R. K., Bernstein L., Hartnett, N. M., & Boone, J. R. (1991). Cancer patterns among Vietnamese immigrants in Los Angeles County. *British Journal of Cancer, 64,* 185–186.

Royce, D., Thyer, B., Padget, D., & Logan, A. (2001). *Program evaluation: An introduction* (3rd ed.). Belmont, CA: Wadsworth/Thompson.

Roysircar, G. (2003). Counselor awareness of own assumptions, values, and biases. In G. Roysircar, P. Arredondo, J. N. Fuertes, J. G. Ponterotto, & R. L. Toporek (Eds.), *Multicultural competencies 2003: Association for Multicultural Counseling and Development* (pp. 15–26). Alexandria, VA: AMCD.

Roysircar, G. (2004a). Child survivor of war: A case study. *Journal of Multicultural Counseling and Development, 32*(3), 168–180.

Roysircar, G. (2004b). Counseling and psychotherapy for acculturation and ethnic identity concerns with immigrants and international student clients. In T. B. Smith (Ed.), *Practicing multiculturalism: Affirming diversity in counseling and psychology* (pp. 248–268). Boston: Allyn & Bacon.

Roysircar, G. (2004c). Cultural self-awareness assessment: Practice examples from psychology training. *Professional Psychology: Research and Practice, 35*(6), 558–566.

Roysircar, G. (2005). Culturally sensitive assessment and multicultural guidelines. In M. G. Constantine & D. W. Sue (Eds.), *Applications of multicultural guidelines.* Boston: Allyn & Bacon.

Roysircar, G., Arredondo, P., Fuertes, J. N., Ponterotto, J. G., & Toporek, R. L. (2003). *Multicultural counseling competencies 2003: Association for Multicultural Counseling and Development.* Alexandria, VA: AMCD.

Roysircar, G., Gard, G., Hubbell, R., & Ortega, M. (2005). Development of counseling trainees' multicultural awareness through mentoring ESL students. *Journal of Multicultural Counseling and Development, 33*(1), 17–36.

Roysircar-Sodowsky, G., & Maestas, M. (2000). Acculturation, ethnic identity, and acculturative stress: Evidence and measurement. In R. H. Dana (Ed.), *Handbook of cross-cultural and multicultural personality assessment* (pp. 131–172). Mahwah, NJ: Lawrence Erlbaum.

Sodowsky, G. R. (1991). Effects of culturally consistent counseling tasks on American and international student observers' perception of counselor credibility: A preliminary investigation. *Journal of Counseling and Development, 69,* 253–256.

Sodowsky, G. R., & Lai, E. W. M. (1997). Asian immigrant variables and structural models of cross-cultural distress. In A. Booth, A. C. Crouter, & N. Landale (Eds.), *Immigration and the family: Research and policy on U.S. immigrants* (pp. 211–234). Mahwah, NJ: Lawrence Erlbaum.

Sue, S., & Morishima, J. K. (1982). *The mental health of Asian Americans.* San Francisco: Jossey-Bass.

Swerdlow, A. J. (1991). Mortality and cancer incidence in Vietnamese refugees in England and Wales: A follow-up study. *International Journal of Epidemiology, 20,* 13–19.

United Nations High Commission on Refugees. (1998). *The state of the world's refugees 1997–1998: A humanitarian agenda.* Washington, DC: Oxford University Press.

U.S. Department of Health and Human Services. (1998). *Initiative on race, one America.* Retrieved October 13, 2001, from http://www.whitehouse.gov/initiatives

U.S. Department of Health and Human Services. (2001a). *Culture, race, & ethnicity: A supplement to mental health: A report of the Surgeon General.* Rockville, MD: Author.

U.S. Department of Health and Human Services. (2001b). *Healthy people 2000: Understanding and improving health.* Rockville, MD: Author.

World Health Organization. (2004, November). *Ottawa Charter for Health Promotion, 1986.* First international conference on health promotion, Ottawa, Canada, 17–21 November. Retrieved December 30, 2004, from http://www.who.dk/AboutWHO/Policy/20010827_2

CHAPTER 25

Social Justice Related to Working With HIV/AIDS From a Counseling Health Psychology Perspective

Christa K. Schmidt, Mary Ann Hoffman, and Nicole Taylor

At the heart of social justice work is a perspective that aims to liberate and transform conditions of living while elevating equity and fairness. Those values correspond to the goals of counseling psychology. Despite ambiguity regarding exactly *how* to systematically integrate a commitment to social justice work into counseling psychology research, training, and practice, the concept is one that has been embraced by many in our field (Fouad et al., 2004; Goodman et al., 2004; Vera & Speight, 2003). These calls to action have resulted in the development of aspirational goals, but have left much work to be done in defining what social justice work actually looks like. Some in the field have attempted to define the theoretical underpinnings of social justice in counseling psychology, its specific activities, and its outcomes (Goodman et al., 2004). This chapter aims to elucidate how social justice can play a role in counseling health psychology, with particular emphasis on HIV and AIDS. In the first section, we will discuss how counseling health psychologists can incorporate a social justice perspective into their work with individuals and communities coping with HIV. Next, we will outline a model of university and community agency partnership (U-CAP) that is mutually beneficial to both the social justice training of counseling psychologists and to the community agencies and individuals receiving services in their communities. We will make specific recommendations for the implementation of this model from the perspective of both community agencies and training programs in counseling psychology. Case examples will be given to illustrate the successful implementation of the model.

Counseling health psychology is one of the many areas that can be informed and enhanced by a social justice perspective. Often, health concerns profoundly affect people's emotional, social, sexual, and vocational functioning and can cause disruptions in life goals and roles (Hoffman & Driscoll, 2000). Viewing health concerns from a broader sociopolitical context may help explain the differences between how men and women, whites and racial minorities, and those of higher versus lower economic status face illness and treatment. For example, a relationship exists between health status (as defined by progress toward health promotion or disease prevention) and income. Individuals from lower income areas with less education are more likely to suffer from certain health problems, such as hypertension, obesity, and problems associated with cigarette smoking, and have limited or no access to preventive care (U.S. Department of Health and Human Services, 1998).

Similarly, environmental factors affect both the acquisition and the outcome of diseases. People living in urban areas, especially those of low socioeconomic status, are at a greater risk for health problems than people living in less populated areas (Speers & Lancaster, 1998). HIV infection is a primary example of this trend, because it is a disease that currently poses the largest threat to poor and disenfranchised communities (Kenagy et al., 2003). For instance, women of color have recently become the fastest growing segment of the population with HIV (Centers for Disease Control Division of HIV/AIDS Prevention, 2002). Thus, using a social justice approach to counseling health psychology must include examining problems and intervening at both the individual and community levels.

Despite what we know about the effects of disease on communities, our knowledge of health is mostly derived from medical and psychological research and practice that focuses on the individual, and often white, middle-class individuals (Mastroianni, Faden, & Federman, 1994). We agree with Adler (2003) and Prilleltensky and Prilleltensky (2003) that counseling health psychology would benefit from less focus on individual factors and a greater focus on the multiple levels of impact on individuals coping with illness, including the community and society levels.

Goodman et al. (2004) conceptualized social justice work as "scholarship and professional action designed to change societal values, structures, policies, and practices such that disadvantaged or marginalized groups gain increased access to these tools of self-determination" (p. 795). Like other areas of social justice work, research and practice of counseling health psychology occur on three levels: the micro, or individual, level; the meso, or community, level; and the macro, or societal, level (e.g., Bronfenbrenner, 1979; Goodman et al., 2004; Moane, 2003; Trickett, 1996). Prilleltensky and Prilleltensky (2003) have devised an approach for psychologists to address the health and wellness of individuals, groups, and communities by addressing issues of power, privilege, and social justice. The basic premise of this approach, known as critical health psychology, is to avoid the tendency of "mainstream" practitioners of health psychology to concentrate too much on the individual and use a reactive mode of intervention. In contrast, Prilleltensky and Prilleltensky favor interventions that address social structures at the community or societal level. Authors in community psychology (Harper & Salina, 2000; Harper, Contreras, Bangi, & Pedraza, 2003) discuss the importance of working within the community to address larger social issues such as oppression and marginalization.

Within counseling psychology, research and interventions directed at the community level fit with the philosophical underpinnings of the profession with its emphasis on prevention and adaptation across the life span of healthy individuals (Gelso & Fretz, 2001). Additionally, working with individuals and their communities speaks to counseling psychology's core value of considering how an individual is influenced by his or her environment and cultural context (Gelso & Fretz, 2001). The overlap between the values of counseling psychology as a field and the benefits of social justice in communities provides a strong rationale for counseling psychologists' work at the community level, which would allow them to affect change at multiple levels.

Applying a Social Justice Perspective to Counseling Health Psychology: HIV/AIDS

We have selected the HIV/AIDS pandemic to illustrate how a social justice approach to counseling health psychology can be integrated into university research and training programs in our field. As professionals working with individuals affected by HIV or AIDS, we have learned that health epidemics have far-reaching effects beyond biomedical symptoms. Physical health and disease also have profound effects on psychosocial, cultural, and political facets of individuals and communities. In the following discussion, we illustrate the impact of HIV and AIDS on individuals, communities, and societies, which provides the backdrop for counseling psychologists' work with this global health concern from a social justice perspective.

The Individual, Community, and Societal Levels of HIV/AIDS Impact

Individuals diagnosed with HIV or AIDS are faced with multiple stressors that can have a large impact on their psychological well-being (Hoffman, 1996). Many who contract HIV are already experiencing chronic burdens that relate to money, housing, work, relationships, and vulnerability to crime (Gurung, Taylor, Kemeny, & Myers, 2004). In a study examining how an HIV-positive diagnosis has further impact on these burdens, Gurung et al. (2004) found that HIV infection appears to increase vulnerability to depressed mood both on its own and by exacerbating the chronic burdens experienced by low-income individuals. Furthermore, individuals who perceived themselves as having higher levels of chronic burdens also experienced lower social support, less optimism, and more avoidant coping. Within gay and lesbian populations as well as in communities of color, the social effects of homonegativity, racism, and oppression can also contribute to distress. Thus, an HIV diagnosis typically compounds the stressors that already exist in an individual's life and makes him or her more vulnerable to poor adjustment through weakened resources. Furthermore, although the emotional impact of HIV/AIDS has been documented, individual responses to the disease range dramatically from having a severe negative response to maintaining emotional health as it existed prior to the diagnosis (Hoffman, 1996). The emotional distress experienced by an individual can vary along several parameters, including prediagnosis level of functioning, stage of disease, time since diagnosis, side effects from medications, and many others (Hoffman, 1996). Therefore, when considering the psychological, emotional, and behavioral impact of HIV or AIDS on individuals, one must consider the coalescence of all disease-related and non-disease-related variables.

Communities are differentially affected by HIV/AIDS. The sociopolitical location, social and sexual networks, sexual practices and patterns, attitudes, beliefs, and overall health status of different socioeconomic and cultural groups within a given community influence the degree to which HIV is both viewed and experienced within different communities (Trickett, 2002). Overall, HIV is rapidly becoming a disease that disproportionately affects young, low-income, minority individuals. The Centers for Disease Control (2002) reported that 40,000 new HIV infections occur each year in the United States, half of which are in individuals younger than 25 years old. Furthermore, although women account for only 30% of new infections, adolescent and adult women represent one of the most rapidly increasing groups infected with HIV, as their rate jumped from 7% to 26% between 1985 and 2002 (National Institute of Allergy and Infectious Diseases, 2004). Additionally, people of color have a disproportionately high representation of HIV infection as 70% of new infections among men were contracted by Black or Hispanic men and 82% of new infections among women were contracted by Black or Hispanic women. Moreover, the majority of new cases are reported in low-income areas (Centers for Disease Control, 2002).

Seventy-five percent of HIV cases among women are transmitted through heterosexual sex and 25% through injection drug use. For men, 15% of cases are transmitted through heterosexual sex, 25% through injection drug use, and 60% through homosexual sex (National Institute of Allergy and Infectious Diseases, 2004). Gender, race/ethnicity, socioeconomic status, and sexual orientation all appear to be important variables to consider when planning interventions that will benefit individuals affected by HIV. However, it is also essential to recognize that these variables overlap within the community, and therefore interventions directed at the "gay community," "poor community," or "heterosexual community" alone will not be entirely effective. It is clear that HIV is having a profound impact at the community level, and socially just prevention interventions can be the first line of defense in working at this level.

Counseling psychologists need to consider the individual, community, and societal implications when working with HIV/AIDS. On an individual level, working with HIV-positive individuals can enhance their quality of life through helping them increase personal resources and overcome depressive symptoms related to the illness. When considering a counseling psychologist's work at the community level, prevention efforts aimed at areas and groups that are disproportionately represented in the HIV statistics can begin to reduce these numbers and strengthen these communities. It is important to maintain awareness that interventions are contextually bound at individual, community, and societal levels, which will keep our work with the HIV/AIDS pandemic focused on our sphere of influence as well as aware of the larger culture of the illness.

University and Community Agency Collaborations

The nature of HIV/AIDS as an individual, community, and societal phenomenon has implications for interventions from a counseling psychology perspective as well as for the training of counseling psychology professionals. We see the opportunity for a reciprocal model of working with individuals and communities affected by HIV/AIDS that enhances both the impact of counseling psychologists from a social justice perspective on the community and the training of counseling psychology students as social change agents. Before outlining this model, we will discuss recommendations for university and community partnerships put forward by psychologists from other disciplines, and the implications for counseling psychologists.

As counseling psychology begins to incorporate a social justice perspective into practice, research, and training applications, examining sister schools of psychology traditionally defined by this viewpoint helps to illustrate how such partnerships between community-based organizations and universities can be developed. One example, described by Trickett and Schmid (1992), outlines three sets of activities that are included in community-level interventions, which could be applied to counseling psychologists' work within the HIV/AIDS community. First, Trickett and Schmid (1992) propose environmental assessment of the community context and individuals within that context. With regard to working with communities affected by HIV/AIDS, this implies that counseling psychologists should first become familiar with the immediate community with which they will be working, as well as the larger social structure within which the community fits. Second, developing collaborative relationships between the researcher or clinician and the setting or community where the intervention occurs is essential (Trickett & Schmid, 1992). By partnering with community-based organizations, counseling psychologists will have the opportunity to work with individuals who are directly coping with the effect of HIV/AIDS, as well as work toward larger-scale prevention efforts within the community. Finally, Trickett and Schmid (1992) suggest that professionals working within the community design interventions through processes that serve the goals of community development by enhancing local resources. For counseling psychologists working with HIV/AIDS, socially just interventions would necessarily include the strengths and resources of the community, such as existing programs, social support networks, and prevalent personal resources.

Using HIV-related organizations as an example, Harper and Salina (2000) present another model from a community psychology perspective, to establish relationships with community-based organizations. They outline an empowerment research agenda that includes community research participants in a collaborative relationship with researchers. They highlight the importance of researchers venturing outside of the traditional university-based settings to interact with the community members who will be the focus of research attention. With regard to HIV-related work, researchers are urged to collaborate with community-based organizations knowledgeable about the unique social, political, religious, psychological, and medical issues and controversies that surround the disease. In doing so, it is presumed that the work of researchers and community-based organizations will be mutually beneficial, ultimately resulting in research that can be applied more directly to individuals in the community.

We propose a model of university and community agency partnership (U-CAP) that builds on Trickett and Schmid's (1992) recommendations and Harper and Salina's (2000) model, but includes recommendations specifically designed for counseling psychologists concerned with social justice. Partnering with community-based organizations is a central component to integrating a health and social justice perspective into counseling psychology programs at universities. The goal of these partnerships, as reflected in the name of our model, is that they are reciprocal and mutually beneficial, in which individuals in the community can receive better services, researchers can develop increased knowledge of populations of interest, and students can receive training in areas beyond those traditionally provided by a university counseling center. Community organizations can benefit from the counseling, evaluation, and consultation services provided by the university. Counseling psychologists can benefit from these relationships by developing interest-specific training opportunities; research outlets; and sites for student placements in clinical, outreach, and research work. In addition, counseling psychologists and trainees can benefit from on-site supervision provided by the community organization, thus creating a true university and community agency partnership. In the first arch of the model, we will describe how individuals and communities will benefit from partnering with counseling psychology programs through counseling, consultation, program evaluation, and research. In the second arch, we will describe how working with individuals and communities affected by HIV/AIDS can greatly enhance the training of graduate students in counseling psychology as socially just scientists and practitioners (see Figure 25.1).

The Impact of U-CAP on the HIV/AIDS Community

A social justice perspective in counseling psychology requires professionals to evaluate what they can do to transform and liberate individuals and communities (Speight & Vera, 2004). From a health perspective, the immediate question is, How can counseling psychologists intervene to change the status quo of this disease and reduce the deleterious effects on the communities who have faced the most severe impact? Partnering with community agencies that are on the front lines of this work is a necessary step to make such a contribution.

University programs that are interested in collaborating with a community agency must first determine what unique and helpful contributions they can make

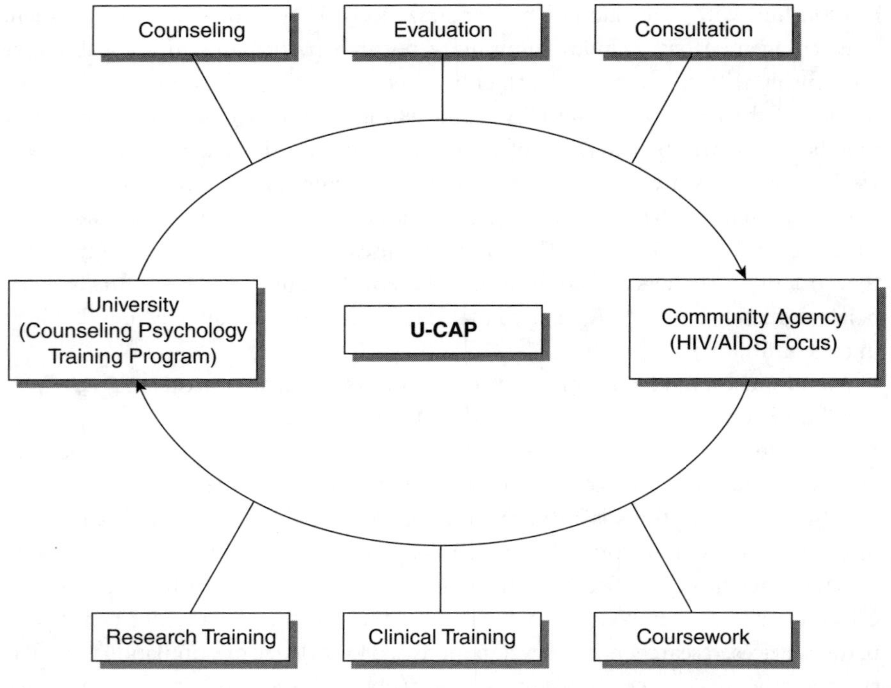

Figure 25.1 Model of University and Community Agency Partnership (U-CAP)

to the individuals served by the organization. As an initial entry point, it would be important to examine the types of counseling services currently offered to individuals served by the agency. In a study examining the challenges to HIV service provision in community settings, social workers and nurses cited mental/emotional health supports for the patients and families to be an important service need (Olivier & Dykeman, 2003). Counseling services, for instance, could be an asset to treatment in community agencies. At the same time, resources to provide such services are often limited within community agencies, making procurement of these services difficult (Beckerman & Rock, 1996). Thus, university programs might contribute by offering a practicum training experience on-site to enhance the services currently being offered, bringing the social work and nursing staff of community agencies into direct contact with a counseling psychology perspective. By having counseling trainees contribute to the counseling services offered at the center, the resources of the agency could be expanded. For example, an organization that currently offers testing services could have advanced practicum students offer follow-up counseling sessions, or conduct ongoing psychoeducational groups for individuals adjusting to different aspects of the illness. Such services would make a collaborative partnership more appealing to the community agency because the individuals they serve would receive direct benefits.

Program assessment and evaluation research represent another important area where counseling psychologists can collaborate with community agencies. A second consideration of the collaboration would be how the community agency currently evaluates the services that it offers. Because counseling psychologists are specifically trained in evaluation, it would be possible to work together with the agency to enhance its current programs and services through evaluation methods. With HIV-related populations, this might include developing measures of drug adherence, psychosocial functioning, and adjustment following participation in the programs and services offered by the agency. If the agency has current evaluation methods already in place, counseling psychologists could offer their services by helping to improve such measures. This evaluation component could relieve some of the burden placed on agency staff to demonstrate their effectiveness and usefulness to their sources of funding, be they public or private.

Consultative and psychoeducational interventions tailored for professionals working with patients and clients with HIV/AIDS represent another entry point for counseling psychologists. In the study mentioned above, the need for in-service HIV education and more HIV-related information was frequently cited by nurses and social workers as one of the services that would be most helpful for those providing care for persons living with HIV/AIDS (Olivier & Dykeman, 2003). In a consultative role, counseling psychologists can serve this function by communicating the implications of research findings directly to the staff of the organization. For instance, a team of counseling psychologists investigating the impact of disclosure of HIV status on the mental health of those diagnosed with the virus would present its findings to the medical and social work staff of the community agency in a roundtable discussion, making specific suggestions and recommendations for discussing disclosure issues with their patients and clients. Such consultation would keep the community agency on the cutting edge of information about HIV/AIDS and the most effective interventions, ultimately enhancing their ability to provide quality services to the community.

Counseling, program evaluation, and consultation are broad areas that counseling psychologists could contribute to community agencies addressing the needs of individuals and communities managing HIV/AIDS. Such services would go beyond the focus on the individual, which is often the case within counseling psychology (Speight & Vera, 2004), and extend the potential impact to the community. By extending such services to community agencies, we would begin to address the questions of how counseling psychologists can contribute to the liberation of individuals and communities from the devastating effects of HIV and AIDS. The following recommendations for implementing a U-CAP program illustrate how counseling programs can begin to establish a socially just agenda in the area of HIV/AIDS by partnering with community agencies.

Summary of Recommendations

- Establish a reciprocal relationship with a community agency focused on addressing the needs of persons living with HIV/AIDS.
- Extend beyond the scope of the university to begin working on the front lines of intervention with HIV/AIDS at the individual and community levels.

- In conjunction with the staff of the community agency, evaluate the types of services that are currently offered.
- Conduct a needs assessment to begin to identify the areas of strength and growth within the agency.
- Examine counseling, consultation, program evaluation, and research programs. Conduct focus groups with different groups of staff (e.g., doctors, nurses, social workers) to obtain a complete picture of what the agency needs are.
- Identify services that could contribute to the service provision of the agency. Build on existing programs and create new programs or areas of development.
- Collaborate with agency staff on all levels to outline program implementation. Identify the requirements of both agency staff and university faculty. Outline the roles of each member of the partnership and specify individuals who will fill those roles.
- Implement programs.
- Evaluate partnership at specified intervals and on an ongoing basis.

Case Illustrations

Counseling psychologists working in university communities can intervene at one or multiple levels of the U-CAP. To show how the university-community collaboration can occur, the following case examples are provided as illustrations of this work.

Case 1: Application to University Faculty

A counseling health psychologist at a university in an urban setting, Sarah Baker, PhD, is advancing her research program in the area of HIV. As part of her research program, Sarah has established a relationship with a community agency focusing on the needs of individuals diagnosed with HIV. When Sarah became interested in socially just research and interventions with individuals and communities coping with the effects of HIV/AIDS, she approached the director of a community agency that is known to offer free testing and health services to low-income individuals, and the director agreed to allow Sarah's research team to collect data at the agency. Sarah's team is investigating the factors that contribute to adherence to antiretroviral therapy, and their findings are expected to have direct implications for service delivery of the community agency. When the results of the study demonstrate that participation in a support group contributes to increased adherence to drug treatment, Sarah and her students present their findings to the agency staff. Following this consultation, Sarah meets with the staff of the agency to determine how such knowledge can enhance the existing programs at the agency.

Case 2: Application to University Faculty

Because many students have expressed interest in obtaining practicum experiences outside of the university counseling center, Brian Jackson, PhD, a counseling psychology faculty member who organizes and structures students' practicum experiences, decides to approach a community agency that is known to offer counseling services to clients diagnosed with HIV and AIDS. Together, Brian and the staff of the agency establish a practicum opportunity for students enrolled in the counseling psychology program at Brian's university. Currently, three students are offering ongoing posttest counseling to individuals who test positive for HIV, as well as facilitating a support group. They receive individual supervision on-site at the agency, as well as group supervision within their academic department. This experience has increased the amount of services the community agency is able to provide and has greatly enhanced the diversity of the practicum experiences available to the students in Brian's program.

The cases of Drs. Sarah Baker and Brian Jackson illustrate how counseling psychology faculty in university settings can contribute to a community agency providing services for individuals affected by HIV/AIDS, thereby promoting a social justice agenda. The second arch of the model describes how counseling training programs will be more prepared to train students in the area of social justice through a U-CAP program.

The Impact of U-CAP on Counseling Psychology Training Programs

According to the American Psychological Association's Office on AIDS (2004), content related to HIV/AIDS should be included in the training of counseling and clinical psychologists because of the profound psychological effect this disease has on individuals living with HIV as well as on their families and communities. Furthermore, psychologists in these disciplines have the expertise to apply theories of behavior change at both the individual and the community level through primary and secondary prevention strategies and behavioral interventions. Certainly, counseling psychologists work with communities that are affected by this disease, but the extent to which they provide specific and targeted interventions and training is unclear. Early in the study of HIV/AIDS, one examination showed that only 19% of APA-approved graduate programs in psychology offered training in this area (Campos, Brasfield, & Kelly, 1989). In a more recent analysis, Anderson, Campos, and Hamid (1998) found that only 14% of graduate programs in psychology offered coursework with a primary focus on HIV/AIDS content. These identified courses primarily centered on counseling individuals diagnosed with HIV or AIDS. In the other 86% of the courses where HIV/AIDS material was included but was not the primary focus, the largest number of courses was most often related to counseling or psychotherapy. In other words, very few courses, if any, with a multicultural, ethics, consultation, or research focus were reported to include HIV/AIDS material even though the subject is entirely relevant to curricula in these domains.

Writings such as those by Hoffman (1991) and Werth (1993) have described how HIV/AIDS material can be added to graduate training programs. For example, Hoffman (1991) suggests multiple ways that HIV/AIDS content can be included in training programs in counseling, including offering a half-day or one-day workshop designed to enhance students' awareness and knowledge of the impact of HIV/AIDS on individuals and communities, incorporating related components within existing courses (e.g., a unit within an ethics course or multicultural course or a clinical component within a practicum), or adding a course devoted exclusively to HIV/AIDS content to the existing curriculum. By demonstrating the multiple ways in which this training can be included, counseling programs may reduce their perception of barriers to implementing HIV/AIDS material and be more likely to make such training a reality for their students. This flexible approach is advocated by the American Psychological Association Office on AIDS as well because it helps overcome common barriers to implementing HIV/AIDS material, such as attempting to add content to already full curricula, finding faculty with expertise to teach a full course, and justifying how much time and resources to devote to this area versus other topics. The U-CAP model presents an important additional step by extending the training arena into the greater community as students become partners as agents of social change.

The inclusion of U-CAP in counseling programs would provide a springboard for HIV/AIDS content in such curriculum areas as coursework, practicum, and research training. Such content would be relevant to the perspectives of multicultural competence and professional issues topics including the effects of social stigma, adjustments to life transitions, and social justice. To give students the theoretical understanding of the impact of HIV/AIDS, multiple courses could incorporate content as it relates to the goals of the course. Then, the partnership with a community agency would provide students with firsthand experience working with individuals, groups, and communities affected by HIV/AIDS in a practicum setting. Finally, this partnership would potentially offer research opportunities to students interested in developing their research interests in counseling health psychology related to HIV/AIDS. Together, the effects of the U-CAP on coursework, practicum, and research training would strengthen the program's commitment to and emphasis on training in social justice.

HIV/AIDS content in counseling psychology coursework should include an emphasis on the effects of the disease on individuals, subgroups, and the larger community, as well as social impacts. By including a U-CAP as part of the curriculum, students will need to be prepared by their coursework to work with individuals and communities within a social justice framework. On an individual level, counseling theory and methods classes have the opportunity to address specific counseling approaches to working with individuals diagnosed with HIV or AIDS. These courses can also include the unique aspects of the disease that may be relevant areas for exploration in therapy. On a community or societal level, courses that focus on broader social issues, such as ethics, multiculturalism, and consultation, contain a natural entry for including HIV-related concerns. Such courses could incorporate the oppression, discrimination, and marginalization of individuals diagnosed with HIV and how these societal forces have an impact on entire communities disproportionately affected by the illness. If students are given the opportunity to consider the complex and multidimensional nature of living with the virus, they will be better prepared to work with these individuals in appropriate and helpful ways.

Another potential contribution of the U-CAP is the enhanced counseling training experience that would come from working with clients at a community agency focused on HIV/AIDS. Ultimately, if students are able to participate in a practicum experience working with the HIV/AIDS community, their theoretical knowledge can be applied in a hands-on experience, allowing them to gain deeper understanding of the individual and community impact of the disease. Because many counseling students receive most of their practicum experience in a university counseling center, the opportunity to work with underserved individuals within the community would provide firsthand experience and understanding of the need and value of social justice in the field. The opportunity to work with individuals and communities coping with HIV/AIDS would provide students with specific knowledge of the issues related to this disease, as well as with a greater understanding of the unbalanced nature of health concerns in our society. Therefore, the type of practicum opportunity a U-CAP could provide would further reinforce training students in our field's commitment to social justice.

Finally, by including a U-CAP program, counseling psychology trainees could investigate a multitude of counseling and health-related questions by collecting research data from individuals affected by HIV/AIDS. For instance, researchers could investigate and enhance knowledge around the changing impact of HIV/AIDS on individuals and communities, effective mental health treatment and prevention efforts, and the extent of the effects of disease-related discrimination and marginalization. Such projects could be conducted within a program using a U-CAP by having students collaborate with the community agency to conceptualize, design, and complete research that will advance both the students' research skills and the community's work with this population. Furthermore, including a counseling psychology perspective in HIV/AIDS research will be invaluable to the advancement of the global understanding of the impact of the illness. To do so, it is important to teach students the methodological and ethical issues related to conducting research with these groups. As counseling psychology programs emphasize the scientist-practitioner model, implementing a U-CAP in the area of HIV/AIDS would give students the experience of a link between their research and clinical skills.

Summary of Recommendations

- Partner with community agencies focused on HIV/AIDS work to create practicum and research opportunities for training purposes.
- HIV/AIDS offers an unusual opportunity to explore not only health and overall functioning, but sexuality and sexual behaviors, substance use, stigma,

discrimination, sexual orientation, social class, race, ethnicity, access to health care, and the intersection of numerous other variables that have defined this pandemic. HIV/AIDS can serve as a template for a number of these topics that can be explored in graduate coursework such as professional issues and multiculturalism classes.

- Counseling psychology professors can help students work with clients with HIV/AIDS through additional clinical experiences, such as externships.
- Didactic portions of practica can also integrate HIV/AIDS into the curriculum. Clinical topic presentations and case presentations about HIV/AIDS will encourage the entire class to think about HIV/AIDS as a clinical issue. Discussing the unique mental health ramifications of the disease will benefit all students.
- Clinical supervisors can help expose counseling psychology graduate students to HIV/AIDS-related issues as well. An important task of supervisors is to help supervisees manage their countertransference to working with individuals with HIV/AIDS. Innovative models of supervision could be explored to allow multiple supervisors and/or consultants when working with clients at outside agencies.
- When applying for an internship, students with an interest in HIV/AIDS-related issues can be encouraged to apply to sites that have an emphasis on populations with HIV/AIDS. Trainees can be encouraged to develop their specialty areas while on internship to further enhance their skills in conducting therapy with clients with HIV/AIDS. According to the American Psychological Association's Office on AIDS, there are currently 15 APA-approved predoctoral internship sites that offer some degree of clinical training in HIV/AIDS.
- Research projects in HIV/AIDS should be encouraged, especially as partnerships with community agencies and organizations.
- Help integrate students' understanding of research and practice by using HIV/AIDS as a model that applies easily to both realms. HIV/AIDS can provide an integrative model to exemplify the scientist-practitioner goals of counseling psychology.

Case Illustrations

In addition to the direct work of counseling psychologists with the community, the U-CAP will provide community impact through its influence on the training of students. The following two case examples demonstrate how students can be active participants and beneficiaries of the U-CAP model.

Case 1: Application to Students of Counseling Psychologists

Samantha is a third-year graduate student in a counseling psychology program. She has an interest in working with individuals with HIV/AIDS in a community mental health center as a future career. As a student, she wants the opportunity to develop her skills as a therapist with those clients on a regular basis, but her practica experiences are focused on the college counseling center at the university where her program is housed.

Samantha decided to seek out a clinical opportunity at a community agency in her area that works with individuals diagnosed with HIV/AIDS. Samantha has been able to see clients with HIV/AIDS in individual therapy and is in the process of starting a therapy group. She is considering doing her dissertation research at the agency and is collaborating with her supervisor to plan research that will be mutually interesting and beneficial to both Samantha and the agency. She is hoping to fill a void in the research by providing her research services to answer a question that will benefit the agency. Samantha has learned a great deal about working with individuals with HIV/AIDS, how a community-based agency is run (which will benefit her as she pursues her career goals), how to exemplify the scientist-practitioner model, and what research is important to community-based HIV/AIDS organizations.

Case 2: Application to Students of Counseling Psychologists

Ben is an advanced doctoral student in counseling psychology. He has pursued his interest in studying the psychological effects of HIV/AIDS by developing a doctoral dissertation on work satisfaction in individuals after their diagnosis with HIV. He collected data for his study at his internship site, a community-based counseling center that focuses on the health concerns of low-income communities. Through his research, he has learned that lower levels of perceived workplace support, higher levels of perceived workplace discrimination (both HIV-related and homophobia), and higher levels of psychological distress are predictive of job dissatisfaction in his sample of HIV-positive and AIDS-diagnosed employed men and women. This has potential implications for employment in persons living with HIV disease.

Through his dissertation work and choice of internship placement, Ben has been able to further his interest in working with HIV/AIDS patients. He has presented his findings to the staff of his internship site, including recommendations on how to work with clients who have been diagnosed with HIV. He is planning to present his findings at the APA convention and to submit them for publication. He has sought out opportunities to further his own training in the area and is an exemplar of the scientist-practitioner model.

Conclusions

HIV/AIDS is a pandemic that has influenced individuals, communities, and entire societies for more than two decades. Counseling psychologists working from a social justice perspective have an opportunity to make a difference by collaborating with community agencies on the front lines of this work. Such collaborations, as illustrated by the U-CAP model, provide a reciprocal, mutually beneficial opportunity for primary and secondary intervention on the individual and community levels of HIV/AIDS as well as in the social justice training of counseling psychology graduate students. These partnerships place the core values of social justice into action within the framework of counseling health psychology. The manner in which HIV/AIDS is addressed can serve as a template for social justice training in counseling psychology programs for future critical social issues.

References

Adler, N. E. (2003). Looking upstream and downstream from the middle of the river: A commentary on Prilleltensky and Prilleltensky. *Journal of Health Psychology, 8,* 211–213.

American Psychological Association Office on AIDS. (2004). *The role of the psychologist in responding to the HIV/AIDS epidemic.* Retrieved November 1, 2004, from http://www.apa.org/pi/aids/hope.html

Anderson, J., Campos, P., & Hamid, G. (1998). *A survey of graduate faculty teaching HIV/AIDS courses.* Washington, DC: American Psychological Association.

Beckerman, N., & Rock, M. (1996). Themes from the frontlines: Hospital and social work with people with AIDS. *Social Work in Health Care, 23,* 75–89.

Bronfenbrenner, U. (1979). *The ecology of human development.* Cambridge, MA: Harvard University Press.

Campos, P. E., Brasfield, T. L., & Kelly, J. A. (1989). Psychology training related to AIDS: Survey of doctoral graduate programs and predoctoral internship programs. *Professional Psychology: Research and Practice, 20,* 214–220.

Centers for Disease Control Division of HIV/AIDS Prevention. (2002, March). *HIV/AIDS among U.S. women: Minority and young women at continuing risk.* Retrieved October 15, 2004, from http://www.cod.gov/hiv/pubs/facts/women.htm

Fouad, N. A., McPherson, R. H., Gerstein, L., Blustein, D. L., Elman, N., Helledy, K. I., & Metz, A. (2004). Houston, 2001: Context and legacy. *The Counseling Psychologist, 32,* 15–77.

Gelso, C., & Fretz, B. (2001). *Counseling psychology* (2nd ed.). Belmont, CA: Wadsworth.

Goodman, L. A., Liang, B., Helms, J. E., Latta, R. E., Sparks, E., & Weintraub, S. R. (2004). Training counseling psychologists as social justice agents: Feminist and multicultural principles in action. *The Counseling Psychologist, 32,* 793–837.

Gurung, R. A. R., Taylor, S. E., Kemeny, M., & Myers, H. (2004). "HIV is not my biggest problem": The impact of HIV and chronic burden on depression in women at risk for AIDS. *Journal of Social and Clinical Psychology, 23,* 490–511.

Harper, G. W., Contreras, R., Bangi, A., & Pedraza, A. (2003). Collaborative process evaluation: Enhancing community relevance and cultural appropriateness in HIV prevention. *Journal of Prevention & Intervention in the Community, 26,* 53–69.

Harper, G. W., & Salina, D. D. (2000). Building collaborative partnerships to improve community-based HIV prevention research: The University-CBO Collaborative Partnership (UCCP) model. *Journal of Prevention & Intervention in the Community, 19,* 1–20.

Hoffman, M. A. (1991). Counseling the HIV-infected client: A psychosocial model for assessment and intervention. *The Counseling Psychologist, 19,* 467–542.

Hoffman, M. A. (1996). *Counseling clients with HIV disease: Assessment, intervention, and prevention.* New York: Guilford.

Hoffman, M. A., & Driscoll, J. (2000). Health promotion and disease prevention: A biopsychosocial model of health status. In R. Lent & S. Brown (Eds.), *Handbook of counseling psychology* (Vol. 3, pp. 532–567). New York: Wiley.

Kenagy, G. P., Linsk, N. L., Bruce, D., Warnecke, R., Gordon, A., Wagaw, F., & Densham, A. (2003). Service utilization, service barriers, and gender among HIV-positive consumers in primary care. *AIDS Patient Care and STDs, 17,* 235–244.

Mastroianni, A. C., Faden, R., & Federman, D. (1994). Women's participation in clinical studies. In A. C. Mastroianni, R. Faden, & D. Federman (Eds.), *Women and health research: Ethical and legal issues of including women in clinical studies* (pp. 36–74). Washington, DC: National Academies Press.

Moane, G. (2003). Bridging the personal and the political: Practices for a liberation psychology. *American Journal of Community Psychology, 31,* 91–101.

National Institute of Allergy and Infectious Diseases (NIAID). (2004). *Fact sheets: HIV/AIDS statistics.* Retrieved October 15, 2004, from http://www.niaid.nih.gov/factsheets/aidsstat.htm

Olivier, C., & Dykeman, M. (2003). Challenges to HIV service provision: The commonalities for nurses and social workers. *AIDS Care, 15,* 649–663.

Prilleltensky, I., & Prilleltensky, O. (2003). Towards a critical health psychology practice. *Journal of Health Psychology, 8,* 197–210.

Speers, M. A., & Lancaster, B. (1998). Disease prevention and health promotion in urban areas: CDC's perspective. *Health Education and Behavior, 25,* 226–233.

Speight, S. L., & Vera, E. M. (2004). A social justice agenda: Ready, or not? *The Counseling Psychologist, 32,* 109–118.

Trickett, E. J. (1996). A future for community psychology: The contexts of diversity and the diversity of contexts. *American Journal of Community Psychology, 24,* 209–229.

Trickett, E. J. (2002). Context, culture, and collaboration in AIDS interventions: Ecological ideas for enhancing community impact. *Journal of Primary Prevention, 23,* 157–174.

Trickett, E. J., & Schmid, K. (1992). The social context of the school: An ecological perspective on school, adolescents in schools, and interventions in schools. In P. Tolan & B. Cohler (Eds.), *Handbook of clinical research and practice with adolescents.* New York: Wiley.

U.S. Department of Health and Human Services. (1998). *Health in America tied to income and education.* Atlanta, GA: U.S. DHHS, Centers for Disease Control Prevention and Health Promotion.

Vera, E. M., & Speight, S. L. (2003). Multicultural competence, social justice, and counseling psychology: Expanding our roles. *The Counseling Psychologist, 31,* 253–272.

Werth, J. L., Jr. (1993). Recommendations for the inclusion of training about persons with HIV disease in counseling psychology graduate programs. *The Counseling Psychologist, 21,* 668–686.

PART VI

Counseling Psychologists in the International Arena

CHAPTER 26

Counseling Psychologists as International Social Architects

Lawrence H. Gerstein

This introductory chapter to this section in the *Handbook* titled "Counseling Psychologists in the International Arena" highlights the history of counseling psychologists working outside of the United States. It also provides an overview of the five chapters in this section. Next, it discusses a framework drawing from the peace psychology literature to comprehend the social justice projects described by the authors. Finally, this chapter concludes by encouraging more counseling psychologists to embrace the role of social architect and participate on interdisciplinary teams designed to provide a host of culturally appropriate and effective services worldwide.

Counseling Psychology and International Settings

Counseling psychology has a long history of offering various services outside of the United States. It has been hypothesized that the root of this effort can be traced to the work of W. Lloyd, E. G. Williamson, D. Super, H. Borow, L. Brammer, and others

Author's Note: I wish to acknowledge Doris Kirkpatrick for her significant contribution to the section on peace psychology found in this chapter.

who helped in the reorganization of Japan's educational system following World War II (Fukuhara, 1989; McWhirter, 2000). Since World War II, an increasing number of counseling professionals have relied on the scientist-professional model, for example, when consulting, teaching, training, and conducting research outside of the U.S. borders. While performing such activities, counseling psychologists have discovered the many personal and professional benefits and challenges of living and working in another country. That is, experiencing the diversity of cultures and people; coping with differences in language; facing structural, environmental, and individual obstacles; learning how psychology and counseling are practiced and taught; acquiring an understanding of unique research methods; and most important, developing new relationships with individuals throughout the world. No doubt, members of our profession who have ventured to foreign countries were greatly enriched and stimulated by their experiences. Hopefully, they also contributed to the enhancement of the country and/or citizens they served.

Lately, not only have a greater number of counseling psychologists pursued international work, but the profession has also vigorously stressed the importance and relevance of such activities (Douce, 2004; Gerstein & Moeschberger, 2003; Gerstein & Ægisdóttir, 2004; Gerstein & Ægisdóttir, 2005a, 2005b, 2005c; Heppner, 2004; Leong & Blustein, 2000; Leong & Ponterotto, 2003; Leung, 2003; McWhirter, 1988; Norsworthy & Gerstein, 2003a, 2003b; Pedersen & Leong, 1997; Ægisdóttir & Gerstein, 2005) to assist international populations, cultures, and countries in need. Members of our profession have been encouraged to broaden their vision and recognize the urgency and the societal, professional, and personal value of international endeavors, especially when considering the interconnectedness between people and countries, and the ease of global communication and travel. Proactive efforts along with work in response to an international request have been discussed.

A growing number of major contributions on the topic of internationalizing counseling psychology have appeared in *The Counseling Psychologist.* An increasing number of symposia have also been hosted at professional counseling conferences. Furthermore, recent leaders (Louise Douce & P. Puncky Heppner) of the Society of Counseling Psychology have declared some aspect of international work as their presidential initiative. A few common themes are articulated in these publications, presentations, and initiatives. First, many counseling professionals have stressed the necessity of relying on culturally appropriate models and strategies of service delivery (e.g., counseling, prevention, consultation, training); policy formulation and implementation; and research methodology (e.g., studies that employ cross-culturally valid theories, procedures, and analyses) when working in international settings. Next, a few professionals have mentioned the importance of designing and implementing effective training models to prepare U.S. counseling psychology students to engage in international work. And third, a number of individuals have pointed out the personal, cultural, and professional dangers of simply applying U.S. models and strategies overseas, and the serious risks of integrating these models and strategies with indigenous frameworks (Gerstein & Moeschberger, 2003; Gerstein & Ægisdóttir, 2004; Leong & Blustein, 2000; Leong & Ponterotto, 2003; Leung, 2003; Norsworthy & Gerstein, 2003b; Pedersen & Leong, 1997; Ægisdóttir & Gerstein, 2005).

As must be apparent from the brief description of the recommendations just mentioned, these suggestions are consistent, in general, with some basic tenets of the multicultural counseling movement: understanding, respecting, and honoring specific cultural norms, values, and behaviors when conceptualizing and implementing various types of counseling interventions, training models, research paradigms, and policies. In fact, international work may be seen as the next stage in the multicultural counseling movement; a movement that now appears to be firmly and securely grounded in serving the individual needs and issues faced by a diverse U.S. population in terms of race, ethnicity, religious belief, sexual orientation, and physical ability.

Given the extensive and systemic nature of these needs, it is understandable that some professionals (Speight & Vera, 2004; Vera & Speight, 2003) in the multicultural counseling movement have now advocated shifting the focus of mental health service from simply assisting the individual to addressing the wider needs of the larger group or community. As such, these scholars have encouraged members of our profession to become more involved in social justice, advocacy, and activist work when attempting to deal with multicultural concerns.

Purpose of International Section

The five chapters found in this section of the *Handbook* are consistent with the proposed new direction for the multicultural counseling movement. They are also congruent with the evolving focus of counseling psychology on international work, particularly the profession's efforts to effectively resolve systemic and structural issues through social justice, advocacy, and activism. As a result, this section of the *Handbook* presents some outstanding international work by a few notable counseling psychologists. Each chapter offers a rich theoretical foundation as a basis for the social justice strategies employed to address the international issue of concern.

The first chapter in this section was written by Sharon Horne and Susan Mathews. For many years, these authors have been consulting with various nongovernmental organizations (NGOs) in Eastern Europe. In this chapter, Horne and Mathews describe their ongoing work with a Hungarian women's rights organization to reduce structural and direct violence toward women. The authors' work is grounded in an integration of a social and counseling psychology perspective on social justice. It is also grounded in an integration of feminist psychology, multicultural counseling principles, peace psychology, and liberation psychology. Horne and Mathews provide training to the leaders of this NGO in the hope that one-on-one violence toward women will decrease in Hungary and that the structural, societal factors reinforcing such violence will be eliminated. The authors clearly articulate their specific roles as international consultants and carefully discuss the importance of respecting the norms and behaviors of other cultures. They also caution counseling psychologists about the serious dangers of exporting Western models of psychology to non-Western countries and cultures.

In the second chapter, Benedict T. McWhirter and Ellen Hawley McWhirter discuss their ongoing consultation and training project in Peñalolén, Chile, that began in 1995. Peñalolén is considered to be a lower- and working-class part of Santiago. The authors have visited this locale each year since the inception of this project, responding to a need in the community to strengthen parenting skills and help reduce oppression, poverty, and various interpersonal and community conflicts. This project is affiliated with a faith education curriculum offered by a local Catholic church. The project is designed as a psychoeducational parenting program for couples and, as such, is called "Mentor Couples." The authors consult and train couples, for example, in parenting and group skills. Some couples then serve as the volunteer leaders of the Mentor program. Basically, the program is structured to improve family communication, closeness, and faith and community participation. The foundation of this program is based in liberation theology, an innovative empowerment model, and cognitive and humanistic theories. Along with a very detailed description of various consulting and training strategies used to increase the effectiveness of Mentor Couples, B. T. McWhirter and E. H. McWhirter openly assess the strengths, shortcomings, and challenges of this project and their work.

Kathryn L. Norsworthy authored the third chapter in this section, with contributions by Ouyporn Khuankaew. As a seasoned, longtime international consultant in South Asia and Southeastern Asia, Norsworthy offers a highly informative and pragmatic description of her innovative work with individuals and groups in Thailand, and with refugee and internally displaced communities of Burma and Cambodia. In this chapter, Norsworthy discusses her collaborative work with local partners to reduce violence against women and HIV/AIDS. She also reports on their joint efforts toward peacebuilding, social justice education, and meeting some other needs of the communities served. To accomplish their goals, Norsworthy and colleagues rely on principles tied to postcolonial studies, feminist psychology, critical theory, liberatory education, and participant action research. In addition to describing her work in Asia, Norsworthy provides an excellent analysis of the hazards of psychological colonialism, neocolonialism, cultural imperialism, and the exportation of dominant U.S. psychology. She also offers a useful overview of ethical issues when engaged in international work and an outline of training, research, and practice implications based on her extensive consulting experiences.

The fourth chapter in this section was written by Scott L. Moeschberger, Alicia Ordóñez, Jui Shankar, and Shonali Raney. These authors introduce a novel and compelling model to conceptualize the process of engaging and carrying out social justice activities. Their social justice model incorporates an awareness, engagement, and action component grounded in a systemic paradigm of nonviolent methods. Three concrete examples of how this model might be employed are discussed. The first example focuses on social justice strategies to reduce and prevent conflict and different forms of violence (structural and direct) in El Salvadoran gangs. In the second example, the individual, interpersonal, societal, and environmental consequences of the damming of the Narmada River in India are described. A strategic plan to effectively address these consequences, including a structure to foster peaceful community development and cohesion, is presented as well. The last example of how this awareness-engagement model might be applied examines the dispute among India, Pakistan, and the people of Kashmir in the context of human rights violations, ethnopolitical conflicts, and military confrontation. Some potential ways that counseling psychologists could assist in helping to lower the tension and violence in this region are also explained.

The final chapter in this section was written by Lawrence H. Gerstein and Doris Kirkpatrick. It provides a brief overview of the literature on nonviolence and its relevance to counseling psychology. Following this, the authors describe in great detail the history of Tibet and the Tibet-China dispute, and the 10-year efforts of an NGO led by the senior author to help Tibetans regain their country. Specific strategies and policies of this NGO, known as the International Tibet Independence Movement (ITIM), are described, as are techniques employed by Gerstein to lead an international movement to achieve Tibet's independence. Throughout the chapter, Gerstein and Kirkpatrick discuss the theoretical models (e.g., Elaboration Likelihood Model, theories of group counseling, organizational behavior, multicultural counseling, volunteerism, telecommuting) and philosophical principles (e.g., Gandhian & Buddhist) serving as the framework for ITIM's activities and the senior author's work. Challenges for this movement and for Gerstein are also highlighted, as are recommendations for future research, training, advocacy, and activism. The importance of counseling psychologists becoming more actively involved in the establishment and maintenance of peaceful communities around the world is stressed as well.

Obviously, each of the five chapters in this section of the *Handbook* describe some type of structural or direct violence and various international efforts by counseling psychologists to peacefully resolve, for instance, personal, interpersonal, community, and ethnopolitical conflicts. Therefore, it seems important to offer an overview of a discipline, peace psychology, devoted to such topics. Perhaps this overview will provide a context to better understand, integrate, and evaluate the specific international social justice work presented in the chapters to follow. It also might help when contemplating and pursuing such work in other settings, cultures, and/or countries.

An Overview of the Peace Psychology Movement

Sometimes, when reminded of the evolution of a movement, it becomes clearer what is currently being done in the field. Peace psychology has grown out of the basic dedication of psychologists to promote the well-being of humans. The commitment to benefiting human life through the effective integration of scientific investigation and effective action, in general, serves as the foundation of applied psychology. This foundation has inspired the viewpoint that psychology can affect society in a way that reduces suffering brought about by violence and gross social inequalities. It is within this tradition that the peace psychology movement emerged.

The beginnings of peace psychology can be traced to many sources, including the founder of American psychology, William James. James favored pragmatic approaches, and this preference translated into a view that individuals could confront the evils of the world through action and that it was their moral duty to do so (Morris, 1950). As a pacifist, James sought alternative strategies to service in the military for developing virtues in young people. In his essay, "The Moral Equivalent of War," James indicated that for the greater good of society, young people ought to be given opportunities for community service as an alternative to military service (James, 1910). James's statements reflected the prevailing national interest in experimentalism and its sense of optimism about the future (Morris, 1950). This positive-mindedness existed in the peace movement developing across the United States during the first years of the 20th century, until the outbreak of World War I (DeBenedetti, 1980).

During World War I, psychologists were employed in the examination of U.S. Army recruits using intelligence tests and job selection tests (Benjamin, DeLeon, Freedheim, & VandenBos, 2003). This application of standardized tests gave psychologists a foothold that advanced the social status of the profession as well as increased the employment opportunities for psychologists through the development of new standardized tests and other consulting opportunities (Smith, 1986). Psychologists were also employed to examine and treat soldiers suffering from various psychopathologies near the end of the war (Benjamin et al., 2003). A notable exception to the general movement to "rally around the flag" following World War I can be found in the writings of William McDougall. McDougall, a social psychologist, claimed that discoveries in science and technology would not ensure peace (Rudmin, 1986). In a foreshadowing of the developments of the nuclear age, he stated,

> And if some physicist were to realize the brightest dream of this kind and teach us to unlock the energy within the atom, the whole race of man would live under the threat of sudden destruction, through the malevolence of some cynic, the inadvertence of some optimist, or the benevolence of some pessimist. (McDougall, 1931, pp. 44–45)

McDougall offered an insightful analysis of the difficulties related to trying to ensure security through massive destructive power.

During World War II, psychologists were again substantially involved in the war effort. Their roles included training; developing propaganda;, surveying attitudes domestically and internationally; examining and testing prisoners of war; and conducting studies of morale, intelligence, and personality (Benjamin et al., 2003). Following World War II, the U.S. government used psychologists to support governmental policies concerning atomic power and weaponry. For example, psychologists worked with government and military officials to develop research and programs aimed at fear reduction, attitude assessment, and the normalization of the public's reaction to atomic issues (Morawski & Goldstein, 1985). Some of the assumptions underlying this effort included the idea that (a) domestic and foreign policy were rooted in psychology; (b) to avoid public hysteria regarding atomic issues, a program of behavioral control was necessary; and (c) nuclear confrontation was inevitable (Morawski & Goldstein, 1985). In support of U.S. government policy, psychologists failed to acknowledge that a fear response in relation to nuclear threats might be appropriate (Morawski & Goldstein, 1985).

Following World War II, fearful of McCarthyism and investigations of antiwar organizations and their members, many psychologists were hesitant to put themselves at professional and personal risk by speaking out for peace (Christie, Wagner, & Du Nann Winter, 2001). However, psychologists' support for the U.S. government's policies began to change during the late 1950s and early 1960s. This change might be reflective of the sociopolitical environment of the United States at this time; that is, the fact that the public more actively challenged the government at this juncture, particularly on issues related to the U.S. policy of deterrence (DeBenedetti, 1980). Deterrence is the policy through which nations ensure their security by taking measures to prevent the hostile actions of another nation. In the United States, this policy reflected the build-up of enormous stockpiles of conventional and nuclear weapons (Christie et al., 2001).

Signaling a change from promoting government policy, psychologists such as Morton Deutsch (1961), Charles Osgood (1961), and Roger Russell (1961) brought attention to alternative policies designed to prevent war and, instead, encourage methods of conflict resolution (in Russell, 1961, a special issue of the *Journal of Social Issues*). Consistent with this new emphasis, the policy of nuclear deterrence was critically examined in several psychological publications (Deutsch, 1961; Milburn, 1961; Osgood, 1959, 1962; Wright, Evan, & Deutsch, 1962). Additionally, psychologists began forming concepts relating to Cold War mentality, such as Bronfenbrenner's (1961) *mirror image*. This concept refers to the idea that views of the enemy are distortions that may be similarly occurring on both sides of a conflict. Osgood (1961) also introduced the concept of Graduated and Reciprocated Initiatives in Tension-Reduction (GRIT), a strategy for reducing international tensions (Russell, 1961).

Following the Nuclear Test Ban Treaty in 1963, the public criticisms of the U.S. government diminished and less attention was given to issues of nuclear disarmament and peace (DeBenedetti, 1980). A few psychologists, however, continued to write in opposition to war and violence (Frank, 1967; Kelman, 1965; Lifton, 1967; Stagner, 1967). Their efforts, though, were overshadowed by other psychologists who were interested in such social issues as "domestic crises surrounding interracial conflicts, the Vietnam War, and the feminist movement" (Morawski & Goldstein, 1985, p. 281).

In the early 1980s, as tensions built between the United States and the Soviet Union, the nuclear disarmament movement took on new energy and interest. The goal of a nuclear freeze on testing, production, and the deployment of new nuclear weapons attracted broad public support to the peace movement (Hogan, 1994). Psychology experienced a resurgence of activity aimed at nuclear disarmament as well (Wagner, 1985). A few examples of this work include psychologists who wrote about conditions such as "nuclear anxiety" (Schwebel, 1982), the effects of the threat of nuclear war on childhood development (Escalona, 1982), and psychological defenses (Nelson, 1985). Special issues of several scholarly journals in psychology were published on the topics of peace and nuclear war (Fiske, Fischoff, & Milburn,

1983; Gordon, 1982; Greening, 1984). Furthermore, efforts to address peace and nuclear disarmament were pursued by the American Psychological Association (APA) when preparing a pamphlet titled "Preventing Armageddon." The cause of peace was also adopted as a theme by several APA divisions (Wagner, 1985).

Although the campaign by psychologists to influence policymakers regarding nuclear disarmament was vigorously championed, there was little effect. As the Soviet Union collapsed and the Cold War ended, the reduced threat of nuclear war changed the focus of peace psychology (Christie et al., 2001). The reconfiguration of political power struggles away from a "bipolar superpower structure" (United States vs. the Soviet Union) has generated a very different system of conflicts in the world (Christie et al., 2001). Instead of two major superpowers exerting influence over numerous allied nations, the United States has become a major power with many minor powers struggling for domination (Huntington, 1999). Problems associated with ethnic, religious, and economic conflicts and disparities, along with issues such as overpopulation and ecological destruction, have gained more attention as sources of violence and war (Christie et al., 2001). Recent incidents of terrorism in the United States and the resulting war on terrorism highlight the changing focus of global politics and concerns for security around the world. These developments have created a need for a transformation of peace psychology to address the diverse sources of violence around the world.

In their edited handbook of peace psychology, Christie et al. (2001) presented a schema for organizing current issues in peace psychology. The authors introduced a four-dimensional model focusing on direct violence, structural violence, peacemaking, and peacebuilding. According to the authors, direct violence, the traditional focus of peace psychology, involves "direct, acute insults to the psychological or physical well-being of individuals or groups," and can range from "intimate relations to the large-scale violence of genocide" (p. 8). Structural violence, based on Galtung's (1969) proposal, was thought to refer to indirect forms of violence that deprive individuals or groups of material and nonmaterial resources and slowly destroy them, such as when people are "socially dominated, politically oppressed, or economically exploited" (Christie et al., 2001, p. 8). Peacemaking was explained as a process to "reduce the frequency and intensity of direct violence" (p. 10), such as when parties enter into conflict resolution negotiations to prevent violence, or when postwar interventions are used to disrupt cycles of violence. Christie et al. (2001) described peacebuilding as efforts to reduce structural violence by pursuing social justice. Peacebuilding occurs when systems are transformed to provide equal opportunities to people. With this four-dimensional model, the authors "present a reconceptualization of peace psychology as a field of research and practical intervention" (p. vii), addressing the increasing areas of interest to a variety of peace psychologists.

A somewhat earlier development in the peace psychology movement greatly contributed to meeting the diverse needs of peace psychologists. In 1990, the Division of Peace Psychology (Division 48) was formed as part of the APA. Thus, the broader profession of psychology recognized the legitimacy of the ongoing efforts of peace psychologists to transform the lives of individuals through attention to the societal issues of violence and inequality.

Conclusion

Obviously, each of the five chapters in this section of the *Handbook* is consistent with the major focus of peace psychologists: designing and modifying policies, programs, and structures to eliminate and prevent violence and inequality throughout the world. Clearly, counseling psychologists are committed to achieving these same outcomes and, as such, share much in common with peace psychologists. In fact, some counseling psychologists, including a number of authors in this section of the *Handbook,* consider themselves to be peace psychologists.

It is hoped that by reading these chapters, a greater number of counseling psychologists will embrace this professional role and pursue the multitude of opportunities to contribute to the worldwide effort to establish and maintain communities, cultures, and nations of peace. Because there are many horrific examples around the world of violence, oppression, inequality, human rights abuses, and border disputes, there is an urgent need for a larger group of diverse and competent professionals to intervene. Given the complexity and diversity of these problems, it is essential that interdisciplinary teams be formed to design and implement a variety of systemic policies, programs, and structures that are culturally appropriate and effective.

As discussed in the chapters to follow, for a strategy, policy, and/or structure to be successful, local professionals and stakeholders in the country or culture of interest must be members and leaders of this team. With their background in multicultural counseling, developmental principles, group counseling, consultation, prevention, and program development and evaluation, counseling psychologists can make a major contribution to this team as well. International social justice work, advocacy, and activism require one to possess a broad, systemic base of knowledge and skills grounded in a deep understanding and appreciation for cultures and diverse structures. Counseling psychologists have the potential to develop this knowledge and skill, and in so doing, also develop the ability to serve as essential social architects on interdisciplinary teams striving to advocate and implement nonviolent solutions. The authors of the chapters in this section of the *Handbook* are excellent role models of such social architects. Hopefully, through their examples, more of you will be inspired to function as social architects on teams that are dedicated to alleviating and preventing direct and structural forms of violence around the world. Then, there will be a greater possibility for peace to prevail in all corners of this planet.

References

Ægisdóttir, S., & Gerstein, L. H. (2005). Reaching out: Mental health delivery outside the box. *Journal of Mental Health Counseling, 27,* 221–224.

Benjamin, L. T., Jr., DeLeon, P. H., Freedheim, D. K., & VandenBos, G. R. (2003). Psychology as a profession. In D. K. Freedheim & I. B. Weiner (Eds.), *Handbook of psychology* (Vol. 1, pp. 27–46). Hoboken, NJ: Wiley.

Bronfenbrenner, U. (1961). The mirror image in Soviet-American relations: A social psychologist's report. *Journal of Social Issues, 17*(3), 45–56.

Christie, D. J., Wagner, R. V., & Du Nann Winter, D. (2001). *Peace, conflict, and violence: Peace psychology for the 21st century.* Upper Saddle River, NJ: Prentice Hall.

DeBenedetti, C. (1980). *The peace reform in American history.* Bloomington: Indiana University Press.

Deutsch, M. (1961). Some considerations relevant to national policy. *Journal of Social Issues, 17*(3), 57–68.

Douce, L. A. (2004). 2003 presidential address: Globalization of counseling psychology. *The Counseling Psychologist, 32,* 142–152.

Escalona, S. K. (1982). Growing up with the threat of nuclear war: Some indirect effects on personality development. *American Journal of Orthopsychiatry, 52,* 600–607.

Fiske, S. T., Fischoff, B., & Milburn, M. A. (Eds.). (1983). Images of nuclear war [Entire issue]. *Journal of Social Issues, 39*(1).

Frank, J. D. (1967). *Sanity and survival in the nuclear age.* New York: Random House.

Fukuhara, M. (1989, August). Counseling psychology in Japan. In J. J. McWhirter (Chair), *Counseling psychology from an international perspective.* Symposium presented at the annual meeting of the American Psychological Association, New Orleans, LA.

Galtung, J. (1969). Violence, peace and peace research. *Journal of Peace Research, 3,* 176–191.

Gerstein, L. H., & Ægisdóttir, S. (2004). *Training international social change agents: Transcending the North American box.* Symposium presented at the 21st Annual Teachers College Winter Roundtable on Cultural Psychology and Education: Strategies for Building Cultural Competence in Psychology and Education, Columbia University, New York.

Gerstein, L. H., & Ægisdóttir, S. (Eds.). (2005a). Counseling around the world [Special issue]. *Journal of Mental Health Counseling, 27,* 95–184.

Gerstein, L. H., & Ægisdóttir, S. (Eds.). (2005b). Counseling outside of the United States: Looking in and reaching out [Special section]. *Journal of Mental Health Counseling, 27,* 221–281.

Gerstein, L. H., & Ægisdóttir, S. (2005c). A trip around the world: A counseling travelogue! *Journal of Mental Health Counseling, 27,* 95–103.

Gerstein, L. H., & Moeschberger, S. (2003). Building cultures of peace: An urgent task for counseling professionals. *Journal of Counseling & Development, 81,* 115–120.

Gordon, E. W. (Ed.). (1982). Forum on the psychological effects of preparing for nuclear war. *American Journal of Orthopsychiatry, 52*(4), 580–645.

Greening, T. (Ed.). (1984). Special peace issue [Entire issue]. *Journal of Humanistic Psychology, 24*(3).

Heppner, P. P. (2004, July). Stronger together: Valuing our diverse strengths. *Society of Counseling Psychology Newsletter,* pp. 2, 21.

Hogan, J. M. (1994). *The nuclear freeze campaign: Rhetoric and foreign policy in the telepolitical age.* East Lansing: Michigan State University Press.

Huntington, S. P. (1999). The lonely superpower. *Foreign Affairs, 78*(2), 35–50.

James, W. (1910). The moral equivalent of war. *McClure's Magazine,* August. Republished in *Peace and Conflict: Journal of Peace Psychology, 1*(1), 17–26.

Kelman, H. (Ed.). (1965). *International behavior: A social-psychological analysis.* New York: Holt, Rinehart and Winston.

Leong, F. T. L., & Blustein, D. L. (2000). Toward a global vision of counseling psychology. *The Counseling Psychologist, 28,* 5–9.

Leong, F. T. L., & Ponterotto, J. G. (2003). A proposal for internationalizing counseling psychology in the United States: Rationale, recommendations, and challenges. *The Counseling Psychologist, 31,* 381–395.

Leung, S. A. (2003). A journey worth traveling: Globalization of counseling psychology. *The Counseling Psychologist, 31,* 412–419.

Lifton, R. J. (1967). *Death in life: Survivors of Hiroshima.* New York: Basic Books.

McDougall, W. (1931). *World chaos: The responsibility of science.* London: Kegan Paul, Trench, Trubner.

McWhirter, J. J. (1988). The Fulbright program and counseling psychology. *The Counseling Psychologist, 16,* 279–281.

McWhirter, J. J. (2000). And now, up go the walls: Constructing an international room for counseling psychology. *The Counseling Psychologist, 28,* 117–122.

Milburn, T. W. (1961). The concept of deterrence: Some logical and psychological considerations. *Journal of Social Issues, 17*(3), 3–11.

Morawski, J., & Goldstein, S. (1985). Psychology and nuclear war: A chapter in our legacy of social responsibility. *American Psychologist, 40,* 276–284.

Morris, L. R. (1950). *William James: The message of a modern mind.* New York: Scribner.

Nelson, A. (1985). Psychological equivalence: Awareness and response-ability in our nuclear age. *American Psychologist, 40,* 549–556.

Norsworthy, K. L., & Gerstein, L. H. (2003a). Counseling and building communities of peace: The interconnections. *International Journal for the Advancement of Counseling, 25*(4), 197–204.

Norsworthy, K. L., & Gerstein, L. H. (Eds.). (2003b). Counseling and communities of peace [Special issue]. *International Journal for the Advancement of Counseling, 25*(4), 197–324.

Osgood, C. (1959). Suggestions for winning the real war with communism. *Journal of Conflict Resolution, 3,* 295–325.

Osgood, C. (1961). An analysis of cold war mentality. *Journal of Social Issues, 17*(3), 12–19.

Osgood, C. (1962). *An alternative to war or surrender.* Urbana: University of Illinois Press.

Pedersen, P., & Leong, F. (1997). Counseling in an international context. *The Counseling Psychologist, 25,* 117–122.

Rudmin, F. (1986). History of peace psychology: Comment on Morawski and Goldstein. *American Psychologist, 41,* 586–588.

Russell, R. W. (Ed.). (1961). Psychology and policy in a nuclear age [Special Issue]. *Journal of Social Issues, 17*(3), 1–87.

Schwebel, M. (1982). Effects of the nuclear war threat on children and teenagers: Implications for professions. *American Journal of Orthopsychiatry, 52,* 608–618.

Smith, M. B. (1986). War, peace, and psychology. *Journal of Social Issues, 42*(4), 23–38.

Speight, S. L., & Vera, E. M. (2004). A social justice agenda: Ready or not? *The Counseling Psychologist, 32,* 109–118.

Stagner, R. (1967). *Psychological aspects of international conflict.* Detroit, MI: Wayne State University Press.

Vera, E. M., & Speight, S. L. (2003). Multicultural competence, social justice, and counseling psychology: Expanding our roles. *The Counseling Psychologist, 31,* 253–272.

Wagner, R. V. (1985). Psychology and the threat of nuclear war. *American Psychologist, 40,* 531–535.

Wright, Q., Evan, W., & Deutsch, M. (Eds.). (1962). *Preventing World War III: Some proposals.* New York: Simon & Schuster.

CHAPTER 27

A Social Justice Approach to International Collaborative Consultation

Sharon G. Horne and Susan S. Mathews

Due to its foundation in prevention and vocational issues, and its emphasis on client strengths, developmental processes, advocacy, and the central role of cultural diversity, counseling psychology has been linked to social justice since its inception (Hartung & Blustein, 2002; Kiselica & Robinson, 2001). Although the social justice mission of counseling psychology tapered off in the mid-1980s, the emerging professional focus on racial and ethnic diversity renewed interest in issues of inclusion (Bingham, 2000), social advocacy (Lee & Walz, 1998), and systematic oppression (the arbitrary and unjust exercise of power by large systems) (Prilleltensky, 1997). Indeed, social justice became a pivotal concept in the reshaping of counseling psychology for the new millennium (Douce, 2004; Fouad et al., 2004); for example, a model of social justice, based on systemic exploration of the role of complex sociocultural and historical forces in fostering privilege and oppression, was infused into the Houston 2001 counseling psychology conference. This prizing of social justice was not only reflective of the developing understanding of the role of culture in shaping mental health, but it was also a result of the changing job market, with a demand for more community-focused, multidisciplinary, and prevention-based consultation practices to address social problems (Helms, 2003). As media and commercial enterprises advance in an evolving global monoculture, counseling psychology increasingly turns its attention to its role in international counseling and psychological concerns.

Although the profession of counseling psychology beyond North America is in its infancy, there are numerous U.S.-trained counseling psychologists who have broadened their scope of practice beyond the United States (e.g., T. Sayger & A. Uruk [Turkey], L. Gerstein [Tibet], B. McWhirter & E. Hawley McWhirter [Chile], K. Norsworthy [Southeast Asia], O. Yakushko [Ukraine]) to include direct services and interventions, research, and consultation. Leong and Ponterotto (2003) have called for the internationalization of counseling psychology by expanding the rubric for methods of psychological science, developing profession-based and Division 17 initiatives, and increasing counseling-program-specific activities. Increasingly, the practice of counseling psychology is emphasizing collaborative consultation (see Horne & Mathews, 2004); the combined increase in attention to consultation, social justice, and internationalization is reshaping the field of counseling psychology. The focus of this chapter is to highlight a social justice approach for counseling psychologists who conduct consultation in international contexts to local professionals who engage in direct clinical services. Specifically, the authors' experience stems from consultation practice in former communist (Soviet sector) states: Hungary, Romania, Uzbekistan, and Russia. A case example will highlight how this approach to social justice has been practiced in central Europe with crisis volunteers and hotline workers. We begin with defining international social justice.

Defining Social Justice in International Contexts

As described by the United Nations General Assembly (2000), cultures of peace require seven crucial elements that may adopt different forms depending on the context; the seven elements are human rights, nonviolence, inclusiveness, civil society, peace education, sustainability, and social justice. Social justice was defined as the "institutionalized equity in distribution and access to material, social, and political resources; truth-telling, reparations, and penalties for infractions; full participation and power-sharing by different groups; gender justice and full participation of women" (Wessells, Schwebel, & Anderson, 2001, p. 351). Within counseling psychology, the term *social justice* most often refers to the practice of challenging oppression by advocating for and ensuring the culturally competent provision of services and interventions to marginalized individuals and groups (Lewis & Bradley, 2000). In accordance with this objective, counseling psychologists are encouraged to be proficient and culturally competent in working with multiple cultural identities, to employ socially just measurement that fosters human integrity and development rather than stigmatization and false categorization, and to challenge stigma and oppression in social services (Lee & Walz, 1998). Counseling psychologists who consult internationally in nonpeaceful communities attend to both the macro social justice issues of structural inequality occurring at the state and large systems levels, and the micro issues of individual inequality and marginalization that may be occurring in the consultation.

This multilayered practice of social justice is challenging to experienced psychologists working with groups that share cultural and linguistic commonalities; however, differences in nationalities and languages present even greater obstacles to collaborative consultation. Whenever there is a convergence of cultures, traditions, and languages, misconceptions, misunderstandings, and, sometimes, conflict are commonplace. Divided societies are exacerbated by patterns of colonial domination (historical patterns of unjust and exploitative ownership by external nations), racism, and economic and political oppression (Wessells & Bretherton, 2000). International interactions within groups can alter power dynamics, social identities, intra- and interpersonal relations, and political meaning. As all societies can be characterized by fluctuating degrees of both consensus and conflict, it is only natural that international relationships may consist of alternating allegiances, insecurities, and engagements.

The practice of social justice can decrease the potential for conflict and can foster the development of peaceful and ongoing relationships. Tyler (2000) likened social justice to the oil within an engine, which allows "the many parts within the engine to interact without the friction that generates heat and leads to breakdown" (p. 117). Despite the current popularity of social justice, Speight and Vera (2004) cautioned that, without a thorough analysis of what a commitment to social change requires, the term *social justice* may become an empty buzzword within counseling psychology. If social justice is defined too broadly or abstractly, it may fail to represent when counseling psychologists actually engage in practices with the ultimate aim of disrupting institutional oppression and domination (Miller, 1999). A definition that is too broad may actually inadvertently support injustice by reinforcing an unjust status quo, allowing *any* psychological processes that lead to positive outcomes to be encompassed within the term *social justice,* or making oppression explicit but not acting upon it or challenging it. As counseling psychologists who wish to see a commitment to social justice become a core element of our profession, we believe that it is necessary to begin articulating the role and practice of social justice, particularly in international consultation. First, we examine social justice in relation to cultural competence and the role of Western hegemony (the domination of one state over another via political and ideological means).

The International Consultant: Is It Possible to Be Culturally Competent?

As counseling psychologists, we prize cultural competency and concur that it is necessary for effective research and practice. However, we question whether competency is sufficient for international work, and whether the very term *competence* appropriately reflects the process and goals of international collaborative consultation. For example, Dean (2001) disputed that cultural competence can ever be achieved, arguing that culture is always in a process of transformation; therefore, only partial understanding is attainable. The problem with cultural competence is located in the metaphor of American "know-how," that is, that knowledge provides a means of control, which is to be aspired to above all else in Western culture. Dean argued for the adoption of a postmodern framework in cross-cultural work; this perspective acknowledges that culture is always changing, and boundaries between and within groups are permeable, so cultural competence can never truly be achieved. It is only possible to be "informed not-knowers" (Laird, 1998, p. 30) who engage in a constant process of gathering information and gaining experience from others, while simultaneously raising self-awareness, sorting impressions, and shifting meanings. As Dean (2001) describes,

> This is not to say that becoming informed about the history and central issues of a particular cultural group at different periods in time is not an important aspect of clinical work. . . . Sources of information can provide a beginning step in the process . . . as long as they don't lead to a presumption of knowledge or competence. Once we presume to "know" about another we have appropriated that person's culture and reinforced our own dominant, egocentric position. I am proposing that we distrust the experience of "competence" and replace it with a state of mind in which we are interested and open but always tentative about what we understand. (p. 629)

In essence, claiming competence and expertise with respect to other cultures may superimpose outside interpretations and understandings onto other cultures. That is not to say that the consultant to Hungary, for example, should not have familiarity with the Hungarian Revolution of 1956, the systemic oppression of the Roma people, or the reconstruction of gender roles in the postcommunist system. The consultant should use this information to engage from an informed place, with openness to understanding how social processes are constructed and experienced within the context at hand. Granted, it is challenging to achieve a place of "informed not-knowing" when the culture and language are not one's own, and the consultant spends only short periods of time in the setting. This dynamic process of becoming culturally aware requires constant reflexivity of openness and understanding that, if successful, leads to greater approximations of shared cultural experience. Developing "informed not-knowing" can strengthen the consulting relationship, provided it is engaged in with care. Consultees generally want consultants to know "enough" so that it is evident they have some contextual understanding, but consultees also wish to retain their expert positions on their experience. Likewise, counseling psychologists should prepare consultees to integrate material and practices that they have to offer, while not discarding historically beneficial methods of helping.

The Western Consultants' Heavy Baggage of Global Hegemony

In order for a positive interaction between consultants and consultees to occur, an awareness of the role of global power is necessary. Historically, countries situated in the West and North have comprised the majority of large global economies that wield unequal financial and political power over countries in the East and South. Western-Eastern and Northern-Southern power differences can affect international collaborations negatively. The danger lies in the prizing of Euro-American training in psychology and Western helping models as superior to the methods of local communities, when Western consultants work in non-Western contexts (Horne & Mathews, 2004). As a result, consultees may defer to outside consultants and accept Western methods at face value, downplaying any successful indigenous practices that may be accessible to the community out of fear of appearing undeveloped (Wessells & Bretherton, 2000). A case in point would be the adoption of individualized psychotherapy to replace meditation simply because it is being practiced in the West. Such a process enacts cultural imperialism (the practice of a more powerful nation to promote its own culture and language through materials, practices, and products in a less powerful nation) by marginalizing the voices of local experience, and perpetuates the deeply rooted social injustice based on North-South and East-West relations. In addition, Western methods may not be applicable in other settings, as they are often derived from individualistic values that may not carry over to more collectivistic or interdependent cultures. For example, non-Western consultees training to become counseling psychologists might be taught that cognitive-behavioral techniques are superior because of their predominance in U.S. programs; such techniques might be ineffective for cultures that prize intuition, emotion, or community support as primary means to foster mental health. In order to ensure that cultural imperialism does not occur, international consultants can work self-critically from a power-sharing partnership model, involving careful listening, consultees' active leadership, building on the resources that local customs and people provide, and development of culturally relevant interventions rather than externally imposed solutions (Wessells et al., 2001). The next section describes a process of international collaboration.

Procedural Justice and a Multicultural-Feminist Approach to Foster Social Justice

Although primarily informed by principles of multicultural and feminist theories, our approach has been significantly guided by social psychology research (e.g., Tyler, 2000), social work (e.g., Dean, 2001), liberation theory (e.g., Freire, 1970), and peace psychology (Christie, Wagner, & Du Nann Winter, 2001). For a thorough review of contributions from educational psychology, consultation, and multicultural and feminist theories, see Horne and Mathews (2004).

The counseling psychology construction of social justice differs from the traditional view of social justice founded within the field of social psychology, which has focused primarily on attitudes and behaviors that contribute to and result from the subjective experience of justice and injustice (Tyler, 2000). For example, social psychology has given primary attention to the requisites for social justice (e.g., what is needed to achieve social justice, illustrations of its implementation through reconciliation and conflict resolution, and practices of peace-building). On the other hand, counseling psychology has emphasized the practice of training psychologists to become adept at practicing social justice and advocacy, as well as consultation. Counseling psychology has focused on the "doing" of social justice, whereas social psychology has emphasized the processes that foster social justice and what perceptions and experiences occur in its presence or absence. In order to conduct collaborative consultation, an understanding of both the how and the why are important. Counseling psychologists need to understand not only how to engage from a social justice framework, but also what factors are necessary to increase the potential for social justice. An important aspect of this understanding is procedural social justice.

Procedural social justice has emerged as a viable process for decision making and conflict resolution and is considered to have more promise for bridging differences than other forms of justice (i.e., relative deprivation theory, distributive social justice) (Tyler, 2000). Procedural social justice is predicated on the belief that people will accept outcomes when those outcomes are fairly decided upon; that is, participants in procedural social justice tend to be satisfied with outcomes and are more willing to accept them voluntarily when they believe that third-party decision-making procedures are fair. Four primary factors influence the perception of fairness as practiced by procedural social justice: opportunities for participation and giving voice, the impartiality of the forum, the belief in the trustworthiness of the leadership, and the extent to which interpersonal relations are engaged in with respect and dignity (Tyler, 2000). An engaged practice of social justice can be of tremendous benefit in creating peaceful working relationships, solving conflicts, and generating solutions. In order for a practice of social justice to be effective, however, the groups or individuals involved must be able to distinguish between judgments that are personally beneficial and judgments that they deem to be just or correct for the situation. They also should have a common understanding of how justice is achieved, and they must be amenable to decisions that they do not find desirable (Tyler, 2000). In international consultation, this practice would require that all the participants (e.g., crisis center counselors) would prioritize group goals (e.g., a crisis center efficiently operated that provides a supportive environment) over any individual needs for accomplishment, that they agree that power sharing and decisions by consensus are the avenue for just resolutions, and that they would be willing to work with results with which they may disagree if the group determines them to be beneficial. Groups and individuals may come together with all of these basic requirements in place; for the most part, however, consultants must employ a strategy of social justice to achieve group mutual agreement on these matters.

Our approach to international work aligns with and extends procedural social justice by putting into practice principles and mechanisms informed by multicultural counseling (a practice that emphasizes cultural context in individual development; counseling psychologists raise awareness of their own cultural values and beliefs, their clients' worldviews, and employ culturally relevant intervention strategies) and feminism (the analysis of how gender influences the ways in which power is distributed, maneuvered, performed, and privileged along cultural and androcentric lines; it emphasizes egalitarianism, women's autonomy, and social activism) (for discussion of the integration of these theories, see Horne & Mathews, in press). For example, in keeping with procedural justice, our approach to consultation prizes participants' perspectives and experiences by providing a space for "voice," and engages in power sharing, which fosters an atmosphere of neutrality and builds trust in leadership. We provide content and experiences of our own to increase participants' trust, and we use a multicultural approach that emphasizes respect for cultural and individual differences and experiences. Prior to describing consultation in practice, we provide a context for the organization (the consultee) in this case.

Case Example: Women's Rights Association of Budapest, Hungary (NANE)

NANE, a Hungarian Women's Rights nongovernmental organization (NGO), was founded in January 1994 and remains the only organization of its kind in the country. NANE's community service is dedicated to ending human rights violations and the threat of violence against women and children through advocacy, personal support services, and public education; in 1999, NANE achieved the status of "highly charitable organization" awarded by the Hungarian government (NANE Women's Rights Association, 1999, p. 1).

NANE volunteers and staff members operate two hotlines—antiviolence and antitrafficking—and offer client services in-person, such as counseling and accompanying victims to seek legal services. NANE also implemented the Peer Education Project, a pilot program in secondary schools designed to prevent gender-based violence. Each year, NANE holds a minimum of two 50-hour training courses to prepare new volunteers to join the organization. Additionally, NANE volunteers lobby and cooperate with other agencies to generate and introduce policy and legal amendment proposals to increase rights and protection for violence victims. Volunteers provide training courses to raise awareness and educate members of other professions who have regular contact with victims of violence. NANE provides public education to increase societal awareness concerning women's rights and the harmful effects of violence through multiple media formats, a public education campaign, and community demonstrations. Finally, NANE translates and publishes Western resources for the Hungarian public on violence against women and trauma (e.g., *Trauma & Recovery* by Judith Herman). In the following section, we highlight the working principles of our approach by describing our relationship with NANE. We initially became involved with NANE through our participation with MOSAIC (Models of Social Action Involving Communities), a nonprofit organization we co-founded to establish grassroots partnerships with women's groups. Beginning in 1997, members of MOSAIC made annual visits through 2002. At times, NANE members visited the United States for training; however, the majority of our consultation took place in Hungary over 2-week periods.

Working Principles of Multicultural Feminist Consultation in International Applications

Setting a Context for Multicultural-Feminist (M-F) Collaboration

One aspect of this approach to collaborative consultation is our emphasis on a commitment to reflexivity, power sharing, and cultural sensitivity. Prior to entering into the consulting relationship, we provide a description of how we approach our work, engaging consultees in a dialogue about the process. We also express a desire for all participants to play active roles, which supports the explicit sharing of value orientations in keeping with feminist theory. In order to gain insight into the consultees' worldviews, we ask for background information about consultees and the organization, relevant terminology, and any additional materials or information they feel would be helpful. With NANE, which began as a feminist organization, we stated the roots of our consultation approach explicitly. In other consultations, when there is no familiarity with multicultural counseling and feminism, we have opted to explain our approach by emphasizing cultural diversity, power sharing, and commitment to equality. For example, NANE operates within a feminist framework that has been influenced by Western feminist writings on nonviolence and experiences of members who have studied feminism. Therefore, from the beginning, NANE was in accord with our approach to consultation. We articulated the ways we would like to engage NANE in the consultation, and they asked informed questions about experiential exercises and their level of involvement, and provided information about what they most desired from consultation and training. This process ensured active participation and investment from NANE members. In keeping with feminist practice, the consultees in NANE set the agenda in collaboration with the consultants. Before beginning collaborative consultation, counseling psychologists should become aware of any biases and values, in keeping with multicultural counseling.

Consultants' Self-Evaluation of Biases and Values

Negotiating the complex interaction of multiple cultures and systems requires international consultants to be self-aware of biases and values. Consultants must take responsibility for conducting a thorough self-examination and seek to be informed about the consultee's culture and language prior to the consultation, so that the burden of cultural education does not fall solely on the consultees. In addition, implementing a feedback process is important to minimize cultural misunderstandings and increase consultants' access to the consultees' experiences, because it is impossible for consultants to learn everything about a consultee's culture. For example, our experiences in Eastern Europe have taught us to implement periodic language check-ins to determine linguistic pitfalls that may have occurred during the consultation process. During our collaboration with NANE, we have been provided with many opportunities to examine our own biases and assumptions, and to discuss them openly with NANE members. As an example, we have had to set aside biases about paid volunteers, an unfamiliar concept in Western societies, which caused us to question volunteers' investment in the organization. Opening up a dialogue helped us to understand the particular economic challenges that nongovernmental agencies face in postcommunist countries. From the start, a written and oral feedback process has been in place with NANE that allows both consultants and consultees the opportunity to comment on the process.

Engaging in Power Sharing

When cultures in transition are experiencing profound distress because of rapid changes, we believe that a tendency to overvalue Western models appears to increase. Non-Western participants may waver in their support for consultation, ranging from profound distrust of anything Western to idealization of Western models and concepts. Only through active power sharing can patterns of domination be disrupted (Wessells & Bretherton, 2000). Therefore, maximizing the success of M-F consultation requires consultants to genuinely share power with consultees. For instance, facilitating consultees' discussions of successes and challenges working in their various roles can provide a culturally sensitive exploration of issues, generation of new ideas, or consensus decision making among consultees. Consultees' experiences should be prioritized, and they should be responsible for agenda setting. Consultants pay close attention to how talking time is divided between consultants and consultees, desiring an outcome in which consultees feel deeply heard. Important issues unique to each consultee group can emerge only when power is shared and consultees are provided with opportunities to articulate their experiences. Conducting joint trainings with local colleagues where the instruction and facilitation are shared equally is the optimal illustration of power sharing.

Consultation with NANE has consisted of trainings in which leadership was shared by or alternated between Western consultants and NANE leaders. This often allowed us an inside look into dynamics and interactions to which we would not otherwise have access, thereby strengthening the consultation overall. Time was structured to allow consultees to voice their experiences, both individually and in groups. For example, brainstorming sessions about the functioning of the organization were employed, participants were asked to write about their concerns, and feedback was encouraged. We paid close attention to the ways that power was produced and enacted in the training. For example, we deliberately turned over facilitation if time had been monopolized by one group, or initiated exercises that involved more passive members. Power sharing requires consultants to factor in more time, in addition to time needed for skills training.

Privileging Consultees' Needs and Goals

M-F consultants must be considerate of consultees' worldviews throughout the process, which includes a willingness to change goals and needs during the consultation. Additionally, when external agents (i.e., granting agencies) determine needs and problems, the proposed goals may not reflect the needs and experiences of the consultees. In such cases, it is critical for consultants to advocate for consultees by providing a final report to the external agent that clearly outlines the rationale for shifting the focus of the training to better satisfy participants' needs, as well as offer suggestions for future trainings that will enhance consultees' progress more effectively.

At the start of each consultation with NANE, joint goals stemming from the organization's needs were established. During one consultation with NANE, for example, the volunteers requested additional training and supervision to enhance their hotline counseling skills. Shortly after the training began, it became apparent that several NANE members were engaged in interpersonal disagreements and tension. As a result, we recommended that the goals of the consultation be readjusted to include conflict resolution, communication skills, and strategies to enhance volunteer retention and accountability. Being an effective consultant requires knowing when to address issues that may eventually become barriers in the process.

Maintaining an Awareness of the Impact of Consultation on Consultants, Consultees, and Clients

M-F consultants recognize that all parties are altered by the collaboration. We directly articulate the ways that our work and personal lives have been affected by the consulting relationship. For example, we may share missed opportunities or ways we have grown from our work with them. In the past, we have shared with NANE that their prioritizing of working with police is something to be admired, when it took many years for crisis centers to work with government agencies in our country. We have expressed high regard for what they accomplish with so few resources, and have shared with them that we have learned the importance of humor in our work. Our attention to the ways that we have been transformed through the consulting interaction honors the voices, attributes, and gifts of the consultees, which is consistent with M-F theories. We model that there are ways of relating beyond hierarchical communication (expert-consultee) by valuing consultees' strengths and experiences as well as what they have taught us (the consultants). For instance, at the close of the consultation or training, we share our impressions, lessons learned, and the new experiences that we intend to incorporate into future training sessions. Our reflections may range from sharing phrases in the local language (e.g., *Egan,* meaning "thank you") that we have acquired, to discussing how we intend to alter a role-play or exercise, to demonstrating our newly acquired repertoire of local dances or phrases. The consultees also report being transformed by the consultation, increasing the importance of creating peer support and networking systems to support their growth and development of newly acquired skills and information (Mathews, Horne, & Levitt, 2005). Because consultees generally work in high-stress environments that necessitate self-care, we advocate for consultees to use the consultation to build on their trust and interdependence with one another to establish ongoing, long-term communication that can continue to serve as a foundation for support, growth, and change.

Our lives have been influenced greatly by NANE, and it has been important to share the ways that that has taken shape. For example, we shared with NANE how we have developed our approach to consultation because of our relationship with NANE members (i.e., including more check-ins, allowing for more humor and downtime, conducting interviews to better understand the process, expanding research endeavors). In addition, we have shared with NANE how we hold them up as an exemplar of a grassroots organization that truly serves victims but engages in effective advocacy and policy change to other crisis centers, both in the United States and Eastern Europe. Finally, we have shared how we feel personally inspired and challenged, as well as energized, to continue nonviolence work by following the example NANE sets, doing the work with so few resources in comparison to Western crisis centers.

Evaluating the Process and Following Up

An M-F approach to consultation requires ongoing research, using both qualitative and quantitative methods, to provide a means for evaluating and documenting consulting activities, as well as expanding the consultation literature. One of the most important tasks for consultants is to evaluate and document the successes and challenges of the consultation process as a means to provide suggestions and new directions for future consulting practices. Consultants may address issues such as knowledge base, counseling effectiveness, morale, self-care, prevention of burnout, and peer support networks. M-F consultation supports the existence of the collaborative relationship as long as it is beneficial to the consultees. This principle emphasizes the importance of follow-up and the potential for long-term maintenance of relationships with consultees by "keeping the door open," maintaining contact via email, planning follow-up meetings, or establishing research partnerships. As part of our ongoing evaluation, Mathews, Horne, and Levitt (2005) conducted a qualitative study exploring NANE members' volunteer identity development and the impact of the consulting relationship. Participants expressed in structured interviews that the most valuable part of the consultation was the attention to the process of the consulting interaction. Participants shared that their experiential participation helped them integrate the information presented and engage in the interpersonal relationships among the members on a more personally relevant level. Our interest in their work beyond the consultation (e.g., research on the process) opened many doors for continued contact on issues beyond what was covered in the consultation. Furthermore, several benefits have emerged from our efforts to maintain a long-term relationship with NANE. For example, we served as consultants to NANE's recent book publishing project by offering translation assistance through email. In addition, we have connected NANE members with crisis workers working in neighboring countries (i.e., Romania). Challenges to ongoing international relationships, however, include financial costs (i.e., travel) and limited time to continue the connection in a meaningful way.

Process Mechanisms for Effective Multicultural-Feminist Consultation

Shifting From Expert to Collaborator

International consultants are often confronted with complex problems in ever-changing contexts, which can increase the tendency to prize and rely on American models as potential curative solutions to social problems. Additionally, consultees' expectations of Western models of consultation can further hinder consultants' efforts to establish collaborative relationships. Therefore, consultants should resist adhering to the expert model by enacting the values of M-F collaboration throughout the consultation process. Specifically, we seek opportunities to give voice to consultees in order to emphasize their expertise and model collaborative practices. For instance, we have been introduced to consultees as "the American experts who are here to help." Consultees often perceive U. S. models of development to be ideal and assume that consultants require no information about their experiences with crisis work. At the same time, some consultees have resisted any overt abandonment of the expert position due to the traditional importance in former Soviet societies to perceived status and title (Richmond, 1992). In an effort to minimize this resistance, we shift indirectly from our expected expert role to a collaborative role by privileging consultees' identities and experiences, encouraging them to actively participate. We often begin by requesting that participants share their names, backgrounds, and experiences, as well as collectively identifying rules for engagement and training goals.

During our consulting work with NANE, we valued the participation and input of all volunteers, regardless of their length of time or level of responsibility in the organization. For example, we integrated experiential exercises into trainings that modeled collaborative practices and power sharing, and provided opportunities for volunteers to actively voice their expertise. Specifically, we encouraged volunteers to draw themes or examples from their own work for these tasks in an effort to make them as culturally relevant as possible. We also make explicit that U.S. models of preventing and reducing violence have failed in a number of ways.

Providing Content Throughout Process

An essential value in the M-F collaborative consultation approach is providing content *throughout* the process. Effective consultation stems from consultants' ability to shift back and forth interactively between process and content (Schein, 1993). For instance, we offer information and expertise when appropriate (e.g., providing comparative statistics concerning violence against women or suggesting aspects that were successful in our previous organizational experiences). During the course of these discussions, we continually seek opportunities to facilitate engagement that will successfully illustrate the concepts, thereby enabling the participants to grasp the content within the process.

Communication across cultures has the potential to create language barriers that may reduce consultants' effectiveness in conveying content. The content we are typically most concerned with is providing skills training for active listening and helping skills for working with victims, making referrals, and providing information about what is known about violence against women. It is important for consultants to be able to shift quickly from the content to process (e.g., language check-ins) to enhance participants' understanding of the information. Furthermore, incorporating experiential role-play or team-building exercises may assist consultants in conveying content through process, which may engage a wider range of learning styles among participants. During one exercise with NANE, a web of thread was woven among participants standing in a circle to symbolize group dynamics and the interconnectedness of volunteers. The pieces of yarn on one side of the circle were cut to collapse the web as a means of illustrating the damaging effects of indirect communication to the organization as a whole. Several NANE volunteers reported that this demonstration conveyed the importance of direct communication to strengthen their organizational dynamics more effectively than the consultants' discussion about communication.

Embedding Advocacy and Social Justice Into the Collaborative Process

Advocacy is intrinsic to the M-F collaborative consultation process. International consulting relationships with nonprofit organizations in transitional societies have taught us that the personal and political elements of advocacy are indistinguishable. We continually seek out opportunities to use a social justice approach by working as change agents with and for our consultees. Specifically, we explore with consultees ways to address social issues of greatest concern to their work or organizations. We also advocate on behalf of our consultees by communicating the important issues that emerged during consultation work with local government officials, journalists, and administrators.

With NANE, we encouraged volunteers to explore how individual, organizational, political, and social barriers impede their organizational goals. For example, volunteers identified fear of working on the hotline (i.e., individual), insufficient supplies and human resources (i.e., organizational), prioritizing of concerns about children's welfare (i.e., political), and a conspiracy of silence around the issue of domestic violence (i.e., social). NANE's priorities shift depending on the context: At times, NANE focused on meeting the safety needs of individual victims of violence, and at other times, volunteers emphasized advocacy initiatives to garner government fiscal support for shelters. However, during the consultation, advocacy goals and initiatives were explored on all levels.

Engaging Consultees and Clients in Exploration of the Larger Context

M-F collaborative consultation necessitates engaging consultees in an exploration of the larger contexts that affect their work, as well as the lives of individuals whom the organization aims to help. In essence, we aim to engage in a consultation that is grounded in the practice of critical consciousness (Christie et al., 2001; Freire, 1970), which may include investigating systemic barriers that support violence and generating alternative solutions for removing these barriers. It is important for M-F consultants to work collaboratively with consultees in this process. Consultees are encouraged to determine specific objectives that enable them to consider the successes and shortcomings of their efforts and suggest new directions for future interventions. M-F consultants also can provide reassurance to consultees by pointing out that some systems may not be open to change (e.g., the government may not have funds at its disposal to support victim services), which is not a limitation that reflects negatively upon the organization's efforts.

One of the roles we played as consultants was to provide networking support to maintain NANE's connection to the larger women's movement in order to sustain volunteers' hope and energy in their work. Because NANE frequently encounters systems that are not open to change (e.g., other nonprofit organizations' resistance to coalition-building with NANE because of competition over local resources), it is important for volunteers not to view these limitations as negative reflections on the organization's success. An exploration of the larger context enabled volunteers to generate new, creative solutions for challenging or removing these barriers, and increased empathy for the limitations on what they as individuals and one organization can achieve. NANE members took stock in their accomplishments (e.g., working hotline for almost 5 years, large numbers of victims and families served) and prioritized future goals (e.g., lobbying the parliament, establishing other centers in other cities). Both consultants and consultees emerged from this process energized.

Limitations, Ethical Considerations, and Implications for Research, Practice, and Training

Both consultants and consultees can contribute to breakdowns in international consultation. Western consultants can experience their access to knowledge and resources as a double-edged sword. Without a doubt, the decades of psychological science and practice in the West can place Western consultants working with these issues in an advantageous place; however, they are at a disadvantage when they believe this information to be factual and applicable to the cultural context within which they are working. It can be challenging to suspend interventions and practices until their application in the local context is explored. More often than not, however, Western consultants do not have sufficient time for exploration or for testing interventions, and consultees may be desperate for a quick fix. Therefore, Western models often are exported as proven practices, even when they constitute poor science or encourage damaging outcomes, despite their good intentions.

The reality of international work can inhibit effective multicultural-feminist practices. Often, Western consultants are providing their own resources for the consultation, or are only partially subsidized. Depending on who is funding the consultation, consultants may find themselves with little control over their schedule and with limited access to all the members of the organization. Time changes, flight delays, and adjustments to diet and climate can take a toll on being open to being informed, understanding, and collaborative. Finally, some individuals are more open to this approach than others. For example, with crisis centers combating violence against women, a multicultural-feminist approach is typically a good fit because most often the centers have a goal of increasing equal opportunities for women; at the same time, they tend to have an awareness of the importance of culture in shaping existing inequalities. However, when we have worked with organizations not founded within a grassroots framework, there has been resistance to this approach. In several instances, some members were compelled to educate the others on violence against women in order to gain credibility within the group; such a process can put Western consultants on the periphery, as they are perceived to be even less trustworthy than nonprofit workers. Therefore, the relationship with consultees can be placed at risk.

Likewise, consultees may find such an approach threatening, and may choose to not participate fully in processes of social change, which typically disrupts the consulting process (Wessells et al., 2001). For example, because of the transition in the former Soviet Union, younger generations appear to be much more open to this style of social change than their elders. As the older generations become more underprivileged and disadvantaged by the changing market structures, there may be more attempts to undermine helping processes that seem alien or Western. In such instances, when internal breakdown has occurred, the Western consultant may not be aware that the process has ground to a halt, but may be able to sense that something is not going quite right. Furthermore, as Wessells and colleagues point out, power sharing may not be achievable when consultees engage in informal norms that maintain the power asymmetry among groups. Indeed, members of marginalized groups may support the privilege of the group in power because of internalized oppression and deeply embedded structural inequalities. In such cases, even the best efforts by a consultant cannot chip away at the entrenched power patterns.

Engaging in international consultation is a relatively new practice for counseling psychologists. As a profession, we need to expand the methods of psychological science to include qualitative (e.g., grounded theory, narrative, ethnography) in addition to quantitative research methodology to internationalize counseling psychology (Leong & Ponterotto, 2003). When using Western instruments and measures, care must be taken to validate and ensure cultural relevance. Counseling psychologists in training conducting international research should be encouraged and supported. Finally, our flagship journals should place international research on par with research focused on domestic issues.

International consultation work necessitates careful consideration of several components of the "Ethical Principles of Psychologists and Code of Conduct" (APA, 2002) in order to ensure ethical practice. First, international consultants are urged to consider their boundaries of competence in consultation carefully, as well as their range of knowledge about the consultees' organization and culture. Consultants are required to obtain appropriate supervision as needed (APA Ethical Standards, 2.01 a–d); although clear standards for preparation and training for international consultants may not be well defined for all situations, consultants are urged to take "reasonable steps to ensure the competence of their work" (APA Ethical Standards, 2.01 e, p. 5). Second, international researchers are ethically bound to avoid exploitative relationships. For instance, researchers obtaining data from consultees in exchange for professional development training or consultation may engage in this type of bartering arrangement only if it is not "clinically contraindicated or exploitative" (APA Ethical Standards, 6.05, p. 9). Additionally, researchers are encouraged to carefully consider ethical guidelines for sharing publication credit with in-country professionals, consultees, and translators (APA Ethical Standards, 8.12, a–b).

Finally, international consultants working across cultural and language barriers may face additional obstacles in the utilization of assessment devices, in protection of consultees' confidentiality, and in the provision of informed consent for participating in consultation and research, particularly if recording devices are involved. As required by APA Ethical Standards 9.02 (b), 8.02 (a) 1–8, 4.02 (a–c), and 4.03, consultants must take special care to disclose the limitations of assessment results if validity and reliability have not been well established for the population, as well as ensure that translation of informed consent procedures, limits of confidentiality, and permission to record, respectively, are clear and accurate. Also, consultants delegating work to translators are encouraged to take

> reasonable steps to (1) avoid delegating such work to persons who have a multiple relationship with those being served that would likely lead to exploitation or loss of objectivity; (2) authorize only those responsibilities that such persons can be expected to perform competently on the basis of their education, training, or experience, either independently or with the level of supervision being provided; and (3) see that such persons perform these services competently. (APA Ethical Standards, 2.05, p. 5)

Finally, prior to the start of their work with consultees, consultants are strongly encouraged to discuss the parameters of the consulting relationship and obtain consultees' written consent for disclosure of the outcomes of the consulting relationship (APA Ethical Standards, 4.06 and 6.06, respectively).

There are many opportunities to expand the training of counseling psychology trainees in international consultation. For example, crisis centers throughout post-communist countries are interested in forming long-term collaborations, in which our students could provide training in supervision and consultation to emerging counselors and psychologists, and vice versa. Our faculty and students could benefit immensely from exchange programs that provide opportunities for practice and partnerships outside of the United States. In fact, an international practicum program is in development at our university. Second, in training counseling psychologists, as a profession we should broaden multiculturalism to include international as well as domestic cultural milieus. Global awareness of psychological issues should be infused in programs similar to the inclusion of multicultural principles. Finally, counseling psychology students are not required to leave the country to engage in collaborative consultation with cultures different from their own; local communities of refugees and immigrants are in need of consulting services, and some programs are engaged in this training (e.g., University of Georgia).

Only by placing culture at the center of focus in collaborative international consultation can patterns of inequality eventually be challenged and power sharing be allowed to emerge to foster social justice and change (Wessells et al., 2001). Counseling psychologists are best positioned not only to challenge their own values and beliefs with regard to cultural expectations and experiences, but to openly engage in a process of understanding international relationships and meaning making. These principles and mechanisms of collaborative consultation provide a foundation for counseling psychologists to prepare for international work from a social justice perspective and model culturally appropriate interventions and practices that challenge structural inequalities.

References

American Psychological Association. (2002). Ethical principles of psychologists and code of conduct. *American Psychologist, 57,* 1060–1073.

Bingham, R. P. (2000). 1999 Division 17 presidential address: Lessons learned at the half century mark. *The Counseling Psychologist, 28,* 143–149.

Christie, D. J., Wagner, R. V., & Du Nann Winter, D. (2001). *Peace, conflict, and violence.* Princeton, NJ: Prentice Hall.

Dean, R. G. (2001). The myth of cross-cultural competence. *Families in Society: The Journal of Contemporary Human Services, 82,* 623–630.

Douce, L. A. (2004). 2003 presidential address: Globalization of counseling psychology. *The Counseling Psychologist, 32,* 142–152.

Fouad, N. A., McPherson, R. H., Gerstein, L., Blustein, D. L., Elman, N. S., Ihle Helledy, K., & Metz, A. J. (2004). Houston, 2001: Context and legacy. *The Counseling Psychologist, 32,* 15–77.

Freire, P. (1970). *Pedagogy of the oppressed.* New York: Seabury.

Hartung, P. J., & Blustein, D. L. (2002). Reason, intuition, and social justice: Elaborating Parsons's career decision making model. *Journal of Counseling and Development, 80,* 41–47.

Helms, J. E. (2003). A pragmatic view of social justice. *The Counseling Psychologist, 31,* 305–313.

Horne, S. G., & Mathews, S. S. (2004). Collaborative consultation: International applications of a Multicultural-Feminist approach. *Journal of Multicultural Counseling and Development, 32,* 366–378.

Kiselica, M., & Robinson, M. (2001). Bringing advocacy counseling to life: The history, issues, and human dramas of social justice. *Journal of Counseling and Development, 79,* 387–397.

Laird, J. (1998). Theorizing culture: Narrative ideas and practice principles. In M. McGoldrick (Ed.), *Re-visioning family therapy* (pp. 93–110). New York: Guilford.

Lee, C. C., & Walz, G. R. (Eds.). (1998). *Social action: A mandate for counselors.* Alexandria, VA: American Counseling Association and ERIC/CASS.

Leong, F. T. L., & Ponterotto, J. G. (2003). A proposal for internationalizing counseling psychology in the United States: Rationale, recommendations, and challenges. *The Counseling Psychologist, 31,* 381–395.

Lewis, J., & Bradley, L. (Eds.). (2000). *Advocacy in counseling.* Greensboro, NC: ERIC/CASS.

Mathews, S. S., Horne, S. G., & Levitt, H. M. (2004). *Feminism across borders: A Hungarian adaptation of Western feminism.* Unpublished manuscript.

Mathews, S. S., Horne, S. G., & Levitt, H. M. (2005). *Feminism across borders: A Hungarian adaptation of Western feminism. Sex Roles: A Journal of Research, 53,* 89–103.

Miller, D. (1999). *Principles of social justice.* Cambridge, MA: Harvard University Press.

NANE Women's Rights Association. (1999).

Prilleltensky, I. (1997). Values, assumptions, and practices: Assessing the moral implications of psychological discourse and action. *American Psychologist, 52,* 517–535.

Richmond, Y. (1992). *From nyet to da: Understanding the Russians.* Yarmouth, MA: Intercultural Press.

Schein (1993).

Speight, S. L., & Vera, E. M. (2004). A social justice agenda: Ready, or not? *The Counseling Psychologist, 32,* 109–118.

Tyler, T. R. (2000). Social justice: Outcome and procedure. *International Journal of Psychology, 35,* 117–125.

United Nations General Assembly. (2000). *Resolution 52/15.* New York: Author.

Wessells, M. G., & Bretherton, D. (2000). Psychological reconciliation: National and international perspectives. *Australian Psychologist, 35,* 100–108.

Wessells, M. G., Schwebel, M., & Anderson, A. (2001). Psychologists making a difference in the public arena: Building cultures of peace. In D. J. Christie, R. V. Wagner, & D. Du Nann Winter (Eds.), *Peace, conflict, and violence* (pp. 350–362). Princeton, NJ: Prentice Hall.

CHAPTER 28

Couples Helping Couples

Consultation and Training in Peñalolén, Chile

Benedict T. McWhirter and Ellen Hawley McWhirter

As this book attests, counseling psychologists and counseling professionals of all varieties have a renewed attention to social justice during the past decade in a manner that is reflective of past emphases on prevention and amelioration of social ills (e.g., Blustein, 2001; Herr & Niles, 1998; Lee & Walz, 1998; Lewis, Lewis, Daniels, & D'Andrea, 1998; O'Brien, 2001; see also *The Counseling Psychologist,* vol. 31). Yet individuals committed to carrying out principles of social justice and advocacy in a systematic fashion have been in the minority within the profession, in part because of a continued focus on the individual in mental health practice, adherence to a belief that counseling is neutral and value-free, and the embeddedness of the profession within mainstream ideology (McClure & Russo, 1996). At the same time, we have always believed that there is an inescapable link between prevention practice, the improvement of public mental

Authors' Note: We thank the many Mentor Couples, friends, and colleagues of San Roque Parish in Santiago, Chile, for their enduring commitment and labor toward building meaningful social change. We also thank Dr. Jeff McWhirter, longtime professor of counseling psychology at Arizona State University, for the many years of personal and professional mentoring and for his review of this chapter. Finally, we dedicate this chapter to our uncle, Robert L. Plasker, C.S.C., for providing both of us with the personal formation that has led us to integrate the principles of liberation theology and social justice into our professional goals, training philosophy, and actions as counseling psychologists.

health, and a commitment to enhance economic and social justice. In this chapter, we describe our efforts to integrate the science and practice of psychology with a commitment to increasing social justice in one community.

Our goal in this chapter is to describe our ongoing consultation and training work in Peñalolén, a poor and working-class sector of Santiago, Chile, that has very limited access to psychological services. Since 1995, we have made yearly trips of 3 to 4 weeks to Peñalolén. We first visited Chile to see Benedict's sister, who was then a student Fulbright Scholar in Chile, and to visit his uncle, a Catholic priest who has spent more than 40 years serving impoverished communities in Chile and Peru. During that visit, we met several couples who were active in the family faith education program coordinated by Benedict's uncle, Father Robert. Their enthusiasm, the opportunity to experience Father Robert's pedagogical praxis with families, and the beauty of Chile combined to draw us back again. The following year, we began providing informal consultation to individuals and couples in Peñalolén. In 1999, several couples requested more formal training to enhance their work as paraprofessionals with other families. In every subsequent visit, we have provided weekend workshops and consultation to the couples (*parejas guias*—literally, "couple guides," hereafter referred to as "Mentor Couples") of the very large San Roque parish. We continued the work described herein and wrote this chapter during a 1-year sabbatical as Fulbright Scholars in Chile. We continue this work today.

In the following sections, we describe the context of our work, the processes and challenges unique to this experience, and background information about our own formation and education. Next, we review elements of Chile's recent history and current situation that are critical to understanding the challenges and environmental limitations faced by the Mentor Couples. We then discuss the family faith education program, our guiding frameworks, and close with a summary and implications.

Overall Context

Authors' Background

Both of the authors have been faculty members of counseling psychology since graduating from Arizona State University in 1992. Benedict majored in theology as an undergraduate student at the University of Notre Dame and participated in a 15-month service-scholar program in Canto Grande, Peru, a slum outside of Lima. While in Peru, he lived with a family; taught manual arts to middle school students; participated in a faith community; and studied economics, politics, Liberation Theology, and Peruvian literature. Liberation theology is one of the guiding frameworks for our current work in Peñalolén, Chile. As the son of a university faculty member, he also lived for a year in Ankara, Turkey, and another year in Sydney and Perth, Australia (J. McWhirter, 1987). Ellen majored in psychology at the University of Notre Dame, with a concentration in Latin American studies. She spent a semester in Mexico studying Spanish, Latin American history, politics, and liberation theology. Following her graduation, she worked in Arizona for several years as a Headstart teacher and as a home education specialist for monolingual Spanish-speaking families with children with developmental disabilities. These experiences were the foundation for her model of empowerment in counseling (e g., E. McWhirter, 1994, 1997, 1998), which is the second guiding framework for our work in Chile. Both of us have had long-term involvement in the social justice applications of our faith. Our families, education, and life experiences have helped to orient us to the sociopolitical history, cultural and religious norms, and economic reality of Chile; these also help us understand our limitations: We do not pretend to have achieved a deep understanding of the complexities of Chile.

Chile's Recent History

Chile has a long history of democracy and was governed by elected presidents until 1973. In 1970, socialist Salvador Allende was elected president, the outcome of mass organization of poor, rural, urban, and working-class Chileans along with university and arts communities (Constable & Valenzuela, 1991; Ensalaco, 2000; Infoplease, 2004). Allende's presidency was marked by trade embargoes, loan refusals, and covert destabilization efforts by the U.S. government that created economic difficulties and growing internal opposition (Kornbluh, 2003). One CIA memo to Henry Kissinger stated, "U.S. policy has been to maintain maximum covert pressure to prevent the Allende regime's consolidation" (Kornbluh, 2003, p. 29). On September 11, 1973, *La Moneda,* the equivalent of the U.S. White House, was bombed. Through a violent military coup, General Augusto Pinochet assumed control of Chile and imposed a strict and brutal dictatorship.

U.S. involvement in engineering and carrying out the coup, support of the Pinochet government, and detailed knowledge of the repressive tactics of the dictatorship have been well documented (e.g., Kornbluh, 2003). Severe military control implemented after the coup included prohibitions against the assembly of groups, strict curfews, and the banning of "leftist" literature, such as the poetry of Pablo Neruda. Tens of thousands of Chileans were expelled from the country (Amnesty International [AI], 2001; Constable & Valenzuela, 1991; Wright & Oñate, 1998). Detentions, disappearances, and murders of Chileans continued well into the 1980s, with documentation of the disappearance, extrajudicial execution, or death under torture of more than 4,000 people between 1973 and 1990 (AI, 2001). Those who worked with the poor in education and social services were frequent targets of repression. After the coup, a number of Catholic priests who served parishes in Peñalolén and other poor areas were arrested, tortured, and/or expelled from Chile. Father Robert was expelled in 1974 on charges of "consciousness-raising."

In 1980, in response to international and internal pressures, Pinochet supervised the writing of a new constitution. It granted him lifetime senator status, but also included periodic referendums on his continued leadership of the country. In a 1988 plebiscite, he was soundly rejected by voters to continue as head of government, and a presidential election was held in 1989. Although retired, at the time of this writing Pinochet remains a member of the senate.

Since the 1989 election, Chile technically has been a democracy. The process of transformation has been slow, however. A 1978 military government decree prevented prosecution for prior human rights violations and serves as a major obstacle to reparation and reconciliation for the crimes committed by the regime (AI, 2001). The failure to bring to justice those who were involved in the many human rights violations has had significant mental health consequences for victims and families of victims (AI, 2001; Lira, 1996). Many who held powerful positions in the military, police, and senate during the dictatorship continue to hold leadership roles.

Peñalolén was heavily affected by the coup and its aftermath because as a poor and working-class area, many residents were active supporters of the Allende government. Villa Grimaldi, *Parque por la Paz* (Park for Peace) is a public park and museum in Peñalolén established on the site of a former detention and torture center. Documentation indicates that at least 4,500 people were detained and tortured at this site alone between 1973 and 1978, and 226 were murdered or, in the absence of a corpse, "disappeared" from this site and were never seen again (see http://www.villagrimaldicorp.cl/). Many of the Mentor Couples with whom we work were teenagers when the coup occurred. One father watched the aerial bombing of La Moneda from his rooftop. Another recalls a particular day when he walked for several blocks counting the mutilated and dismembered bodies of more than 40 men and women on a single street in Peñalolén; gunfire, corpses, street abductions, suspicion, and fear became part of his daily life at age 14.

Although most members of the parish of San Roque were opposed to Pinochet, we do hear diverse political viewpoints. Favorable references tend to emphasize supply shortages and disorganization experienced under Allende and conclude with, "This country had no head or feet until Pinochet; he put things in order." Another position is expressed as "I didn't like the socialists, and the dictatorship was tough, but no one in my family ever got killed; I think some of the bad things got exaggerated." The effects of family silence about the dictatorship—a common survival strategy—may be summarized in the reflections of one taxi driver:

> I don't care who's in charge. During Pinochet, the only bad thing my parents ever said about him was that he shouldn't kill so many people. It didn't affect me. I'm not political, I just want to work and be left alone.

Most of the time, Mentor Couples simply do not talk about the dictatorship.

Contemporary Chile

Today in Chile, literacy rates (95%) and life expectancy (76 years) are higher than those of most of Latin America (World Bank Group, 2003; World Fact Book, 2001). However, one document reported that half of Chilean women have experienced violence in their relationship with a partner (34% of which was physical violence), and after a 1994 law on intrafamily violence went into effect, the number of court cases increased from nearly 1,500 in 1994 to nearly 75,000 in 1999 (U.S. Department of State, 2004). The 2003 unemployment rate was 9.2% (Infoplease,

2004); in 2000, 22% of the population lived below the poverty line (World Fact Book, 2001). On average, women with university training make only 53.4% of the earnings of their male counterparts. There are no laws prohibiting sexual harassment (U.S. Department of State, 2004).

One of the most striking aspects of Chilean life is the daily work schedule. The legal workweek is 6 days (48 hours), and the maximum workday is 10 hours (U.S. Department of State, 2004). But these are often exceeded, and commute times in the huge and congested city of Santiago are often more than an hour each way. Space shortages force many schools to operate a double schedule, with half of the students in school until 7 p.m. The Mentor Couples typically spend two or three evenings per week in meetings in their faith communities, facilitating their education groups and other leadership activities. These meetings begin between 8 and 9 p.m.

The practice of psychology in Chile has changed rapidly since the 1989 elections. National attention is increasingly directed to prevention and intervention for alcoholism, drug addiction (7.6% of Chilean adolescents use coca-based drugs) (Organization of American States, 2000), and domestic violence. The past 15 years (postdictatorship) have seen the institution of the National Mental Health Policy (1993), the National Substance Abuse Policy (1993), and the National Mental Health Program (1999)—quite recent compared with nations such as Argentina and Mexico, in which mental health policies were initiated in 1957 and 1984, respectively. According to the World Health Organization (2002), there are 3.9 psychologists (with a bachelor's or master's degree) per 100,000 people in Chile. By comparison, there are 26.4 psychologists (with a master's or doctoral degree) per 100,000 in the United States. Few Chileans will see a psychologist in their lifetime.

Meanwhile, the characteristics of a global free-market economy have accompanied a huge increase in consumerism and individualism in Chile. Imported products replace indigenous equivalents. The social messages of such an economy, which have the merchandising and advertising look of the United States, are juxtaposed with the fact that very few Chileans have the economic power to achieve the lifestyle and self-image that is being sold.

Long work hours, high unemployment, a lack of access to psychological services, and the social effects of the economy combine to present numerous challenges to the families of Peñalolén. The family faith education program of San Roque parish offers a unique avenue through which to assist couples to develop critical skills and competencies that will help them and their families to meet the challenges of the contemporary Chilean social context.

Family Faith Education Program

San Roque's family faith education program, developed in Chile, is founded on the notion that parents are the ideal educators and models for their own children (Decker, 1996). The primary program goal is to prepare parents with the information, skills, and support they need to teach and model their faith to their children, as well as to enhance family communication, discipline, and closeness. The program is organized around four of the seven Catholic sacraments or sacred milestones: entry into the Catholic community, reconciliation, oneness with God, and mature commitment to practice of the faith. Therefore, parents participate in the faith education curriculum corresponding to the sacrament that they wish their child to receive, ranging in duration from 6 weeks to 2 years. Mentor Couples present the weekly parent curriculum, while young adults facilitate weekly meetings for the children addressing similar, developmentally appropriate content. Regularly scheduled family group activities enhance family communication, closeness, and faith and community participation. Mentor Couples are volunteers who already completed the curriculum. Our work has been to serve as consultants and trainers for them.

Each Mentor Couple works with a group of 6 to 12 parent couples (with some groups considerably larger). Both parents are required to participate when possible. In the case of single mothers (or fathers), a male (or female) godparent or close relative is encouraged to participate to provide children with exposure to both male and female role models of faith. The Mentor Couples facilitate the same group of parents for the duration of the curriculum, so for those in the 2-year curriculum, close and enduring relationships are forged. As such, group members often seek the counsel of Mentor Couples for support and assistance with family crises.

The Mentor Couple experience is transformative. Couples typically begin leading their first group with much apprehension and doubt, and find that they have many strengths and skills to share. The majority of the couples have not had access to formal education beyond high school, many did not complete high school, and they consistently face significant economic difficulties. Many Mentor Couples meet weekly with other Mentor Couples to provide mutual support, solve problems, and nurture their own faith development.

Workshop and Training Content

When we were asked by the couples to provide formal training, we met with them in small groups to learn about their preparation, the nature of the difficulties they experienced as group leaders, and the techniques that they typically used to address problems (an assessment strategy typical of most consultation models). Their preparation largely focused on content rather than delivery or managing group dynamics. Problems that they described included lack of experience in facilitating groups; difficulty responding to members' behaviors (such as arriving late, disrupting the group, monopolizing the group, attacking the leaders); couple members experiencing a marital crisis that is played out in the group; members who seem disinvested; conflict within the Mentor Couple associated with differences in style or skills; disagreement over how to respond to couples' requests for relationship assistance; Mentor Couples feeling burned out, stressed, and developing an imposter syndrome ("How can we help them when we fight all the time?") or resentment ("all this time and energy for others but no time to nurture our own relationship"). Mentor Couples responded to these issues with a variety of strategies and perceived effectiveness. They expressed a desire for a more systematic way to address these issues and for ways to help families, because they often are the sole contact for families in crisis.

After elaboration, clarification of terms (especially important given the language differences), and checking on the accuracy of our perceptions, we suggested some general themes for a series of workshops, which were received very positively: group facilitation skills, listening and communication skills, and problem-solving skills. The first workshop we offered focused on communication skills (listening, communicating accurate messages, providing feedback); stages of group development (forming, norming, storming, performing); and group facilitation strategies (e.g., discussed in Corey & Corey, 1997; Yalom, 1995). In a subsequent workshop, we focused on conflict resolution, mediation, and problem-solving skills. Next, we provided training in working with couples in crisis, added the Stages of Change model (Prochaska & DiClemente, 1992), and included principles of and strategies in motivational interviewing (Miller & Rollnick, 2002). Each of these workshops took place over the course of a weekend, and each was repeated until approximately 40 couples received the same basic content. These initial workshops took place over the course of 3 years. Since then, we have continued to develop and deliver workshops to enhance previous themes and to provide new workshops based on requests (such as strategies for effective parenting and enhancing relationship intimacy). Of course, we frequently have follow-up consultations with individual Mentor Couples to assist them with their groups, as well as with their own marriage and family difficulties.

Guiding Frameworks and Models for the Workshops

Both of us blend humanistic and cognitive behavior theories in our practice. We emphasize empathy, genuineness, the importance of self-concept, and belief in the strengths and capabilities of the Mentor Couples. We also consistently address the role of perceptions and attributions in creating and resolving problems. Two additional frameworks provide interdisciplinary elements to our work: liberation theology (Gutiérrez, 1971), and the empowerment model (E. McWhirter, 1994). Elaboration of each of these is incorporated with further description of the workshops and consultation work.

Liberation Theology

Liberation theology refers to an approach to the practice of theology centered on a "preferential option for the poor" that emerged from two pivotal conferences within the Catholic church: the second Vatican Council in Rome (1962–1965) and the conference of Latin American bishops in Medellín, Colombia, in 1968 (Berryman, 1987). Since then, a number of variations of liberation theology have been described (Allen, 2000). Our focus here is on Latin American liberation theology, of which the most important principles are the option for the poor (that is, that the Church must align itself with the poor in their demand for justice) and institutional violence (that ignoring poverty, and the conditions of injustice that perpetuate poverty, is a form of violence) (Allen, 2000). The theology of liberation also includes premises that the historical context of a people must continuously inform the practice of theology, that solidarity with the poor means addressing their physical and psychological oppression, and that liberation (and human salvation) involves not just spiritual dimensions but the active pursuit of justice and human rights (Boff & Boff, 1987; Gutiérrez, 1971). Liberation theology is a reaction against, and a Christian response to, the problem of the suffering of the poor; God is viewed as one who accompanies the poor as they seek fuller humanity and justice. Gustavo Gutiérrez, one of the founders of liberation theology, described "the poor" in the context of liberation theology as persons who are "insignificant," without social weight, and often invisible. They are insignificant because of their skin color, gender, or lack of resources, or because they speak a language or have customs that the dominant group considers inferior.

Tenets of liberation theology guide our conceptualization of "the poor" and broaden our attention beyond spiritual well-being to physical and psychological well-being. Liberation theology is reflected in our critical, positive appraisement of the faith education program as one that nurtures family strengths by increasing communication, enhancing Catholic family identity, broadening the family's base of support, and providing families with skills and resources that will enrich their own and other families. Tenets of liberation theology help us be mindful of the means by which religion (and counseling) can serve to oppress or pacify people. Rather than reinforcing passivity, families in the faith education program are encouraged to be active, critical, and questioning of their faith. Parents also critically reflect on dimensions of their family life such as family meals, professed versus lived values, and work and family conflicts.

Liberation theology is not just discussed by theologians but is also lived in communities. In the late 1960s, thousands of groups of Latin American Christians began meeting in small groups to reflect on the meaning of the Bible in their everyday realities, and continue to do so today. These groups, Comunidades Eclesial de Base (Christian Base Communities, or CEBs), engage in reflection on their realities, followed by action that is guided by principles of faith, justice, and love (Boff & Boff, 1988; B. McWhirter, McWhirter, & McWhirter, 1988). The family catechesis groups are parallel to CEBs. For example, several years ago, one catechesis group became very focused on biblical messages about hunger. Based on their reflection, they organized an ongoing, bi-weekly project to bring food to people living under bridges in central Santiago. To accommodate work and family demands, they gather at midnight.

Like many psychologists, during our training we heard numerous recommendations that the topic of religion be avoided completely in therapy. This recommendation is at odds with current recognition of the roles of culture, community, and spirituality as resources for clients (e.g., APA, 2002). A strengths-based approach to counseling requires identification of resources and supports. For many people, and certainly for the Mentor Couples, this includes religious beliefs. Our role with the couples requires that we continuously reflect on the messages that we are communicating overtly and covertly. However, because they are participants in a faith-based program, our experience and knowledge of Catholicism is an important part of what we bring to the work. We attempt to be transparent about our attitudes and beliefs, what we are not sure about, and varying interpretations of Catholic teachings. As family members of their pastor, we are sometimes presumed by the Mentor Couples to know everything that the pastor knows, and to agree with everything that the pastor says. We frequently highlight distinctions between psychology and theology, between our role and the pastor's role, and between his approach and our approach. These efforts are essential to practicing in compliance with the ethical principles of fidelity and responsibility and justice, and the standards of competence and multiple relationships.

Empowerment Model

An empowerment model is the other major guide for our work in Peñalolén. We define empowerment as

> the process by which people, organizations, or groups who are powerless or marginalized: (a) become aware of the power dynamics at work in their life context, (b) develop the skills and capacity for gaining some reasonable control over their lives, (c) which they exercise, (d) without infringing upon the rights of others, and (e) which coincides with supporting the empowerment of others in their community. (E. McWhirter, 1994, p. 12)

This model, derived from community psychology, social work, and education literatures, also guides our clinical training (E. McWhirter & McWhirter, in press). The "5 Cs of empowerment" (E. McWhirter, 1998) illustrate implementation of the model; they are collaboration, context, critical consciousness, community, and competence.

Collaboration includes power and process dimensions of our consulting relationship. Our participation was not imposed but was initiated by the Mentor Couples themselves. They defined the problems and challenges and help shape the training content and process. We do not attempt to be "just one of the folks," nor highlight our status as university professors. We use our many natural connections as Catholics, as a married couple, and as parents while acknowledging our differences in history, socioeconomic status, education, and culture. We attempt to minimize hierarchy by explicitly recognizing and engaging their knowledge, experience, and wisdom.

Throughout this chapter, we highlight the context—the second C—of our work with the Mentor Couples. Family life was affected by the dictatorship in countless ways. People felt a chronic sense of vulnerability because the accusation of a disgruntled neighbor could lead to arrest and detention. The curfew made many community activities more difficult (Constable & Valenzuela, 1991; Rajevic, 2000). Half a generation of Chileans was raised under the repression of the dictatorship. Returning exiles found adjustment very difficult and often were unable to recover marriage and family relationships after the forced separation (Wright & Oñate, 1998). Children born after 1970 are often unaware of what their parents experienced. Many parents disengaged from political and community participation for their children's safety and now lament their offsprings' lack of participation. As they attempt to promote communication and self-nurturance among other families, many of the Mentor Couples express doubt and guilt about how they managed their own parenting. We placed stronger emphasis on supporting positive self-concept and family identity as these contextual factors emerged.

The third C of empowerment, critical consciousness, refers to individuals' ability to critically examine their life contexts and the dynamics of those contexts, and to become active participants in constructing their lives rather than viewing themselves as passive objects of circumstance (Freire, 1970; Gutiérrez, 1971; Martín-Baró, 1994). We constantly attempt to enhance our understanding of the dynamics and consequences of oppression, privilege, power, culture, and religion, in the context in which the couples and the program operate; to incorporate that awareness into our work; and to facilitate critical consciousness among the couples. Mentor Couples vary in critical consciousness but tend to be very aware of dynamics associated with the Catholic Church as an institution (e.g., hierarchy, sexism); with their faith experience (e.g., individualism vs. collectivism); and with the effects of social forces, such as materialism.

Our attention to power dynamics has to include that a priest (in a predominantly Catholic nation), who is also Benedict's uncle, supervises and guides the family catechesis program. His approach to leadership (i.e., democratic and decentralized; trust and challenge people and they will rise to the challenge); the people's perceptions of his role as a priest (i.e., he must be listened to; "he speaks for God"; he should tell us what to do); and people's assumptions about us as relatives of the priest (i.e., they must be listened to; we have to pretend we like them), as well as people's perceptions of us as U.S. psychologists (they can solve all problems quickly; they have no problems; they don't know anything about our problems; they will be pompous and boring); combined with our perceptions of our approach, our actual approach, our relationship with Benedict's uncle, and our varied relationships with the couples, are all part of those dynamics. One way we attend to those dynamics is through our post-workshop reviews. Rather than asking, "Did we miss something?" our question is, "What did we miss?" We review interactions that we didn't understand and try to identify how issues of power, culture, or language might have influenced what transpired. Most important, we regularly seek, overtly acknowledge, and use the Mentor Couples' feedback. During and subsequent to workshops, we consciously attempt to reward criticism, questions, and challenges from the Mentor Couples.

Community, the fourth C, means that empowerment goes beyond individual accrual of skills or power to include being connected with, and contributing to the empowerment of, one or more communities. The Mentor Couples are members of a parish community and view their catechesis groups and Peñalolén as important communities. A community provides a sense of identity, belonging, history, and resources, and it requires contribution in return. This concept incorporates three essential elements of community: interdependence and mutual support, belonging, and shared meanings (Krause, 2001). As Mentor Couples work with other couples in their parish, they develop a stronger sense of identity as a family, as a couple, as leaders, and as members of a faith community. As in any community, there are personal rifts among the Mentor Couples. Most of these tensions are the result of indirect criticism, gossip, and accusations of mishandling responsibilities. When couples bring these dynamics to our attention, we encourage them to exercise their skills in listening, providing feedback, and problem solving.

Competence is the final C of empowerment. We approach our work here with deep respect for the skills, experience, and wisdom of the Mentor Couples, and view this as essential for compliance with the ethical standard of competence. For example, one couple reported that for years following the coup, their catechism groups included members of the military and couples traumatized by the detention, expulsion, or disappearance of family members or friends. They conducted their groups in two languages, overtly delivering the curriculum and covertly providing support to those suffering in silence. A phenomenal degree of skill was required to carry out this work over time, under threat, and while the Mentor Couple negotiated their own difficulties. Our goals for the Mentor Couples include increasing their effectiveness, enjoyment, and confidence in leading groups, as well as enhancing their awareness of many unrecognized skills that they already possess. Not surprisingly, many of the participants equate their lack of formal education with the absence of skills, a notion that diminishes as they successfully engage in experiential skills activities. Couples with more experience become co-teachers, as they take responsibility for facilitating the learning of newer colleagues. We work to incorporate the notion of "paraprofessional" into their identity, to reinforce the legitimacy of their skills and knowledge. Finally, one of the key skills we address in each workshop is to acknowledge and reinforce the skills of the other couples with whom they are working. The practice of giving and receiving compliments enhances community and mutual respect.

Other Details

For each workshop, we provide handouts that summarize main concepts. Chileans edit each handout as Chilean Spanish is highly colloquial. As we present the material, participants provide additional corrections, enhancing the meaningfulness of the content. In every workshop, one or more couples has taken on the responsibility of asking questions to clarify content that they believe others might not have understood (typically because our vocabulary or our illustrations were not effective). Experiential activities and skills practice are a part of every workshop. We open each workshop with coffee and visiting, allowing those who work late an extra buffer of time, and we offer a light meal to close each session, usually at 10:30 p.m. Sharing a meal is a valued and meaningful experience in Chile.

Naturally, there are many cultural differences to address in workshop content and experiential activities. For example, we have observed that when a workshop participant presents a specific problem (e.g., "One of the fathers in our group came to the class drunk"), there is a typical response. One or more workshop participants responds (in a caring and concerned manner) by laying out exactly how to respond to the problem. This typically consists of a 3- to 5-minute testimonial monologue on how the speaker has responded successfully to the same (or a somewhat similar) problem. These monologues tend to generate competitive, critical, or "yes, but . . ." responses from other workshop participants. At the same time, the testimonial is a valued social practice that increases insights into the personal experiences of others, increases universality, and conveys a genuine desire to assist one another. Therefore, rather than attempting to eliminate testimonials, we focus on timing, asking that people first reflect back the concerns of the person who brings up the problem, recognize the unique and common elements of the problem, and elicit information about what solutions have been attempted thus far.

Liberation theology and the empowerment model have been important in guiding our consultation and training work. Oppression, privilege, and power are explicitly and implicitly addressed in both. Both liberation theology and the empowerment model highlight dynamics of dependency, control, and passivity, which characterize the history of relationships between members of dominant and nondominant groups. Using liberation theology and empowerment as our guides leads us to continually acknowledge that we are vulnerable to recreating those very same dynamics. When we debrief after a workshop, we identify instances of our own behavior that contradict liberation and empowerment. We are willing to struggle with the tension around this contradiction because we believe that it is ultimately most useful for our Mentor Couples, for their couple groups, and for our own personal growth. Liberation theology and the empowerment model conceptualize people as participating in a journey that can lead to liberation. We are glad to have such good company along the road.

Implications and Conclusion

Our consultation and training work in Peñalolén, Chile, is work in progress. It is work that consistently evokes feelings of awe, confusion, frustration, and excitement. There are moments in which we feel completely perplexed and unable to communicate in any language. There are other moments we would describe as "communion," in which we feel deeply connected to the lives, work, and hearts of the Mentor Couples. Over the years, the stark movements from feeling very skillful to feeling like a beginner, feeling fluent to nonlingual, and from feeling useful to feeling like impediments have blended into a smoother rhythm of recognizing our strengths and limitations.

As such, one of the principal implications of our work has been our own increased critical consciousness of our limitations as psychologists and of the weaknesses of a contemporary paradigm in applied psychology. We have found, for instance, that many of our assumptions about what makes interventions effective are borne out within this particular cultural context, whereas other assumptions do not hold up to the challenges of different culture, language, and socioeconomic status. We have also found that the cultural (and, as an extension, ethnic) implications of our work are always deeply connected with the historical power and memory of people within their specific political environments. Within the field of psychology, we, too, often ignore, or only give lip service to, these contexts (Prilleltensky & Nelson, 2002). We have been concerned for some time with how traditional psychological science and practice is, at best, limited, and many times is oppressive in its application (E. McWhirter, 1994; J. McWhirter, McWhirter, McWhirter, & McWhirter, 1993). What we have learned is that psychological practice can be socially transformative, but only if we are aware of our own limitations, self-serving needs, and the small battles within and between our specialties in psychology that keep us pretending that we do more than we actually do. It is clear to us that what we have learned from our associates and friends who are the Mentor Couples far outweighs what we have provided to their community.

What implications for training and practice can be derived from this experience? First, we view counseling psychology's attention to multicultural competence as an essential foundation for international consultation and training, and, as such, social justice work. Second, because interdisciplinary perspectives have been critical to our effectiveness, we consider interdisciplinary training to be crucial to the formation of counseling psychologists. For example, theology, history, economics, and political science have expanded our understanding of Chile's context in critical ways. These and many other areas (e.g., anthropology) would also be rich sources for strengthening the foundation of psychological work that contributes to justice. Efforts to streamline and narrow training in psychology, often driven by the need to reduce costs, must consider the importance of enhancing critical thinking via study in other disciplines. We suggest that training programs require courses that enhance interdisciplinary thinking, and that approved continuing education for practicing psychologists include exposure to contemporary thinking in other disciplines as well. Third, we support cultural and language immersion experiences, both for students in training programs and as an important criterion for student selection. Counseling psychologists could work with their university's international programs to support summer cultural and language immersion experiences for students. Finally, our appreciation for living out the complexity of our code of ethics has deepened in this international setting. We have had to negotiate multiple relationships, have deepened our understanding of the multiple levels of "respecting individual and cultural differences," and have learned a great deal about the ways in which people in a different country and culture define and live in human dignity. We suggest that ethical case study problem-solving strategies in training programs highlight with greater frequency the cultural, political, and language implications of ethical responses of psychologists in service delivery and research activities.

Although we see rich potential for counseling psychology as a discipline to enhance social justice efforts around the world, we also recognize the damage done when knowledge is decontextualized, presumed superior, and imposed by members of a dominant group. Perhaps humility supersedes the importance of any other attitude instilled in training; it should accompany all of the skills and knowledge we attempt to convey to master's and doctoral students. The opportunity to engage in this ongoing work has renewed our enthusiasm for counseling psychology training and practice. We have seen how our work in Chile can increase the skills and psychological mindedness of wonderfully committed and hard-working people whose goal of helping others is at the forefront of their actions. They are the true creators of social change, one family at a time. The skills and knowledge that counseling psychologists enjoy can be powerful tools in promoting social justice, especially when we share them with the people who are already engaged in transforming and strengthening their communities.

References

Allen, J. L., Jr. (2000). Key principles of liberation theology. *National Catholic Reporter, 36*(31), 16–17.

American Psychological Association. (2002). *APA ethical principles of psychologists and code of conduct.* Retrieved March 15, 2004, from http://www.apa.org/ethics/code2002.html

Amnesty International. (2001). *Chile: Testament to suffering and courage: The long quest for justice and truth.* Retrieved May 1, 2004, from http://web.amnesty.org/library/print/ENGAMR220142001

Berryman, P. (1987). *Liberation theology: The essential facts about the revolutionary movement in Latin America and beyond.* New York: Pantheon.

Blustein, D. L. (2001). Extending the reach of vocational psychology: Toward an integrative and inclusive psychology of work. *Journal of Vocational Behavior, 59,* 171–182.

Boff, L., & Boff, C. (1987). *Introducing liberation theology.* New York: Orbis.

Boff, L., & Boff, C. (1988). *A concise history of liberation theology.* New York: Continuum International Publishing Group.

Constable, P., & Valenzuela, A. (1991). *A nation of enemies: Chile under Pinochet.* New York: Norton.

Corey, M. S., & Corey, G. (1997). *Groups: Process and practice* (5th ed.). Pacific Grove, CA: Brooks/Cole.

Decker, C. (1996). *Catequesis familiar: Su métodología.* Santiago: Instituto de Catequesis.

Ensalaco, M. (2000). *Chile under Pinochet: Recovering the truth.* Philadelphia: University of Pennsylvania Press.

Freire, P. (1970). *Pedagogy of the oppressed.* New York: Seabury.

Gutiérrez, G. (1971). *A theology of liberation: History, politics and salvation.* Maryknoll, NY: Orbis.

Herr, E. L., & Niles, S. G. (1998). Career: Social action on behalf of purpose, productivity, and hope. In C. G. Lee & G. R. Walz (Eds.), *Social action: A mandate for counselors* (pp. 117–156). Alexandria, VA: American Counseling Association.

Infoplease. (2004). *Chile.* Retrieved April 17, 2004, from http://infoplease.com/ipa/A0107407.html

Kornbluh, P. (Ed.). (2003). *The Pinochet file: A declassified dossier on atrocity and accountability (a National Security archive book).* New York: The New Press.

Krause, J. M. (2001). Hacia una redefinición del concepto de comunidad (Toward a redefinition of the concept of community). *Revista de Psicología, 10*(2), 49–60.

Lee, C. G., & Walz, G. R. (Eds.). (1998). *Social action: A mandate for counselors.* Alexandria, VA: American Counseling Association.

Lewis, J., Lewis, M., Daniels, J., & D'Andrea, M. (1998). *Community counseling: Empowerment strategies for a diverse society* (2nd ed.). Pacific Grove, CA: Brooks/Cole.

Lira, E. (Ed.). (1996). *Reparación, derechos humanos y salud mental (Reparation, human rights, and mental health).* Santiago de Chile: Ediciones ChileAmerica CESOC.

Martín-Baró, I. (1994). Writings for a liberation psychology. In A. A. Aron & S. Corne (Eds.), *Writings for a liberation psychology.* Cambridge, MA: Harvard University Press.

McClure, B. A., & Russo, T. R. (1996). The politics of counseling: Looking back and forward. *Counseling & Values, 40*(3), 162–175.

McWhirter, B. T., McWhirter, E. H., & McWhirter, J. J. (1988). Groups in Latin America: Comunidades eclesial de base as mutual support groups. *Journal for Specialists in Group Work, 13*(2), 70–76.

McWhirter, E. H. (1994). *Counseling for empowerment.* Alexandria, VA: American Counseling Association.

McWhirter, E. H. (1997). Empowerment, social activism, and counseling. *Counseling & Human Development, 29*(8), 1–11.

McWhirter, E. H. (1998). An empowerment model of counsellor training. *Canadian Journal of Counselling, 32*(1), 12–26.

McWhirter, E. H., & McWhirter, B. T. (in press). Grounding clinical practice in an empowerment model. In Aldarondo, E. (Ed.). *Promoting social justice through mental health practice.* Mahwah, NJ: Lawrence Erlbaum.

McWhirter, J. J. (1987). A counseling psychologist in Turkey. In A. P. Dudden & R. R. Dynes (Eds.), *The Fulbright experience, 1946–1986* (pp. 181–183). New Brunswick, NJ: Transaction Books.

McWhirter, J. J., McWhirter, B. T., McWhirter, A. M., & McWhirter, E. H. (1993). *At-risk youth: A comprehensive response.* Pacific Grove, CA: Brooks/Cole.

Miller, W. R., & Rollnick, S. (2002). *Motivational interviewing: Preparing people for change* (2nd ed.). New York: Guilford.

O'Brien, K. M. (2001). The legacy of Parsons: Career counselors and vocational psychologists as agents of social change. *Career Development Quarterly, 50,* 66–76.

Organization of American States. (2000). *Chile: Evaluation of progress in drug control.* Inter-American Drug Abuse Control Commission, OAS–CICAD MEM. Retrieved June 15, 2003, from http://www.cicad.oas.org/InformesMEM/Ing/Chileeng_fin.pdf

Prilleltensky, I., & Nelson, G. (2002). *Doing psychology critically: Making a difference in diverse settings.* London: Macmillan/Palgrave.

Prochaska, J. O., & DiClemente, C. C. (1992). Stages of change in the modification of problem behaviors. In J. O. Prochaska (Ed.), *Progress in behavior modification* (pp. 184–218). New York: Academic Press.

Rajevic, P. (2000). *El libro abierto del amor y el sexo en Chile (The open book about love and sex in Chile).* Santiago: Planeta.

U.S. Department of State. (2004). *Country reports on human rights practices: Chile.* Retrieved April 17, 2004, from http://www.state.gov/g/drl/rls/hrrpt/2003/27890.htm

World Bank Group. (2003). *Chile data profile.* Retrieved April 17, 2004, from http://devdata.worldbank.org/external

World Fact Book. (2001). *Chile economy 2001.* Retrieved February 5, 2004, from http://www.photius.com/wfb2001/chile/chile_economy.html

World Health Organization. (2002). *Atlas: Country profiles on mental health resources.* Retrieved June 13, 2003, from http://mh-atlas.ic.gc.ca/

Wright, T., & Oñate, R. (1998). *Flight from Chile: Voices of exile.* Albuquerque: University of New Mexico Press.

Yalom, I. D. (1995). *The theory and practice of group psychotherapy* (4th ed.). New York: Basic Books.

CHAPTER 29

Bringing Social Justice to International Practices of Counseling Psychology

Kathryn L. Norsworthy with contributions by Ouyporn Khuankaew

Bringing Social Justice to International Practices of Counseling Psychology

Increasing numbers of Western counseling psychologists are traveling across international borders to teach, consult, or conduct research, especially in countries outside the West. In August 2000, postmodernist psychologist Kenneth Gergen gave an invited address for the American Psychological Association titled "From Psychological Colonialism to Creative Collaboration." He challenged Western psychologists working internationally to continue to search for approaches that do not objectify, or "other," those with whom we collaborate—that do not bring the politics of domination and subordination into our relationships and partnerships outside the West. He charged us with transcending the current dualism and power dynamics of the "I–you or us–them" relationship in our international activities by moving

Authors' Note: The authors wish to express deepest respect for and solidarity with collaborators from Burma, Thailand, Cambodia, and Tibet, who participated in the workshops discussed in this chapter. We also gratefully acknowledge funding for these projects provided by a McKean grant and Jack B. Critchfield grants through Rollins College, Winter Park, Florida. We sincerely appreciate the important comments and input from Lisa Tillmann-Healy, Deena Flamm, and Margaret McLaren.

to a more human, less ethnocentric stance—a stance that is based in solidarity and mutuality, and that centers local wisdom and indigenous systems in a collaborative process of defining problems and needs and creating culturally relevant solutions.

As a white, Western, counseling psychologist working in the Global South (those parts of the world often hierarchically defined as "Third World"; thus, Global North refers to countries of the West), I find important meaning in Kenneth Gergen's words. Although I have traveled extensively in Southeast and South Asia over the past 18 years, it has only been in the past 8 years that I have been working regularly in the region, collaborating with local partners from the region in activist research and consultation projects. At the invitation of individuals and groups from Thailand, the refugee and internally displaced communities of Burma, and Cambodia, we offer workshop formats for addressing local problems and building communities of social change. The projects, focusing on violence against women, HIV/AIDS, peace-building, social justice education, community-based feminist counseling, and other locally defined needs, take place in a variety of contexts, with grassroots, nongovernmental, and governmental workers as well as with academics and activists. My primary working partnership is with Ouyporn Khuankaew, a Thai feminist activist and educator who lives in Chiang Mai, Thailand. Together, we have taken up the challenge of developing models and practices of activist research and consultation based on principles drawn from a range of disciplines, including postcolonial studies, feminist psychology, critical theory, liberatory education, and participant action research. We are concerned with the application of principles from these theoretical perspectives within our relationship and between partner groups and/or individuals and ourselves.

From my standpoint as a counseling psychologist, I write this chapter with the aim of discussing contextual, theoretical, and experiential elements of this social justice work in Southeast Asia. Because psychological colonization and neocolonialism are often inherent in the work of Western psychological "experts" and volunteers working outside the West (Lugones & Spelmann, 1983), particularly in the Global South, I will include an overview of these concepts particularly in relation to the internationalization of counseling psychology. By centering my experiences, the evolving relationship between Ouyporn and me, and the relationships between our local collaborators and us, I will illustrate the importance of taking a "decolonizing" approach to this kind of cross-cultural work. Via excerpts from conversations and interviews, Ouyporn and other friends from the region will share their more candid thoughts, feelings, and experiences about this process.

The Foundation: Postcolonial Analysis

Taking a decolonizing stance and constructing power-sharing models of collaboration involves first drawing on work from postcolonial studies to deconstruct the processes and practices of colonialism, imperialism, and psychological colonization. Such a power analysis helps situate the United States and U.S. psychology globally in relation to Thailand and other countries of the Global South and brings the lens of power to the social and political processes and practices within the country in which the consultation or research is taking place. This section presents important background in postcolonial theory in relation to the formation of Global North/South working partnerships and includes relevant commentary from Ouyporn and other local collaborators.

The Voices From Asia

As I forge valued relationships and alliances with colleagues and friends from Thailand, Burma, Cambodia, India, and Tibet, I come closer to their daily lives. They speak more candidly, and I become privy to their experiences with Westerners working in the region. As we come to trust one another more deeply, my local collaborators and partners convey their stories of difficulties and frustrations with many Western volunteers and professionals who come to "help."

For example, Ying, a 31-year-old woman from an ethnic minority group of Burma, living in exile in Thailand, says, of a Westerner who is the director of a nongovernmental organization (NGO) devoted to the issues of the people of Burma:

> The western man is the boss of my friend, who is a woman from Burma. They work in an NGO for Burma people. He doesn't ask her anything about the people; he just does what he likes. She feel very uncomfortable because she knows what he wants is not good for them, but because he is so high, so educated, she dare not to tell him. (Personal communication, 2001)

Myo, a 43-year-old man from Burma living in exile along the Thai border, holding a PhD from a well-respected U.S. university, tells the following:

> When I do workshops with some westerners, they only treat me like a translator. They don't bother to ask about the context of the group we are working with. They don't plan with me, or involve me in the process. Yet, it is up to me to make the group understand and respond well to their training activities. It is like I am essential, yet invisible. (Personal communication, 2000)

Surapee, a 48-year-old Thai consultant to Western NGOs working in Thailand, reveals that

> a few years ago, some western experts came to Thailand to do the workshop on gender. At that time, we do not have that word or concept in our vocabulary. The westerners got very frustrated, and thought we were slow. They forgot that, at some point, in their own country nobody talked about gender very much. They tried to push the group, but the group needed time to discuss and work out their own understanding of these ideas in the way that is appropriate for our society. (Personal communication, 2000)

Colonialism, Imperialism, and Psychological Colonization

The testimonies of Ying, Myo, and Surapee all illustrate elements of a "colonizing mentality" on the part of the Westerners to whom they refer. Historically, colonialism has involved nation-states' traveling to new territories, overtaking land and people, and establishing colonies controlled by the colonizing government (Said, 1993). This expansionism has been supported by imperialism, whereby a country views itself as superior and uses this belief to justify exerting sovereign control over another culture or country. In contemporary feminist psychology literature, colonialism is defined as "a system of domination characterized by social patterns or mechanisms of control which maintain oppression and which vary from context to context" (Moane, 1994, p. 252). Thus, although colonialism may involve occupation of another country or culture, it can also be psychological. Due to globalization (international economics and its attendant pressures to extinguish difference in favor of the Western, and largely U.S., dominant world paradigm), powerful forces of influence and control can be exerted and maintained through means other than physical colonization, such as through the influences of media, economic policies, and Western psychology.

Cultural imperialism (Said, 1993) enforces colonization by exerting the dominant values, practices, and meanings within the colonized context. This renders the perspectives of the colonized invisible while simultaneously negatively stereotyping and "othering" (objectifying) the colonized group. Colonization and imperialism involve universalizing a dominant group's experience and culture, and establishing dominant perspectives and behavior as the norm and as representative of what is "human" (Lugones & Spelman, 1983; Young, 2000). The dominant group is the agent of influence, change, and definition, whereas the subordinate group finds itself disempowered and without self-determination. Colonialism and imperialism have interrelated social and psychological effects on the colonizers and the colonized.

Irish feminist psychologist Geraldine Moane (1994) has offered a valuable discussion of the mechanisms of imperious colonization and its effects on colonizers and colonized alike. According to Moane (1994), common mechanisms of colonization include physical coercion, economic exploitation, sexual exploitation, political exclusion, control of ideology and culture, and fragmentation (divide and conquer). Through these processes, the colonizer is established as the authority and as powerful, independent, and rational. The colonized are infantilized and defined as childlike, passive, intellectually inferior, dependent, and excessively emotional (Nandy, 1983). Because of the overwhelming power differential and the exertion of control by the colonizers over the minds, bodies, and spirits of those colonized, many colonized individuals internalize these negative qualities. This internalization leads to disruptions in identity development, and members of the colonized group often develop feelings of inferiority and self-hatred (Moane, 1994). According to Memmi (1965), those who are colonized may develop attitudes of dependency and ambivalence toward the colonizers, including feelings of hate, fear, admiration, affection, and sometimes identification. At the same time, the colonizers depend on the colonized for their status and identity, survival and comfort while simultaneously projecting their disowned aspects onto the colonized group. Thus, there is interdependency between the colonizers and the colonized that leads to ambivalence for each group with regard to the other. Enforced by the colonizers, a kind of social and psychological complementarity develops that can become deeply entrenched and difficult to change (Kenny, 1985).

Understanding colonization and imperialism helps to contextualize relationships of countries and people from the Global South and the Global North, particularly in terms of the impact of globalization and capitalization on societies and cultures in both regions. Recognizing how U.S. psychology is embedded in this context is an ethical issue for psychologists from the Global North traveling to the Global South to work. The ethical principles of the American Psychological Association (1992) guide psychologists to "respect the fundamental right, dignity, and worth of all people." This principle is foundational in considering the exportation of U.S. psychology via research, consultation, and activism.

Exportation of U.S. Psychology

The United States occupies a dominant social and political location at the global level, whereby U.S. economics, politics, media, and corporate policies and practices have profound influences. Many of our fellow global citizens outside this country view the United States as imperialistic, oppressive, and colonizing. Others have idealized or, at best, hold ambivalent feelings about, our country and, by default, about us when we enter their spaces. U.S. counseling psychologists traveling outside our own country, particularly to the Global South, to consult, teach, research, or engage in activist activities are likely to encounter these sentiments. We need to understand the dynamics of colonization in order to form relationships based on power sharing and to avoid replicating colonizing social and political patterns (Cheung, 2000; van Strien, 1997). Furthermore, it is critical that we recognize that our own profession is implicated.

Dominant U.S. psychology is based in values and worldviews that privilege culturally defined Western dominant identities and values, such as individualistic, White, masculine, heterosexual, and middle and upper class (Fox & Prilleltensky, 2001). U.S. counseling psychologists, drawing from liberation, feminist, and multicultural theories and practices, have voiced strong concerns about the applications of hegemonic frameworks of U.S. psychology with minority group members in the United States (Arredondo, 1999; Fox & Prilleltensky, 2001; Sue & Sue, 2003). Increasingly clear is the need for critical reflection before exporting U.S. psychology in general, and counseling psychology in particular, to other parts of the world.

In the same ways that members of dominant groups within this country can be blinded by their privilege and dominant social location, U.S. counseling psychologists working internationally can be unaware of the power dynamics in play within research, consultation, or practice relationships crossing cultures and national boundaries. We run the risk of not recognizing the power and privilege we hold simply by virtue of a nationality backed by U.S. economic, political, and military policies and practices. This power is compounded by our special knowledge, skills, and access to resources needed by those with whom we are working.

For example, regarding Westerners going to Thailand to work or do research, Ouyporn reports,

> The way the western expert comes in often is exactly the way we see the government going into the villages and developing the people. For example, mostly the experts who come first, become advisors, and stay at the top level, are male . . . western. And all these Thai government people will go to them. And they give technical advice, so that already reinforces the idea that men know how to develop society and the idea of being expert. This is everywhere in the world. When you have high education, when you are a man, when you are white, you have opportunities to really develop yourself into a certain status in society. And then you are invited to come and, even with good intentions, you assume the role of expert. But before that, in Thailand, the government already considers themselves experts, going to every village and fixing the problems of the village, disregarding the wisdom of the local people. So when this model is reinforced it makes it harder to dismantle the top-down, trickle down model of the expert. It is hard for me to say this is only the mistake of the western expert, because you can see that this already exists in this culture. (Personal communication, 2002)

As Ouyporn clearly points out, most countries are built around patriarchal systems of structural oppression (United Nations Commission on the Status of Women, 1998). As such, when privileged Westerners travel to other countries to work, we are entering hierarchical systems where the government and members of dominant social groups (e.g., well educated, upper class, male, etc.) define reality and take on a paternalistic role, prescribing what is best for the "children." "Experts" from the Global North enter such a system with power and privilege in relation to our social identities as well as based on membership in a dominant global entity whose policies and practices typically have profound influence on the everyday lives of people from that country. When the "expert" holds a colonial mentality and operates without understanding the local culture and without consciousness regarding his or her power and privilege, he or she is strengthening the preexisting dynamics of oppression, domination, and subordination in relation to race/ethnicity, class, gender, and other social locations within the country. The "expert" is engaging in practices of psychological colonization.

For example, at a recent U.S. psychology conference, several activists from the Philippines were discussing their concerns during a meeting of international women.

> The academics from the west come to our country and go straight to the universities. This is a problem because, while the academics and government professionals have a lot of influence on us in terms of what practices we should use, where funding will be directed, and who can do our jobs, we have little, if any, influence in the other direction. It is one way, top down. So the western academic just reinforces a system that is already exclusive and in which we have no voice. (Personal communication, 1998)

Regarding research practices, several ethnic minority women leaders of Burma attending one of our workshops complained about an influential research report written by a Westerner about the situation in their country.

> We don't know where she got her information. She said things that were not true, and did not show what is happening as it really is. She didn't tell about the difficulties of the ethnic groups of Burma—how they are targeted by the SLORC (current military dictatorship) for torture and forced labor. The westerners, they only want to come over and study us and go home and publish their article or get their degree. They benefit from our problems. (Personal communication, 1999)

Existing Perspectives on Decolonization, Power Sharing, and Creative Collaboration

Deconstruction of the processes and practices inherent in colonization, imperialism, patriarchy, and the attendant power dynamics offers essential information for the Western counseling psychologist working internationally, particularly in the Global South. The next step is to put this knowledge into practices of power sharing and creative collaboration. Lillian Comas-Diaz (1994) reminds us that an integrated approach that is aware of contexts of colonization, ethnicity, race, and gender must be at the center of practices that are liberating, decolonizing, and empowering.

Specifically, for Western psychologists enculturated and educated in a U.S. context, the APA has recently passed the "Resolution on Culture and Gender Awareness in International Psychology," based on the work of a task force led by Joy Rice and Mary Ballou (2002). This document challenges Western psychologists to become aware of the potential for processes of psychological colonization and neocolonialism in our international work and to become aware of and act differently from historical processes of global imperialism and colonialism. We are reminded to engage in continued efforts at unlearning the colonizing and hegemonic attitudes, principles, and practices we have internalized as U.S. citizens and in our psychology training programs. Rice and Ballou (2002) emphasize five principles for bringing social justice values to our international work:

1. Understanding experiences of individuals in diverse cultures and contexts
2. Respect for pluralism based on differences
3. Awareness and analysis of power
4. Critical analysis of Western perspectives
5. International and interdisciplinary social-cultural perspectives

It is also important for Western psychologists and colleagues from outside the West to understand decolonization from the perspective of those occupying the "colonized" position. Lillian Comas-Diaz (1994) outlines five steps in the process of decolonization from the perspective of those on the receiving end of colonialism:

1. Recognizing the systemic and societal context of colonialism and oppression—becoming aware of the colonial mentality
2. Correcting cognitive errors that reinforce the colonized mentality and acknowledging ambivalence
3. Self-asserting and reaffirming racial and gender identity and developing a more integrated identity
4. Increasing self-mastery and achieving autonomous dignity
5. Working toward transformation of self and/or the colonized condition (see Comas-Diaz, 1994, for a more complete discussion of the decolonization process)

Clearly, in Global North/South partnerships, we all have a part in the process of unlearning the "colonized mentality" and developing a power-sharing approach to consultation, research, and activism. For the Westerner traveling to the Global South as a consultant or "helper," understanding this process is critical in being deliberate about engaging in methods and practices that do not reinforce colonization and dehumanization, but, rather, support decolonization, power sharing, and empowerment of ourselves and local collaborators.

Ouyporn describes her perspective on this issue along with the potential impact of moving to a power-sharing framework:

> For me, it is hoping and asking western people who come with good intentions to be aware of their power, to be humble, to come here and feel like we are equal, we are friends, and we can learn from each other. I think this is going to change the way the government will think about its own people here, if westerners can come with this attitude. Especially in Thailand now it is very common that the Thai government and Thai society in general are looking up to westerners as the experts, as better than us, richer than us, more developed than us. So if people from the west start changing their attitude and their actions, it will influence change in our culture too. (Personal communication, 2002)

Toward a praxis of decolonization, power sharing, and creative collaboration, Ouyporn and I see the "colonized mentality" in our local partners, our Western colleagues, and us. Thus, everyone has a stake in the transformation of these relationships, in the interest of peace, justice, and becoming more fully human.

Our Journey

The following narrative, including comments by Ouyporn, briefly chronicles our journey in establishing a North/South partnership in light of the previously discussed issues. These reflections testify to my original positionality in the relationship with Ouyporn and the ways our relationship has evolved over the course of the past 8 years.

Orlando, Florida, 1997: I am going to work in Thailand with Ouyporn Khuankaew. According to her letters, she is a feminist activist who works with nongovernmental and grassroots groups around South and Southeast Asia. We are planning to do a workshop with a Thai group on violence against women, one of my areas of expertise. Ouyporn will be the translator. Informed by my feminist and multicultural education, my 12 years of regular travel to Asia, and my 5 years of living abroad in several European countries, I know that there is much I don't know about the culture in which I am about to work. I also know that, as an educated professional from the United States and because of the ways the U.S. is situated globally, I symbolize resources and information as well as imperialism and arrogance, that kind of know-it-all attitude that comes with privilege. I know that my discipline, psychology, is grounded in White, masculine, middle and upper class, heterosexual U.S. values and experiences.

Chiang Mai, Thailand, 1997: Ouyporn tells me later that she also has questions and apprehensions because she has worked with Westerners extensively. She is wondering what kind of "farang" (Thai for Westerner) I will be. She is particularly skeptical because I am an academic. She senses from our prior communication that I may have things to contribute, but will I recognize that she also is capable and skillful? Will I listen when she offers ideas? Will I operate from an ethnocentric perspective in the workshops and in my relationship with her, thus behaving as if she and her culture are inferior and invisible? Will our relationship replicate the dynamics of the New World Order? What will she have to give up in order to benefit from my potential contributions? What will be the impact of her choice to sponsor me with "her people"? She recalls, "I decided to tag along and see what would happen."

Bangkok, Thailand: We meet in person on December 24, 1997. Ouyporn, Thai, a woman of color from the Global South, an activist experienced with people from the West; me, a White woman, a Western counseling psychologist from the Global North, a novice at working in the region. In our correspondence, we establish that we both are feminists sharing a common spiritual tradition, Buddhism, and that the values of both of these philosophies are central in our lives. Yet, we each have our own concerns about embarking on this new journey and are cautiously optimistic about our agreement to collaborate.

Though this is not my first trip to Thailand, I find myself continuously encountering novel experiences. I feel that how I respond to each new situation will impact my developing relationship with my new friend and colleague. My ability to tolerate a high degree of ambiguity and uncertainty while asserting myself at appropriate times seemed to be of paramount importance on my end.

Our work does not begin totally grounded in values of mutuality and collaboration since I am to be the workshop leader and Ouyporn is to serve as the translator. However, during this first workshop I notice that Ouyporn seems to be including her own thoughts during translation. She explains that she wants the group to understand more clearly and then she reviews what she added. I am regularly both grateful for and amazed by Ouyporn's wisdom and skill in clarifying and elaborating on the topics we are exploring. Sometimes she uses an idea I offer the group to emphasize a point that she believes, based on the culture and context, to be particularly important. Periodically, after a long period of working hard, she spontaneously announces to the group "Time for a game!" After a rousing round of "elephant, skunk, palm tree" or "earthquake," games involving movement and group contact, everyone settles in more receptively to the next activity.

In the evenings we talk more. I learn that Ouyporn herself does training: women's leadership, community organizing, non-violence, and conflict resolution, traveling all over the region to work with different groups. It is very clear that I am working with an extremely bright, capable, assertive, and talented woman with whom I share many common life experiences, values, commitments, a Buddhist spiritual tradition, and a working poor/working class background. We also have differences, from those as obvious as race and ethnicity, mother language, enculturation processes, age, physical size, education level, and location in the global "village," to more subtle ones such as communication styles and worldviews related to coming from individualistic vs. collectivist societies.

Ouyporn and I each believe we are the one who initiated the conversation about shifting the dynamics of our relationship. In actuality, Ouyporn was already co-facilitating the workshops; we just hadn't made it explicit. We frankly discuss our feelings of dissatisfaction with our respective roles in the first workshop and agreed that it would be much more exciting and congruent for us to operate consistently with our feminist and engaged Buddhist principles. Thus, we embark on a new course, committing to a shared partnership between the two of us and with workshop participants and local partners. The partnership requires regular reflection on our work with one another and establishing a similar process with our collaborators. This commitment involves continuous work on trust building and honesty and has the potential to be liberating and transformational, for both of us and for our local collaborators.

Analysis of the Journey

An analysis of the previous narrative reveals something about how Ouyporn and I each entered the relationship with one another, and how the relationship has transformed over a 8-year period. When initially embarking on this journey, I was clearly naïve. Though I did show some awareness in that first encounter with Ouyporn and our local collaborators of the importance of understanding how my identities and experiences would inform and impact how I engaged with our Thai collaborators, I still made assumptions that I would be the person who would "teach the workshop" on that first trip. Ouyporn's experience, knowledge, and skills came to light while the workshop was in process. I seemed surprised that she, too, had extensive training and practice in workshop facilitation and that she would know better than me how best to engage with the group. She, on the other hand, assumed the role of "translator," admitting that she thought she might be able to learn something, though she was also apprehensive and cautious due to her previous experiences with Westerners. She held power through her knowledge of the Thai language, her cultural access to the participants as a Thai, and her ability to reframe or add ideas to mine when we conducted the workshop. When we brought the power arrangements to the surface, we both enthusiastically embraced the change, and later Ouyporn commented to me, regarding our efforts,

> I cannot do it alone . . . it has to come from you too. And that is why the whole thing about interconnectedness works with us, because I know when we work together, at first people will still look at me like the translator for you. Because, one, the language that is used is English, so there is already that power; second, your being white; third, your being the academic. I am aware of it and I think what helps is when you are supporting us rather than reinforcing this power difference. This part must come from you because you are the one who has that power. It won't work if only I try to work on that with you or with the group. I think with the group it will come as a result of how we work together and how we present the workshop and ourselves, because whatever we do will reflect; people will see it. This is how our relationship connects to the group. Our actions are interconnected with everyone in the circle. (Personal communication, 2002)

Theoretical Framework

The previous section illustrates significant dynamics of the relationship between Ouyporn and me. There is a particular emphasis on our ongoing efforts to address the power elements between us, our efforts at taking a decolonizing stance with one another and with our local collaborators. In addition to drawing on postcolonial studies, our emerging activist research and consultation approach is informed by overlapping principles from the disciplines of liberation theory (Freire, 1970; Ivey, 1995; Martín-Baró, 1994); feminist theory (Brown, 1994; hooks, 1994; Landrine, Klonoff, & Brown-Collins, 1995; Worell & Johnson, 1997); critical theory (Agger, 1998; Kincheloe & McLaren, 2000; Matsuda, 1995; Schor, 1996; West, 1993); and participant action research methodologies (Herr, 1995; Kemmis & McTaggart, 2000). Liberation theory, as discussed by Paulo Freire (1970) and Ignacio Martín-Baró (1994), challenges conventional perspectives in education and psychology by taking the position that those most subordinated in society are capable of defining and analyzing their own situations and engaging in social transformation aimed at their own liberation. Liberation theory encourages a structural analysis of all forms of oppression from the perspective of those in oppressed positions; thus, the voices of the poor are centered as the authorities of their own lived experience. Furthermore, there is recognition that everyone is caught in the "web of oppression" and that everyone has a stake in addressing his or her own internalizations of oppression as well as the external manifestations if we are all going to be truly free. In using a group approach, practices of liberation theory involve beginning with the experiences of group members and supporting them in articulating the issues or concerns based on their cultural and sociopolitical contexts. Facilitators use a problem-posing, dialogic approach to support this process and work collaboratively, offering frameworks within which the wisdom of the group can emerge as the members attempt to find solutions and directions for social change. Through this kind of process, group members cultivate a critical consciousness (Freire, 1970) whereby they can reflect on their lived experiences, analyze them, and then take appropriate action to address the systems of oppression and domination that are contributing to their social and political subordination.

Contemporary feminist psychology, as articulated in the ground-breaking edited volume *Shaping the Future of Feminist Psychology* (Worell & Johnson, 1997), brings in the importance of gender and its interactions with other aspects of identity, such as race, ethnicity, class, sexual orientation, age, ability/disability, and spiritual tradition, as a central organizing principle in human lives. The implication here is that experience must be contextualized to truly understand its complexities and meanings, and that, like liberation theory, the individual holds authority in defining his or her experiences and the meanings of them. There is an emphasis in feminist theory on analyzing power in relationships and in contexts as an essential part of meaning making and in developing solutions to problems. Laura Brown (1994) poses two core values, diversity and antidomination, in guiding feminist theory and practice. Valuing diversity means recognizing multiple perspectives and multiple standpoints as important and necessary to fully represent the complexity of a situation or an issue. Antidomination values call for active efforts to oppose, interrupt, and change situations and systems based in oppression and subordination.

Like feminist theory, as an emancipatory discipline, critical theory (Agger, 1998; Kincheloe & McLaren, 2000; Matsuda, 1995; Schor, 1996; West, 1993), an amalgamation of the agreements and disagreements of a multitude of scholars, also analyzes the ways that power operates within a society, particularly in terms of who gains and who loses, from individual and group perspectives. Thus, there is an interest in the study of privileged groups, those who benefit from the social and political power arrangements, as well as the ways in which those who seek emancipation journey through this process (Kincheloe & McLaren, 2000). Because these systems of inequality tend to be naturalized within a society and at the global level, critical theory is useful because it calls for an interrogation and questioning of these structures of "normality," in terms of the human costs. With a strong emphasis on reflexivity, criticalists make explicit their values and assumptions as they enter into research and praxis, recognizing that there is no "objective" stance. Thus, a critical theorist/practitioner makes no apologies for grounding his or her work principles of justice, liberation, and transformation of oppressive social and political systems. Simultaneously, she or he will also recognize that other variables, such as social locations and identities, cultural background, and social and political context, influence perception and must be consistently reflected upon in terms of how one is influenced and influencing others.

Participant action research methodologies share common ground with liberatory, feminist, and critical theory in the commitment to a participant-centered approach that strives to facilitate local actors in (a) defining their own questions,

(b) engaging in discourse and activities aimed at examining the questions more deeply, (c) generating and acquiring the knowledge and skills to address their needs and/or the needs of the community or society, and (d) implementing the plans generated by local actors to address the questions and concerns coming out of the research process. Brinton Lykes (2001), based on her work with grassroots women from the highlands of Guatemala, stresses the importance of recognizing the activist researcher as "other"—an outsider—and that this positionality has an impact on the research process. In the Freirian spirit, she reminds us that our work needs to be done in solidarity with the research community rather than on behalf of the local actors, and that the research process needs to offer something of value to the community of participants. Michelle Fine and colleagues (in press) discuss Maori scholar Linda Tuhiwai Smith's (1999) emphasis on drawing knowledge and meaning from indigenous customs and practices and incorporating this wisdom into the meaning-making and action phases of a project. Fine et al. also stress that the research project should equip local collaborators to carry on after the activist researcher has concluded the "official" project—the passing of the torch.

All of these theoretical and practice frameworks describe various ways in which participants in a project are centralized, that their knowledge and wisdom is privileged, that they define their own predicaments and solutions in collaboration with facilitators or researchers, and that the work leads to action and social change. Furthermore, through the praxis of this decolonizing methodology, everyone is humanized and transformed by the process.

Our Work

Based on the previously described theoretical contributions, we are developing a methodology with the goals of (a) facilitating analysis and problem solving based on participants' cultural and community contexts, (b) collaboratively developing culturally relevant solutions and action plans for social change, and (c) preparing participants to take the liberatory workshop methodology back to their home communities (see Norsworthy & Khuankaew, 2004, for a more detailed description of the workshop theory and methodology and examples of its implementation with women from the refugee communities of Burma).

The Process

Anchored in these values, Ouyporn and I devote our efforts to facilitating experiences that undermine and disrupt the enactment of psychological colonization and neocolonialism. As workshop facilitators, we recognize that we hold particular sources of power and privilege that are important for us to acknowledge and regulate. Thus, at the outset of each workshop, we explicitly articulate our desire to be co-learners and co-constructors of knowledge arising from a collaborative process. We describe our main role as one of offering questions and experiences that support the emergence of the wisdom of the group.

As members of a Thai/U.S. partnership, we are devoted to engaging in a power-sharing relationship between the two of us and with group members. As such, we engage in continuous reflection regarding our collaboration. This "radical reflexivity" helps all of us to analyze the power dynamics within our relationships and to transform those dynamics that might undermine mutuality and collaboration. When we see group members discounting their own or other group members' contributions, we explicitly emphasize our belief that everyone's wisdom is valid and important rather than only that of the facilitators. At times, we as a facilitation team may analyze group dynamics and make subtle shifts in our facilitation dynamics. For example, early on we noticed that local collaborators would often direct their questions, attention, and group contributions to me, the White Westerner, and systematically leave Ouyporn out of the conversation. We determined that this was a good time to practice decolonization through such strategies as my deliberately turning to Ouyporn or breaking eye contact with the group rather than reinforcing the behavior. At times, I would become the recorder and Ouyporn the facilitator of the discussion. We also use a more direct approach in addressing dynamics that do not support power sharing, such as encouraging our collaborators to deconstruct and challenge any ideas and practices, theirs and ours, based in oppression and domination. We are committed to processing our experiences honestly within our partnerships, even when the feedback involves difficult dialogues. For example, periodically I can slip into the Western "expert" role and begin to define reality for everyone or go into extended lecture mode, as I have been so enculturated to do. Ouyporn has shared with me how she feels in these circumstances and the ways that her own and the group's agency and authority is undermined when I do this. On the other hand, I have shared my feelings of exclusion when Ouyporn has left me out for an extended period by speaking Thai with the members of a Thai group and not letting me know crucial elements of the interaction that influence how we will proceed in a workshop.

Examples of Projects in Action

Two examples of our work are The Feminist Counseling Project and Social Action Trainers Project. In each of these projects, at the request of local collaborators, we have worked together with groups from Thailand, Burma (in exile), and Cambodia using a methodology that integrates the previously discussed theoretical principles and practices. The Feminist Counseling Project involves supporting local groups that have identified specific mental health issues, such as posttraumatic stress, in developing justice-based community response systems that can be carried out using a peer counseling approach (because of the lack of availability of "professionals" or because counseling psychology and other applied disciplines are not part of the culture). Local collaborators first define the problem from their cultural, social, and political perspectives; analyze the root causes of the problem using a critical feminist lens; and then develop solutions and action plans for how to address the problem and do the necessary social change work to remove the conditions under which the problem would arise (e.g., transforming systems that support and reinforce violence into systems grounded in power-sharing values). We as facilitators develop processes and stimulus experiences that support the group in accessing their already existing knowledge and wisdom about their own lives in order to generate theory as well as solutions. Although we may contribute our thoughts and ideas during group reflections, ultimately the group members themselves make the final decisions and take responsibility for seeing that their action plans are implemented.

For example, in working with a group of women from Burma living in exile in Thailand, we came together in a remote location to work on the issue of violence against women in their communities using a workshop format. As facilitators, Ouyporn and I initially supported the group in building a safe container for the subsequent, and more emotionally challenging, parts of the workshop. We carefully observed the development of the group trust and solidarity, and followed this initial phase with an invitation to explore more deeply the forms of violence against women that the women have encountered in their contexts and to analyze the root causes and systemic factors supporting the violence. Together, the group members, Ouyporn, and I delved into our experiences as women who live in societies in which gender-based violence is structuralized and institutionalized, and in which sexist and misogynist attitudes and values underlie and permeate these interlocking systems. A major area of exploration was how power and privilege factor into these oppressive systems and support the use of violence against women to maintain them. After deconstructing structural violence against women and its manifestations at the individual, family, community, organizational, and sociopolitical levels, the group was ready to tackle the challenging task of how to address the issue. Significant time was spent brainstorming and evaluating the costs, benefits, and feasibility of a range of options focused at each of the previously mentioned levels. Each woman developed an action plan for how she and the allies from her community would address the problem of violence against women. Group members identified the need for further knowledge and skills in particular areas, including learning basic counseling skills for supporting trauma survivors. Thus, for this particular workshop, the remainder of the workshop was devoted to basic peer counseling training with a segment on understanding the effects of gender-based trauma. Additionally, during the workshop, participants and facilitators investigated contextually and culturally relevant means of offering these services so that women would be more likely to access them. Informal counseling networks were much preferred over culturally taboo formalized options. Thus, many women planned to start sewing circles or "tea circles," during which conversation could emerge spontaneously. Other women discussed visiting survivors at home and offering support as women cooked meals or cared for children.

As exciting as the workshop itself were the plans for implementation and the reports the women gave upon their return for follow-up capacity building and support. One woman successfully spearheaded a movement leading to the development of a legal process for perpetrators of domestic violence in the refugee camp in which she resided. Another woman began having conversations in her community about violence against women and offered peer counseling to several of her neighbors, with very positive results. A couple of group members did mini-workshops with local women's groups on the topic and led a very useful consciousness-raising and informational campaign. Many of the women reported that they were continuing their own "unlearning oppression" work as well as parenting their children into more flexible gender roles.

One of the areas identified by the women as important to them in their continued capacity building was to learn the liberatory workshop methodology that Ouyporn and I used with them. Thus, the second project, Social Action Trainers, emerged. In this workshop series, we invited workshop participants to articulate their experiences of the previous workshops with us and in workshops using different methodologies. The group members deconstructed the elements of the workshops in relation to facilitator stance, behavior, and attitudes. They also noted elements of the methodology, including types of activities, how the activities were introduced, who was centered in the methodological process, and from where the knowledge originated. We also explored the role of the facilitators in relation to knowledge production. Finally, together we analyzed the power dynamics within the group, and how power was used and for what purpose.

The next phase of the workshop involved participants and facilitators together setting goals and workshop outcomes. From there, Ouyporn and I designed a workshop based on both our own knowledge and skill set in relation to our methodology while keeping the desires and goals of group members at the center of the plan. Over the course of the workshop, participants deepened their understanding of gender-based violence while discovering and learning through the participant-centered experiential approach the theory and practice of this liberatory methodology for social change.

In keeping with the value of power sharing and the goal of decolonization, as a group we regularly reflected on the power dynamics within the group and checked ourselves in terms of our uses of power as a means of supporting empowerment. This radical reflexivity occurred between Ouyporn and I as facilitators, both publicly and privately; among group members; and between the group and us as facilitators. As with the feminist counseling workshop, at the close of the Social Action Trainer workshop, each group member took away an action plan based on her own community needs and agreed to come back and report on her progress in carrying it out. Once again, the women returned full of stories of how they had successfully facilitated groups in their communities and about new projects that had sprung from their work. One woman who did a workshop on violence against women in her area planted the seeds for the development of a women's crisis center and a human rights documentation project to record the stories of women who were assaulted and abused by members of the Burma military and the Thai police. Another pair of women who did a workshop with their own organization reported that the workshop had been well received and precipitated a ripple effect of women pledging to break the silence about rape and partner abuse within their refugee camp communities and to take an empowering stance when reaching out to survivors and ongoing victims.

Ouyporn and I were also transformed through the facilitation of these and the other workshops and projects in which we have been involved. First, through regular opportunities to reflect on our partnership, our understanding of how to operate from a decolonizing, empowering stance with one another and with the groups and individuals with whom we work became more complex. Through our engagement in these processes, our own relationship has been enriched and our emotional bond deepened. We experience a greater degree of effectiveness in our work together and independently from one another. Our work is not always easy, so the strength of our commitment to our relationship, which we both feel is based in love, compassion, mutual respect, and empowerment, has been critical in getting us through the challenging times.

For me, in addition to doing my own ongoing "unlearning oppression" work, this has meant a continuous practice of letting go of my ego while holding on to my integrity as a counseling psychologist and activist with knowledge and skills that may be of some value to my sisters and brothers from Southeast and South Asia. It has involved following feminist, multicultural, and liberation values of decentering myself in the learning process in the service of supporting collaborators in finding their own voices to language their experiences and having them heard; in accessing their own knowledge, wisdom, and solutions; and, as bell hooks (1994) has suggested, in engaging in education, research, and activism as practices of freedom.

From an ethical perspective, a number of questions emerge in carrying out liberatory international work involving Global North/South "border crossings." For example, can Western psychologists challenge local practices when they are oppressive to women, gays and lesbians, or ethnic minority people? If so, what are the best ways to do so? Our work demonstrates the importance of Western psychologists partnering with local collaborators who can serve as cultural informants and equal partners in all activities and determine if and how to bring in an oppression analysis. Furthermore, on the issue of dual relationships, how do we address the tensions of our very Western-based ethical imperative to avoid them when local cultural models prescribe that one must be regarded as a friend or family member in order to be trusted and allowed to interview or conduct projects such as ours? Feminist psychologists (Grossman et al., 1997; Lykes, 2001) and qualitative researchers, particularly ethnographers (Tillmann-Healy, 2003) and participant action methodologists (Fine, Weis, Weseen, & Wong, 2000), have offered very useful commentaries on the ethics of "relational" models and practices. Finally, in North/South collaborative projects, how do we manage the power differentials so that our collaborators feel empowered to assert their authority when we as Western partners are veering off-track in our understandings of the local situations, cultural practices, problems, and solutions?

Joy Rice and Mary Ballou (2002) remind us of our feminist principles of mutuality and power sharing in addressing these questions. They emphasize the importance of psychologists interrogating and addressing power differentials and the ways they undermine true collaboration. Furthermore, when we are involved in international work we need to acknowledge that we are learning and contributing simultaneously. Rice and Ballou (2002) also pose several questions as we develop criteria for assessing how successfully we bring together ethics and social justice in our international work:

> Does it help? Whose way is it? Who does it help? What and which group does it privilege? Are the voices of all in the chorus? Is the theory or method congruent with the experience of the people or does it serve to promote an entrenched authority or group? (p. 5)

Ethically, international counseling psychologists need to pursue theoretical, research, and practical frameworks that are culturally relevant and liberatory. Yet U.S. counseling psychology continues to struggle with ethnocentrism, isolation, cultural encapsulation, and hegemony (Douce, 2004; Leung, 2003; Marsella, 1998; Pederson, 2003). Recent special issues of *The Counseling Psychologist* (July 2003, January 2004) have been devoted to critiquing U.S. counseling psychology and articulating recommendations for bringing justice values into theory and practice within the profession both in the United States and internationally (for international perspectives, see Leong & Ponterotto, 2003; Leung, 2003; Takooshian, 2003).

Implications and Future Directions for Practice, Training, and Research

The work presented in this chapter represents a step forward in implementation of some of these recommendations within an international context. Ouyporn and I have seen firsthand how using a methodology drawn from postcolonial studies, liberation, feminist, critical, and participant action frameworks is truly emancipatory for everyone—researchers, facilitators, and local collaborators alike. The ripple effect is evident; when we experience this kind of process, we are transformed, and we are likely to replicate the process in other spheres of our lives.

Postcolonial analysis offers a useful lens for understanding U.S. colonialism and imperialism and how, as a profession, U.S. psychology is implicated, particularly in our efforts to internationalize. Ouyporn and I demonstrate how taking a decolonizing approach in our work abroad involves addressing our own "colonial mentality," ethnocentrism, cultural encapsulation, power, and privilege while taking into account the effects of colonization on those in the colonized position. We hope that readers can see the importance of bringing the postcolonial analysis of counseling psychology into our master's- and doctoral-level training program curricula as a way of preparing future counseling psychologists to address the problems of U.S. psychological hegemony when designing international research projects or engaging in international collaboration.

Furthermore, our framework is designed to promote horizontal collaboration (rather than vertical) between U.S. counseling psychologists and partners from other parts of the world, particularly the Global South. Marsella (1998) and Leung (2003) encourage this kind of power sharing between counseling psychologists across international borders. We also demonstrate why U.S. counseling psychologists need to partner with local actors who are not in counseling psychology, partly because the field is not institutionalized in many parts of the world. Counseling psychologists need to come out of the ivory tower in order to deepen our understandings of the lived experiences and contexts of our international research and practice communities and in order to engage in true solidarity work with partners on the ground. Ouyporn and I strongly urge Western counseling psychology training programs to include local and international service learning components as a way of offering trainees firsthand experiences in collaboration and partnership. These projects need to be closely supervised and preceded by solid training in ethical international and cross-cultural practice so that trainees can develop the critical consciousness necessary to conduct research, consultation, and activism from a foundation of justice-based cultural and gender sensitivity.

Our framework centers indigenous wisdom and attendant practices (see Pederson, 2003) as important and valid in defining problems and developing solutions. Rice and Ballou (2002) point out that "valuing others' history and world views, their ways of knowing, their organizing and functioning, and their standpoints is critical" (p. 2) in understanding the experiences of individuals in diverse cultures and contexts. Counseling psychology needs to continue the move toward valuing multiple epistemologies and sources of knowledge, including interpretive, ethnographic, participant action, and other forms of qualitative research. Although quantitative methodologies can be useful, they are neither the only nor the preferable means of answering many important questions emerging in the 21st century. Qualitative methodologies aimed at centering and amplifying the experiences and voices of the research and practice communities as authorities over their own lives serve as liberatory vehicles for groups that have been historically and/or globally devalued and silenced.

Finally, we hope readers recognize that grounding the practice of international counseling psychology in principles of empowerment, mutuality, and relationship helps us all appreciate our global interconnectivity and see that U.S. psychology is not the standard for the rest of the world. As Louise Douce (2004) reminds us, "We, as counseling psychologists, cannot be in this circle holding hands if we choose to stand in the middle as the first, best, and only voice in counseling psychology" (p. 150). Only through creative collaboration and a deep commitment to enacting values of peace and justice in our international theories and practices can we become a truly relevant discipline worldwide.

References

Agger, B. (1998). *Critical social theories: An introduction.* Boulder, CO: Westview.

American Psychological Association. (1992). Ethical principles of psychologists and code of conduct. *American Psychologist, 47,* 1597–1611.

Arredondo, P. (1999). Multicultural counseling competencies as tools to address oppression and racism. *Journal of Counseling and Development, 77,* 102–108.

Brown, L. S. (1994). *Subversive dialogues: Theory in feminist therapy.* New York: Basic Books.

Cheung, F. M. (2000). Deconstructing counseling in a cultural context. *The Counseling Psychologist, 28*(1), 123–132.

Comas-Diaz, L. (1994). An integrative approach. In L. Comas-Diaz & B. Greene, *Women of color: Integrating ethnic and gender identities in psychotherapy.* New York: Guilford.

Douce, L. (2004). Society of Counseling Psychology Division 17 of APA presidential address 2003: Globalization of counseling psychology. *The Counseling Psychologist, 32*(1), 142–152.

Fine, M., Torre, M. E., Boudin, K., Bowen, I., Clark, J., & Hylton, D., et al. (in press). Participatory action research: From within and beyond the prison bars. In P. Camic, J. E. Rhodes, & L. Yardley (Eds.), *Qualitative research in psychology: Expanding perspectives in methodology and design.* Washington, DC: American Psychological Association.

Fine, M., Weis, L., Weseen, S., & Wong, L. (2000). For whom? Qualitative research, representations, and social responsibilities. In N. K. Denzin & Y. S. Lincoln (Eds.), *Handbook of qualitative research* (2nd ed., pp. 107–131). Thousand Oaks, CA: Sage.

Fox, D., & Prilleltensky, I. (2001). *Critical psychology: An introduction.* Thousand Oaks, CA: Sage.

Freire, P. (1970). *Pedagogy of the oppressed.* New York: Herder & Herder.

Grossman, F. K., Gilbert, L. A., Genero, N. P., Hawes, S. E., Hyde, J. S., & Maracek, J. (1997). Feminist research: Practice and problems. In J. Worell & N. G. Johnson (Eds.), *Shaping the future of feminist psychology: Education, research, and practice* (pp. 73–91). Washington, DC: American Psychological Association.

Herr, K. (1995). Action research as empowering practice. *Journal of Progressive Human Services, 6*(2), 45–58.

hooks, b. (1994). *Teaching to transgress: Education as the practice of freedom.* New York: Routledge.

Ivey, A. (1995). Psychotherapy as liberation: Toward specific skills and strategies in multicultural counseling and therapy. In J. G. Ponterotto, J. M. Casas, L. A. Suzuki, & C. M. Alexander (Eds.), *Handbook of multicultural counseling* (pp. 53–72). Thousand Oaks, CA: Sage.

Kemmis, S., & McTaggart, R. (2000). Participatory action research. In N. K. Denzin & Y. S. Lincoln (Eds.), *Handbook of qualitative research* (2nd ed., pp. 567–605). Thousand Oaks, CA: Sage.

Kenny, V. (1985). The post-colonial personality. *The Crane Bag, 9,* 70–78.

Kincheloe, J. L., & McLaren, P. (2000). Rethinking critical theory and qualitative research. In N. K. Denzin & Y. S. Lincoln (Eds.), *Handbook of qualitative research* (2nd ed., pp. 279–313). Thousand Oaks, CA: Sage.

Landrine, H., Klonoff, E. A., & Brown-Collins, A. (1995). Cultural diversity and methodology in feminist psychology: Critique, proposal, empirical example. In H. Landrine (Ed.), *Bringing cultural diversity to feminist psychology: Theory, research, and practice* (pp. 55–75). Washington, DC: American Psychological Association.

Leong, F. T. L., & Ponterotto, J. G. (2003). A proposal for internationalizing counseling psychology in the United States: Rationale, recommendations, and challenges. *The Counseling Psychologist, 31*(4), 381–395.

Leung, S. A. (2003). A journey worth traveling: Globalization of counseling psychology. *The Counseling Psychologist, 31*(4), 412–419.

Lugones, M. C., & Spelmann, E. V. (1983). Have we got a theory for you! Feminist theory, cultural imperialism and the demand for "the woman's voice." *Women's Studies International Forum, 6,* 573–581.

Lykes, M. B. (2001). Activist participatory research and the arts with rural Maya women: Interculturality and situated meaning making. In D. L. Tolman & M. Brydon-Miller (Eds.), *From subjects to subjectivities: A handbook of interpretive and participatory methods* (pp. 183–199). New York: New York University Press.

Marsella, A. J. (1998). Toward a "global-community psychology": Meeting the needs of a changing world. *American Psychologist, 53,* 1282–1291.

Martín-Baró, I. (1994). *Writings for a liberation psychology.* Cambridge, MA: Harvard University Press.

Matsuda, M. (1995). Looking to the bottom: Critical legal studies and reparations. In K. Crenshaw, N. Gotanda, G. Peller, & K. Thomas (Eds.), *Critical race theory: The key writings that formed the movement* (pp. 63–79). New York: New Press.

Memmi, A. (1965). *The colonizer and the colonized.* Boston: Beacon Press.

Moane, G. (1994). A psychological analysis of colonialism in an Irish context. *The Irish Journal of Psychology, 15*(2 & 3), 250–265.

Nandy, A. (1983). *The intimate enemy.* Oxford, UK: Oxford University Press.

Norsworthy, K. L., & Khuankaew, O. (2004). Women of Burma speak out: Workshops to deconstruct gender-based violence and build systems of peace and justice. *Journal for Specialists in Group Work, 29*(3), 259–283.

Pederson, P. (2003). Culturally biased assumptions in counseling psychology. *The Counseling Psychologist, 31*(4), 396–403.

Rice, J., & Ballou, M. (2002). *Cultural and gender awareness in international psychology.* Washington, DC: American Psychological Association, Division 52, International Psychology, International Committee for Women.

Said, E. W. (1993). *Culture and imperialism.* New York: Knopf.

Schor, I. (1996). *When students have power: Negotiating authority in a critical pedagogy.* Chicago: University of Chicago Press.

Smith, L. T. (1999). *Decolonizing methodologies: Research and indigenous peoples.* London: Zed.

Sue, D. W., & Sue, D. (2003). *Counseling the culturally diverse: Theory and practice* (4th ed.). New York: Wiley.

Takooshian, H. (2003). Counseling psychology's wide new horizons. *The Counseling Psychologist, 31*(4), 420–426.

Tillmann-Healy, L. M. (2003). Friendship as method. *Qualitative Inquiry, 9,* 729–749.

United Nations Commission on the Status of Women. (1998). *Thematic issues before the Commission on the Status of Women.* Report of the Secretary General. ECN.619985.

van Strien, P. J. (1997). The American "colonization" of northwest European social psychology after World War II. *Journal of the History of the Behavioral Sciences, 33*(4), 349–363.

West, C. (1993). *Race matters.* Boston: Beacon.

Worell, J., & Johnson, N. G. (1997). *Shaping the future of feminist psychology: Education, research, and practice.* Washington, DC: American Psychological Association.

Young, I. M. (2000). Five faces of oppression. In M. Adams, W. J. Blumenfeld, R. Castañeda, H. W. Hackman, M. L. Peters, & X. Zuniga (Eds.), *Readings for diversity and social justice* (pp. 35–49). New York: Routledge.

CHAPTER 30

Counseling Psychology and Nonviolent Activism

Independence for Tibet!

Lawrence H. Gerstein and Doris Kirkpatrick

Throughout the world, the call for nonviolent solutions to various community, ethnic, religious, and nationalistic conflicts, for example, has steadily grown. Perhaps this increased interest in nonviolent solutions has materialized, in part, because of the rise in extensive media coverage of violence and its traumatic effects around the world; the actual increase in different forms of violence; and/or the greater number of individuals, communities, and nations experiencing the firsthand and secondary devastating consequences of the aftermath of violence. Regardless of the explanation, since the 1960s there has been a concerted effort led by politicians, diplomats, human rights activists, religious leaders, professionals affiliated with a host of disciplines, various nongovernmental organizations, and groups of laypeople to implement and reinforce peaceful strategies to resolve conflicts and violence among people and between nations. Clearly, although the global effort to pursue nonviolence has become stronger, it is unfortunate that the historic reality of confronting violence with violence has basically remained constant in current-day situations worldwide. As a result, there continues to be an urgent need to implement innovative and practical theories and strategies designed to resolve violence through peaceful means. Counseling psychologists can play an important role in helping to meet this need.

Authors' Note: We wish to thank Sarah Blankenship for her library research related to the focus of this chapter.

In this chapter, therefore, we briefly review the main theories of nonviolence, related research, and psychometric measures designed to assess this construct. Next, as a case in point, we discuss the senior author's (Lawrence H. Gerstein's) efforts and challenges leading an international, nonviolent movement designed to peacefully return Tibet to the Tibetans. We articulate some of the theoretical principles guiding, in part, this effort as well. Additionally, the importance of interdisciplinary collaboration and teamwork is stressed. Moreover, we mention some ethical issues to keep in mind when pursuing a peaceful resolution to the Tibet-China dispute. We also speculate about the current and ultimate effect of this nonviolent movement on creating peace between China and India, and the movement's possible influence on the future stability and political integrity of Taiwan, Southern Mongolia, and Eastern Turkestan. We conclude this chapter by outlining some future directions (i.e., practice, theory, research, and training) for counseling psychologists in terms of their possible contribution to establishing and maintaining communities, cultures, and nations of peace.

Overview of Literature on Nonviolence

Not surprisingly, the scholarly literature on nonviolence exists in many different disciplines, including peace studies, history, theology, anthropology, political science, peace psychology, and other social sciences (e.g., Bonta, 1993; Boulding, 2000; Christie, Wagner, & Du Nann Winter, 2001; Erikson, 1969; Sharp, 1973). There has been a great deal of writing and research in psychology, however, on violence and aggression. Interestingly, there has been very little corresponding material in psychology on the topic of nonviolence (Mayton, 2001). Although there is a paucity of literature in psychology on nonviolence, a few authors have produced some important publications.

Leroy H. Pelton (1974), in his book *The Psychology of Nonviolence,* introduced a basic overview of the psychological aspects of nonviolence and the capacity to use nonviolent resistance to change minds. Similarly, Vinod K. Kool (1990) incorporated a collection of 30 papers from a symposium on nonviolence held in 1988 in his book *Perspectives on Nonviolence.* This book offered an introduction to the history, key concepts, theoretical foundations, and some empirical research in the area of peace psychology. A second book by Kool (1993), *Nonviolence: Social and Psychological Issues,* included papers from a symposium on nonviolence organized in 1992. This book presented an empirical foundation for psychological research on nonviolence.

A more comprehensive overview of nonviolence and also the discipline of peace psychology was provided by Daniel J. Christie and colleagues (2001) in their book *Peace, Conflict, and Violence: Peace Psychology for the 21st Century.* This volume contained contributions from numerous authors, covering four main themes current in peace psychology: violence, social inequalities, peace making, and the pursuit of social justice. Christie et al.'s book focuses on psychological topics, but includes multidisciplinary viewpoints and multiple contexts of relevance. Finally, Rachel

M. MacNair (2003) published the most recent edition to texts on nonviolence in a book titled *The Psychology of Peace: An Introduction (Psychological Dimensions to War and Peace)*. MacNair reviewed the literature on the psychology of nonviolence, highlighting the cause-and-effect nature of violence and its counterpart, nonviolence. This introductory text also includes an excellent overview of the concepts in peace psychology, results of empirical research, and recommendations for future research.

Theories and Research on Nonviolence

Although there is a paucity of literature in psychology on nonviolence, there are several psychological theories, models, and approaches focusing on this concept. They include value theory, peacebuilding approaches of women, and Kurt Lewin's model of force field analysis. Gandhi's writings and activities have also been discussed in relation to conceptualizing nonviolence. In this section of the chapter, we briefly highlight each of these frameworks and provide an overview of pertinent research.

Value Theory

Values have been proposed as a basis for attitude formation by several researchers (e.g., Hofstede, 1980; Rokeach, 1973; Schwartz, 1994). Value theory has been proposed as a theoretical framework for studying values that influence cognitive or emotional reactions. The assumption of this theory is that a universal content and structure exist in value systems across cultures. The main proponents, Schwartz and colleagues (Schwartz, 1994; Schwartz & Bilsky, 1987, 1990; Schwartz & Sagiv, 1995), defined values as "desirable goals, varying in importance, that serve as guiding principles in people's lives" (Sagiv & Schwartz, 1995, p. 438). This theory postulates that values are organized around particular motivational types: power, achievement, hedonism, stimulation, self-direction, universalism, benevolence, tradition, conformity, and security (for descriptions of each, see Sagiv & Schwartz, 1995). For example, when one is forgiving, this promotes the preservation and enhancement of the welfare of people with whom one is in frequent personal contact. This value is thought to be associated with benevolence. The 10 motivational types are further organized into groups called higher-order value types that combine two or more of the basic 10 values. These higher-order value types are "opposes openness to change" (self-direction and stimulation); "conservation" (conformity, tradition, and security); "self-transcendence" (universalism and benevolence); and "self-enhancement" (achievement and power) (Sagiv & Schwartz, 1995).

A connection between value theory and nonviolence was made by Mayton, Diessner, and Granby (1996). In terms of nonviolence, it is thought that when one possesses self-transcendent values such as broad-mindedness, wisdom, equality, unity with nature, helpfulness, and forgiveness, this is a sign of the understanding, protection, and enhancement of the welfare of people close to us, as well as the welfare of all people and nature (Schwartz, 1992). Transcendent values and the value type *conformity* have been associated with nonviolent tendencies (Mayton, 1994; Mayton et al., 1996).

Mayton and colleagues (1996) have examined which values were prized by individuals who showed a predisposition toward nonviolent methods. Participants in this study were asked to complete two assessments, the Nonviolence Test (Kool & Sen, 1984) and the Values Questionnaire (Schwartz, 1992). Results indicated that the *universalism* and *benevolence* value types were consistent with the values of individuals who expressed predispositions toward using nonviolent strategies for conflict resolution. These value types, the researchers argued, were consistent with the Gandhian concepts of *ahimsa* and *tapasya.*

The potential heuristic value of value theory would seem to be strong. Value theory represents a method for linking moral concepts or values with actions. It provides a basis for examining social values that exist and motivate action. This operationalizing of value schemas serves to strengthen our ability to examine and elaborate on nonviolence and the values that contribute to nonviolent philosophy and behavior. Clearly, such a theory can lead to the development of new ideas, concepts, and peaceful strategies to resolve conflict.

A potential weakness of value theory is that there are potential cross-cultural differences in value structures even though some researchers have claimed that the theory is valid across cultures (Schwartz, 1994; Schwartz & Sagiv, 1995). In other words, does this theory truly represent a universal value structure? The differences and similarities between the value structures of various cultures and groups need further study.

Peacebuilding Approaches of Women

Another model recognizes that gender has an impact on peacebuilding and can contribute to our understanding and evaluation of peacebuilding practices. In their research regarding peacebuilding approaches of women, McKay and Mazurana (2001) described how women were pursuing nonviolent approaches to social change that were different from men's approaches. Women's approaches to peacebuilding often involve emphasis on the processes of relationship building, cooperation, networking, psychosocial and spiritual processes, and the reconciliation of human relationships (Mazurana & McKay, 1999). Attempts to pursue structural peacebuilding appear to be less emphasized by women. Instead, women prefer pursuing psychosocial processes, such as recovering from trauma or constructing more peaceful and just relationships and behaviors (McKay & Mazurana, 2001).

McKay and de la Rey (2001) offered support for this assertion. In their study of 16 female South African leaders of organizations involved in peacebuilding, the investigators examined how "women view peacebuilding within their own country and culture" (p. 241). McKay and de la Rey used a feminist participatory research design. Participants were from various parts of South Africa who attended a workshop planned to elicit their perspectives on peacebuilding. Data from the audiotaped sessions were analyzed, as were data gathered on the artifacts of the workshop. Analysis of data involved transcribing and examining the dialogue as well as conducting a thematic analysis of drawings produced by the women. As expected, results indicated that peacebuilding for these women was a psychosocial process involving, for example, relationship building, teamwork, networking, grassroots work, advocacy, communicating, and nurturing one another. Participants also connected peacebuilding with physical, psychological, and spiritual health. This study demonstrated the significance of encouraging females to develop peacebuilding strategies to achieve peace.

Kurt Lewin's Model of Force Field Analysis

Kurt Lewin (1938, 1948, 1951) developed a model for conceptualizing change in systems that may be useful when examining how forces interact with one another to build nonviolent communities. According to Lewin, force field analysis is a status that exists between driving forces that act to change the status and resistant forces that act to resist change. These forces are thought to operate in direct opposition to one another.

Norsworthy and Gerstein (2003a) argued that force field analysis can be applied to the goal of building nonviolent communities. For example, they claimed that mental health professionals could assess the opposing and supporting forces associated with establishing and maintaining peaceful communities. They reported that results of such an assessment could be used to develop strategies to strengthen the supporting forces in an effort to achieve the desired goal. Additionally, they stated that these results could be employed to construct interventions designed to reduce or eliminate the forces that restrain or undermine the existence of peaceful communities. To date, there is no research to support Norsworthy and Gerstein's (2003a) assumptions about how Lewin's force field analysis model can be employed to establish nonviolent communities.

Gandhian Principles

The term *nonviolence* is strongly associated with Gandhi, who promoted nonviolence as both a philosophy and a political strategy (Harak, 2000). Gandhi discussed a number of concepts as a basis for this approach. The first concept, Satya, is a striving for the truth. According to Gandhi, humans are limited in their perception of the truth. Because humans are prone to error, they see things from a faulty perspective, and therefore, they have no right to act violently toward others (da Silva, 2001). The second concept, Ahimsa, is nonviolence in its earliest form. According to Indian tradition, nonviolence as a goal is related to love of or compassion for all life. It is believed there is a kinship of life among all living creatures, and violent action, such as war, is wrong because it disrupts all life, not just human life. According to Gandhi (1983), "To see the universal and all-pervading Truth face to face one must be able to love the meanest of creation as oneself" (p. 504). Ahimsa refers to a refusal to do harm or allow injury because of the belief in the sacredness of life (Pelton, 1974).

To address potentially violent situations in a way that promotes nonviolence, Gandhi espoused Satyagraha, the use of nonviolent "soul force" or "truth force." This meant pursuing truth with insistent will, but without physical violence (da Silva, 2001). The fourth concept, Tapasya, means "self-suffering." According to Gandhi, suffering is a necessary condition for Satyagraha. To achieve social resistance, one must be ready to sacrifice comfort, personal safety, or even one's life. According to this philosophical view, enduring suffering instead of reacting violently is a way to interrupt a cycle of violence.

The operationalization of a system or philosophy of peace is a major strength of this model. By taking the concept of nonviolence and providing a more distinctive characterization of what constitutes nonviolent philosophies and actions, Gandhi advanced the pursuit of nonviolence. Furthermore, Gandhi's approach provides an active posture for nonviolence advocates. From this perspective, nonviolence is a pragmatic, action-oriented choice that offers an alternative to violence. Gandhi's articulation of the principles of nonviolence offers hope in terms of an alternative to violence and a practice that meets the human yearning for peace.

Gandhi's model of nonviolence (Gandhi, 1951) as discussed earlier appears to be more of a philosophy than a theory, and therefore, it presents some obstacles to researchers seeking to test it. However, research does exist linking Gandhi's model to nonviolence. Political scientists such as Joan Bondurant (1965), Richard Gregg (1966), and Gene Sharp (1960, 1973, 1979) have examined the effects of Gandhian concepts on political and social change. For example, Sharp's book *The Politics of Nonviolent Action* (1973) is regarded as definitive in its field for its analysis of techniques of nonviolence. Sharp presents a strongly pragmatic approach to nonviolence, which is in some respects different from the more principled tone of Gandhi's writings.

Two major drawbacks present themselves regarding Gandhi's model of nonviolence. First, as just mentioned, the model is more of a philosophy than a theory, and consequently, it is difficult to verify or falsify. Second, although nonviolent protests have been pursued following Gandhi's concepts, this has only been practiced sporadically and may as yet lack historical evidence. Gandhi's practices and doctrines may represent ideals that are difficult to implement; however, his vision of victory through nonviolence has relevance to the current world and should continue to be studied.

Measures of Nonviolence

A few researchers have attempted to measure aspects of nonviolence, particularly in relation to Gandhi's framework. Currently, there are five objective instruments designed to identify characteristics of nonviolence: the Pacifism Scale (Elliott, 1980), the Gandhian Personality Scale (Hasan & Khan, 1983), Nonviolence Test (Kool & Sen, 1984), Multidimensional Scale of Nonviolence (Johnson et al., 1998), and the Teenage Nonviolence Test (Mayton, Weedman, Sonnen, Grubb, & Hirose, 1999). These measures seek to assess nonviolent attitudes and behaviors and nonviolent tendencies in personality (Mayton et al., 2002). An overview of each will now be presented.

The Pacifism Scale (55 Likert items) was developed by Elliott (1980) to assess attitudes related to pacifism. Elliott derived his concept of pacifism from Gandhian philosophical principles; specifically, the components of Satyagraha, Ahimsa, and

Tapasya. From these components, Elliott posited that measuring attitudes toward physical nonviolence, psychological nonviolence, active value orientation, and locus of control would most closely match the Gandhian concept of pacifism (Elliott, 1980). The Pacifism Scale is considered to have adequate reliability, but there are no data on its validity.

Qamar Hasan and Shamsur Khan (1983) constructed the Gandhian Personality Scale (29 Likert items) to describe Gandhian or nonviolent personalities. Six factors are linked with the scale: machiavellianism/anti-machiavellianism, authenticity, cynicism/anti-cynicism, openness to experience and tolerance, tenderness and generosity, and trust in human nature. There is insufficient information regarding the psychometrics (e.g., reliability, validity) of this scale.

The Nonviolence Test (65 forced-choice items) was developed by Kool and Sen (1984) to assess attitudes related to nonviolence. Like the Pacifism Scale, this measure was designed around the Gandhian principles of nonviolence discussed previously. The device is intended to show that individuals with nonviolent predispositions display a more rational, self-controlled approach than individuals with violent predispositions (Kool, 1993). This measure appears to be reliable and valid.

Johnson et al. (1998) introduced the 80-item Multidimensional Scale of Nonviolence to assess six different components of nonviolence: direct nonviolence, systems-level nonviolence, compassion and connection, indirect oppression, nonviolence toward the planet, and spirituality. Reliability and validity have been established for this measure.

Finally, the Teenage Nonviolence Test (55 Likert items) was developed by Mayton et al. (1999) to measure attitudes related to nonviolence in adolescents. Previously, there had not been an instrument of this kind available for use with this population (Mayton, 1999). This measure contains six subscales. The first three subscales, physical nonviolence, psychological nonviolence, and active value orientation, are derived from Elliott's (1980) work. The next two subscales (Satyagraha and Tapasya) assess Gandhian principles, and the final subscale targets helping and empathy. Reliability for this scale is inconsistent, but there are data to support its validity (Konen et al., 1999).

Background of an Activist

Up to this point in the chapter, we briefly reviewed some theories, research, and measures linked with nonviolence. Now, our attention will focus on the senior author's (Lawrence H. Gerstein's) background as a social activist and his efforts to help bring about a nonviolent solution to the Tibet-China conflict. For the sake of making this discussion more intimate, this text will be presented in a first-person voice rather than third person.

Being an activist and an academic can be a very challenging balancing act for me. The necessity of taking immediate action to confront a new human rights violation, emerging catastrophe, upcoming legislative initiative, and/or international crisis or development can often interfere with the expectations and responsibilities of my daily academic life.

One can speculate based on career development theories (e.g., Social Learning Theory of Krumbolz, Vocational Typology Theory of Holland, Trait Theory of Roe) why some counseling psychologists become social activists and others do not. It might be informative to discuss what shaped my interest in social activism. Throughout my life, I was exposed to various individuals committed to eliminating the inequities of society. For instance, my paternal grandmother, Anna Gerstein, served as a nurse at a local hospital assisting indigent individuals, and my paternal grandfather, Daniel Gerstein, founded the first restaurant union in New York City in the 1940s to protect the workers from unfair labor practices, ensure a competitive wage, and establish reasonable employment benefits. Later, in the mid-1950s, this same grandfather started a union to protect and represent the needs and interests of building employees. Moreover, my father, Melvin Gerstein, rose to the office of president of this union in the mid-1970s. Each of these unions represented a diverse ethnic population of members both from the United States (e.g., African Americans, Native Americans) and from abroad (e.g., Cubans, Puerto Ricans, Haitians, Jamaicans, Eastern Europeans, Central Americans). It should be noted that while in college, I worked as a representative for the building employees union, addressing members' concerns and collecting dues.

My father was also extremely active in the political arena in New York State as well as serving as one of the founders and long-time supporters of his Temple. Similarly, my mother, Helen Gerstein, was a tireless leader of the Temple's sisterhood. Members of my extended family were also deeply rooted in social causes. For instance, my cousin, Janet Levy, was part of the inner group of activists in the 1950s involved in the women's movement.

As must be apparent from this brief overview, I was exposed to many close family members invested in social justice, activism, and advocacy. These persons served as powerful role models shaping my own evolving interest and dedication to such work. During family gatherings, much of the discussion would center on the needs and human rights of the oppressed and underprivileged, issues of ethnic groups in the United States, international affairs, and domestic and national politics.

My attraction to activism and social justice was also greatly influenced by the civil unrest, social and political movements, counterculture, and scholarship of the 1960s. As a teenager during the 1960s, I participated in many different types of demonstrations and causes. My first exposure to Buddhism occurred during this time as a result of reading Hermann Hesse's *Siddhartha*. Furthermore, I became more interested in Asia because of the worldwide popularity of Chairman Mao Tse-Tung's "Red Book," and President Nixon's historic visit to China.

Upon entering college, I planned to become an attorney. After working in law firms, however, I realized that I did not fit in such an environment. It was at this time that I became aware of my desire to become a professor. I eventually earned a BBA in public administration, but decided to pursue a graduate degree in rehabilitation counseling instead of political science, thinking the former would more closely match my interests at the time—serving the mental health needs of individuals. As a master's student, I also developed a deep appreciation for Zen Buddhism and Jewish Mysticism.

After practicing in a mental health center for a number of years, I decided to pursue a doctoral degree. All through my Ph.D. program, I was uncertain about whether to major in counseling or social psychology. Ultimately, I focused on both, because I appreciated the pragmatic helping framework of counseling psychology and the theoretical and empirical foundation of social psychology's pursuit of interpersonal relationships and group behavior.

It was during my doctoral training (1979–1983) that I once again became involved in social justice work. This time, though, I focused my attention on a marginalized professional group. For many years, with one of my doctoral cohorts, David K. Brooks, Jr., I co-led the effort to pass counselor licensure laws in each state of the United States. Through this work, I acquired an understanding of the legislative process, lobbying, coalition building, organizational leadership, public relations, and grassroots development. The skills I learned as a leader of the counselor licensure movement were invaluable and have greatly influenced my current activist endeavors.

Given my role models during my formative years, the events of the 1960s, and my graduate school interests and learning experiences, it is not surprising that, as an academician, I have integrated social justice, advocacy, and activism into my research and service. For the most part, since becoming a professor, I have pursued the following topics: loneliness, altruism in the workplace, cross-cultural helping, human rights abuses, cross-cultural behavior and methodology, ethnopolitical conflicts, and nonviolent approaches to disputes.

Perhaps the most important person shaping my interest in activism, other than my family members, entered my life in the mid-1980s. I first met Taktser Rinpoche (His Holiness The Dalai Lama's oldest brother) at a lecture on Tibet He was giving in Indianapolis. Rinpoche had just recently returned from a trip to Tibet and was sharing disturbing images and horrific stories about the current situation in His country. Along with being very moved by Rinpoche's lecture, I was quite taken by His demeanor and personality, especially because Rinpoche was in His late 60s at the time. This was the first time that I had been in the presence of a reincarnated Lama, heard about the extensive destruction in Tibet, and learned about the details of China's illegal and brutal occupation of Tibet in 1959.

Like a flash of light, I immediately realized that I wanted to become better acquainted with Rinpoche. I then began to visit with Rinpoche at the Tibetan Cultural Center in Bloomington, Indiana, a center founded by Rinpoche to protect, preserve, and promote Tibetan culture and Tibetan Buddhism, and to educate people about the history and current situation in Tibet. Rinpoche and I spent many hours drinking tea, telling jokes, laughing, swapping tales, talking politics, discussing the Tibet-China conflict, and simply conversing about life! Over time, I developed an understanding of the basic tenets of Tibetan Buddhism and culture, and more important, established a very close relationship with Rinpoche.

Among many discoveries, I learned that Rinpoche, at the age of 8 years old, was recognized by the 13th Dalai Lama (previous Dalai Lama) as the 24th incarnate of Taktser Rinpoche's spirit. Furthermore, I discovered that at the young age of 27, Rinpoche became the Abbott (or head) of Kumbum Monastery in Tibet, which was composed of more than 4,000 monks.

Unfortunately, after a very brief period of time as Abbott, Rinpoche was forced out of Kumbum. Located in Amdo, or the Eastern part of Tibet, right next to China's border, Kumbum was one of the first areas to be invaded by the army of the People's Republic of China (PRC). When the PRC arrived in 1949, few people in Lhasa (Tibet's capital) knew of the invasion. The PRC held Rinpoche under house arrest in the monastery, sleeping in His room and following Him 24 hours a day. The PRC demanded that Rinpoche travel to Lhasa, denounce the Tibetan government, and denounce His younger brother, His Holiness The 14th Dalai Lama (current Dalai Lama), who was then about 15 years old. Moreover, the PRC demanded that Rinpoche kill His brother, The Dalai Lama. In return for these actions, the PRC promised Rinpoche that He would become the PRC government leader of Tibet.

After months of denying the PRC's request, Rinpoche realized that someone needed to go to Lhasa to inform The Dalai Lama of the fact that the PRC had invaded Tibet. So, Taktser Rinpoche pretended to agree with the PRC's demands and set off with 1,000 Tibetans and more than 10,000 animals for Lhasa, hoping He could escape His captors. Sure enough, Rinpoche was successful, and He was one of the first Tibetans to inform His Holiness The Dalai Lama of the seriousness of China's invasion. Sadly, when Taktser Rinpoche pretended to agree with the PRC, He had also broken His vows as a monk; a consequence He had already accepted before informing the PRC of His decision. Because of this, He gave back His vows as a monk.

Unfortunately, neither His Holiness The Dalai Lama nor the Tibetan officials accepted the seriousness or urgency of Rinpoche's report. As a result, Rinpoche decided in 1950 that He would leave Tibet and attempt to educate the world about the atrocities in Tibet and the actions of the PRC. As one of the first, if not the first, high-profile Tibetans to go into exile, Taktser Rinpoche traveled the world meeting government and United Nations officials to establish support for Tibet. Sadly, no one listened, and the situation in Tibet worsened. Taktser Rinpoche was also the first Tibetan to settle in the United States after the PRC invasion in 1949.

Hearing Rinpoche's story and learning more about the atrocities in Tibet, I was primed to help Tibetans regain their country. In the early 1990s, Rinpoche asked me to serve as a leader of the Indiana Tibet Committee. Without hesitation, I agreed to this honorable request. Later, in 1995, Rinpoche and I co-founded the International Tibet Independence Movement (ITIM). Before discussing the mission and activities of ITIM, and my role, it might be helpful to provide some basic information about Tibet, explain in much greater detail the Tibet-China conflict, and describe the tragedy in Tibet.

History of Tibet

Tibet is a country that shares a western border with India, an eastern border with China, a southern border with Nepal, Bhutan, Sikkim, and Myanmar (Burma), a northeastern border with Outer Mongolia, and a northwestern border with East Turkestan. Tibet is considered the highest plateau in the world, with an average elevation of more than 12,000 feet. The tallest mountain in the world, Mount Everest, is located in both Tibet and Nepal. In terms of land mass, Tibet is as large as western Europe. Historically, most Tibetans were nomads and farmers. The majority of Tibetans continue to live this type of lifestyle. Religion has always played an important role in Tibetan life, influencing every aspect of the culture and society. In fact, until 1959, Tibet was ruled by a theocracy—a political hierarchical system that His Holiness The 14th Dalai Lama was in the process of changing when He was forced into exile to India in 1959.

Before 1959, Tibet was an independent nation that was isolated from the rest of the world. Its geographic location, rugged terrain, high altitude, and the lifestyle and philosophy of its people contributed to this reality. From the inception of their ethnic race, Tibetans have been fiercely independent yet strongly interconnected to their family, community, culture, monastic institutions, and country, rendering a relationship with the "outside" world unnecessary.

Given their deeply held Buddhist beliefs, Tibetans have an unwavering respect for the environment, nature, and all sentient beings. They do not believe in disturbing the environment and therefore frown upon mining, fishing, deforestation, or any activity that disrupts a natural setting. Furthermore, they condemn the killing of any sentient being, including insects! However, unlike what most people believe, Tibetans are rabid red meat (sha) eaters, but they usually do not eat fowl. The high plateau of Tibet limits the availability of different foods, especially fruits and vegetables. Moreover, Tibet's altitude brings with it frigid weather conditions. Consequently, to keep warm and to obtain enough protein, Tibetans have survived historically on beef, cheese (chhura), roasted barley (tsampa), yogurt (zho), and potatoes (zhogho). One yak, sheep, goat, or cow can feed many Tibetans, and in part, this outcome serves as a rationale for killing these animals. Tibetan Buddhists, however, will not kill or slaughter these animals themselves. Instead, Tibetan Muslims carry out these functions. Prayers are recited during this process as well as when eating any foods. Tibetan Buddhists offer each of their meals to all sentient beings in order that they may feel nourished and relieved of suffering. Thus, Tibetan Buddhists eat not for themselves, but to benefit all other living creatures.

Although some people want to believe that Tibet was a type of Shangri-La before 1959, and is even such a place now, reality suggests something different. The theocratic feudal system oppressed some members of the society, and economic poverty was blatantly apparent. Furthermore, regional warlords and kings controlled most of the resources and dictated policies to the masses. Even with these shortcomings, Tibetans generally remained happy and content with their lives, respecting one another's roles and position in society.

Illiteracy was also rampant among the laypeople. Many monks, on the other hand, were able to obtain an education and develop reading and writing skills, particularly the skills necessary to practice their religion. The monastery operated as a multifunctional institution training and housing the monks; serving as a place of worship for monastics and laypersons; and providing a host of social, medical, educational, legal, and other services to the local communities. In fact, the monastery served as the focal point for an entire geographic locale. Along with the functions just mentioned, the monastery operated as a museum housing religious artifacts and other cultural items of significance.

The Tibet-China Conflict

In 1949, life in Tibet began to change considerably. At this time, Mao Tse-Tung rose to power in China. Mao believed that Tibet had always been a part of China. This belief was based, in part, on the marriage of the Tibetan King, Songsten Gampo, to the Chinese Princess, Wen Cheng, during the Tang period (618–907). Mao thought that this marriage was evidence of Tibet belonging to China. It should be noted, though, that Tibet has a recorded history of statehood extending back to 127 B.C.

Chairman Mao, however, claimed it was time to reunite Tibet, Southern Mongolia, and East Turkestan with the motherland. He also argued that the Tibetan people needed to be liberated from the oppressive theocratic feudal system operating in Tibet. Furthermore, Mao claimed that religion was poison! Thus, in 1949, Mao's People's Liberation Army (PLA) began invading Tibet and the other countries just mentioned. At the time of China's illegal invasion in 1949, Tibet possessed all the attributes of an independent country recognized by international law, including a defined territory, a government, tax system, unique currency and language, unique postal system and stamps, army, and the ability to carry out international relations.

By 1959, the PLA had successfully invaded Tibet and established its control in Tibet's capital city, Lhasa. Soon after the massive Tibetan uprising in Lhasa on March 10, 1959, His Holiness The 14th Dalai Lama escaped to India, where He has remained ever since.

Tragedy in Tibet

The so-called liberation of Tibet was not peaceful. PLA tanks and heavy artillery were used to fight the poorly equipped Tibetan army, to battle the Tibetan nomadic warriors, and to subdue the masses in the larger cities. Since Tibet's invasion, more than 1.2 million Tibetans have died at the hands of the PLA and PRC police. In addition, more than 6,000 monasteries have been destroyed or severely damaged, with only 16 standing in some form or another. The number of monks and nuns has also been significantly reduced. Those who have remained as monks and nuns have been forced to sign statements denouncing His Holiness The Dalai Lama and the Tibetan government in exile, and endorsing the legitimate rule of Tibet by China's central government.

There has also been widespread environmental destruction in Tibet. Forests have been destroyed; corrosion and mudslides have become more frequent; water has been contaminated; precious minerals have been mined, including huge quantities of uranium; large amounts of nuclear waste have been dumped in the rivers; and exotic and endangered species have been hunted and killed. Moreover, Tibet has become a major platform for China's nuclear weapons; a highly disturbing irony given that Tibetans, as mentioned earlier, do not believe in killing and prefer to solve problems through nonviolence.

The daily life of Tibetans has changed drastically as well. They lack even the most basic human rights—the ability to speak freely, congregate in large groups, read what they wish, listen to particular radio and television broadcasts, and practice various rituals and behaviors unique to their culture. In schools, Chinese is the main language, and Tibetan history and culture is rarely taught. Furthermore, there is no religious freedom in Tibet. All monasteries are under the careful eye of China's police or the PLA. In fact, in the larger cities, there are surveillance cameras everywhere. It is illegal for Tibetans to own or display a picture of His Holiness The Dalai Lama. If they are caught, they face unspecified time in prison. Certain religious practices, especially those connected to His Holiness, are forbidden. Thus, Tibetans are not permitted to recite long life prayers for His Holiness or to celebrate His Holiness's birthday either in private or in public places.

Forced sterilization of women is a common practice in Tibet, as is forced abortion and unspeakable forms of torture (e.g., raping women and nuns with electric cattle prods, hanging people over fire for hours, ordering individuals to kneel in broken glass, pouring ice cold water over people during the height of winter). These strategies are used to control the Tibetan population in Tibet. At the same time, China has been involved in a huge transfer of Chinese individuals to Tibet. Given that China has not allowed any fact-finding missions to Tibet by reputable organizations (e.g., United Nations, Human Rights Watch), it is difficult to accurately estimate the size of the population in Tibet. In the larger cities, however, the Tibetan exile government has claimed that the Chinese population outnumbers the Tibetan population in some instances by a 2 to 1 margin. The effect of this population distribution has been devastating for the Tibetans in terms of, for example, not being able to protect their cultural values, beliefs, and behaviors. Many young and middle-aged Tibetans living in the major cities have adopted Chinese habits, values, and behaviors.

The top government and business leaders in Tibet are Chinese. As a result, Tibetans lack power, the ability to make important decisions, and financial wealth. Tibetans employed by the PRC government in Tibet are required each week to attend an "education" session where they publicly denounce His Holiness The Dalai Lama and the Tibetan exile government, and acknowledge that Tibet has always been a part of China. To further humiliate and control Tibetans, the PRC has imported prostitution, gambling, karaoke bars, alcohol, and drugs to Tibet. This action has had a devastating effect on the culture, particularly for younger Tibetans.

Obviously, China has engaged in a systematic effort to control and reshape Tibet. It is hard to understand how their strategies and policies are "liberating" Tibetans. In fact, the PRC's treatment of Tibet and Tibetans can be considered cultural genocide.

To the outside observer, it appears that Tibetans in Tibet have conformed to China's rules, regulations, and norms. This is not surprising, because Tibetans inside Tibet are extremely limited in their ability to change the current political structure. They are outnumbered and without weapons, and they lack the financial resources and infrastructure to make a significant impact on their brutal oppressor. On the inside, however, Tibetans still have a deep feeling, admiration, and respect for His Holiness The Dalai Lama, whom they continue to perceive as their spiritual and political leader. Privately, Tibetans also have a strong appreciation for their unique culture, a clear understanding they are not Chinese, and a dogmatic belief that Tibet belongs to Tibetans. Perhaps because of their deep religious beliefs and the clarity of what is in their hearts, most Tibetans are able to effectively manage and display an outside face and hide their inside face. They have relied on those of us in the exile world to speak the truth (Satya) about the atrocities in Tibet and to engage in actions to secure independence (rangzen) for their country.

Activism and Tibet

Until the early 1990s, however, few laypeople, organizations, diplomats, and governments were knowledgeable about Tibet and/or took action to address the Tibet-China conflict. For instance, I recall some reactions I heard when displaying a "Free Tibet" banner while hosting an informational table for Tibet at a Lollapalooza Music Festival in 1994 headlined by the Beastie Boys. A number of concert goers asked me, "Can I have my free 'Tibb bit' please?" "Who is this 'Free Tibet' you are talking about?" "How do I get my 'Free Tie Bet'?" and "Free 'To bet' on what?" Interestingly, my experience was not unique, as other Tibet activists reported similar situations during this time period.

Since the mid-1990s, there has been a steady rise in awareness concerning Tibet and action on behalf of Tibet. Many more people now recognize the word Tibet, can pronounce it, understand that Tibet is a country, and are engaged in the struggle to resolve the conflict between Tibet and China. There is no doubt this substantial increase in worldwide attention regarding Tibet has resulted, for the most part, because of the extensive travels of His Holiness The Dalai Lama and His Holiness's engaging, warm, compassionate, kind, sincere, respectful, intelligent, and altruistic personality and demeanor.

Interest in Tibet has also resulted from greater activity among numerous governments and nongovernmental organizations (NGOs) worldwide that have implemented policies and strategies, for example, to help solve the Tibet-China conflict, secure the release of Tibetan political prisoners, eliminate human rights abuses, and prevent the destruction of the environment on the Tibetan plateau. Furthermore, hundreds of Tibet support groups (TSGs) have been formed composed of thousands of supporters committed to achieving similar objectives to those just mentioned. Hundreds of Tibetan associations (TAs) made up of exiled Tibetans are pursuing these objectives as well. It should also be noted that almost all of these TSGs and TAs are invested in nonviolent strategies to accomplish their goals. This is not surprising, because His Holiness The Dalai Lama has strongly advocated employing nonviolence to resolve the Tibet-China conflict, and these organizations are greatly influenced by His Holiness's philosophy, strategy, and recommendations, which are grounded in Gandhian and Buddhist principles and actions (His Holiness The Dalai Lama, 1999). In part, His Holiness contends that violence might bring about a temporary solution to the Tibet-China conflict, or any conflict for that matter, but ultimately such violence would beget more violence, leading to heightened animosity and struggles between Tibet and China. Therefore, although it may take longer to resolve the issues between Tibet and China by relying on nonviolent strategies (Ahimsa), His Holiness believes that the eventual solution would be permanent and less destructive to the Tibetans, Chinese, other sentient beings, and the environment.

The Structure of ITIM

One TSG that has closely adhered to His Holiness's and Gandhi's nonviolent approach is the International Tibet Independence Movement (ITIM). As stated earlier in this chapter, ITIM was co-founded by His Holiness The Dalai Lama's oldest brother, Taktser Rinpoche, and Lawrence H. Gerstein on March 18, 1995, to secure Tibet's independence using nonviolent methods. ITIM has evolved as a grassroots, not-for-profit 501(c)3 organization headquartered in Fishers, Indiana. Seven individuals from different parts of the United States, including one Tibetan, serve on ITIM's Board of Directors. For the past 8 years, I have served as the president of ITIM. Each month, the Board meets via a free telephone conference call scheduled through www.freeconference.com. During these 90-minute meetings, the Board discusses and establishes policies, strategies, and resources for various campaigns and activities, and examines and makes decisions about the infrastructure of the organization. Board members also share progress reports concerning their responsibilities and accomplishments. All Board members are expected to lead working committees (four standing and four ad hoc) designed to establish and implement different campaigns and activities, and fulfill the infrastructure needs of the organization. A cadre of local volunteers also serves on these committees and carries major responsibility for achieving the mission. Efforts to achieve ITIM's mission as well as other information is also communicated through a quarterly newsletter, *Rangzen Voice,* that can be found online (www.rangzen.org).

Along with the Board of Directors, there is also an ITIM Advisory Board. This Board is composed of 11 individuals (including six Tibetans and one Taiwanese). Advisory Board members live in the United States, India, Taiwan, and Australia. Their role is to provide critical feedback and input regarding ITIM's objectives, policies, campaigns, and activities. Given their diverse backgrounds and locations, Advisory Board members play a unique role in the operations and aspirations of the organization. This Advisory Board carries out its responsibilities via e-mail and, on occasion, telephone.

Over the years, ITIM has established a strong base of international support among laypeople, TSGs, TAs, and the Tibetan government in exile located in Dharamsala, India. Currently, ITIM has approximately 20,000+ worldwide supporters. As evidence of this support, the ITIM Web site (www.rangzen.org) averaged more than 131,000 hits per month for the year 2004.

Given the extensive nature of ITIM's support, it is noteworthy that, except for very brief periods of time, ITIM has always been a completely volunteer organization. Local volunteers and ITIM Board members meet for 2 hours in person every 2 weeks. These meetings are designed to strategize and evaluate campaigns and activities, assign and review roles and responsibilities, and accomplish concrete tasks. Although an agenda is developed prior to each biweekly meeting, urgent issues and campaigns sometimes take precedence, or participants introduce topics that require attention. Every attempt is made to also enjoy each other during the course of the meeting, have fun when possible, meet the various needs of the participants, establish a good fit between the participants' skills and interests and the identified tasks or responsibilities, and accomplish the stated goals (Ellis, 2002; Little, 1999). Furthermore, an effort is made to welcome new volunteers, help them feel connected to the long-standing members of the group, ascertain their motivation for attending, educate them about ITIM and its activities, and explore their interest and willingness to serve on various ITIM working committees (Clary, Snyder, & Ridge, 1992; Clary et al., 1998; Ellis, 2002; Little, 1999).

As the leader of the monthly ITIM Board meeting and the biweekly volunteer meeting, in part I facilitate the discussions, keep the group focused on task, reinforce cooperation between those in attendance, promote creative problem solving, strive to strengthen cohesion in the group, empower participants' involvement, attempt to balance the needs of the participants with the objectives of the organization, honor the cultural differences between the participants, and make every effort to provide the participants with a rewarding experience. This requires an understanding of group behavior and dynamics (Corey & Corey, 2002; Forsyth, 1999; Yalom, 1995), organizational behavior (Gerstein & Shullman, 1992), and grassroots organizations (Adams, 1991; Robertson & Lewallen, 1975); an appreciation for the role and needs of volunteers (Ellis, 2002; Little, 1999; McCurley & Vineyard, 1998); and knowledge about telecommuting (Baruch, 2000; Gills, 2003; Manoochehri & Pinkerton, 2003; Potkin, 1999; Potter, 2003) and cultural behaviors, values, and issues. Not all counseling psychologists have the skills to effectively lead such a diverse group of individuals. One must be able to demonstrate, for example, sophisticated group process skills; the ability to encourage, shape, and reward highly specialized skills among the participants; and the skills to reinforce collaboration among a culturally diverse group of volunteers. Obviously, facilitating this type of group is quite different from leading a traditional counseling group. Therefore, it is critical that one adhere to the APA ethical principles, particularly those related to doing no harm, scope of practice, competence, and engaging in group and consultation activities.

Along with leading the meetings and serving on some committees, I also coordinate e-mail correspondence, volunteers, media campaigns, public relations, fund raising, educational resources and programs, ongoing and periodic major human rights campaigns, and high-visibility advocacy events. Some of these will be discussed in detail later in the chapter. One task that I perform, however, will be mentioned briefly now.

Since the inception of ITIM, I have been actively engaged in an effort to network and coordinate with other groups that are also oppressed by the PRC. As stated earlier, Tibet was not the only country invaded by the PLA beginning in 1949. Southern Mongolia and East Turkestan were also captured. Like Tibet, Mao argued that these countries were historically part of China. Thus, it was Mao's intention to "reunite the motherland" when he ordered the illegal occupation of all these countries. The new flag of China introduced by Mao reflected this intention. Each of the five stars is considered significant. One star stands for the Han people; one star for Tibet; and one star each for Southern Mongolia, East Turkestan, and Manchuria. The remaining task for the PRC to fulfill Mao's motherland policy is integrating Taiwan into mainland China.

Given the situation just outlined, I have developed collaborative relationships with the leaders of various organizations committed to securing independence for each of the countries mentioned above, along with groups advocating for democracy in China. This has entailed drawing from the social psychological research on intergroup cooperation such as the Realistic Group Conflict Theory (Sherif, 1966) and the Contact Hypothesis (Allport, 1954; Pettigrew, 1998) and then formulating and implementing mutually acceptable policies and strategies to achieve the desired goals. Face-to-face meetings, telephone conversations, and e-mail correspondence have made it possible to establish and maintain collaboration among the leaders. To be an effective contributor to this team of high-profile activists, it is essential to demonstrate culturally appropriate behaviors and knowledge of the history of each country's background and struggle.

The numerous committed, dedicated, and talented volunteers and Board members of ITIM have helped the organization achieve many of its goals. They have been tireless in their effort to return Tibet to the Tibetans. Each joined the organization for his or her own particular reason. Some have been motivated, for example, by their interest in Buddhism, social justice, and/or human rights; their exposure to His Holiness The Dalai Lama or Taktser Rinpoche; their contact with Tibetan monks, Tibetan nuns, Tibetan laypersons, or Tibet supporters; or their attendance at a Tibet function. Regardless of their reason, most have volunteered countless hours on behalf of the Tibetan people and the cause of regaining Tibet. Although there has been a degree of turnover among the ITIM volunteers and Board members, the working group of volunteers has remained rather stable, and the composition of the Board has changed very little over time. More important, the overwhelming majority of volunteers who have chosen to be less involved in the day-to-day activities of ITIM have continued to keep abreast of the Tibet situation and have contributed in less active ways (e.g., sending e-mails on behalf of political prisoners, educating others) to the movement.

ITIM Projects and Campaigns

Since the inception of ITIM in 1995, the organization has implemented many large-scale, international projects and campaigns, including an education and employment service known as Rangzen House to assist Tibetans who wish to improve their lifestyles. One major signature campaign of ITIM was designed to free a teenager who was first abducted in Tibet by the PRC when He was 6 years old. In 1995, His Holiness The Dalai Lama recognized Gendun Choekyi Nyima as The Panchen Lama. As soon as this happened, the PRC kidnapped the boy, His family, and some senior monks close to this spiritual leader. Ever since, no one has been able to see or talk to these individuals, including officials of the United Nations, Amnesty International, Human Rights Watch, and the U.S. State Department. For Tibetan Buddhists, The Panchen Lama is the second most important spiritual leader to The Dalai Lama, and He is responsible for leading the search to find the reincarnation of the next Dalai Lama. Since His capture, ITIM has coordinated worldwide postcard and monthly e-mail campaigns to various PRC leaders and NGOs to either demand His release or request assistance with His case.

Along with its ongoing Panchen Lama campaign, ITIM is well known for its "Marches for Tibet's Independence." Since 1995, ITIM has coordinated 11 walks and bicycle rides for Tibet's independence covering approximately 3,190 miles (5,132.7 kilometers) in 327 days. I have served as the overall coordinator of each of these projects with the assistance of an ITIM Board subcommittee. These walks and rides have occurred on the East and West Coasts of North America, in the Midwest, and across two Canadian borders. The longest walk happened in 1997 and began at the PRC Embassy in Toronto and ended at the United Nations in Manhattan, New York. This walk took 90 days over a distance of about 650 miles (1,045.8 kilometers). Twelve people, including Taktser Rinpoche, who was 75 years old, and Palden Gyatso (Tibetan monk and former political prisoner), who was in his mid-60s, served as core participants of this grueling walk through the mountains of upstate New York. This walk happened during the height of the winter, and on many days, the walkers were knee deep in snow. I recall Rinpoche commenting on these conditions when asked why He wanted to walk in the middle of winter, especially from Toronto, "This is more like Tibet! Our suffering is nothing like what they are experiencing in Tibet. This is easy compared to what they go through every day. We should experience some pain. We have it good in exile. This is not supposed to be some vacation."

Despite the cold weather and snow, along the way numerous others joined the walk for a few hours, a day, or a weekend. Upon reaching Manhattan via the George Washington Bridge, more than 1,000 Tibetans and supporters walked the final miles to the United Nations, stopping traffic in the busy streets and educating motorists and pedestrians along the way. Like all of ITIM's other walks and bike rides since 1997, one of its most important objectives was achieved—being interviewed on the different radio services (e.g., Radio Free Asia, Voice of America, Voice of Tibet) broadcast inside of Tibet and heard by those willing to risk their lives hearing the news. It is clear that Tibetans in Tibet who heard the participants interviewed or learned of these interviews were greatly inspired by the simple act of walking or riding a bike.

Another important objective for these projects is educating the public through the local media and by simply walking in a community. Walking 10 to 18 miles each day makes it possible to be seen on numerous occasions by many passing motorists. All of the walkers carry a Tibetan flag, U.S. flag, Canadian flag (when in Canada), or sign with a distinct message. To observe the proper protocol in the United States, an attempt is made to have the lead walker carry the U.S. flag. Deciding on a message and how to phrase it to maximize on its receptivity is challenging. Based on the Elaboration Likelihood Model (ELM) (Petty & Cacioppo, 1981, 1986), ITIM has purposely kept each message understandable and simple (e.g., Free Tibet, China Out of Tibet), and focused on an action (e.g., Boycott China's Goods, Honk for Tibet) or a specific strategy, such as connecting with a local population. For example, during a 3-day, 55-mile walk in Florida following the barrage of hurricanes in September 2004, one of the Tibetans carried a sign that read, "Tibetans Love Florida." While on an 11-day, 200+-mile walk from Indianapolis to Chicago in December 2004, a participant held a sign that stated, "Hoosiers for Tibet." One needs to take into consideration the characteristics of the potential audience (e.g., cognitive complexity, education, socioeconomic status); their knowledge and attitudes about the topic (e.g., Tibet); their motivation; and their ability to receive, process, and evaluate the message when deciding on the text (Petty & Cacioppo, 1981, 1986).

Regardless of the message, careful attention must be paid to the color and size of the text, the background color and size of the sign, and the placement and inclusion of any images. Understanding the proper creative contrast and balance between the text, background, and any images is critical. As motorists often are traveling at more than 40 miles per hour, it is essential that each message is crisp, bright, and easily read. The walkers are always greatly inspired each time a motorist, especially a truck driver with his or her loud horn, responds positively to the 20- by 24-inch "Honk for Tibet" sign where the message is in large white letters and the background is a bright red.

Creating an effective sign does not ensure that the message will be received. A very challenging aspect of these walks is to make certain participants maintain enough distance (about 15 feet is ideal) between each other so that a motorist has the opportunity to even see a sign if he or she is able or interested. Often, participants become preoccupied socializing with each other while walking. When this happens, two, three, or more participants group together and their signs become unrecognizable by the passing motorists. More important, while socializing, the participants can become less mindful of the motorists and endanger themselves and the passing vehicles. The onsite walk coordinator must remind participants to spread out and, at the same time, allow them opportunities to build trust, closeness, and support, especially because most walkers are unfamiliar with each other prior to commencing the event. For some participants, they experience their time on the route as a walking meditation.

Another way that the walkers or bike riders attempt to educate the public is through presentations at local schools (e.g., middle and secondary); universities; churches; Buddhist centers; and wellness facilities (e.g., yoga institutes, holistic health centers). Ideally, these presentations are arranged prior to beginning a walk or ride by identifying potential sites along the route. Presentations typically last for 90 minutes, with sufficient time allotted for questions and in-depth discussion. Again, relying on the ELM, an understanding of the local culture, and the audience's knowledge about Tibet, a presentation might include showing a brief video about the persecution of Tibetan nuns, playing a longer video about the missing Panchen Lama, offering a lecture by the walkers or riders on various aspects of the Tibet situation, hosting a panel discussion composed of local leaders and the participants, or sharing a Buddhist teaching or performance. An example might be informative at this point.

While bike riding for Tibet through the mountains of Pennsylvania in April 2004, the riders stopped to make presentations at various high schools, universities, and churches. When planning this bike ride, it became apparent that many individuals along the route were devastated by the closing of manufacturing companies and the outsourcing of jobs. Furthermore, it was discovered that the route would take the riders right near the crash site of Flight 93 in Shanksville on September 11, 2001. Realizing the depressed economic condition of the residents in this rural area of Pennsylvania and the hardship experienced by the families living in Shanksville, ITIM decided to emphasize during all presentations the importance of "Buying American," and "Boycotting China's Goods." The riders also genuinely expressed their compassion and remorse to those in attendance. Additionally, the riders organized an interdenominational prayer service with local residents and religious leaders at the crash site, and they offered traditional Tibetan objects as a way to show respect for the victims of Flight 93.

One other way that the walkers or riders promote their message is by staying in local churches, homes, or Buddhist centers, where they have many formal and informal opportunities to communicate with the congregants, staff, local residents, and neighborhood businesspeople. Over the years, the Unitarian Church has been the most receptive to housing the walkers or riders. Methodist, Catholic, and Presbyterian churches as well as the Society of Friends have also welcomed them. Again, an attempt is made to prearrange lodging before a walk or ride begins. It is very humbling and encouraging to realize that churches all around North America have been willing to open up their doors so that 6 to 30 strangers can sleep on their floor, cook meals, use their facilities, and disturb the daily rituals of the institution for up to 4 days. This is even more impressive when one recognizes that the mission of the walk or bike ride is often totally unrelated to the mission of the particular church.

One final way that the message of a walk or bike ride is publicized is through ITIM's Web site. Each day, highlights of the walk or ride and revealing images are posted to the site. Prior to and during such a project, various listservs are notified that these daily updates will be posted. In this way, thousands of people around the world can "participate" in the walk or bike ride as it progresses. As mentioned earlier, the ITIM Web site averaged 131,000 hits per month in 2004. Contrast this with the number of Web site hits (269,000+) during April 2004 when ITIM coordinated a 15-day, 600+-mile "Bike Ride for Tibet's Independence" from Washington, DC, to Toronto, and the number of hits (210,000+) during December 2004 when an 11-day, 200+-mile march from Indianapolis to Chicago took place. It is evident from examining these numbers that such events have a widespread impact. On occasion, ITIM has even received e-mails from Tibetans inside of Tibet indicating they are following the walk or bike ride and are inspired by the effort. This is highly significant, because the PRC monitors all e-mails, and the individual sending the e-mail can be imprisoned for his or her action. Needless to say, ITIM has also received hate and threatening e-mails from people in China during various walks and bike rides. Furthermore, there is concrete evidence that the U.S. government and military keep track of such projects as well, for instance, by visiting the ITIM Web site.

Planning, organizing, and implementing a march or bike ride for Tibet is an enormous undertaking that can be quite expensive. It requires the energy, commitment, time, and talent of many local and site-specific volunteers operating as a functional team. A core group of volunteers located in Indiana arrange housing and presentations, connect with the media, obtain approval from law enforcement in the targeted area, and establish the logistics (e.g., map the path; identify medical facilities, restaurants, shopping centers, landmarks, etc.) of the route. A group of volunteers along the route must be recruited as well to assist with many of the same tasks just mentioned. Additionally, these persons help network the walkers or riders with local organizations that share a common interest in social causes. Overall, these key individuals serve as hosts or guides in their communities, and their efforts greatly contribute to the overall success of a project.

Another person who has a major role in the success of such projects is the onsite coordinator. This person, in part, coordinates communications (e.g., assigns tasks to participants; interacts with local supporters, support groups, media, law enforcement, and the public; facilitates nightly briefings; supports and encourages the participants), finances (e.g., manages collection and distribution of funds, maintains records), and logistics (e.g., manages the schedule, housing, presentations), and also monitors the health and safety of the participants. He or she is also responsible for driving the support vehicle that accompanies the participants along the entire route.

Each walker or rider has responsibilities as well. For example, participants prepare food, maintain the equipment and vehicle, clean the lodging facility, and staff the merchandise and informational table. To be selected as a core walker or rider, an individual must be physically healthy, committed to independence for Tibet, willing to pursue truth without physical violence (Satyagraha), motivated to assist with tasks, able to function on a team, patient, tolerant, and willing to "live on the road" with limited resources for an extended period of time! The self-suffering (Tapasya) for the cause of Tibet pales in comparison to the impact of the project. Beyond educating people about Tibet, the participants often experience the deep personal satisfaction of serving on a team where everyone, for 24 hours a day, is focused on the same goals. Indeed, this is a rare opportunity for the participants to channel all of their energy on a common, honorable mission.

Challenges of ITIM and the Tibet Movement

Like most not-for-profit organizations, ITIM has faced challenges. It is difficult to recruit enough talented volunteers, motivate such persons to remain actively involved in the organization, and maintain cohesiveness in the working group when there is turnover among the members (McCurley & Vineyard, 1998). Having a full-time, paid director and other staff members would most probably resolve some of these problems. A full-time director would also be helpful with capacity building; providing stability for the organization; and coordinating ongoing outreach, networking, fund raising, and campaign development and implementation. Interestingly, most ITIM volunteers possess few skills securing funds and have expressed limited willingness to pursue this task. Consequently, ITIM has had difficulty raising funds on an ongoing basis. This has made it challenging to fully support the infrastructure of the organization and to feel secure in long-term planning. However, ITIM has been extremely successful obtaining extensive financial support for its major projects (e.g., walks).

Long-distance communication between the Board members is also a challenge at times (Manoochehri & Pinkerton, 2003; Potkin, 1999), as is managing an equitable distribution of the roles and responsibilities of these individuals. Each Board member balances ITIM tasks, activism on behalf of Tibet, a full-time job, and family responsibilities. All the Board members, however, strive to respect the ebb and flow of one another's investment and ability to effectively manage his or her ITIM workload.

There are also many challenges in the entire Free Tibet movement. With more than a thousand TSGs and TAs worldwide, communication and decision making can be quite challenging. Even with the Internet, it is often difficult to communicate in a timely and meaningful fashion (Manoochehri & Pinkerton, 2003; Potkin, 1999). Language and cultural differences complicate this process even further. TSGs also vary greatly in their missions, resources, and ability to accomplish various objectives. When you add to these challenges the fact that not one country has openly stated that Tibet is illegally occupied by China, it becomes apparent that there are many forces blocking a solution to the Tibet-China conflict. Even India, which has probably the most to gain from Tibet once again becoming a peaceful nation, has succumbed to the influence and demands of China. India's "sleeping elephant" must awaken and generate the will and strategies to peacefully tame China's "dragon," so the Tibetan "snow lion" can rightfully return to its historic position of authority in Tibet.

One reality about China's strength and control of Tibet cannot be stressed enough. China's communist government has no respect for human rights, and it restricts the freedom of all its people. Therefore, the Tibet movement takes issue with the PRC government and not the average citizen of China. The movement's effort is directed at affecting the PRC government and, at the same time, helping the Chinese people to secure democracy. This means, in part, dialoguing with mainland Chinese individuals whenever possible, even in the United States, and discussing with them the principles and benefits of democracy and the history and current situation in Tibet from both their perspective and that of the Tibet movement. Increased contact between such individuals can change attitudes. Learning each other's perspective may result in reevaluating attitudes toward the other group and bring about attitude change (Allport, 1954; Pettigrew, 1998). Establishing and maintaining dialogue is a very challenging task, but one that is essential if the Chinese and Tibetans are to live peacefully as neighbors in the future. Documents, Web sites, newspapers, and visual materials have been prepared in the Chinese language to facilitate achieving this goal, and forums have been held where Chinese and Tibetan individuals can meet and share their views and aspirations.

Obviously, China is a formidable opponent that has a great deal of leverage around the globe. With more than 1.3 billion people, it represents the largest potential marketplace in the world. To penetrate this marketplace, many companies and countries are constantly jockeying for trading rights with China. Furthermore, China exports numerous products that almost always are less expensive than what can be purchased in other countries. As an exercise, investigate where your shoes; telephone; toaster; clothing; and, if you are from the United States, your American flag are manufactured. You will be surprised to discover that almost everything you own and purchase was made in China, and in some cases, even the apple juice you drink!

Currently, China can be considered an economic superpower. In the not-so-distant future, it will also become a military superpower as it reinvests its economic profits in the further development of military technology and hardware. Clearly, China's strength and philosophy of governance represents one of the greatest challenges faced by the Tibet movement. The strong belief in the movement, however, is that over time, nonviolence will succeed in returning Tibet to the Tibetans and freeing the Chinese citizens of the oppressive PRC regime.

Counseling Psychology and Nonviolent Activism: Future Directions

As must be apparent from this chapter, counseling psychologists can play a unique role in helping to solve various conflicts around the world through nonviolence (Gerstein & Moeschberger, 2003; Kirkpatrick, Raney, Shankar, & Gerstein, 2004; Norsworthy & Gerstein, 2003a, 2003b). Our profession's historic emphasis on a developmental perspective, social justice, multiculturalism, group work, community interventions, prevention, and consultation make it uniquely suited to address systemic injustices, inequality, and the effects of violence. Obviously, societal inequalities and injustices often arise from conditions in the environment. As counseling psychologists have learned more about the environment, they have displayed a renewed appreciation for the importance of social justice activities guided by developmental, multicultural, group dynamic, and systemic principles and strategies (Blustein, McWhirter, & Perry, 2005; Fouad et al., 2004; Goodman et al., 2004; Kiselica, 2004; Speight & Vera, 2004; Vera & Speight, 2003).

For counseling psychology, social justice can be conceived as expanding professional activities beyond individual counseling to include being active in the community through social advocacy or community interventions (Vera & Speight, 2003). This perspective fits quite well with the framework of peace psychology. For instance, counseling psychology's strong emphasis on multiculturalism fits with the aims of peace psychology as it seeks to address issues of diversity in all its forms: ethnic, racial, religious, physical makeup, and sexual orientation. In fact, the emergence of societal violence is often deeply rooted in multicultural concerns (Willis, 2004). Of late, counseling psychology has placed greater importance in terms of theory, practice, research, and training on targeting multicultural issues at the societal level (Vera & Speight, 2003).

As can be seen from this chapter, counseling psychology's emphasis on group work, community interventions, and consultation can also be valuable when engaged in peacebuilding activities. From a focus on lessening tension and conflict at an individual or small group level, it is logical to see how the direction of counseling psychology could be modified to integrate research, theory, and practice to address a host of conflicts expressed in the broader society. Carl Rogers exemplified this shift in direction as he consulted with various international groups, holding forums and therapeutic, community-based group sessions to promote peace and conflict reduction in such places as South Africa during the 1980s (Whiteley, 1987).

Consistent with the work of Rogers, currently, there is a strong movement to internationalize the field of counseling psychology (Douce, 2004; Gerstein & Moeschberger, 2003; Gerstein & Ægisdóttir, 2004, Gerstein & Ægisdóttir, 2005a, 2005b, 2005c; Heppner, 2004; Leong & Blustein, 2000; Leong & Ponterotto, 2003; Leung, 2003; Norsworthy & Gerstein, 2003b; Pedersen & Leong, 1997; Ægisdóttir & Gerstein, 2005). Our profession is looking to see what role it will play in the increasingly interconnected global community (McWhirter, 1988). As violence and social injustice continue to plague the world, it is hoped that greater interest in promoting the cause of peace will challenge our profession to increase its awareness, understanding, and skills to engage in efforts to build and maintain communities of peace, thereby reducing or preventing various forms of violence. Some recommendations to accomplish this objective will now be discussed briefly.

Practice

Unfortunately, there are many incidences of structural (e.g., militarism, human rights abuses, globalism) and direct (e.g., war, genocide, weapons of mass destruction) forms of violence around the world. Counseling psychologists can help to alleviate or prevent these types of violence by serving, for example, as group leaders; policymakers; and program planners, implementers, trainers, and evaluators. This work, however, must be pursued on interdisciplinary teams composed of a diverse group of "local" professionals and laypersons. Through such collaboration, it becomes possible to integrate culturally sensitive, effective, and indigenous theories and strategies to establish and maintain peaceful solutions designed to reduce or prevent the occurrence of violence.

Along with the roles just mentioned, counseling psychologists can seek opportunities to become involved with different organizations dedicated to building and maintaining communities of peace. Organizations such as the United Nations, Amnesty International, Human Rights Watch, and Refugees International employ psychologists to assist with their various policies and programs. In fact, APA has a formal relationship with the United Nations. Many other not-for-profit groups around the world hire psychologists to address the antecedents and consequences of violence. Furthermore, most organizations offer extern and intern experiences to psychology graduate students.

Research

There are an infinite number of research studies on violence and nonviolence that warrant our attention. For instance, there is a need to conduct further research on values theory and the Gandhian model of nonviolence discussed much earlier in this chapter. The relationship between values, personality characteristics, and nonviolence could be explored in greater depth, as could the effectiveness of employing Gandhian principles (e.g., Ahimsa, Satyagraha) to resolve conflict.

Additionally, many of the theories on nonviolence focus on individual variables (e.g., values). Therefore, there is a great need to construct and test theories that address macro issues. That is, the influence of environmental, cultural, and economic factors on the presence of violence and nonviolence and the successful implementation of peaceful solutions. It would be ideal to rely on an interdisciplinary framework (e.g., psychology, anthropology, political science, economics, environmental architecture) when constructing and employing such theories.

There is also a need to investigate the effects of war and cultural genocide on individual behavior. The incidence and type of trauma experienced by persons subjected to these situations could be examined, as could their coping mechanisms. One current study in progress, for example, is looking at the effects of China's illegal occupation of Tibet on Tibetan women's adjustment to living in exile (Raney, 2005).

There are other research questions related to the Tibet movement that counseling psychologists could pursue. Here are a few. First, do walks/bike rides for Tibet increase knowledge about Tibet, a willingness to join the movement, and a boycott of China's products? Next, can mainland Chinese individuals' attitudes be changed through exposure to messages based on the ELM? And third, what are the differential effects of various strategies designed to increase understanding between Tibetans, Chinese, East Turkestanians, Mongolians, and Taiwanese?

Training

To conduct the research just briefly outlined and to engage in the various professional roles highlighted earlier requires counseling psychology students and professionals to not only master some of the core knowledge and skills traditionally found in our curriculum (e.g., group and multicultural counseling), but also to pursue other learning experiences. Courses in applied and basic social, organizational, and community psychology would be helpful, as would classes in peace studies, consultation, anthropology, political science, economics, and qualitative methodology. Field experiences are essential. Extern and intern placements or employment positions in NGOs and/or government agencies worldwide, for instance, would be ideal. Opportunities to integrate coursework and field work are also important because such a curriculum or training experience requires an ability to process and think clearly and carefully across different disciplines. Achieving such an integration is a complex task involving a great deal of time and motivation, and exposure to effective role models and mentors.

Conclusion

There is little doubt that striving to develop and foster communities of peace represents an exciting opportunity for counseling psychologists. This type of work is highly important and essential as different forms of violence are rampant throughout the world. There is an urgent need for more social architects to bring about peaceful solutions to various conflicts between people, cultures, and countries. Such architects are also required to help reinforce current nonviolent strategies employed to resolve conflicts.

Historically, counseling psychologists focused on helping individuals, couples, families, and small groups to find inner peace. Of late, as discussed in this chapter, a number of counseling psychologists have expanded their emphasis to establish and maintain peace between much larger groups of individuals. This perspective fits well with our profession's commitment to prevention, improving the quality of life, and serving the basic needs of a diverse multicultural, international population.

If a greater number of counseling psychologists pursue such work, the incidence of systemic direct and structural violence around the world will decrease. As a result, we will help protect, preserve, and enhance the citizens and environment of the planet. Contributing to the accomplishment of this outcome is a daunting challenge. Counseling psychologists possess the philosophical framework and many of the fundamental skills to meet this challenge successfully. What remains to be seen is whether there are enough of us willing and able to demonstrate the passion and vision to confront peacefully the worldwide atrocities of violence afflicting communities, cultures, and nations. To promote and help create worldwide peace requires great sacrifice and potential risk. We are convinced that counseling psychologists are primed to grasp this opportunity. Therefore, in the years ahead, we fully expect counseling psychologists to serve as members of interdisciplinary teams of social architects committed to building and maintaining peaceful communities, cultures, and nations.

References

Adams, T. (1991). *Grass roots: How ordinary people are changing America.* New York: Carol.

Ægisdóttir, S., & Gerstein, L. H. (2005). Reaching out: Mental health delivery outside the box. *Journal of Mental Health Counseling, 27,* 221–224.

Allport, G. W. (1954). *The nature of prejudice.* Cambridge, MA: Addison-Wesley.

Baruch, Y. (2000). Teleworking: Benefits and pitfalls as perceived by professionals and managers. *New Technology, Work and Employment, 15*(1), 34–60.

Blustein, D. L., McWhirter, E. H., & Perry, J. C. (2005). An emancipatory communitarian approach to vocational development theory, research, and practice. *The Counseling Psychologist, 33,* 141–179.

Bondurant, J. V. (1965). *Conquest of violence: The Gandhi philosophy of conflict.* Berkeley: University of California Press.

Bonta, B. (1993). *Peaceful peoples: An annotated bibliography.* Metuchen, NJ: Scarecrow Press.

Boulding, E. (2000). *Cultures of peace: The hidden side of history.* Syracuse, NY: Syracuse University Press.

Christie, D. J., Wagner, R. V., & Du Nann Winter, D. (2001). *Peace, conflict, and violence: Peace psychology for the 21st century.* Upper Saddle River, NJ: Prentice Hall.

Clary, E. G., Snyder, M., & Ridge, R. (1992). Volunteers' motivations: A functional strategy for the recruitment, placement, and retention of volunteers. *Nonprofit Management and Leadership, 2,* 333–350.

Clary, E. G., Snyder, M., Ridge, R. D., Copeland, J., Stukas, A. A., Haugen, J., & Miene, P. (1998). Understanding and assessing the motivations of volunteers: A functional approach. *Journal of Personality and Social Psychology, 74,* 1516–1530.

Corey, M. S., & Corey, G. (2002). *Groups: Process and practice* (6th ed.). Pacific Grove, CA: Brooks/Cole.

da Silva, A. (2001). Through nonviolence to truth: Gandhi's vision of reconciliation. In R. G. Helmick & R. L. Petersen (Eds.), *Forgiveness and reconciliation: Religion, public policy, & conflict transformation* (pp. 295–317). Philadelphia, PA: Templeton Foundation Press.

Douce, L. A. (2004). 2003 presidential address: Globalization of counseling psychology. *The Counseling Psychologist, 32,* 142–152.

Elliott, G. C. (1980). Components of pacifism. *Journal of Conflict Resolution, 24,* 27–54.

Ellis, S. J. (2002). *The volunteer recruitment book (and membership development).* Philadelphia: Energize.

Erikson, E. H. (1969). *Gandhi's truth on the origins of militant nonviolence.* New York: Norton.

Forsyth, D. R. (1999). *Group dynamics* (3rd ed.). Pacific Grove, CA: Brooks/Cole.

Fouad, N. A., McPherson, R. H., Gerstein, L., Blustein, D. L., Elman, N., Helledy, K. I., & Metz, A. J. (2004). Houston, 2001: Context and legacy. *The Counseling Psychologist, 32,* 15–77.

Gandhi, M. (1951). *Selected writings.* London: Faber and Faber.

Gandhi, M. K. (1983). *The story of my experiments with truth.* New York: Dover.

Gerstein, L. H., & Ægisdóttir, S. (2004). *Training international social change agents: Transcending the North American box.* Symposium presented at the 21st Annual Teachers College Winter Roundtable on Cultural Psychology and Education: Strategies for Building Cultural Competence in Psychology and Education, Columbia University, New York.

Gerstein, L. H., & Ægisdóttir, S. (Eds.). (2005a). Counseling around the world [Special issue]. *Journal of Mental Health Counseling, 27,* 95–184.

Gerstein, L. H., & Ægisdóttir, S. (Eds.). (2005b). Counseling outside of the United States: Looking in and reaching out [Special section]. *Journal of Mental Health Counseling, 27,* 221–281.

Gerstein, L. H., & Ægisdóttir, S. (2005c). A trip around the world: A counseling travelogue! *Journal of Mental Health Counseling, 27,* 95–103.

Gerstein, L. H., & Moeschberger, S. (2003). Building cultures of peace: An urgent task for counseling professionals. *Journal of Counseling & Development, 81,* 115–120.

Gerstein, L., & Shullman, S. (1992). Counseling psychology and the workplace: The emergence of organizational counseling psychology. In S. Brown & R. Lent (Eds.), *Handbook of counseling psychology* (2nd ed., pp. 581–625). New York: Wiley.

Gills, T. L. (2003). Managing the virtual workforce requires knowledge of communication behavior. *Communication World, 20*(5), 10–12.

Goodman, L. A., Liang, B., Helms, J. E., Latta, R. E., Sparks, E., & Weintraub, S. R. (2004). Training counseling psychologists as social justice agents: Feminist and multicultural principles in action. *The Counseling Psychologist, 32,* 793–837.

Gregg, R. B. (1966). *The power of nonviolence.* New York: Schocken.

Harak, G. S. (Ed.). (2000). *Nonviolence for the third millennium.* Macon, GA: Mercer University Press.

Hasan, Q., & Khan, S. R. (1983). Dimension of Gandhian (nonviolent) personality. *Journal of Psychological Researches, 2,* 100–106.

Heppner, P. P. (2004, July). Stronger together: Valuing our diverse strengths. *Society of Counseling Psychology Newsletter, 2,* 21.

His Holiness The Dalai Lama. (1999). *Ethics for the new millennium.* New York: Riverhead.

Hofstede, G. (1980). *Culture's consequences: International differences in work-related values.* Thousand Oaks, CA: Sage.

Johnson, P., Adair, E., Bommersbach, M., Callandra, J., Huey, M., Kelly, A., et al. (1998). *Non-violence: Constructing a multidimensional attitude measure.* Paper presented at the annual meeting of the American Psychological Association, San Francisco.

Kirkpatrick, D., Raney, S., Shankar, J., & Gerstein, L. H. (2004, October). *Approaches to social justice in three international settings: Tibet, India, and South Africa.* Symposium presented at the First Annual Gandhian Nonviolence Conference, Memphis, TN.

Kiselica, M. S. (2004). When duty calls: The implications of social justice work for policy, education, and practice in the mental health professions. *The Counseling Psychologist, 32,* 838–854.

Konen, K., Mayton, D. M., Delva, Z., Sonnen, M., Dah, W., & Montgomery, R. (1999). *The Teenage Nonviolence Test: Concurrent and discriminant validity.* Paper presented at the annual meeting of the American Psychological Association, Boston.

Kool, V. K. (1990). Toward a theory of the psychology of nonviolence. In V. K. Kool (Ed.), *Nonviolence: Social and psychological issues* (pp. 1–24). New York: University Press of America.

Kool, V. K. (Ed.). (1993). *Nonviolence: Social and psychological issues.* Lanham, MD: University Press of America.

Kool, V. K., & Sen, M. (1984). The Nonviolence Test. In D. M. Pestonjee (Ed.), *Second handbook of psychological and social instruments* (pp. 48–55). Ahmedabad, India: Indian Institute of Management.

Leong, F. T. L., & Blustein, D. L. (2000). Toward a global vision of counseling psychology. *The Counseling Psychologist, 28,* 5–9.

Leong, F. T. L., & Ponterotto, J. G. (2003). A proposal for internationalizing counseling psychology in the United States: Rationale, recommendations, and challenges. *The Counseling Psychologist, 31,* 381–395.

Leung, S. A. (2003). A journey worth traveling: Globalization of counseling psychology. *The Counseling Psychologist, 31,* 412–419.

Lewin, K. (1938). *The conceptual representation and the measurement of psychological forces.* Durham, NC: Duke University Press.

Lewin, K. (1948). *Resolving social conflicts: Selected papers on group dynamics, 1935–1946.* New York: Harper.

Lewin, K. (1951). *Field theory in social science: Selected theoretical papers* (D. Cartwright, Ed.). New York: Harper Torchbooks.

Little, H. (1999). *Volunteers: How to get them, how to keep them.* Naperville, IL: Panacea.

MacNair, R. (2003). *The psychology of peace: An introduction.* Westport, CT: Praeger.

Manoochehri, G., & Pinkerton T. (2003). Managing telecommuters: Opportunities and challenges. *American Business Review, 21*(1), 9–17.

Mayton, D. M. (1994). *Values and nonviolent personality predispositions: A replication of correlational connections.* Paper presented at the annual meeting of the American Psychological Association, Los Angeles.

Mayton, D. M. (1999). *Teenage nonviolence: How do we define and measure it?* Paper presented at the Sixth International Symposium for Contributions of Psychology of Peace, San José, Costa Rica.

Mayton, D. M. (2001). Nonviolence within cultures of peace: A means and an end. *Peace and Conflict: Journal of Peace Psychology, 7*(2), 143–156.

Mayton, D. M., Diessner, R. & Granby, C. D. (1996). Nonviolence and human values: Empirical support for theoretical relations. *Peace and Conflict: Journal of Peace Psychology, 2*(3), 245–253.

Mayton, D. M., Susnjic, S., Palmer, B. J., Peters, D. J., Gierth, R., & Caswell, R. N. (2002). The measurement of nonviolence: A review. *Peace & Conflict, 8*(4), 343–355.

Mayton, D. M., Weedman, J., Sonnen, J., Grubb, C., & Hirose, M. (1999). *The Teenage Nonviolence Test: Internal structure and reliability.* Paper presented at the annual meeting of the American Psychological Association, Boston.

Mazurana, D., & McKay, S. (1999). *Women and peacebuilding.* Montreal, Quebec: International Centre for Human Rights and Democratic Development.

McCurley, S., & Vineyard, S. (1998). *Handling problem volunteers.* Darien, IL: Heritage Arts Publishing.

McKay, S., & de la Rey, C. (2001). Women's meaning of peacebuilding in post-apartheid South Africa. *Peace and Conflict: Journal of Peace Psychology, 7*(3), 227–242.

McKay, S., & Mazurana, D. (2001). Women as peacebuilders. In D. Christie, R. Wagner, & D. Du Nann Winter (Eds.), *Peace, conflict, and violence: Peace psychology in the 21st century.* Upper Saddle River, NJ: Prentice Hall.

McWhirter, J. J. (1988). The Fulbright program and counseling psychology. *The Counseling Psychologist, 16,* 279–281.

Norsworthy, K. L., & Gerstein, L. H. (2003a). Counseling and building communities of peace: The interconnections. *International Journal for the Advancement of Counseling, 25*(4), 197–204.

Norsworthy, K. L., & Gerstein, L. H. (Eds.). (2003b). Counseling and communities of peace [Special issue]. *International Journal for the Advancement of Counseling, 25*(4), 197–324.

Pedersen, P., & Leong, F. (1997). Counseling in an international context. *The Counseling Psychologist, 25,* 117–122.

Pelton, L. H. (1974). *The psychology of nonviolence.* New York: Pergamon.

Pettigrew, T. F. (1998). Intergroup contact theory. *Annual Review of Psychology, 49,* 65–85.

Petty, R. E., & Cacioppo, J. T. (1981). *Attitudes and persuasion: Classic and contemporary approaches.* Dubuque, IA: Brown.

Petty, R. E., & Cacioppo, J. T. (1986). *Communication and persuasion: Central and peripheral routes to attitude change.* New York: Springer-Verlag.

Potkin, H. (1999). How to communicate with telecommuters. *Harvard Management Communication Letter, 2*(5), 4–7.

Potter, E. E. (2003). Telecommuting: The future of work, corporate culture, and American society. *Journal of Labor Research, 24*(1), 73–85.

Raney, S. (2005). *The endangered lives of women: Peace and mental health among Tibetan refugee women.* Unpublished research, Ball State University, Muncie, IN.

Robertson, J., & Lewallen, J. (1975). *The grass roots.* San Francisco: Sierra Club Books.

Rokeach, M. (1973). *The nature of human values.* New York: Free Press.

Sagiv, L., & Schwartz, S. H. (1995). Value priorities and readiness for out-group social contact. *Journal of Personality and Social Psychology, 69,* 437–448.

Schwartz, S. H. (1992). Universals in the content and structure of values: Theoretical advances and empirical tests in 20 countries. *Advances in Experimental Social Psychology, 25,* 1–65.

Schwartz, S. H. (1994). Are there universal aspects in the structure and content of human values? *Journal of Social Issues, 50*(4), 19–45.

Schwartz, S. H., & Bilsky, W. (1987). Toward a universal psychological structure of human values. *Journal of Personality and Social Psychology, 53,* 550–562.

Schwartz, S. H., & Bilsky, W. (1990). Toward a universal psychological structure of human values: Extensions and cross-cultural replications. *Journal of Personality and Social Psychology, 58,* 878–891.

Schwartz, S. H., & Sagiv, L. (1995). Identifying culture-specifics in the content and structure of values. *Journal of Cross-Cultural Psychology, 26,* 92–116.

Sharp, G. (1960). *Gandhi wields the weapon of moral power: Three case studies.* Ahmedabad, India: Navajivan.

Sharp, G. (1973). *The politics of nonviolent action.* Boston: Porter Sargent.

Sharp, G. (1979). *Gandhi as a political strategist.* Boston: Porter Sargent.

Sherif, M. (1966). *In common predicament: Social psychology of intergroup conflict and cooperation.* Boston: Houghton Mifflin.

Speight, S. L., & Vera, E. M. (2004). A social justice agenda: Ready or not? *The Counseling Psychologist, 32,* 109–118.

Vera, E. M., & Speight, S. L. (2003). Multicultural competence, social justice, and counseling psychology: Expanding our roles. *The Counseling Psychologist, 31,* 253–272.

Whiteley, J. (Ed.). (1987). Carl Rogers and the person-centered approach to peace [Special issue]. *Counseling and Values, 32*(1).

Willis, D. G. (2004). Hate crimes against gay males: An overview. *Issues in Mental Health Nursing, 25,* 115–132.

Yalom, I. D. (1995). *The theory and practice of group psychotherapy* (4th ed.). New York: Basic Books.

CHAPTER 31

Moving From Contact to Change

The Act of Becoming Aware

Scott L. Moeschberger, Alicia Ordóñez, Jui Shankar, and Shonali Raney

A discussion of the topic of social justice presupposes a critical feature—awareness. We are using the term *awareness* in a way similar to Perls (1973) and Stevens (1973). It refers to an increased understanding of the self in relation to the world and is closely tied to an integrated sense of personal identity. We view such awareness as integral to the identity formation of a counseling psychologist who strives for social justice. The focus of this chapter is to shed light on factors that influence an individual or group to care about social justice, and the critical role of awareness in moving toward social justice. To accomplish this, we will share from personal experience in understanding and engaging in issues related to injustice. Injustice is a term that can be used to describe any situation that is deemed unfair and is used in this context to describe political, social, and economic situations where one group wields power over another with outcomes that are detrimental to the parties without power. Through the examples of conflict in Salvadoran gangs, the effects of damming the Narmada River in India, and the Kashmir conflict, we will discuss this concept of awareness in connection to the model we propose. Inspiring students, counseling psychologists, and citizens to engagement in these issues is a multifactor process that relies on an awakening and growth of awareness. Out of awareness flows engagement and participation, which contribute to a spiral of increasing awareness. In this chapter, we will set forth a theory of engagement with the need for social justice. We will examine three illustrations to demonstrate how this approach is relevant in a variety of contexts. Each example discusses counseling psychologists who, through the process of their training, became aware of injustices, began to engage with these situations, and developed roles to foster change.

Our model for awareness and engagement ultimately strives to facilitate change. In each context that is discussed, one can identify movement through four components: (a) contact with a reality of oppression (where one group abuses the power held over another group) and conflict (a common outcome of oppression, where an oppressed group fights back with whatever means it deems most effective; it is recognized here that the seeds of conflict are complex and often involve wrongs by both parties that then deteriorate into violence); (b) increasing awareness, formulating an efficacy to create change, and understanding the role of self in relation to this change; (c) developing a deeper understanding of the historical and social contexts in the situation; and (d) engaging and participating in the process of change. Although we have identified four distinct categories, the components are not linear in progression but instead continually interact with and influence each other.

In understanding how the field of counseling psychology relates to the field of social justice, it is important to consider the ethical implications inherent in diverse settings. As we discuss this model and examples we have encountered, we are motivated by a desire for a world where there is justice. However, we cannot assume that all parties will agree on what is considered "just" in any given situation. There will always be disagreement about how justice can be defined and quantified. To address this tension, we will briefly refer the reader to Garcia, Cartwright, Winston, and Borzuckhowska (2003), who proposed the Integrative Transcultural Model that attends to cultural variables involved in ethical dilemmas. Psychologists using this model need to possess certain attitudes that are imperative in the ethical decision-making process. These attitudes include reflection, or awareness of their own feelings, values, and skills; attention to context, such as institutional policy, society, and culture; balance, which involves weighing issues presented by all individuals concerned; collaboration, or inviting all parties to participate in the decision process; and tolerance, or acceptance of diverse worldviews. As well as considering carefully the ethical principles as outlined by the American Psychological Association (APA) Code of Conduct, it is also important to be aware of the cultural expectations that may exist, as well as any ethical guidelines or codes specific to that country. For example, many cultures view gift-giving as a sign of hospitality and trust, and to refuse such a gift could be considered offensive. On the other hand, APA guidelines would discourage the acceptance of gifts, so context and circumstances in other countries must be weighed with discretion. Confidentiality is always a key value for counseling psychologists, but it can become an issue of not just emotional safety but physical safety amidst the tenuous issues of advocacy in some countries.

Contact With Conflict or Injustice

The first factor in this model describes an initial direct or indirect contact with a reality of oppression or conflict. The individual may directly experience the situation or learn about it through someone else's experience. Consider, for example, conflicts that receive a lot of media attention. The Palestinian who is not able to get to work because of being stopped at checkpoints, the Israeli who loses someone through a suicide bombing, and the Palestinian who loses someone through a retaliatory attack—all inescapably experience conflict in a direct way. Their friends in the United States may learn about the situations through hearing their stories, and others may learn of what is happening through the media or in the classroom. If we take a moment to look around, we are surrounded by these situations, both at home and abroad; however, we do not understand or react to every one of them. We may hear a report on the news about an incident of racism or we may have a friend who is not taken seriously at work because she is a woman. We may experience such injustice firsthand. Many people feel overwhelmed at the sheer amount of conflict and injustice in the world and feel helpless to act. Other conditions need to occur.

Becoming Aware

Awareness is not an end-product but an ongoing experience that stems from one's interaction with oneself and with the surrounding world (Stevens, 1973). It does not occur in isolation. Increasing awareness can happen in a variety of ways, but always includes attentiveness to circumstances, a choice to watch and listen rather than turn away. It usually starts with an encounter with a social condition that is experienced as unfair (as described in the previous section). In this encounter, a personal investment is felt. In other words, I (or someone I care about) am (is) affected by this injustice. I cannot or will not ignore it. The investment is emotional because injustice implicitly has a negative effect on well-being. There can also be physical, economical, social, and vocational implications of the particular injustice. This leads me to devote energy to seeing change occur, a process that is facilitated by certain conditions. This motivation is buoyed by an optimistic sense that change is possible, that engagement is worthwhile, that involvement makes sense and is consistent with personal and cultural beliefs of what is just or fair, even if there is social pressure against it (Armitage, Conner, Loach, & Willetts, 1999; Conner, Warren, Close, & Sparks, 1999; Courneya, Bobick, & Schinke, 1999). Chances of involvement are further increased if the person feels socially responsible for the harmful consequences of injustice (Zelezny, Chua, & Aldrich, 2000). A person who recognizes his or her own skills and resources will feel more empowered to contribute to social causes (Fetterman, 2001; Yeich, 1996). Another motivating factor is a perceived control over the volitional choice to engage (that it is an intentional act of will, rather than something that happens to him or her) (Strube & Berry, 1985).

One's role is shaped by a self-perception that includes perceiving oneself as an activist (one who takes action to spur social change) or a person who contributes, and is also shaped by previous experience with the issues or some form of social action. An honest assessment will acknowledge two internal forces: one that wants to recognize the need for action and another that wants to ignore it and avoid the inevitable sacrifice that would come with engagement in social action. Through reflection, the individual avoids guilt and dogmatism, but identifies values and small steps of action that are not overwhelming, which the individual can then offer as an initial contribution (Watkins, 1988). This may include things like learning more about a situation, discussing it with family and friends, or writing a letter to the editor of a local paper. Once a person has come into contact with an issue of injustice and has become aware of some of the dynamics, the next significant factor is to better understand the context of history and culture.

Understanding Historical and Contextual Factors

Context is key to understanding the dynamics of a situation where there is conflict or oppression—historical, social, and individual contexts. An individual or group may choose actions that seem self-defeating, counterproductive, or even pathological. Rather than labeling such actions as resistant or flawed, the counseling psychologist needs to conceptualize the person (or group) in context, identifying structural sources and differentiating them from individual sources of the problem. A structural issue is one that is inherent in the very institutions (or structures) of a society. For example, a child may not succeed academically because of a low genetic capacity for learning (individual source), or a child may not succeed academically because that child attends a school in a community with few resources to devote to education. Some argue that understanding this, more than a theoretical matter of fashion, is a social responsibility, because disciplines that locate the source of problems solely on the individual contribute to a structural violence as they ignore the structural factors that hinder people's development (Freire, 1970; Martín-Baró, Aron, & Corne, 1994).

In considering this idea, it is important to have an understanding of systems. A systemic approach is crucial to areas of social justice; it tends to be concerned with the negative effects of oppression within a system, rather than a more traditionally narrow approach of problems within an individual. Systems are complex structures that occur within the context of roles, boundaries, power differentials, and history. Each system might reflect its own unique configuration with its own perceived historical origins. The components of a system such as culture, religion, ethnic identity, and language are interconnected such that a change in any one part will effect change in other parts of the system. Bronfenbrenner (1979) described systems that are embedded within a complex of systems; thus, there is a nesting of systems within systems. Beginning with the microsystem (e.g., home), there is a connectedness with the larger exosystem (e.g., the community), and ultimately the macrosystem (society at large). Each system possesses its own set of beliefs and values for its members and the systems with which it interconnects.

A conceptualization that takes context into account may challenge the dominant cultural discourse, developing what is known as a "critical consciousness" (Freire, 1970). This involves contact with the reality of the situation and those living in the midst of it and the development of an awareness beyond the "official discourse." This usually occurs by identifying the needs of those less powerful or less fortunate and by hearing their voices. This often stands in contrast with the "official view" of the problem and is guided by a universal striving for justice for all.

From Awareness to Engagement

The final component of the model involves identifying and engaging/participation. This involves activism (which then feeds further awareness). Solutions evolve from multiple voices and a collaborative effort to construct social change. The counseling psychologists' contribution may be that of helping conceptualize and give a voice to all the parties, but an effective solution does not come directly from the counseling psychologist, but from the orchestration of various resources and voices. The counseling psychologist may be involved in this process of engagement at a number of levels.

Lederach (1998) identified several possibilities, drawn from reconciliation movements, for the roles a counseling psychologist may take: top-level leadership, middle-ranged leadership, and grassroots leadership. Top-level leadership would pertain primarily to world leaders and individuals in prominent positions who would be able to directly influence change at the policy level. Typically, this level would be limited to exceptional situations dealing with executive leadership of organizations or other groups. Middle-ranged leadership functions primarily in the sphere of training others for involvement and being a key spokesperson on these issues. Examples of work at this level include problem-solving workshops, training in conflict resolution, and peace commissions. Grassroots leadership encompasses active social involvement through direct involvement in commissions, grassroots training, prejudice reduction, and psychosocial work in posttrauma. The latter two roles will be highlighted within the case studies that follow.

A primary goal in this process of activism is the empowerment of the oppressed, which is inspiring a "sense of personal responsibility and collective efficacy" (Webster & Perkins, 2001, p. 355). This involves enhancing their access and power over resources basic to their needs. This is accomplished through enhancing their knowledge and ability to cooperate with others in the transformation of injustice. The result of this process is that members of oppressed groups gain greater control and influence over their present and future circumstances. All of these components we have introduced (contact, awareness, understanding historical and social contexts, and engagement) involve effective service to the oppressed, a challenge to structural violence, the formulation of problems from the perspective of the oppressed, and a new praxis involving the transformation of structural injustice (Martín-Baró et al., 1994).

Personal Illustrations From Three Counseling Psychologists in Training

In the following three examples, we attempt to show how each one of us views his or her role within a specific setting. Although each one is unique in setting and context, we hope to demonstrate our experiences in light of the aforementioned components of the awareness model described. In addition, we provide practical examples of what the process of engagement would look like in each setting.

A Peaceful Approach to Conflict Resolution Between Salvadoran Gangs (Alicia Ordóñez)

Like many other Salvadorans, my contact with the phenomenon of gangs occurred through direct, everyday encounters in the street or indirectly through the news. Mere contact, however, did not stimulate my awareness. I studied psychology at a university that made an explicit commitment to building a more just society and advocating for the oppressed. The interaction with others in this environment influenced my inclination to bear in mind the system as I strive to make sense of individual or group behavior. The following paragraphs will offer an application of the awareness model to the participation a counseling psychologist could have in the process of striving for a peaceful resolution to the gang conflict.

Understanding Historical and Contextual Factors

A review of historical and contextual factors emphasized for me the need to look beyond the individuals involved and address the structural factors that enable the gang phenomenon. El Salvador is a Central American country with a history of war, where violence and availability of arms are high. The problem of gangs has become an increasingly alarming issue for the past 15 years. It is estimated that there are more than 40,000 gang members in El Salvador (Ayala, 2003). There are two dominant hypotheses attempting to explain this phenomenon (Ayala, 2003). The first one contends that gang activity started with the deportation from the United States of hundreds of young people with a history of delinquent behavior. Immigrants escaping war and poverty, forced to cut off their roots and social support, faced racial discrimination and other social and economic disadvantages. In this context, many young people joined gangs in an attempt to develop a sense of belonging and gain respect. The second hypothesis argues that deportation is one of many other structural and situational factors that alienate and marginalize big sectors of the Salvadoran population and push youth to join gangs.

There is a great deal of research (e.g., Branch, 1999; Esbensen, Deschenes, & Winfree, 1999) on why people join gangs; in El Salvador, gangs tend to attract young people in highly populated urban areas. These communities tend to be low income and have little access to basic services, they have high unemployment rates, they have high levels of community and family violence, and they exhibit conditions of social exclusion.

Peaceful efforts to solve this problem have been uncoordinated and stem mainly from nongovernmental sources. Some include attempts to control small weapons (Perez, 2003), technical skills training, and educational scholarships (Ayala, 2003). The strongest governmental efforts, criticized as punitive, aim at incarcerating gang members (Castro & Marroquin, 2003).

From Awareness to Engagement

For a counseling psychologist, engagement in the process of building a peaceful solution would involve the use of scientific knowledge to help conceptualize the conflict and design interventions attending to the systemic nature of the problem. As the awareness model suggests, to accomplish this I would need to differentiate the structural and individual sources of violence. A helpful approach in this regard would be to identify direct violence and structural violence levels, which operate together and therefore require complementing strategies (Christie, Wagner, & Du Nann Winter, 2001).

Direct violence involves actions that directly hurt the physical and psychological well-being of individuals or groups, such as the direct aggression between gang members. Interventions at this level should target the reduction and prevention of violence using peace-making strategies. An effective approach would rely on the knowledge that the other party has power to inflict damage, but shares values and is willing to give up something to attain a common good (Baron & Byrne, 2000; Christie et al., 2001). In this example, I could assist in the facilitation of a negotiation process between gangs. The process would involve the acknowledgment of the other gang as a threat, but also the identification of shared needs for self-determination, more access to opportunities, and generally a better quality of life, not only for gang members but also for their respective communities (e.g., the needs to have access to basic services and to decrease poverty and marginalization). This intervention would rely on the already existing strength of heightened commitment to group membership, but it would expand this sense of membership by identifying the gang members with their barrios, beyond the gang. Reconciliation could be promoted by asking participants to make a video of their history of struggle, the needs in their barrios, and their process of reconciliation. Gangs could then be encouraged to share experiences and promote the duplication of the model in other marginalized communities. In addition, this level would involve concrete actions from the gangs, community, nongovernmental organizations, and the government to sanction nonviolence. The community can be encouraged to research and learn from other communities where gang violence has been successfully discouraged, such as the rural areas. To be sustainable, these efforts need to be accompanied by structural interventions.

Structural violence is defined in terms of an unjust social configuration where some individuals are systematically deprived of their human rights and limited in the satisfaction of their basic needs, as a function of others' maintenance of their privileges (Christie et al., 2001). Strategies at the structural level would seek the transformation of unjust structures that put low-income youth at risk to engage in gang violence. These strategies require the empowerment and active involvement of the oppressed individuals. For example, based on the diagnostic video, gang members could propose reforms in the educational system so the Ministry of Education can meet their needs for training, and community members could implement organizational strategies proven successful in other communities at preventing gang violence. Other actions should be directed toward government entities and agencies with economic and educational policy-making and law-making capacity to enhance social and economic opportunities for youth development.

For a counseling psychologist, networking would be a key strategy in the search for peaceful solutions. My role would include middle-range leadership and assistance in the synchronization of efforts by various agents. Some actions would include writings to sensitize the public opinion and key agents (e.g., policymakers, government, community members, gang members) about the problem from the perspective of the oppressed, consultation to agencies working on research and policy proposals, and support for activism efforts (e.g., by sharing scientific information about nonviolent strategies and successful local experiences for conflict resolution). Participation in these efforts with other agents would, in turn, help further increase my awareness and develop a more complex critical consciousness.

Damming Sustainable Development? (Jui Shankar)

"hamara gaon mein hamara raj!" ("our rule in our villages")

(Parajuli, 1996, p. 38)

I am Indian. I heard about the dambuilding on the Narmada River while I was growing up. News reports, private discussions, and even chance meetings with various activists brought the events closer to my life; however, at that time none of this seemed connected to my realm of learning or experiences. Now, training to be a counseling psychologist in the United States, far away from India and my community, I have been finding ways of relating my learning here to community development back in India. Community building is an extension of the need for peaceful cultures within Indian society—peaceful toward each other, including women, children, and the environment. Because of the interdependency among resources and people, this requires recognition of the need for education, clean drinking water, and sustainable development. As an illustration, I will discuss how my sense of social responsibility is piqued by the awareness of contributions that counseling psychologists can make to community development; possible areas to which we can contribute; ways in which we can join local activists to promote social justice; and, finally, implications for research and training. This is the beginning of my awareness.

Understanding Historical and Contextual Factors

The Narmada River originates in the central Indian state of Madhya Pradesh and flows westward through the states of Maharashtra and Gujarat. The developmental project involves harnessing the waters of the Narmada and her 41 tributaries by building more than 3,000 dams (Roy, 1999). Although some of the smaller dams have been built, the most visible large dam is the 455-foot-high Sadar Sarovar Project in Gujarat, whose construction has sputtered along since 1961 and then began in earnest in 1987 with a World Bank loan of $450 million (Udall, 1995). Concerns over the construction of the Sadar Sarovar Project initially brought many environmental organizations to the forefront, and then other nongovernmental organizations began to examine more closely the resettlement issues of the estimated 1,000,000 people to be displaced (Cernea, 1988; Dwivedi, 1999). People and activists have continued to mobilize protests, gather information from the various resettlement offices, and disseminate important information about people's rights and the costs of the Sadar Sarovar Project (Dwivedi, 1999).

From Awareness to Engagement

Beginning with an awareness and then contact with the controversy over the construction of this dam, I, along with other students of counseling psychology and counseling psychologists, am now faced with decisions of responsibility toward these communities and the social movement associated with this struggle. Systemic changes are needed when so many are affected and so much is at stake. Recognizing how to enter the system, what services might be needed, and the implementation of these needed services is crucial; simultaneous with these considerations is the concern that our work must not perpetuate modes of oppression that might already exist within this context.

Often, the question is—how? How is this all possible? And more important, how is this related to counseling psychology? An integral component of counseling psychology is the promotion of psychological wellness for people and communities through a life-span developmental framework. Contemporary training in counseling psychology supports training in sophisticated research designs, methodological diversity, and multicultural work. Thus, counseling psychology offers a base for gaining a systems perspective and incorporating learning from other disciplines (e.g., political science, sociology, and anthropology), expanding our ability to understand, practice, and research a variety of systems.

Often, the system we choose to enter might be overwhelming, and thus, starting work at the local level and incorporating indigenous solutions begins the process of social justice. To begin, it is important to recognize mental health concerns and possible crises that arise with displacement issues, such as a shift to minority status, socioeconomic disadvantage, and the need to preserve one's identity amid the chaos. Some researchers have suggested that displaced persons develop an alternative culture while attempting to settle into a new environment (Atlani & Rousseau, 2000; Brody, 1994), and thus, counseling psychologists working with displaced persons would have to consider the effects of the new living conditions and the possible need to provide basic necessities such as food, water, and shelter. Once we are able to establish the provision of basic living conditions, we would have to move beyond traditional mental health counseling to serve as consultants, advocates, and advisors (Atkinson, Thompson, & Grant, 1993) to begin the process of social change.

Our most valuable resource comes from our training in relationship building with our clients (Horvath & Greenberg, 1994), which are skills that might be transferred to build and establish collaborative and constructive relationships with the different stakeholders, such as the affected communities, local and national activists, and state and central governments. Relationships such as these might, for example, assist in negotiations and policy development among these stakeholders to promote and create potential solutions to the social problem of displacement and resettlement. Such actions might support interdependent relationships among not only the different stakeholders but also with the larger social system of political and economic issues, culture, and society (Bronfenbrenner, 1979).

Continual participation in mediating and encouraging stakeholders to remain engaged in the process might enable us to find ways of encouraging necessary measures that incorporate community-based resource management and rural development, such as the provision of clean drinking water, adequate health care services, and schools. While the state governments and community are engaged, we would also initiate collaborations between the states and the affected communities to negotiate sustainable solutions for the Sadar Sarovar Project. Stemming from these discussions is also the recognition that although development projects are instituted to serve the people, the very people whom they are meant to serve are kept out of the planning. Thus, we could not only encourage but insist that at this stage of agenda setting, all of the various stakeholders (e.g., the people, the state governments, the financial institutions, and the policymakers) engage in discussions that lead to collaborations that promote well-being in the community. Based on discussions and investigations, and the use of sociological, anthropological, and psychological methodologies, policy implementation might potentially be delineated and appropriate courses of action taken. Such steps would not only ensure constant development but also safeguard communities and thus establish good but important best practices in development.

War in the Clouds: The Kashmir Conflict (Shonali Raney)

Hum kya chahtey? Azaadi! (What do we want? Freedom!)

—Popular slogan in the Kashmir valley (Bose, 2003)

As a counseling psychologist-in-training, I cannot recall one specific moment where I first heard about the conflict in Kashmir. Born and raised in Mumbai, India, I spent most of my life knowing about the existence of the Kashmir situation but realizing little of the ways in which I might be able to contribute to a possible resolution of this conflict. My awareness was shaped by the coming together of my identity as an Indian, a counseling psychologist-in-training, and most important, a human rights advocate. As counseling psychologists building cultures of peace, we understand that peace agreements are essential for conflict resolution to occur. Before peace agreements can occur, however, we must understand structural factors that contribute to the ongoing violence and the resulting marginalization and concerns of the people. This section will highlight some of these concerns along with my personal exploration of possible roles I could take as a counseling psychologist.

Understanding Historical and Contextual Factors

In 1947 when the British were leaving India, Kashmir was still one of the disputed territories where there was no resolution as to which nation would gain accession. On October 27, 1947, Kashmir was formally made a part of the Indian territory. However, a small part of western Kashmir was still in the hands of the Pakistanis, who named it Azad Kashmir or independent Kashmir. Through the 1950s and 1960s, Kashmir's autonomy was slowly taken away, with the Central Indian government gaining increasingly more control over the state. On July 2, 1972, India and Pakistan signed the Simla Accord, under which it was agreed that there would be a cease-fire line, and a promise was made to resolve what had come to be known as the

Kashmir issue through peaceful means. However, the final discussion and settlement of Kashmir was postponed for another date, and this settlement never took place. As a result of political discontent, several militant groups emerged, including the Jammu and Kashmir Liberation Front (JKLF) and the Muslim United Front (MUF), among others. To combat these militant groups, the central government intervened again, and this led to the governor's rule being declared on January 19, 1990. This marks the beginning of widespread atrocities on the part of the Indian government and the neglect of human rights. The human rights violations included shooting of unarmed demonstrators, civilian massacres, and summary executions of detainees. As a result of these violations, 100,000 Hindu Kashmiris, known as Pandits, and thousands of Muslims left the Kashmiri valley. At the present time, however, Kashmir still continues to fight for its independence.

One approach to solutions has focused on increased involvement of the United Nations (UN) in the Kashmir dispute (Nabi Fai, 2000). Psychologists have often served as consultants to the United Nations and have worked toward developing appropriate standards, integrating psychosocial perspectives, and developing mental health programs as part of U.N.-based activities (Wessells, Schwebel, & Anderson, 2003). Other solutions include using counseling psychologists to contribute to public dialogue instead of only the political participants who would ordinarily have a say in conflict resolution. Counseling psychologists can play an important role as experts in the psychological dimensions of social justice issues. Wessells et al. (2003) described this consciousness-raising process as sensitization, which begins with the propagation of psychological knowledge and tools that dispute previously held notions about the causes of war. This process of reframing allows for newer perspectives on old problems and the use of networks and mass media to carry the message of peace to a wider audience.

As a means to reach this wider audience, counseling and peace psychologists have the power to influence policies with respect to human rights violations in Kashmir. The gross human rights violations discussed earlier have led to an increase of more than 10 times the number of psychiatric symptoms as the population exhibited before the conflict began. These symptoms have been blamed on fear and high levels of stress (Kumar, 1999). Counseling psychologists can step in at this point and prevent the pathologizing of individuals who have experienced such high levels of stress and conceptualize individuals in the context of the structural violence. Social injustice has also been demonstrated by the unwillingness on the part of the Indian government to offer the same democratic freedom to Kashmir that the rest of the country receives (Ganguly, 1997). Counseling psychologists can serve as activists, mobilizing and empowering the people of Kashmir to push for fundamental democratic rights.

From Awareness to Engagement

Counseling psychologists play an important role in conflict resolution and in the peace building. To this end, counseling psychologists can facilitate collaborative dialogue between all three disputed parties—the peoples of India, Pakistan, and Kashmir—toward more power sharing. Such partnership results in paying close attention to the needs of the people in the Kashmir valley and encouraging the local people to participate in the decision-making process. In the process of moving from theoretical understanding to practice, I would define my role as a counseling psychologist on a number of different levels. First, I could see myself as a peace psychologist trying to reduce ethnic tension in the region of Kashmir. In order to do this, I would first have to be a part of the community to understand the dynamics that are unique to this culture, knowing that as a Hindu, I will have a different perspective.

Another role would be sharing a voice in some way, to communicate to India, Pakistan, and especially the international community the atrocities suffered by the Kashmiris by the hands of the Indian armed forces and the Muslim militant groups. Also, there is a need to highlight the environmental degradation that has occurred as a result of the continued violence over five decades. I also see myself playing a big role in working with victims of trauma, both adults and children, who have lost their homes, their families, and possibly their identities. Last but not least, I see myself playing a part in educating the women about their rights and finding ways to stand up for what they need. As an Indian, I was always in contact with the reality of the Kashmir situation, especially after its exacerbation in the early 1980s. However, as a counseling psychologist-in-training, I believe that it is my responsibility to learn more about not just the oppression and the extent of human rights abuses, but also the ways in which counseling psychologists can contribute to the processes of healing and reconciliation. It must be noted that counseling psychologists need to understand the historical and social contexts of the situation before any intervention is proposed. This requires me to understand the plight of the Kashmiri people and the struggles they face in the context of the partition between India and Pakistan. Finally, as an instrument of change and a future counseling psychologist, I need to collaborate with social workers, lawyers, and doctors (along with other potential allies) to foster action that extends from the grassroots to shift toward policies that engender peace.

Final Summary

These three examples have provided a glimpse into our journey toward social action. In each illustration, there are strands of the four components of our model of awareness. We came in contact with some kind of social injustice. Our awareness was increased, and we understood our connection to these issues. We pursued a deeper understanding of the history and culture surrounding the situations. Finally, we became involved through engagement at some level.

The world is full of unfairness and injustice, but there are also those who will wage tirelessly for a better world. However, they sometimes need to be inspired to move through this process of awareness. There is a tremendous opportunity to facilitate this during the training of counseling psychologists. It begins with exposing students (or others with a young interest in these areas) to the realities of injustice. Needs exist all around us. We should be willing not only to meet needs but also to take a deeper look at why the needs exist, and to encourage others to do the same.

We should examine the unintended or intended negative consequences of the systems and structures that exist in our own communities. We may even be the beneficiaries of structural injustice. We may have access to resources and opportunities because someone else is being denied a living wage, a safe place to live and work, and opportunities to improve their lives. This may be happening in our own backyard, or it may be out of sight in another part of the world, where the environment is degraded or factory conditions are unfair, to meet the demands of the North American market.

Effective involvement requires an awareness of social structures, historical context, and oppressive systems. It requires study and effort to understand issues that are often complex. This should be part of the training of future professionals, and also the subject of ongoing research. Within our training paradigms, we must focus not only on meeting individual needs, but also on the individual in a context (see Gerstein & Moeschberger, 2003). Interdisciplinary training (e.g., anthropology, sociology, political science, and economics) would help achieve this by developing a broader understanding of how counseling psychologists can engage in creating social change. Likewise, researchers must rely on more qualitative methodologies (Gerstein & Moeschberger, 2003) to gain a more descriptive and holistic representation of the problem. These could likely integrate methods from other disciplines that would lead to both a macro (economic data, policy analysis) and micro (field notes, ethnographies) approach to data collection.

There is much work to be done to reach a better understanding of the most effective course toward a peaceful world. Foundational to this work is how to spur those in the field of counseling psychology to take active involvement in this process. This chapter has discussed one model and built on the available research of the factors that influence involvement. There is more to be discovered about the best way to motivate and inspire counseling psychologists to invest energy in social action. A good starting point is for training programs to model this kind of investment and for research efforts to focus on issues and define problems from the perspective of the oppressed. We must take time to look past immediate economics and listen to the voice of those affected by the ripples that extend from these issues. Who are the stakeholders in political and social decisions, and how can we help ensure that they have a voice? This, again, is not a matter of charity; it is a social responsibility for counseling psychologists.

References

Armitage, C. J., Conner, M., Loach, J., & Willetts, D. (1999). Different perceptions of control: Applying an extended Theory of Planned Behavior to legal and illegal drug use. *Basic and Applied Social Psychology, 21,* 301–316.

Atkinson, D. R., Thompson, C. E., & Grant, S. K. (1993). A three-dimensional model for counseling racial/ethnic minorities. *The Counseling Psychologist, 21,* 257–277.

Atlani, L., & Rousseau, C. (2000). The politics of culture in humanitarian aid to women refugees who have experienced sexual violence. *Transcultural Psychiatry, 37,* 435–449.

Ayala, E. (2003). *Pandilleros: Matar o morir por el barrio* [Gang members: Kill or die on behalf of the neighborhood]. Retrieved April 13, 2003, from http://www.Latinoamerica-online.it/paesi2/salvador-03.html#pandilleros

Baron, R. A., & Byrne, D. (2000). *Social psychology* (9th ed.). Boston: Allyn & Bacon.

Bose, S. (2003). *Kashmir: Roots of conflict, paths to peace.* Cambridge, MA: Harvard University Press.

Branch, C. W. (1999). Pathologizing normality or normalizing pathology? In C. W. Branch (Ed.), *Adolescent gangs: Old issues, new approaches* (pp. 197–211). Philadelphia, PA: Brunner/Mazel.

Brody, E. (1994). The mental health and well-being of refugees: Issues and directions. In A. J. Marsella, T. Bornemann, S. Ekblad, & J. Orley (Eds.), *Amidst peril and pain: The mental health and well-being of the world's refugees* (pp. 57–68). Washington, DC: American Psychological Association.

Bronfenbrenner, U. (1979). *The ecology of human development: Experiments by nature and design.* Cambridge, MA: Havard University Press.

Castro, C., & Marroquin, D. (2003). Ninos recibiran trato de adultos [Children will be treated as adults]. *La Prensa Grafica.* Retrieved August 31, 2003, from http://www.archive.laprensa.com.sv/20030725/nacion/nacion5.asp

Cernea, M. M. (1988). *Involuntary resettlement in development projects: Policy guidelines in World Bank–financed projects.* Washington, DC: The World Bank.

Christie, D. J., Wagner, R. V., & Du Nann Winter, D. (2001). *Peace, conflict, and violence: Peace psychology for the 21st century.* Englewood Cliffs, NJ: Prentice Hall.

Conner, M., Warren, R., Close, S., & Sparks, P. (1999). Alcohol consumption and the theory of planned behavior: An examination of the cognitive mediation of past behavior. *Journal of Applied Social Psychology, 29,* 1676–1704.

Courneya, K. S., Bobick, T. M., & Schinke, R. J. (1999). Does the Theory of Planned Behavior mediate the relation between personality and exercise behavior? *Basic and Applied Social Psychology, 21,* 317–324.

Dwivedi, R. (1999). Displacement, risks and resistance: Local perceptions and actions in the Sadar Sarovar. *Displacement and Change, 30,* 43–78.

Esbensen, F. A., Deschenes, E. P., & Winfree, L. T. (1999). Differences between gang girls and gang boys: Results from a multisite survey. *Youth & Society, 31,* 27–53.

Fetterman, D. M. (2001). *Foundations of empowerment evaluation.* Thousand Oaks, CA: Sage.

Freire, P. (1970). *Pedagogy of the oppressed.* New York: Seabury.

Ganguly, S. (1997). *The crisis in Kashmir: Portents of war, hopes of peace.* Cambridge, U.K.: Cambridge University Press.

Garcia, J. G., Cartwright, B., Winston, S. M., & Borzuckhowska, B. (2003). A transcultural integrative model for ethical decision making in counseling. *Journal of Counseling and Development, 81,* 268–277.

Gerstein, L. H., & Moeschberger, S. (2003). Building cultures of peace: An urgent task for counseling professionals. *Journal of Counseling & Development, 81,* 115–120.

Horvath, A. O., & Greenberg, L. S. (1994). *The working alliance.* New York: Wiley.

Kumar, S. (1999). Mental health problems increase as health care in Kashmir collapses. *Lancet, 353,* 908.

Lederach, J. P. (1998). *Building peace: Sustainable reconciliation in divided societies.* Washington, DC: United States Institute for Peace.

Martín-Baró, I., Aron, A., & Corne, S. (1994). *Writings for a liberation psychology.* Cambridge, MA: Harvard University Press.

Nabi Fai, G. (2000). Only a solution in Kashmir will bring peace and security to all of South Asia. *Washington Report on Middle East Affairs, 19,* 48–50.

Parajuli, P. (1996). Ecological ethnicity in the making: Developmentalist hegemonies and emergent identities in India. *Identities, 3,* 15–59.

Perez, C. (2003, March 4). *Desarme de pandillas* [Disarming of gangs]. Retrieved April 10, 2003, from http://www.desarme.org

Perls, F. S. (1973). *The Gestalt approach and eyewitness to therapy.* Palo Alto, CA: Science and Behavior Books.

Roy, A. (1999). *The cost of living.* New York: The Modern Library.

Stevens, J. (1973). *Awareness: Exploring, experimenting, experiencing.* New York: Bantam.

Strube, M. J., & Berry, J. M. (1985). Attributional and emotional concomitants of control relinquishment. *Basic and Applied Social Psychology, 6,* 205–220.

Udall, L. (1995). The international Narmada campaign: A case study of sustained advocacy. In W. F. Fischer (Ed.), *Toward sustainable development: Struggling over India's Narmada river* (pp. 201–227). Armonk, NY: M. E. Sharpe.

Watkins, J. (1988). Imagination and peace: On the inner dynamics of promoting peace activism. *Journal of Social Issues, 44,* 38–57.

Webster, L., & Perkins, D. D. (2001). Redressing structural violence against children: Empowerment-based interventions and research. In D. J. Christie, R. V. Wagner, & D. Du Nann Winter (Eds.), *Peace, conflict, and violence: Peace psychology for the 21st century.* Englewood Cliffs, NJ: Prentice Hall.

Wessells, M., Schwebel, M., & Anderson, A. (2003). Psychologists making a difference in the public arena: Building cultures of peace. In D. J. Christie, R. V. Wagner, & D. Du Nann Winter (Eds.), *Peace, conflict, and violence: Peace psychology for the 21st century.* Englewood Cliffs, NJ: Prentice Hall.

Yeich, S. (1996). Grassroots organizing with homeless people: A participatory research approach. *Journal of Social Issues, 52*(1), 111–121.

Zelezny, L. C., Chua, P. P., & Aldrich, C. (2000). Elaborating on gender differences in environmentalism. *Journal of Social Issues, 56,* 443–457.

PART VII

Policy and Legislative Change

CHAPTER 32

Social Action in Policy and Legislation

Individuals and Alliances

Rebecca L. Toporek

> Why do we not honor what we can do? Part of the reason is that "virtue" is often defined as the ultimate commodity, something exclusive, like a Porsche or a perfect figure, that only the rich and famous have access to. "Virtue" is defined as so outside of normal human experience or ability that you'd think, if you were doing it right, you'd know, because camera crews and an awards committee would appear on your lawn. (Goska, 2004, p. 49)

One objective of this *Handbook* is to encourage counseling psychologists to see themselves as actors in the resolution of oppression and injustice. As indicated in her essay on political paralysis, Goska (2004) suggests that one of the reasons we may hesitate to attempt large-scale action against injustice is that we tend to view people who are visibly involved in political advocacy as exceptional people possessing qualities that are outside the norm. It is our intention in this section of the *Handbook* to present illustrations of political activity undertaken by counseling psychologists within organizations and public policy in an effort to bring this type of action to a more personal level.

Repeatedly, discussions around social justice in psychology emphasize the need for political action (e.g., Humphreys, 1996; Kiselica, 2004; Toporek & Reza, 2001; Vera & Speight, 2003). Meara and Davis (2004) noted that one of the major accomplishments of the Houston 2001 National Counseling Psychology Conference was to highlight the role of counseling psychologists in political advocacy. Given the extent of social problems and injustice, there is a plethora of venues for political involvement in the interest of fairness, equity, justice, and human rights. Advocacy, in the service of social justice, may be considered along a continuum with individual client empowerment on one end and social action on the other (Toporek, 2000; Toporek & Liu, 2001). The professional action taken by counseling psychologists may fall anywhere on the continuum and include activities such as facilitating client self-advocacy or empowerment through educating, skill building, and role playing; advocating within a system for particular clients or client groups; or social action that includes advocating for structural and policy change. Counseling psychologists are involved in the full range of different approaches, from individual empowerment efforts (e.g., Morrow et al., chapter 17) to international human rights advocacy (e.g., Gerstein & Kirkpatrick, chapter 30).

As an introduction and overview to the section on social action in legislation and policy, this chapter will describe efforts ranging from institutional change within psychology to federal legislative efforts. The two chapters that follow this overview chronicle the careers of four counseling psychologists and their experiences engaging in extensive legislative work.

Organizational Change

Counseling psychologists have been involved in significant organizational change efforts both inside and outside the profession. Internal efforts include changes in organizational structures, policies, and practices of psychology (e.g., guidelines for multicultural practice). Examples of external efforts include advocacy for workplace and education policies that significantly influence people's lives, such as antidiscrimination, sexual harassment, and fair hiring and promotion policies.

Within the Profession

Within counseling psychology, there have been efforts, sometimes sponsored by professional associations and sometimes initiated by individuals or groups of psychologists who have recognized a need for organizational change. A few examples include increased equity in representation in organizational leadership and governance, adoption and implementation of standards and guidelines for increasing professional competence regarding marginalized populations, modifying accreditation and ethical standards to increase the relevance of the profession, and advocating within professional organizations to take public positions on human rights issues.

Recognition of the inadequacy of practice and training standards for relevant and ethical service to marginalized groups (e.g., women, minorities, and LGBT clients) has resulted in various efforts to institutionalize standards that would delineate appropriate assessment and interventions for these groups as well as competencies needed by counseling psychologists serving these groups. Competence, as an ethical imperative, stipulates that psychologists must be proficient and knowledgeable in areas that are relevant to their clients. The establishment of standards provides guidance in defining and demonstrating competence. Many of these efforts were initiated or sponsored by leaders within the American Psychological Association (APA) and the American Counseling Association (ACA) and carried out by task forces made up of organization members. For example, Allen Ivey, during his presidency in Division 17 from 1979 to 1980, charged a task force to develop a set of multicultural guidelines and competencies (Sue et al., 1982). This effort was revisited with a charge from Thomas Parham, president of the Association of Multicultural Counseling and Development (AMCD) in 1990–1991, to refine these competencies and advocate for their adoption within the structures of ACA. In 1994, Beverly O'Bryant, president of ACA, advocated for the adoption of the multicultural competencies. In response to criticism that the competencies were too vague, the Professional Standards Committee of AMCD developed a document that operationalized the multicultural competencies, providing examples and strategies for competency development (Arredondo et al., 1996).

In 2003, the ACA formally adopted the Multicultural Counseling Competencies. The Executive Board of AMCD facilitated two publications advancing the implementation of the multicultural counseling competencies (Roysircar, Arredondo, Fuertes, Ponterotto, & Toporek, 2003; Roysircar, Sandhu, & Bibbins, 2003). These publications, supported organizationally by both AMCD and ACA, provided further elaboration and expansion of the inclusiveness of the definition of multiculturalism to include issues of religion, immigrant cultures, women's issues, LGB concerns, and physical disability.

Parallel to the work in ACA to implement the multicultural competencies, a task force of Division 17 of APA—including psychologists who were involved in the original development of the multicultural competencies, psychologists who had been involved in writing guidelines for other marginalized populations (e.g., women, LGBT, disabilities), as well as other committed psychologists—developed the Multicultural Guidelines (APA, 2003b). These were adopted by Division 17 in 2003 and have become standards for training and practice.

This example illustrates the notion that institutional change is a lengthy process, often involving several successive groups and leaders who become involved at different points in time to advocate for a vision as well as to integrate improvements in actual implementation in order to institutionalize social change. Although adoption of these guidelines has been a significant achievement in increasing equity in access and relevant treatment in counseling, the issue of implementation still presents considerable challenges.

Another example of a professional association leadership initiative was a task force to develop a set of competencies for advocacy in counseling by Jane Goodman, president of ACA, in 2002. This task force was charged with defining advocacy within the context of counseling and proposing a model of competencies that could guide professional counseling practice and facilitate counselors in taking a more active role in addressing social justice issues. The Advocacy Competencies outlined by the task force (Lewis, Arnold, House, & Toporek, 2002) were adopted by the

American Counseling Association in 2003. Expanding on the advocacy model proposed by Toporek (2000) and the community counseling model described by Lewis, Lewis, Daniels, and D'Andrea (1998), the Advocacy Competencies are described using two dimensions: (a) "micro"- and "macro"-level advocacy, and (b) "acting with" and "acting on behalf" of clients. Advocacy that reflects "acting with" the client or client communities ranges from micro-level advocacy to macro-level advocacy and respectively includes "client/student empowerment," "community collaboration," and "public information." Advocacy that represents "acting on behalf" of clients or client communities respectively includes "client/student advocacy," "systems advocacy," and "social/political advocacy." A full description of the Advocacy Competencies may be accessed through the ACA Web site.

Counseling psychologists have also been significant contributors to the public positions taken by the APA regarding controversial concerns such as the Policy on Conversion Therapy (Haldeman, 2003) and supporting civil marriage for same-sex couples and opposing discrimination against same-sex parents (Winerman, 2004). These efforts have gained strength through coalition building with other divisions in APA. For example, formal organizational initiatives to address social justice concerns include APA's Divisions for Social Justice (DSJ). The DSJ was formed in 1999 as a coalition of APA divisions invested in supporting and encouraging social justice initiatives (APA, 2003a). The coalition is composed of representatives from Divisions 17 (Society of Counseling Psychology); 9 (Society for the Psychological Study of Social Issues); 27 (Society for Community Research and Action); 35 (Society for the Psychology of Women); 39 (Psychoanalysis); 43 (Family); 44 (Society for the Psychological Study of Lesbian, Gay and Bisexual Issues); 45 (Society for the Psychological Study of Ethnic Minority Issues); 48 (Society for the Study of Peace, Conflict and Violence); and 51 (Society for the Psychological Study of Men and Masculinity). The activities of the DSJ have thus far been focused in three areas: (a) convention programming, (b) nominations and elections, and (c) strengthening the working connection between the member divisions and the Public Interest Directorate. To this end, they have sponsored symposia and town hall meetings at conventions as well as initiated conversations with Public Interest Directorate (2004) to call attention to social justice issues and advocate for action.

Within ACA, there has also been a recognized need for a formal organization to address broad issues of oppression inclusive of LGBT, ethnic and racial oppression, gender, disabilities, and human rights. In 1998, a group of concerned counselors came together in a 2-day meeting at ACA headquarters in Alexandria, Virginia, to discuss the need for ACA to more formally address social justice issues. Out of that meeting, several strategies were initiated, including the formation of a division within ACA devoted specifically to addressing social justice issues and issues of marginalization across groups. Since that time, Counselors for Social Justice (CSJ) has moved from its status as a special interest group to a fully institutionalized division given a swell in membership. Since its inception, the group has sponsored A Day of Learning, focused on social justice and human rights issues at ACA conventions, and has sponsored public demonstrations promoting peace and various human rights issues. At the 2005 convention, the group also sponsored a Day of Action, designed to provide a service to the community in which the convention was held. In addition, CSJ regularly posts and sponsors learning activities, political advocacy information and resources, and collaborative efforts with other organizations via the organization Web site and electronic newsletter. In the spring of 2005, CSJ collaborated with Psychologists for Social Responsibility in sponsoring a conference in Portland, Oregon, devoted to social justice issues and social action.

External Organizations

An example of an organization that functions both within and outside professional organizations is the National Institute of Multicultural Competence (NIMC), whose mission is to implement the Multicultural Counseling Competencies and the Multicultural Guidelines consistently throughout all training programs and practice. Although members of this organization include past and current leaders in both ACA and APA, this organization was formed separately from the professional associations for a variety of reasons. First, it was recognized that leadership changes frequently within the organizations, and to maintain a consistent focus on competencies, there was a need for a group that could extend beyond individual leadership terms. Second, it was recognized that in addition to organizational leadership and initiatives, there was a need for extensive efforts to facilitate the implementation of competencies that would require the grassroots support and work of many individuals, and go beyond those involved in active positions in the professional associations. Third, it was recognized that the professional organizations, at any one time, may have numerous initiatives and areas of concern and may not focus the amount of attention needed in order to implement the competencies.

Psychologists for Social Responsibility is a private, nonprofit corporation whose mission is to apply "psychological knowledge and skills to promote peace with social justice at the community, national and international levels" (Psychologists for Social Responsibility, 2005). Specific areas of advocacy and attention include conflict resolution and violence prevention; facilitating positive changes for victims and survivors of violence; advocacy for human needs and human rights; and the application of psychological knowledge in public policy at local, national, and international levels.

There are numerous examples of counseling psychologists' initiatives aimed at promoting organizational change in a myriad of environments. For example, Fassinger and Gallor (chapter 19) provide a full description of the progression of organizational policy changes in workplace equity. Counseling psychologists as educators and administrators can influence educational policy. One example is advocating for changes to increase access, diversity, and inclusion in the college and university environments (P. Arredondo, personal communication, 2005). Other examples include advocacy for domestic partner benefits within one's workplace, policies to protect whistle-blowers (Johnson & Chope, in press), and advocacy for clearer discrimination complaint resolution processes (Toporek & Reza, 2001).

Federal and State Legislation

Legislative efforts represent broad-scale impact that counseling psychologists may have regarding issues that affect clients. Sometimes, legislative involvement stems from and is supported by our professional associations, whereas at other times, it may be initiated through our employment or personal involvement.

Legislative Action Through Professional Associations

There are numerous examples of psychologists who have been active in federal legislation and policy as representatives of APA regarding issues such as promoting increased funding for mental health of college students (Ablasser, 2004) and racial and ethnic health disparities legislation (APA Public Policy Office, 1995). Bobbie Celeste (Shullman, Celeste, & Strickland, chapter 33) describes her work in legislation as a psychologist advocate within a state psychological association, and Robert McPherson (McPherson, chapter 34) provides an in-depth look at his statewide work specifically regarding managed care legislation.

Legislative Action and Public Policy

Counseling psychologists have expertise in research, counseling, administration, education, and consultation. In each of these arenas, there is the potential to inform public policy either as a member of professional associations or within the scope of one's employment. Although there are numerous examples of individual and group efforts of counseling psychologists, I have chosen just a few in each of these areas.

Throughout the feminist and multicultural movements, numerous counseling psychologists have advocated for the importance of orienting research toward influencing public policy (e.g., Bingham, 2003; Enns, 1993). Vera and Speight (2003) described Transformative Participatory Evaluation research, a form of methodology in which the counseling psychologist partners with marginalized communities to work toward goals of political empowerment, emancipation, and social justice. Shullman (Shullman et al.) describes testifying before Congress and presenting research findings informing congressional debates regarding issues such as gender equity. Likewise, the Surgeon General's Report on Mental Health (U.S. Public Health Service, 1999) was informed, in part, on research conducted by counseling psychologists.

The application of expertise in counseling and mental health issues to legislation can be seen in the recent development of the Campus Care and Counseling Act (H.R. 3593/S. 2215), later combined with the Youth Suicide Prevention bill and renamed the Garrett Lee Smith Memorial Act (S. 2634). Along with the APA Education Directorate's Public Policy Office, three members of APA and Division 17, Sherry Benton, Jim Campbell, and Emil Rodolfa, used their experience in college student mental health and treatment to help draft and support legislation that would potentially result in new federal revenues for prevention and treatment (Ablasser, 2004).

The grassroots advocacy campaign that partnered the APA Committee on Ethnic Minority Affairs with APA's Public Policy Office is an example of the application of mental health expertise to racial and ethnic health disparities legislation (Greene, 2004). This effort brought groups of counseling psychologists and counseling psychology students together with legislators to discuss concerns about problems with legislation that was being proposed.

Training for Legislative Involvement

The Public Policy Office of APA has created a guide for getting involved in the federal advocacy process (APA Public Policy Office, 1995). The purpose of this guide is to encourage psychologists to become involved in the political process and to do so more effectively. The guide presents readers with a basic understanding of the structure of federal law- and policy-making bodies and processes as well as appropriate mechanisms for voicing concerns. In addition, the Public Policy Office also sponsors regular advocacy training workshops for psychologists who are interested in becoming involved.

Although some counseling graduate programs are beginning to integrate practica and internships in advocacy and policy (e.g., Talleyrand et al., chapter 4), these opportunities are still somewhat rare. The APA Congressional Fellows program provides a unique venue through which postdoctoral psychologists can learn and contribute to public policy at the federal level (Chamberlin, 2004). A major goal of the fellowship program is to give psychologists the opportunity to apply their specialized content knowledge, practical expertise, and methodological training to policy making by placing them in the offices of members of Congress or congressional committees in positions such as policy analysts on topics such as health care, veterans' issues, suicide, mental health, and public safety, to name a few.

Introduction to the Policy and Legislation Section

> Even in a seemingly losing cause, one person may unknowingly inspire another, and that person yet a third, who could go on to change the world, or at least a small corner of it.
>
> (Loeb, 2004, p. 6)

In this section of the *Handbook*, we present two chapters that provide the reflections of four counseling psychologists who have been involved in various aspects of political advocacy. They have each emphasized that in writing these chapters, they hope to provide a personal perspective regarding legislative and public policy involvement rather than spotlight themselves as exceptions. As indicated in the quote by Loeb (2004), although change is slow and sometimes overwhelming, individual actions accumulate and inspire. The earlier description of the adoption and implementation of the multicultural competencies illustrates that institutional change is rarely the result of one individual or even a group of individuals. Each effort builds and supports subsequent efforts, eventually resulting in substantive change. It is in this spirit that we present this section of the *Handbook.* By presenting these personal stories, we hope to provide support for those who are currently involved in policy and legislative social justice work as well as provide a glimpse into the personal and professional development of four counseling psychologists.

Sandra Shullman, Bobbie Celeste, and Ted Strickland share their personal stories of their political and personal development from three different perspectives (Shullman et al., chapter 33). Sandra describes her evolution of increased involvement in public policy through efforts to bring research and psychological literature to public policy decisions. As a consultant and educator, Sandra draws upon her content knowledge relevant to such social justice topics as sexual harassment, as well as her knowledge of systems and organizations. Bobbie Celeste recounts her professional career as a psychologist-advocate for a state psychological association. This blend of political knowledge, lobbying, and psychology demonstrates the integration of interdisciplinary expertise in the interest of social justice. Finally, Ted Strickland describes his personal and professional development culminating in his experiences as a U.S. Congressman addressing issues of social justice. He adeptly integrates current psychological theory and the political process and provides inspiration regarding the potential in all of us for involvement in legislation and policy.

Robert McPherson has been involved in statewide initiatives in Texas advocating for issues related to consumer rights and psychological practice. In his chapter (McPherson, chapter 34), Robert provides a personal backdrop for his own development and subsequent involvement in influencing Texas law regarding managed care and its influence on clients and psychologists. This work is influenced by his continued role as an educator and administrator within a counseling psychology graduate program.

Conclusion

The vastness of social challenges facing humanity requires large-scale intervention. Although the expertise of counseling psychologists is well suited to individual empowerment and local community involvement, likewise, much of this expertise can, and should, be applied on a broad scale. Public policy decisions such as welfare reform, gender equity, same-sex marriage and adoption, and homelessness must be informed by knowledge that comes from the communities most affected. Counseling psychologists, with expertise in consulting, communicating, researching, and direct service, are in a unique position to serve as that bridge.

References

Ablasser, C. (2004). Creating healthy campuses: APA members successfully promote psychological services at colleges and universities. *APA Monitor on Psychology, 5*(10), 66–67.

American Psychological Association. (2003a). Division spotlight. *Monitor on Psychology, 34,* 71.

American Psychological Association. (2003b). Guidelines on multicultural education, training, research, practice, and organizational change for psychologists. *American Psychologist, 58,* 377–402.

American Psychological Association Public Policy Office. (1995). *Advancing psychology in the public interest: A psychologist's guide to participation in federal advocacy process.* Retrieved on February 21, 2005, from http://www.apa.org/ppo/ppan/piguide.html

Arredondo, P., Toporek, R., Brown, S. P., Jones, J., Locke, D. C., Sanchez, J., & Stadler, H. (1996). Operationalization of the multicultural counseling competencies. *Journal of Multicultural Counseling & Development, 24,* 42–78.

Bingham, R. P. (2003). Fostering human strength through diversity and public policy: A counseling psychologist's perspective. In W. B. Walsh (Ed.), *Counseling psychology and optimal human functioning* (pp. 279–295). Mahwah, NJ: Lawrence Erlbaum.

Chamberlin, J. (2004). Policy in the making: Through APA's Congressional Fellowship Program, five psychologists are learning the ins and outs of Capitol Hill. *Monitor on Psychology, 35*(7), 46.

Enns, C. Z. (1993). Twenty years of feminist counseling and therapy: From naming biases to implementing multifaceted practice. *The Counseling Psychologist, 21*(1), 3–87.

Goska, D. V. (2004). Political paralysis. In P. R. Loeb (Ed.), *The impossible will take a little while* (pp. 47–62). New York: Basic Books.

Greene, L. V. (2004). Grassroots campaign seeks to combat disparities. *Monitor on Psychology, 35*(3), 56–57.

Haldeman, D. C. (2003). APA's policy on conversion therapy: A brief history. *Division 44 Newsletter, 19*(1). Retrieved March 22, 2005, from http://www.apa.org/divisions/div44/v0119nu1.htm#APA's%20Policy%20On%20Conversion%20Therapy:%20A%20Brief%20History

Humphreys, K. (1996). Clinical psychologists as psychotherapists. *American Psychologist, 51,* 190–197.

Johnson, R. A., & Chope, R. C. (in press). How can a career counselor work with a whistle-blower? *Journal of Career Development, 31*(4).

Kiselica, M. (2004). When duty calls: The implications of social justice work for policy, education, and practice in the mental health professions. *The Counseling Psychologist, 32*(6), 838–854.

Lewis, J. A., Arnold, M. S., House, R., & Toporek, R. L. (2002). *Advocacy competencies: Task Force on Advocacy Competencies.* Alexandria, VA: American Counseling Association. Electronic version available at http://www.counseling.org/Content/NavigationMenu/RESOURCES/ADVOCACYCOMPETENCIES/advocacy_competencies1.pdf

Lewis, J. A., Lewis, M. D., Daniels, J. A., & D'Andrea, M. J. (1998). *Community counseling: Empowerment strategies for a diverse society* (2nd ed.). Pacific Grove, CA: Brooks/Cole.

Loeb, P. R. (2004). *The impossible will take a little while.* New York: Basic Books.

Meara, N. M., & Davis, K. L. (2004). Houston 2001 National Counseling Psychology Conference: Making a difference for the specialty. *The Counseling Psychologist, 32*(1), 99–108.

Psychologists for Social Responsibility. (2005). *Psychologists for Social Responsibility: Building cultures of peace.* Retrieved March 29, 2005, from http://www.psysr.org/

Roysircar, G. S., Arredondo, P. A., Fuertes, J., Ponterotto, J., & Toporek, R. L. (2003). *Multicultural counseling competencies 2003: AMCD.* Alexandria, VA: Association of Multicultural Counseling and Development.

Roysircar, G. S., Sandhu, D. S., & Bibbins, V. (Eds.). (2003). *Multicultural competencies: A guidebook of practices.* Alexandria, VA: Association of Multicultural Counseling and Development.

Sue, D. W., Bernier, J. E., Durran, A., Feinberg, L., Pedersen, P., Smith, E., & Vazquez-Nutall, E. (1982). Position paper: Cross-cultural counseling competencies. *Counseling Psychologist, 10,* 45–52.

Toporek, R. L. (2000). Creating a common language and framework for understanding advocacy in counseling. In J. Lewis & L. Bradley (Eds.), *Advocacy in counseling: Counselors, clients, and community* (pp. 5–14). Greensboro, NC: Caps Publications.

Toporek, R. L., & Liu, W. M. (2001). Advocacy in counseling psychology: Critical issues of race, class, and gender. In D. B. Pope-Davis & H. L. K. Coleman (Eds.), *The intersection of race, class and gender in counseling psychology* (pp. 385–413). Thousand Oaks, CA: Sage.

Toporek, R. L., & Reza, J. V. (2001). Context as a critical dimension of multicultural counseling: Articulating personal, professional, and institutional competence. *Journal of Multicultural Counseling and Development, 29*(1), 13–30.

U.S. Public Health Service. (1999). *Mental health: A report of the Surgeon General: Executive summary.* Available at http://www.surgeongeneral.gov/library/mentalhealth/home.html

Vera, E. M., & Speight, S. L. (2003). Multicultural competence, social justice, and counseling psychology: Expanding our roles. *The Counseling Psychologist, 31,* 253–272.

Winerman, L. (2004). Timely action. *Monitor on Psychology, 35*(1), 48.

CHAPTER 33

Extending the Parsons Legacy

Applications of Counseling Psychology in Pursuit of Social Justice Through the Development of Public Policy

Sandra L. Shullman, Bobbie L. Celeste, and Ted Strickland

No volume on social justice and counseling psychology would be complete without addressing the role of counseling psychologists in the development of public policy. Whereas Frank Parsons's social justice legacy has been directed at the actual counseling-related work of the vocational counselor, it is important to consider how the development of public policy could or should fit with the counselor's role. O'Brien (2001) defined social justice work as "actions that contribute to the advancement of society and advocate for equal access to resources for marginalized or less fortunate individuals in society" (p. 66). Indeed, it is the political and public policy arenas that often define the priorities and determine the extent of the dedicated resources for publicly funded social justice programs and social change practices.

At times, counseling psychology colleagues have expressed disdain with political and public policy development processes. They have been heard to say things such as, "I couldn't talk to those sorts of people" or "I don't have time to get involved in public policy" or "I am not interested in politics." The irony is that many counseling psychologists work in programs funded by initiatives developed in the political and public policy arenas. It would seem illogical to assume that those counseling psychologists who implement such programs would not, could not, or should not contribute to their initial development.

This chapter will highlight approaches taken by three counseling psychologists to become involved in public policy and political efforts so that readers can consider viable alternatives for their own involvement in such processes. In preparing this chapter, we were asked to write our experience in our own voice. It is hoped that every counseling psychologist can find some specific way(s) in which they can influence the nature of public discourse about topics vital to both clients and their professional colleagues. Those illustrated here are designed to create a vision of a spectrum of involvement for counseling psychologists rather than presuming a specific or prescriptive approach.

Counseling Psychologist as On-the-Job Advocate: All in a Day's Work

One of the authors of this chapter (Shullman) has been involved in advocacy for social justice issues as a professional in the course of her everyday work for more than 30 years. In her own words, here is the story of her involvement:

> In the early part of my career, I served as a university administrator (Assistant Dean of Students) in a student services function. Professionally, I became an active member of the National Association for Women Deans, Administrators and Counselors (NAWDAC) because many of the then-current and previous senior women leaders in student services at our institution had held significant leadership roles in NAWDAC. In the 1970s, I became involved on my campus in the development of a women's studies program and an extended program of women's services. As the Equal Rights Amendment moved to center stage in public policy discourse, I recognized (as did NAWDAC) that equal rights for women under the U.S. Constitution was foundational to all other women's development efforts. I worked at the state level with other colleagues to prepare educational materials and to contact our local legislators about passage of the Equal Rights Amendment in Ohio. In the process, I was asked by NAWDAC to testify before the state legislature. I had never done this before, but I wanted to do what I could to help. I prepared a statement, practiced, and presented at the legislative hearing. The hearing itself was handled quite respectfully, and I felt I had done my best. The real debate occurred in the rotunda of the state capitol as I was leaving. Someone from the opposition who had heard my testimony threw down the verbal gauntlet. I found myself transported to the center of the conversation and discovered that the appropriate points and words came very easily. From that point on, I knew that, as long as I was prepared and cared about an issue, I could do a reasonable job of testifying and representing my group. As I completed these activities, it became obvious to me that there were great needs and opportunities for professionals to work in such an arena on other issues of importance to clients, students, and colleagues. I continued this work for a number of years and had the satisfaction of being present when the governor of Ohio signed the Equal Rights Amendment.

In the late 1970s, I became a member of the American Psychological Association and found an immediate home with the then-named Division 17 Committee on Women (now the Section on Women). Not coincidentally, the Division 17 Committee on Women was at that time involved with other APA groups to formulate a larger response to the determined resistance to passage of the Equal Rights Amendment. Work during this period led to my later involvement in research on a variety of women's issues.

Ironically, while the Equal Rights Amendment is still not part of the U.S. Constitution, many public policies addressing work and benefits have been altered to reflect gender equity. This lack of final passage of the ERA as a national constitutional amendment points out the reality that sometimes the pursuit of one public policy issue may result in a different (but also important) impact and influence than initially intended. For example, I went on to work on some of the earlier sexual harassment research on the incidents and dimensions of sexual harassment in academia and the workplace (Fitzgerald & Shullman, 1993; Fitzgerald et al., 1988; Shullman, 1992a, 1992b; Shullman & Watts, 1990). As this research became available, numerous attorneys, human resources executives, and university administrators contacted our research group for information. Requests for invited addresses increased. Several members of the research team got involved in forensic activities as treatment specialists, expert witnesses, or case consultants. Some of this research is now widely cited in legal briefs throughout the U.S. judicial system. I also continued work at the state level to present psychological evidence and provide legislators with current scientific information relevant to women's issues such as sexual harassment, choices related to pregnancy, and women's employment opportunities.

Having been involved with APA groups on a number of legislative initiatives, I volunteered to be the first federal advocacy coordinator for Division 17, following the establishment by the APA Practice Directorate of an elaborate advocacy network for state and provincial psychological associations in the 1990s (other directorates at APA now offer similar options). In this capacity for 10 years, I served as the liaison between Division 17 and the APA for advocacy at the federal level around issues such as mental health parity, inclusion of psychology in federal graduate medical education funding, patient rights, and patient access to care for all Americans. I also joined my state psychological association (the Ohio Psychological Association), where I found a number of like-minded souls across a variety of psychological disciplines. Eventually, I came to co-chair the state advocacy efforts for the Ohio Psychological Association, where we addressed parity for mental health in the health insurance system, a range of patient rights protections in the health care system, hospital privileges for psychologists, and a variety of issues related to discrimination and unfair treatment of targeted client populations.

All of these efforts were worked into my "regular" job as a counseling psychologist. Most of this work seemed so intertwined with my daily professional responsibilities that it would have been hard to compartmentalize them totally.

My social justice advocacy activities involved sending letters, making telephone calls, sending e-mails, meeting with legislators (or legislative staff), testifying, developing information and research summaries, giving invited presentations, debating, training others to advocate, making and soliciting financial contributions, and persuading other colleagues to get involved. All of these activities were direct extensions of skills I had developed and used in the course of my practice. I was not (and still am not) a professional politician or public policy maker, but I have been able, over the course of time, to contribute at least some small amount to movement at both national and state levels on a number of social justice issues.

I believe strongly that good public policy is good for both psychology and those whom psychology serves. I have personally experienced the importance of psychologists becoming active citizens in the advocacy process, advocating for client populations who cannot advocate as well for themselves, and advocating for psychological knowledge and practice to be centrally included in public policy debate and development. Psychological science is critical to the development of sound public policy in innumerable arenas. Personal passion and professional commitment are vital to ensuring that such science-based, sound public policy is the outcome of the political process. I see it as part of my personal and professional role in our country to be part of making that happen. Whenever I hear myself saying, "Someone ought to do something about this . . . ," I have learned to ask myself what I should be doing about it first rather than waiting and hoping or assuming someone else indeed will do it all for me. That is both the responsibility and privilege of being a professional and representing your colleagues.

I have learned much about myself, our profession, those in need of services, and the legislative and regulatory processes of my country and community in the pursuit of social justice. Some of the key learning includes the following:

1. Psychologists have developed skills that can be useful in advocacy for vulnerable people and public policy. The skills of counseling psychologists can be used well outside the four walls of professional offices.

2. Those in need of services, especially those in the behavioral health arena, are especially vulnerable and can be easily overlooked in the public policy arena without our help.

3. The legislative and regulatory process, both locally and nationally, can be influenced by our collective efforts, especially if each counseling psychologist makes a personal commitment to be involved in some tangible way over time. Issues, attitudes, and approaches can be changed over time as long as the work is viewed more like a marathon than a sprint.

4. Involvement in advocacy provides great opportunities for professional growth. Advocacy experiences have become the incubator for trying out a variety of tasks; experiencing the pressure of working under adversity; enhancing worldviews through exposure to diverse individuals, groups, and cultures; and seeing the intensity of advocacy efforts come to fruition.

Counseling Psychologist as Lobbyist and Advocate: Going Professional

Another author of this chapter (Celeste) has been involved in paid professional advocacy since 1997, serving as the director of professional affairs for her state psychological association. This position, developed with seed money from the Practice Directorate of the American Psychological Association, is a paid psychologist-advocate position. This section traces the course of a second psychologist's development as a social justice advocate in her own voice:

> A concern for social justice issues, particularly the civil rights and antiwar movements, drew me to politics in the 1960s. As a college student, I participated in antiwar marches, civil rights initiatives, political campaigns, and college protests. When civil rights legislation was passed and the war in Vietnam ended, it reinforced my belief that social justice work could change public policy.
>
> My first paid social justice work was as a U.S. Peace Corps volunteer in the Fiji Islands. This early immersion into a Pacific Island country exposed me to new worldviews and gave me an opportunity to experience a communal rather than individualistic culture. I also learned to use approaches in my work aimed at empowering the Fijians with whom I worked. These techniques used by multicultural and feminist psychologists have been identified as elements of social justice work (Goodman et al., 2004). These strategies include "ongoing self-examination, sharing power, building on strengths, and leaving clients with the tools for social change" (p. 798).
>
> My next paid advocacy position was with a coalition lobbying the governor and state legislature to increase state aid to families with dependent children. The effort was successful and was followed by paid work for a presidential candidate. My next years were spent professionally as a counselor, but I volunteered in a number of local, state, and national campaigns. My husband and I devoted hours to his campaign as the Democratic nominee for the U.S. Senate and his brother's campaigns and public service as the lieutenant governor and governor of Ohio. These campaigns offered an effective outlet for social justice work and provided an opportunity to give emotional support and counsel to family and campaign workers living in the political spotlight.
>
> With two children mostly raised, I began my doctorate in counseling psychology, which led to my professional advocacy position as a licensed psychologist. The Ohio Psychological Association (OPA) recruited me for a newly created part-time position, Director of Professional Affairs, because of my combination of political experience and professional training as a psychologist. The role of Director of Professional Affairs includes being a registered lobbyist for the association, monitoring the introduction of new bills, researching current laws and regulations, writing position papers, meeting with legislators to describe psychology's position on pending legislation, attending legislative hearings, and recruiting psychologists to give testimony before committees. Because policy is also made in regulation as well as in

legislation, monitoring changes in the executive branch of government and following the rule-making process after a bill has passed is also a required aspect of advocacy. I am also an advocate for psychologists as they struggle with managed care and insurance coverage and reimbursement difficulties.

In preparation for lobbying efforts, I work closely with the association director and volunteer board member psychologists to develop and implement policy initiatives. Given that psychology is a small player in the state legislative arena, we join forces with coalitions representing social service groups, health care providers, and mental health advocates. We are fortunate to have several legislators who were trained as psychologists and who provide helpful insight and guidance to our lobbying efforts.

My other advocacy activities include training psychologists to be advocates. This involves writing articles for the newsletter, organizing advocacy workshops at state conventions, planning statehouse lobbying events for psychologists as well as sending action alerts and preparing information for the Web site. Training future psychologists to be advocates is essential, and I make a point of reaching out to graduate students whenever possible. In conjunction with The Ohio State University counseling psychology program, I have supervised five counseling graduate students in practicum placements and served as summer external placement supervisor for a predoctoral intern. I also speak regularly about advocacy to graduate psychology programs throughout Ohio. The state association works closely with the Ohio Psychological Association Graduate Students (OPAGS), providing them with guidance and opportunities to participate in state and federal advocacy activities.

Working closely with the APA Practice Directorate, I participate in advocacy training and lobbying on Capitol Hill. Raising money for the APA Practice Directorate's political action committee, AAP-Plan, and OPA's political action committee is also part of my portfolio as a Director of Professional Affairs for a state psychology association. This position also involves participation in Division 31 (The State Psychological Association Affairs), which shares ideas for building strong associations and effective advocacy programs.

Public policy issues at the state level parallel those at the national level. I assist the state association leadership and staff in work to promote access to mental health services for all citizens, the rights of gay and lesbian couples to have domestic partnerships, the protection of psychologists' scope of practice, children's right to medical care without parent relinquishment, client protection from sexual exploitation by mental health providers, privacy of mental health records, and provider protection legislation. During the economically tight budget times of the period following the economic downturn in 2000, maintaining mental health services for adults who have Medicaid insurance continues to be a significant issue.

Although lobbying may seem far removed from the work and training of counseling psychologists, the required skills are ones emphasized in the professional training of the counseling psychologist: listening, building relationships, articulating arguments, interpreting data, reading technical material, understanding research implications, and analyzing data. The skill base as doctoral-level social scientists make counseling psychologists well suited to work in the public policy arena. Relationships and data are valuable commodities in politics, and psychologists are experts in both areas. In addition, lobbyists rely heavily on their reputation for trustworthiness to achieve continuing success. Psychologists' training in confidentiality and ethics is highly transferable to advocacy within the field of lobbying.

Psychologists' understanding of the change process in psychotherapy also has parallels in the public policy arena. Clinicians learn to be patient with clients as they slowly practice new behavior, to be satisfied with incremental change, and to be respectful of people with significantly different viewpoints. Psychologists also learn that they can't "win them all." Some clients are not ready or able to make needed changes, or changes accomplished one year are undone the following year. Creating change in the public policy arena is similar. Patience, satisfaction with incremental change, and respect for differences are all necessary ingredients for successful policy development work.

Another similarity between psychotherapy and lobbying is the relationship between scientific facts and motivation to change. Clients may know the facts and understand the logic of a prescribed change, but they need to be emotionally ready to implement the change. Legislators are the same way. Data to support the new policy are necessary but will not be sufficient to convince policymakers to institute a public policy change. What is needed is emotional readiness from their own experience or from that of their constituents and colleagues. Strong citizen action, combined with supportive data, eventually is persuasive in the public policy arena. Counseling psychologists can participate effectively in both functions, providing the research basis for action and providing the citizen input through activities such as those described in this chapter.

An especially frustrating aspect for psychologists involved in social advocacy has been the reluctance of a significant number of psychologists to become involved in the political process. Training programs could address this deficit by increasing students' exposure to the political process. Once aware of the opportunities and challenges, most students are eager to participate and come back again and again to advocacy activities, such as legislative visits at the statehouse. Exposing students to policy development could take many forms. For example, possible class assignments for students could include visiting the city council or the state legislature; inviting politicians to speak with students; compiling psychological research findings about a current public policy debate; preparing testimony and writing letters to support legislation; volunteering to work in campaign or legislative offices; learning about electronic advocacy sites; and volunteering at state, provincial, or territorial psychological association conventions.

Faculty could belong to their state, provincial, or territorial psychological association and encourage students to join. Public policy as it applies to licensure and supervision could be included in the pre- and postdoctoral internship training because students often stay in the state in which they do their internships. If our training programs expose students to the public policy process and reward their involvement, they may leave graduate school prepared to make public policy work part of their professional identity.

Working as a Director of Professional Affairs with a state association is one possible avenue for those interested in affecting public policy. This position is not unique to Ohio; 18 state psychological associations have similar part-time, paid psychologist-advocate positions (Sullivan, personal communication). The APA Practice Directorate is encouraging state associations to develop these political advocacy positions in an effort to enhance psychology's voice in state and federal policy making.

Counseling Psychologist and Minister as Public Official: A Christian in the Lion's Den

Ted Strickland, a third co-author, was the first psychologist (a counseling psychologist) to be elected to the U.S. Congress. He has been officially involved in political advocacy for social justice issues since 1975. His interests in helping those suffering from economic and social hardships, however, began much earlier. Strickland describes in more depth his autobiographical journey in a book titled *Psychology and Public Policy: Balancing Public Service and Professional Need* (Lorion, Iscoe, DeLeon, & VandenBos, 1996). The interested reader is referred to this chapter in its entirety for a description of his views on the unique role psychologists can offer in service to public officials, the value of psychological knowledge for policymakers, and psychology's untapped potential as a policy profession.

Given that few (but a growing number of) psychologists have made a successful run for public office, a brief summary of Congressman Strickland's political journey in his own words may be helpful to the reader:

> My journey into political advocacy for social justice officially began in 1976 when I interrupted work on my doctoral dissertation to run for the U.S. Congress. Perhaps I just wanted to avoid finishing my dissertation, but I believe the greater influence came from all that went on during the Watergate hearings. I remember wanting to be a part of righting the wrongs of that time.
>
> From my earliest memories, I felt a deep compassion for those suffering from economic and social hardships. As the eighth of nine children born into a steelworker's family from the Appalachia area of Ohio, I learned the importance of family unity and commitment to deal with these hardships.
>
> As far back as I can remember, politics was important to my father. He was particularly grateful for the policies of Franklin Delano Roosevelt during the Depression and the fair labor laws and safety standards passed in the years that followed. Without the decent wages gained through the labor movement, I'm not sure how our family could have fought back from the devastation of a flood and a fire that destroyed our home and everything in it. Watching my family's struggle to build back after the fire left an indelible impression on me

of how hardships can come to people through no fault of their own and how frightening vulnerabilities can be without someone to lean on.

While my dad worried about keeping our family fed and clothed, my mother quietly saw to it that I went to college. There was no question in the hearts of her children that she loved all of us equally, but she was especially proud of my interest in the ministry and the way I enjoyed opportunities for formal learning.

Initially, my ministerial actions had more to do with Christian witnessing than promoting social justice issues. However, a year after I was ordained, I moved from my ministry in a local church and began work in a Methodist Children's Home. It was there that my first interests in psychology emerged. Several of the children had been sexually and emotionally abused or were dealing with teenage drug addiction. It didn't take me long to realize that these children needed a level of help and expertise beyond my Thursday night chapel service. With that awareness, I returned to college and enrolled in a counseling psychology program at the University of Kentucky.

Up until that time in my life, I held strong social and theologically conservative views. However, in my graduate studies, I gravitated toward the humanistic viewpoints of such psychologists as Carl Rogers and Abraham Maslow. I believe my movement from fundamentalist leanings toward humanism largely happened because it proved to be more consistent with the values I learned from my parents than what I experienced in seminary. For example, consider the early political influence of my father, who saw government as having a role in helping people, and the unconditional love and acceptance my mother showed not only to each of her nine children, but also to the others around her. Her spirit was like the woman who said, "I don't like to criticize anyone else's children because I don't know what my own are doing."

My ministerial and psychology training merged when I worked with seriously disturbed public offenders—first in the emergency unit of a community mental health center, then as a lobbyist for mental health legislation, and finally as a psychologist on the mental health unit of a maximum security prison. In these roles, I was an outspoken advocate for the poor and mentally ill, arguing against, in my mind, a societal press that did not want to provide for these individuals in any therapeutic or rehabilitative way. The frustration I felt led to a growing interest in a political career and the possibility of changing the system from the inside out through public legislation.

I finally got my chance in 1992 when I was elected to the U.S. House of Representatives after losses in 1976, 1978, and 1980. My district is politically conservative, and the strategy of my opponents continues to be to paint me as a liberal or, as Caprara and Zimbardo's (2004) recent article suggests, a "center-leftist" as opposed to a "center-rightist."

Taking a moment to review Caprara and Zimbardo's (2004) tentative findings is useful in that they provide some insight into the fundamental differences underlying values supporting the opposing political views expressed in our current public policy debates. According to Caprara and Zimbardo, my votes as a center-left politician would be influenced by inherent traits and values such as Friendliness (concern and sensitiveness or kindness toward others) and Openness (broadness of one's own cultural interest and exposure to new ideas, people, and experiences). My concerns would be about equality and social justice with an emphasis on values such as solidarity, social policies, and civil rights. At the higher-level value, my type includes openness to change (self-direction and stimulation, independence of thought, feeling, and action) and self-transcendence (universalism and benevolence with an emphasis on accepting others as equals and a concern for their welfare).

The inherent traits and values of "center-right" voters and politicians include a significantly high degree of Energy (level of activity, vigor, and assertiveness) and Conscientiousness (self-regulation in both proactive and inhibitory aspects). Generally, the traditional concern of the political right wing is recognition of individual achievements and social order. They tend to hold values such as entrepreneurship, business freedom, order, self-control, and security. Higher-level value types include conservative (security, conformity, submissive self-restriction, preservation of traditional practices, and protection of stability) and self-enhancement (power and achievement or the pursuit of one's own success, and dominance over others).

Although Caprara and Zimbardo (2004) caution against overinterpretation because of small sample sizes and the difficulty experienced in eliciting meaningful responses, my personal experiences suggest that their findings are intuitively sound. I firmly believe that center-leftists shoulder the lion's share of social justice work as defined by Parsons. But in the larger political perspective, I also accept the necessity of vigorous interplay between respective values if we are to have a strong system of checks and balances for competing interests. In the best of a democracy, center-rightists' resistance to change slows the pace to levels that reduce the risk of chaos and confusion in our society. On the other side, if center-leftists did not promote change and adaptations, we would experience stagnation and nongrowth. Thus, both have an important role in the well-being of a shared world.

Unfortunately, the positive aspects of these differing values and traits are lost in many of our political campaigns. Too many campaigns are not about who is best suited to serve, but who can win. Consequently, many representatives in government today are mediocre at best, and those supportive of social justice issues are increasingly underrepresented. Why? One explanation is voter turnoff. With the rancor and meanness of campaigns, some protest by simply not voting. The increasingly conservative leaning of the United States suggests that the center-leftist voters may be the ones who stay home on Election Day.

Using Caprara and Zimbardo's (2004) work, it is possible that the traits of Friendliness and Openness attributed to center-leftists are trumped by the Energy and Conscientious traits of the center-rightists. For example, sensitiveness or concern about hurting someone's feelings gets in the way when the debate is emotionally charged, and the opposition feels free to show vigor and assertiveness without regard for the impact on others. Unfortunately, emotionally charged arguments tend to center on socially divisive issues. As history instructs us, social justice never has and never will come without courage in the face of adversity.

Therefore, a first step counseling psychologists can take toward a strong role in the development of public policy is to stay engaged when the negative rhetoric comes.

A second step is to contact legislators with concerns—preferably in person. Most members enjoy constituent visits to both their Washington and district offices. They especially appreciate attendance at any town hall meetings or forums they sponsor in their home areas. As a member of Congress, I'm grateful to psychologists not only because they helped elect me to Congress, but also because they make me a better public servant than I would be without their insight. Representatives learn important and relevant information from direct service people, and this knowledge and insight are crucial to good decision making and the development of effective public policy initiatives.

Finally, I would like to provide examples of how my background as a counseling psychologist influences my work in Congress—work that I believe falls in the category of social justice. First, as a rule, for any legislation that is introduced, my staff and I carefully examine it for fairness to those who live in rural areas and low-income areas. This particularly manifested itself in vocational training programs and funding for resources meant to relieve the impact of long-term rural and urban poverty. I am a strong advocate for parity for mental health care in the insurance system, the Childrens Health Insurance Program (CHIPS)—with an ultimate vision of universal health care coverage for every citizen in our great nation. Tapping back into my early work with public offenders, my staff and I collaborated with others of a similar interest and created legislation to encourage the use of mental health courts as an alternative to the sole use of the criminal justice system to address mental health and criminal justice issues.

The other major areas of social justice that concern me as a legislator are veterans' rights and the safety of our troops in harm's way. After learning of the ways in which the rights of our veterans are being neglected, I received special permission to serve on the Veterans' Affairs Committee. Currently, I'm fighting to help veterans receive needed VA benefits as well as trying to ensure that all of our soldiers in Iraq are protected with proper body armor, uparmored Humvees, and other essential equipment.

Congressman and Dr. Strickland challenges his psychological colleagues to consider "how you can be a psychologist and support policies that prohibit your clients from making decisions for themselves, especially related to employment, education, and health care." He encourages us, as psychologists, to consider new models of service delivery and new forms of training that can make differences in people's lives, thinking beyond the confines of our offices.

Ted Strickland is not the only psychologist to take his skills and training as a psychologist into elected office. The list of psychologist-state legislators grows each year. These dedicated psychologists on both sides of the political aisle work on education, mental health reform, and issues of social justice in statehouses across the country. Their stories and career paths as psychologist-legislators have been well documented in the American Psychological Association journal *Professional Psychology: Research and Practice.* The narratives of these psychologists add breadth and depth to the picture of how psychologists can contribute special expertise to legislative deliberations (Barnhart, 2002; Blanchard, 2002; Buffmire, 1995; Celeste, 2000; Geake, 1995; Heldring, 1995; Kennemer, 1995; Miller, 2002; Sullivan, 1999; Sullivan, McNamara, Ybarra, & Bulatao, 1995; Walley, 1995).

Conclusions and Recommendations

This chapter has illustrated and highlighted the role of the counseling psychologist in the development of public policy for social justice and has suggested different paths for counseling psychologists in actively influencing public policy to achieve social justice. Without prescribing any specific role, several recommendations and suggestions can be made for involvement in the political/public policy-making process.

1. Support the public policy efforts of national professional organizations. The American Psychological Association advocates for public policy issues through each of its directorates—Public Interest, Education, Practice, and Science—as well as through the centralized APA Public Policy Office. The American Counseling Association also advocates for a number of social justice concerns. Issues of particular interest to counseling psychologists are often addressed at the federal level by these groups. Recent sample efforts have included parity for psychological services in health insurance plans, welfare-to-work legislation, federal support for college and university counseling centers, psychologist inclusion in graduate medical education resources, and mental health courts as alternatives for addressing criminal substance abuse issues. Other national groups, such as the Association of Black Psychologists, the Latino/Latina Psychological Association, and the Association of Asian Psychologists, are also involved in advocating for a number of social justice public policy issues.

2. Support the public policy efforts of state, territorial, and provincial professional organizations. State, territorial, and provincial psychological associations, for example, also work on public policy efforts at the state level. Also, a number of the national groups (such as the minority psychological associations) have corresponding state chapters. Efforts by such groups often involve targeted populations with specific needs, such as vocational training applicants, welfare-to-work populations, and other health and human services issues. Recently, several such groups have provided key psychological knowledge to legislators and policy makers around issues such as same-sex marriage and family situations, minority health care disparities, child development and custody issues, and approaches to addressing senior citizen needs. State and provincial psychological associations, like national groups, may file amicus briefs in various legal cases, outlining the key psychological issues

and current research findings that may support a court's proceedings. In such filings, research summaries are prepared to educate policy and decision makers.

3. Support political action and political giving groups that support social justice issues of personal and professional concern. Professional psychological organizations also develop independent political action organizations so that funds can be solicited for various issues and/or candidates supportive of particular social justice issues. At times, psychologists express skepticism about becoming involved in such political giving processes because they may feel that supporting a candidate who supports one of their public policy issues means they also have to agree with all positions the candidate may take. It is important to remember that virtually no public policy maker, whether in an elected or administrative position, is likely to take positions completely congruent with any one constituent. Compromise is inherent to the public policy-making process, and support for issues may well involve some reasonable levels of such compromise.

4. Psychologists may have much to contribute as active public policy makers. Counseling psychology cannot always rely on existing public policy to cover significant social justice issues. Sometimes, it is critical to be directly involved in the dialogue involving policy development. This can be done by testifying in front of public policy-making bodies, presenting relevant psychological research about the issues being addressed. Psychological expertise is often overlooked in public policy debate and lost in a quagmire of presumed "common sense." Such common sense often runs counter to evidence-based scientific findings and can result in disastrous public policy.

5. Psychologists can have more influence on the design of better public policy than we might think. Many psychologists likely assume that they can't make a difference or they have little to contribute to the development of public policy initiatives. As this chapter hopefully demonstrated, psychologists who focus efforts on specific issues can often have tremendous influence on public policy development. Getting to know specific policy makers, talking to policy makers about one specific topic, and preparing materials on specific topics to educate policy makers can have a tremendous influence on the framing of public policy at its earliest stages of development.

6. Some aspects of public policy development related to social justice issues can be accessed only from the inside out. While all of the preceding suggestions are excellent means of influencing social justice issues in the public policy arena, there is also a significant need to have the voice of counseling psychology involved in the actual internal debates of such legislative and public policy bodies. This could include serving as staff or advisor to a public official, or actually running for office and becoming a public official. Much of the significant debate about social justice issues can take place out of the public spotlight. At times, there is no substitute for having psychological knowledge immediately at hand in the middle of a closed policy deliberation. Such roles could also include becoming appointed to various public policy boards, commissions, and committees.

7. Support other psychologists who are willing to involve themselves in the public debate about social justice issues. Colleagues who work to influence public policy need the support and encouragement of those doing psychological work in social justice. Such support is also needed for those who do the direct service work in social justice areas. The recognition that all of these roles are critical in the goal of achieving social justice would take the discipline of counseling psychology one step closer to achieving its full potential.

8. It is well documented that, among the helping and health professions, psychologists raise relatively little money to support causes and candidates (AAP Advance, Spring, 2002, p. 6). It is in the arena of power and monetary resource brokering where psychologists are least trained to function effectively. This lack of preparation contributes to the reaction by many psychologists, who find lobbying and raising money for candidates and political action committees somewhat distasteful. In other professions, students are taught to join their professional associations, become political participants, and contribute financially to their organizations' political action committees. Political advocacy is an important part of their professional identity, and they look to their state and national associations to lead the way in this arena. Many professional development courses do provide information about federal and state policies.

9. The realm of social advocacy and politics and the development of public policy is fraught with compromises and dilemmas. Many psychologists view such situations as ethical nightmares. Professional seminars could help prepare students for the real dilemmas involved in trying to formulate good public policy, especially when extreme compromise may be involved at any given point in time or alliances with persons or groups with antithetical views in other areas may be required for situational effectiveness. Ethical case studies involving social advocacy and public policy formation could provide helpful resources for the education of psychologists and their preparation for the public policy arena.

All of the co-authors of this article chose counseling psychology because of its focus on individual strengths and its emphasis on the "remediation and prevention of personal, interpersonal, vocational and educational concerns" (Brown & Lent, 1992, p. xi). It appears that, at its core, counseling psychology provides a framework that nourishes the development and involvement of psychologists in social advocacy and public policy development.

References

Association for the Advancement of Psychology. (2002, Spring). Comparison of health care professions political giving performance. *The AAP Advance,* 6.

Barnhart, P. N. (2002). The accidental politician. *Professional Psychology: Research and Practice, 33,* 281–284.

Blanchard, J. (2002). At home in a strange land. *Professional Psychology: Research and Practice, 33*(3), 285–288.

Brown S. D., & Lent, R. W. (Eds.). (1992). *Handbook of Counseling Psychology* 2nd ed.) New York: Wiley.

Buffmire, J. A. (1995). Are politics for you? *Professional Psychology: Research and Practice, 26,* 453–455.

Caprara, G. V., & Zimbardo, P. G. (2004). Personalizing politics: A congruency model of political preference. *American Psychologist, 59*(7), 581–594.

Celeste, B. L. (2000). We must be the change we want to see in the world: Psychologists in the statehouse. *Professional Psychology: Research and Practice, 31,* 469–472.

Fitzgerald, L. F., & Shullman, S. L. (1993). Sexual harassment: A research analysis and agenda for the 1990s. *Journal of Vocational Behavior, 42,* 5–27.

Fitzgerald, L. F., Shullman, S. L., Bailey, N., Richards, M., Swecker, J., Gold, Y., Ormerod, M., & Weitzman, L. (1988). The incidents and dimensions of sexual harassment in academia and the workplace. *Journal of Vocational Behavior, 32,* 152–175.

Geake, R. R. (1995). Practical tips for getting involved in politics. *Professional Psychology: Research and Practice, 26,* 463–464.

Goodman, L. A., Liang, B., Helms, J. E., Latta, R. E., Sparks, E., & Weintraub, S. R. (2004). Training counseling psychologists as social justice agents: Feminist and multicultural principles in action. *The Counseling Psychologist, 32,* 793–837.

Heldring, M. B. (1995). Running for political office: If at first you don't succeed . . . *Professional Psychology: Research and Practice, 26,* 449–452.

Kennemer, W. N. (1995). Psychology and the political process. *Professional Psychology: Research and Practice, 26,* 456–458.

Lorion, R. P., Iscoe, I., DeLeon, P. H., & VandenBos, G. R. (1996). *Psychology and public policy: Balancing public service and professional need.* Washington, DC: American Psychological Association.

Miller, D. (2002). Advancing mental health in political places. *Professional Psychology: Research and Practice, 33,* 277–280.

O'Brien K. M. (2001). The legacy of parsons: Career counselors and agents of social change. *Career Development Quarterly, 50*(1), 66–76.

Shullman, S. L. (1992a, August). *Sexual harassment training: Intervention in context.* Proceedings of the American Bar Association annual meeting, Section of Labor and Employment Law, San Francisco.

Shullman, S. L. (1992b, March). *Sexual harassment training interventions: Contextual factors.* Proceedings of Sex and Power Issues in the Workplace: A National Conference to Promote Men and Women Working Productively Together, Bellevue, WA.

Shullman, S. L., & Watts, B. G. (1990). Sexual harassment in higher education: Legal aspects. In M. A. Paludi (Ed.), *Ivory power: Sexual harassment on campus.* Albany: SUNY Press.

Sullivan, M. J. (1999). Psychologists as legislators: Results of the 1998 elections. *Professional Psychology: Research and Practice, 30,* 250–252.

Sullivan, M. J., McNamara, K. M., Ybarra, M., & Bulatao, E. Q. (1995). Psychologists as state legislators: Introduction to the special section. *Professional Psychology: Research and Practice, 26,* 445–448.

Walley, P. B. (1995). Lucky dogs. *Professional Psychology: Research and Practice, 26,* 459–462.

CHAPTER 34

Confessions of an Abiding Counseling Psychologist

Robert H. McPherson and Clare Reilly

"What's the problem?"

"Well we're getting a royal screwin' by an insurance company."

"What type of policy?" I ask.

"It's a medical policy," she says. "We bought it five years ago, Great Benefit Life, when our boys were seventeen. Now Donny Ray is dying of leukemia, and the crooks won't pay for his treatment . . . Well, pardon my French, but they're a bunch of sumbitches."

"Most insurance companies are," I add thoughtfully, and Dot smiles at this.

(A liberal excerption from John Grisham's fictitious novel *The Rainmaker*)

This chapter tells two stories with unfinished endings. The first is a coming-of-age story about one man's aspirations to be an abiding counseling psychologist on matters of social justice. The second story provides an abbreviated and selective historical account of the evolution—and now hopeful

Authors' Note: Much of this chapter is written in the voice of the first author, who assumes full responsibility for any inaccuracy of fact or interpretive bias that follows. He gratefully acknowledges the contributions of the second author, who provides the reader with a cogent synthesis of managed care and its reform in the United States. Finally, both authors express their gratitude to Rebecca Toporek and Nadya Fouad for their patient guidance, comments, and editorial expertise.

devolution (Newman, 2004)—of the U.S. managed care system. It is the intersection of these stories that may provide the reader with an example of one psychologist's participation in matters of political advocacy on an important and continuing social justice issue affecting our profession and those we attempt to help.

A Brief Family History

Although it is often said that all politics are local, it is equally true that all politics are personal. What follows is part autobiographical and part confessional. It is a rendering of my professional drift toward participation in psychological association service and political advocacy efforts on behalf of psychological practice. The story is not particularly awe-inspiring, but will perhaps reassure the reader that some good can be accomplished through political involvement, and that an average psychologist can make a contribution to the cause.

This story starts with my family. My father was a high school dropout and a decorated, 20-year career Marine sergeant turned self-taught—via a home correspondence course—furniture upholsterer. My mother was one of five children born to a poor West Texas cotton farmer. She graduated from high school, became a homemaker, and eventually joined the family's small upholstery business as a seamstress. Mom always voted Democrat—when she voted—until Ronald Reagan ran for president. Dad grew up tough, short, skinny, and poor on the outskirts of Boston. He has never declared a political party. Dad would likely be best classified as an independent; most certainly, he has been independently minded and opinionated about most things in his 80 years of living. Politics were rarely discussed in my family, but there was generally profane disdain in our house for politicians of all persuasions.

As the eldest of four brothers, my early childhood was characterized by the multiple moves of a military family, with the bulk of my education occurring in the public schools of Southern California, then Lubbock, Texas. I eventually became a self-funded, first-generation college graduate from Texas Tech University, majoring in education. With diploma in hand, I had only two job offers: teaching health and coaching baseball in Big Springs, Texas, or directing a peer counseling program at Ector High School, a low-income minority school in Odessa, Texas. I chose the latter, where I also completed a master's degree in school counseling at the University of Texas of the Permian Basin. I eventually moved to The Big City—Houston—and completed a PhD in counseling psychology at the University of Houston. Counseling psychology has been my professional identity for the duration of my professional life, but I must first confess to my readers, whom I assume are mostly liberal-minded counseling psychology colleagues, that my wife is a Big "C" Clinical psychologist in private practice. We have a 9-year-old daughter, a son who recently entered the army (a second confession) against my objections, and a daughter currently working as a legislative aide for senior Republican Senator Pat Roberts of Kansas (yet a third confession).

My children experienced my engagement in professional association service and political advocacy through accounts of my frequent travel to the state capitol, and more painfully, from my all-too-frequent absences from their school and extracurricular events stemming from these same trips to Austin. Their familial exposure to matters political more recently include an occasional political fundraiser for both Democratic and Republican candidates hosted in our home on behalf of the Houston Psychological Association. Like my family of origin, their mother and I did not espouse a strong political partisan in our house, although it might be more accurately stated that we were moderate in our political views, with she leaning more to the right and me to the left of the middle of the silent majority.

My children seem to have cut their own path ideologically, politically, and spiritually. My son, John, considers himself a patriot, inspired to be a Special Forces soldier from stories told by and about his Marine Corps grandfather (my father) and by the terrorist attack of September 11. John tolerated several semesters of college life to appease his parents, then enlisted when he could so without our signature. I recently watched ambivalently—pride for his accomplishments and terror for his safety—as he was honored in a military graduation ceremony. I tried reassuring myself with, "This has been his dream, and his Strong Campbell scores did match exceptionally well with the military profile."

He also finds politics boring and refuses to join the bantering in which his older sister and I sometimes engage on matters of public policy, political ideology, and political correctness. And I must confess that at 25, his sister's knowledge and influence on matters affecting the social welfare, defense, economic, and health care concerns of our society far exceeds that of their father. The simple virtue of my sense of social justice is no match for her articulate ideology and command of factual information. Some observers of the Washington political scene lament that our nation's capital is run by 20-year-olds; I take great pride, and assurance, that my Sara is standing so near the helm.

Survivor's Guilt

As is true for many of the baby boomer generation, the evolution of my political ideology began naïvely and idealistically, in part, by the student activism movement in the late 1960s and early 1970s, and in response to my own unexpressed fear of the Vietnam War and anger about the draft. More germane to the purposes of this chapter, my adult efforts at political activism—or in the politically correct vernacular of counseling psychology, social justice—were initially stirred by the musical lyrics of the day (i.e., "Four Dead in Ohio"), and by the antiwar and peace activities of the mostly college students I observed on television while I was in high school.

My freshman year in college at Texas Tech coincided with the final stages of the last military draft in U.S. history. I recall sitting in yet another painful botany lecture with some 400 or so other students; many had transistor radios pressed against their ears to learn of their military fate via the lottery number assigned to their birthdays. Low numbers meant a high likelihood of being drafted. I have not won a lottery since, but that day I learned that my draft lottery number was 324, which meant that I would not be headed to Vietnam but could otherwise continue an unimpressive start to my lifelong career in the academy. That same year, I became a self-declared champion foosball player, a better than average pool hustler in the student union, and a "frat rat."

Reflectively, I wish I had been more engaged in the peace movement of the times, but truthfully, I was just relieved to have dodged the bullets, landmines, fraggings, and fire bombs of Southeast Asia. I was reasonably content working long hours at two jobs, going to college, playing intramural sports, contemplating the possibilities afforded by the "Pill," and occasionally drinking too much beer. In the years that followed that memorable botany class in which I earned a well-deserved "D," it was an enlightened fraternity brother who eventually pushed me toward more noble notions of career aspiration and social responsibility.

My friend nicknamed himself Hawkeye after the *M*A*S*H* character. His real name was Tommy Allen. He was the most intelligent person who befriended me in college, and we became college roommates and lifelong friends. We both began our professional careers teaching in low-income, minority high schools in Texas. We were an unlikely pair. Tom was extroverted and the eldest son of college-educated folk. His father was a college history professor, his mother a schoolteacher. He was—and still is—wonderfully passionate about living, helping others, and learning. My parents were simply relieved when I graduated from Lubbock High School and would have been proud if I had stayed on with the family-owned upholstery business on 34th Street in Lubbock. I was introverted, laid-back, and an academic underachiever who typically took the path of least resistance.

I had stumbled my way into Tech with a small ($250) journalism scholarship—I had been both athlete and co-sports editor for my high school newspaper—but eventually I changed my major from mass communications—I hated typing and deadlines—to education. Along the way, I arose at 4:30 each morning to deliver the *University Daily* newspaper to campus dormitories and office buildings, continued working a large portion of most days at Banner Upholstery, attended classes intermittently, and enjoyed the limited social life of a very poorly funded "fraternity man." In the summers, I "escaped" the dust and dry heat of West Texas to work as a counselor at a summer camp on Lake LBJ near Austin.

My friend, Hawkeye, majored in English, was a Rhodes scholar nominee, and eventually attended law school and was selected editor of the *University of Texas Law Review* some years later. Tom chided me to study, introduced me to the world of student government politics, proofread my term papers when I dared let him, and more important, challenged my shallow attempts at intellectualism and shamed me for my lack of social action. I eventually became a teacher education major at his prodding. At the time, he was the only English major, and I the only teacher education major, amid the entire male Greek (i.e., fraternity) population enrolled at Texas Tech (this is not so much a confession, but rather a badge of honor I wear proudly).

By chance, I eventually discovered the world of counseling by way of a flyer posted in the stairwell of the university administration building announcing a new program called Guidance Associate Studies. After my first course in this program designed to train assistant school counselors, I became hooked on psychology, and counseling specifically. I became a voracious reader, attended class regularly, and began to take my education and my future more seriously. Admittedly, motivated in large part by my own needs for recognition and achievement, I also began demanding more stimulating and challenging instruction from my education professors—"I don't want to learn how to make pretty bulletin boards, show me how to help people!" I also eventually entered the world of student government, where I demanded greater relevancy in my training, pressed for student evaluations of instructors, and advocated for dedicated space for student organizations in the College of Education.

In my self-righteous zeal, it seemed to me that most of my peers were passive and unappreciative of my revolution against the mediocrity and irrelevancy of the "Mickey Mouse" curriculum called teacher education. Ironically, and fortunately for me, a number of my professors, including the college dean, encouraged my efforts and actually colluded with me and a handful of other upstarts to make a difference in our college. Indeed, it has been my experience throughout my professional life that well-intended, if not naïve, brinkmanship is often welcomed by those whom I might first believe to be the "enemy."

Saving the World

I eventually graduated from college and moved to Odessa, where I headed the peer counseling program at Ector High School. Ector High is now a middle school, having been closed by Health, Education, and Welfare (HEW), a former government agency, with claims that Odessa had failed to successfully integrate its public school system. As an aside, if you have read the book or seen the movie *Friday Night Lights,* you might be bemused to know that Odessa solved its integration problems, in part, by demoting Ector High to a middle school and bussing the school's better Black athletes to football powerhouse Permian High School, featured in the film. The other students were sent to Odessa High School.

Ector High was on the south side of the city's railroad tracks, where my students were much poorer than I had ever been as a college student, where our "college-bound" (e.g., Odessa Community College) seniors were reading at the sixth-grade level, and where my peer counseling students were routinely stopped by the police when we ventured north of the tracks to attend district-wide meetings with peer counselors from Odessa and Permian High Schools. I still have a vivid memory of sitting in the backseat of the car of one of my favorite students, a beat-up "low rider," when we were stopped by one of Odessa's finest. My African American students sitting on either side of me in the backseat sported Afro coiffed hair that seemed to cover the full width of the car's rear windshield, whereas the proud Mexican American owner of the low rider sported shoulder-length hair and a headband.

> The police officer asked, "What are you boys doin' outta school and on this side of town?"
>
> "We are goin' to a meeting for peer counselors. We're with our teacher," replied our driver, pointing back to me.

The officer's complexion and expression changed like a kaleidoscope—from confident glare, to befuddlement, and finally disparagement, as he leaned into the car, peering through his reflective sunglasses at my smiling white face amid the kinky hair and dark-skinned students beside me. He finally let us pass after checking everybody's school ID, including mine, and giving the driver a warning about driving a car without proper shock absorbers.

I tell my graduate students today that those 3 years in Odessa were my equivalent to the Peace Corps—and like most Peace Corps volunteers, I learned much more from my high school students than I ever gave back. I learned about racism on both sides of the tracks. I learned to do counseling while walking around because my high school "clients" preferred to talk to me in the safety of the halls, the cafeteria, and at athletic and other social events rather than face the stigma associated with seeing me in the "counselor's office." And I also learned that there are unintentional consequences of doing good.

A report I authored revealing a substantial achievement gap between the reading levels of students from Ector High versus students from the city's other two high schools was leaked to the local press, then used as minor supportive evidence in the HEW investigation. I had hoped the report would lead to more instructional resources for my students and to the feeder schools to our high school. Instead, Permian High School added to its already legendary status as a 4-AAAA football dynasty.

My first wife's (another confession) acceptance into graduate school pulled us away from spectacular sunrises and sunsets of West Texas, and 3 years after leaving college to save the world, we packed our U-Haul truck and drove to Houston a bit more humble and eager to be something "more" than schoolteachers. The move to Houston also reunited me with my friend Tom Allen, who was teaching English to inner-city middle school kids by day and volunteering for the local ACLU chapter by night. I soon entered the doctoral program at the University of Houston (UH), where I took up my pattern of student advocacy activities, leading a charge for student representation at program and departmental committee faculty meetings, and launching a personal quest to transform our counselor education program into a counseling psychology, APA-accredited equivalent program. Four years later, I left Houston to complete my internship at Texas A&M, then returned to the UH as a member of the counseling center staff and coordinator of the learning support and tutorial service, where I procrastinated on the final defense of my dissertation while waiting for a degree change (PhD), name change (counseling psychology), and positive accreditation notice from the APA.

Life After Graduate School

Finally a graduate and now a full-time faculty member at UH, I was drafted onto the Houston Psychological Association legislative committee by a former supervisor who knew of my student advocacy activities. I was quickly drawn into real-world political campaigning, and 3 years later was standing before a joint committee of the Texas state senate and house members as a Texas Psychological

Association board member, testifying in favor of maintaining the doctoral standard for the independent practice of psychology. I was now making my transition from student education reformist to professional practice advocate.

Concurrently, managed care was finally gaining momentum in the early 1990s in Texas and was soon to become a major challenge in the care of my clients and to the livelihood of psychologists. As an elected leader of the Texas Psychological Association, I became aware that there was a pressing need for psychologists to be involved at a legislative level to address some of the problems created for clients by managed care.

A Story of Mismanaged Care

This second story is a more formal and much less personal narrative about the managed care movement in the United States and tells of Texas's efforts to address some of its ills.

The system of health care in the United States has been subject to many transformations throughout the latter half of the past century. Like many cultural trends, the trends in health care administration have seen changes nearly every decade (Bachman, 2004). In the early 1900s, health care costs were relatively low and doctors were often able to care for patients without payment. In the 1920s, private health insurance was created to cover some of the higher medical costs, but very few citizens were inclined to pay for insurance when the cost of health care was generally still so inexpensive (Anders, 1996). In the 1940s and 1950s, employer-sponsored health care became increasingly popular. In the 1960s, the federal government involved itself in health care with the creation of both Medicare and Medicaid. In the 1970s, the passage of the Employee Retirement and Income Security Act (ERISA) exempted corporate employee benefit plans from regulation by state laws, which proved to have a major effect on the future of health care. Finally, in the 1980s, managed care came onto the scene (Bachman, 2004), having a monumental influence on the health care industry and, in turn, the administration of mental health services.

In order to understand the impact that managed care has had on health care, it is important to be familiar with the context in which it emerged. When it first arrived, managed care was the brilliant answer to the question of how to contain rapidly rising health care costs. The increasingly expensive costs of health care were, in part, the result of employer-organized health insurance. In the years following World War II, as a reaction to strict wage controls induced by the outbreak of the war, many companies implemented employer-organized health insurance as a means of attracting potential workers. During the 1940s and 1950s, labor unions and corporations became the primary advocates for and providers of health insurance for workers. As corporations increasingly used health insurance benefits to draw employees to their companies, the insurance packages they offered grew bigger and better. A movement within the field of psychology to receive fee-for-service reimbursement began in the 1960s and continued through the 1980s. Finally, professional psychology became insurance viable, as corporations expanded their coverage to include mental health services. Psychological practitioners began to shift their focus from a "collaboration, consultation, and prevention model to a direct service model, where time spent in clinical contact would be reimbursable by insurance" (Rae, 2004, p. 48).

The impact that employer-organized health insurance had on the health care industry was enormous. Corporate-provided insurance, combined with other factors, resulted in rising health care costs that became virtually unaffordable for the companies paying the bills. Even the federal government began to suffer from the effects of rising health care costs, as the creation of Medicare and Medicaid had made it a major provider of health insurance for the elderly and the poor, respectively. The cost increases were brought about by several factors. First, in the years following World War II, major technological advances in the medical field resulted in improved, but extremely costly, methods of treating medical conditions (Newman & Dunbar, 2000). Many community hospitals turned into virtual "medical centers" full of expensive diagnostic equipment that required, in addition to highly skilled nurses, a large work force of technicians. Part of this craze could also be seen in the medical schools and teaching hospitals that encouraged physicians to specialize in diseases that were difficult to cure and costly to treat (Anders, 1996).

An additional reason for the rising health care costs was that doctors had begun to pump up their caseloads to make the most of the fee-for-service reimbursements (Anders, 1996). They took on more patients in order to receive payments from a greater number of health insurance plans. They also began to excessively treat their patients, either because they believed they had a responsibility to do everything possible for their patients or because they knew that the more they treated, the more they would be paid. Regardless of their motivation, this drove medical bills so high that insurance companies grew suspicious of the medical profession. Studies were conducted examining regional variations in how often doctors conducted the same surgical procedures; these studies often showed that doctors in a given region were on a "surgery binge," conducting specific surgeries at a much higher rate than doctors in other parts of the country, without any evidence that patients in their area were any sicker. Several other studies revealed that a high percentage of surgeries conducted across the nation had actually been unnecessary. Many people pushed for health care reform, arguing that doctors could no longer be trusted, as they were "operating far too often, treating patients as financial piñatas to be cut open for profit" (Anders, 1996, p. 24). Psychologists were not above these kinds of practice growth strategies. Testing and patient hospitalizations grew rapidly in the 1980s and 1990s.

Patients also contributed to the rising costs in health care as the view of health care shifted from being a privilege to a right. If advances in medicine could help prevent or alleviate a medical condition, then people wanted these advances to somehow help them. Because employer-provided insurance insulated employees from the costs of health care, they were never forced to see the financial implications of this attitude. Additionally, it became apparent that the mere increase in availability of medical services (via additions to employer insurance packages) seemed to generate an increase in demand by employees. For example, when Chrysler changed their insurance packages to include mental health services, their employees' use of these services increased fivefold, even though there was no evidence of an increase in the number of workers with mental disturbances (Anders, 1996).

As a result of these factors, by the late 1970s, both corporate America and the U.S. federal government were looking for some way to alleviate the egregious costs of health care. It became apparent that the only feasible way to deal with rising health care costs was to "intervene before doctors ever saw a patient" (Anders, 1996, p. 25). Managed care was essentially designed to be a moderator between doctors and patients, monitoring costs as well as treatments. Its primary concern was to lower costs, supposedly without a loss in quality or effectiveness of treatment. It had been decided that medical and mental health professionals could no longer be trusted to make cost-effective health care decisions. Therefore, third-party experts were enlisted to make these decisions for them. Corporations began employing managed care plans to serve as a common link between insurance providers, health professionals, and employees. Eventually, it became the general consensus across the nation that managed care was the only way to solve the cost problem in health care.

Managed care, in its traditional form, operates on the basis of a "supply-control model: control costs by limiting the supply of care" (Bachman, 2004, p. 15). This is done in a number of ways. First, patients' access to health care providers is restricted. Each managed care company creates its own treatment network, which includes only those doctors and treatment facilities that are deemed capable and trustworthy of delivering quality health care at a reasonable cost. The manner in which these treatment networks are run varies depending on the version of managed care to which one belongs. For example, health maintenance organizations, or HMOs, require that patients use only the services of prearranged groups of doctors and hospitals if they want to receive any insurance coverage at all. There is also great variability among HMOs; for example, some operate on a "staff model" in which all health care providers are directly employed by the HMO, others enlist certain independent practitioners who agree to follow the managed care "rules." Other, less restrictive versions of managed care, such as preferred provider organizations, or PPOs, simply encourage members to use a prearranged group of doctors and hospitals in order to receive greater insurance coverage. In cases where members choose to use the services of doctors that are not part of their managed care treatment network, they are often ineligible for insurance coverage and are forced to pay out-of-pocket for their health care. This issue is particularly salient in emergency situations, when patients are required to use only the services of a previously selected hospital if they wish to be eligible for insurance coverage. One can imagine that in such circumstances, patients' restricted access to providers becomes a crucial issue.

In addition to ensuring cost-effective treatment, provider networks serve another managed care function. Out of the prearranged group, patients are required to choose a primary care physician. From that point on, the elected primary care physician plays a major role in that patient's health care. Managed care organizations are based on the idea of preventive care, which is placed primarily in the realm of these primary care physicians, who serve as the managed care "gatekeepers" (Newman & Dunbar, 2000). It is their task to prevent and detect medical conditions before they become serious enough to be costly. Primary care physicians also function as the barrier between patients and specialists, including psychologists, whose services cost much more than the less expensive visits to the gatekeeper. Without approval of the primary care physician, and sometimes even the managed care organization itself, patients are not allowed to visit specialists or have costly medical tests performed. The difficulty in getting past the gatekeepers reduces the chances that patients will attain access to services that cost more than managed care organizations are willing to spend.

However, ultimately, the efforts of managed care organizations to reduce the costs of health care suffered from greed, the same motivation it was intended to address. Indeed, over time, managed care acquired as many opponents as it once had supporters, if not more. George Anders (1996), a senior special writer for *The Wall Street Journal,* reveals in his book *Health Against Wealth* the harsh realities of managed care. He includes detailed accounts of managed care gone wrong, citing heart-wrenching tales: a family whose child underwent several amputations as a result of the managed care barriers to emergency medicine; a woman whose managed care company denied her request for a bone marrow transplant when she was in a critical stage of breast cancer, despite appeals from her doctors, who believed the transplant would save her life; a doctor in a rural area who struggled to squash an epidemic of a rare and deadly disease, shigellosis, because the managed care company refused to pay for the medical cure. In addition to relating real-life anecdotes, Anders comments on the dysfunction that has arisen because managed care brings corporate values and market forces into the health care industry. The incompatibility of the two worlds of business and medicine resulted in damaging health care practices.

The field of mental health had not been immune to the damaging effects of managed care policies. Anders (1996) writes, "Mental health spending is a favorite cost-cutting target of managed care plans. Many have cut overall spending in half, which may leave . . . patients without the care that their doctors or family members believe they need" (p. 77). In most cases, mental health care is "provided as a 'carve-out' benefit from a more comprehensive benefit package" (Roberts & Hurley, 1997, p. 10). Carve-out refers to the situation in which an employer contracts with two separate health care companies, one that manages only medical coverage and one that manages only mental health coverage. These specialized companies are called managed behavioral health care organizations, or MBHOs.

The managed care attack on mental health services was not completely unfounded. As was the case with doctors, many mental health professionals had begun to exploit the fee-for-service system to which they had become accustomed. They earned a reputation for greed and dishonesty, much like the surgeons who were performing excessive procedures. The result was that employers hired carve-out companies specializing in mental health to ensure that they were not being duped into paying exorbitant fees for unnecessary services.

Mental health carve-outs are run in much the same way as the managed care organizations that oversee medical care. The primary goal is the same, cutting costs, and the manner in which this is done is similar—third-party overseers. The overseers, like the medical management directors and teams, have restricted the freedoms of both patients and doctors. Patients' access to mental health services is limited, psychologists' ability to determine the course of treatment for their patients is hindered, and the unique aspects of each patient are put to the wayside while the carve-outs decide for the psychologists and the patients the type and length of treatment that will be administered. Managed behavioral health care organizations, like HMOs and PPOs, have depersonalized the administration of care. In the field of mental health, the personal aspect of the services delivered is often cited as the most important factor in successful treatment.

Generally, short-term treatment is the only form of treatment covered by managed care and is only accessible when approved by the MBHO. Stories noting inadequate mental health care include managed care's denial of treatment to a man who requested counseling for his 3-year-old daughter, who had been raped; to a man having suicidal thoughts; to a mother hearing voices telling her to kill her children; and to adults with severe substance addictions. Obtaining approval for treatment has become much more difficult in the managed care world—an obstacle that has mental health professionals worried about the feasibility in helping those who truly need it.

In addition to these horror stories, numerous authors have cited problems for clients in receiving adequate mental health care because of managed care systems (Karon, 1995), and that vulnerable populations have been affected most significantly. La Roche and Turner (2002) noted that racial/ethnic minority individuals face financial and cultural barriers to accessing mental health services through managed care as well as inadequate quality and inappropriateness of services. Furthermore, they noted that provider and consumer awareness was problematic, especially for individuals having limited English skills or who were unfamiliar with bureaucratic systems of health services. A few other examples of populations adversely affected by managed care in mental health include children (Busch & Horowitz, 2004), clients with eating disorders (Franco & Erb, 1998), and youth in the juvenile justice system (Thomas, Gourley, & Mele, 2004).

This concern also raised ethical issues for counseling psychologists as recognized by a special issue of *The Counseling Psychologist* examining concerns over ethical issues related to counseling practice through managed care (Cooper & Gottlieb, 2000; Tjeltveit, 2000; Younggren, 2000). Similarly, the 2001 Houston Conference of the Society of Counseling Psychology designated a workgroup to address managed care as one of 10 critical issues facing the profession (Blustein, Elman, & Gerstein, 2001).

In addition to affecting clients, managed care affects psychologists' lives in a number of ways (Rupert & Baird, 2004). Among the most salient stressors are cost-cutting (resulting in decreased salary and reimbursement), external constraints on patients' treatment, and increased paperwork required by managed care organizations. Rupert and Baird's study also showed that professional psychologists who had a high number of managed care caseloads worked longer hours, had more client contact, received less supervision, reported more negative client behaviors, experienced more stress, were less satisfied with their incomes, and were more emotionally exhausted than those with fewer managed care caseloads. Thus, managed care is hurting not only the patients, but also the professionals.

Accordingly, as a result of the growing disenchantment with managed care, there has been an increase in government regulation aimed at correcting the negative effects of cost containment on the delivery of health care services (Newman & Dunbar, 2000). Both the federal government and most state governments have become involved in the fight against the abuses of managed care. One of the most prominent issues in recent years has been that of health insurer liability (NCSL online: Cauchi & Coleman, 1998), especially regarding cases where managed care organizations deny care. In the event that denial of care has damaging effects, the question to be asked is, Who is and who should be responsible for medical outcomes in the managed care system? Many states have passed legislation that allows enrollees to hold their health plan responsible for medical complications that result from their plan's failure to exercise "ordinary care." These types of consumer protection laws have come in several forms. Some states have passed legislation that simply overrides managed care "hold harmless" clauses that render doctors and hospitals, as opposed to the health plan, liable for medical damages. Other states have passed legislation that requires managed care treatment directors to be licensed physicians who are held fully responsible for treatment decisions made by the plan. Still other states have passed legislation that allows enrollees to sue their HMOs for medical malpractice. Unfortunately, it has also been the case that the needs of patients requiring mental health have often been overlooked in this kind of legislation—such was the case in Texas.

The Texas Challenge

In 1997, Texas became the first state to pass explicit "right to sue" legislation, and it is here that the personal story and the managed care story intersect. It was believed that by allowing plan participants to sue their health plans, managed care organizations would become more responsive to their consumers (Butler, 2000). Although the effects of managed care had been felt in Texas for several years before the legislation was passed, it took some time for the necessary advocacy groups to come together and for the timing within the legislature to be just right. In 1995, the Texas Medical Association initiated a bold, long-term strategy to address some of the major grievances of managed care. After much lobbying by policy advocates, the members of the legislature agreed to take on the issue of managed care. The nation's first comprehensive legislation became effective September 1, 1997.

Although it is likely that the Texas Medical Association (TMA), with its very powerful and well-funded political action committee, could have facilitated the passage of this legislation on its own, the eventual effort included an unprecedented coalition of both consumer advocacy groups and other nonmedical physician health care provider associations as support.

Unfortunately, the originally proposed legislation to reform managed care excluded psychologists and other nonphysician (i.e., non-MDs and ODs) health care providers from critical components of the bill. I was serving as president of the Texas Psychological Association at the time, and although my first reading of the legislation suggested that "patient" included those with mental illness or who sought mental health services, we soon discovered, following an offer to support the legislation, that the bill sponsors did not intend this to be the case. Through the strategic and coordinated efforts of our lobbyist, Lisa Ross, and our association executive director, David White, we pulled together a coalition of other mental health provider groups and successfully negotiated with the TMA and the legislature the inclusion of the mental health professions and, more important, our patients in the package of bills designed to protect patients and place at least some accountability and legal liability on the shoulders of managed care companies.

It is worth noting here that the actions of the Texas Psychological Association on this front have often been attributed to me exclusively. Most certainly, I had the good sense to encourage the hire of our lobbyist over some considerable reluctance and resistance by some members of our Association Board. Their reticence to hire Ms. Ross stemmed from her marriage to the lead lobbyist of the state medical association and fear that she would compromise our very premature efforts to advance prescription authority for psychologists in 1997. I argued persuasively that Ms. Ross was an exceptionally talented and "hungry" lobbyist, and second, that her relationship with her TMA lobbyist husband could be beneficial to our other causes. Although politics may make for strange bedfellows, it is also possible that bedfellows can make for unexpected political gains. Most certainly, Ms. Ross's relationship with her husband assisted our ability to gain support from the TMA, and it was her astute political acumen and political alliances, along with those of David White, that aided our efforts and ultimately the passage of a comprehensive managed care reform and patient protection legislative package that included mental health providers, their services, and, most important, their patients and clients. I was but one member of the team, and my job was to serve as the official spokesperson for the state psychological association.

With that clarification (or confession), there were several important components to Texas's legislation. First, it eliminated the defense often used by health plans that they were not liable for medical malpractice because of "corporate practice of medicine" laws. These laws prohibited organizations not owned by physicians from employing physicians, thereby prohibiting them from practicing medicine. Therefore, managed care companies claimed that they could not be sued for medical malpractice because as corporations they were, in effect, barred from practicing "medicine" (Butler, 2000). Second, Texas's legislation established a specific standard of liability for managed care plan decisions, the "ordinary care" standard (SB 386, Sec 88.001, 10). If a health plan fails to use "ordinary care" in denying or delaying payment for care recommended by a health care provider, the plan is liable. Third, the Texas legislation created "independent review organizations" to which plan enrollees could appeal disputes over plan coverage. Also included in the 1997 legislation was a clause that prohibited health plans from removing a health care provider from its plan for advocating on behalf of a patient and a clause that declared "hold harmless" clauses as per the third-party payer void.

The federal government has looked to Texas to understand the impact of liability legislation. Congress often depends on states to provide the testing ground for national reform, and Texas provides a concrete example of the effects of liability legislation. Supporters of health plan liability say that Congress must only look to Texas to see how their worst fears, such as defensive medicine, increased premiums, and a flood of lawsuits, are unfounded (Aston, 2001). In the managed care system, most parties have felt the effects of liability legislation. Physicians, psychologists, and other health care providers have noticed tangible improvements in their ability to practice, some saying that the biggest change is the move away from the automatic denial of treatment. Others feel empowered, especially by the legislation that prohibits managed care from retaliating against providers who advocate on behalf of their patients (Aston, 2001).

On the other side of the liability debate, there are worries that liability legislation will force managed care to practice "defensive medicine"—approving potentially unnecessary procedures to avoid litigation. It has also been argued that defensive medicine will result in a boost in insurance prices. However, in 2001, four years after the passage of the liability legislation, the premium increases in Texas have been consistent with those nationwide. Opponents also fear that liability legislation will lead to a flood of lawsuits. However, Texas's independent review system has proven effective in countering this possibility. Because patients' claims are typically dealt with effectively in the review process, there is often no need to file a lawsuit. Those who support liability legislation point to the low numbers of suits as proof that the prediction of massive amounts of litigation were groundless (Aston, 2001).

Although the Texas legislation has had a decided impact on managed care reform, it is not without its problems. The ability to reduce the risks inherent in managed care is limited by a powerful federal bill. The Employee Retirement and Income Security Act, or ERISA, passed in 1974, was designed to establish uniform federal standards for pension and employee plans, including those offered through private-sector employers and unions. The purpose of providing a single federal law governing these plans, including health plans, was to keep employers from having to comply with several conflicting states' rules as well as a federal rule (Rakich & Ledbetter, 2000). Having the single overriding federal law has had negative effects on states' abilities to regulate. Because any state laws "relating to" employer benefit plans, including health plans, are preempted under ERISA, states have limited power to pass legislation to control employer-based insurance. It is because of ERISA that Texas's 1997 legislation was not fully upheld in the 5th Circuit U.S. Court of Appeals. Although some avenues of placing responsibility for damages on health plans were left open, the Court ruled that ERISA does not permit the patients to file lawsuits if a health maintenance organization determines that requested treatment was not medically necessary or was not covered by the patient's plan. The Court also ruled that state law could not regulate the independent review boards. Thus, because the legislation "related to" employer benefits plans, ERISA preempted the Texas statute (Aston, 2001). Essentially, the Texas statute's power was limited by the Circuit Court's decision as a result of ERISA.

Across the nation, ERISA has hindered states' abilities to regulate health plans. Because federal law takes precedence over state laws, states have been unable to successfully establish laws that place full liability on managed care organizations for negligence and malpractice. The result is that enrollees in "ERISA plans" have very little power when it comes to forcing responsibility onto their managed care plans. Patients who suffer harm as a result of the misadministration of health care by their managed care organization find themselves with no viable cause of action because they are legally unable to sue (Rakich & Ledbetter, 2000). Further, in June 2004, the U.S. Supreme Court ruled that employee-sponsored managed health care plans were not liable for negligent decisions about health care because when the plan decides to deny benefits, it is only applying the terms of an insurance contract, not making a medical decision (Mariner, 2004). Mariner asserts that this decision reinforces the inability of ERISA to protect patient rights in health care. Because only Congress can amend ERISA, there has been a recent push by managed care reform advocates for legislation on the federal level.

There continue to be battles regarding client and practitioner rights and managed mental health care. For example, APA recently joined a class action lawsuit against managed care companies under racketeering statutes (Holloway, 2004).

Conclusion

In 1997, psychology became my political party. I remain a part-time staff member of the Texas Psychological Association as Director of Professional Affairs, serving frequently as a spokesperson for the profession before the legislature. David White remains our Executive Director, and I assist him and our new lobbyist with the development of political strategy, briefs and white papers for distribution to the legislature, and often with the education and sometimes necessary prodding of psychologists to engage in the political process on behalf of the profession and our clients. I derive great professional satisfaction from this work and have come to recognize the value to the professional association in having a psychologist with long-term relationships with the legislature.

Our battle to maintain the doctoral standard for the independent practice of psychology and to reserve the use of the title "psychologist" to those with doctoral training continues today. Last month, a conservative Republican state legislator from Houston surprisingly introduced a mental health parity bill that would require insurance companies to match mental health coverage and benefits with those offered for physical ailments. We also continue to counter the excessive profiteering motives of managed care companies as we seek to include psychologists in "prompt payment legislation" that would fine those third-party payers who inappropriately and purposefully withhold or deny payment of services rendered. Indeed, the American Psychological Association and its state affiliates remain continuously engaged in the support or opposition of hundreds of pieces of legislation that affect the profession and our clients.

If the chapters in this book have touched you in some way and/or you have been reluctant to engage in the political aspects of your profession, we offer the following three very simple suggestions and encouragement:

1. Just show up at your next local or state psychological association business meeting and simply say, "What can I do to help?" If members are the lifeblood of a professional association, volunteers are the very heart of the organization. Volunteer and you will most certainly be put to work. Do the work you have been assigned, and

you will be given more work to do. There are far too few psychologists working on behalf of too many colleagues and far too many clients. The work is, in fact, endless, but the satisfaction in giving back to the profession and affecting public policy is exponentially satisfying.

2. If you can't show up, send a check. Whether you make the check payable to a psychological political action committee or directly to a candidate of your choosing, know that money is as much a part of the political process as kissing babies . . . and just as important. The communication of ideas in the political process, whether it be part of the campaigning process, the lobbying process, or the educational process of fellow psychologists, the public, or the politicians, is expensive. Political campaign and political action committee contributions (at least at the level psychologists can afford) do not buy votes, but they do ensure that your voice, the voices of psychologists, and, most important, the voices of those least able to advocate for themselves—our clients—can be heard among the bellowing and belching of corporate interests like managed care.

3. Vote. Vote often. Let the candidates of your choice—psychologists need friends on both sides of the legislative aisle—know that you vote and that you are a psychologist.

References

Anders, G. (1996). *Health against wealth: HMOs and the breakdown of medical trust.* Boston: Houghton Mifflin.

Aston, G. (2001, May 28). Texas trial: HMO liability law. *American Medical News.* Retrieved July 6, 2004, from http://www.ama-assn.org/amednews

Bachman, R. (2004). Consumer-driven healthcare: The future is now. *Benefits Quarterly, 2,* 15–22.

Blustein, D., Elman, N., & Gerstein, L. (2001, August). *Executive report on social action groups.* National Counseling Psychology Conference, Houston, TX.

Busch, S. H., & Horowitz, S. M. (2004). Access to mental health services: Are uninsured children falling behind? *Mental Health Services Research, 6*(2), 109–116.

Butler, P. (2000). *ERISA preemption primer.* Washington, DC: Alpha Center. Retrieved July 6, 2004, from http://www.ncsl.org/programs/health/liable.htm

Cauchi, R., & Coleman, G. (1998). *Special briefing: Health insurer liability.* Retrieved July 6, 2004, from http://www.ncsl.org/programs/asi/briefing.htm

Cooper, C. C., & Gottlieb, M. C. (2000). Ethical issues with managed care: Challenges facing counseling psychology. *The Counseling Psychologist, 28*(2), 179–236.

Franco, D. L., & Erb, J. (1998). Managed care or mangled care: Treating eating disorders in the current healthcare climate. *Psychotherapy: Theory, Research, Practice, Training, 35*(1), 43–53.

Holloway, J. D. (2004). Psychology joins class action lawsuit against managed care. *Monitor on Psychology, 35*(10), 34.

Karon, B. P. (1995). Provision of psychotherapy under managed health care: A growing crisis and national nightmare. *Professional Psychology: Research and Practice, 26*(1), 5–9.

La Roche, M. J., & Turner, C. (2002). At the crossroads: Managed mental health care, the ethics code, and ethnic minorities. *Cultural Diversity and Ethnic Minority Psychology, 8*(3), 187–198.

Mariner, W. K. (2004). The Supreme Court's limitation of managed care liability. *New England Journal of Medicine, 351*(13), 1347–1352.

Newman, R. (2004). Leading psychology forward: Staying the course in uncertain times. *Professional Psychology: Research and Practice, 35*(1), 36–41.

Newman, R., & Dunbar, D. (2000). Managed care and ethical conflicts. *Managed Care Quarterly, 8*(4), 20–32.

Rae, W. A. (2004). Financing pediatric psychology services: Buddy, can you spare a dime? *Journal of Pediatric Psychology, 29*(1), 47–52.

Rakich, J. S., & Ledbetter, R. K. (2000). Managed care liability and ERISA preemption. *Managed Care Quarterly, 8*(1), 28–37.

Roberts, M. C., & Hurley, L. K. (1997). *Managing managed care.* New York: Plenum.

Rupert, P., & Baird, K. (2004). Managed care and the independent practice of psychology. *Professional Psychology: Research and Practice, 35*(2), 185–193.

Thomas, J., Gourley, G. K., & Mele, N. (2004). The impact of managed behavioral health care on youth in the juvenile justice system. *Archives of Psychiatric Nursing, 18*(4), 135–142.

Tjeltveit, A. C. (2000). There is more to ethics than professional codes of ethics: Social ethics, theoretical ethics, and managed care. *The Counseling Psychologist, 28*(2), 242–252.

Younggren, J. (2000). Is managed care really just another unethical Model T? *The Counseling Psychologist, 28*(2), 253–262.

PART VIII

Future Directions

CHAPTER 35

Future Directions for Counseling Psychology

Enhancing Leadership, Vision, and Action in Social Justice

Rebecca L. Toporek, Lawrence H. Gerstein, Nadya A. Fouad, Gargi Roysircar, and Tania Israel

Injustice, oppression, and inequality abound within the United States and internationally, presenting counseling psychologists with a plethora of avenues through which to apply their knowledge, training, and expertise. As has been illustrated throughout this *Handbook,* this involvement may take a variety of forms and venues. The goal of this chapter is to highlight the themes that seem to cross the varied settings, problems, and methodological and theoretical approaches taken by each of the authors. We then highlight future directions for counseling psychologists with respect to theory, research, practice, training, and policy. Finally, we acknowledge the challenges that arise for counseling psychologists engaged in social justice activities.

Central Themes in Social Justice Work

A number of themes emerge from the work described by the counseling psychologists in this *Handbook:* community involvement, interdisciplinary collaboration, multilevel or systemic approaches, pace of change, and commitment to service. An explication of these themes can provide some guidance and a structure for future directions in theory, practice, research, training, and policy linked with social justice initiatives.

Community Involvement

Throughout this *Handbook,* it was absolutely clear that the persons and communities who were affected most by oppression or injustice had the capacity and knowledge that were necessary to understand their problems as well as the specifics of a solution. We are convinced that these individuals or communities were not atypical in this regard. In fact, we contend that all persons and communities have the potential to accurately assess and contribute to the effective resolution of their challenges regardless of context and issue. Therefore, engaging various stakeholders (e.g., individuals, communities, organizations) both domestically and internationally is critical for practical and ethical reasons, not the least of which is increasing the probability of the desired outcome.

The old adage that the client is the expert on his or her problem can also be extended to communities. We must assume that the community possesses a unique and informed perspective of its situation (Toporek & Williams, chapter 2) and demonstrate this respect for the expertise of the community and the client. Engaging the community is not only essential in defining the problem or challenge and setting goals, but it is also necessary to provide a history regarding previous attempts to alleviate problems and understanding the sociohistorical context. As demonstrated in this *Handbook,* counseling psychologists can partner with stakeholders, sharing their theoretical background, professional and financial resources, expertise in consultation, communication, multicultural issues, vocational and group behavior, and large systems. Cultural sensitivity and comprehensive collaboration are central in respecting the community's expertise (Norsworthy, chapter 29). Horne and Mathews (chapter 27), for example, discussed in great detail their successful effort to involve individuals, governmental agencies, and organizations in the development and modification of programs offered by crisis volunteers and hotline workers to assist oppressed women in Hungary. Similarly, McWhirter and McWhirter (chapter 28) described their long-standing initiative to empower couples in Chile to serve as paraprofessionals and mentors of couple enhancement and enrichment groups.

Not surprisingly, there can be problems (e.g., failure to accurately understand the issue, rejection or failure of the solution, negative effect on the culture) when stakeholders are not involved in the entire intervention process. Cosgrove (chapter 15) emphasized the damaging and pathologizing effects on homeless mothers when researchers and public policy makers neglect to include their voices. She noted that well-intentioned center psychologists have perpetuated victim-blaming perspectives regarding homelessness because their research and recommendations have focused on the individual level rather than systems, and that this, in part, has resulted because the voices of affected communities have not taken center stage in the process.

The concept of the culturally encapsulated counselor (Wrenn, 1962, 1985) can be extended to describe the potential danger that arises when excluding stakeholders from the process and also operating out of one professional perspective. Such danger is particularly apparent when a perspective is applied to a population or community without its consultation. Even when a population or community is involved in the intervention process, there are inherent dangers. For example, international clientele might willingly and/or blindly embrace U.S. models of service delivery. Such models, however, may be inappropriate or even destructive to the target culture. Therefore, counseling psychologists must be extremely mindful of the dangers of employing U.S. models in other countries, with special attention focused on the subtle impact of these models on the behaviors, attitudes, values, structures, and policies of the culture being served (see Gerstein & Kirkpatrick, chapter 30; Horne & Mathews, chapter 27; Norsworthy & Khuankaew, chapter 29). At the very least, counseling psychologists need to honor, respect, and value communities and other cultures, and the local people's abilities to help in the process of designing and implementing their own solutions.

Community involvement allows psychologists to gain a more complete understanding of who the community is and its complex and diverse perspectives and needs. This was the central thesis of Morrow, Hawxhurst, Montes de Vegas, Abousleman, and Castañeda (chapter 17) in their examination of the herstory of feminist therapy, social justice, and multiculturalism. Notably, Whitcomb and Loewy (chapter 16) emphasized that in developing advocacy groups for LGB issues, a concentrated effort was made to ensure that the groups reflected more than the needs and goals of "White, middle-class, out, gay men." Juntunen et al. (chapter 21), in their discussion of welfare reform and improving services provided to recipients of welfare, stressed the importance of grounding interventions within the needs of the community, citing ineffective practices that may otherwise occur.

Interdisciplinary Collaboration

Another overarching theme that appears in this *Handbook* is the importance of various forms of collaboration. Links across disciplines are critical to increase the likelihood of identifying and employing multidimensional approaches to a range of complex social justice issues. It is notable that numerous other professions, such as social work, public health, law, anthropology, community psychology, political science, ethnic studies, and women's studies, have substantial history and knowledge regarding effective social justice strategies. As an example of this, Santiago-Rivera, Talka, and Tully (chapter 14) provided a notable discussion regarding the central role that epidemiology, public health, social welfare, and nursing have had in confronting environmental racism.

The tendency of disciplines to function in isolation reflects an aspect of cultural encapsulation that can reduce the effectiveness of interventions and increase the potential for redundancy. Disciplinary bias may also communicate an attitude of elitism and arrogance to communities and other social change agents. This can be seen in the discussion provided by Juntunen et al. (chapter 21) regarding interagency collaboration necessary for welfare-to-work interventions. Among other positive effects, interdisciplinary collaboration minimizes the danger of myopic perspectives that can result when a problem is conceptualized and approached from one vantage point. Increasing our knowledge of other disciplines and foundational assumptions can create synergy and "formidable alliances." This outcome was described by Toporek and Chope (chapter 20) as an essential ingredient in the rise of partnerships in social entrepreneurship as a way to reduce social programs' dependency on public support and also reduce the instability and vulnerability that emerged from such dependency.

One type of collaboration can be seen in the use of interdisciplinary team approaches where each party brings expertise, training, credibility, and resources to address different aspects of a problem. For example, in the chapter on health education among Vietnamese refugees, Huynh and Roysircar (chapter 24) discussed the successful work of teams composed of psychiatrists, medical professionals, educators, social workers, and psychologists when providing comprehensive health treatment and education. Similarly, a unique aspect of the domestic violence intervention described by Bell and Goodman (chapter 12) involved the use of interdisciplinary teams bridging the legal system and social services to respond to the needs of both the victim and the offender.

Throughout the *Handbook,* numerous examples were offered illustrating how counseling psychologists might join, form, and participate on such teams. Gerstein and Kirkpatrick (chapter 30), for instance, suggested that counseling psychologists acquire excellent experience in interdisciplinary teamwork through employment and internship opportunities with human rights organizations, the United Nations, the U.S. State Department, diplomatic corps, Amnesty International, Human Rights Watch, Refugees International, international consulting firms, and the Peace Corps. These organizations can provide counseling psychologists with practical experience in forming and maintaining interdisciplinary and interagency alliances as well as outstanding international experience. In his work promoting a peaceful solution to the Tibet-China conflict, Gerstein (Gerstein & Kirkpatrick) expressed how this type of interdisciplinary collaboration is essential to raise public awareness about human rights violations and motivate individuals to take appropriate nonviolent action. McPherson and Reilly (chapter 34) noted the importance of collaborating with other professional organizations to enhance the strength needed to address problems in managed care and increase the likelihood of achieving successful legislation.

Collaboration between people and among organizations also represents another way in which the resources and expertise are multiplied. For example, Schmidt, Hoffman, and Taylor (chapter 25) and O'Brien et al. (chapter 5) introduced models of collaborative efforts between universities and community agencies. Both models increase training opportunities related to specific social issues as well as increased personnel and expertise available when addressing concerns such as HIV/AIDS and domestic violence, respectively.

Because many social issues are complex and result from oppression and privilege that are embedded in multiple systems, a great deal of expertise and resources are necessary to effect change. One alternative to effectively addressing the complexities and challenges of these types of issues is involving members of multiple disciplines (e.g., counseling psychology, community psychology, program evaluation, political science, qualitative methodology, epidemiology, medicine, anthropology) on social justice teams. These members should represent both sides of the scientist-practitioner continuum, working, as Fassinger and Gallor (chapter 19) described, to develop a scientist-practitioner-advocacy approach.

Multidisciplinary collaboration, however, brings its own set of challenges—disparate professional languages, traditions, and techniques—but it is precisely this diversity that is needed to comprehend and successfully intervene in the systemic layers and contexts of prevention, promotion, and social justice research and practice. Furthermore, funding agencies are increasingly encouraging large, longitudinal, multisite, and/or multidisciplinary efforts that concentrate diverse resources to develop powerful, innovative, and exciting interventions, policies, and research paradigms. It is hoped that in the next decade, an expanding body of evidence and experience will change the complexion of prevention, promotion, and social justice from a visionary campaign of isolated professionals—rooted primarily in compelling ideology—to a multidisciplinary science and practice grounded in a strong empirical and experiential basis.

Multilevel or Systemic Approaches

Another theme emerging from the social justice work featured in this *Handbook* is the ability of counseling psychologists to conceptualize and intervene at multiple levels and within multiple systems. As mentioned earlier, most social justice issues are complex and involve diverse individuals and other (e.g., communities, organizations) stakeholders, along with various aspects of the context, environment, and structure linked with the stated concern. More often than not, many systems, both human and nonhuman, are connected to the concern. Thus, counseling psychologists must be competent in understanding the dynamic interplay between a host of factors comprising the system. They must also be skilled in designing and implementing interventions and policies that maximize appropriate systemic solutions. For example, when discussing social class oppression, Hopps and Liu (chapter 23) asserted that counseling psychologists must recognize the micro-level impact of their involvement in the health care system as well as their responsibility to advocate for change at a systems level. Likewise, a number of chapters included ecological models of intervention to illustrate multisystemic approaches in international work (Moeschberger, Ordóñez, Shankar, & Raney, chapter 31), school prevention (Roysircar, chapter 6), family enrichment (McWhirter & McWhirter, chapter 28), and environmental racism (Santiago-Rivera, Talka, & Tully, chapter 14).

Multilevel activity can also occur within a profession and an organization. Part of the notable social change in addressing LGB issues, for example, came through efforts within the American Psychological Association (APA) to advocate for public statements regarding LGB rights (Whitcomb & Loewy, chapter 16). Furthermore, the fairly recent creation of the Divisions for Social Justice of the APA (Toporek, chapter 1) reflects an even more significant shift in the philosophy and commitment of the psychology profession to social justice. The psychologists within APA leading this effort are pursuing social justice issues within APA governance (e.g., working together to appoint social justice–oriented individuals to APA committees, working with and supporting APA's Public Interest Directorate) and advocating for ongoing social justice–related research, action, and public policy (e.g., supporting social justice efforts of various APA divisions).

Changes in workplace policies (Fassinger & Gallor, chapter 19) and public policy (e.g., Juntunen et al., chapter 21; McPherson & Reilly, chapter 34; Shullman, Celeste, & Strickland, chapter 33) influence individuals through large-scale systemic change. Fassinger and Gallor described the problems perpetuated by trying to resolve oppression and discrimination by working only with individuals facing these forms of injustice. Strickland (Shullman et al.) noted that his work with individual clients and families raised his awareness that these problems could not be solved by individual interventions alone. This motivated him to become involved in making legislative changes by becoming an active participant in Congress. Similarly, Shullman noted that the research and training that she received regarding gender equity clarified the need to become an advocate for these issues, raising the awareness of those involved in government and public policy. The collaboration and legislative efforts needed to improve consumer and practitioner rights in the face of managed care was chronicled by McPherson and Reilly. Similarly, Hopps and Liu discussed the need to reexamine the system within which we work as counseling psychologists and the importance of intervening at a systems level while maintaining a consciousness of our tendency to rely on previously oppressive systems and tools to challenge the oppression.

Finally, the need to provide training to work in multiple levels of intervention was also noted throughout the *Handbook* and specifically explicated by Talleyrand, Chung, and Bemak (chapter 4) in their description of their training program. They described the efforts within their program to pay careful attention to all levels of intervention throughout the curriculum, practicum, and internships.

The Pace of Change

The seriousness of human rights issues, poverty, violence, and oppression fosters a sense of urgency, yet few substantive and lasting changes can be made rapidly. Therefore, another theme emerging from this *Handbook* is patience, persistence, and the value of pursuing small steps when trying to bring about change or implement new solutions, particularly in international settings (Gerstein & Kirkpatrick, chapter 30), but also in local environments (e.g., Toporek & Chope, chapter 20). Given the multisystemic nature of many social problems, there are multiple focal points of potential intervention. Not all of these possible points, however, are viable targets for promoting change, and some features of a system might be more amenable to change than others. In addition, when selecting a focal point of change in a community, one must select an entry point that allows the community to adapt to change in ways that ensure forward movement and empowerment (e.g., Gerstein & Kirkpatrick; McWhirter & McWhirter; Vera et al.). Rapid changes risk imposing solutions that are ill-fitted and not derived from the community, and they can result in a new form of oppression (Cosgrove, chapter 15; Juntunen et al., chapter 21). The projects described in this *Handbook* reflect the theme of pacing one's interventions and the need to build relationships first (e.g., Horne & Mathews; Norsworthy; Toporek & Chope). Tied to this theme is the importance of assessing and understanding the problem and particular worldview, then working in a committed, collaborative, multicultural way toward resolution (Thompson et al., chapter 8). Most of the projects discussed in this *Handbook* evolved over years and sometimes decades. Shullman et al. (chapter 33) noted a similar issue at the legislative level and emphasized that psychologists need to understand that legislative change is a long-term process and may require compromises. This long-term commitment provides the opportunity for justice to take hold and community power and self-determination to be sustained.

Commitment, Fidelity, and Veracity

Another theme throughout descriptions of social justice work presented in this *Handbook* reflects the need to honor commitments to affected communities. Toporek and Williams (chapter 12) discussed ethical issues related to commitments, informed consent, and nonmaleficence in terms of systems interventions. The effects of interventions when applied systemwide have the potential to influence a number of people and systems, often including those who may not have been informed of the intervention or the goals. Therefore, concerns about the influence of the intervention may be far reaching and may have ripple effects that are unexpected (Pope, 1990). Kiselica and Robinson (2001) urged caution when making promises that cannot be kept and further asserted that counseling psychologists must make certain to accomplish what they had promised. Bell and Goodman (chapter 12) provided an interesting example of this in terms of the responsibility of social justice researchers who are conducting program evaluations to inform the program that the outcomes may not necessarily reflect their expectations. Thus, promises of supportive evidence from social justice–oriented research and program evaluation should not be made a priori.

Aspects of honesty and veracity have been noted in a number of chapters in this *Handbook*. For example, McWhirter and McWhirter (chapter 28) described the necessity of clarifying their values and beliefs in their work affiliated with a Catholic community in Chile. These authors stressed the importance of distinguishing their beliefs from those of the church leaders in order to minimize the danger of misperception or undue perceptions of assigned power by association. This issue of fidelity, or trust, is pivotal with respect to work in marginalized communities for whom psychology, as an establishment, has not been a trusted ally. This has been true as well regarding the perceptions of Westerners working in non-Western countries. Norsworthy & Khuankaew (chapter 29) emphasized that an important aspect of building relationships in Thailand involved understanding historical contact with Westerners as well as clarifying how she may be able to work in trustworthy ways. Similarly, for many communities, veracity or honesty in intentions has also been questionable. Historically, there may be some distrust of researchers from various disciplines (e.g., anthropology and ethnology) given the exploitative and harmful use of research results or the research process (Marker, 2003). Although there is less discussion about this type of influence by a counseling psychology researcher, communities may not distinguish disciplines. Rather, if experiences with outside researchers have been perceived by the community to be harmful, there is a likelihood for distrust of all outside researchers. In addition, traditional research methods have not been inclusive enough of the community's goals, and thus a community may not feel as though its needs are being properly served (Cosgrove; Fassinger & Gallor).

Another issue that can lead to distrust in communities is the instability of public and private grant funding for projects (Pope, 1990). Although most of these projects are intended to provide, and indeed do provide, positive benefit, they are often short lived given changes in public policy, funding, and the attrition of project leaders (Toporek & Chope). Because it is often not possible to continue indefinitely in a community, and because it is often desirable for a community to gain a level of self-advocacy skills, Goodman et al. (2004) asserted that a major goal of social justice work is to leave clients "with tools for social change" (p. 798). This goal was illustrated throughout the *Handbook* (e.g., McWhirter & McWhirter).

The chapters in this *Handbook* offer rich and innovative scientist-professional perspectives of social justice work. Clearly, they provided many concrete, useful examples of how to engage in social justice activities based on an interdisciplinary and multicultural framework of theory and practice. The major themes just discussed capture, in part, the commonalities in the social justice work described by the various authors. These themes and other topics addressed in this *Handbook* provide a foundation for the recommendations to follow. We have grouped these recommendations to focus on future directions in theory, practice, research, training, and policy linked with social justice initiatives. Hopefully, this discussion will contribute to the advancement of various social justice activities among counseling psychologists and, more important, contribute to a broad, multidisciplinary, systemic effort to reduce and prevent a host of social injustices and inequities.

Future Directions

Theory

Unfortunately, within counseling psychology, there has been limited attention to theories related to different forms of oppression and social justice. While there is increasing awareness of contextual factors that influence human development (e.g., Ivey, Ivey, Myers, & Sweeney, 2005), career choice (e.g., Lent & Brown, 1996), and other aspects of wellness, the extent to which these models have become foundational in our field is limited. As in traditional counseling, theory is important to the enterprise of prevention, promotion, and social justice. Theory enables teasing out active ingredients from confounding variables. Theory permits the measurement, for example, of proximal and distal indicators. In terms of social justice, a theory can identify relevant risk and protective factors, which then become potential targets for intervention and policy development and implementation. An intervention or policy, for instance, may aim to prevent discrete illnesses (e.g., HIV/AIDS, post-traumatic stress disorder related to torture and war) among the public or to promote broad competencies (e.g., wellness promotion model, racial consciousness) among mental health providers.

Furthermore, as mentioned by Gerstein, there is a great need for theories that are cross-culturally valid, effective, and systemic. Counseling psychology's relevance in international settings, for example, would be enhanced by developing theories that viably integrate U.S. and non-U.S. models of psychology and counseling. In addition, attention is needed to identify appropriate roles for members of interdisciplinary teams serving diverse clientele around the world.

Developing workable, culturally sensitive theories and models for understanding and addressing social justice issues from a counseling psychology perspective presents a significant challenge and area for future growth. The heuristic value of existing theories in diverse disciplines (e.g., anthropology; political science; economics; architecture; and social, community, peace, and organizational psychology) can contribute significantly to theory development in counseling psychology. Diverse disciplines also provide a wealth of important resources for designing and implementing culturally appropriate, effective, and systemic solutions.

Practice

Along with the need to develop new theories of social justice work, it is essential that counseling psychologists interested in this type of work carefully examine the nature and scope of their practice. To be an effective social change agent, it is important to define practice as inclusive of individual, group, and systems interventions. In addition, the diverse roles of counseling psychologists in practice must also be acknowledged and embraced, including therapist, counselor, advocate, social change agent, educator/trainer, consultant, policy developer and implementer, and so on (Toporek & Liu, 2000). As we have learned from the chapters in this *Handbook,* to be most effective, counseling psychologists must move beyond micro-level interventions, recognize the range of types of oppression and the intersections among these oppressions, focus on privilege as well as oppression, and receive training that prepares them for these roles.

The example of posttraumatic stress disorder (PTSD), diagnosis, and treatment demonstrates the complexity of scope of practice and acknowledgment of micro and macro perspectives of etiology as well as intervention (Huynh & Roysircar, chapter 24). Is PTSD an individual or social disorder? Research on victims of political persecution indicates that individual symptoms of trauma often do not match up to the criteria of the clinical diagnosis of PTSD. In addition, the term *disorder* implies that the victim is at fault instead of the perpetrators of the trauma, and that can add to the alienation that individuals suffering political persecution already experience. PTSD should be thought of as occurring within a social context. The concept of PTSD is also limited in that in areas of political persecution and war, it is not only individuals but also families and communities that experience traumatic events. This raises the question of whether or not whole families and communities should be considered as traumatized, including villages, townships, communities of fishermen, and thousands of orphans, as in the recent tsunami natural disaster in South and Southeast Asia. Similarly, people who suffered tremendous psychological and physical trauma as a result of Hurricane Katrina may also be affected at individual, family, and systems levels, not only because of the effects of the hurricane, but also because of the repercussions of the problematic disaster response systems. Furthermore, subsequent questions raised about the role of racism and social classism on the media's coverage and the governmental response to the tragedy may have contributed to the trauma experienced by those affected by this disaster. Finally, criticism of the use of the words *post* and *disorder* includes the fact that some traumatic events are not limited to a certain event in time that has already passed.

When designing an intervention or policy, counseling psychologists must consider the scope of the strategy (universal, selected, secondary, tertiary); the level of the target variable (individual or micro-, exo-, or macrosystem); and the timing of the strategy. Moreover, communities serve as the context for most preventive interventions and policies, so practitioners and researchers must learn to navigate within communities and to serve local needs. Counseling psychologists can safeguard the rights of all participants by minimizing coercive methods of influence; involving the public in choices about program design and implementation; and carefully evaluating prevention, promotion, and social justice programs.

Counseling psychologists can also support community organizing and activism. For example, conflicts may occur within marginalized communities because of within-group differences. In particular, individuals at various stages of identity development may have differing goals, agendas, and approaches to working with allies. Counseling psychologists can use their professional group, consultation, and multicultural skills to help marginalized communities understand these differences; find common ground; and construct and implement effective, appropriate, community-based solutions.

Consistent with such skills and a focus on prevention is the importance of working to create nonoppressive environments. These efforts entail working not only with marginalized groups, but also with people who have privilege. Counseling psychologists can provide support and training for allies, that is, individuals who are committed to social justice for groups of which they are not members. Another essential element is working with people who are unaware of their privilege to help them gain insight into the dynamics of oppression, including the ways that they and others are hurt by living within an oppressive society. This will also entail helping individuals who are members of marginalized groups to gain awareness of the ways in which they may experience privilege as well as oppression.

Support for marginalized individuals can help them cope with oppression, and advocacy can help to address the systemic mechanisms of oppression. It is equally important to help people to recognize the dynamics, impact, and possible means of combating oppression. Consciousness-raising, educational interventions, and political strategizing can help communities develop the resources, insight, motivation, and tools to challenge oppression and inequality.

Advocacy is another area of practice that has historically received minimal attention from the profession of counseling psychology. As is evident from various experiences shared in this *Handbook*, counseling psychologists can make significant contributions in advocating for self-sufficiency, systemic justice, and equitable resource distribution. Advancing practice and training with the hope that counseling psychologists learn and apply skills for political advocacy is essential so that work in, for example, vocational psychology informs policy rather than having to take a reactive, remedial, or reparative stance.

Overall, based on the chapters found in this *Handbook*, there is a dire need to establish models of intervention and policies that are broadly based and that address institutional change and social advocacy in the vocational, educational, health, international, and mental health arenas. Establishing counseling psychologists as individual advocates as well as placing them in organizations committed to promoting and securing political and/or legal modifications in society can advance the cause of social justice. For example, Whitcomb and Loewy described efforts within the APA to counter antigay movements. On a legislative level, Shullman et al. and McPherson described their roles statewide and nationally both inside and outside of government regarding issues such as gender equity, consumer rights, managed care, and other issues. Other organizational efforts could be pursued by counseling psychologists, for instance, spearheading an initiative to enhance the infrastructure in the Society of Counseling Psychology (Division 17) designed to network counseling psychologists and students around the world. This could lead to greater international collaboration on social justice activities.

Research

Throughout this *Handbook*, there were many excellent recommendations offered with respect to conducting social justice research. Community involvement appeared as a consistent theme within the recommendations. Community involvement is integral when determining appropriate and relevant social justice research questions. Often, a researcher pursues a line of research that is consistent with established theory or a research agenda (Cosgrove; Pope-Davis, Liu, Toporek, & Brittan-Powell, 2001). However, these research questions may not be meaningful to the population whom the research is intending to benefit. As was discussed to some extent in each of the earlier chapters, community-driven research questions with direct and immediate benefits to the community enhance the ability of counseling psychologists to make substantive social change through research. As Fassinger and Gallor pointed out, part of advocacy is asking the right questions.

There is a plethora of research questions that would inform both counseling psychology and the general public on social justice issues. Here are a few examples. What works in counseling for clients from low socioeconomic backgrounds? How and when should we integrate mental health and work? What is the role of work in psychological health across socioeconomic status groups? What is the cross-cultural validity of various prevention and psychoeducational programs developed within the United States that are based on North American models of psychology and counseling? How are U.S. counseling psychologists perceived and evaluated by the stakeholders receiving services outside of the United States? What is the outcome to the clientele served of networking providers around the world? What are the expectations of the clientele served in different countries, and how do these expectations differ from expectations in the United States? What is the long-term effect of implementing nonviolent solutions in terms of establishing and maintaining peaceful communities, cultures, and countries? Investigation of these and other questions could help to inform counseling psychologists and interdisciplinary intervention teams regarding the cultural relevance and impact of international interventions. In addition, this type of research may provide the necessary support needed for endorsement by human rights groups and other organizations who may serve as allies.

Along with these questions and topics, there is another area deserving research attention. One of the powerful shifts in research is moving the focus from the "victim" or the "oppressed" to focusing on environmental issues, privilege, or the oppressor. Examples of this shift can be seen in research investigating the influence of racism on White people (e.g., Spanierman & Heppner, 2004) and theory concerning the effect of heterosexual privilege on heterosexual identity development (Mohr, 2002; Worthington, Savoy, Dillon, & Vernaglia, 2002). Greater attention is thus needed on research that investigates contextual variables that maintain injustice and inequity.

There is also an urgent need to enhance the use of community-centered and empowerment-oriented research methods such as participatory action research. The wisdom and experience of disciplines such as social work, community organizing, applied social psychology, and public health can be beneficial when considering how these methods may apply to the research approach of counseling psychologists. Furthermore, increased interdisciplinary collaborative research efforts are needed. This type of approach would allow for many different aspects of social problems to be addressed in a coordinated way. Moreover, it would increase the likelihood of engaging communities in collaborative research endeavors designed to address their specific concerns. Research methodologies that incorporate a community service component would serve to increase the probability of equity, whereby the research results could benefit not only the professionals carrying out the project but also the community. This type of research approach may also increase the likelihood that the community will maintain a level of trust that the counseling psychologist or research group is working toward resolving issues that are important to the community.

Prevention, promotion, and social justice research is faced with a myriad of complex measurement issues. As a science, this type of research sits astride the intersection of life-span development; epidemiology; and counseling, community, health, multicultural, and liberation psychologies. Longitudinal modeling, sampling challenges, the problems of levels of analysis, combining data from multiple informants (see Huynh & Roysircar, chapter 24), qualitative analysis, skewed data, and small effect sizes—all call for sophisticated measurement and analytic techniques. Coping with these problems frequently requires skills that exceed the methodological repertoire of the average counseling psychology researcher. It is recommended that there be allocation of resources to train entry-level and mid-career counseling psychologists in prevention, promotion, and social justice research methodology. If some of these resources are directed to disseminating prevention methodology into doctoral-level curricula, more counseling psychology researchers may be in a position to conduct the sophisticated research needed.

Finally, future social justice research must also focus on influencing policy and practice by affecting the bottom line, increasing the impact of research findings by framing the research with direct policy implications, and ensuring that research results are promoted in the popular media. It is important to understand that most policy changes come about when institutions are financially affected. For instance, policy change is more likely to occur if results from research demonstrate the economic impact, for example, when discriminatory practices are perpetrated.

Training

In order for counseling psychologists to perform as competent social justice agents, they need training in group work, consultation, multicultural counseling, prevention, community development, research, and program evaluation and development. Acquiring an in-depth understanding of multiple and alternative roles as well as of organizational dynamics and community organizing is important as well.

More specifically, counseling psychologists need to obtain knowledge about issues facing marginalized and oppressed communities, along with an appreciation and respect for diverse cultures and dynamics. To practice as effective social change agents, counseling psychologists must be able to demonstrate highly advanced consultation, advocacy, outreach, and action research skills. Furthermore, counseling psychologists need to broaden their perspective about their professional role. No longer will they be able to define "practice" only as therapy; rather, counseling psychologists must expand their vision of practice to encompass a range of activities that promote social justice and systemic change. Moreover, counseling psychologists need to learn how to operate as effective members of interdisciplinary teams.

Integrating interdisciplinary collaboration into training programs can be done in a variety of ways both in academic courses and in the field. For example, courses in community psychology, applied social psychology, organizational behavior, political science, anthropology, qualitative methods, economics, international relations, program evaluation, and development could be integrated into the curriculum. To increase international competence, for instance, core course assignments could link interests in international work. Greater opportunities could be developed for field practica and internships at nongovernmental organizations (NGOs), international consulting firms, and in a country of interest. Programs could also encourage the acquisition of a second language.

Existing training programs need to focus much more on building and sustaining community partnerships as well as teaching students consultation and organizational change skills (Talleyrand et al., chapter 4). Eventually, cultural competence for domestic and international counseling and social justice activities will be embedded in doctoral training programs to the extent that there can also be a greater emphasis on continuing education. The systematic implementation of multicultural competencies (Arredondo et al., 1996; Sue, Arredondo, & McDavis, 1992) and APA's Multicultural Guidelines (APA, 2003) would help ensure that cultural context is respected and integrated into social justice and counseling.

To increase the ability of counseling psychologists to adequately address social justice issues related to employment, more content is needed in training programs regarding laws related to employment fairness, discrimination, affirmative action, welfare reform, and facilitation of institutional change. In addition, training for skill development is needed in vocational psychology in such areas as confronting discrimination, working with whistle-blowers, and preventing workplace violence. Training programs also need to prepare students to offer effective treatments for clients from low socioeconomic backgrounds, including helping these clients to understand the role of work in their psychological health. Students must be trained to comprehend and confront the fundamental assumptions that sustain subtle biases in the workplace. In particular, students must learn about the external causes of these biases such as sexism, racism, ageism, homophobia, and heterosexism, and they must develop the skills to effectively address these biases.

One initiative that could enhance the opportunities that students have for appropriate training in social justice work would be to include more explicit language in the APA accreditation standards around social justice, systems intervention, activism, and advocacy training. Developing a set of competencies in these areas could help ensure consistency. An example is provided by the Advocacy Competencies (Lewis, Arnold, House, & Toporek, 2001) adopted by the American Counseling Association. One existing area that could be appropriately expanded is APA's Committee on Accreditation guidelines, Domain D and Domain A5, Individual and Cultural Diversity. These domains could be expanded to include attention to social justice concerns and training to reflect issues of oppression more broadly by recognizing field placements that actively train students to address issues of social class and diversity on a systems level. In addition, expansion of APA accreditation of internship sites that provide social justice training would be a significant improvement.

Policy

As must be apparent from this chapter and the others in this *Handbook,* it is essential that counseling psychologists network and lobby at the grassroots level and at the managerial level with various NGOs, the United Nations, and governmental agencies worldwide to establish and modify policies and structures related to direct and structural forms of violence (e.g., violence toward women, children, refugees). Division 17 could also work to establish relationships with international consulting firms, the United Nations, and NGOs that are engaged in social justice, advocacy, and activism. All these recommendations will require a great deal of time; energy; resources; and interpersonal, structural, cultural, and technological sophistication.

Counseling psychologists should be more involved in briefing legislators on social justice topics (Juntunen et al., chapter 21; McPherson, chapter 34; Shullman et al., chapter 33) either as a representative of counseling psychology professional organizations, independent researchers, or directly as legislators or politicians. Fortunately, there are opportunities in our profession for gaining training in legislative advocacy (APA Public Policy Office, 1995). In addition, some counseling graduate programs are providing related training (Toporek & McNally, chapter 3). There is, however, a significant need for increased activity in this area.

Our own internal policies and structures needed to be modified as well. To produce a larger number of social change agents, counseling psychology programs need to value and reward faculty and students for social justice, advocacy, and activism work (Helms, 2003). Likewise, there needs to be greater recognition in the Society of Counseling Psychology for such work.

Structural accountability and reward systems within the profession, as well as in larger systems such as universities, agencies, and government, present other factors that influence social justice work. For example, social justice scholarship is realized through the creation or enhancement of community-based programs evidenced by the dissemination of knowledge in formats useful to the community, not necessarily highly refereed, top-tier journal publications. This type of information generation may be problematic because it is far from certain whether a person seeking tenure or promotion in a research university can obtain such academic rewards through non-peer-reviewed outlets. Such community products may not be regarded as valued university successes, and the grants might not be regarded as well-spent money. Consequently, the implication is that social justice outreach has to develop a balance between promoting access and accountability and, on the other hand, ensuring its sustainability through products associated with traditional academic performance.

Being socialized to pursue ethereal knowledge as a necessary product for the tenure and promotion system, many faculty members are rarely committed to remain in the community beyond the time that is supported by funding to do applied research. Hence, it is not surprising that social justice–oriented faculty face skepticism in the local community about their interest in the lives of the community members. Many in the community believe that the university will exploit them, and that the community will be a site of university activity only so that grants may be won, publications written, or students trained. Because the work of the faculty raises the hopes of the community, the departure of the university makes matters worse than before the university arrived. The lack of commitment of the university to sustain the work in the community causes the community to be frustrated, angry, and distrusting of the university. These negative outcomes bring us back to the rationale for the creation of social justice advocacy—to transform knowledge into actions that are deemed valuable by communities and for the benefit of the communities as stakeholders.

There is evidence that the conditions in universities may be changing, resulting in the potential for societal conditions and reward structures to align to create top-level interest in actions that promote social justice. In February 1999, the Kellogg

Commission on the Future of State and Land Grant Universities reported that community engagement through outreach scholarship is essential in garnering the public support that state and land grant institutions must have to survive. Accordingly, a zeitgeist may be emerging to encourage university leaders to respond to the current social pressures for greater value-added contributions of higher education to the matters of everyday life affecting the communities within which they are embedded.

Challenges for Social Change Agents

Given the extent and challenge of societal problems that exist, and the potential for counseling psychologists to be involved in attempting to alleviate oppression and injustice in so many ways, it seems important to focus some attention on the well-being of counseling psychologists operating as social change agents. In part, the extent to which counseling psychologists actually engage in social justice work, rather than passively idealizing it, may hinge on personal and contextual factors. The two areas that seem relevant to consider are personal development and self-care of the psychologist-change agent.

Personal Development

Much of this *Handbook* has focused on professional development such as training, interdisciplinary collaboration, and expansion of the ways in which counseling psychologists confront and address social justice issues. There is also a need to acknowledge that social justice work involves a level of personal commitment and skill that goes beyond the typical professional scope. In this context, personal development refers to the advancement of the counseling psychologist as a person in ways that augment or enhance her or his ability to effectively respond to challenges, competently engage in diverse arenas, and maintain integrity in the face of difficult work. Consoli and Machado (2005) described the need for psychologists to engage in "personal elongation exercises" or "specific activities that speak of the therapists' intention to stretch their latitude of acceptance by exposing themselves to alternative ways of conceptualizing human strengths and struggles as well as human change and stability processes" (p. 429). Within this vein, we would like to touch on a few recommendations for personal development: the need for mentors and role models, supportive networks, self-awareness and reflection, personal involvement in communities, and travel and immersion experiences.

Mentors and role models are essential for doing social justice work, particularly international and anti-oppression work. It is important to affiliate with competent and experienced social change agents when entering a new arena or problem, gaining insight, consultation, and clarification of one's perspectives or worldview. A counseling psychologist should not work on his or her own or in isolation from other professionals. This is important not only for the acquisition of appropriate skills, but also for support and feedback.

Self-awareness and reflection is another necessary activity for personal development. As with multicultural competence development, self-awareness is critical in social justice work, given that biases, beliefs, and personal histories influence our work, sometimes positively and sometimes negatively. Without awareness, it is more difficult to approach social justice activities with the best interests of the client(s) at the forefront. Although passion, anger, and frustration can be potent fuel for difficult social justice work, these emotions can also interfere with self-care, sound judgment, and cooperative alliances. Mentors can be instrumental in providing the social change agent with valuable insight about their intentions and personal motivations, and how their worldview may influence their perception of the issue as well as the way they approach the problem or solutions.

Personal involvement in diverse communities is a different prospect in several ways from professional involvement in a community and provides the potential for great benefit in expanding one's worldview. One significant difference between engagement as a professional and engagement as a person is that of power. When a counseling psychologist enters a community as a professional, there is some level of power, safety, and security that goes along with that position and stance regardless of the reality of that perception or the credibility ascribed by the community. When one enters and participates with a community as a person, without the professional garb and directive, the possibility of experiencing a sense of vulnerability and humility is greater.

One's ability to understand a community and culture is greatly enhanced by the personal experience of existing in that world. Traveling as a cultural observer and participant provides an excellent way to learn about cultures, people, and different environments, thereby increasing one's cultural competence as well as one's ability to effectively engage in social justice work, particularly in an international arena. There are an infinite number of diverse opportunities around the world and the United States to perform as a social change agent. Along with travel, one's competence can be strengthened by pursuing many other activities (e.g., reading, visiting museums, participant observation, associating with local people) to learn about cultures. When engaged in international or immersion work, it is critical to maintain and display a sense of humility. Be humble, positive, and hopeful!

Self-Care

One of the issues raised by Helms (2003) regarding the difficulty of implementing social justice in counseling psychology was the lack of institutional support and financial compensation for such work. Although pro bono work is expected per the ethical code of the APA, there are also financial constraints, particularly for those counseling psychologists who come from less economically advantaged backgrounds. Hence, the people who have personal experience with oppression also tend to be the ones with the least amount of resources to give back. This imbalance of resource allocation and financial infrastructure for social justice work in our profession can result in an overextension of the self and neglect of self-care. A few recommendations for increasing self-care include developing and selecting mentors, acknowledging and allowing for sources of strength such as spirituality or other forms of inspiration and joy, recognizing varying needs throughout one's life cycle, and accepting the fact that there will be times in life when one can give more and times when one must focus on immediate family and personal needs. Although we are well trained to teach and coach others on maintaining a balance of a healthy physical, emotional, relational, and spiritual life, we may not follow our own advice. Numerous resources can help with this, including tools of meditation, mindfulness, community support, and even therapy.

To accomplish these recommendations, there may need to be changes in one's work life to increase the value that is given to social justice work. For example, accreditation, tenure and promotion, and public policy must change to facilitate counseling psychologists' contributions in social justice work. Achieving these outcomes requires extensive effort, time, and institutional commitment and support. It is critical, however, that in the meantime, counseling psychologists operating as social change agents maintain their health, well-being, and stamina as well as that of their families and communities. This will help to ensure that such persons remain involved in long-term efforts to reduce and prevent social injustice, oppression, discrimination, violence, and other forms of inequity and societal challenge.

Conclusion

As must be rather obvious from this chapter as well as the other chapters in this *Handbook*, there are numerous challenging and diverse societal and community issues throughout the world requiring the urgent and immediate attention of competent and effective counseling psychologists and other professionals trained as social change agents. Stellar examples of counseling psychologists tackling such issues were presented in this *Handbook*. Without a doubt, there are many other counseling psychologists not featured in this *Handbook* who are engaged in equally important social justice activities. Hopefully, in the not-so-distant future, we will become more aware of the models driving their work and their unique social change strategies to solve systemic problems.

Clearly, it is no longer sufficient or appropriate to simply address human and community problems through a reliance on individual-oriented interventions and solutions. In fact, such interventions may be ineffective and even harmful to the clientele served. To avoid this outcome, counseling psychologists must now be trained as scientist-professionals to think and act systemically based on a multidisciplinary, multicultural model of conceptualization and action. Preparing counseling psychologists to function as systemic social change agents takes on even greater importance if one assumes, as we do, that societal and community problems around the globe will not only increase in the years ahead, but will also become more complex and difficult to address through micro-interventions implemented by professionals acting without the assistance of multidisciplinary teams.

Given the reemergence of social justice work as a vital aspect of the profession of counseling psychology, there may be opportunities for our future graduates to be better prepared to perform as competent and effective systemic thinkers, researchers, and change agents serving the social justice needs of diverse cultures, communities, and even nations. As discussed in this *Handbook*, many aspects of our doctoral training programs will need to be modified to prepare such professionals. At the very least, the curricula must be designed so that students acquire a multidisciplinary and systemic perspective through coursework, research, and fieldwork.

It is encouraging and exciting to witness and experience the energy surrounding the reinvigoration of social justice activities in the counseling psychology profession. As our profession further evolves and matures, thankfully, it appears we are becoming much more comfortable and willing to openly and actively embrace this aspect of our historic roots—that is, pursuing strategies and policies to preserve and enhance communities and the society at large, and activities designed to confront social injustice, inequity, discrimination, violence, and oppression. Hopefully, this *Handbook* will help facilitate and inspire greater numbers of counseling psychologists to embrace this legacy and pursue the training and experiences necessary to function as effective social change agents. Counseling psychologists who follow this path will be in a position to make a unique and significant contribution to multidisciplinary teams designed to modify and/or strengthen the fundamental fabric and structure of our communities and cultures. Ultimately, this can only help to enhance the quality of life for all people around the globe.

References

American Psychological Association Public Policy Office. (1995). *Advancing psychology in the public interest: A psychologist's guide to participation in federal advocacy process.* Retrieved on February 21, 2005, from http://www.apa.org/ppo/ppan/piguide.html

Arredondo, P., Toporek, R., Brown, S., Jones, J., Locke, D., Sanchez, J., & Stadler, H. (1996). Operationalization of multicultural counseling competencies. *Journal of Multicultural Counseling and Development, 24*(1), 42–78.

Consoli, A. J., & Machado, P. P. P. (2005). Las psicoterapeutas, ¿nacen o se hacen? Las habilidades naturales y adquiridas de las psicoterapeutas: Implicaciones para la selección, capacitación y desarrollo profesional [Psychotherapists, are they born or made? Psychotherapists' natural and acquired skills: Implications for selection, training and professional development]. In H. Fernández-Alvarez & R. Opazo Castro (Eds.), *La integración en psicoterapia: Manual práctico [Integration in psychotherapy: A handbook]* (pp. 385–451). Madrid, Spain: Paidós.

Goodman, L. A., Liang, B., Helms, J. E., Latta, R. E., Sparks, E., & Weintraub, S. R. (2004). Training counseling psychologists as social justice agents: Feminist and multicultural principles in action. *The Counseling Psychologist, 32*(6), 793–837.

Helms, J. E. (2003). A pragmatic view of social justice. *The Counseling Psychologist, 31*(3), 305–313.

Ivey, A., Ivey, M. B., Myers, J., & Sweeney, T. (2005). *Developmental counseling and therapy: Wellness over the lifespan.* Boston: Houghton Mifflin.

Kiselica, M. S., & Robinson, M. (2001). Bringing advocacy counseling to life: The history, issues, and human dramas of social justice work in counseling. *Journal of Counseling & Development, 70,* 387–397.

Lent, R. W., & Brown, S. D. (1996). Social cognitive approach to career development: An overview. *Career Development Quarterly, 44*(4), 310–321.

Lewis, J., Arnold, M. S., House, R., & Toporek, R. L. (2001). *Advocacy Competencies: American Counseling Association Task Force on Advocacy Competencies.* Retrieved July 19, 2005, from http://counselorsforsocialjustice.org/advocacycompetencies.html

Marker, M. (2003). Indigenous voice, community, and epistemic violence: The ethnographer's "interests" and what "interests" the ethnographer. *International Journal of Qualitative Studies In Education, 16*(3), 361–375.

Mohr, J. J. (2002). Heterosexual identity and the heterosexual therapist: An identity perspective on sexual orientation dynamics in psychotherapy. *The Counseling Psychologist, 30,* 532–566.

Pope, K. S. (1990). Ethics and malpractice: Identifying and implementing ethical standards for primary prevention. *Prevention in Human Services, 8*(2), 43–64.

Pope-Davis, D. B., Liu, W. M., Toporek, R. L., & Brittan-Powell, C. S. (2001). What's missing from multicultural competency research: Review, introspection, and recommendations. *Cultural Diversity and Ethnic Minority Psychology, 7*(2), 121–138.

Spanierman, L. B. & Heppner, M. J. (2004). Psychosocial Costs of Racism to Whites Scale (PCRW): Construction and initial validation. *Journal of Counseling Psychology, 51*(2), 249–262.

Sue, D. W., Arredondo, P., & McDavis, R. J. (1992). Multicultural counseling competencies and standards: A call to the profession. *Journal of Counseling and Development, 70,* 477–486.

Toporek, R. L., & Liu, W. M. (2001). Advocacy in counseling psychology: Critical issues of race, class, and gender. In D. B. Pope-Davis & H. L. K. Coleman (Eds.), *The intersection of race, class and gender in counseling psychology* (pp. 385–413). Thousand Oaks, CA: Sage.

Worthington, R. L., Savoy, H. B., Dillon, F. R., & Vernaglia, E. R. (2002). Heterosexual identity development: A multidimensional model of individual and social identity. *The Counseling Psychologist, 30,* 496–531.

Wrenn, C. G. (1962). The culturally encapsulated counselor. *Harvard Educational Review, 32,* 444–449.

Wrenn, C. G. (1985). Afterword: The culturally encapsulated counselor revisited. In P. Pedersen (Ed.), *Handbook of cross-cultural counseling and therapy* (pp. 323–329). Westport, CT: Greenwood.

Author Index

Aanstoos, C. M., 26
Abeles, N., 347
Ablasser, C., 494
Acevedo, M. J., 157, 158
Ackerland, S., 124
Ackerlind, S. J., 124
Adair, E., 447, 448
Adams, E. M., 124
Adams, K., 299
Adams, M., 38, 39
Adams, T., 457
Adelsheim, S., 121
Adeola, F. O., 188
Adler, N. E., 318, 320, 322, 359
Ægisdóttir, S., 378, 465
Agger, B., 431, 432
Agyeman, J., 185
Akbar, N., 19, 20, 21
Akwesasne Task Force on the Environment, 188, 191
Albee, G. W., 41, 87
Alcorn, J., 41
Alderfer, C. P., 284
Aldrich, C., 474
Alexander, C. M., 46
Ali, S. R., 318, 319, 320
Allen, J. L., Jr., 412
Allen, T. D., 284
Allport, G. W., 458, 463
Allred, E. N., 187
Alston, R. J., 177
Altmaier, E. M., 5
American Lung Association, 341–342
American Psychiatric Association, 217, 219, 239, 341, 348, 351
American Psychological Association, 4, 5, 6, 7, 8, 17, 18, 19, 20, 21, 22, 23, 31, 32, 40, 86, 125, 135, 136, 137, 151, 176, 219, 220, 227, 232, 233, 262, 263, 267, 268, 298, 299, 314, 367, 370, 384, 402, 413, 425, 491, 492, 494, 495, 546, 547
Amick, B. C., III, 322
Amnesty International, 408, 409
Anders, G., 520, 521, 522, 523
Anderson, A., 118, 119, 122, 389, 392, 402, 403, 482
Anderson, D. J., 157
Anderson, E. A., 201
Anderson, J., 298, 367
Anderson, L., 201, 210
Anderson, M. Z., 252
Anderson, N. B., 320, 326
Anderson, N. J., 4
Anderson, T. L., 298
Andrus, M., 325
Annan, J. R., 101
Annie E. Casey Foundation, 121
Antioch College, 77
Antonio, A. L., 266
Archer, J., 62
Arctic Monitoring and Assessment Programme, 187
Armitage, C. J., 474
Armstead, C. A., 326
Armsworth, M. W., 5
Arnold, M. S., 31, 491, 546
Aron, A., 475, 476
Arredondo, P., 5, 17, 49, 86, 132, 133, 135, 141, 155, 191, 193, 278, 283, 339, 347, 425, 491, 492, 546
Asch, A., 171, 172, 235
Aston, G., 527
Atkinson, D. R., 25, 87, 131, 133, 134, 139, 151, 232, 279, 282, 480
Atlani, L., 480
Ayala, E., 477

Bachman, R., 156, 157, 520, 522
Badgett, M. V. L., 266

Baer, N., 166
Bagg, B., 67
Bahniuk, M. H., 284
Bailey, N., 501
Baird, K., 524
Baker, D. B., 40
Baker, L., 70
Ballou, M., 233, 427, 437, 439
Baluch, S. P., 6, 290
Bangi, A., 360
Banyard, V. L., 202, 206
Barak, O., 322
Barlow, C. E., 314
Barnett, O. W., 157
Barnhart, P. N., 509
Baron, R. A., 478
Barrett-Conner, E., 341
Barry, M., 104
Bartels, K. M., 272
Barton, C., 126
Barton, J. A., 185, 194
Baruch, Y., 457
Bassuk, E. L., 201
Bassuk, S. S., 201, 322
Basta, J., 157
Bates, S. R., 341
Bechtel, M. A., 64
Beck, A. T., 303
Beck, F. O., 108
Beckerman, N., 364
Becker-Schutte, A. M., 226
Beckstead, A. L., 216, 225
Belknap, J., 157, 158
Bell, E., 190
Bell, L. A., 38, 39
Bell, M. E., 157, 158, 159, 160, 162, 164
Bellinger, D., 187
Bemak, F., 47, 53, 133, 134
Bendell, D., 322
Benishek, L. A., 71
Benjamin, L. T., 40
Benjamin, L. T., Jr., 382
Bennet, S. K., 151
Bennett, J. L., 171
Bennett, L., 157, 162
Bennett, M., 7
Bennett, P., 322
Berglund, M. L., 89
Berk, L. E., 132, 136, 138, 139
Berkeley Planning Associates, 172
Berkman, L. F., 322
Bernier, J. E., 5, 151, 491
Bernstein L., 342
Berry, J. M., 474
Berry, M. F., 100
Berryman, P., 412
Berube, M., 175
Best, A., 330
Betz, N. E., 5, 252, 261, 300
Bhati, K. S., 277
Bibbins, V., 491
Bielstein Savoy, H., 226
Bieschke, K. J., 71, 225
Biever, J. L., 135
Biglan, A., 83, 97
Bilsky, W., 444
Bindman, A. B., 326
Bingham, R. P., 118, 252, 277, 283, 388, 494
Bird, J. A., 341, 342
Black, K., 82
Blair, S. N., 314
Blanchard, J., 509
Blank, R. M., 296
Blasi, G. L., 210
Blustein, D. L., 2, 5, 6, 17, 18, 46, 47, 118, 155, 251, 252, 276, 277, 300, 314, 358, 378, 388, 406, 464, 465, 524
Bobick, T. M., 474
Boehnlein, J. K., 341, 342, 349
Boff, C., 413
Boff, L., 413
Bolden, M. A., 6, 290
Bommersbach, M., 447, 448
Bond, J. T., 266
Bondurant, J. V., 447
Bonilla, N. T., 341, 342
Bonta, B., 443
Boone, J. R., 342
Bornstein, D., 290
Borow, H., 3
Borzuckhowska, B., 473
Bose, S., 481
Bosma, L., 331
Boudin, K., 433
Boulding, E., 443
Bouma, J., 322
Bowen, I., 433
Bowman, P., 91
Bowman, P. J., 21
Bowman, S. L., 231, 234, 235, 252
Boyce, T., 318, 322
Boyce, W. T., 320
Boyd, C., 347
Boyd-Franklin, N., 31
Boykin, K., 225
Boyle, M. H., 320
Brabeck, M., 46

Brack, C. J., 151
Bradley, L., 190, 389
Brady, S. S., 322
Branch, C. W., 477
Brantlinger, E., 180
Brasfield, T. L., 367
Bray, J. H., 329, 330
Brennan, A. F., 156, 157
Bretherton, D., 390, 392, 396
Brittan-Powell, C. S., 543
Brody, E., 480
Broman, C. L., 87
Bromley, J. L., 119
Bronfenbrenner, U., 39, 78, 80, 131, 132, 155, 359, 383, 475, 480
Brooks, G. C., 4
Brooks-Gunn, J., 93, 191
Brown, ?., 512
Brown, C., 299
Brown, L. S., 20, 22, 25, 231, 234, 239, 431, 432
Brown, M. T., 277
Brown, N. J., 185, 194
Brown, S., 546
Brown, S. D., 277, 285, 540
Brown, S. P., 5, 49, 193, 492
Brown-Collins, A., 431
Browning, C., 151
Brownlee, K., 44
Bruce, D., 359
Brunner, E., 321
Bruns, C. M., 237, 238
Bruyere, S. M., 262, 265, 266
Bryant, B., 186, 189, 190
Brydon-Miller, M., 203
Buchanan, S., 172
Buchholz, K., 330
Buckley, M. J., 60
Buckner, J. C., 201
Buffmire, J. A., 509
Buhrke, R. A., 151, 217
Bulatao, E. Q., 509
Bullard, R. D., 185, 186, 189, 193, 194
Bullock, H. E., 202, 319
Burke, J., 325, 329
Burman, E., 205
Burr, V., 207
Busch, S. H., 524
Bush, I. R., 298
Butler, L. M., 119
Butler, P., 525, 526
Butler, S., 241
Byars-Winston, A. M., 252
Byrne, D., 478
Cacioppo, J. T., 459, 460
Cahill, S., 157, 265, 269, 270
Callandra, J., 447, 448
Camacho, T., 320, 326
Camic, P. M., 340
Campbell, C., 131
Campbell, J., 166
Campbell, W. K., 322
Campos, P. E., 367
Canadian Psychological Association, 19, 21, 22
Cantor, J., 223
Capitanio, J. P., 225
Caprara, G. V., 507, 508
Cardemil, E., 131
Carnine, D., 97
Carnoy, M., 103
Carpenter, D., 188
Carroll, D., 322
Carroll, L., 223
Carter, P. L., 320
Carter, R. T., 6, 17, 102, 191, 277
Cartwright, B., 473
Casaburri, N., 174
Casas, J. M., 132, 139, 191
Caspi-Yavin, Y., 347
Cass, V. C., 151, 173, 224
Castellanos, L. P., 124
Castellazzo, G., 320
Castro, C., 326, 477
Caswell, R. N., 447
Catalano, R. F., 89, 134
Cauchi, R., 525
Cavett, A. M., 300
Celeste, B. L., 509
Centers for Disease Control & Prevention, 341, 359, 361
Cernea, M. M., 479
Chakiris, B. J., 276
Chamberlin, J., 495
Chan, C., 225
Chang, M. J., 266
Chanpong, G. F., 172
Chassin, L., 138
Chattes, L. M., 87
Chaves, A. P., 155, 277
Cheatham, H. E., 252
Cheek, D., 2
Chen, E., 320
Chen, E. C., 151
Chen, J., 322, 326, 327
Chen, Y. J., 342
Cheng, T., 296, 297
Chen-Hayes, S. F., 190

Chesler, P., 233
Chesney, M. A., 318, 322
Cheung, F. M., 425
Chomsky, N., 344
Chope, R. C., 493
Christie, D. J., 118, 119, 122, 124, 383, 384, 392, 400, 443, 478
Chronister, K. M., 299
Chua, P. P., 474
Chung, R. C.-Y., 53, 133, 134
Chung, Y. B., 217, 223, 252
Chwalisz, K., 40
Cianciotto, J., 265, 269, 270
Cicchetti, D., 78
Claire, T., 320
Clancy, C. M., 322, 325
Clark, J., 433
Clark, L., 185, 194
Clark, R., 320
Clark, V. R., 320
Clary, E. G., 457
Clay, D., 328
Close, S., 474
Close, W., 252
Clow, R. B., 300, 304
Coatsworth, J. D., 94
Cochran, S. D., 217
Cockerham, W. C., 320, 326
Cohen, L., 166
Cohen, S., 318, 322
Coker, D., 158
Cole, E. R., 318, 319, 320
Coleman, G., 525
College Board, 104
Collins, K. S., 338, 339, 340, 341, 343, 345
Collins, N. M., 2, 3, 49, 119, 155
Comas-Díaz, L., 232, 234, 427, 428
Comilang, K., 46
Commission on Chronic Illness, 79
Committee on Ways and Means, U.S. House of Representatives, 295
Conduct Problems Prevention Research Group, 80
Conner, M., 474
Connolly, D., 202, 203, 204
Consoli, A. J., 546
Consortium for Policy Research in Education, 104
Constable, P., 408, 414
Constantine, M., 86
Contreras, R., 360
Conway, M. A., 173
Cook, D. A., 44, 49
Cook, E. P., 252, 283
Cook, K. J., 158
Cook, S. W., 303
Cooper, C. C., 524
Cooper, H., 320
Cooperman, A., 268
Copans, S. A., 133
Copeland, J., 457
Copman, S., 155
Corcoran, E., 260
Corey, G., 412, 457
Corey, M. S., 412, 457
Corne, S., 475, 476
Cornoni-Huntly, J., 321
Cosgrove, L., 207
Courneya, K. S., 474
Cowan, J., 284
Cowen, E. L., 79, 81, 82
Coyte, P. C., 325
Cozzarelli, C., 202
Creagh, M. G., 278
Crimmins, E. M., 322, 323, 326, 329
Croizet, J. C., 320
Crosby, T., 138, 139
Cross, W. E., Jr., 173
Croteau, J. M., 252
Crouse, J., 103
Csikszentmihalyi, M., 82
Cureton, J., 63
Curry, M. A., 172

Dadds, M. R., 139
Dah, W., 448
Daher, C., 326
Daiger, D., 303
Dana, R. H., 349
D'Andrea, M., 7, 17, 23, 44, 49, 63, 64, 87, 406, 492
Daniel, J. H., 347
Daniels, J., 44, 49, 63, 64, 406
Daniels, J. A., 7, 23, 87, 492
Darley, J. G., 3, 277
Darus, H. J., 284
da Silva, A., 446, 447
D'Augelli, A. R., 151, 173, 216, 217
Davey-Smith, G., 322
Davidson, L., 201
Davidson, N., 321
Davidson, W. S., 157
Davies, A. B., 284
Davis, G. Y., 104
Davis, H. V., 277
Davis, K., 45
Davis, K. L., 489
Davis, L., 329, 330

Davis, L. J., 170
Davis, S., 260
Davis, T., 325
Dawes, A., 118
Day, J. D., 24
Dean, C. W., 158
Dean, R. G., 390, 391, 392
DeBenedetti, C., 382, 383
Decker, C., 410
de la Rey, C., 445
DeLeon, P. H., 270, 354, 355, 382, 506
Delgado, R., 235, 236
Delgado Bernal, D., 235, 236
Delgado-Romero, E. A., 173
DeLoach, C. P., 171
Delva, Z., 448
Delworth, U., 4, 174
Densham, A., 359
Denton, N. A., 104
Deschenes, E. P., 477
Deutsch, M., 383
Diaz, J., 112
Dibble, R., 330
Dichiser, T., 299
DiClemente, C. C., 412
Diego, M., 322
Diemer, M. A., 155, 277
Diessner, R., 444, 445
Dillon, F. R., 226, 544
DiMatteo, M. R., 329
Distefano, T. M., 252
Dixon, D., 294, 297, 300
Dixon, D. N., 5
Dokecki, P., 23, 32
Donnelly, D. A., 158
Donovick, P. J., 322
Doty, M. M., 338, 339, 340, 341, 343, 345
Douce, L. A., 151, 378, 388, 438, 439, 465
Dowd, E. T., 5
Downing, N. E., 176, 177
Downs, M. A., 187, 188
Dreyfoos, J., 117
Driscoll, J., 314, 359
Dryfoos, J. G., 96
Du, N., 342
Duffy, K. G., 132, 133, 140, 141, 347
Dumont, M., 138
Du Nann Winter, D., 383, 384, 392, 400, 443, 478
Dunbar, D., 521, 522, 525
Duncan, G. J., 191
Dunlop, S., 325
Dunn, J., 78
Dunston, K., 318, 319, 320
Durran, A., 5, 151, 491
Dutton, M. A., 157, 162
Dwivedi, R., 479
Dworkin, S. H., 151
Dyche, L., 135
Dykeman, M., 364, 365

Earls, F., 121
Earp, A. L., 326
Easterbrooks, M. A., 201
Eaves, L., 78
Eby, L. T., 284
Edwards, J. N., 338, 339, 340, 341, 343, 345
Edwards, S., 294, 297, 300
Edwards, S. A., 5
Eggen, D., 157
Egner, M., 296
Eitsen, D. S., 207, 210, 211
Elarth, A. M., 341
Elias, M. J., 81
Elliott, D., 119
Elliott, G. C., 447, 448
Elliott, J. E., 252
Elliott, R., 3
Ellis, S. J., 457
Elman, N., 2, 6, 17, 18, 118, 155, 314, 358, 388, 464, 524
Embaye, N., 223
Emrich, C., 261
Engel, G., 314, 344, 345, 346, 347
Enner, S. T., 83
Enns, C. Z., 151, 233, 494
Ensalaco, M., 408
Epel, E. S., 320
Epstein, D., 158, 159, 160, 162
Equality North Dakota, 217
Erb, J., 524
Erez, E., 157, 158
Erikson, E. H., 443
Esbensen, F. A., 477
Escalona, S. K., 383
Espín, O. M., 232, 234
Esten, G., 176
Estey, M., 172, 178
Evan, W., 383
Evans, B., 185
Evans, G., 326
Evans, G. D., 131
Everson, S. A., 322, 324
Ewart, C. K., 326
Eyler, J., 60, 65

Faden, R., 359
Fairfax, D., 88

Faiver, C. M., 65
Fang, S.-R., 44
Fassinger, R. E., 40, 71, 225, 252, 258, 261, 270, 272
Faul, K., 299
Faust, S., 342
Federal Register, 344
Federman, D., 359
Feeney, A., 321
Feinberg, L., 5, 151, 491
Feinstein, J. S., 321, 323, 325, 326
Feldman, J., 321
Feminist Therapy Institute, 19, 22, 241
Ferris, J., 231, 234, 235
Fetterman, D. M., 474
Field, T., 322
Fine, M., 171, 172, 202, 216, 235, 433, 437
Finkel, S. E., 192
Finkelberg, S. L., 5
Fischer, A. R., 272
Fischoff, B., 383
Fisher, C. B., 102
Fiske, S. T., 383
Fitzgerald, L. E., 4
Fitzgerald, L. F., 158, 252, 300, 501
Flannery, D., 60, 63, 65, 67
Flay, B. R., 97
Flewelling, R. L., 83
Flynn, C., 133, 138
Flyvbjerg, B., 203
Foley, C. C., 171
Folkman, S., 318, 322
Follingstad, D. R., 156, 157
Fondacaro, M. R., 41, 118
Ford, D. A., 158
Ford, D. L., 278
Fordham, S. A., 104
Forsyth, D. R., 457
Foscarinis, M., 210
Foster, S. L., 39
Fouad, N. A., 2, 5, 6, 17, 118, 155, 191, 252, 276, 277, 283, 314, 358, 388, 464
Foucault, M., 203
Fountain, J., 299
Fox, D., 41, 425
Fox, D. R., 155, 156, 200
Fox, R. E., 220
Fox-Piven, F., 202
Frable, D. E. S., 318, 319
Franco, D. L., 524
Frank, J. D., 383
Franklin, J. H., 100
Franks, P., 322, 325
Freedheim, D. K., 382
Freire, P., 105, 106, 237, 241, 392, 400, 415, 431, 432, 475
Fretz, B., 360
Fretz, B. R., 4
Freund, K., 325
Frey, L. L., 133, 138
Friedan, G., 23, 32
Friedman, D. H., 201, 203
Friedman, M. J., 355
Frye, M., 118
Fuertes, J., 491
Fuertes, J. N., 86, 135, 151, 339, 347
Fukuhara, M., 378
Fukuyama, M. A., 173
Furlong, M. J., 132, 139

Gabalac, N. W., 233
Gajar, A., 172
Galassi, J. P., 123
Galinsky, E., 266
Gallagher, K., 299
Gallagher, L., 89
Gallagher, L. A., 155, 277
Gallardo-Cooper, M., 191
Gallo, L. C., 320
Galster, G., 103
Galtung, J., 384
Gandhi, M. K., 446, 447
Ganguly, S., 482
Garbarino, J., 89
Garber, J., 133, 138
Garcia, J. G., 473
Garcia, R. M., 60
Garcia-Vazquez, E., 121, 122, 123
Gard, G., 142, 339
Gardner, G. T., 135
Gardner, M. K., 191
Garmezy, N., 285
Garnets, L., 217
Gates, G., 266
Gaventa, J., 203, 205
Gay, Lesbian, Straight Education Network, 124, 125
Gaylord, C. E., 190
Geake, R. R., 509
Geis, G., 4
Gelso, C., 360
Genero, N. P., 437
Gerrity, E. T., 355
Gerstein, L., 2, 5, 6, 7, 17, 18, 118, 155, 314, 358, 378, 388, 446, 457, 464, 465, 484, 524
Gibbons, L. W., 314
Gierth, R., 447

Gilbert, L. A., 437
Gilboa, A., 322
Giles, D. E., 60, 65
Gilfoyle, N. F. P., 219
Gill, T. M., 322
Gillespie, K. N., 64
Gilliam, F., 108
Gilligan, C., 173
Gills, T. L., 457
Gilroy, P. J., 223
Goffman, E., 170, 171, 178
Gold, M. R., 322, 325
Gold, S., 175, 179, 180
Gold, Y., 501
Goldman, N., 323
Goldstein, P., 298
Goldstein, S., 382, 383
Gomez-Marin, O., 341
Gondolf, E. W., 166
González, R. C., 135, 276
Goodchilds, J., 217
Goodman, D., 39
Goodman, E., 322
Goodman, L. A., 6, 7, 23, 25, 26, 27, 28, 31, 39, 40, 41, 63, 155, 156, 157, 158, 159, 160, 162, 164, 165, 358, 359, 464, 503, 540
Goodwin, J., 151
Gordon, A., 359
Gordon, E. W., 384
Goska, D. V., 489
Gottlieb, M. C., 524
Gourley, G. K., 524
Government Accountability Office, 258, 259, 264
Grace, M. C., 187
Graham, C. A., 201
Graham, S., 299
Graham-Bermann, S. A., 202, 206
Granby, C. D., 444, 445
Grant, S. K., 25, 87, 279, 282, 480
Grau, N., 121, 122, 123
Green, B. L., 157, 187
Green, L. W., 330
Greenberg, L. S., 480
Greene, B., 175, 176, 225
Greene, L. V., 495
Greening, T., 384
Greer, M. L., 190
Gregg, R. B., 447
Grella, C. E., 320
Grey Wolf, I., 60, 65, 66, 67
Grieger, I., 46
Griffin, P., 38, 39
Grossman, F. K., 437
Grossman, K., 186
Grove McCrea, L., 119
Grubb, C., 447, 448
Grumbach, K., 326
Grzywacz, J., 331
Guerney, B. G., 124
Gueron, J. M., 297
Guerra, R., 226
Guindon, M. H., 170
Gunther, J., 119
Gurung, R. A. R., 360
Gustitus, C., 157
Gutiérrez, G., 412, 413, 415

Haan, M., 320, 322, 326
Hackett, G., 5, 232
Hage, S., 45, 87
Hage, S. M., 5, 6, 7, 118, 119
Hahn, H., 172, 178
Hahn, M. E., 4
Hains, A. A., 252
Hakuta, K., 266
Haldeman, D. C., 219, 492
Hall, C., 285
Hall, R. L., 175, 176
Hallman, W., 186
Ham, M. D. C., 191
Hamid, G., 367
Hamilton, G., 297, 298, 304
Hancock, K. A., 217
Hanna, F. J., 170
Hanna, W. J., 171, 172
Hansen, J. C., 5
Hansen, L. S., 4, 276, 284
Harachi, T. W., 134
Harak, G. S., 446
Harding, A. K., 190
Harding, S., 203
Hargrove, D. S., 131, 283
Harley, D. B., 175
Harmon, L. W., 252
Harnett, P. H., 139
Harper, G. W., 360, 362, 363
Harris, A. P., 236
Harris, C., 39
Harrison, C. B., 87
Hart, C., 322
Hartnett, N. M., 342
Hartung, P. J., 2, 46, 47, 251, 252, 276, 388
Harvard Civil Rights Project, 90
Hasan, Q., 447, 448
Haskins, R., 296

Hassouneh-Phillips, D., 172
Hauenstein, A. L., 277
Hauff, E., 342
Haugen, J., 457
Haukkala, A., 322
Hause, E. S., 156, 157
Hauser, P. M., 320, 321
Haverkamp, B. E., 23, 31
Hawes, S. E., 437
Hawkins, J. D., 89, 134
Hawley, S. T., 326
Hawxhurst, D. M., 231, 233, 240
Hays, R. D., 329
Hayward, M. D., 322
Head, J., 321
Healey, K., 158
Healey, S., 179, 180
Heck, R., 63, 64
Heesacker, M., 41
Heldring, M. B., 509
Helkala, E., 322
Helledy, K. I., 2, 5, 6, 17, 118, 314, 358, 464
Helms, J. E., 4, 5, 6, 7, 23, 25, 26, 27, 28, 31, 39, 40, 41, 44, 49, 50, 101, 102, 103, 104, 105, 107, 113, 119, 155, 156, 157, 173, 287, 358, 359, 388, 464, 503, 540, 547, 649
Hemingway, H., 322
Hendy, H. M., 157
Hensler-McGinnis, N., 63
Heppner, M. J., 252, 283, 303, 544
Heppner, P. P., 303, 378, 465
Hepworth, D. H., 193
Herek, G. M., 225
Herman, J., 355
Hernandez, D., 49
Hernandez, M., 138, 139
Hernandez-Reif, M., 322
Herr, E. L., 3, 276, 277, 300, 406
Herr, K., 431
Hershberger, S. L., 151, 216, 217
Hershey, L., 178
Hill, C. E., 61
Hill, C. L., 31
Hill, E., 103
Hill, H., 296, 297
Hill, L., 341
Hill, M., 233
Hill, S. E. K., 284
Hinton, W. L., 342
Hirose, M., 447, 448
Hirschel, J. D., 158
Hoffman, M. A., 314, 359, 360, 361, 368
Hofstede, G., 444
Hogan, J. M., 383
Holland, D., 139
Holland, J. L., 303
Holleman, M. C., 329, 330
Holleman, W. L., 329, 330
Holloway, J. D., 528
Hollway, W., 207
Holmes, B., 330
Hong, G. E., 191
Hoofien, D., 322
hooks, b., 113, 202, 431, 437
Hopkins, N., 259
Hopps, J., 318, 319, 320, 327, 328
Horne, S. G., 389, 392, 393, 398
Horowitz, R. I., 322
Horowitz, S. M., 524
Horvath, A. O., 480
House, J. S., 320, 322, 326, 327
House, R., 31, 190, 491, 546
Howard, K. A., 252
Howland, C. A., 171, 172
Hubbell, R., 142, 339
Huey, M., 447, 448
Huff, R., 345, 354
Hughes, D. L., 338, 339, 340, 341, 343, 345
Hughes, R. B., 151, 171, 172
Human Rights Campaign, 267
Human Rights Watch, 216
Humphreys, K., 489
Hunt, A., 186, 188
Huntington, S. P., 384
Hurley, J., 331
Hurley, L. K., 523
Hurst, J. C., 4, 174
Hutchison, I. W., 158
Hyde, J. S., 437
Hylton, D., 433

Ibrahim, F. A., 282
Ickovics, J. R., 320, 322
Ihle Helledy, K., 155, 388
Imhoff, A. R., 261
Infoplease, 408, 409
Ingram, R. E., 139
Instituto Oscaro Romero, 237
Isaac, K., 101, 105, 112
Iscoe, I., 354, 355, 506
Israel, T., 152, 223, 226, 232, 235
Ives, B. I., 338, 339, 340, 341, 343, 345
Ivey, A., 431, 540
Ivey, A. E., 2, 3, 49, 119, 155, 191
Ivey, M. B., 540

Jackson, J., 2, 118, 155
Jacoby, B., 60
Jakubowski-Spector, P., 4
James, W., 382
Jamieson, N. L., 341
Janoff-Bulman, R., 201
Jans, L., 172
Jarjoura, D., 320, 321, 322
Jarvis, M. J., 322
Jasper, J. M., 151
Jenkins, C. N., 341, 342
Jensen, M., 191
Jobin-Davis, K., 5
Johnson, A., 299
Johnson, G. S., 193
Johnson, I. M., 157
Johnson, N. G., 431, 432
Johnson, P., 447, 448
Johnson, R. A., 493
Jones, J., 5, 49, 193, 492, 546
June, L., 174
Juntunen, C. L., 5, 131, 133, 134, 139, 252, 277, 294, 300

Kachgal, M. M., 219
Kaczmarek, P., 123
Kagan, N., 5
Kahn, R. L., 318, 322
Kalbfleisch, P. J., 284
Kampa-Kokesch, S., 252
Kampert, J. B., 314
Kamradt, B., 132
Kaplan, G. A., 320, 322, 324, 326
Kaplan, J., 63
Kaplan, S., 329
Karon, B. P., 524
Kaschak, E., 238
Kauff, J., 296, 297
Kauhanen, J., 322
Keita, G., 158
Kelley, R. D. G., 100
Kelly, A., 447, 448
Kelly, D. B., 278
Kelly, J. A., 367
Kelman, H., 383
Kemeny, M., 360
Kemmis, S., 431
Kemp, A., 157
Kemp, S. P., 191
Kenagy, G. P., 359
Kendler, H. H., 40
Kennemer, W. N., 509
Kenny, D. A., 266
Kenny, M., 46, 89, 126
Kenny, M. E., 155
Kenny, V., 425
Khan, S. R., 447, 448
Khanna, A., 44
Khuankaew, O., 433
Kincheloe, J. L., 105, 431, 432
King, K. D., 231, 235
Kinzie, J. D., 341, 342, 349
Kirby, K. M., 223
Kirkpatrick, D., 464
Kiselica, M., 2, 39, 388, 489
Kiselica, M. S., 23, 24, 25, 26, 44, 53, 256, 270, 464, 539
Kitagawa, E. M., 320, 321
Kitsantas, A., 53
Kitzinger, C., 207, 233
Klebanov, P. K., 191
Kleiner, A. J., 233
Kleinman, J., 321
Kline, M., 345, 354
Klitzing, S. W., 202
Klonoff, E. A., 431
Knight, S. J., 340
Koblinsky, S. A., 201
Kocot, T. G., 157
Koegel, P., 201, 210
Konen, K., 448
Kool, V. K., 443, 445, 447, 448
Korman, M., 232
Kornbluh, P., 408
Koss, M. P., 158
Kottler, J. A., 135
Kraft, M. K., 298
Krause, J. M., 415
Kravatz, D., 231, 233
Kravetz, D., 207
Kravitz, R., 329
Kretchmar, M. D., 61
Krieger, N., 320
Krieglstein, M., 158
Krumboltz, J. D., 284
Kuehl, S. J., 219
Kuhn, C., 322
Kumar, S., 482
Kunz, G., 326
Kuper, B. D., 131
Kuriloff, P., 319, 320

Ladany, N., 86
LaFromboise, T. D., 39, 191, 286
Lagace, M., 266
Lai, E. W. M., 340
Laird, J., 391
Lancaster, B., 359

Land, H., 121
Landrine, H., 232, 235, 431
Lane, D. M., 261
Lantz, P. M., 320, 322, 326, 327
La Roche, M. J., 524
Larry P. v. Riles, 22
Larsen, J. A., 193
Larson, L. M., 64
Larson, R., 89, 90
Lasso, B., 134
Latta, R. E., 6, 7, 23, 25, 26, 27, 28, 31, 39, 40, 41, 155, 156, 157, 165, 358, 359, 464, 503, 540
Lavelle, J., 347, 350
LaViolette, A. D., 157
Lawrence and Garner v. Texas, 219
Leach, J. J., 276
Lease, S. H., 216
Ledbetter, R. K., 527, 528
Lederach, J. P., 476
Lee, C. C., 7, 44, 49, 388, 389
Lee, C. G., 406
Leighninger, L., 194
Leischow, S., 330
Lenk, K., 331
Lent, ?., 512
Lent, E. B., 300, 305
Lent, R. W., 277, 285, 540
Lentz, E., 284
Leonard, A. S., 268
Leong, F. T. L., 252, 277, 283, 378, 389, 402, 438, 465
Leong-Grotz, K., 326
Lepkowski, J. M., 320, 322, 326, 327
Lerman, H., 22
Lerner, R., 88, 89, 141
Lerner, R. M., 46, 102
Leung, P. K., 341, 342, 349
Leung, S. A., 378, 438, 465
Lev, A. I., 223
Levin, S., 266
Levine, A., 63
Levine, M., 38, 39
Leviton, A., 187
Levitt, H. M., 398
Levy, A., 121
Lewallen, J., 457
Lewin, K., 446
Lewis, E., 100
Lewis, J., 31, 190, 389, 406, 546
Lewis, J. A., 7, 23, 87, 491, 492
Lewis, M., 406
Lewis, M. D., 7, 23, 87, 492
Li, L. C., 31
Liang, B., 6, 7, 23, 25, 26, 27, 28, 31, 39, 40, 41, 155, 156, 157, 358, 359, 464, 503, 540
Liazos, T. C., 219
Lickers, H., 186, 188
Liddle, B. J., 217, 277
Liddle, M. C., 31
Liebow, E., 201
Liessmann, C., 125
Lifton, R. J., 383
Lima, L., 284
Limbert, W. M., 319
Lin, K. M., 342
Lin, T., 325
Lindy, J., 187
Linsk, N. L., 359
Lipman, E. L., 320
Lira, E., 409
Lisi, D., 172
Little, H., 457
Littman, R. A., 277
Liu, W. L., 279, 282, 283, 284
Liu, W. M., 18, 19, 22, 23, 24, 25, 31, 233, 318, 319, 320, 490, 541, 543
Lloyd, S., 157
Loach, J., 474
Locke, D., 49, 546
Locke, D. C., 5, 193, 492
Loeb, P. R., 495
Loewen, J. W., 100, 112
Logan, A., 352, 353
Logue, E. E., 320, 321, 322
Lonczak, H. C., 89
Long, J. A., 322
Lonsdale, S., 172
Looman, C. W., 322, 326
Lopez, R. E., 2
Lopez, S. J., 315
Loprest, P., 296
Lorde, A., 239, 257
Lorion, R. P., 354, 355, 506
Loseke, D. R., 157
Lott, B., 202, 320
Love, B., 4
Lu, F. G., 342
Lubell, M., 192
Lueschen, G., 326
Lugones, M. C., 422, 424
Lundberg, A., 185, 186
Luzzo, D. A., 277
Lykes, M. B., 433, 437
Lynch, J. W., 320, 322, 324
Lynch, K., 191
Lynn, F. M., 302

Machado, P. P. P., 548
Mackenbach, J. P., 322, 326
MacNair, R. M., 444
Maestas, M., 342
Maestas, M. V., 133
Mahoney, J., 132
Makuc, D., 321
Malatu, M. S., 322
Mander, A. V., 233
Manese, J. E., 191
Manfredi, C., 326
Manoochehri, G., 457, 463
Maracek, J., 437
Marcia, J. E., 78
Marecek, J., 26, 207, 231, 233
Mariner, W. K., 528
Marker, M., 540
Marmot, M. G., 321, 322
Marroquin, D., 477
Marsella, A. J., 355, 438
Marshall, K. G., 277
Martell, R. F., 261
Martikainen, P., 322
Martín-Baró, I., 118, 194, 196, 415, 431, 475, 476
Martinson, K., 298
Marullo, S., 60, 63, 65, 67
Massey, D. S., 104
Masten, A. S., 94
Mastroianni, A. C., 359
Masuda, M., 342
Mathews, H. F., 326
Mathews, S. S., 389, 392, 393, 398
Matsuda, M., 431, 432
Matthews, A. K., 326
Matthews, C. R., 216
Matthews, K. A., 320, 322
Maty, S. C., 324
Maughan, B., 78
Mayfield, R., 123, 124
Mays, V. M., 2
Mayton, D. M., 443, 444, 445, 447, 448
Mazurana, D., 445
McCabe, R. E., 314
McCarn, S. R., 225
McChesney, K. Y., 210
McClure, B. A., 406
McCracken, D., 265
McCurley, S., 457, 462
McDavis, R. J., 5, 44, 49, 132, 133, 141, 278, 283, 546
McDavis, S., 49
McDougall, W., 382
McDowell, T., 44
McFarlane, T., 314
McGlynn, E., 329
McHugh, J. L., 219
McIsaac, W., 325
McKay, S., 445
McKenzie, E. B., 157
McKinlay, J. B., 325
McLaren, P., 431, 432
McLaren, P. L., 105
McLellan, B., 232, 234, 236, 240
McLeod, K. C., 157
McMahan, S., 331
McMichen, P. J., 151
McNally, C. J., 119
McNamara, K. M., 509
McNamee, S. J., 150
McPhee, S. J., 341, 342
McPherson, R. H., 2, 6, 17, 118, 155, 314, 358, 388, 464
McRae, M., 231, 234, 235
McTaggart, R., 431
McWhirter, A. M., 117, 417
McWhirter, B. T., 117, 413, 414, 417
McWhirter, E. H., 39, 117, 277, 299, 408, 412, 413, 414, 417, 464
McWhirter, J. J., 117, 378, 407, 413, 417, 465
Meara, N. M., 24, 489
Medley, R., 138, 139
Mele, N., 524
Melton, G. B., 216
Memmi, A., 424
Mendez, J. L., 131, 133, 140
Mero, R. P., 320, 322, 326, 327
Mertens, D. M., 142
Mesch, G., 331
Metz, A., 358
Metz, A. J., 2, 5, 6, 17, 118, 155, 314, 388, 464
Meyer, J., 78
Michael, R. S., 109
Middleton, R. A., 175
Miene, P., 457
Milburn, M. A., 383
Milburn, T. W., 383
Milem, J. F., 266
Miles, T. P., 322
Miller, D., 390, 509
Miller, J. B., 150
Miller, R. K., 150
Miller, S. L., 157
Miller, W. R., 412
Mills, D. H., 5
Mills, K. I., 263, 264, 266, 268

Mintz, L. B., 272
Miranda, J., 342
Mirowsky, J., 322
Mishler, E. G., 210
Mitchell, J., 326
Mngadi, S., 177
Moane, G., 155, 359, 424
Mobley, M., 194, 195
Moeschberger, S., 5, 378, 464, 465, 484
Mohai, P., 186, 189, 190
Mohr, J. J., 151, 226, 544
Mollica, R. F., 347, 350
Montgomery, R., 448
Moore, L. J., 341, 342, 349
Morawski, J., 382, 383
Morgan, K. M., 201
Morishima, J. K., 348, 349
Morrill, W. H., 4, 174
Morris, L. R., 382
Morrow, S. L., 216, 225, 231, 233, 240
Morse, G., 186, 188
Moskowitz, M., 325
Moss, N. E., 320
Mrazek, P. J., 97
Muller, E. N., 192
Mullin, K., 155
Munger, R. G., 341
Murdock, N. L., 41
Murry, S., 105
Musick, M. A., 320, 322
Myers, H., 360
Myers, J., 540
Myers-Lipton, S. J., 65

Nabi Fai, G., 482
Nandy, A., 424
NANE Women's Rights Association, 394
Napoli, P. J., 277
Nardo, A. C., 109
National Association of Social Workers, 19, 21, 22
National Center for Children in Poverty, 78
National Coalition for the Homeless, 201
National Gay and Lesbian Task Force, 267, 269
National Institute of Allergy and Infectious Diseases, 361
National Mental Health Policy, 410
National Mental Health Program, 410
National Science Board, 259
National Science Foundation, 259, 260
National Substance Abuse Policy, 410
National Telecommunications and Information Administration, 276
Needleman, H. L., 187
Nelson, A., 383
Nelson, G., 41, 118, 417
Nelson, L. H., 203
Nelson, M. K., 301
Nemeroff, C., 238
Neville, H., 87
Neville, H. A., 5, 44, 194, 195
Newman, R., 515, 521, 522, 525
New Mexico Department of Health, 121
Ng, P., 157
Nguyen, D., 342, 348, 349
Nichaman, M. Z., 314
Nieves, L. A., 187
Nightengale, D. S., 296
Niles, S. G., 3, 276, 277, 300, 406
Nishimura, B., 138, 139
Nobles, W., 19, 20, 21
Nolan, C. M., 341
Nordal, K. C., 133
Norsworthy, K. L., 5, 378, 433, 446, 464, 465
North, F., 321
Nosek, M. A., 151, 171, 172
Nutt, R. L., 151
Nutting, P. A., 322, 325

Oakes, J. M., 319
Obear, K., 267
O'Brien, ?., 499
O'Brien, C. T., 296
O'Brien, K. M., 40, 61, 63, 251, 252, 258, 272, 283, 299, 406
O'Byrne, K. K., 119
Oetting, E. R., 4, 174
Ogden, D. W., 219
Ohnishi, H., 282
Olivier, C., 364, 365
Olkin, R., 171, 178, 180
O'Malley, M. S., 326
Omari, S. R., 320
Oñate, R., 408, 414
Opp, K. D., 192
Ordway, L., 329
Organization of American States, 410
Ormel, J., 78
Ormerod, M., 501
O'Rourke, B., 172
Ortega, M., 142, 339
Osgarby, S. M., 139
Osgood, C., 383
Ostrove, J. M., 318, 319, 320

O'Sullivan, C., 158
O'Sullivan, M. J., 134
Overholt, A., 288

Pace, D., 174, 179
Padget, D., 352, 353
Paffenbarger, R. S., Jr., 314
Paikoff, R., 93
Palinkas, L. A., 187, 188
Palmer, B. J., 447
Palmer, L. K., 7, 41
Palmer, P., 235
Palombi, B., 174, 179
Parajuli, P., 479
Parham, T. A., 44, 49, 191
Park, J., 71
Parker, I., 205
Parker, R., 325
Parker, W. M., 62
Parsons, F., 3, 256, 277, 299
Patel, C., 321
Patel, S., 63
Paterson, D. G., 277
Patterson, C. J., 216
Patterson, D. G., 3
Paulanka, B., 342, 343, 345
Pavelski, R., 132
Pavetti, L., 296
Payton, C. R., 22
Pedersen, P., 5, 151, 378, 438, 439, 465, 491
Pedersen, P. B., 49
Pedraza, A., 360
Peller, G., 103, 104, 113
Peltier, B., 123, 124
Pelton, L. H., 443, 446
Peplau, L. A., 217
Perales, N., 202
Perez, C., 477
Perez, P., 155, 193, 225
Perkins, D. D., 476
Perkins, D. V., 38, 39
Perkins, R., 233
Perloff, J. N., 201
Perls, F. S., 472
Perry, J. C., 464
Peters, D. J., 447
Peterson, G. W., 303
Peterson, K., 269
Peterson, N., 276
Peterson, R., 109
Petrosino, A., 119
Petterson, J. S., 187, 188
Pettigrew, T. F., 458, 463
Petty, R. E., 459, 460
PFLAG, 125
Pham, C. T., 342
Phillips, J. C., 272
Phillips, M., 103, 331
Phillips, S. D., 5, 261
Phinney, J. S., 173
Pickett, T., Jr., 318, 319, 320
Pickles, A., 78
Pieterse, A. L., 6, 290
Pietrofesa, J. J., 4
Piette, J., 326
Pilisuk, M., 185
Pinderhughes, R., 190
Pindus, N., 296
Pinkerton T., 457, 463
Plomin, R., 78
Polakow, V., 201, 211
Polek, D. S., 156, 157
Polivy, J., 314
Polowy, C. I., 219
Ponterotto, J. G., 46, 86, 135, 151, 191, 339, 347, 378, 389, 402, 438, 465, 491
Pope, K. S., 26, 27, 28, 280, 539, 540
Pope, M., 252, 277
Pope-Davis, D. B., 23, 233, 320, 543
Porche-Burke, L., 118
Porter, N., 22
Poteet, M. L., 284
Potenza, M. T., 64
Potkin, H., 457, 463
Potter, E. E., 457
Potter, J., 207
Powell, L. C., 104
Power, P. G., 303
Prentice, M., 60
Price, J. M., 139
Price, R. H., 88, 89
Prilleltensky, I., 7, 23, 26, 32, 38, 39, 41, 118, 173, 174, 179, 180, 181, 237, 257, 258, 270, 359, 360, 388, 417, 425
Prilleltensky, O., 7, 41, 171, 173, 174, 177, 179, 180, 181, 359, 360
Prince, J. P., 252
Prineas, R. J., 341
Prochaska, J. O., 412
Prosperi, D. C., 121
Provost, M. A., 138
Psychologists for Social Responsibility, 493
Purnell, L., 342, 343, 345

Rachal, K., 294, 297, 300
Rachal, K. C., 5
Rae, W. A., 521
Rajevic, P., 414

Rakich, J. S., 527, 528
Rallis, S. F., 97
Ralph, J., 103
Ranchor, A. V., 322
Raney, S., 464, 466
Rapoff, M. A., 327
Rasheed, S., 231, 234, 235
Ratts, M., 17
Rawlings, E. I., 157
Reardon, R. C., 303
Reczycki, M., 347, 350
Redding, R., 216
Redman, P., 216
Reedy, D., 299
Reese, L. E., 87, 123, 124
Reeser, L. C., 194
Regoli, M. J., 158
Reichert, M. C., 319, 320
Reiss, D., 88, 89
Reivich, K., 131
Ren, X. S., 322
Reynolds, A. L., 151
Reza, J. V., 44, 87, 489, 493
Rhoads, R. A., 62, 63, 68
Rhodes, N. R., 157
Rice, J., 190, 276, 427, 437, 439
Rice, J. K., 151, 299
Richards, M., 501
Richardson, M. S., 252, 300
Richie, S. D., 131
Richmond, Y., 399
Rideout, C. A., 272
Ridge, R. D., 457
Ridley, C. R., 31, 233
Riger, A., 176, 179
Riger, S., 158
Riley, A. W., 322
Riley, C., 341, 342, 349
Ringwalt, C. L., 83
Rintala, D. H., 171, 172
Ritter, J., 138
Roarke, A. E., 5
Roberts, M. C., 523
Robertson, J., 322, 457
Robins, L., 121
Robinson, M., 2, 23, 24, 25, 44, 53, 256, 270, 388, 539
Rock, M., 364
Rogers, W., 329
Rogovsky, E., 171, 172
Rokeach, M., 444
Rollins, C. W., 175
Rollnick, S., 412
Romano, J., 87
Romano, J. L., 5, 119, 219
Rooney, S. C., 226
Root, M. P., 277, 282
Rose, G., 321, 322
Rosenthal, R., 201
Ross, C. E., 322
Ross, R. K., 342
Rossi, P. H., 319
Rossman, G. B., 97
Roth, M., 325
Rothblum, E., 217
Roush, K. L., 176, 177
Rousseau, C., 480
Rowe, W., 151
Roy, A., 479
Royce, D., 352, 353
Roysircar, G., 86, 133, 135, G., 142, 225, 339, 340, 347, 349, 354, 491
Roysircar-Sodowsky, G., 133, 138, 342
Rubicon Programs, 288
Rubin, L., 238
Rucker, T., 322, 325
Rudmin, F., 382
Rudolph, S., 299
Ruiz De Esparaza, C., 139
Rupert, P., 524
Rush, A. K., 233
Russell, G. M., 235
Russell, J., 187, 188
Russell, R. W., 383
Russo, N. F., 158
Russo, T. R., 406
Rutledge, L. L., 156, 157
Rutter, M., 78
Ryan, J. A., 89

Sackett, L. A., 156
Safe Schools Coalition, 125
Sagiv, L., 444, 445
Said, E. W., 424
Salahuddin, N., 70
Salina, D. D., 360, 362, 363
Salonen, J. T., 322
Saltzman, L. E., 156, 157
Samler, J., 4
Sampson, J. P., Jr., 303
Sanchez, J., 5, 49, 193, 492, 546
Sanderman, R., 322
Sandhu, D. S., 491
Santiago-Rivera, A. L., 185, 186, 188, 191
Sarason, S. B., 38
Satterwhite, P., 166
Saunders, D. E., 303
Saunders, D. G., 156, 157

Savoy, H. B., 544
Sawhill, I., 296
SCANS, 302
Schanberg, S., 322
Schatzlein, J., 172
Schechter, S., 157
Schein, ?., 399
Schell, A., 187
Schell, M. J., 326
Schewel, M., 482
Schill, T. R., 303
Schillinger, D., 326
Schinke, R. J., 474
Schlossberg, N. K., 4, 5
Schmid, K., 362, 363
Schmidt, L. D., 24
Schmitz, B., 63
Schooler, C., 322
Schor, I., 431, 432
Schuck, K., 277
Schwartz, S. H., 444, 445
Schwebel, M., 383, 389, 392, 402, 403
Schweder, A., 132
Schwirian, K., 331
Schyb, I., 298
Scott, J., 62
Scullion, K., 121, 123
Scurfield, R. M., 355
Sealand, N., 191
Sears, S. F., Jr., 131
Seccombe, K., 202
Sedlacek, W. E., 4
Seeman, T. E., 323, 326, 329
Seligman, M., 131
Seligman, M. E. P., 82
Sellergren, S. A., 326
Sen, M., 445, 447, 448
Serrano-García, I., 38
Shankar, J., 464
Shannon, C., 298
Sharp, G., 443, 447
Shema, S. J., 322
Sherbourne, C. D., 329
Sherif, M., 458
Shermis, S. S., 7
Sherwood, G., 174
Shi, L., 325
Shinn, M., 210
Shipley, M. J., 321, 322
Shoben, E. J., Jr., 4
Shochet, I. M., 139
Shullman, S., 457
Shullman, S. L., 501
Siahpush, M., 322
Silva, D., 121
Silver, M., 321
Simon, A., 225
Simon, J. G., 322
Simon, N. P., 4
Simonoff, E., 78
Sinacore-Guinn, A. L., 239, 243
Sinaiko, A. R., 341
Singh, G. K., 322
Sipps, G. J., 65
Sirin, S., 277
Skiba, R. J., 109
Slattery, S. M., 71
Sleeter, C. E., 63
Smith, B. H., 131, 133, 140
Smith, C., 158
Smith, D., 341, 342, 349
Smith, E., 5, 491
Smith, E. J., 151
Smith, E. M. J., 232
Smith, G. D., 321, 322
Smith, L. T., 433
Smith, M. B., 26, 382
Smith-Arnold, M., 190
Snell-Johns, J., 131, 133, 140
Snow, D. A., 201, 210
Snyder, C. R., 315
Snyder, M., 457
Sodowsky, G. R., 340
Solberg, V. S., 252
Soleck, G., 318, 319, 320
Solomon, S. E., 172
Sonnen, J., 447, 448
Sonnen, M., 448
Spaeth, J. L., 326
Spanierman, L. B. 544
Sparks, E., 6, 7, 23, 25, 26, 27, 28, 31, 39, 40, 41, 155, 156, 157, 358, 359, 464, 503, 540
Sparks, P., 474
Speer, D. C., 95, 96, 97
Speers, M. A., 359
Speight, S. L., 6, 7, 45, 49, 60, 63, 86, 87, 118, 119, 153, 155, 156, 193, 200, 237, 358, 363, 365, 379, 390, 464, 489, 494
Spelmann, E. V., 422, 424
Spitzer, R. L., 221
Sprinthall, N. A., 5
Stadler, H., 5, 193, 492, 546
Stagner, R., 383
Stamler, V. L., 174
Stamm, B. H., 133
Stansfeld, S., 321, 322

Starfield, B., 322, 325
Stattin, H., 132
Steer, R. A., 303
Stefancic, J., 235, 236
Steff, M. E., 121
Steiner, R., 121, 122, 123, 124
Steinitz, V., 210
Stevens, J., 472, 474
Stiffman, A., 121
Stoddard, S., 172
Stodden, R. A., 173
Stokols, D., 330, 331
Stoltenberg, C., 41
Stoltzfus, S., 124
Strage, A. A., 61
Strickland, B. R., 2, 118
Stronks, K., 322, 326
Strozier, A. L., 303
Strube, M. J., 474
Stukas, A. A., 457
Styron, T. H., 201
Suchday, S., 326
Sue, D. W., 5, 49, 87, 118, 132, 133, 141, 151, 170, 171, 178, 179, 180, 181, 191, 278, 283, 331, 425, 491
Sue, S., 348, 349
Sugden, G. J., 65
Sullivan, C. M., 157
Sullivan, M. J., 509
Sundberg, N. D., 277
Super, D. E., 277
Susnjic, S., 447
Sutton, S. E., 191
Suzen, D., 300
Suzuki, L. A., 64
Swanberg, J., 266
Swecker, J., 501
Sweeney, M. L., 303
Sweeney, T., 540
Sweet, S. G., 172, 178
Swerdlow, A. J., 342
Syme, S. L., 318, 322, 329
Szymanski, E., 172

Tagler, M. J., 202
Takooshian, H., 438
Talley, K. D., 207, 210, 211
Talley, W. B., 170
Talleyrand, R. M., 53, 277
Taluc, N., 157
Tan, C., 157
Tanney, M. F., 5
Taranto, R. G., 219
Tatum, B. D., 104, 106, 149, 150
Taussig, C., 82
Taylor, R. J., 87
Taylor, S. E., 360
Tazuma, L., 342
Teasley, M., 190
Tenney, K., 338, 339, 340, 341, 343, 345
Terrance, C., 299
Thoennes, N., 156
Thomas, D. A., 284
Thomas, J., 524
Thomas, K. R., 172, 179, 180
Thompson, A. S., 3, 277
Thompson, C. E., 5, 7, 25, 44, 87, 101, 102, 105, 107, 112, 279, 282, 480
Thompson, D. A., 231, 234, 235
Thomson, R. G., 171
Thurman, P., 191
Thyer, B., 352, 353
Tien-Li Loke, N., 158
Tierney, 131, 133, 134, 139
Tillmann-Healy, L. M., 437
Timmer, D. A., 207, 210, 211
Tjaden, P., 156
Tjeltveit, A. C., 524
Tobler, N. S., 83
Tomes, H., 26
Toomey, T., 331
Toporek, R. L., 5, 18, 19, 22, 23, 24, 25, 31, 44, 49, 86, 87, 135, 190, 193, 279, 282, 283, 284, 339, 347, 490, 491, 492, 541, 543, 546
Torkelson Lynch, R., 172, 179, 180
Torre, M. E., 433
Torres, D., 138, 139
Toulouse, A. L., 64
Townsend, P., 321
Tran, C. G., 342
Transgrud, H., 299
Trickett, E. J., 359, 361, 362, 363
Trimble, C., 237, 238
Trimble, J. E., 191
Trueba, H. T., 172
Trutko, J., 296
Turner, C., 524
Turrell, G., 322
Twenge, J. M., 322
Tyler, L. E., 4
Tyler, T. R., 390, 392, 393

U.S. Census Bureau, 260, 262, 268
U.S. Conference of Mayors, 201
U.S. Congress, 295
U.S. Department of Education's Office for Civil Rights, 123

U.S. Department of Health and Human Services, 317, 321, 322, 325, 326, 330, 338, 343, 354, 359
U.S. Department of State, 409, 410
U.S. Public Health Service, 494
Udall, L., 479
Unger, D. G., 186
United Nations Commission on the Status of Women, 426
United Nations General Assembly, 389
United Nations High Commission on Refugees, 349
Urban Institute Study, 201
Ussher, J. M., 203

Vaglum, P., 342
Vakil, E., 322
Valenzuela, A., 408, 414
Valian, V., 261, 262
van de Mheen, H., 322, 326
Van den bos, G. R., 354, 355, 382, 506
van der Meer, J. B., 322
van Ryn, M., 325, 329
Van Sertima, I., 100
Van Slyke, B., 71
Van Slyke, E. J., 71
van Strien, P. J., 425
Vasquez, M., 118, 264
Vasquez, M. J. T., 5, 232
Vazquez, L., 124
Vazquez-Nutall, E., 5, 151, 191, 491
Vera, E. M., 6, 7, 45, 49, 60, 63, 86, 87, 118, 119, 123, 124, 153, 155, 156, 193, 200, 237, 358, 363, 365, 379, 390, 464, 489, 494
Vernaglia, E. R., 544
Vernon-Jones, R., 138, 139
Vessey, J., 331
Vineyard, S., 457, 462

Wade, K. A., 119
Wade, R. C., 60
Wagaw, F., 359
Wagenaar, A., 331
Wagner, R. V., 383, 384, 392, 400, 443, 478
Waldo, M., 121, 122, 123, 124, 125, 126
Waller, J., 322
Walley, P. B., 509
Walsh, M. E., 46, 123
Walsh-Bowers, R., 39
Walz, G. R., 44, 49, 388, 389, 406
Wandersman, A., 186
Wang, F., 326
Wang, V. O., 23, 32
Wangsgaard Thompson, B., 235
Ward, C. M., 283
Ward, K., 60, 63, 65, 67
Wardle, J., 322
Warnecke, R., 359
Warren, R., 474
Warter, E., 126
Washington, E. D., 138, 139
Watkins, J., 475
Watson-Armstrong, L. A., 172
Watts, B. G., 501
Watts, R. J., 7, 38, 39
Weaver, K., 296
Webster, L., 476
Webster's Dictionary, 1
Weedman, J., 447, 448
Wei, M., 314
Weinberg, D., 41, 118
Weintraub, S. R., 6, 7, 23, 25, 26, 27, 28, 31, 39, 40, 41, 155, 156, 157, 358, 359, 464, 503, 540
Weis, L., 216, 437
Weiss, B., 187, 325
Weissberg, R. P., 81
Weitzman, L., 231, 234, 235, 501
Welfare Law Center, 276
Wells, M., 151
Wendell, S., 170, 177, 178, 180
Wernette, D. R., 187
Werth, J. L., Jr., 368
Weseen, S., 437
Wessells, M. G., 389, 390, 392, 396, 402, 403, 482
West, C., 431, 432
Wetherell, M., 207
Wettersten, K. B., 299
Whaley, G. L., 276
Whitcomb, D. H., 223
White, I., 321
White, L. E., 202
Whitefield, K., 139
Whitehead, M., 321
Whiteley, J., 465
Whiteley, J. M., 4
Wilkinson, A. V., 202
Wilkinson, S., 207
Will, G. F., 202
Willetts, D., 474
Williams, D. R., 67, 320, 322, 325, 326, 327
Williams, M., 325, 326
Williams, R. L., 4
Willis, D. G., 464
Willmott, L., 176

Wilson, C., 326
Wilson, L., 158
Wilson, R., 264
Wilson, S. E., 325
Winerman, L., 492
Winfree, L. T., 477
Wing, A. K., 236
Winston, S. M., 473
Wintram, C., 241
Witt, W. P., 322
Wolfson, P. R. Q., 219
Wong, F. Y., 132, 133, 140, 141, 347
Wong, L., 437
Worell, J., 431, 432
World Bank Group, 409
World Fact Book, 409, 410
World Health Organization, 342, 410
Worthington, R. L., 5, 223, 225, 226, 252, 277, 300, 544
Wrenn, C. G., 535
Wright, B. A., 171
Wright, Q., 383
Wright, T., 408, 414

Yalom, I. D., 412, 457
Yando, R., 322
Yang, Y., 322
Yarris, E., 174
Ybarra, M., 509
Yeich, S., 203, 205, 474
Yllö, K., 157, 166
York, E., 242, 243
Young, C. G., 44
Young, E. M., 172
Young, I. M., 149, 204, 424
Young, K., 121
Young, M. E., 171
Youngflesh, A., 67
Younggren, J., 524

Zanglis, I., 132
Zayas, L. H., 135
Zelezny, L. C., 474
Zigler, E., 82
Zimbardo, P. G., 507, 508
Zorza, J., 158
Zytowski, D. G., 251

Subject Index

Ableism, 149, 261
Access to health care providers, restricted, 522
Access to mental health services:
- ensuring equal, 20
- limited, 524

Action research, 207, 306, 313
Action research projects, community-based, 315
Action research skills, 545
Activism, 81, 108, 114, 153, 218, 219, 235, 238, 242, 379, 381, 385, 425, 428, 437, 439, 449, 450, 476, 479, 542, 546, 547, 563
- as practice of freedom, 437
- awareness and, 476
- empowerment of the oppressed, 476
- navigating conflicts between academia and, 223–224
- schooling of Black children and, 103–105
- Tibet and, 455–456, 463
- *See also specific forms of activism*

Activist activities, 24, 425
Activist allies, 225
Activist consultation, 422
Activist groups, 189, 218
Activist research, 422
- consultation approach, 431

Activist researcher, 433
Activists, 24, 109, 166, 218, 225, 242, 244, 422, 426, 437, 479, 482
- high-profile, 458
- *See also specific types of activists*

ACT UP, 224
Administration of Environmental Programs on Indian Reservations, 190
Adolescent physical/emotional well-being, social class and, 322
Adult Learning Center, 305
Advocacy, 2, 4, 6, 7, 8, 9, 11, 18, 23, 24, 25, 26, 29, 30, 31, 48, 52, 54, 97, 119, 120, 139, 142, 186, 237, 238, 256, 258, 267, 271, 272, 279, 283, 284, 332, 379, 380, 385, 388, 392, 394, 398, 400, 406, 446, 449, 450, 457, 473, 502, 504, 542, 543, 545, 546
- about equality in work, 251
- against racism, 5
- asking right questions, 543
- definition, 18
- embedding into collaborative process, 400
- for client populations, 502
- for psychological knowledge/practice in public policy debate/development, 502
- for women, 4
- in counseling, 23
- internships, 495
- macro-level, 492
- micro-level, 492
- paid professional, 503
- within professional organizations, 22
- *See also specific types of advocacy*

Advocacy counseling, 270
- competencies, 491

Advocacy counselors, 44, 57
Advocacy efforts, 267, 271
- collaborative, 195, 196

Advocacy goals, 265, 266, 272, 400
Advocacy groups, 31, 525, 535
Advocacy intervention, evaluating law school-based, 162–164
Advocacy model, 282–283, 492
Advocacy process, psychologists becoming active citizens in, 502
Advocacy programs, 162, 163, 166
Advocacy resources, 279
Advocacy roles, nontraditional, 40

Advocacy skills, 273
Advocacy training, 495, 504, 546
Advocacy work, 13, 50, 547
Affirmative action:
  battle over, 262
  college admissions and, 262
  effects of dismantling, 137
  higher education and, 263
  Supreme Court decision upholding, 266
African American activism:
  in Bloomington (IN), 108
  See also Black activism
African American environmental protests, Warren County (NC), 189
Age Discrimination Act, 279
Ageism, 149, 546
  working to combat, 1
Agency for Toxic Substances and Disease Registry, Minority Health Initiative of, 190
AIDS outreach programs, 223–224
Aid to Families with Dependent Children, 202, 295
Alliances, 8, 9, 10, 81, 104, 108, 192, 278, 284, 289, 346, 423, 512, 526, 536, 549
American Counseling Association, 47, 152, 223, 491, 492, 493, 510
  Advocacy Competencies, 31, 491–492, 546
  Association for Gay, Lesbian and Bisexual Issues in Counseling, 223
  Code of Ethics, 223
  Counselors for Social Justice Division, 54, 492–493
  Multicultural Counseling Competencies, 491
American Multicultural Counseling Association, 152
American Psychiatric Association, 215, 219
American Psychological Association, 222, 267, 298, 384, 421, 491, 493, 494, 501, 528, 537
  advocates for school acceptance of LGB youth, 270
  Committee on Accreditation, 220
  Committee on Ethnic Minority Affairs, 494
  Congressional Fellowship Program, 41, 495
  Division for Social Justice, 492, 537–538
  Division of Counseling Psychology (Division 17), 4, 8, 220, 389, 491, 492, 494, 501, 543, 546
Division of Family (Division 43), 492
Division of Peace Psychology (Division 48), 384
Division of Psychoanalysis (Division 39), 492
Education Directorate, 220, 494, 510
Ethical Principles of Psychologists and Code of Conduct, 17–22, 32, 135, 136, 402, 403, 425, 457, 473, 549
expansion of accreditation standards, 546
Guidelines on Multicultural Education, Training, Research, Practice, and Organizational Change for Psychologists, 86, 233, 135, 314, 491, 546
multicultural competencies, 176
Office on AIDS, 368, 370
policy, 217
Practice Directorate, 501, 503, 504, 506, 510
Public Interest Directorate, 219, 492, 510, 538
Public Policy Office, 495, 510
public positions on LGB issues, 220
relationship with United Nations, 465
School to Work task force, 252
Science Directorate, 510
Section for Ethnic and Racial Diversity, 7, 8, 152
Section for Lesbian, Gay, and Bisexual Awareness, 7, 8, 136, 152, 220, 223, 226
Section for Prevention, 8
Section for the Advancement of Women, 7–8, 152, 234
Section for Vocational Psychology, 8
Section for Women, 501
Society for Community Research and Action, 492
Society for the Psychological Study of Ethnic Minority Issues (Division 45), 152, 492
Society for the Psychological Study of Lesbian, Gay, and Bisexual Issues (Division 44), 152, 220, 223, 226, 492
Society for the Psychological Study of Men and Masculinity (Division 51), 492
Society for the Psychological Study of Social Issues (Division 9), 492
Society for the Psychology of Women (Division 35), 152, 492

Society for the Study of Peace, Conflict and Violence (Division 48), 492
Special Interest Group on Social Justice, 8
State Psychological Association Affairs (Division 31), 504
2003 Amici Curiae brief, 219
American School Counselors Association, 47
Americans with Disabilities Act, 172, 175, 265, 279
misperceptions of, 266
AmeriCorps, 284
Amnesty International, 408, 459, 465, 536
Antibilingual education legislation, 137
Anti-Defamation League, 123
Anti-discrimination laws, sexual orientation and, 267
Anti-domestic violence activists, 157
Antigay movements, APA efforts to counter, 543
Antiracism strategies, 102
Anti-racist activists, 218
Anti-Semitism, 149
Antisodomy laws, 219
Antiwar activities, 516
Antiwar movement, 503
Antiwar organizations, 383
Applied social psychology, 544, 545
Approval for treatment, obtaining, 524
Asexual objectification, 171
Asian American Psychological Association, 152
Asian Americans:
alternative health care, 341
need for interpreter when seeking health care, 340
stigmatization of mental health problems among, 348
See also Cambodian refugees; Vietnamese refugees
Assessment counseling competency, 2
Association for Gay, Lesbian, and Bisexual Issues in Counseling, 152
Association for Women in Psychology, 152
Association of Asian Psychologists, 510
Association of Black Psychologists, 152, 510
Ethical Standards of Black Psychologists, 19–21
Association of Multicultural Counseling and Development, 491
Professional Standards Committee, 491
Aubry, Rick, 288
Awareness, 472
activism and, 476
as ongoing experience, 474
definition, 472
identity formation of social justice-striving counseling psychologist and, 472
increasing, 474–475
Awareness and engagement model, 473, 478, 483
becoming aware, 474–475, 483
identifying and engaging participation, 476, 483
initial contact with reality of oppression or conflict, 473–474, 483
understanding historical/contextual factors, 475, 483

Ball State University, cultural diversity/ social justice issues in counseling psychology training program, 46
Baton Rouge cancer alley/toxic corridor, Black residents in, 188
Battered women's syndrome, 232
Bay Area Homelessness Project, 287
Beck Depression Inventory, 303
Beers, Clifford, 44
Bias and discrimination, minimizing effects of, 20–21
Biases and values, consultants' self-evaluation of, 395–396
Bicultural struggles, misdiagnosis and, 239
Big Brother/Big Sister mentoring program, 271
Biopsychosocial focus on mental and physical health, 314, 331
emphasizing with clients/patients, 329
mechanisms and pathways, 320
Biopsychosocial model, 344–345, 346, 347
Southeast Asian Refugee Service and, 344–346
Black activism, 103, 104, 108
See also African American activism; Black children, activism and schooling of
Black children, activism and schooling of, 103–105
Black nationalism, 103, 104
Black Report, 321
Blaming the victim, battered women and, 157
Block grants, 295

Border disputes between nations, attempting to resolve, 1
Bosnia Reconstruction Program, 346
Boston College:
  cultural diversity/social justice issues in counseling psychology training program, 40, 46
  Institute for the Study and Promotion of Race and Culture (ISPRC), 47
  "Tools for Tomorrow" intervention, 46
Breadwinners Institute, 3
Brown v. Board of Education, 104
Buddhism, 349, 429, 449, 458
  principles and actions, 455
  Tibetan, 450
Buhrke, Robin, 219
Bush administration, 258

California domestic partner registry, 269
California medical schools, minority enrollment in, 263
Cambodian Mutual Alliance Association, 346, 350, 352, 353
Cambodian refugees, 315–316, 339, 346
  Cambodian Holocaust related psychiatric disorders, 348
  depression and anxiety, 349
  dual diagnosis of PTSD and major depression, 351
  health education and level of confidence in health, 351
  intergenerational transmission of trauma, 341
  posttraumatic stress disorder, 341
  prevalence of PTSD, 349
  psychosomatic problems, 348
Campus Care and Counseling Act, 494
Campus Contact, 60
Canadian Code of Ethics for Psychologists, 19
  respect, 20
  responsibility, 21
  social action, 22
Cancer, social class and, 326
Cardiovascular disease, social class and, 324
Career counseling, 3, 4, 11, 52, 120, 277, 278, 281, 283, 285–290, 299, 300, 304, 545
  See also Vocational/career counseling
Career education programs, school-based, 252, 270–271
Carve-out benefits, 523
Case consultants, 501
Center for Multicultural Human Services, 47
Central characteristic/spread, 171
Change, pace of, 533, 538–539
Charity model of intervention, 313
Child care programs, benefits of instituting, 266
Child care, mandatory on-site, 270
Child care policy, national, 299
Child development issues, 510
Child labor, 251
Childrens Health Insurance Program, 509
Chile:
  adolescent drug abuse, 410
  consumerism, 410
  contemporary, 409–410
  daily work schedule, 410
  domestic violence, 409, 410
  individualism, 410
  lack of access to psychological services, 410
  National Mental Health Policy, 410
  National Mental Health Program, 410
  National Substance Abuse Policy, 410
  number of qualified psychologists in, 410
  poverty, 410
  practice of psychology in, 410
  recent history, 408–409
  substance abuse prevention/intervention, 410
  unemployment, 409, 410
  See also Family faith education program (Peñalolén, Chile); Peñalolén (Chile), consultation and training work in
China, 443, 451, 453, 454, 457–458, 461, 463–464
Chinese Americans, lack of confidence in doctors, 340–341
Choekyi Nyima, 458
Christian Base Communities, 413
Church of Jesus Christ of Latter-Day Saints, 243
Citizen action, 505
Civil marriage for same-sex couples, APA position on, 492
Civil protection orders, 162
Civil rights, counseling psychologists advocating for, 2
Civil Rights Act, 175
Civil rights movement, 4, 111, 151, 189, 240, 503

Civil society, 390
Civil unions, 269
Class-bound values and assumptions, 134
Classism, 149, 202, 261, 300, 305, 315
social class and, 320
Client action/activism, 242
Client goals, adherence to, 280
Client/student advocacy, 492
Clinton, Bill, 202, 338
Cognitive-behavioral techniques, 392
Cold War:
end of, 384
mentality, 383
Collaboration, 9, 10, 26, 31, 41, 51, 62, 69, 70, 89, 126, 131, 133, 152, 159, 165, 174, 194, 204, 205, 206, 210, 211, 220, 237, 273, 289, 299, 313, 316, 330, 365, 366, 372, 392, 395, 397, 399, 403, 414, 422, 428, 429, 433, 434, 437, 438, 439, 457, 458, 465, 473, 481, 521, 534, 538
community, 492
creative, 427, 428, 439
hospital-ethnic community, 346
institutional, 288
interdisciplinary, 13, 120, 166, 339, 443, 533, 535–537, 545, 548
international, 391, 392, 438, 543
multidisciplinary, 537
university-community, 366, 557
vertical, 438
Collaborative consultation, international, 388–404
Collaborative relationships, 135, 362, 399, 458
Collective interest model, 192
Collective sphere, 173, 174
College and university counseling centers, 363, 367, 369, 371
federal support for, 510
College Board National Task Force on Minority High Achievement, 103
Colonial domination, 390
Colonialism, 422, 424, 427, 438
Colonization, 424, 425, 427
common methods of, 424
Colonized mentality, 428
Columbine High School shootings, 94
Coming out, 224–225
LGB counseling psychologists, 225
Commitments:
ethical issues related to, 539
honoring to affected communities 539
Commonwealth Fund study, 338, 339, 340
Communities:
prevention work and, 82
underserved, 86, 87
See also Marginalized communities, historically; Oppressed communities
Communities, outreach with urban, 89–95
program curriculum, 91–92
program implementation challenges, 92–95
program participants and design, 90–91
Communities of color, 361
mental health disparities in, 87
Communities of peace, 5, 443, 466
Communities of social change, building, 422
Community, 415
expertise of, 534
Community Abuse Prevention Services Agency “women’s music” project, 242–243
feminist multicultural aspects of, 243
Community action, 242
Community activism, 5, 107, 153
Community activists, 88, 206
Community-based feminist counseling, 422
Community-based program outreach, 88–89. *See also* Communities, outreach with urban
Community-based resource management, 480
Community-based social change, 242
Community building, 479
Community capacity-building, 95
Community-centered research methods, 544
Community empowerment, 539
Freire’s model, 105
principles, 141
Community engagement, outreach scholarship and, 548
Community interventions, 464
safeguarding rights of participants, 542
Community involvement, 533, 534–535
research, 543
Community-level interventions:
designing interventions through processes serving community development goals, 362
developing collaborative relationships, 362
environmental assessment, 362

Community Model of Embeddedness, Interdependence, Intradependence and Evolution, 174–180
  embeddedness, 173, 175–176
  evolution, 173, 179–180
  evolution of the Cube, 174–175
  interdependence, 173, 176–177
  intradependence, 173, 177–179
  model of the Cube, 174
Community organizing, 544
  counseling psychologist support of, 542
Community outreach, 87
  importance of evaluation, 95
  programs, 96
Community partnerships, 302–303
  training for building/sustaining, 545
Community psychology, 38, 39, 41, 118, 130, 132–137, 278, 360, 362, 414, 466, 535, 537, 545
  access, 133
  common multicultural factors, 131, 133–136
  cultural experiences, 133–134
  ethical considerations, 136–137
  organizational multicultural competence, 134
  provider multicultural competence, 135–136
Community self-advocacy skills, 540
Community support, 550
Competence, 20, 23–24, 25, 28, 30, 32, 37, 78, 81, 82, 137, 179, 280, 289, 313, 390, 391, 414, 416, 457, 490, 491, 546, 549, 554, 558, 566
  assessing, 273
  boundaries, 402
  international, 545
  limits, 253, 280
  See also Cross-cultural; Multicultural competence
Comprehensive collaboration, 534
Comunidades Eclesial de Base, 413
Confidentiality, 69, 95, 136, 141, 473
  limits, 403
  psychologists' training in, 505
Conflict resolution, 392, 393, 481, 482
  methods, 383
  training, 476
Conscientization, 237, 238, 240
Consciousness raising, 26, 158, 231, 238, 240–241, 408, 482, 543
  campaigns, 436
  ethical issues and, 26
  feminist, 233
  movement, 241
Constitution, U.S., 150, 175, 500, 501
  equal protection clause, 265
  14th Amendment, 269
Constructive relationships, 480
Consultation, 11, 54, 80, 109, 120, 124, 126, 140, 141, 152, 158, 160, 166, 173, 174, 177, 181, 272, 278, 281, 289, 306, 313, 329, 363, 364, 365, 366, 368, 369, 378, 379, 385, 389–403, 407, 411, 412, 417, 418, 422, 423, 425, 428, 431, 439, 457, 464, 466, 479, 494, 521, 534, 535, 542, 545, 548
  counseling competency, 2
  maintaining awareness of impact on consultants/consultees/clients, 397–398
Consultees, 391, 392, 395, 398, 399, 400–401, 402, 403
  consultants advocating for, 396
  consultants being considerate of worldviews of, 396
  privileging needs and goals, 396–397
Consumer rights issues, legislative action and, 543
Contact Hypothesis, 458
Corporation for National Service, 60
Council for the Accreditation of Counseling Related Education Programs, 45
Counseling competencies, 13, 173
  cross-cultural, 5
  multicultural, 49, 86, 135, 173, 194, 278, 491, 493, 554
Counseling for social justice, 235, 237, 238
Counseling graduate programs, 55, 272, 367, 495, 547
Counseling health psychology, 314, 315, 316, 317, 358, 359, 360, 368, 372
Counseling program-specific activities, 389
Counseling psychologist/minister:
  as public official, 506–510
Counseling psychologists, 1, 2, 3, 4, 5, 6, 7, 8, 9, 10, 11, 12, 13, 18, 20, 21, 22, 23, 24, 25, 26, 31, 32, 37, 38, 40, 44, 77, 79, 80, 117, 119, 120, 121, 122, 123, 124, 126, 130, 137, 149, 151, 152, 153, 155, 156, 157, 158, 159, 166, 167, 173, 174, 175, 177, 178, 179, 180, 181, 186, 190, 191, 192, 193, 194, 196, 200, 201, 212, 215, 216, 217, 218, 219, 220, 222, 223, 224, 225, 226, 227, 237, 251, 252, 253, 256, 270, 271, 277, 278, 279, 282,

285, 287, 288, 289, 290, 294, 299, 305, 316, 358, 360, 361, 362, 363, 364, 365, 366, 367, 370, 372, 377–385, 388, 389, 390, 391, 392, 393, 395, 402, 403, 406, 418, 421, 425, 438, 439, 442, 443, 449, 457, 464, 465, 466, 467, 472, 473, 476, 479, 480, 481, 482, 483, 484, 489, 490, 492, 493, 494, 495, 496, 499, 500, 502, 504, 505, 509, 510, 524, 533, 534, 535, 536, 537, 538, 539, 540, 541, 542, 543, 544, 545, 546, 547, 548, 549, 550, 551
as lobbyists/advocates, 503–506
as on-the-job advocates, 500–502
as organizational change agents, 5
as social architects, 377ER 26
briefing legislators on social justice topics, 547
employment of, 4
oppression issues addressed by, 151
peaceful communities and, 381
Counseling psychology, 46, 551
accredited doctoral programs, 40
interest in social justice/social action/advocacy, 1–2, 5, 6–7, 8, 12–13
internationalizing, 378
preference for medical models emphasizing individual/remedial therapy, 2, 5
shift toward advocacy for, 2, 5
Counseling psychology training:
advocacy tracks in, 273
to work in multiple levels of intervention, 538
Counseling Self-Estimate Inventory, 64
Counselor licensure movement, 450
Counterstorytelling, 236
Covenanters, 108
Creative collaboration, 421, 427, 428, 439
Critical consciousness, 26, 400, 414, 415, 417, 432, 439, 475, 479
Critical health psychology, 359–360
Critical/liberation psychology, 237
Critical psychology, 41, 236–237
Critical race/gender theories, 238
Critical race theory, 235–236, 237
definition, 235
movement, 235
Critical theories, 235–236, 238. *See also* Critical theory; Critical race theory
Critical theory, 12, 380, 422, 431, 432, 438
feminist, 236
Latino/a critical theory, 236
Cross-cultural communication, ultimate goal of effective, 134
Cross-cultural competency, 63, 64
perceived, 66
Cross-cultural counseling, 5, 232, 554
See also Cross-Cultural Counseling Competency model
Cross-Cultural Counseling Competency model, 5, 151
Cross-cultural empathy, 135
Cultural competence, 166, 195, 232, 278, 331, 390–391
increasing through traveling, 549
Cultural competencies, 53, 60, 176, 347
Cultural competency, 390
Cultural deficit, 132
Cultural diversity, 388
Cultural education, 395
Cultural encapsulation, 438, 535
Cultural genocide, 454
Cultural identity groups, 138–139
Cultural imperialism, 380, 392, 424
oppressed groups and, 149
Culturally aware, dynamic process of becoming, 391
Culturally competent community programming, 346–354
evaluation of participant confidence in health promotion, 350–352
HP curriculum syllabus, 347–349
outcome or summative evaluations, 353–354
participants, 347
process or formative evaluation, 352–353
suggested program evaluation model for HP curriculum, 352
Culturally relevant intervention strategies, 393
Cultural scapegoating, 204
Cultural sensitivity, 395, 534
Cultural values misunderstandings, misdiagnosis and, 239
Culture, role of in shaping mental health, 388
Cultures of peace, 114, 389, 481
Custody issues, 510

Dalai Lama, The, 450, 451, 452, 453, 454, 455, 456, 458, 459
DARE, 83
Davis, King, 190
Decision-making dilemmas, social justice career choices and, 281

Decolonialism, 104
Decolonization, 427, 428, 434, 436
  five steps in process of from perspective of the decolonized, 428
Decolonizing approach, 433, 438
Deep poverty, 296
Defense of Marriage Act, 268
  challenges to, 269
Defensive medicine, liability legislation and, 527
Delayed-treatment groups, 96
Demystification, 238, 240
Depression, Great, 251, 506
Deterrence, 383
Developmental contextualism, 89
Developmental systems theories, 102
  relationism and, 102
Diabetes, social class and, 324
Diplomatic corps, 536
Direct violence, 384
Disability rights movement, 151
Disciplinary bias, 535
Discourse analysis, 207, 210. *See also* Federal policy on homelessness, discourse analysis of
Discrimination, 3, 5, 7, 13, 20, 21, 51, 92, 103, 108, 113, 125, 150, 173, 175, 177, 180, 189, 193, 201, 202, 204, 206, 211, 215, 218, 220, 222, 223, 235, 236, 237, 238, 240, 252, 253, 258, 261, 263, 264, 265, 266, 267, 269, 273, 277, 278, 279, 281, 282, 284, 289, 316, 338, 369, 370, 371, 492, 493, 501, 538, 546, 550, 551
  helping clients deal with, 281–283
  See also specific types of discrimination
Discrimination lawsuits, workplace, 266
Distributive justice, 313
Distributive social justice, 393
Distrust in communities, researchers,' 540
Diversity, 39, 49, 60, 70, 71, 137, 234, 256, 270, 271, 432, 464
  areas of human, 11
  awareness, 223, 237
  celebrating, 233
  client, 24
  cultural, 46, 378, 388, 395, 546
  definition, 175
  ethnic, 21, 67, 166, 180, 388
  human, 81, 216, 227, 237, 272, 273
  in discipline, 330
  in theory, 330
  racial, 66, 67, 166, 180
  respecting, 136, 173, 174, 234
  socioeconomic, 66
  valuing, 432
  within-group, 354
Diversity education in schools, 270–271
Doctoral training programs, 551
Domestic partner benefits, 263–264, 270
  as recruiting incentive, 266
Domestic violence, 10, 42, 52, 60, 61, 62, 64, 66, 67, 68, 69, 159, 160, 165, 208, 242, 244, 296, 298, 400, 410, 435, 536
  homelessness and, 71, 208
Domestic violence intervention, use of interdisciplinary teams, 536
Domination, systems of, 432
Drift hypothesis, 322

East Turkestan, 443, 451, 453, 457, 458
Ecological model, Bronfenbrenner's, 39, 78, 80, 131, 132
  exosystem, 131
  macrosystem, 131
  mesosystem, 131
  microsystem, 131
Ecological model for contextualizing multicultural counseling psychology processes, Neville and Mobley's, 194–196
  exosystem, 195
  individual/person system, 195
  macrosystem, 195
  mesosystem, 195
  microsystem, 195
Ecological models of intervention, 537
  See also Ecological model, Bronfenbrenner's; Ecological model for contextualizing multicultural counseling psychology processes, Neville and Mobley's
Economic disparities, digital divide and, 276
Economic oppression, 390
Economic systems, actively working to change, 1
Education, 90–91, 139, 190, 207, 216, 271, 297, 475
  engaging in advocacy through, 271
  equal access to, 26, 54
  poor, 296
  public, 22
  regulating access to, 4
  social change in secondary, 77
Educational counseling, 3
Educational discrimination, 261
Educational equity, importance of legal change in mandating, 265

Educational interventions, 543
Educational opportunities, increasing access to, 1
Educational opportunity structures, 262
Educational psychology, 123, 124, 392
Egalitarianism, 393
Ego-dystonic homosexuality, 217
Ego identity development, adolescent, 136
Elaboration Likelihood Model, 380, 459, 460, 466
Employee Retirement and Income Security Act, 520, 527, 528
Employee-sponsored managed health care plans, 528
Employment, barriers to, 281
Employment advocacy, 286
Employment disparities, digital divide and, 276
Employment Non-Discrimination Act, 267
Employment opportunities, women's, 501
Employment Stabilization Project, 3, 251
Employment Stabilization Research Institute, 277
Empowerment, 1, 18–19, 31, 81, 113, 137, 173, 174, 240, 241, 242, 243, 279, 282, 284, 330, 428, 436, 437, 439, 476, 478, 490, 496, 539
  collective, 114
  community, 105, 141, 280, 330
  cultural, 9
  definitions, 19, 240, 414
  education and, 340
  ethnic minority group lack of, 340
  facilitating, 28
  of school children, 130
  of students, 56
  political, 494
  See also Empowerment model
Empowerment model, 257, 408, 412, 414–416, 417
  5 Cs of empowerment, 414–416
Empowerment-oriented research methods, 544
Environment, striving to protect, 2
Environmental activism, 186, 191–192
  external efficacy, 192
  internal efficacy, 192
  role of social justice and advocacy in, 190–191
Environmental advocacy, 191, 196
Environmental behavior models, multicultural, 2
Environmental contamination, 190
  ethnic minorities and health and, 187–189, 196
  exclusionary nature of policies dealing with, 186
  heightened public awareness about, 186
  studies on impact of in Native American communities, 187–188, 190
Environmental factors:
  acquisition of diseases and, 359
  outcome of diseases and, 359
Environmental issues, research on, 544
Environmental justice, 185, 188
  framework, 193–194
Environmental movement, 186, 189–190
  tribal lands and, 190
Environmental Protection Agency, 190
Environmental racism, 10, 153, 186–187, 189, 192, 193, 196, 537
  addressing common causes and effects, 194
  confronting, 535
  definition, 186
  public health/nursing interventions, 194
  social work interventions and, 193, 194
  sociopolitical problems associated with, 194
Epistemic psychopolitical validity, 258
Equal Access Act of 1984, 265
Equal Benefits Ordinance (San Francisco), 264
Equal Employment Opportunity Act (Title VII), 279
Equal Employment Opportunity Commission, 279
Equal Rights Amendment, 500, 501
Equity goals:
  expert testimony training and, 270
  legislative efforts and, 270
  research and, 270
Ethical codes, 19–23
  respect, 19–20
  responsibility, 19, 20–21
  social action, 19, 21–23
Ethical decision making, 137
  process, 473
Ethical decision making models, 31–32
  need for research on impact of different, 32
Ethical issues and social justice, counseling psychology and, 23–28
  competence, 23–24, 25
  do no harm, 23, 27–28

dual roles and professional boundaries, 23, 25
informed consent, 23, 26–27, 29–30
managed care and, 524
politicizing of social justice, 23, 25–26
worldview and assumptions, 23, 24–25
Ethical practice, 280
See also Client goals, adherence to; Competence, limits of; Informed consent
Ethics, psychologists' training in, 505
Ethnic diversity, 388
Ethnic identity, minority youth and, 136
Ethnocentrism, 438
Ethnographers, 437
Ethnographic research, 439
Ethnographies, 484
Ethnography, 402
Ethnopolitical conflicts, resolving, 1, 7, 13
Euro-American training in psychology, 391–392
Evaluation, 95–97
formative, 83, 95, 142, 352–353
summative, 83, 95, 351, 352, 353–354
Evaluation practices, unfair work, 261
Exosystem risk factors, 78, 79
Experiential role-play exercises, 399
Experimentalism, 382
Expert witnesses, 501
Exxon Valdez oil spill disaster, 188

Fairness, perception of, 393
Family catechesis groups, 413
Family enrichment, 537
Family faith education program (Peñalolén, Chile), 407, 410–411
Catholic sacraments and, 411
primary program goal, 410
Family leave policies, liberal, 270
Family Self-Sufficiency program, 300
Federal advocacy process, 495
Federal policy on homelessness, discourse analysis of, 205–210
homelessness as disease, 209–210
homelessness as uncontrollable event/natural disaster, 209
war-like solutions for homelessness problem, 210
Fee-for-service reimbursement, 520–523
Feminism, 171, 234, 235, 238, 243, 393, 395
multiculturalism and, 234, 243
third wave, 237, 238
Feminist activists, 422, 429, 559
Feminist changes, counseling psychologists advocating for, 2, 4
Feminist Counseling Project, The, 434
Feminist critical theory, 236
Feminist group work, 241
Feminist identity development, five-stage model of, 176
Feminist movement, 172, 238, 383, 494
Feminist multicultural counseling/psychotherapy for social justice, 231, 232, 235, 238, 240, 241, 242–245
analysis of power in psychotherapy, 240–241
consciousness-raising/conscientization/demystification, 240
feminist multicultural perspectives on assessment and diagnosis, 239–240
herstory and evolution of 232–235, 535
implementing 238–242
importance of group work to empower clients, 241
music of Utah battered women, 242–243
political action/activism, 241–242
premise, 242
training, 243
University of Utah Women's Resource Center, 243–245
Feminist multicultural counselors/therapists, 232, 236
working for social justice, 235, 239, 240, 241
Feminist multicultural group counseling, 240
Feminist multiculturalperspectives on assessment and diagnosis, 239–240
cultural systems and structures, 239
cultural values, 239
gender socialization, 239
trauma, 239
See also Feminist therapy
Feminist participatory research, 445
Feminist psychologists/therapists, 237, 238, 241, 244, 437, 503
Feminist psychology, 380, 422, 425, 432, 438
Feminist psychology framework, environmental activism and, 191–192
Feminist-run shelter programs, 158
Feminists, 157, 234, 235, 244, 429
second wave, 238
third wave, 238

Feminist theories, 392
Feminist theory, 395, 431, 432
antidomination and, 432
contemporary, 238
diversity and, 432
Feminist therapy, 233, 238
goals, 233
grassroots origins, 231
herstory of, 231, 535
movement, 234
professionalization of, 237
Feminist Therapy Code of Ethics, 241
social action, 22
Fidelity, working in marginalized communities and, 539
Field notes, 484
Field research counseling competency, 2
Flexible work arrangements, 270
Flextime, 270
Force field analysis model, Lewin's, 444, 446
goal of building nonviolent communities and, 446
Free Tibet movement, 463
See also Tibet movement
Functional literacy, 112

Gandhian Personality Scale, 447, 448
Gandhian principles of nonviolence, 446–447, 448, 455
Ahimsa, 445, 446, 447, 456, 466
drawbacks to, 447
Satya, 446, 455
Satyagraha, 446, 447, 448, 462, 466
Tapasya, 445, 446–447, 448, 462
Garrett Lee Smith Memorial Act, 494
Gender equity, public policy decisions on, 496, 543
Gender gap, corporate strategies to close/eliminate, 265
Genocide, 384, 465
George Mason University Counseling and Development (C&D) Program, 45, 47–56
accreditation, 55
collaborative research projects, 53
curriculum and training, 50–53
ethics training, 53
faculty recruitment, 49, 50
field experience opportunities, 51–52
internships sites, 47, 52
local/national/international partnerships, 54
mission statement development, 49
research and professional development activities, 53–55
social justice training recommendations based on, 55–56
student recruitment, 50
technology training, 53
theoretical framework and mission, 49
transformation challenges, 54–55
Gerstein, Lawrence H., 456
Glass ceiling, 261
Globalism, 465
Globalization, 424, 425
of manufacturing occupations, 276
service occupations, 276
Global North, 422, 425, 426, 429
"experts," 426, 434
Global North/South
"border crossings," 437
partnerships, 423, 428, 437
Global power, awareness of role of, 391
Global South, 422, 425, 427, 429, 438
Goodman, Jane, 491
Governmental structures, actively working to change, 1
Graduated and Reciprocated Initiatives in Tension-Reduction (GRIT), 383
Graduate medical education resources, psychologist inclusion in, 510
Grant funding, trust and instability of public and private, 540
Grassroots activism, 218, 225
Grassroots advocacy, 494
Grassroots framework, 401
Grassroots groups, 429
Grassroots leadership, 476
Grassroots movement, 197
Grassroots organizations, 398, 457
Grassroots partnerships, 394
Grassroots support, 493
Grassroots training, 476
Grassroots work, 446
Grassroots workers, 422, 433
Grounded theory, 402
Group behavior, 534
Group counseling, 132, 385, 466
feminist multicultural, 240
Group counseling theory, 380
Group dynamics and intervention counseling competency, 2
Group solidarity, 435
Group trust, 435
Group work, 464
importance of to empower clients, 241

Guidelines on Multicultural Education, Training, Research, Practice and Higher education:
counseling psychologists and, 4
Gyatso, Palden, 459

Harvard Program in Refugee Trauma, 316, 317, 339, 345–346, 349, 351, 352, 353, 354
Depression/Torture Screening Instrument, 353
Health Promotion Confidence Evaluation Form, 347, 350, 351, 353
Torture Screening Instrument, 347
Hate crimes, 123
Hazardous materials exposure, social class and, 326
Hazardous wastes, health issues associated with exposure to, 186
Head Start, 78
Health:
barriers to for racial/ethnic minorities, 338
racial gap in, 322
social class and, 319, 322, 323
Health care:
barriers to for racial/ethnic minorities, 338
employer-sponsored, 520
minority disparities in equality of, 339
minority disparities in utilization of, 339
poverty and high cost of, 339–344
Health care administration trends, 520
Health care decisions, physician-influenced, 325
Health care educational opportunities, 326
Health care industry, 325, 520, 521, 523
Health care management, passivity in, 328
Health care system, 315, 323, 326, 328, 331, 332, 354, 537
Asian Americans and, 339, 354
cultural competence of those within, 331
culturally sensitive, 338
failure to communicate, 328
increasing agency within, 328
inequalities, 321
interaction with, 325
mental health care services in, 355
mistrust of, 326
negotiating, 330
patients' rights protections in, 501
social class and, 11
universal, 325
Health Disparities Report, 322
Health education, 11, 60, 316, 332, 339, 340
access to, 339
community, 316
culturally competent, 343
curriculum, 346
Vietnamese refugees and, 339–340, 351, 352, 354, 536
Health insurance, 263, 341, 520
corporate-provided, 521
employer-organized, 520, 521
inadequate, 87, 339
low income and access to, 339
quality of, 325
Vietnamese refugees and, 339
See also Health insurance system, parity for mental health in; Health insurer liability
Health insurance system, parity for mental health in, 501, 510
Health insurer liability, 525
Health literacy, 325
about diabetes, 326
levels, 325, 326
research, 328
Health maintenance organizations, 326, 328, 522, 524, 525
Health-problem risk, urban living and, 359
Health Promotion Curriculum, 345, 346, 347, 348, 349, 350, 352, 353, 354
curriculum syllabus, 347, 354
participants, 347
pilot implementation, 351
Health promotion theory, 330
Health psychology, 11, 120, 314, 315, 330, 359
integrative model of social justice/multicultural/biopsychosocial framework, 314
See also Counseling health psychology
Health Resources and Services Administration, 119
Health risk behaviors, 323
prevention and intervention, 331
social class and adult, 322
Health risk information, access to, 326
Health status, income and, 359
Healthy People 2000 initiative report, 338
Hegemony, 438
Helms, Janet E., 47

Heritage learning of Africans/African Americans/Others, promoting, 107, 109, 112
restoring historical memory and, 111–113
See also Heritage Project
Heritage Project, 83–84, 101, 105–107, 108, 109, 110, 111, 112, 113, 114
as critical qualitative research study, 105
goals, 105
Heritage School component, 106, 107
teacher training component, 106
workshops/consultations component, 106
Hesse, Hermann, 449
Heterosexism, 149, 232, 236, 261, 546
Heterosexual identity development theory, heterosexual privilege and, 544
Higher Education Act (Title IX), 279
Historical memory, restoring, 107
promoting heritage learning of Africans/African Americans/ others and, 111–113
HIV/AIDS, 380, 536, 541
applying social justice perspective to counseling health psychology and, 360
communities differentially affected by, 361
groups at risk for, 313
impact of, 316
impact of U-CAP on HIV/AIDS community, 363–365
impact on communities, 360'
impact on individuals, 360
individual/community/societal levels of impact, 360–366
modes of transmission, 361
projects, 422
recommendations, 365–366
societies, 360
university and community agency collaborations, 362–363
working with communities affected by, 362
See also HIV/AIDS patients
HIV/AIDS patients:
age, 361
emotional impact, 361
multiple stressors of, 360–361
people of color, 361
HMOs. *See* Health maintenance organizations
Home-based interventions, 139
Homeless, working with, 1
counseling psychologists and social justice in, 2
ethical issues involved in studying, 203
Homeless activists, 210, 211
Homeless mothers:
damaging/pathologizing effects on, 534
implications for public policy and creating strength-based services, 210–211
needs and experiences of, 203–205
negative stereotyping of, 204, 205
stigmatizing of, 204, 211
Homelessness, 296
as otherness, 210
different types of, 208
ethical issues involved in studying, 203
images evoked by, 209
public policy decisions on, 496
sociopolitical context of, 203
solving, 208
victim-blaming perspectives and, 534
Homelessness, discourse analysis of federal policy on, 205–210
homelessness as disease, 209–210
homelessness as uncontrollable event/natural disaster, 209
war-like solutions for homelessness problem, 209, 210
Homeless women, use of dysfunctional/ avoidant coping by, 202
See also Homeless mothers; Homelessness
Home-work interface, norms and policies complicating, 261
Homonegativity, 261, 361
Homophobia, 216, 239, 546
internalized, 216
psychoeducational approaches to coping with/combating, 226
working to combat, 1
Homosexuality, stresses resulting from social stigma of, 136
minority youth and, 136
Housing and Urban Development, 300
Housing Authority Family Self-Sufficiency Program, 302
Houston Psychological Association, 516, 519
Human behavior models, multicultural, 2

Human rights, 22, 390
Human rights abuses, 482
counseling psychologists confronting, 3, 13
developing and implementing strategies to eliminate, 1–2
Human rights activists, 442
Human rights advocacy, international, 490, 493
Human Rights Campaign, 267, 270
Human rights groups, ally support from, 544
Human rights issues, long-term change and, 538
Human rights organizations:
employment opportunities in, 536
internship opportunities in, 536
Human Rights Watch, 454, 459, 465, 536
Humor:
as integral part of therapeutic relationship, 135
Hungary, 389
consultant to, 391
Hurricane Katrina:
community posttraumatic stress disorder and, 542
racism in government response to, 542
social classism in media coverage of, 542

IBM, domestic partner benefits offered by, 266
Identity development, 542
Identity Pride stage, 151, 224
Illness, homelessness and chronic, 208
Immersion experiences, 548
Immersion work, 549
Immigrants, adolescent, 133
acculturative stress, 133
depression, 133
language barrier, 133–134
suicide, 133
Imperialism, 422, 424, 425, 427, 429, 438
Inclusion, 388
development of model of, 173–174
See also Community Model of Embeddedness, Interdependence, Intradependence and Evolution; Inclusion, full
Inclusion, full:
LGBT people, 270
of women, 270
people of color, 270
people with disabilities, 270
poor people, 270
Inclusiveness, 390
India, 451, 452, 453, 456, 463, 481, 482, 483
Indiana University, 83–84, 108–109
School of Education, 107
Indigenous Women of North America, 190
Indochinese Psychiatric Clinic (Boston), 347
Inequality, 533
challenging, 543
Inequity, 550
Information processing strategy, cognitive-emotional, 102
Informed consent, 253, 280
full, 24, 31
parental, 137
procedures, 403
systems interventions and, 539
Initiative on Race, 338
Injustice, 472, 489, 533, 534, 548
counseling psychologists confronting, 3, 7, 13
In-service prevention training with school personnel:
promoting social justice through, 124–126
Safe School Project, 124
Supporting Teachers Supporting Student program, 125–126
Institutional change, focusing on, 285–288
service learning on the street, 286–287
social entrepreneurship, 287–288
Institutionalized discrimination, 150
Institutionalized racism, 112
counseling psychologists as change agents to prevent, 2
Institutional oppression, 216, 390
Integrated Corporation for Cultural and Social Development, 112
Integrative Transcultural Model, 473
Interdisciplinary collaboration, 443, 533, 535–537, 548
integrating into training programs, 545
Interdisciplinary collaborative research, 544
Interdisciplinary intervention teams, 544
Interdisciplinary team approaches, 536
Interdisciplinary training, counseling psychologist, 484
International Association for Counselling, 54
International collaboration, 391, 392, 438
International collaborative consultation, 390
International consultants, 395, 398

culturally competent, 390–392
protection of consultees' confidentiality, 403
provision of informed consent for participating in consultation and research, 403
utilization of assessment devices, 403
International consultation, 390, 402
consultants and consultees contribution to breakdowns in, 401
International consulting relationships, 400
International counseling psychologists, 438
International counseling psychology, 439
principles for bringing social justice values to, 427
International human rights advocacy, 490
International interactions within-group, 390
International interventions:
cultural relevance of, 544
impact of, 544
Internationalization of counseling psychology, 389, 422
Internationalizing counseling psychology field, 465
International Tibet Independence Movement, 380, 451
projects and campaigns, 458–462
structure of, 456–458
Tibet movement and challenges of, 462–464
Internet use policies, addressing on-line hate/harassment and, 271
Internet Web sites, social justice organizations,' 284
Internships, 284
Interpretive research, 439
Interventions:
indicated, 79–80
multicomponent preventive, 80
selective, 79, 80
universal, 79, 80, 81
Interview skills, practicing, 302
Intimate partner violence, 156–158
seeking systemic change for victims of, 156, 158–159
Intimate partner violence services, Haitian immigrant women and, 164–166
Ivey, Allen, 491

James, William, 381
Jammu and Kashmir Liberation Front, 482
Japan, post-WWII educational system reorganization of, 378
Jewish Mysticism, 449
Job coaching, 300
Job-first programs, 297
Job Service, 302, 305
Job shadowing assignments, 302
Job sharing, 270
Job tracking, 261

Kashmir. *See* Kashmir conflict
Kashmir conflict, 472, 481–483
awareness and engagement, 482–483
understanding historical and contextual factors, 481–482
Kellogg Commission on the Future of State and Land Grant Universities, 547–548
Kobe Earthquake Program, 346
Ku Klux Klan, 108

Labor movement, 151, 506
Latina/o critical theory, 236
Latino/Latina Psychological Association, 510
Lawrence and Garner v. Texas, 219
Lawrence v. Texas, 269
Law school-based advocacy intervention, evaluating, 162–164, 166
Legal advocacy, 30
Legislation, federal and state, 494–495
legislative action and public policy, 494–495
legislative action through professional associations, 494
training for legislative involvement, 495, 547
Legislative advocacy, 196, 220, 547
Legislative process, influencing, 2
Lesbian/gay/bisexual/transgender advocacy, 216, 218, 226, 227, 268, 493
Lesbian/gay/bisexual/transgender communities, 224
building of support networks, 218
Gay Pride celebrations, 218
heterosexual counseling psychologist allies of, 225, 226
targeted activism, 218
Lesbian/gay/bisexual/transgender identity development, understanding models of, 224–225
Lesbian/gay/bisexual/transgender individuals:
activism, 218, 224–225
activist community, 218

activists, 218, 224
anti-harassment/nondiscrimination regulations, 265
domestic partnerships, 504, 510
federal employees, 268
fight for domestic partner benefits, 268
finding support through professional organizations, 222–223
full inclusion, 270
heterosexual allies, 225–227
influencing public opinion concerning, 220–221
mental health profession oppression against, 217
navigating conflicts between activism and academia, 223–224
non-LGB allies, 225–226
oppression of, 216–217
populations, 361
recent history of affirmation/advocacy for, 216
special considerations for LGB counseling psychologists, 224–225
strategies for surviving and thriving, 221–227
systematic discrimination of, 215
systematic oppression of, 215
U.S. military and, 216, 220
workers, 262
Lesbian/gay/bisexual/transgender issues:
counselor didactic training in, 272
developing advocacy groups for, 535
social change in addressing, 537
Lesbian/gay/bisexual/transgender rights movement, 151
APA public statements for, 537
Lesbian/gay/bisexual/transgender social action, models of counseling psychologists engaged in, 217–219
community organizing, 218
Lesbian/gay/bisexual/transgender social policy and legislation, influencing, 219–220
Lesbian/gay/bisexual/transgender students, 267
anti-discrimination/harassment policies, 265
Massachusetts initiative, 265
Lesbian/gay/bisexual/transgender youth, 216, 264–265
alcoholism among, 217
antisocial adaptation strategies, 217
extreme social isolation of, 216
homophobic remarks and, 124
legislative protection of in schools, 269
physical harassment of, 264
risk for mental health problems, 217
self-harmful adaptation strategies, 217
suicidal risk, 151
suicide among, 216, 217
threats of attack against, 216
verbal abuse/harassment of, 216, 264
See also Safe School Project
Lesbians, work-related inequities and, 261
Liberation psychology, 38, 235, 236–237, 238, 380, 425, 438
Liberation theology, 379, 407–408, 412–414, 417
Liberation theory, 392, 431–432
Liberatory education, 380, 422
Licensing, market demands of:
as social justice training challenge, 40, 41
Lobbying, psychotherapy and, 505
Long-range collaborative initiatives, trust-building through, 88
Los Angeles domestic partner benefits law, 264
Lotus Corporation domestic partner benefits, 264
Loyola University Chicago, cultural diversity/social justice issues in counseling psychology training program at, 46

Macro-level advocacy, 492
Macrosystem risk factors, 78–79
Managed behavioral health care organizations, 523, 524
short-term treatment, 524
Managed care, 520, 522
addressing problems in, 536
adverse effects on counseling professionals, 524
legislative efforts needed to improve consumer and practitioner rights in the face of, 538, 543
supply-control model, 522
Managed care, market demands of:
as social justice training challenge, 40, 41
Managed care abuses, government fight against, 525
Managed care environment, 2, 5

Managed care in mental health, populations adversely affected by, 524
Managed care organizations, 522, 523, 525, 528
Managed care plans, 522
Managed care system, 515, 524, 527
Mann, Horace, 77
Manpower Demonstration Research Project, 297
Manpower utilization, underdeveloped countries and, 277
Mao Tse-Tung, 453, 457–458
  "Red Book," 449
Marginalization, 10, 149, 151, 175, 258, 360, 369, 389, 478, 481, 492
  counseling psychologists confronting, 3, 7, 8, 25
Marginalized communities, 9, 10, 149, 151, 153, 478, 494, 539, 542
  historically, 86
  response of counseling psychology to concerns of, 151–152
  trust issues/conflicts/within-group differences, 539, 542
Marginalized groups, 7, 8, 111, 123, 150, 151, 155, 175, 202, 261, 359, 390, 402, 490, 542
  inequitable vocational lives of, 261
  See also Marginalized professional groups
Marginalized individuals, 11, 63, 150, 151, 152, 153, 389, 542
Marginalized professional groups, 450
Marquette University:
  cultural diversity/social justice issues in counseling psychology training program, 46
  minority student recruitment and retention approach for counseling psychology program, 46
Marriage Protection Act, 268–269
Maslow, Abraham, 507
Massachusetts:
  educational program to make schools safe for LGBT youth, 265
  same-sex marriage in, 268
Mathematics Policy Research, Inc., 297
Mathers Museum of World Cultures, 106
MBHOs. *See* Managed behavioral health care organizations, 523
McCarthyism, 383
McDougall, William, 382
Medicaid, 520, 521
  mental health services for adults with, 504
Medical malpractice, HMOs and, 525
Medicare, 520, 521
Medication management:
  in individual psychotherapy, 330
  in support groups, 330
Meditation, 550
Mental health care in insurance system, parity for, 509
Mental health carve-outs, 523
Mental health courts, 509, 510
Mental health field, damaging managed care policies and, 523
Mental health providers, steps to facilitate clients'/patients' access to care, 328
Mental health resources, racial/ethnic minority underutilization of, 133
Mental health services, 87, 121, 138, 233, 305, 317, 355, 520, 523, 524, 525
  access to, 504
  community, 134
  employer health insurance coverage, 522
  insurance coverage of, 521
Mentor Couples, 11, 379, 406, 407, 409, 410, 411, 412, 413, 414, 415, 416, 417, 418
Mentoring programs, 271
Mentors, 26, 261, 284, 466, 534, 548, 549
  lack of for business women, 261
  need for, 548
  peer, 141
Micro-level advocacy, 492
Microsystem risk factors, 78
Militarism, 465
Mindfulness, 550
Minorities, 3, 141, 175, 263, 317, 338, 340, 343–344, 490
  access to mental health services, 317
  Asian, 339
  availability of mental health services, 317
  ethnic, 4, 82, 131, 132, 133, 136, 141, 175, 186, 252, 253, 313, 332, 338
  health care disparities, 354, 510
  racial, 359
  underrepresented in mental health research, 317
Mirror image, concept of, 383
Mollica, Richard, 349
Monastery, Tibetan, 452–453
More Pie Initiative, 8, 152
Mormonism, 243

Mortality, social class and, 320–321
MOSAIC (Models of Social Action Involving Communities), 394
Multicultural awareness, 64–65
Multicultural Awareness, Knowledge, and Skills Survey, 64
Multicultural competence, 5, 130, 193, 279, 282, 316, 368, 418
  development, 549
  organizational, 134
  provider, 135–136
  working to promote, 1
Multicultural competencies, 57, 176, 193, 278, 491, 495
  advocacy for adoption of, 491
  systematic implementation of, 546
Multicultural competency literature, major themes in, 233
Multicultural counseling, 9, 25, 39, 45, 49, 51, 86, 120, 135, 151, 153, 194, 232, 233, 234, 235, 385, 393, 395, 466, 545
  career counseling competencies, 278
  competencies, 86, 135
  early training in, 233
  impetus for, 232
  principles, 380
  tenants of movement, 379
  theories, 283, 380
Multicultural counselors, 244
  feminist, 232, 236
Multicultural education, 63, 71
  as social justice work, 62–63
  goal of, 63
Multicultural-feminist collaboration, 395, 399, 400
  advocacy in, 400
  providing content throughout process, 399–400
Multicultural-feminist consultants, 397
  considerate of consultees' worldviews, 396
Multicultural-feminist consultation:
  importance of follow-up, 398
  maintaining long-term relationship with, 398
  research and, 398
  working principles of in international applications, 395–398
Multicultural-feminist consultation, process mechanisms for effective, 398–401
  shifting from expert to collaborator, 398–399
Multicultural-feminist theories, 397
Multiculturalism, 39, 45, 48, 49, 54, 55, 62–63, 71, 84, 119, 120, 173, 174, 175, 176, 180, 181, 232, 234, 238, 243, 256, 369, 403, 464, 491, 535
  definition, 62
  expanded definition of, 491
  feminism and, 234, 243
  women with disabilities embedded in, 176
Multicultural issues, 534
  at societal level, 464
Multicultural learning in service learning course, evaluation of, 63–68
  discussion of findings, 64–68
  method, 64
Multiculturally competent counselors, 86
Multicultural movement, 494
Multicultural psychologists, 503
Multicultural psychology, 425
Multicultural Relationship Skills workshops, 125
  addressing prejudice through, 123–124
Multicultural theories, 289, 392
Multicultural therapists, 237
Multidimensional Scales of Nonviolence, 447, 448
Multidisciplinary/multicultural model of conceptualization and action, 550
Multidisciplinary teams, 550, 551
Multilevel/systemic approaches, 533, 537–538
Multiple cultural identities, working with, 390
Multiple role conflict, 261
Multisystemic youth development programs for urban youth, building, 86–97
Muslim United Front, 482
Mystification, 240
My Vocational Situation, 303

NANE, 534
  antitrafficking hotline, 394
  antiviolence hotline, 394
  consultation with, 396, 397
  establishing needs-based joint goals with, 397
  feedback process with, 396
  feminist framework, 395
  leaders, 396
  members, 395
  paid volunteers, 395–396
  Peer Education Project, 394

qualitative study on members' volunteer identity development and impact of consulting relationship, 398
sharing with, 397–398
shifting priorities, 400
volunteers, 394, 400
Narmada River damming (India), sustainable development and, 472, 479–481
awareness to engagement, 480–481
understanding historical and contextual factors, 479
National Academy of Sciences, 260
National Association for Women Deans, Administrators and Counselors, 500
National Association of School Psychologists, 270
National Association of Social Workers, 219
Code of Ethics, 19
responsibility, 21
social action, 22
Texas Chapter, 219
National Healthcare Disparities Report, 321, 325
National Institute of Multicultural Competence, 493
Multicultural Counseling Competencies, 493
Multicultural Guidelines, 493
National Latino/a Psychological Association, 152
National People of Color Environment Leadership Summit, first, 189
environmental justice principles, 189–190
National Violence Against Women Survey, 156
Nation building, 1
Nations of peace, 443
Native Americans, 108, 150
Nazi medical experiments on Jews, 344
Neighborhood associations, 330–331
Neocolonialism, 380
Nepal, 451, 452
New World Order, 429
Nixon, Richard: historic visit to China, 449
No Child Left Behind Act, 269
Nondiscrimination laws, 217
Nongovernmental organizations, 442, 455, 459, 466
in Eastern Europe, 380, 394, 478, 479, 546
Nonmaleficence, systems interventions and, 539
Nonoppressive environments, working to create, 542
Nonviolence, 390
measure of, 447–448
Nonviolence literature, overview of, 443–444
Nonviolence Test, 445, 447, 448
Nonviolence theories and research, 444–447
Gandhi's writings/activities, 446–447
Lewin's model of force field analysis, 446
peacebuilding approaches of women, 445–446
Value theory, 444–445
Nonviolent activism, future directions for counseling psychology and, 464–466
practice, 465
research, 465–466
training, 466
Nuclear anxiety, 383
Nuclear deterrence, 383
Nuclear disarmament, 384
movement, 383
Nuclear Test Ban Treaty, 383
Nuclear war, threat of, 384
Nursing home care, 326, 328

Obesity:
medical model and, 314
prevention, 314
social class and, 324
O'Bryant, Beverly, 491
Occupational opportunities, increasing access to, 1
Occupational opportunity structure, 257, 262
exclusionary, 257
Occupational segregation, 261
Occupational stereotypes, 261
Ohio Psychological Association, 501, 503
Graduate Students, 504
Ohio State University, The, 3
counseling psychology program, 504
Old boy networks, 261
Oppositional identity, black children in white schools and, 104
Oppressed communities, 87, 545
accessibility of traditional psychological/counseling services, 87
historically, 86

mental health needs of, 81, 97
potential for paternalism, 25
serving, 20, 21, 86
Oppressed groups, 18, 21, 102, 114, 149, 175, 180, 476
exploitation of, 149
serving, 21
Oppressed individuals, 478
Oppression, 10, 13, 19, 21, 26, 32, 38, 39, 42, 57, 63, 67, 71, 78, 81, 101, 103, 105, 109, 112, 118, 119, 149, 152, 153, 170, 176, 177, 178, 179, 180, 193, 215, 232, 233, 234, 235, 236, 237, 238, 240, 241, 257, 258, 261, 270, 278, 322, 341, 360, 361, 369, 379, 385, 388, 389, 390, 391, 402, 413, 415, 417, 424, 426, 428, 431, 432, 434, 436, 437, 448, 473, 475, 480, 483, 489, 492, 533, 534, 536, 537, 538, 539, 540, 541, 542, 543, 546, 548, 549, 550, 551
addressing systemic mechanisms of, 542
combating, 543
challenging, 543
counseling psychologists confronting, 3, 7, 13
eliminating, 7
impact on individuals and communities, 150–151
internalized, 261
long-term change and, 538
maintenance of, 150
multiple systems of for women, 261
of LGB individuals, 216–217
psychological stressors and, 151
self-blame of internalized, 258
systematic, 388
systems of, 432
women with disabilities and, 171–173
Oppression psychology, 38
Oppressor, research on, 544
Organizational behavior models, multicultural, 2
Organizational behavior theory, 380
Organizational change efforts, counseling psychologist, 490–493
external organizations, 493
for adoption/implementation of standards/guidelines increasing professional competence about marginalized populations, 490
for increased equity in organizational leadership/governance representation, 490
for modifying accreditation/ethical standards to increase profession's relevance, 490
for professional organizations to take public positions on human rights issues, 490
to institutionalize standards that delineate appropriate assessment/intervention for underserved groups, 490
within counseling psychology profession, 490–493
Organizational Change for Psychologists, APA, 5
Ostendorf, Henry, 286
Othering, 107, 111, 202, 424
Otherness, 149, 150
homelessness as, 210
seven categories of, 149
Outreach and prevention counseling competency, 2
Outreach programs, 89, 92, 94, 132
interventions, 132–133

Pacifism Scale, 447–448
Pakistan, 482, 483
Panchen Lama, The, 458, 459, 460
campaign, 459
Parental notification laws, 269
Parham, Thomas, 491
Parsons, Frank, 3, 44, 46, 251, 256, 277, 499, 508
Participant action frameworks, 438
Participant action methodologists, 437
Participant action research, 12, 205, 380, 422, 431, 432–433, 439
Participatory action research, 153, 203, 242, 544
Patient rights protections in health care system, 501
Patriarchy, 427
Peace, promotion of, 119
Peace activities, 516
Peace agreements, 481
Peacebuilding, 380, 384, 392, 422, 445, 482
activities, 464
women's approaches to, 445–446
Peace commissions, 476
Peace Corps, 47, 52, 503, 519, 536
Peace education, 390
Peacemaking, 384, 443
Peace movement, 517
Peace psychologists, 385, 482, 483

Peace psychology, 377, 380, 381, 384, 392, 443, 444, 464
 reconceptualization of, 384
Peace psychology literature, 377
Peace psychology movement, 381–382, 384
Peer mentor programs, 141
Peñalolén (Chile), consultation and training work in, 417–418, 539
 communication skills/stages of group development/group facilitation strategies workshop, 412
 conflict resolution/mediation/problem-solving skills workshop, 412
 Mentor Couples, 407, 409, 410, 411, 412, 413, 414, 415, 416, 417, 418
 postworkshop reviews, 415
 working with couples in crisis/principles of and strategies in motivational interviewing workshop, 412, 534
 workshop and training content, 411–417
 See also Chile; Empowerment model; Family faith education program (Peñalolén, Chile); Liberation theology
Penn State University, cultural diversity/social justice issues in counseling psychology training program of, 46
People of color:
 full inclusion, 270
 HIV/AIDS and, 361
 mental health concerns, 151
 salary/wage inequities, 262
 work-related inequities, 262
 See also Women of color
People's Liberation Army (PLA), 457
 invasion of Tibet, 453–454
People's Republic of China (PRC), 451, 457, 458, 461, 463, 464
 government in Tibet, 454
 See also Tibet-China conflict
People with disabilities, 151, 175, 179, 180, 257
 full inclusion, 270
 work-related inequities, 262
Personal elongation exercises, counseling psychologists and, 548
Personal involvement in communities, 548
Personal Responsibility and Work Opportunity Reconciliation Act, 294, 295, 296, 297, 298, 306, 307
Personal sphere, 173, 174
Phronesis, 203, 205, 212
Policy, future of counseling psychology, 546–548
Political action/activism, 241–242
Political action and giving groups, supporting social justice issues of personal and professional concern, 511
Political action organizations, professional psychological organizations,' 511
Political activism, 231, 233, 238, 241–242, 516
Political advocacy, 489, 490, 493, 495, 506, 512, 515, 543
 for social justice, 506–510
Political emancipation, 494
Political empowerment, 494
Political oppression, 390
Political paralysis, 489
Political prisoners, advocating for the release of, 1
Political/public policy-making process recommendations/suggestions, 510–512
Political strategizing, 543
Political systems, actively working to change, 1
Politics of compassion, 210
Policy analysis, 484
Positive-mindedness, 382
Positive youth development, 89–90
Positive youth development program, example of, 90–95
 challenges, 93–95
 components, 91
 goals and activities, 90
 language barrier, 90–91
 parent sessions, 91–92
 participant characteristics, 90
 teacher consultations, 92
Postcolonial studies, 422–423, 431, 438
Posttraumatic stress disorder, 541–542
 community, 542
 family, 542
 Hurricane Katrina and community-wide, 542
 torture-related, 541
 2005 Southeast Asia Tsunami, 542
 war-related, 541, 542
Poverty:
 long-term change and, 538
 mortality and living in, 326
 See also Poverty, high cost of health care and; Poverty line

Poverty, high cost of health care and, 339–344
cultural misunderstandings/poor communication with health care providers, 340
ethical considerations, 343–344
lack of health care prevention service, 339–340
low confidence in overall health/health care provider, 340–341
need for group prevention service for Southeast Asian refugees, 343
Southeast Asian refugee health problems, 341–342
Vietnamese refugees' health knowledge/practices, 342–343
Poverty line, 296
African Americans living below, 322
impact of living below, 320
Latinos living below, 322
Power, 417
Power dynamics, 233, 234–235, 257, 390, 414, 415, 421, 425, 427, 434, 436
client-therapist, 238, 240
Power in psychotherapy, analysis of, 240–241
Powerlessness, oppressed groups,' 149
Power sharing, 130, 389, 393, 394, 395, 396, 399, 402, 403, 425, 427, 428, 434, 435, 436, 437, 438, 482
engaging in, 396
models of collaboration, 422
partnership model, 392
relationships, 425, 434
values, 435
PPOs. *See* Preferred provider organizations
Practice, future counseling psychology, 541–543
diverse roles, 541
inclusiveness, 541
Praxis, 241, 432, 433, 476
Pre-employment training, 297
Preferred provider organizations, 522
Pregnancy, choices related to, 501
Prejudice, addressing through multicultural relationship skills workshops, 123–124
Prejudice reduction, 476
Prevention, 2, 5, 10, 21, 31, 45, 55, 79, 80, 82, 83, 84, 89, 117, 118, 119, 120, 127, 137, 141, 174, 192, 242, 244, 314, 315, 345, 347, 348, 360, 378, 385, 406, 464, 467, 512, 537, 541, 542
community, 81, 82
issues, 388
primary, 79, 82, 87, 89, 132, 330
programs, 87
secondary, 79, 132, 330, 346, 367
social justice and, 118–119
tertiary, 79, 133
See also Prevention, barriers to; Prevention interventions
Prevention, barriers to, 119–120
counseling course work overload, 120
individual-oriented counseling psychology students, 119–120
lack of skilled interdisciplinary collaborations, 120
reimbursement methods, 119
Prevention and social justice in New Mexico's schools, pressing needs for 120–126
needs/resources assessment, 121
promoting prevention through social justice training in teacher education, 122–124
promoting social justice through in-service prevention training with school personnel, 124–126
social justice service learning outreach to public school students, 122
Prevention interventions, 313, 314
versus reparative interventions, 315
Prevention research, complex measurement issues, 544
Prevention research methodology, need for training in, 545
Prevention science, 94
Prevention work and research, ethics of, 82–84
Prevention work with youth:
protective factors, 78
risk factors, 78
Preventive care, 522
Preventive interventions, 344
Preventive medicine, lack of knowledge of, 328
Primary care physicians, 522–523
Primary intervention, 316
Primary prevention interventions, 132, 137, 330
Principles for the Counseling and Therapy of Women, 272
Priority: Home!, 207–209, 210, 211
Prison reform, counseling psychologists and, 4

Privacy of mental health records, 504
Privilege, 25, 57, 62, 71, 77, 78, 132, 150, 157, 202, 233, 234, 235, 236, 237, 240, 241, 273, 320, 359, 388, 415, 417, 425, 426, 429, 433, 435, 438, 502, 521, 536, 541, 542, 544
heterosexual, 226, 544
male, 158
of the group, 402
white, 54
Privileged groups, 432
Problem-solving workshops, 476
Pro bono work, 21, 271
Procedural justice, multicultural-feminist approach to foster social justice and, 392–401
working principles of multicultural feminist consultation in international applications, 395–398
Procedural social justice, 393
Process evaluations, 352
Professional insularity, relative:
as social justice training challenge, 40, 41
Professional limitations, psychologist awareness of, 23–24
Professional practice advocate, 520
Profession-based initiatives, developing, 389
Program accreditation criteria, as social justice training challenge of, 40
Program evaluation, strategies for successful, 95–97
Program fidelity, 94
Programmatic interventions, 285
Programmatic vocational intervention, 253
Programmatic work-related interventions, 252
Project HOPE, 301, 302, 304, 305, 306
challenges and opportunities, 304–305
considerations for counseling psychology training and research, 305–306
impact of, 303–306
implications for training and research, 305–306
stage 4, 302
stage 1, 301, 303
stage 3, 301–302
stage 2, 301
Protective factors, 79
Provider protection legislation, 504
Psychiatric disability, homelessness and, 208
Psychic income, 286
Psychoeducation, 300, 313, 330–331
as holistic endeavor, 328
Psychoeducational parenting program, 379
Psychoeducational programming counseling competency, 2
Psychological colonialism, 380
Psychological colonization, 422, 424, 426, 427, 433
Psychological counselors:
in-service training by, 271
preservice training by, 271
supporting efforts of students/clients involved in organizational change activities, 271
Psychological direct service model, 521
Psychological distress, social class and, 324
Psychological hegemony, 438
Psychological measurement, 4
Psychological neocolonialism, 422, 427, 433
Psychological services in health insurance plans, parity for, 510
Psychologist-advocate, 496
for state psychological association, 496
Psychologist-legislators, 509–510
Psychologists:
hospital privileges for, 501
protection of scope of practice, 504
Psychologists for Social Responsibility, 493
special areas of advocacy, 493
Psychology:
exportation of U.S., 425–427
feminist criticism of mainstream, 232, 233
Psychosocial competence, 313
Psychosocial work in posttrauma, 476
Public health, 406–407
history, 315
Public information, 492
Public policy, 12, 47, 51, 95, 153, 189, 203, 210, 237, 276, 278, 288, 290, 315, 489, 493, 494, 495, 496, 499, 500, 502, 503, 506, 509, 510, 511, 512, 516, 529, 538, 540, 550, 560
counseling psychologist influence on framing of, 511
government and, 538
influencing, 95
on homelessness, 211
role of counseling psychologists in development of, 499

Public policy efforts:
state/territorial/provincial professional organizations, 510
state/territorial/provincial psychological associations, 510
Public policy makers, counseling psychologists as, 511

Qualitative assessment/evaluation, 142, 165, 304
Qualitative research, 32, 53, 56, 64, 104, 105, 163, 201, 206, 242, 290, 300, 306, 398, 398, 402, 439, 466, 484, 537, 544, 545
Quantitative assessment/evaluation, 57, 142
Quantitative research, 32, 40, 53, 56, 64, 290, 306, 398, 402, 439
Queer theory, 236

Race, social class and, 322, 332
Racial consciousness, 104, 113, 541
raising, 104
Racial differences in intelligence, "scientific" discourse about, 257
Racial diversity, 66, 166, 388
Racially diverse educational environments, positive outcomes for college students in, 266
Racial/ethnic minority individuals, 104, 524
counseling psychologists' advocacy for, 4
cultural barriers to accessing mental health services through managed care, 524
financial barriers to accessing mental health services through managed care, 524
inadequate quality and inappropriateness of services, 524
Racial identity, 5
assessment, 107–109
continuum, 107
definition, 101
Racial identity development, 101, 102, 107
assessing racial climate, 107–109
confronting dissonance, 107, 110–111
group settings and, 102
keys to facilitating, 107–111
maintaining caring perspective, 107, 109–110
organizations and, 102
Othering, 107, 111
schools and, 102
Racial Identity Interaction Model, Helms's Racial Identity Theory and, 100, 101–103
Racial identity statuses, 102
Racial identity theory, 81, 101, 105, 106. *See also* Racial Identity Theory, Helms's
Racial Identity Theory, Helms's, 100–105, 107, 113
Racial Identity Interaction Model and, 101–103
See also Heritage Project
Racial-social activism, 81, 100, 105, 107
school-based, 101
See also Heritage Project
Racism, 5, 28, 42, 44, 51, 65, 66, 67, 92, 100, 101, 102, 103, 104, 105, 107, 109, 110, 111, 112, 113, 132, 138, 149, 150, 151, 153, 160, 202, 232, 235, 236, 239, 261, 323, 361, 390, 474, 519, 542, 544, 546
as sociopolitical ill, 101
as topic in history books, 112
combating, 1, 5, 6, 110
dealing with through cultural identity groups, 138–139
deep structure of, 104
evolved manifestations of, 111
Hurricane Katrina and, 542
influence on White people, 544
in school settings, 81, 106
preventing institutional, 2
See also specific forms of racism
Radical feminism, 235
Radical feminist multicultural counseling for social justice, concepts and principles related to, 235–238
counseling for social justice, 237
critical theories, 235–236
liberation/critical psychology, 236–237
third-wave feminist psychotherapy, 237–238
Radical reflexivity, 434, 436
Radio Free Asia, 459
Rangzen House, 458
Realistic Group Conflict Theory, 458
Reconciliation, 392, 409, 411, 445, 478, 483
Reconciliation movements, 476
Reflexivity, 395
Reframing process, 482
Refugees International, 465, 536
Rehabilitation Acts:
1992, 172
1973, 172

Relational models and practices, ethics of, 437
Relational sphere, 173, 174
Relationism, developmental systems theories and, 102
Relationship building training, 480
Relationship Enhancement principles, 124
Relative deprivation theory, 393
Religious oppression, 149
Remediation, 117, 174, 279, 314, 316, 324, 327, 512
Reparative therapies, 219
Research, future counseling psychology, 543–546
Research on fiscal issues, social change through, 265–267
Resources, provision of:
  to be used in socially responsible ways, 271
  to shape institutional practices, 271
  to support organizations pursuing social justice aims, 271
Résumé, developing or refining, 302
Reverse discrimination, 263
Right to medical care without parent relinquishment, children's, 504
Rinpoche, Taktser, 450, 451, 456, 458, 459
Risk constellations, 78, 80
Risk-disease prevention, wellness promotion versus, 81–82
Risk factors, 78–79
Rogers, Carl, 465, 507
Role models, 56, 68, 78, 141, 385, 411, 449, 450, 466
  need for, 548
  positive, 284
Romania, 389, 398
Roosevelt, Franklin Delano, 506
Roving Résumé Writers, 286–287
Rubicon Programs, Inc., 287, 288
Rubicon Employment Services, 288
Rubicon Enterprises, 288
Russia, 389

Sadar Sarovar Project, 479, 481
Safe School Project, 124
Salvadoran gangs, peaceful approach to conflict resolution between, 472, 477–479
  awareness to engagement, 477–479
  educational scholarships, 477
  incarcerating gang members, 477
  negotiation intervention between gangs, 478
  small weapons control, 477
  technical skills training, 477
  understanding historical and contextual factors, 477
Same-sex marriage and adoption:
  legalization of, 268
  public policy decisions on, 496
Same-sex parents, APA opposition to discrimination against, 492
San Francisco Human Rights Commission, 264
San Francisco State University Counseling Department program, 286
SCANS skills, 301–302
School dropout, 83, 515
  after-school transportation services and decrease in, 134
  New Mexico, 121
School-based prevention programs, 139
  assets to effective service delivery, 130–131
  integrative theory of ecological setting, 130, 131–132
School prevention, 130, 137, 537
School to Work movement, 252
School-to-work transition, 277, 300
Scientist-practitioner-advocacy approach, 537
Scientist-practitioner-advocate model of training and professional contribution, 272, 277, 537
Scientist-practitioner continuum, 537
Scientist-practitioner model, 55, 272, 369, 371
  as social justice training challenge, 40
Scientist-professional model, 378
Secondary prevention interventions, 79, 132, 141, 316, 330, 346, 347, 367
Selective interventions, universal interventions versus, 79–81
Self-advocacy, 30, 282, 283, 490, 540
Self-awareness and reflection, 548, 549
Self-sufficiency, barriers to, 301
Senior citizens:
  addressing needs of, 510
  social class and, 322
Sensitization, 482
Service, commitment to, 533, 539–540
Service delivery, international embracing of U.S. models, 535
Service learning, 10, 39, 80, 117, 206, 285, 286, 439
  as experiential education, 60
  as mechanism for social change, 60

cross-cultural awareness/skills and, 60, 64–65
definition, 60
ethical issues related to 68
"in the streets" program, 286–287
outreach to public school students, 122
personal development and, 60
See also Roving Résumé Writers
Service learning courses in counseling psychology programs:
guidelines for implementing, 69–70
See also Service learning domestic violence course, innovative
Service learning domestic violence course, innovative, 59–60, 61–62
cross-cultural competence training, 61
didactic and experiential learning topics, 61
evaluation, 62
Helping Skills Model, 61
readings/service analysis reflection papers/seminars, 62
service projects, 62
volunteer shelter work, 61–62
Service learning model, social justice training through, 42
Sex education in schools, 270–271
Sexism, 1, 42, 149, 150, 176, 202, 232, 236, 261, 415, 546
Sexual abuse/assault, 239
Sexual assault crisis advocacy training, 244
Sexual exploitation by mental health providers, client protection from, 504
Sexual harassment, 280, 410, 490, 496
in academia, 501
workplace, 501
Sexual orientation:
as psychological construct, 226
Sexual orientation conversion, 219
Shadowing, 284, 302
Shadow jobs, 261
Simla Accord, 481
Skills training, 138, 288, 295, 297, 300, 301, 313, 396, 399, 477
Slaves, 108, 150
Social action, 2, 7, 8, 9, 18, 19, 21–23, 26, 37, 63, 101, 103, 104, 105, 109, 112, 114, 149, 152, 153, 186, 203, 244, 256, 279, 289, 299, 449, 474, 483, 484, 490, 493, 517
racial, 102
school-based, 101
Social action groups, 6, 8, 18
Social action on environmental justice, toward a framework for, 192–196
Social Action Trainers Project, 434
workshop, 436
Social activism, 70, 81, 100, 104, 105, 107, 108, 151, 393, 449
for lesbian and gay individuals, 151
identity development for members of marginalized groups and, 151
Social activists, 3, 25, 70, 449
Social advocacy, 3, 5, 7, 29, 57, 256, 388, 464, 505, 512, 543
Social Capitalism Resource Center, FastCompany's, 290
Social change, 10, 12, 31, 32, 47, 49, 52, 56, 59, 60, 61, 63, 68, 70, 71, 77, 83, 127, 136, 205, 217, 219, 232, 233, 241, 242, 257, 258, 265, 266, 273, 280, 283, 284, 289, 295, 303, 368, 390, 402, 418, 432, 433, 434, 436, 445, 447, 474, 476, 480, 484, 491, 537, 540, 543
Social change agents, challenges for counseling psychologists as, 548–550
personal development, 548–549
self-care, 549–550
Social change agents, helping clients consider becoming professional, 283–285
develop plan for contextual/cultural support, 284
develop strategies for increasing opportunities and decreasing barriers, 284–285
develop strategies for strengthening resilience, 285
identify life goals/career options, 284
identify mentors/role models/allies, 284
understand client's contextual cultural framework, 283
Social class, 20, 25, 28, 29, 111, 272, 277, 316, 318, 319, 320, 321, 322, 324, 326, 327, 330, 332, 370, 546
adolescent physical and emotional well-being and, 322
adult health risk behaviors and, 322
as psychological construct, 319–320
cancer and, 326
cardiovascular disease and, 324
dangerous jobs and, 326
diabetes and, 324
difficulty with activities of daily living and, 324
exposure to hazardous materials and, 326
fetal development and, 324
graded effects of across stratification range, 320
health and, 315, 319, 322, 323, 324, 326

health care and, 11
integrating into practice, 319
macro-level mechanisms, 323; micro-level mechanisms, 323
mortality and, 320–321
obesity and, 324
poor traumatic brain injury prognosis and, 324
predictive of poor knowledge/understanding/misinformation about medical conditions, 327
psychological distress and, 324
race and, 322, 332
senior citizens and, 322
social support and, 324
socioeconomic status and, 319–320
subjective health rating and, 324
subjective life expectancy and, 324
Social class in psychology, role of, 318–319
causes and contributors, 324–332
community-level interventions, 329–331
definitional issues in foundational literature, 323
foundational literature, 320–323
macro-level factors, 325–327
micro pathways in foundation literature, 323
social class as psychological construct, 319–320
social justice intervention, 327–329
specific interventions, 331–332
Social classism, Hurricane Katrina and, 542
Social class oppression, 63, 71, 537
Social control, government as instrument of, 216
Social Enterprise Alliance, 290
Social entrepreneurship, 285, 287–288, 290
partnerships in, 536
Social injustice, 490
Social institutions, actively working to change, 1
Social justice, 1, 2, 3, 5, 6, 7, 8, 9, 10, 11, 12, 13, 17, 18, 23, 24, 32, 37, 38, 41, 42, 44, 45, 46, 47, 48, 49, 51, 52, 53, 54, 55, 56, 57, 60, 71, 77, 79, 80, 84, 117, 118, 119, 120, 121, 122, 123, 124, 126, 127, 130, 136, 152, 155, 156, 157, 173, 174, 175, 176, 177, 179, 180, 181, 186, 190, 191, 192, 193, 215, 219, 220, 222, 223, 224, 226, 227, 232, 235, 236, 237, 239, 242, 243, 244, 251, 256, 270, 276, 277, 278, 280, 281, 282, 283, 285, 287, 289, 290, 294, 295, 313, 314, 316, 317, 332, 358, 359, 363, 367, 368, 369, 372, 379, 380, 384, 388, 389, 390, 392, 393, 403, 406, 407, 418, 437, 443, 449, 450, 458, 464, 472, 473, 475, 479, 480, 489, 490, 493, 494, 499, 502, 509, 510, 511, 512, 514, 516, 535, 537, 538, 540, 541, 543, 545, 547, 549
applying models of training in counseling psychology to, 39–40
counseling psychology graduate students, 317
Davis's definition, 45
defining in international contexts, 389–390
definitions, 1, 390
facilitating clients through dilemmas of, 281
politicizing of, 25–26
practice of, 28–31
rejuvenation of role as a notable force in counseling psychology, 277
working definitions of, 18–19
See also Social justice advocacy
Social justice, foundations for practicing from place of, 278–281
complex roles, 278, 279
cultural competence, 278–279
interdisciplinary contributions, 278
social justice resources, 278, 279
Social justice activism, 222, 224
Social justice activists, 277
Social justice advocacy, 190, 464, 490, 500, 502
activities, 502
counseling psychologists and, 1–2, 5, 6–7, 8, 12–13
See also Social justice
Social justice education, 380, 422
goal, 38
Social justice initiatives, 540
Social justice interventions:
community level to reduce social class disparities, 329–331
specific, 331–332
Social justice leadership, 37
Social justice research methodology, need for training in, 545
Social justice service learning outreach, New Mexico public school students and, 122
service learning activities, 122
See also Service learning
Social justice teams, 537
Social justice training in counseling psychology:
challenges for, 40–41
contributing to, 41–42
setting context for, 38

Social justice training recommendations:
adjunct faculty/field supervisors, 55–56
assessment and evaluation, 56
empowerment of students, 56
faculty retreats, 55
partnership building, 56
See also George Mason University Counseling and Development (C&D) Program
Social justice vision, 37
Social justice work, 2, 6, 8, 9, 11, 18, 20, 24, 25, 31, 40, 41, 47, 52, 53, 54, 56, 77, 110, 118, 130, 155, 156, 165, 167, 215, 217, 221, 223, 224, 225, 237, 257, 271, 272, 278, 279, 280, 284, 285, 358, 359, 381, 385, 418, 422, 450, 496, 499, 503, 508, 546, 547, 548, 549, 550
central mission, 278
central themes, 533–541
conceptualization of, 155
definitions, 60, 499
macro level, 155, 156
meso level, 155, 156
micro level, 155, 156, 158
multicultural education as, 62–63
See also Change, pace of; Community involvement; Interdisciplinary collaboration; Multilevel/systemic approaches; Service, commitment to
Social Learning Theory, 449
Social literacy, 112
Social oppression:
definition, 170
Roush model of ending, 177–178
women with disabilities and, 171–172
See also Oppression
Social/political advocacy, 492
Social psychology, 392
Social psychology research, 392
Social responsibility, 479
Social stigma, people with disabilities and, 170
Social support, social class and, 324
Social work, 392
Society of Counseling Psychology, 7, 223, 226, 378, 547
list-serve, 222
Society of Indian Psychologists, 152
Socioeconomic status:
health care access and, 325
health insurance coverage and, 325
social class and, 319–320
Sodomy laws, 269
Texas, 269
Southeast Asian Refugee Health Problems, 341
Southeast Asian refugees, 316, 338–355
attitudes regarding mental health, 349
chronic diseases, 348
concept of PTSD assessment, 355
infectious diseases upon arrival in United States, 341
lung cancer, 342
Massachusetts, 339
psychosomatic illness, 349
PTSD prevalence, 355
reasons for implementing health promotion program for, 343
smoking, 341–342
trauma and torture effects, 349
trauma survivors, 346
various cancers, 342
See also Cambodian refugees; Vietnamese refugees
Southern Mongolia, 443, 453, 457, 458
Southern Poverty Law Center, 123
Soviet Union, collapse of, 384
Stages of Change model, 412
Stereotyping, oppression and, 150
Strength-based shelters, 203, 211
Strengths-based counseling approach, 413
Stress-diathesis model, 78
Structural injustice, 484
Structural issues, 475
Structural oppression, patriarchal systems of, 426
Structural violence, 384
Student activism, 516
Student advocacy, 492, 519
Student-centered prevention projects, 77
Students of color, reaching level of "critical mass," 46
Students with learning barriers, identification and referral of, 123
Substance abuse, homelessness and, 208
Suicide, 216, 495
adolescent immigrants, 133
attempts, 136
LGB youth and, 217
rates, 133
rural boys, 133
teen, 121
Summative evaluations, 95, 351, 352, 353–354
Supportive networks, 548
Surgeon General's report, 317, 494

Sustainability, 389, 547
Systemic change efforts, challenges in promoting:
  adapting to shifts in nature of role/task, 159
  considering potential negative consequences, 159
  dealing with, 161
  negotiating divergent perspectives/value orientations in collaborations, 159
Systemic change efforts, counseling psychologists and, 166
Systems, 6, 7, 9, 11, 13, 49, 52, 65, 120, 131, 156, 194, 195, 196, 207, 211, 295, 319, 327, 384, 388, 395, 400, 401, 435, 446, 475, 480, 484, 496, 534, 537, 539, 547. *See also specific types of systems*
Systems advocacy, 492
Systems of care model, 132

Taiwan, 443, 458
Teacher education, promoting prevention through social justice training in, 122–123
Teachers College, Columbia University, 3
Teaching roles, counseling psychologist, 38
Team-building exercises, 399
Teenage Nonviolence Test, 447, 448
Teen pregnancy, New Mexico, 121
Telecommuting theory, 380
Temporary Aid for Needy Families programs, 295, 296, 297, 303, 304
Tenure criteria, traditional academic:
  as social justice training challenge, 40, 41
Terrorism, 384
Tertiary prevention interventions, 133, 141
Texas:
  HMO liability legislation, 526–527
  "right to sue" legislation, 525
  statewide initiatives advocating for consumer rights issues and psychological practice, 496
Texas Medical Association, 525, 526
Texas medical schools, minority enrollment in, 263
Texas Psychological Association, 519–520, 525, 526, 528
Thailand, trust and building relationships in, 539–540
Third National Conference for Counseling Psychology, 5
Third World. *See* Global South
Theory, future counseling psychology, 540–541
  cross-culturally valid, 541
  culturally sensitive, 541
  diverse disciplines and, 541
Tibet, history of, 451–453
Tibet activists, 455
Tibetan associations, 455, 456, 463
Tibetan Buddhism/Buddhists, 450, 452, 459
Tibetan Muslims, 452
Tibet-China conflict, 380, 443, 448, 450, 451, 453–456, 463, 466, 536
Tibet movement, 462–464, 466, 553. *See also* Free Tibet movement
Tibet support groups, 455, 456, 463
Time-out tenure tracks, 270
Title IX, 264, 265
  lawsuits related to safe educational environments for LGBT youth, 264
Tolerance of diverse worldviews, 473
Torture Survivors Program, 346
Toxic waste facilities, ethnic minority community locations of, 186, 187, 188–189, 190
Training, future of counseling psychology, 545–546, 548
  acquisition of a second language, 545
  action research skills, 545
  advocacy skills, 545
  appreciation/respect for diverse cultures/dynamics, 545
  community development, 545
  community organizing, 545
  consultation, 545
  employment law, 546
  field practica/internships at nongovernmental organizations, 545
  group work, 545
  interdisciplinary team members, 545
  multicultural counseling, 545
  obtaining knowledge about issues facing marginalized/oppressed communities, 545
  organizational change skills, 545
  organizational dynamics, 545
  outreach skills, 545
  prevention, 545
  program evaluation and development, 545
  research, 545
  treating low-SES clients, 546
  understanding of multiple and alternative roles, 545
  vocational psychology, 546
  welfare reform law, 546

Training models, applying counseling psychology to social justice, 39–40. *See also* Social justice training in counseling psychology
Training programs, counseling psychology:
case study in incorporating social justice in, 44
incorporating social justice curricula, 32
models of social justice training in, 45–47
See also George Mason University Counseling and Development (C&D) Program; Training, future of counseling psychology
Training roles, counseling psychologist, 38
Trait Theory, 449
Transformative action, 196
Transformative interventions, 103
Transformative Participatory Evaluation research, 494
Transformative psychopolitical validity, 270
Travel experience, 548, 549
Treatment goals, health care provider-patient conflict, 327
Treatment specialists, 501
Tripartite model, 278, 282
Trust, working in marginalized communities and, 539
Trust building, 430
challenge of in community-based programs, 88–89
Trust in leadership, 394
Tsunami disaster (2005 Southeast Asia), posttraumatic stress disorder and, 542
Tuskegee syphilis study, 344
Tyler, Leona, 256, 277

U.S. Civil Rights Commission, 279
U.S. Committee for Refugees, 47
U.S. Department of Education, 119
U.S. Department of Labor, 3
Employment and Training Administration, 297
U.S. Department of State, 459, 536
U.S. Office of Refugee Resettlement, 52
U.S. Supreme Court, 528
U.S. Terrorism Recovery Program, 346
Underserved racial/ethnic groups, distrust of outsiders in, 88
Underutilization of community mental health resources, 141
United Church of Christ Commission for Racial Justice report, 186
United Nations, 451, 454, 459, 465, 482, 536, 546
Universal interventions, selective interventions versus, 79–81
Universal school prevention program, mission statement of, 130, 137–142
access, 130, 139–140
evaluation, 130, 142
staffing and organization, 130, 140–141
University and Community Agency Partnership (U-CAP) program: HIV/AIDS and, 316, 317, 362–363, 370, 372
case examples, 365–367, 370–371
impact on counseling psychology training programs, 367–368, 369
impact on HIV/AIDS community, 363–365
University-community agency models of collaborative efforts, 536
University of California, Berkeley, 263
University of California, Los Angeles, 263
University of California Regents, 263
University of Kentucky counseling psychology program, 507
University of Michigan, 266
affirmative action in law school admissions, 263
University of Missouri–Columbia, 3
University of North Dakota Department of Counseling, 302
University of Oregon counseling psychology program:
counseling center, 277
ecological approach, 40
University of Pittsburgh domestic partner benefits, 264
University of Utah's Women's Resource Center, 243–244
counselor training, 244
Unlearning oppression work, 437
Urban Institute, 297
Utah Coalition Against Sexual Assault, 244
Uzbekistan, 389

Value-based prevention projects, 77
Values, attitude formation and, 444
Values Questionnaire, 445
Value Theory, 444–445, 466
motivational groups, 444
motivational types, 444
nonviolence and, 444–445
potential heuristic value of, 445
potential weakness of, 445
Vermont, civil unions in, 269
Veteran's Administration, 3
Veteran's rights, 509

Victim Informed Prosecution Project, 159–161, 163, 166
participating in, 159–162
Victimization/pathology model, 202–203
Vietnamese American Civic Association, 346, 350, 352, 353
Vietnamese Americans:
health insurance coverage rate, 339
poverty rate, 339
rating their health care, 340, 341
Vietnamese refugees, 315–316, 339, 346
acculturative stresses, 342
acquisition of health information, 340
depression and anxiety, 349
dual diagnosis of PTSD and major depression, 351
health education among, 536
health education and level of confidence in health, 351
health problems, 342
herbal remedy use, 342
intergenerational transmission of trauma, 341
lack of health knowledge, 342
mental health problems, 342
posttraumatic stress disorder, 341, 349
psychosomatic problems, 348
risk of chronic cardiovascular and gastrointestinal diseases, 345
Vietnam War trauma, 341, 348
women's cancers, 342
Vietnam War, 383, 516
trauma, 341, 348
Violence, 550
long-term change and, 538
Violence against women, 380, 435
projects, 422
Violence and aggression:
as social justice concern, 119
oppressed groups and, 149
preventing, 123–124
Vista, 284
Vocational advancement, people of color and, 257
Vocational barriers, 277
Vocational behavior, 534
Vocational/career advocacy, 252, 253, 256
Vocational counseling, 3, 4, 277. *See also* Career counseling
Vocational counselors, 499
Vocational guidance, 277
movement, 251
Vocational identity, 303
depression and, 306
Vocational issues, 388
Vocational meritocracy, 262
Vocational program development, social justice-oriented, 285
Vocational psychologists, 251–252
Vocational psychology, 251, 253, 299, 300, 304
social justice and, 299–300
Vocational Rehabilitation Act, 3
Vocational testing and counseling, bias in, 261
Vocational training, 510
programs, 509
Vocational Typology Theory, 449
Vocations Bureau (Boston, MA), 251
Voice of America, 459
Voice of Tibet, 459
Volunteerism theory, 380

Wage gaps, 260
War on poverty, 4
War on terror, 384
War trauma, political refugees and, 315–316, 317
Weapons of mass destruction, 465
Web of oppression, 431
Welfare recipients, voices of, 300
Welfare reform, 277, 294, 295–298
counseling psychologists and, 5
improving services, 535
movement, 253
psychology's response to, 298–299
public policy decisions on, 496
welfare-to-work programs, 297–298
Welfare reform policies, 202
criticism of, 202
Welfare Reform Task Force, 305
Welfare to Work Act, 202
Welfare-to-work grants, 296
Welfare-to-work interventions, interagency collaboration necessary for, 536
Welfare-to-work program, 253, 294, 304, 510
grounded in vocational and counseling psychology, 300
transitioning clients and mental health issues, 306
Well-being/ability to perform, psychologist awareness of, 24
Wellness promotion, risk-disease prevention versus, 81–82
Wellness promotion model, 541
Wellness promotion programs, 81–82
general, 81
selected, 81

Western hegemony, 390
Western models of consultation, 399, 401
Whistleblowers, working with, 546
Whistle-blowing, 281
White feminist therapy movement, 234, 235
Whitehall Studies, 321
Women, 150
  career barriers, 1
  college professors, 260
  college students, 259, 260
  corporate leadership roles, 260
  counseling psychologists' advocacy for, 4
  entry into nontraditional careers, 258–259
  full inclusion, 270
  salaries/wages, 261
  workplace and, 258
Women of color, 150, 234
  in psychology and social work, 234
  in STEM fields, 260
  systemic barriers to career development, 261
  wages, 261
  work-related inequities and, 261
Women of Color of North America, 190
Women's autonomy, 393
Women's movement, 151, 231, 401, 449
Women's Rights Association of Budapest, Hungary, 394–401, 534. *See also* NANE
Women with disabilities:
  acknowledging personal limitations, 178
  as "the other," 178
  common mistakes therapists make with, 176
  determining relationship to dominant culture, 177
  double handicap, 171
  isolation of, 179
  limited social options, 171
  marginalized, 177
  marriage and, 171
  self-acceptance, 178
  social justice for, 174–175
  social marginalization, 175
  social oppression of, 170, 171–172, 178
  socioeconomic status, 172
  stereotyping of, 171
  systematic rolelessness, 172
  vulnerability to abuse, 172
  work-related inequities and, 261, 262
  See also Women with disabilities, college-level
Women with disabilities, college-level, 172–173
  body image workshops, 177
  discrimination, 173, 175
  prejudice, 175
  social stigma, 173
  See also Women with disabilities
Work:
  advocacy about, 251
  double standards for behavior/accomplishment, 261
  equal access to for all, 251
  equality of, 251
  rights to, 251
Working-class people, U.S., 276
Working-class women, work-related inequities and, 261
Workplace advocacy, 490
Workplace benefits, extension of to unmarried or "domestic" partners, 263
Workplace climates, "chilly," 261
Workplace discrimination, 261, 277
  based on sexual orientation, 267
  confronting, 546
Workplace equity, importance of legal change in mandating, 265
Workplace harassment, 261
Workplace policies, changes in, 538
Workplace resources, inequities in distribution of, 261
Workplace tokenism, 261
Workplace violence, 261
  preventing, 546
Work preparation program, community-based 301–302
Work psychology, 251
World War II veterans, counseling psychologists working with, 2, 4
Wraparound model, 132

YMCA, 78, 132, 134
Youth Suicide Prevention bill, 494
YWCA Women in Jeopardy Program, 244

Zen Buddhism, 449

About the Editors

Rebecca L. Toporek, Ph.D., is an Assistant Professor in the Department of Counseling, Career and College Counseling Specializations, at San Francisco State University. Her research and writing interests include social justice and multicultural supervision and training, advocacy competencies, attitudes toward race and poverty, systemic interventions in discrimination, and career and college counseling. She was a co-editor of the *Handbook of Multicultural Competencies* and is a co-editor of an emerging electronic journal of social justice in counseling and psychology. Rebecca developed and maintains the Multicultural Competence and Social Justice Professional Development and Resources Webtool and is a founding member of Counselors for Social Justice of the American Counseling Association. She received her doctorate degree in counseling psychology from the University of Maryland, College Park. Her most important roles include mother, partner, sister, daughter, friend, colleague, teacher, ally, community member, and global citizen.

Lawrence H. Gerstein, Ph.D., is a Professor of Psychology and Director of Doctoral Training in Counseling Psychology at Ball State University, Muncie, Indiana. He has published over 75 scholarly articles and book chapters, and is active in professional organizations serving on numerous editorial boards and committees. Professor Gerstein's academic expertise is in community, peace, and family psychology, and consultation and research methodology. He is a Fellow of the Society of Counseling Psychology of the American Psychological Association. Gerstein was honored with the Carl D. Perkins Government Relations Award from the American Association for Counseling and Development, and the Kitty Cole Human Rights Award from the American Counseling Association. Professor Gerstein earned his Ph.D. in counseling and social psychology from the University of Georgia in 1983. Professor Gerstein became involved in the Tibet Movement in the 1980s when Taktser Rinpoche (His Holiness The Dalai Lama's oldest brother) requested his help. Gerstein co-founded the International Tibet Independence Movement (ITIM) with Rinpoche. Since 1998, Gerstein has been the president of ITIM (www.rangzen.org), which is a not-for-profit volunteer organization comprised of over 20,000 supporters around the world dedicated to returning Tibet to the Tibetans through nonviolent action.

Nadya A. Fouad, Ph.D., is a professor in the Department of Educational Psychology at the University of Wisconsin–Milwaukee and training director of the Counseling Psychology program there. She was president of Division 17 from 2000 to 2001, and previously served as vice president for Diversity and Public Interest (1996–1999). She is chair of the Council of Counseling Psychology Training Programs (2003–2007). She serves on the editorial boards of the *Journal of Counseling Psychology, Journal of Vocational Behavior, Career Development Quarterly,* and the *Journal of Career Assessment.* She has published articles and chapters on cross-cultural vocational assessment, career development, interest measurement, cross-cultural counseling, and race and ethnicity. She has served as co-chair (with Patricia Arredondo) of the writing and implementation team with Division 45 of the Multicultural Guidelines, which were approved by APA in August 2002 and published in the *American Psychologist* in May 2003.

Gargi Roysircar is the Founding Director of the Antioch New England Multicultural Center for Research and Practice (www.multiculturalcenter.org) and Professor in the Department of Clinical Psychology, Antioch New England Graduate School. She does research on the interface of acculturation and ethnic identity with the mental health of immigrants and ethnic minorities, worldview differences between and within cultural groups, multicultural competencies and training in professional psychology, and multicultural assessment and instrumentation. She has authored several journal articles and chapters on these topics. Her recent co-edited books are *Multicultural Competencies: A Guidebook of Practices (2003)* and *Multicultural Counseling Competencies 2003: Association for Multicultural Counseling and Development (2003).* Gargi Roysircar has recently been involved in tsunami recovery efforts in Tamil Nadu, India, and is now focusing on education in disaster trauma and psychosocial skills specific to disaster work. She is a Fellow of the American Psychological Association (APA) and a Past President of the Association for Multicultural Counseling and Development. She is the editor of the *Journal of Multicultural Counseling and Development.* She was awarded the 2002 Extended Research Award of the American Counseling Association.

Tania Israel is an Associate Professor in the Counseling, Clinical, and School Psychology Program at the University of California, Santa Barbara. She received her doctoral degree in counseling psychology from Arizona State University in 1998, and was honored with the Barbara Kirk Award for Outstanding Graduate Student Research from the Society of Counseling Psychology and the Glen E. Hubele National Graduate Student Award from the American Counseling Association. She received a 5-year career development grant from the National Institute of Mental Health to develop her research on counseling services for lesbian, gay, bisexual, and transgender clients. She is the recipient of awards for her service to the UCSB Resource Center for Sexual and Gender Diversity and for her work with the Peace Education Project of Santa Barbara. She is the current Membership Chair and past newsletter editor for the Section for the Advancement of Women of the Society of Counseling Psychology. Her first act of social justice occurred at age 4 when she wrote a letter to President Nixon asking him to stop the war in Vietnam. She continues her dedication to social justice through her scholarship, teaching, mentoring, and service related to feminism, sexuality, marginalized individuals, intersecting identities, and social change.

About the Contributors

Tamara M. Abousleman is a doctoral student in the counseling psychology program at the University of Utah. She earned her B.A. in psychology at Pomona College in 1993. Her current scholarly pursuits include feminist multicultural therapy outcomes and outcomes measurement and qualitative research on career issues of women with HIV. Her counseling expertise includes a focus on issues particular to being a woman or an adolescent girl in U.S. society and the impact that multicultural (broadly defined) issues have on all people. As a biracial, middle-class feminist, she is beginning a process of integrating multiple sources of knowledge, information, and wisdom into her professional and personal activities.

Eve M. Adams is an Assistant Professor and Director of Training for the Counseling Psychology Ph.D. Program at New Mexico State University. She received her doctorate in counseling psychology in 1988 from The Ohio State University and has served as a psychologist at the University of Akron's Counseling and Testing Center. Eve serves on the editorial board for the *Journal of Counseling Psychology* and has served on the *Journal of Counseling and Development* editorial board. Her research interests are multicultural identity development, gender role beliefs, sexual orientation, and career development. Her teaching interests are supervision, counseling skills, assessment, and career counseling.

Dorienna M. Alfred (Harris) is a Psychological Resident at the University of Missouri Counseling Center in Columbia, Missouri. Her areas of research include chronic illness in women of color and applications of racial identity theory to teacher and counselor training.

Margret E. Bell, Ph.D., recently received her doctorate from the Department of Counseling, Developmental, and Educational Psychology at Boston College. Focusing her research on victims' reactions to trauma and community and justice system responses to domestic violence, she has spent time in a number of settings providing counseling and advocacy services to victims as well as working on domestic violence public policy issues. Her research has been honored with awards from the Association for Women in Psychology, the Society for the Psychological Study of Social Issues, and the American Psychological Association's Divisions 35 and 12.

Fred Bemak is currently a Professor and the Program Coordinator for the Counseling and Development Program in the Graduate School of Education at George Mason University. He has done extensive work in the areas of social justice and mental health, working in 30 countries and throughout the United States. Fred is a former Fulbright Scholar, a Kellogg International Fellow, and a recipient of the International Exchange of Experts and Research Fellowship through the World Rehabilitation Fund. At George Mason University, Fred has facilitated the development of master's and doctoral training programs that emphasize multiculturalism, social justice, leadership, and advocacy and has been working with these issues for more than 30 years.

Carrie L. Castañeda is a doctoral candidate in the counseling psychology program at the University of Utah. She completed her predoctoral internship at the UC Davis counseling center, where her emphasis was the academic track of the Multicultural Immersion Program. Carrie works to make the spirit of social justice present in her clinical and research interests through a focus on the provision of multiculturally competent services to traditionally underserved populations. Her current research qualitatively examines the childhood experiences of Mexican heritage women who acted as language and cultural brokers for their parents and community.

Angela M. Cavett is a practicing psychologist at Badlands Human Service Center in Dickinson, North Dakota, and is an adjunct professor at Dickinson State University. She received her Ph.D. in counseling psychology from the University of North Dakota. Professional interests include child and adolescent therapy; play therapy; attachment issues; ethics; psychologists' involvement in social change; and career aspirations of underserved groups, including welfare recipients and felons.

Bobbie L. Celeste, Ph.D., serves as the Director of Professional Affairs for the Ohio Psychological Association and counsels and consults with individuals and groups. A graduate of the Counseling Psychology program at The Ohio State University, she is active with the Society of Counseling Psychology, serving two terms as their Federal Advocacy Coordinator. In recognition of her work on behalf of professional psychology, she received the American Psychological Association Karl F. Heiser Presidential Award in 2004. She is a member of APA Divisions 17, 31, 35, 45, and 52.

Robert C. Chope is Professor of Counseling at San Francisco State University, where he coordinates the Career Counseling Program. He is also the founder of the Career and Personal Development Institute in San Francisco, a practice that he has had for more than 25 years. Dr. Chope received his Ph.D. from the University of Minnesota, Department of Psychology. He is a licensed psychologist and a licensed marriage and family therapist, as well as the author of *Dancing Naked: Breaking Through the Emotional Limits That Keep You From the Job You Want* and *Shared Confinement: Healing Options for You and the Agoraphobic in Your Life,* both published by New Harbinger Publications. His newest book is *Family Matters: The Influence of the Family in Career Decision Making* (Pro-Ed, 2005). He is a fellow of the National Career Development Association (NCDA), winner of the 2002 Robert Swan Lifetime Achievement in Career Counseling Award, and a winner of the 2004 NCDA Outstanding Career Practitioner of the Year award.

Rita Chi-Ying Chung is an Associate Professor in the Counseling and Development Program, College of Education and Human Development, George Mason University. Her research focuses on social justice and multiculturalism through the psychosocial adjustment of refugees and immigrants, interethnic group relations and racial stereotypes, coping strategies in dealing with racism and its impact on psychological well-being, cross-cultural and multicultural issues in mental health, and cross-cultural achievement motivation and aspirations. Dr. Chung has lived and worked in the Pacific Rim, Asia, and Latin America.

Rhanda B. Clow is Training Director in the University Counseling Center at the University of North Dakota. She received her Ph.D. in counseling psychology from the University of North Dakota. Her primary professional interests include training, counselor supervision, suicidality, experiential learning, clinical and training outcomes, and the welfare-to-work transition. Her current research is on training competencies and outcomes. Other research and clinical interests include personality disorders, psychological assessment, and administration.

Lisa Cosgrove, Ph.D., is a clinical and research psychologist in the Graduate School of Education at the University of Massachusetts at Boston. She has published numerous articles and book chapters on critical psychology, research methods, feminist therapy, and theoretical and philosophical issues related to clinical practice. Her scholarship includes work in the areas of community psychology, social policy, women and homelessness, and the aftermath of trauma. Dr. Cosgrove's research has been supported through grants from NIMH (to the Murray Center of the Radcliffe Institute, Harvard University) and from the University of Massachusetts. She recently co-edited *Bias in Psychiatric Diagnosis* (Rowman & Littlefield) with Paula Caplan.

Brian Daly is a Clinical Child Psychology Intern at the University of Maryland School of Medicine/VA Maryland Health Care System. He is currently working on his doctoral degree in the APA-approved program in Counseling Psychology at Loyola University Chicago. He received a master's degree in counseling psychology from Boston College and a master's degree in general psychology from Boston University. Mr. Daly has research interests related to risk and protective factors for urban children of color, the impact of poverty on the development of young children, prevention and clinical interventions for minority children and families, and university-community collaborations.

Rachel E. Darrow is a third-year doctoral student in counseling psychology at the University of North Dakota. She received her Bachelor of Arts from the University of Wisconsin–Eau Claire. Her primary research interests include secondary traumatic stress and posttraumatic stress disorder. Her professional goals and interests include supervision, consultation for secondary traumatic stress in the workplace, program development, and disaster relief work. She is also interested in volunteering abroad for Doctors Without Borders.

M. Meghan Davidson, Ph.D. is currently a Research Assistant Professor in the Department of Educational, School, and Counseling Psychology at the University of Missouri–Columbia. She earned her doctoral degree in counseling psychology from the University of Missouri–Columbia, and her dissertation consisted of constructing sex-specific scales to measure adolescent attitudes regarding dating relationships in an effort to create appropriate evaluation tools for sexual assault and relationship violence prevention. Her research interests include prevention, sexual assault and domestic violence, multicultural issues broadly defined, and career development. Dr. Davidson was awarded the Council of Counseling Psychology Training Programs (CCPTP) Outstanding Graduate Student Award in 2003.

Sherri L. (Murry) Edwards is the staff psychologist at the Lawton VA Outpatient Clinic in Fort Sill, Oklahoma. As a practitioner and researcher, Dr. Edwards's primary interest is bridging the gap between science and practice relative to mental health and health promotion of African Americans. She completed her dissertation on the self-efficacy of pre-service teachers in the Heritage Project. She maintains a small private practice, including consultation in HIV prevention and evaluation.

Ruth E. Fassinger received her Ph.D. in psychology from The Ohio State University in 1987 and is a Professor in the Counseling Psychology Program at the University of Maryland. Her scholarly work is in the psychology of women and gender, sexuality and sexual orientation, the psychology of work, and advocacy and social justice issues. She is an APA Fellow in Divisions 17, 35, and 44; has served as Vice President for Scientific Affairs in Division 17 and Secretary-Treasurer in Division 44; and currently serves on the editorial boards of *Psychology of Women Quarterly* and *Journal of Counseling Psychology.* She has received numerous awards for her scholarship, teaching, and professional contributions, and maintains a therapy practice specializing in issues related to gender and sexuality.

Susanna M. Gallor is a doctoral student in counseling psychology at the University of Maryland, College Park. She is a student affiliate in the Society of Counseling Psychology, the Society for the Psychological Study of Lesbian, Gay, and Bisexual Issues, and the Society for the Psychological Study of Ethnic Minority Issues. She was previously a Student Representative for the Section for Lesbian, Gay, and Bisexual Awareness as well as the Maryland State Advocacy Coordinator within the American Psychological Association Graduate Student Advocacy Coordinating Team. Her research interests include lesbian and gay issues, social support, the intersections of multiple identities, and multicultural training and competence.

Patricia G. Garcia is a predoctoral student in counseling psychology at the Indiana University School of Education in the Department of Counseling and Educational Psychology. She holds a master's degree in counseling and a master's degree in biochemistry. She has completed her internship with a specialization of diversity issues at Ball State University Counseling Center. Patricia is a native of Argentina and immigrated to the United States 13 years ago. Her research interests focus on issues of oppression in general and more specifically on the impact of racism on interpersonal and psychological well-being. Currently, she is studying the intersection between spiritual development and racial identity development as it applies to White counselors and psychologists.

Rufus Gonzales is a doctoral candidate in counseling psychology at Loyola University Chicago. He has previously earned a Master's of Education in Counseling and Personnel Services from the University of Maryland at College Park (1997) and a Bachelor of Fine Arts in Graphic Design from the University of Illinois at Urbana-Champaign (1995). His research interestes include subjective well-being in urban youth and resilience in Latino populations.

Lisa A. Goodman is an Associate Professor in the Department of Counseling, Developmental, and Educational Psychology at Boston College. She is co-chair of the American Psychological Association's Task Force on Male Violence Against Women and former James Marshall Public Policy Research Fellow at APA. Her research focuses on institutional and community responses to intimate partner violence; the role of coercion in domestic violence; and the effects of violence against underserved women, including homeless, low-income, and severely mentally ill populations. In recent years, she and her students have become interested in alternative models of mental health intervention, especially for low-income women.

Adam Guilmino is a fourth-year doctoral student in the counseling psychology program at the University of North Dakota. He received his bachelor's degree from Loyola University of New Orleans. His dissertation focuses on career success among Native American populations. Other research interests include the school-to-work transition, students' engagement in high school, and domestic violence awareness and work needs of domestic violence survivors. Upon graduation, Adam plans to practice in a community mental health clinic in a rural community serving underrepresented clientele.

Donna M. Hawxhurst is a staff consultant at the University of Utah's Women's Resource Center (WRC), where she also acts as training coordinator for the Feminist Multicultural Counseling Training Practicum. She received her Ph.D. in counseling psychology at Arizona State University in 1972 and has worked primarily as a practitioner, teacher, and consultant for most of her professional life, always welcoming opportunities to collaborate with her partner, Sue Morrow, in projects directed toward social justice. A longtime feminist therapist and activist, she has been committed to integrating a broad multicultural perspective into her life and her work. Her own cultural lenses and worldview have been enormously influenced by her identity as a White, middle-class, lesbian feminist and by her involvement since the early 1960s in civil rights and social justice movements.

Nancy Hensler-McGinnis, M.A., is pursuing a doctorate in counseling psychology at the University of Maryland, College Park. Her first research involvements included qualitative studies on women's career development. More recently, Nancy's clinical experiences at the Center for Posttraumatic Disorders (Psychiatric Institute of Washington) and as the campus victim advocate for survivors of sexual assault and relationship violence have furthered her commitment to integrating counseling practice with cross-disciplinary and culturally attuned theory and research, specifically in the areas of violence against women, trauma recovery, and women's health.

Mary Ann Hoffman is a Professor in the counseling psychology program, Department of Counseling and Personnel Services, at the University of Maryland. She received her Ph.D. in psychology from the University of Minnesota with a specialty in counseling psychology. Her primary areas of research and writing are the psychosocial aspects of chronic disease and wellness, psychotherapy process and outcome, and counselor training and supervision. She is the author of a book titled *Counseling Clients With HIV Disease: Assessment, Intervention, and Prevention* (Guilford, 1996), which was designated by Doody's rating service as one of the top health/medical books of 1997. She is the author or co-author of more than 40 other book chapters, journal articles, and monographs. She has presented more than 60 papers at international and national conferences. She is the Associate Editor of *The Counseling Psychologist* and a Fellow of Division 17 (Society of Counseling Psychology) of the American Psychological Association. She is the 2002 recipient of the Dorothy Booz Black Award for Health Counseling Psychology (Society of Counseling Psychology) of the American Psychological Association.

Joshua A. Hopps is a graduate student in counseling psychology and neuropsychology at the University of Iowa and is currently working at the University of Iowa Hospitals and Clinics. He is interested in the interface between the health care system and individuals from different cultural and social class groups at the individual and systemic levels. Other interests include neuropsychological testing with culturally diverse individuals and trends in referrals for neuropsychological testing throughout the history of the subspecialty. He and his wife are expecting their first child.

Sharon G. Horne is an Associate Professor of Counseling Psychology at the University of Memphis. Her research and teaching interests include gay, lesbian, bisexual, transgendered issues and gender, as well as domestic violence and international social justice concerns. She has lived and worked in many postcommunist countries, including Russia, Romania, Hungary, and Uzbekistan, as well as in West Africa.

Uyen K. Huynh is a clinical psychologist specializing in developmental disabilities and traumatic brain injury. Her research focuses on refugee mental health and public policy. She is currently working on a book on disaster mental health relief work.

Cindy L. Juntunen is a Professor in the Department of Counseling at the University of North Dakota. She received her Ph.D. in counseling psychology from the University of California at Santa Barbara. Her primary research interest includes vocational psychology, with an emphasis on the work and social needs of marginalized groups. Her work has focused on the school-to-work transition, the welfare-to-work transition, and vocational needs and issues for American Indian populations. Her current research is addressing the integration of vocational and emotional needs among disenfranchised populations. Other research and teaching interests include supervision, feminist therapy, and ethical decision making.

Jennifer Kaplan is a doctoroal student in the counseling psychology program at the University of Maryland.

Ouyporn Khuankaew is the director of the Thailand-based organization International Women's Partnerships for Peace and Justice. Ouyporn and Kathryn Norsworthy work individually and collaboratively in Asia and the United States on projects devoted to building communities of peace and justice within grassroots communities and with governmental and nongovernmental groups.

Doris Kirkpatrick, M.A., is a student in the counseling psychology doctoral program at Ball State University. She is specializing in the study of Peace Psychology and has presented on this topic at several conferences, including the First Annual (2004) Gandhian Nonviolence Conference, Memphis, TN. Current areas of research and clinical interest to her include the development level, and stalking research.

William M. Liu, Ph.D., is Assistant Professor of Counseling Psychology at the University of Iowa. He received his doctorate from the University of Maryland at College Park. His research interests are in social class, classism, poverty, homelessness, men and masculinity, and multicultural competencies. He is co-editor of the *Handbook for Multicultural Competencies in Psychology and Education,* and he is on the editorial review boards for *The Counseling Psychologist, Cultural Diversity and Ethnic Minority Psychology, Psychology of Men and Masculinity, Journal of Multicultural Counseling and Development,* and the *Clinician's Research Digest.*

Michael I. Loewy grew up in Los Angeles; did his undergraduate work in sociology and psychology at University of Nevada, Las Vegas; and received his master's degree and Ph.D. in counseling psychology at University of California, Santa Barbara, in 1994. He has been a Professor of Counseling and Counseling Psychology since then. Dr. Loewy's career has been focused on teaching and supervising graduate students in clinical training and theory as well as research. His primary interest and emphasis is multicultural competence. All of his research and teaching reflects his passion for social justice and serving the underserved and underrepresented.

Susan S. Mathews obtained her doctorate in counseling psychology from the University of Memphis. She pursued advanced clinical training in the counseling centers at the University of Minnesota and The Ohio State University. Dr. Mathews has worked as a licensed psychologist in the Psychological and Career Counseling Unit at the University of Memphis since 2003. Her clinical interests include women's issues, emotional change, relational violence, sexual orientation/identity, and supervision/training. Her research interests also include international consultation, particularly in Eastern Europe, as well as implementing qualitative methods to explore therapeutic outcome and effectiveness.

Christopher J. McNally is currently a doctoral candidate in the Collaborative Program in Counseling Psychology at the University of Akron. A 3-year appointment to Ohio's largest community mental health board furthered his commitment to social justice–training environments, the subject of his doctoral dissertation research. He completed his psychology internship at the Counseling and Consultation Service of The Ohio State University and has served the Society of Counseling Psychology as Student Affiliate Group Co-Chair. Related interests include constructivist and postmodern approaches to psychotherapy and cultural interpretation, philosophical and historical foundations of psychology, and the psychology/public policy interface.

Robert H. McPherson is Executive Associate Dean and Professor at the University of Houston where he teaches a mental health public policy course. He and Stewart Pisecco are co-founders of a software company providing behavioral management programs for schools and mental health facilities. Former president of the Texas and Houston Psychological Associations, and former chair of the Council of Counseling Psychology Training Programs, Bob is an APA Fellow, a member of the National Academies of Practice, and recipient of the APA Karl Heiser Award for his legislative efforts. He is current Director of Professional Affairs and APA Council representative for the Texas Psychological Association.

Benedict T. McWhirter, Ph.D., is an associate professor in the counseling psychology program at the University of Oregon, where he has served for most of his tenure as Director of Training. Among his scholarship activities, he co-authored *At-Risk Youth: A Comprehensive Response* (3rd ed., 2004, Brooks/Cole). His scholarship focuses on at-risk youth, college student development, training issues, and multicultural competence within these areas. He was named a 2004 Fulbright Scholar to Chile, where he taught at the Universidad del Desarrollo (University of Development) in Santiago, conducted research on Chilean youth and their families, and provided pro bono community consultation and training.

Ellen Hawley McWhirter, Ph.D., is an associate professor in the counseling psychology program at the University of Oregon. A recipient of the Fritz and Lynn Kuder Early Career Scientist-Practitioner Award, Dr. McWhirter authored *Counseling for Empowerment* (1994, ACA Press) and co-authored *At-Risk Youth: A Comprehensive Response* (3rd ed., 2004, Brooks/Cole). She was a 2004 Fulbright Scholar to Chile, conducting research on Chilean youth, providing consultation and training in the community, and serving as a visiting professor to the Universidad de Chile in Santiago. Her scholarship focuses on empowerment in counseling, training, and consultation, and on adolescent vocational development.

Scott L. Moeschberger, M.A., is a Ph.D. candidate from Ball State University where he received the Benjamin V. Cohen Peace Fellowship to conduct research on reconciliation in Northern Ireland. He recently completed his pre-doctoral internship at the University of Missouri–Columbia. Currently he works for Taylor University as the On-site Academic Director for the Irish Studies Program in Greystones, Ireland. His travels for humanitarian and research work have taken him to Northern Ireland, Ireland, Russia, Kenya, and Albania. His current research is focused on empathy, forgiveness, and social justice in post-conflict communities.

Ana Y. Montes de Vegas is a doctoral candidate in the counseling psychology program at the University of Utah. She is currently completing a predoctoral internship at the University of Hawaii, Manoa. She completed a practicum at the University of Utah's Women's Resource Center. Her academic interests include multicultural and gender issues, student leadership, and stereotype development. Her research interests include ethnic identity and acculturation, standardized testing, feminist/multicultural supervision, and stereotypes. She has a strong commitment to teaching, psychotherapy, research, and outreach.

Melissa Morgan received a Bachelor of Arts degree in psychology from Southwestern University in 1991 and a Master of Arts degree in clinical psychology from Stephen F. Austin State University in 1996. She is currently pursuing a Ph.D. in counseling psychology at Loyola University Chicago. She is a Teaching Fellow for the School of Education and teaches such courses as Identity and Pluralism and Adolescent Psychology. Ms. Morgan's research interests include the study of cross-cultural resilience and subjective well-being.

Susan L. Morrow is an associate professor in the counseling psychology program at the University of Utah. She earned her Ph.D. in counseling psychology at Arizona State University in 1992. Her scholarly interests include multicultural, gender, and lesbian/gay/bisexual/transgender (LGBT) issues and qualitative research methodology. Her academic interests have been informed by her herstory of activism in the civil rights, women's liberation, peace, and LGB movements since the 1960s. Her counseling expertise includes a focus on women, adult survivors of childhood trauma, and LGB issues. As a European American, middle-class, lesbian feminist, she is committed to an ongoing and often complicated process of integrating multicultural issues into her consciousness and writing. She has been partners in life, work, scholarship, and politics with co-author Donna Hawxhurst for 30 years.

Alisa Matteson Mundt, Psy.D., received her doctorate degree in clinical psychology from the Illinois School of Professional Psychology in Chicago. She also studied rehabilitation counseling at the University of South Florida in Tampa, and she completed her predoctoral internship at Grand Valley State University in Michigan. She is currently completing her postdoctoral fellowship at Health and Psychological Services at William Rainey Harper College in Illinois. She is an Adjunct Professor at Argosy University in Chicago. Her interests include the multicultural aspects of disability, college/university counseling, professional development, and psychoanalytic theory/practice.

Kathryn L. Norsworthy is a licensed counseling psychologist and Cornell Distinguished Professor of Graduate Studies in Counseling, Rollins College, Winter Park, Florida. She is also the executive director of the U.S.-based nongovermental organization (NGO) Ahimsa International: Projects for Peace, Justice and Mindful Living. Ouyporn Khuankaew and Kathryn work individually and collaboratively in Asia and the United States on projects devoted to building communities of peace and justice within grassroots communities and with NGO and governmental groups.

Karen M. O'Brien, Ph.D., is an Associate Professor in the Department of Psychology at the University of Maryland. Her interests include conducting applied research that can be used to advance the vocational success of at-risk populations or promote the functioning of adoptive families. Dr. O'Brien serves on the Board of Directors for House of Ruth, a program for battered and homeless women and their children in Washington, DC. She developed a service learning course focused on domestic violence that included the placement of more than 25 student advocates in volunteer positions at the House of Ruth.

Alicia Ordóñez graduated as a psychologist from the Universidad Centroamericana "José Simeón Cañas," El Salvador. She worked at its psychology department and coordinated its psychology clinic. Alongside traditional counseling services, the clinic collaborated in different projects and movements to address needs identified by vulnerable sectors. She also offered independent consultant services to national and international organizations working for human and children's rights. This line of work included doing research to unveil structural injustice and influence policy making. She graduated with a double master's degree in pre-clinical and educational psychology and is completing her doctorate in counseling psychology at Ball State University, Indiana.

Barbara J. Palombi is the director of the Counseling and Career Development Center at Grand Valley State University, Allendale, Michigan. She received her Ph.D. from Michigan State University and has recently received a diploma in counseling psychology from the American Board of Professional Psychology. Her writing emphasis is on professionals and students with disabilities.

Sheetal Patel, M.A., is a doctoral candidate in counseling psychology in the Department of Counseling and Personnel Services at the University of Maryland. Her professional interests include violence against women, the acculturation and adaptation experiences of children from immigrant families, and vocational interventions for at-risk populations. Sheetal was enrolled in Dr. O'Brien's service learning course on domestic violence, and conducted her undergraduate honors thesis on assessing the growth and learning of students who completed this course.

Shonali Raney is a graduate student at Ball State University. She works as part of a voluntary organization with different underprivileged groups, including projects such as working in the rural areas of India, interacting with individuals with disabilities, street children and the children of prostitutes, and highlighting a social issue each year through a poster exhibition. Shonali has also worked in a grade school providing counseling and helping the school make counseling services available.

Clare Reilly is a second-year counseling psychology doctoral student and Cullen Presidential Scholar at the University of Houston. She graduated with honors from Rice University with an undergraduate degree in psychology. Clare is a member of Phi Beta Kappa and was the recipient of the Rice University John W. Brelsford Award for outstanding contributions in psychology. She received an APA Student Travel Award to present her research at the 2004 APA Annual Convention in Hawaii. Her research interests include etiological factors in eating disorders, adult attachment theory, and romantic relationship processes.

Venessa Rempel is a doctoral student in counseling psychology at the University of North Dakota, where she also received her M.A. in counseling. Her research interests include religion and spirituality in the counseling process and performance anxiety. Currently, she is examining musical performance anxiety and how it interacts with anxiety sensitivity and vocational identity to predict career success among classically trained musicians.

Azara L. Santiago-Rivera, Ph.D., is an Associate Professor in the Department of Educational Psychology, Counseling Psychology program at the University of Wisconsin–Milwaukee. She earned a doctorate in counseling from Wayne State University, Detroit, Michigan. Her publications and research interests include multicultural issues in the counseling profession, bilingual therapy, and the impact of environmental contamination on the biopsychosocial well-being of Native Americans. She has presented on these topics at major conferences and has published in such journals as the *Journal of Professional Psychology: Research and Practice,* the *Journal of Counseling and Development,* the *Journal of Community Psychology,* the *Journal of College Student Development,* and the *Latino Research Review.*

Christa K. Schmidt, Ph.D., is a visiting Assistant Professor in Counseling Psychology at the University of Maryland, College Park. She completed her doctorate at the University of Missouri–Kansas City in 2004, has presented her research at multiple conferences, and published in scholarly journals. As an early career counseling health psychologist, Christa's research program is focused on the impact of chronic and terminal illness on individuals, families, and communities. Her work with women with HIV, cancer patients and their families, and the training of counseling psychology graduate students as social change agents all informed her contribution to this innovative publication in counseling psychology.

Jui Shankar, M.A., is a third-year doctoral student in the Department of Counseling Psychology and Guidance Services at Ball State University, Muncie, Indiana. Her research interests include community-based solutions for peacebuilding between groups, social justice, nonviolence, and sustainable development. As a recipient of the Benjamin V. Cohen Peace Award (2003–2004), she conducted interviews with Hindus and Muslims in India in an attempt to understand their solutions for peace in their communities. She is currently working on extending this study for her dissertation.

Sandra L. Shullman is the Managing Director of the Columbus office of the Executive Development Group, an international leadership development and consulting firm, and graduate faculty in the Psychology Department at Cleveland State University. She received her Ph.D. in counseling psychology from The Ohio State University. Dr. Shullman co-authored *Performance Appraisal on the Line* and has written and presented extensively on organizational development and management, career development, self-esteem and motivation, diversity management, sexual harassment, and AIDS. She is Past President of the Ohio Psychological Association and was recently elected to the Board of Directors of the American Psychological Association.

Ted Strickland is currently a United States Congressman representing the State of Ohio. The son of a steelworker, and one of nine children, Ted received a B.A. in History from Asbury College in Kentucky, a Master of Divinity from Asbury Theological Seminary, and a doctoral degree in counseling psychology in 1980 from the University of Kentucky. Professionally, Ted has served as a minister, a psychologist, and a college professor. He was the director of a Methodist children's home, an assistant professor of psychology at Shawnee State University , and a consulting psychologist at the Southern Ohio Correctional Facility (SOCF). During his last five terms in Congress, Ted has fought to secure a meaningful prescription drug benefit under Medicare and to reform the managed care industry; fought to protect American industry and jobs from unfair foreign competition; and been tireless in his advocacy for full funding of promised veterans' health programs.

Kristin Talka is a fourth-year doctoral student in the Department of Educational and Counseling Psychology at the University at Albany, State University of New York. As a graduate student, she has been afforded the wonderful opportunity to work with Dr. Azara Santiago-Rivera as a supervisor. Through their work together in the division of Counselors for Social Justice of the American Counseling Association, Dr. Santiago-Rivera introduced her to the area of social justice and advocacy in the counseling profession. Social justice and advocacy is now a large part of her identity and work as a psychologist in training. Ms. Talka has conducted clinical work in community mental health centers, Rensselaer Polytechnic Institute's College Counseling Center, and the Albany VAMC. She enjoys conducting neuropsychological testing with brain-injured patients as well as serving as a graduate assistant at her university's career center. In addition to the area of social justice research, she is working on her dissertation, focusing on men's fears of intimacy in romantic relationships. Once she receives her Ph.D., she is looking forward to pursuing a career as a psychologist in a college counseling center as well as continuing to serve.

Regine M. Talleyrand is an Assistant Professor with the Counseling and Development Program in the Graduate School of Education at George Mason University. Dr. Talleyrand completed her Ph.D. in counseling psychology from the University of Maryland in August 2001. Her research focuses on the use of racial identity theory and acculturation in the development of physical and mental health models for people of color. She has served as an ad hoc reviewer for the *Journal of Counseling Psychology, The Counseling Psychologist,* the *Assessment Journal,* and the *Journal of Black Psychology.*

Nicole Taylor, M.A., is a doctoral student in the counseling psychology program, Department of Counseling and Personnel Services, at the University of Maryland. Her master's thesis focused on coping styles in daughters of women with breast cancer, which reflects her primary area of interest in counseling health psychology, chronic disease and its impact on families, social justice, and the psychosocial aspects of genetic disease. She is a 2004–2005 University of Maryland research fellowship recipient.

Charu Thakral is currently working on her Ph.D. in counseling psychology at Loyola University Chicago and received her MS in clinical psychology at Illinois State University. She is presently completing her doctoral-level internship at Children's Memorial Hospital in Chicago. Her research interests include areas of study ranging from subjective well-being to stress, coping, and resilience in ethnic minority children and adolescents. Her teaching and clinical interests include advocacy and education in areas of multicultural counseling and competence.

Chalmer E. Thompson is Associate Professor in the Department of Counseling and Educational Psychology at Indiana University, Bloomington. She is also a licensed psychologist. Her areas of research include critical psychotherapy process research and the development of racial identity theory as applied to a range of contexts, including professional development training for teachers, supervision, and classroom settings with people of all ages. She is also the founder of the Heritage Project.

Amy W. Tully, MSEd, LPC, is currently completing a Ph.D. in counseling psychology at the University at Albany, State University of New York. She has provided psychotherapy, career counseling, and crisis intervention services within community mental health clinics, hospitals, and higher education settings. Her experience also includes program development, administration, and teaching undergraduate and graduate courses. Amy has conducted presentations at national and regional conferences on topics such as developing multicultural competencies in counseling and administration and facilitating academic and career decision making.

Elizabeth Vera is an Associate Professor in Counseling Psychology at Loyola University Chicago in the School of Education. She received her Ph.D. in 1993 from The Ohio State University. In 2002, Dr. Vera received the Fritz and Lynn Kuder Early Career Scientist-Practitioner Award from Division 17 of the American Psychological Association. Dr. Vera's recent publications are in the areas of prevention, urban adolescents, and social justice issues in psychology. She teaches classes in Prevention, Human Development, Adolescence, Family Therapy, and Multicultural Issues.

Michael Waldo received a bachelor's degree in psychology from the University of California, Berkeley, and a doctorate in counseling psychology from the University of Utah. He completed internships at the University of Utah Counseling Center and the Veterans Administration Medical Center in New Orleans. He has served as a faculty member at the University of Maryland and Montana State University, and is currently a professor with the Counseling and Educational Psychology Department at New Mexico State University. He served as chair of the Society of Counseling Psychology's Prevention Section. Dr. Waldo supports the legalization of gay marriage.

David H. Whitcomb is on the faculty at the University of North Dakota, where he is the training director of the M.A. in Counseling program. His research focuses on the intersection of sexual orientation and gender roles, the scholarship of teaching and learning, and health issues for gay, lesbian, bisexual, and transgender (GLBT) persons. His social justice work includes running the first HIV prevention workshop in North Dakota for gay and bisexual men and being an officer and founding member of Equality North Dakota, the state's first GLBT human rights group.

Robert A. Williams, Ph.D., is an Assistant Professor of Counseling at San Francisco State University and is the Coordinator of the Marriage and Family Therapy Specialization in the Department of Counseling. He was awarded a NIMH grant in 2004 to study cultural protective factors against drug abuse and delinquency in African American adolescents in low-income communities. His clinical specialties focus, among other areas, on developing group interventions to appropriately empower adolescents when in conflict with adults and peers. His interest in culture-specific and systems approaches is integral to his approach to therapy, education, research, community involvement, and ethics.